Principles of
MacroEconomics

second edition

John E. Sayre
Capilano College

Alan J. Morris
Capilano College

Contributor
James Sentance
University of Prince Edward Island

 **McGraw-Hill
Ryerson**

Toronto Montréal New York Burr Ridge Bangkok
Bogotá Caracas Lisbon London Madrid Mexico City
Milan New Delhi Seoul Singapore Sydney Taipei

McGraw-Hill
Ryerson Limited
A Subsidiary of The **McGraw-Hill** *Companies*

Principles of Macroeconomics
Second Edition

ISBN: 0-07-560463-9

1 2 3 4 5 6 7 8 9 10 TRI 8 7 6 5 4 3 2 1 0 9

Printed and bound in Canada

Photo Credits: Images on pages 80, 158, and 342 copyright © 1998 PhotoDisc, Inc.

Statistics Canada information is used with permission of the Ministry of Industry, as Minister responsible for Statistics Canada. Information on the availability of the wider range of data from Statistics Canada can be obtained from Statistics Canada's Regional Offices, its World Wide Web site at *http://www.statcan.ca*, and its toll-free access number 1-800-263-1136.

Care has been taken to trace ownership of copyright material contained in this text. The publishers will gladly take any information that will enable them to rectify any reference or credit in subsequent editions.

About the Cover: A special thank you to the *National Post* for allowing the use of an article from *The Financial Post* of November 18, 1998. With so many economics instructors telling us that their goal is to have students be able to understand the everyday implication of economic matters, we felt it fitting to use an image showing how current issues become clear with the study of economics.

Senior Sponsoring Editor: Lynn Fisher
Associate Editor: Jenna Wallace
Production Editor: John Eerkes
Production Co-ordinator: Nicla Dattolico
Cover Design: Dave Murphy/ArtPlus Ltd.
Page Layout: Leanne Knox/ArtPlus Ltd.
Printer: Trigraphic Printing Ottawa Limited

Canadian Cataloguing in Publication Data

Sayre, John E., 1942–
   Principles of macroeconomics

2nd ed.
Includes index.
ISBN: 0-07-560463-9

1. Macroeconomics. I. Morris, Alan J. (Alan James). II. Title.

HB172.5.S29 1999   339   C99-930221-3

With love to Jeannie
who helped me get started,
and to
Clélie
who helped me finish
(JES)
and
To the ones I love:
Brian, Trevor, and Jean
(AJM)

About The Authors

Alan Morris, though loath to admit it, first worked as an accountant in England, where he became an Associate of the Chartered Institute of Secretaries and obtained his first degree in 1971 in Manchester, U.K. He subsequently obtained his Master's degree at Simon Fraser University, B.C., in 1973. He worked on his doctorate at Leicester University, U.K., and returned to work in business in Vancouver, B.C., until his appointment at Capilano College in 1988. He currently resides in North Vancouver with his wife and two sons and is an avid devotee of classical music, mountaineering, soccer, and beer. To his knowledge, he has never been an adviser to the Canadian government.

John E. Sayre earned a B.S.B.A. at the University of Denver and an M.A. from Boston University. He began teaching principles of economics while in the Peace Corps in Malawi. He came to Vancouver to do Ph.D. studies at Simon Fraser University and ended up teaching at Capilano College for the next 30 years. As a balance to the rigours of economics, John is an avid cyclist who enjoys reading popular accounts of the exciting developments in quantum physics, following the Blue Jays, and golfing.

Photograph by Jan Westerdrop

Contents

Chapter 3   Measuring National Income   79

Chapter 4   Growth, Unemployment, and Inflation   115

Contents

Preface

Over the years, we have become increasingly convinced that most economics textbooks are written to impress other economists as much as they are to enlighten beginning students. Such books tend to be encyclopedic in scope and intimidating in appearance. It is small wonder that the average student too often emerges from an economics course feeling that the discipline really does earn its reputation of being daunting and unapproachable. The study of economics is challenging, but our experience is that students can also see it as intriguing and enjoyable if the right approach is used. It is our belief that this right approach starts with a really good textbook that is concise without sacrificing either clarity or accepted standards of rigour.

In writing this text we attempted to stay focused on five guiding principles. The first is to achieve a well-written text. We have tried to write as clearly as possible, to avoid unnecessary jargon, to keep sentences to a reasonable length, and to avoid unnecessary abstraction and repetition.

Our second principle has been to avoid an encyclopedic text. It seems that in an effort to please everyone, textbook authors often include everything. The result is that students have difficulty in separating the important principles of economics from mere applications and illustrations of those principles. In contrast, we have made a conscious decision to stay focused on time-honoured principles and to spend the necessary effort to explain those principles thoroughly.

Our third principle is to put the emphasis on student learning. Many years of teaching the principles courses have convinced us that students learn economics "by doing economics." To this end, both review questions and self-test questions are positioned throughout each chapter. This encourages students to apply what they have just read and gives them continuous feedback on their comprehension of the material being presented. Further, we feel that we offer the most comprehensive Study Guide on the market—eight different types of questions, and up to sixty questions for each chapter. In addition, each chapter's Study Guide begins with a section of study tips that are much more than the standard fare of pointing out the chapter's highlights.

The fourth principle is to avoid problems of discontinuity that can occur when different groups of authors do separate parts of a total package. To this end, we are the sole authors of the entire package of material—text, Study Guide, instructor's manual, and test bank.

Finally, we have tried to ensure that as much care and attention has gone into the ancillary materials as went into the writing of the text.

Few things are more satisfying than witnessing a student's zest for learning. We hope that this textbook adds a little to this process.

To the Students

So, one may well ask, why are you taking a course economics? For many of you, the obvious answer to this question is: "Because it is a requirement for the program or educational goal that I have chosen." Fair enough. But there are other good answers to this question. It is a simple truth that if you want to understand the world around you, then you have to understand some basic economics. So much of what goes on in the world today is driven by economic considerations, and those who know no economics often simply cannot understand why things are the way they are. In this age of globalization, we are all becoming citizens of the world and we need to function effectively in the midst of enormous changes that are sweeping across almost every aspect of the social/political/economic landscape. You can either be part of this, and all the opportunities that come with it, or not part of it because you can't make any sense of it.

It is quite possible that you may be a little apprehensive because you have heard that economics is a difficult subject. Nonetheless, we are convinced that almost any student can succeed in economics. But it will require some real work and effort. Here are some tips on the general approach to this course that you might find helpful. First, read the Economics Toolkit that appears at the beginning of the book. The section titled "Canadian Reality" gives basic information on Canada and its economic picture. "Graphing Reality" gives a quick lesson on graphs, which are an essential part of economics. These two sections will give you a solid foundation on which to build your economics knowledge.

Second, before each lecture quickly look over the chapter that will be covered. At this point you don't need to worry about the glossary boxes, the self-test questions, or the Study Guide. Third, take notes as much as you can in the lecture, because it is the process of forcing yourself to express ideas *in your own words* that is a crucial stage in the learning process. Fourth, re-read the chapter, again taking notes and using your own words (don't just copy everything word for word from the text). While doing this, refer to your classroom notes and try to integrate them into your reading notes. Having done this, you are now ready to take on the Study Guide. As painful as it may be for you to hear this, we want to say loud and clear that you should do all of the questions in the Study Guide. You may be slow at first, but you will be surprised at how much faster you become in later chapters. This is a natural aspect of the learning process. It might be helpful for you to get together with one or two other students and form a little study group that meets once or twice a week to do economics Study Guide questions. You will be amazed at how explaining an answer to a fellow student is one of the most effective learning techniques there is. If you ever come across a question that you simply can't understand, this is a sure sign that you need to approach your instructor (or teaching assistant) for help. Don't get discouraged when this happens, and realize that it will probably happen more in the beginning of your process of learning economics than later on in the semester. We are convinced that if you follow this process consistently, beginning in the very first week of class, you will succeed in the course—and not only succeed, but most likely do well. All it takes is effort, good time management, and consistent organization.

Finally, a great deal of what becoming educated is all about involves gaining self-confidence and a sense of accomplishment. Getting an A in a "tough" economics course can be a great step in this direction. We wish you all the best.

Contents

We have not divided the text into different sections since, in many ways, such a sectioning would be arbitrary and really of no great significance. After all, macroeconomics is a very integrated subject and many important themes appear and reappear throughout.

The first chapter of *Principles of Macroeconomics* is much the same as Chapter 1 of the companion volume to this text, *Principles of Microeconomics*, but with an abbreviated section on production possibilities and an added discussion of seven economic goals that a society might legitimately pursue. Chapter 2 is a streamlined, basic introduction to supply and demand analysis for students who have taken microeconomics or who need a refresher. Chapter 3 focuses on the circular-flow-of-income model and national accounting, while Chapter 4 is a discussion of economic growth, unemployment, and inflation.

Chapters 5 develops a model of aggregate expenditures in which the idea of expenditures equilibrium is introduced. Chapter 6 then moves beyond this expenditure model by introducing both prices and productivity within the framework of aggregate demand and supply analysis. We see this as the pivotal chapter in the text.

The next two chapters discuss money, banking, and the money market. Chapter 9, which is the same as Chapter 13 of *Principles of Microeconomics*, presents the theory of trade and protectionism. Chapter 10 explores the way in which exchange rates are determined and how the balance of payments is constructed.

This particular organization ensures that the student has a grounding in the determination of national income as well as money and trade before the discussion of policy, which occurs in Chapters 11 and 12. Chapter 11 presents contrasting views on the purpose of fiscal policy, while Chapter 12 does the same for monetary policy.

Chapter 13 brings economic theory and reality together by looking at how economics and world events interreacted throughout the twentieth century. The last chapter, Chapter 14, takes a bold, but we hope interesting, look at the future.

Textbook Features

We have provided a number of features to help the student come to grips with the subject matter. **Glossary** terms indicate the first use of any term that is part of the language of economics. The term itself is in bold print and the definition is provided in the margin. The page number on which the definition appears is supplied at the end of the chapter for quick and easy reference, and a complete glossary of terms appears at the end of the book.

Review boxes contain very straightforward questions that cover the most basic material of each chapter. Students should be able to answer these questions directly from the text and must master these basics before they will be able to comprehend the more abstract concepts that are at the heart of economics.

Added Dimension boxes identify material that is either general information or supplementary material that we hope adds a little colour to the student's reading.

Self-Test question boxes have been integrated into the text and are scattered at important points throughout each chapter. Their purpose is to give students immediate feedback on how well they understand the more abstract concept(s) discussed. In doing this, we have tried to establish what we believe to be a minimum standard of comprehension that all students should strive to achieve. Students can check their own progress by comparing their answers with those in the Answer Key, which is included with the book.

Study Guide Features

We believe that answering questions and doing problems should be an active *part of the learning process*. For this reason, we chose to integrate a complete **Study Guide** under this same cover. Thus a Study Guide section, with pages screened in colour, immediately follows each chapter. We were careful to write the questions in the Study Guide to cover all the material, but *only* the material, found in the text itself. We have chosen a colourful, user-friendly design for the Study Guide sections, and we hope this will encourage significant student participation.

Within each Study Guide section we begin with **Study Tips**, our suggestions to the students for managing the material in the chapter. Next comes the **Key Problem**. This problem encompasses the fundamental idea or ideas in the chapter. Students are then given the opportunity to really test their understanding with an additional, very similar, problem called **More of the Same**.

The **Translations** section requires students to translate a graph or other mathematical material into words or to translate words into a mathematical presentation. Next, we reinforce the Review Questions and Glossary boxes from the text with a true–false section entitled **Are You Sure?** These questions obviously require students to make a choice, but if they choose false, they are required to explain why. Then comes a series of multiple-choice questions entitled **Choose the Best**. These questions increase in difficulty and in number of optional answers offered as the student works through the twenty questions. A number of shorter questions follow in a section imaginatively entitled **Other Problems**.

The answers to all the Study Guide questions, as well as answers to the self-test questions found in the text itself, can be found in the **Answer Key**, included with the text under a separate cover. We chose to provide the answers in this way so that the student can have the text open to the question page and the Key open to the answer at the same time.

The **Unanswered Questions** in the Study Guide section contain a number of short essay, analytical, and numerical problems for which there are no answers in the Key. Instructors therefore have the option of using these questions for exams, out-of-class assignments, or other types of tests. The answers to the analytical and numerical questions are found in the *Instructor's Manual to accompany Principles of Microeconomics and Principles of Macroeconomics*.

Finally, this edition includes new **Web-Based Activities**, written by Dale Box at the University College of the Fraser Valley. These questions are included to give students the opportunity to apply what they've learned through the exciting and dynamic World Wide Web. The web addresses were correct at the time of printing, but these may change; changes to any addresses will be posted on McGraw-Hill Ryerson's *Principles of Macroeconomics* website.

Supplements For Instructors

Instructor's Manual

There are three parts to each chapter of the *Instructor's Manual*. First is a brief overview of the chapter, with some rationale for the topics included. Second is a description of how we think the material found in the chapter is best presented. Between the two of us, we have taught the macro principles course over two hundred times, and we pass on helpful hints gained from this extensive experience to instructors who may not have been at it so long. More-experienced instructors who have found a comfortable groove will simply ignore these suggestions.

The third part contains the answers to the analytical and numerical questions that appear in the Unanswered Questions section of the Study Guide. We have not included answers to the essay questions of this section because a basic answer can be found directly in the text and a more sophisticated answer would become rather subjective.

Computerized Test Bank

Much effort went into writing the *Test Bank to accompany Principles of Macroeconomics* in order to ensure that the questions cover all topics in the textbook, but *only* those topics. Questions are written in plain English and in true question form to minimize any misunderstanding by students as to what is being asked. There are approximately one hundred questions per chapter. They come in the order of the topics covered in the chapter and include a mixture of both four- and five-answer questions. In addition, certain clearly marked questions are repeats of multiple-choice questions from the Study Guide section. This gives the instructor the option of including multiple-choice questions on an exam that students have, or have not, seen before.

Instructors receive special software that lets them design their own examinations from the test bank questions. It also lets instructors edit test items and add their own questions to the test bank. A printed version of the test bank is available to instructors upon request.

PowerPoint® Presentations

Instructors who adopt *Principles of Macroeconomics*, Second Edition, receive, on request, a PowerPoint presentation package. This package includes a complete file of PowerPoint "slides" for each chapter, as well as a PowerPoint Viewer to display and print this material from the instructor's computer. Each file has several slides relating to the chapter, including some graphs and figures from the text.

Acknowledgements

We wish to thank the following economists who participated in the formal review process during the creation and revision of this book: Terri Anderson, Fanshawe College; Doug Beatty, Lambton College; Dale Box, University College of the Fraser Valley; Larry Brown, Selkirk College; Tom Chambers, Canadore College; Brian Coulter, University College of the Fraser Valley; Greg Flanagan, Mt. Royal College; Bill Gallivan, University College of Cape Breton; Barbara Gardner, SAIT; David Gray, University of Ottawa; Dean Haggerty, Sir Sandford Fleming College; Ibrahim Hayani, Seneca College; James Hnatchuk, Champlain College; Lionel Ifill, Algonquin College; Peter Jacobs, Champlain College; Witold Jankowski, Lakehead University; Cheryl Jenkins, John Abbot College; Peter Kaglik, Red River Community College; Susan Kamp, University of Alberta; Zafar Kayani, University of Northern British Columbia; Peter Kennedy, Simon Fraser University; Joe Luchetti, Sault College; Sharam Manouchehri, Grant MacEwan College; Chris McDonnell, Malaspina University College; Mark Moore, University of British Columbia; Martin Moy, University College of Cape Breton; Paul Pieper, Humber College; Neil Ridler, University of New Brunswick – Saint John; Joe Selby, College of the Rockies; James Sentance, University of Prince Edward Island; Cal Shaw, George Brown College; William Sinkevitch, St. Clair College; Ken Strand, Simon Fraser University; and Bob Weil, Sir Sandford Fleming College.

We wish to give a special acknowledgement to Jim Sentance of the University of Prince Edward Island, who helped us refocus our first attempts at rewriting both the two policy chapters, as well as the penultimate chapter. Jim insisted that we remain relevant and historically accurate, while still leaving us room for the development of the important principles.

We would like to acknowledge our colleagues in the Economics Department of Capilano College—Nigel Amon, Ken Moak, and Mahak Yaseri—for their encouragement and vigilance in spotting errors and omissions in the first edition. Numerous colleagues in other departments also gave us encouragement, and sometimes praise, which is greatly appreciated.

The administration at the college were very accommodating and supportive, while the staff of the computer services and social sciences division were always helpful and provided badly needed help when requested.

John Eerkes's editing has been superb, while Susan Calvert at McGraw-Hill Ryerson has offered excellent professional skills.

We appreciate the work of Clélie Rich, who read a close-to-final draft and helped clarify ambiguities while spotting many errors.

Most particularly, we wish to acknowledge the professionalism and continued faith shown in us by our Associate Editor. It was Jenna Wallace who recognized the potential of this book, and it was she who guided us through the pitfalls inherent in any second edition. Jenna put her heart and soul into every detail of this book's development. Her work went far beyond the norm, and her talents became more apparent at every stage. In addition, she set very high standards for us but never wavered in her belief that we would meet them.

In the end, of course, whatever errors or confusions remain are our responsibility.

Finally, we wish to acknowledge the help and support of our families, who patiently and good-humouredly took over many additional tasks in order to provide us with "free" time. We are deeply moved by this support.

Economics Toolkit

Some students take economics because it is a requirement for a program they have chosen or a degree that they are working toward. Some are interested in a career in business, and taking economics seems like a natural choice. Some even take it because they think that they might like it. Whatever might be the reason you chose to take it, we are glad that you did and hope that you will not be disappointed. Economics is a challenging discipline to learn, but it is also, potentially, one of the most rewarding courses you will ever take. The logic and analysis used in economics is very powerful, and successfully working your way through the principles of economics over the next semester will do for your mind what a serious jogging program will do for your body. Bon voyage!

The Canadian Reality

The Land

Canada is a huge country—in fact, it is the second-largest country on this planet. It contains 7 percent of the world's land mass. It stretches 5600 kilometres from the Atlantic to the Pacific Oceans and encompasses six time zones. Ontario alone, which is the second-largest province after Quebec, is larger than Pakistan, or Turkey, or Chile, or France, or the United Kingdom. Canada's ten provinces range in size from tiny Prince Edward Island to Quebec, which is nearly 240 times as large. In addition, its three territories–the Northwest Territories, the Yukon, and the recently formed Nunavut—demand that we describe this country's reach as from sea to sea to sea.

Within Canada there are at least six major mountain ranges: the Torngats, Appalachians, and Laurentians in the East, and the Mackenzie, Rocky, and Coast ranges in the West, each of which rivals the European Alps in size and grandeur. In addition, Canada has vast quantities of fresh water—9 percent of the world's total—in tens of thousands of lakes and numerous rivers, of which the St. Lawrence and the Mackenzie are the largest.

Canada is richly endowed in natural resources, including gas, oil, gold, silver, copper, iron ore, nickel, potash, uranium, zinc, fish, timber, and, as mentioned above, water—lots of fresh water. The conclusion is inescapable: Canada is a big, beautiful, and rich country.

The People

The word *Canada* comes from the Huron–Iroquois word meaning *village*. In a sense this is very appropriate, because big as the nation is geographically, it is small in terms of population. Its 30 million people make up only 0.5 percent of the world's population. In fact, there are more people in California or in greater Tokyo than there are in the whole of Canada. Interestingly, Canada's population growth rate, at 1.1 percent, is the highest among the G-8 countries of the world primarily because of Canada's high rate of immigration. Thirty-six percent of Canadians live in the province of Ontario, and 25 percent in Quebec. On the other hand, Prince Edward Island has a population of only 140 000, which is less than that of the cities of Sherbrooke, Quebec, or North Vancouver, B.C.

Despite the popular images of the small Maritime fishing village, the lonely Prairie grain farmer, or the remote B.C. logger, Canada is, in fact, an urban nation. A full 77 percent of Canadians live in what Statistics Canada calls "urban" areas. There are four Canadian metropolitan areas with populations of over one million: Toronto, with 4.3 million; Montreal, 3.3 million; Vancouver, 1.8 million; and Ottawa–Hull, 1.1 million. It is also true that the vast majority of the 30 million Canadians live in a narrow band stretching along the border with the United States, which, incidentally, is the longest unguarded border in the world.

Approximately one half of the Canadian population of 30 million are active in the labour force. The labour-force participation rate for males is 73 percent, and for females, 58 percent.

Multiculturalism

Within this vast, thinly populated country there is a truly diverse, multicultural mix of people. This reality was officially recognized in 1988 when Parliament passed the Multiculturalism Act.

There are two official languages in Canada, yet 18 percent of Canadians speak a language other than English or French. In fact, sixty languages are spoken in this country. In each year of the 1990s, more than 200 000 new immigrants arrived in Canada. Over 15 percent of all Canadians are first-generation immigrants. In both Toronto and Vancouver, over one half of the students in the public school system are from non–English-speaking homes. There are over 100 minority-language publications in Toronto, and Vancouver has three daily Chinese-language newspapers.

Canada's First Nations people number 533 000 (1.8 percent of the total population), and almost half of them live in Ontario.

Government

Canada is a constitutional monarchy with a democratic parliament made up of the House of Commons, with 301 elected members, and the Senate, with 104 appointed members. In addition to Parliament, the other two decision-making divisions of the federal government are the cabinet, comprised of the prime minister and his or her twenty-five (or so) ministers and their departments, and the judiciary, which includes the Supreme, Federal, and Tax courts.

Just as there are two official languages in this country, Canada has two systems of civil law—one uncodified and based on common law in English Canada, and the other as codified civil law in Quebec. Canada's constitution, the Canadian Charter of Rights and Freedoms, came into being in 1982, a full 115 years after Confederation created the country in 1867.

The fact that Canada is a confederation of ten provinces results in the federal government sharing responsibilities with the provinces. For example, while the federal government has jurisdiction in national defence, international trade, immigration, banking, criminal law, fisheries, transportation, and communications, the provinces have responsibility for education, property rights, health, and natural resources. Inevitably, issues arise from time to time that do not fit neatly into any one of these categories, with the result that federal–provincial disputes are a continuous part of the Canadian reality.

Canada the Good

Most Canadians are well aware that they live in a good country. But perhaps many don't realize just how good. The average household income is currently over $54 000, which puts the Canadian living standard sixth in the world behind that of the United States, Switzerland, Luxembourg, Germany, and Japan.

The United Nations maintains a "Human Development Index" that uses other factors in addition to average income levels, including crime rates, life spans, income distribution, and the presence of human rights. This index ranks Canada as the number one nation in the world in which to live. One reason for this high ranking is that Canadian governments spent $1700 per person on health care (in 1994, a representative year), which is nearly 10 percent of the country's gross domestic product (GDP), a measure of the total output of all goods and services.

Nearly 65 percent of Canadians own their homes, well over 90 percent are literate, and 15 percent of all Canadians have access to the Internet. All three of these statistics are among the highest in the world.

Canada the Odd

Canada *is* a good country in which to be born or to have emigrated to. However, it does have its oddities. In 1965, 98 years after its "birth," it was decided that Canada really should have a national flag. The Parliamentary selection committee set up to choose one received no less than two thousand designs, and the flag debate was acrimonious, to say the least. Today, however, most Canadians seem quite comfortable with the Maple Leaf. The English-language lyrics of Canada's national anthem, "O Canada," were formally approved only in 1975. Canada adopted the metric system of measurement in the 1970s, but the imperial system is still in wide use; for example, Statistics Canada still reports the breadth of this country in miles, we still sell lengths of wood as "2 × 4s" (inches), and football fields are still 110 yards long.

In this bilingual country, it is odd to note that there are more Manitobans who speak Cree than British Columbians who speak French. In this affluent country of ours, it also interesting to note that 4 percent of Canadian homes are heated exclusively by burning wood. Canada has an official animal—the beaver.

On a more serious note, it is a sad fact that the trade of many goods, and even some services, between any one province and the United States is freer than trade between provinces. There is an interesting history concerning trade patterns in North America. At the time of Confederation, trade patterns on this continent were mostly north–south. The Maritimes traded with the New England states, Quebec with New York, Ontario with the Great Lakes states to its south, and the West Coast traded with California. Canada's first prime minister, John A. Macdonald, was also elected as its third, after having lost his first re-election bid, on the basis of a campaign promise known as the National Policy. This policy had three aspects: a) to build a railway to the West Coast and coax British Columbia into joining Canada; b) to offer free land to new immigrants on the prairies in order to populate this area; and c) to force trade patterns into a east–west mode by erecting a tariff wall against U.S. imports. British Columbia did join Confederation; people did come to Manitoba, Saskatchewan, and Alberta; and the pattern of trade did become more east–west.

So was the National Policy a success? Some would argue yes, pointing out that it built a nation and that just possibly Canada, as we know it, would not exist today without it. Others aren't so sure and would argue that it set back Canada's development by encouraging and protecting new, less efficient industries through the creation of a branch-plant economy. This occurred because American firms that had previously exported to Canada simply jumped over the tariff walls and established Canadian branch plants. This in turn promoted Canadian regionalism and aggravated relations between regions because both the West and the Maritimes felt that most of the economic benefits of the National Policy favoured central Canada.

In any case, as a result of the North American Free Trade Agreement (NAFTA) of 1992, trade with the United States (and Mexico) is now without tariffs and north–south trade patterns are re-emerging. Historically, Canadian policy has come full circle. However, the interprovincial trade barriers between provinces, which were built piece by piece over 100 years, still remain.

The Economy

Canada is among the ten largest economies in the world, despite its small population. In 1997, Canada's GDP was $856.1 billion. This figure can be broken down as illustrated in **Table P.1**.

TABLE P.1

Category	Amount ($ billion)
Personal expenditures	505.4
Investment spending	146.9
Government spending	186.8
Exports	344.5
Less imports	(329.4)
Statistical discrepancy	1.9
Total GDP	856.1

Source: Adapted from Statistics Canada, CANSIM database, matrix 6548.

The provincial breakdown of this 1997 GDP figure of $856.1 billion is shown in **Table P.2.**

TABLE P.2

Province	GDP ($ billion)	% of Total
Newfoundland	10.9	1.3
Prince Edward Island	2.9	0.3
Nova Scotia	20.4	2.4
New Brunswick	17.2	2.0
Quebec	185.4	21.7
Ontario	347.2	40.6
Manitoba	29.2	3.4
Saskatchewan	28.3	3.3
Alberta	101.2	11.8
British Columbia	109.4	12.8
Yukon	1.1	0.1
Northwest Territories (pre-Nunavut)	2.9	0.3

Source: Adapted from Statistics Canada, CANSIM database, matrices 9015–9026.

Note that Ontario, with 36 percent of the nation's population, produces 40.6 percent of its GDP.

In most years, the economy grows and the GDP figure rises. To accurately compare growth in GDP, however, we need to use a common set of prices so that a simple rise in prices isn't confused with an actual increase in the output of goods and services. Using *real* GDP figures, which corrects for any inflation, accomplishes this. **Table P.3** looks at some recent real GDP figures, using 1992 prices.

TABLE P.3

Year	Real GDP ($ billion)	Increase ($ billion)	% Increase
1993	716.1	—	—
1994	744.2	28.1	3.9
1995	760.3	16.1	2.2
1996	769.7	9.0	1.2
1997	799.1	29.4	3.8

Source: Adapted from Statistics Canada, CANSIM database, matrix 6549.

Next, let's look at an industry breakdown of Canada's GDP in **Figure P.1.**

FIGURE P.1 Canada's GDP at Factor Costs, 1997

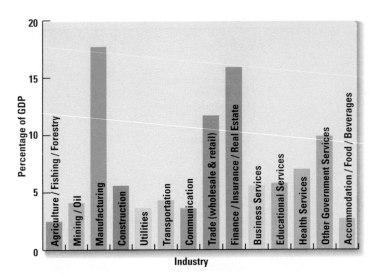

Source: Adapted from Statistics Canada, CANSIM database, matrix 4677.

This information is helpful in many ways. For example, it is certainly time to put to rest the idea that Canada is a resource-based economy and that Canadians are simply "hewers of wood and drawers of water," as many of us were taught in school. In fact, agriculture/fishing/forestry and mining/oil make up less than 7 percent of our economy's GDP. Another figure that makes the same point is that only 5.6 percent of working Canadians are in primary industries, which is dramatically down from 13 percent a quarter of a century ago.

In contrast, one can marshal an argument that Canada is a quite sophisticated and technologically advanced economy. For example, it is not generally recognized that Canada was the world's third nation to go into space with the Alouette I satellite in 1962. Canadian industries pioneered long-distance pipeline technology, and Canada is a world leader in several areas of aviation, including turboprop, turbofan, and fire-fighting aircraft, not to mention the well-known Canadarm used on space shuttles. Canada is also a world leader in commercial submarine technology, and it routinely maintains one of the world's longest and most efficient railway systems. One can also point to many outstanding Canadian companies that are truly world leaders in technology and performance, including Bombardier in transportation equipment, Ballard Power in fuel cell technology, SNC Lavalin in aluminum plant design, Northern Telecom in cellular communications, Trizec Hahn in real estate development, and Magna International in automobile parts manufacturing.

Exports: The Engine that Drives the Economy

Exports are a fundamental part of the Canadian economy. Over 40 percent of its GDP is exported, which makes Canada one of the world's greatest trading nations. Exports to the United States alone directly support over 1.5 million Canadian jobs, and a $1 billion increase in exports translates into 11 000 new jobs. Again, contrary to historical wisdom, only 20 percent of Canadian exports are resources—this figure was 40 percent a quarter of a century ago.

Figure P.2 breaks down the $344 billion of Canadian exports in 1997 into nine categories.

FIGURE P.2: Canada's Exports by Category, 1997

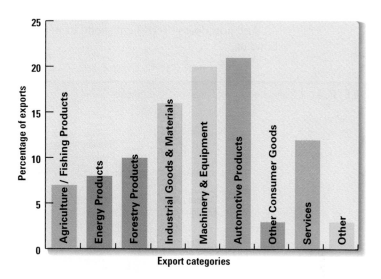

Source: Adapted from Statistics Canada, CANSIM database, matrices 3685 and 3651.

A Mixed Economy

As we enter the twenty-first century, the market system dominates most of the world's economies, and Canada is no exception to this. Yet, government also plays a big role in our economy. For example, in the fiscal year 1996–97 the three levels of government collected $327.6 billion in tax revenue, which represents over 38 percent of Canada's 1997 GDP. **Figure P.3** shows the sources of this revenue.

FIGURE P.3: Tax Revenue for All Canadian Governments, 1997

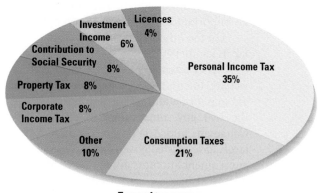

Source: Adapted from Statistics Canada, CANSIM database, matrix 3315.

The largest single source of the government's tax revenue, 35 percent, was personal income taxes. Consumption taxes include, most significantly, the GST (goods and services tax) and the PST (provincial sales tax) as well as gasoline, alcohol, and tobacco taxes, customs tax, and gaming income. These indirect taxes accounted for 21 percent of total revenue. Thus we can see that a majority of the government's tax revenue comes from individual Canadians in the form of direct income taxes or consumption taxes.

And how does government spend its nearly $330 billion of tax revenue? Figure P.4 shows us.

FIGURE P.4: Expenditures by All Canadian Governments, 1997

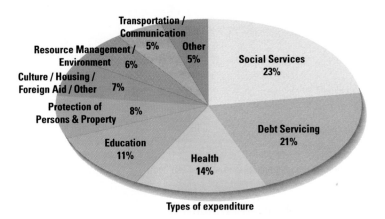

Types of expenditure

Source: Adapted from Statistics Canada, CANSIM database, matrix 3315.

Here we see that government's largest single category, which is 23 percent of spending, was on payments to individuals. The lion's share of this expenditure, 68 percent, was social assistance (welfare) payments. Thus we see that a large percentage of spending by government is an attempt to direct income to poorer Canadians. Since it is all Canadians who pay for most of these expenditures, we can see that the government is actively involved in *transferring* income from higher-income to lower-income families and individuals. This income distribution role is seen by many Canadians as an important function of government.

On the other hand, some Canadians take the view that government has gone too far in its interventionist role and yearn for less government involvement in the economy. They often point to the United States as an example of a economy in which both welfare, unemployment, and pension payments to individuals and direct government aid to poor regions of the country are lower. The difference in the general approach of the two governments may well lie in historical differences in the attitudes of Canadians and Americans toward government. Over the years, Canadians, by and large, have trusted governments to act in their best interest and been more tolerant of government attempts at income redistribution. Americans, on the other hand, have a history of being suspicious of big government and have repeatedly rejected attempts to expand its role. The recent rejection in the United States of attempts to implement a national health-care policy is an example. Another is the Canadian government's direct aid to cultural endeavours, including the funding of a national television and radio network, while no such efforts exist in the United States.

Interest on the national debt was the second-largest category of spending, at 21 percent. Over the years, government has borrowed over $800 billion to finance budget deficits, and the interest paid on this borrowing totalled $75.8 billion in 1997. Most Canadians believe that expenditures on health (the universal medical plan) and education make up government's largest spending categories. However, though these two are large—a combined total of 25 percent—they rank only third and fourth. The fifth category, protection of persons and property, includes expenditures on police, fire departments, the court system, and prisons. The sixth category includes a host of items such as culture (the Canada Council), housing, foreign affairs, immigration, labour, and research.

This completes our brief look at the Canadian economic reality. We hope that it has helped to fill in some of the gaps in your knowledge of the country. We are confident that you will come to know your country much better after a thorough grounding in the principles of economics, for, in a very real sense, economics is about understanding and improving on what we already know.

Graphing Reality

Let's face it: a lot of students hate graphs. For them a picture is not worth a thousand words. It may even be true that they seem to understand some economic concepts just fine until the instructor draws a graph on the board. All of a sudden, they lose confidence and start to question what they previously thought they knew. For these students, graphs are not the solution, but the problem. This section is designed to help those students overcome this difficulty. For those other, more fortunate, students who can handle graphs and know that they are used to illustrate concepts, a quick reading of this section will help reinforce their understanding.

It's probably true to say that if an idea can be expressed clearly and precisely with words, then graphs become an unnecessary luxury. The trouble is that from time to time, economists find themselves at a loss for words and see no other way of getting a certain point across except with the use of a graph. On the other hand, by themselves, graphs cannot explain everything; they need to be accompanied by a verbal explanation. In other words, graphs are not a substitute for words, but a complement. The words accompanied by a picture can often give us a much richer understanding of economic concepts and happenings.

Graphing a Single Variable

The graphing of a single variable is reasonably straightforward. Often economists want to concentrate on a single economic variable, such as Canada's exports, or consumers' income, or the production of wine in Canada. In some cases they want to look at the composition of that variable, say different categories of exports. In other cases they are interested in seeing how that variable changed over a period of time, say total exports for each of the years 1992 through 1997. In the first instance, we would be looking at a *cross-section*; in the second instance we are looking at a *time series*.

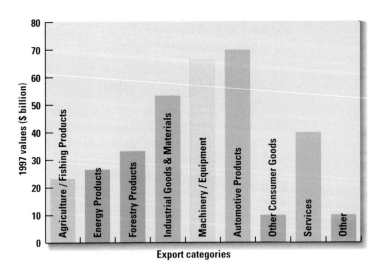

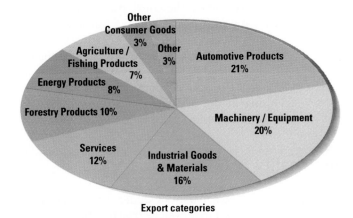

Cross-Sectional Graphs

One popular way of showing cross-sectional data is in the form of a **pie chart**. Figure G.1A, for instance, shows the composition of Canada's exports for 1997 in terms of the type of goods or services that Canada sells abroad.

FIGURE G.1A Composition of Canadian Exports, 1997

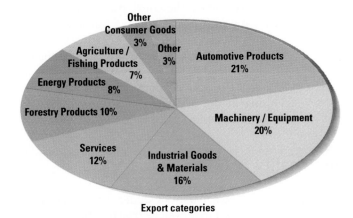

Export categories

The size of each slice indicates the relative size of each category of export. But the picture by itself is not always enough. We have added the percentage of total exports that each type represents. Notice, however, that there are no dollar amounts for the categories.

Alternatively, the same information could be presented in the form of a **bar graph**, as in Figure G.1B.

FIGURE G.1B Composition of Canadian Exports, 1997

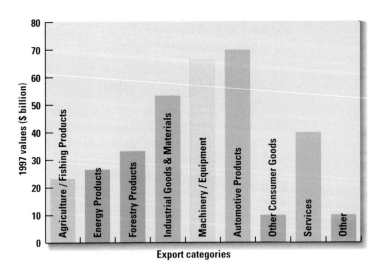

Looking at the bar graph, you'll notice that it's possible to estimate the dollar amounts, but it would be difficult to know the percentage share of the category without a lot of tedious calculation.

Time-Series Graphs

Time-series data can also be presented in the form of a bar graph. **Figure G.2A** shows a bar graph of how the dollar amount of Canada's total exports (ignoring its composition) has changed over a six-year period.

FIGURE G.2A: Total Canadian Exports, 1992–97

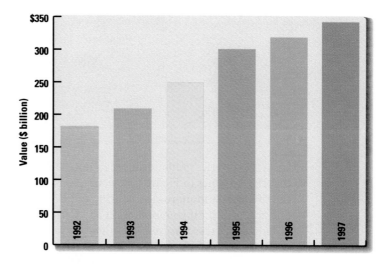

The same information can be presented in a **line graph**, as is done in **Figure G.2B**.

FIGURE G.2B: Total Canadian Exports, 1992–97

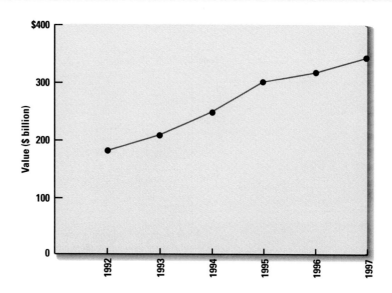

Note that, in both cases, the years (time) are shown on the horizontal axis; early years are on the left, and later years on the right. This is because graphs are always read from left to right.

Graphing Two Variables

Things get a little trickier when we want to deal with two variables at the same time. For instance, suppose we want to relate Canada's disposable income, which is the total take-home pay of all Canadians, and the amount spent on consumer goods (these numbers are in billions and are hypothetical). One obvious way to do this is with a table, as is done in **Table G.1**.

TABLE G.1

Year	Disposable Income	Spending on Consumer Goods
1993	$100	$ 80
1994	120	98
1995	150	125
1996	160	134
1997	200	170

A time-series graph, using the same data, is presented in **Figure G.3**. You can see that the two lines in Figure G.3 seem to be closely related, and that is useful information. However, to more clearly bring out the relationship we could plot them against one another. But if you look again at Table G.1, you will see that there are really three different variables involved: the time (six years), the values of disposable income, and the values of spending. However, it is very difficult to plot three variables, all three against each other, on a two-dimensional sheet of paper.

FIGURE G.3: Disposable Income and Spending on Consumer Goods, 1993–97

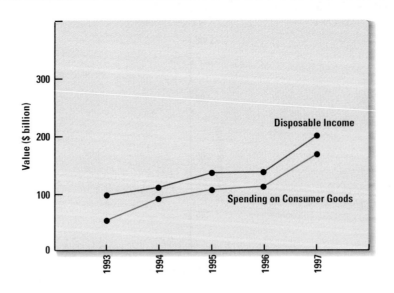

Instead, in **Figure G.4**, we will put disposable income on the horizontal axis (also called the X-axis), and consumer spending on the vertical axis (also called the Y-axis) and indicate time with written notation. There is a rule about which variable goes on which axis, but we will leave that for later chapters.

Next, we need to decide on a scale for each of the two axes. There is no particular rule about doing this, but just a little experience will enable you to develop good judgement about selecting these values. We have chosen to give each square on the axes the value of $20. This can be seen in Figure G.4.

FIGURE G.4: Spending on Consumer Goods

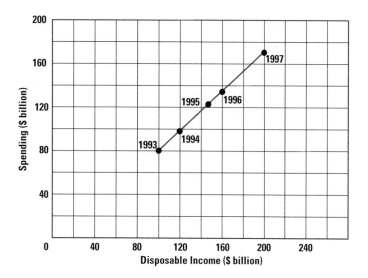

We started plotting our line using the 1993 data. In that year disposable income was $100 and consumer spending was $80. Starting at the origin (where the vertical and horizontal axes meet), which has an assigned value of zero, we move five squares to the right. Now from an income of $100, we move up vertically four squares, arriving at a value of $80 for consumer spending. This is our first plot (or point). We do the same for 1994. First, we find a value of $120 on the horizontal (disposable income) axis and a value of $98 (just less than five squares) on the vertical axis. Where these two meet gives us our second point to plot. We do the same for the three next years, and join up the five points with a line. Notice that the relationship between income levels and consumer spending plots as a straight line.

Direct and Inverse Relationships

Next, if you look back at Table G.1, you will see that disposable income and consumer spending rise together over time. When two variables move together in this way, we say that there is a **direct** relationship between them. Such a direct relationship appears as an upward-sloping line. On the other hand, if you see that two variables move in opposite directions, so that as one variable increases, the other variable decreases, we say there is an **inverse** relationship between them. In that case plotting the two variables together would result in a downward-sloping line.

(When we talk about upward- and downward-sloping, by the way, remember that we are reading the graphs from left to right.)

One last point: the income–consumer-spending line in Figure G.4 is a straight line. There is no reason this has to always be the case. Some data might plot as a straight line, and other data might be non-linear when plotted (as in Figure G.3). Either, of course, could still be downward- or upward-sloping.

Measuring the Slope

As you proceed with this course, you will find that you need to go a bit further than merely being able to plot a curve—in economics, by the way, all lines are described as curves, whether they are linear or non-linear. You will also need to know just how steep or how shallow the line is that you have plotted. That is, you will need to measure the slope of the curve. What the slope in effect shows is how much one variable changes in relation to the other variable as we move along a curve. In graphic terms, this means measuring the change in the variable shown on the vertical axis (known as the **rise**), divided by the change in the variable shown on the horizontal axis (known as the **run**). The rise and the run are illustrated, for our disposable income/consumer spending example, in **Figure G.5**.

FIGURE G.5: Rise Over Run

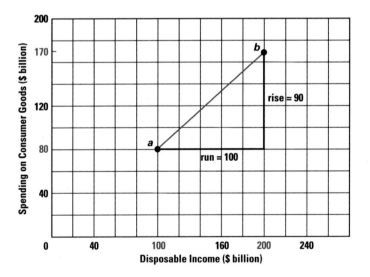

Notice that as we move from point *a* to point *b*, consumer spending increases by 90 (from 80 to 170). This is the amount of the rise. Looking along the horizontal axis, we see that disposable income increases by 100 (from 100 to 200). This is the amount of the run.

In general, we can say:

$$\text{Slope} = \frac{\text{Rise}}{\text{Run}} = \frac{\text{Change in the value on the vertical axis}}{\text{Change in the value on the horizontal axis}}$$

Specifically, the slope of our line is therefore equal to:

$$\frac{+90}{+100} = 0.9$$

Figure G.6 shows four other curves, two upward-sloping and two downward-sloping, with an indication for each on how to calculate the various slopes. In each case we measure the slope by moving from point *a* to point *b*.

FIGURE G.6: Four Different Slopes

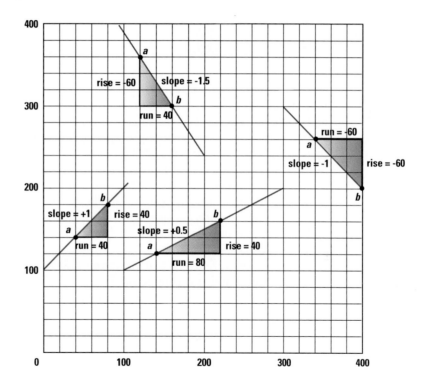

Graphs and Logic

There are some potential problems in illustrating data with graphs. For example, the relationship between income and consumer spending in Table G.1 is hypothetical, since we created it to plot well on a graph. However, any real-world relationship between two variables may not be as neat and simple. Data doesn't always plot into a nice straight line. Even more seriously, we can never be totally certain of the *nature* of the relationship between the variables being graphed. There's often a great danger of implying something that's not there. You need therefore to be on guard against a number of logical fallacies. Suppose for instance that you were doing a survey of women's clothing stores across the country. Reviewing the data you have collected, you notice that there seems to be a close relationship between two particular sets of numbers: the rent paid by the owners of the store and the average price of wool jackets sold. The data is shown in **Table G.2**.

TABLE G.2

Monthly Rent (per 100 m²)	Average Jacket Price
$1500	$80
1600	90
1700	100
1800	110
1900	120
2000	130

The higher the monthly rent, the higher the price of jackets charged in that store. It seems clear, therefore, that the higher rent is the *cause* of the higher price, and the higher price is the *effect* of the higher price. After all, the store owner must recoup these higher rent costs by charging a higher price to her customers. If you think this, then you are guilty of the logical fallacy of **reverse causality**. As you will learn in economics, although the rent of premises and product prices are indeed related, the causality is the other way around. Because stores in certain areas can charge higher product prices, this usually leads to landlords charging those stores higher rents. Higher prices, therefore, are the cause, and high rents the effect. This is not obvious, and suggests that using raw economic data without sound economic theory can lead to serious error.

A second logical fallacy is that of the **omitted variable**, which can also lead to confusion over cause and effect. **Table G.3** highlights this error. Here we see hypothetical data on rates of alcoholism and the on annual income levels of individuals:

TABLE G.3

Income Levels ($)	Alcoholism (per thousand of population)
Below 10 000	40
10 000 – 19 000	35
20 000 – 29 000	30
30 000 – 29 000	25
40 000 – 49 000	20
Over 50 000	15

There certainly seems to be a very close relationship between these two variables. Presented in this form, without any commentary, one is left to wonder if low income causes alcoholism or if alcoholism is the cause of low income. Some people with low incomes may drink in order to try to escape the effects of poverty. Or is it that people who drink to excess have great difficulty in finding or keeping a good job? In truth, it is possible that neither of these views is true. Simply because two sets of data seem closely related doesn't necessarily imply that one is the cause of the other. In fact, it may well be the case that both are effects of an omitted variable. In the above example, it is possible, for example, that both high alcoholism and low incomes are the result of low educational attainment.

A third fallacy can occur when people see a cause and effect that doesn't really exist. This is known as the fallacy of **post hoc, ergo propter hoc**, which literally means after this, therefore because of this. That is to say, it is a fallacy to believe that just because one thing follows another, the one is the result of the other. For example, just because my favourite soccer team always loses whenever I go to see them doesn't mean that I am the cause of their losing!

There is a final fallacy you should guard against, a fallacy, unfortunately, that even the best of economists commit from time to time. This is the **fallacy of composition**, which is the belief that because something is true for the part, it is true for the whole. You may have noticed, for instance, that fights occasionally break out in hockey games. These fights often occur in the corners, which makes them difficult to see. The best way for the individual to get a better view is by standing, and of course when everybody stands, then most people cannot see. Thus, what is true for a single fan—standing up to see better—is not true for the whole crowd. Similarly, a teacher who suggests that in order to get a good grade, a student should sit at the front of the class is also guilty of the same kind of logical fallacy!

We hope that this little primer on Canada and on graphing has been helpful. It is now time to move on to the study of economics.

The Economic Problem

What's ahead... In this first chapter we introduce you to the study of economics and hope to arouse your curiosity about this fascinating discipline. We will define economics, examine three fundamental economic questions, discuss the methodology and language of economics, and make the distinction between macro- and microeconomics. Next, we do a quick development of the production possibilities for a nation and, finally, put the focus on macroeconomics by discussing seven macroeconomic goals and offering an overview of some important economic disputes.

Jon and Ashok are both avid soccer fans and play for local teams. They both like old movies, chess, and *Star Trek*. They are both seventeen years of age, neither has a steady girlfriend, and both are vegetarians. The other thing they have in common is that their fathers are in banking. Jon's father is the executive vice-president of customer relations for the Royal Bank in Toronto. Ashok's father is a night janitor at a branch of the Bank of India in the dock area of Bombay. All of these points are relevant in forming a mental picture of a person, but you will probably agree that a person's economic circumstances are the most relevant of all. In truth, economics is one of the most relevant subjects you study.

What might you expect from a course in economics? Well, it will not help you balance your cheque book and may not be directly helpful in your choice of the right stock to buy. But the study of economics will give you a broad understanding of how a modern market economy operates and what the important things are within one. If you see yourself as a budding businessperson, the study of economics can offer some general insights that will be helpful. Yet you will not find specific tools or instructions. Economics is an academic discipline, not a self-help or how-to course. The common conception that economics is about money is only partly true. We study money, but more in the sense of what it is and the effects of different central-bank money policies, than in the sense of how to make it. The study of economics may not help you to function better in the world in any specific sense, but it will probably help you to understand better how the world functions.

Scarcity, Choice, and Technology

Economists put a great deal of emphasis on scarcity and the need to economize. Individual households face a scarcity of income and therefore must budget expenditures. Most individuals also face a scarcity of time and must somehow decide where to spend time and where to conserve it. In the same sense, an economy as a whole has limited productive resources and must allocate those resources among competing uses.

Productive resources is a term that economists use interchangeably with the term **factors of production** or, sometimes, simply "inputs." Factors of production are traditionally divided into four categories: land, labour, capital and enterprise. **Land** is defined as anything natural, such as fertile soil, deep harbours, good climate, or minerals in the ground. **Labour** refers to a broad spectrum of human effort, ranging from that of a skilled naturopathic physician to that of a construction labourer. **Capital** is made up of the tools, equipment, factories, and buildings used in the production process. Finally, **enterprise** is that very special human talent that is able to put abstract ideas into practical application.

Economists see such productive resources (the factors of production) as *scarce* in the sense that no economy has sufficient resources to be able to produce all of the goods and services everyone wants. This is not to say that there aren't some people who would say that they have all that they want, but there are millions of people who possess a seemingly endless list of wants, and millions more like them waiting to be born. Since the economy cannot produce all that everyone wants, the resources available for production are scarce, and some kind of mechanism must be put into place to *choose* what will be produced and, thereby, by implication, what will not be produced. And this is why economics is sometimes called the *science of choice*.

The term *technology* means the process of using the factors of production, in one of an infinite variety of combinations, to create physical goods and services of an endless variety of types. The output of these goods and services gives the citizens of an economy the ability to meet their wants and needs. In this sense, an economy that produces a large quantity of goods and services is more successful than one that is able to produce only a small quantity.

The success or failure of any economy depends a great deal on whether the individuals, firms, and institutions within it can make the necessary choices in order to adapt to the technological and social changes that inevitably occur over time. For example, we have seen that economies that use an economic system which relies on

factors of production: the productive resources that are available to an economy, categorized as land, labour, capital, and enterprise.

land: any natural resource that can be used to produce goods and services.

labour: human physical and mental effort that can be used to produce goods and services.

capital: all human-made resources that can be used to produce goods and services.

enterprise: the human resource that innovates and takes risks.

Some industry insiders say there are just too many choices for consumers shopping for music these days. Some labels have so many acts on their roster that they can't give them the proper attention.

individual choice and enterprise (for example, Canada, the United States, Japan, and Germany) continue to enjoy success while economies that, until recently, relied on centrally controlled systems (such as Poland, Hungary, and the USSR) faltered.

Another aspect of choice that economists consider important is that any society, much like an individual household, always has a choice between consumption now or in the future. A household could choose to consume less now and save more, enabling it to consume more in the future. Societies that consume less now can use scarce productive resources to build more capital goods and services with which to produce even more consumer goods and services *in the future*. We will return to this point later in this chapter.

Economics: A Definition

In the light of this discussion we can now venture a definition of economics:

> Economics is the study of the allocation of scarce resources to produce goods and services that are used to maximize human satisfaction in the face of unlimited human wants.

macroeconomics: the study of how the major components of an economy interact; it includes the topics of unemployment, inflation, interest rate policy, and the spending and taxation policies of government.

microeconomics: the study of the outcomes of decisions by people and firms through a focus on the supply and demand of goods, the costs of production, and market structures.

We now need to make the distinction between macro- and microeconomics. Many colleges and universities offer a separate course for each of these subjects, but this is not always the case. **Macroeconomics** is the study of how the major components of the economy, such as total investment spending or exports, interact; it includes most of the topics a beginning student would expect to find in an economics course. These include unemployment, inflation, interest rates, tax and spending policies of government, and national income determination. **Microeconomics** studies the outcomes of decisions made by people and firms and includes topics like supply and demand, the study of costs, and the nature of market structures. This distinction can be described metaphorically as a comparison between the use of a wide-angle lens and a telephoto lens of a camera. In the first instance we see the big picture. In the second instance a very small part of that big picture appears in much more detail.

Is Economics Relevant?

As we enter the twenty-first century, we find ourselves living in a society filled with a host of problems and a wide variety of issues that bombard us every day in the media and dominate many of our conversations. Will Quebec separate from the rest of Canada? Will governments reduce their spending on education, and will this drive up the cost of tuition? Are the threats to our environment too serious for us to adequately cope with them? What kinds of jobs will there be in the future, and will there be enough of them to meet the aspirations of our youth? Will Canada's health care system continue to meet people's expectations? Will this country's history of tolerance toward minorities continue, or will prejudice and hatred raise their ugly heads? Will a seemingly endless number of new special-interest groups begin to tear at the fabric of our stable and democratic system of governance? Will productivity in Canada grow rapidly enough for Canadian firms to thrive in an increasingly globalized marketplace?

These questions are broad and diverse. Yet there is an economic dimension to every one of them. In fact, economics is one of the *most relevant* subjects that a student might study. Strangely, however, not everyone shares this view. There are a variety of reasons for this. One is that people often see economics as being too theoretical. However, let's remember that the most effective way to say something intelligent about nearly all the issues of the day is to use theory and abstraction. Another observation that students often make about the discipline of economics is that it seems too narrow in its focus. Yet a precise focus is sometimes needed to identify cause and effect.

Trying to understand economic theory can be challenging and certainly does not come easily, but the rewards, in terms of a better understanding of the world in which we live, are great. Economics is the study of ideas, and in a very real way this is the most important thing that a student can pursue. One of the most famous of twentieth-century economists, John Maynard Keynes, said:

> The ideas of economists, both when they are right and when they are wrong, are more powerful than is commonly understood. Sooner or later, it is ideas, not vested interests, which are dangerous for good or evil.[1]

The Three Fundamental Questions of Economics

A broad perspective on the discipline of economics can be obtained by focusing on what can be called the three fundamental questions of economics: what, how, and for whom? That is, economics is about what gets produced, how it is produced, and who gets it.

What to Produce?

Underlying the question of what should be produced is the previously mentioned reality of scarcity. Any society has only a fixed amount of resources at its disposal, and therefore must have a system in place to make millions of decisions about production. For example, should 50 new military helicopters be produced, or should the limited resources available be used to produce 10 new hospitals with (or without?) research facilities for the study of genetics? Should society exploit natural resources faster to create more jobs and more tax revenue, or slower to conserve these resources for the

---

[1] John Maynard Keynes, *The General Theory* (1936).

Canapress

In this 1995 protest in Toronto, parents walked with children to protest day-care cuts proposed by the Ontario government.

future? Should human effort, capital, and land be directed toward more preschool day-care facilities so that women are not so tied to the home? Or, instead, should those same resources be directed toward increasing the number of graduate students studying science and technology so that the Canadian economy can win the competitive international race in the twenty-first century?

No economist would claim to have the *right* answer to even one of these questions. That is no more the role of an economist than it is of any other member of society. What the economist can do, however, is identify and measure both the benefits and the costs of any one answer—of any one choice.

Let's review what we have said so far.

> **In the face of people's unlimited wants and society's limited productive resources, choice becomes a forced necessity. Because of these choices, the decision to produce one thing means that some other thing will not be produced.**

opportunity cost: the value of the next-best alternative that is given up as a result of making a particular choice.

This last point is so fundamental that economists have invented a special term to identify it: **opportunity cost**. For instance, suppose that the production of 50 new helicopters carries a price tag of $5 billion. In the conventional sense, that is their cost. However, economists would argue that it is more revealing to measure the cost of the helicopters in terms of the 10 hospitals that can't be built because the helicopters were produced. Opportunity costs can thus be defined as what must be given up as a result of making a particular choice; in this case, the hospitals instead of the helicopters. In addition we should recognize that the $5 billion could be spent on other things besides hospitals—say, colleges and universities or mass-transit systems. At this point society would presumably choose what it considers to be its *next-best* alternative. Thus our definition of opportunity costs needs to be modified to: the next-best alternative that is given up as a result of making a particular choice.

Why is it better to think of costs in terms of opportunity cost rather than simply as money payments? Economists argue that using the concept of opportunity costs captures the true measure of any decision. If we use money payments as the true measure, then we seemingly have unlimited means to produce goods, since governments can always print more money. But no matter what any government might wish, any society has only a limited amount of resources. When we realize this, there is no such thing as a "free lunch"—any decision (to produce helicopters, for example) necessarily means less of something else (hospitals). Recognizing that there are opportunity costs involved also forces us to rethink our idea of what we mean by "free." Simply because money does not change hands does not mean that a product is free. A free lunch is never free, because the provision of any meal involves the use of resources which could have been put to some other use.

The concept of opportunity cost can be applied not only at the level of the overall society, as we just saw, but also at the individual level. For the individual, the constraint is not the limited quantity of productive resources but, instead, a limited amount of income. For example, you could think of the cost of going to two movies on the weekend as the sacrifice of one new CD. If you want to think of both of these choices (two movies or one CD) as each costing about $16, that is fine. But thinking of the one as costing the other is often more effective. In general, your income will not allow you to have everything you may want, so you are forced to make choices about what you buy. And the cost of these choices can be measured in what must be given up as a result of making the choice. In the same sense, a society faces a similar set of choices imposed not by limited income but by a constraint on the quantity and quality of the factors of production available.

How to Produce?

Let's move on to the second fundamental economic question that every society must somehow answer: what is the most appropriate technology to employ? We could reword this question by asking: how should we produce what we choose to produce?

For example, there are a variety of ways to produce 10 kilometres of highway. At one extreme, a very labour-intensive method of production could be used involving rock crushed with hammers, roadbed carved from the landscape with shovels, and material moved in wheelbarrows. The capital equipment used in this method is very minimal. The labour used is enormous, and the time it will take is extensive. At the other extreme, a very capital-intensive method could be used involving large earth-moving and tarmac-laying machines, surveying equipment, and relatively little but highly skilled labour. In between these two extremes are a large variety of capital–labour mixes that could also produce the new highway.

The answer to the question of how best to build the highway involves, among other things, knowing the costs of the various resources that might be used. Remember that technology means the way the various factors of production are combined to obtain output. The most appropriate technology for a society to use (the best way to combine resources) depends, in general, on the opportunity costs of these resources. Thus, in the example above, the best way to build a highway depends on the opportunity costs of labour and of capital as well as the productivity of each factor.

For Whom?

We are now ready to move to the third fundamental economic question that every society must somehow answer: for whom? Here we ask: how should the total output of any society's economy be shared among its people? Should it involve an equal share for all, or should it, perhaps, be based on people's needs? Alternatively, should it be based on the contribution of each member of society? If so, how should this contribution be measured—in numbers of hours, or in skill level, or in some other way? Further, who should define what is an important skill and which ones are less important?

Wrapped up in all this is the question of the ownership of resources and whether it is better that certain resources (like land and capital) be owned by society as a whole or by private individuals. In short, the "for whom" question (as well as the "what" and "how" questions) cannot be adequately addressed unless we look at the society's attitude toward the private ownership of resources and the question of who has the power to make crucial decisions.

Thus, you can see that in addressing the "for whom" question, other questions about the fairness of income distribution, incentives, and the ownership of resources all come into play. John Stuart Mill pointed out, nearly 150 years ago, that once an economy's goods are produced and the initial market distribution of income has occurred, society can intervene in any fashion that it wants to redistribute such income; that is, there are no laws of distribution other than the ones that society wants to impose. Whether this observation by Mill gives enough consideration to the incentive for productive effort remains an open question to this day.

Thus, to a large extent the way in which each of the three fundamental questions is answered by a society depends on how that society organizes itself. We will now turn to a discussion about this topic.

ADDED DIMENSION

John Stuart Mill: Economist and Philosopher

John Stuart Mill (1806–73) is considered the last great economist of the classical school. His *Principles of Political Economy*, first published in England in 1848, was the leading textbook in economics for 40 years. Raised by a strict disciplinarian father (James), John Stuart began to learn Greek at the age of three, authored a history of Roman government by eleven, and studied calculus at twelve, but didn't take up economics until age thirteen. Not surprisingly, this unusual childhood later led to mental crisis. Mill credited his decision to put his analytical pursuits on hold and take up an appreciation of poetry as the primary reason for his recovery. He was a true humanitarian who held a great faith in human progress, had a love of liberty, and was an advocate of extended rights for women.

Types of Economies

Throughout history, humankind has coordinated its economies by using some blend of the four Cs: cooperation, custom, command, or competition. Thousands of years ago, members of small groups of hunter-gatherers undoubtedly relied on cooperation with each other in order to survive the dual threats of starvation and predators. They decided cooperatively what work needed to be done, how it was to be done, and who was to obtain what share of the produce. On the other hand, European feudal society in the Middle Ages was dominated by custom, which dictated who performed which task—sons followed the trade of their fathers—and implied that traditional technology was superior to new ways of doing things. Also, serfs were required, by tradition, to share a portion of their produce with the feudal lord.

One need only think of an ancient civilization, such as Egypt 4000 years ago, as an example of how society answered the three fundamental questions by using the command method. There, most of the important economic questions were answered by the orders of those in power, such as the pharaohs and priests. In this century, command has been the prevailing coordinating mechanism in fascist and communist regimes in which a central committee (or presidium) makes most of the fundamental economic decisions.

Market societies, such as we see in most of the industrial countries around the globe today, did not begin to emerge until approximately 200 years ago. Here we find a large role played by competition, while the roles of custom and cooperation have faded. Yet, in small ways we can still witness the role of custom. For example, there are probably as many people in a typical movie theatre audience who use the restrooms as there are people who eat popcorn. However, the theatre charges for the popcorn but not for the use of the restrooms. Why? Because it is customary. The command aspect certainly appears in market societies, in the form of government involvement in the economy. As an aside, it is interesting to note that tradition and command totally replace the use of competition within the family unit, even in the most market-oriented societies.

12-Hour Clock
(each hour = 1000 years)

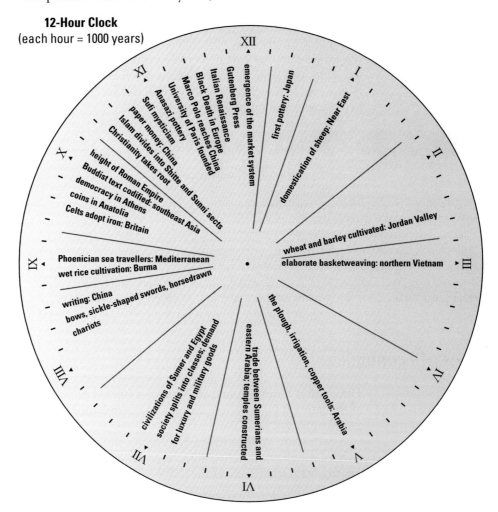

To a large extent the essence of each of these different blends of the four Cs is found in the patterns of ownership and control of the factors of production. It is important to note that ownership of the factors doesn't always mean control over them. Land and capital were communally owned by the people in the former Soviet Union, but control of them was in the hands of a very few powerful Communist Party officials. Conversely, what we call capitalism today stresses the private ownership of the factors of production, but society's laws often place extensive controls on how they can and cannot be used.

wages: the payment made and the income received for the use of labour.

interest: the payment made and the income received for the use of capital.

rent: the payment made and the income received for the use of land.

profit: the income received from the activity of enterprise.

Most modern economies today are referred to as mixed economies because they comprise elements of the two dominant types: command and competition. In such an economy, incomes are earned through the payment of **wages, interest, rent,** and **profits** to the private owners of the factors of production: labour, capital, land, and enterprise. The higher the market value of the factor of production owned by a person, the more income that individual receives. Thus the "for whom" question is answered by the distribution of ownership of the factors of production that the market considers valuable. The "what" question in a modern market economy depends on the way that people choose to spend their income, since it is this spending that makes up the demand for the various goods and services. The "how" question is answered by firms finding the most appropriate technology to produce their output, knowing that success brings profits and that if they fail to do this they will not long be in business.

The Methodology and Language of Economics

Let's now turn to a brief discussion on the methodology used in economics. Earlier, we discussed the *concept* of opportunity cost. We used the word concept, but we could have conveyed the same meaning with the word *idea*. Concepts (or ideas) become the building blocks for the more general terms *theory* or *principle*. In building a theory, a concept is first identified as a hypothesis. Consider, for example, the hypothesis that people will buy more of a good if its price falls. Along with this simple hypothesis, we need to define the terms involved, such as, what is the price we are considering—wholesale? retail? an average over time? a sale price? Also, we need to ask under what conditions this hypothesis is true: for every type of product or just certain types? any time of the year or only certain times? After the terms have been clearly defined and conditions (assumptions) spelled out, the hypothesis is ready to be tested with empirical data gathered by observing actual events. On the basis of this test of data, the theory is accepted, revised, or rejected.

In addition to terms like concept, principle, and theory, you will also find that the discipline of economics has developed its own very specialized language. When we think about this, it really shouldn't be a surprise since every specialty, from sailing to the arts, from pottery to chemistry, has its own language. Such specialized language is, in fact, quite necessary because the development and use of concepts, as well as the use of logic to draw conclusions, often requires language that is either not in general use or requires a more precise definition than is generally understood. As you proceed with your study of economics, the point that you need to first learn the language of economics cannot be overemphasized. Only then will you begin to understand the concepts of economics.

There may be times when the beginning student will think that economics is very abstract and theoretical. If this happens, try to remember that the purpose of theory is analogous to the purpose of a map—to compress a mass of detail down into a highly summarized, but manageable, form. Just as a map on the scale of 1:1 is useless, so too would be a theory that tries to explain every possible reality all at once. Building good theories involves identifying basic underlying relationships between crucial variables and reaching conclusions that point us in the right direction to answer important questions.

To better accomplish this task, economists often build models. Let's look at what we mean by this. Imagine walking into the sales office of a condominium project under construction. Part of the sales presentation is a model of the entire project sitting on a table. You would have no trouble recognizing the model as a representation of what the building will eventually look like. This is true despite the fact that many of the details, such as the elevators, furniture, and appliances, are absent from the model.

Similarly, an economic model uses a scaled-down version of that big picture. However, economists cannot construct a physical representation as is used in the example of the building. Instead, the level of abstraction is even greater, in that the model is all on paper and in the form of concepts, numbers, equations, and graphs. The economist's model also ignores the details that really aren't that important. Constructing such models helps us to understand important relationships between variables.

A Simple Model: The Circular Flow

We can take even the little bit that we have learned so far and build a very simple model of the whole economy. We use **Figure 1.1** to help us.

FIGURE 1.1 The Circular Flow

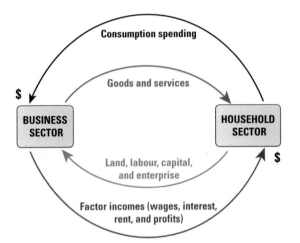

Figure 1.1 identifies two sectors in the economy: the business sector and the household sector. In a market economy like Canada the four factors of production, which we spoke of earlier, are owned by individuals who make up the household sector. These factors flow to the business sector, as represented by the red line identifying land, labour, capital, and enterprise. The business sector uses these factors to produce goods and services, which then flow to the household sector, as shown in green. Now of course, the business sector must pay for the use of the factors of production. These factor payments, in the form of wages, interest, rents, and profits, shown in blue, represent expenditures to the firms, but become income to individuals in the household sector.

And what do people do with their income? They pay for the goods and services that they have received from the business sector. This payment, shown in black, is called consumption spending. Again, expenditures to households become income for businesses. These income expenditures are made with money and are thus referred to as financial flows.

Needless to say, our economy is far more complex than this. However, even a very simple model like this can help us to better understand how it works. Chapter 3 will take this circular flow model several steps further. What we need to always remember is that every model is an abstraction from reality. It doesn't intend to capture all possible relationships or details. In fact, it is often true that the more realistic we try to make our models, the more complex and thus the more confusing and distracting they become.

Agreements and Disagreements in Economics

At some point in the past, you may have heard jokes about economists, such as, "What do you get when you put five economists in the same room? Six opinions." Economists do often disagree with each other. This is a natural by-product of a discipline that is part science and part art. An important reason for such disagreement is that economists, just like all other people, have a particular set of values that they have accumulated over a lifetime, and these values vary, sometimes radically, from person to person. Nonetheless, if each of us uses the scientific method in developing our arguments, then lively debate can be fruitful, despite the different value systems with which we started.

It is also true, however, that there is wide agreement among economists on many questions, and this is remarkable given that economists ask a wide variety of questions, many of which do not get asked in other disciplines. For example, why do firms produce some goods internally and buy others in the market? Why do nations sometimes both export and import the same good? Why does society provide some things to children without charge (education) but not other things (food)?

To help sort out the kind of thing that economists will probably agree on, and what they may well disagree on, we need to make the distinction between what is called *a positive statement* and a *normative one*. Positive statements are assertions about the world that can be tested by using empirical data. Normative statements are based on a value system of beliefs and cannot be tested by using empirical data.

An example of a positive statement would be: The quantity purchased of any commodity will rise if its price falls. There will be little or no disagreement among economists on the importance of this kind of statement, and all will agree that such a statement can be verified with data. An example of a normative statement is: Canadians should save more. Such a statement is normative because it implies a definite value judgment and cannot be verified. This does not make such a statement unimportant, but it does mean that there is likely to be much more disagreement over it.

When building new theories and principles within the discipline, economists tend to work with positive ideas and statements and avoid the normative ones. None of this implies that economists should not enter the legitimate debate over controversial issues, such as the benefits and costs of free trade, but they should be careful and use only sound economic principles in their thinking and then clearly identify the points at which they leave the positive behind and enter the world of normative judgment, advocacy, and value systems.

SELF-TEST

1. Below is a list of resources. Indicate whether the resource in question is land (N), labour (L), capital (K), or enterprise (E):
   A) A bar-code scanner in a supermarket.
   B) Fresh drinking water.
   C) Copper deposits in a mine.
   D) The work of a systems analyst.
   E) The first application of CD-ROM technology to an economics textbook.
   F) An office building.

2. Identify each of the following statements as positive or normative:
   A) The government should reduce its budget deficit by cutting its spending.
   B) If the price of apples rises, then the quantity of oranges bought will increase.
   C) Monopolies tend to set prices higher than would exist in competitive markets.
   D) The economic cost of cleaning up the environment is too high.
   E) Higher-income Canadians should be willing to share their wealth with lower-income Canadians.

REVIEW

1. Identify the four factors of production.
2. Distinguish between macroeconomics and microeconomics.
3. What are the three fundamental questions in economics?
4. Define opportunity costs.
5. What are the four Cs that humankind has used to organize its communities?
6. Identify the four payments to the factors of production.
7. What are the building blocks of a theory?
8. Identify the physical and financial flows in the circular flow model.

Production Possibilities

Let's now construct another very simple model of a country's production possibilities. This allows us to return to a point that we made earlier, that every economy is faced with the constraint of limited resources. Imagine a society that produces only two products—cars and wheat. First, we want to figure out what this economy is capable of producing if it works at maximum potential. What exactly does this mean? Well, it certainly means that it is making use of all its resources: the labour force is fully employed, and all of its factories, machines, and farms are fully operational. But it means more than this. It also means that it is making use of the best technology of which it is aware and is working as efficiently as possible. So what, then, is it capable of producing? Since it can produce either cars or wheat, the output of each depends on how much of its resources it devotes to each. **Table 1.1** shows six possible output combinations, as well as the percentage of the economy's resources used in producing each combination. These possible outputs are labelled A through F.

TABLE 1.1 Production Possibilities for Cars and Tonnes of Wheat (millions of units)

	CARS		WHEAT	
Possible Outputs	% of Resources Used	Output	% of Resources Used	Output
A	0	0	100	20
B	20	10	80	19
C	40	18	60	17
D	60	24	40	13
E	80	28	20	8
F	100	30	0	0

The finite resources available to this economy allow it to produce up to a maximum of 20 tonnes of wheat per year, if 100 percent of its resources are used in wheat production. Notice that this can be done only if no cars are produced (combination A). At the other extreme, a maximum of 30 cars per year can be produced, if all available resources are used in car production. This, of course, would mean that no wheat is produced (combination F). There are many other possible combinations in between these two extremes, and Table 1.1 identifies four of these (B, C, D, and E).

production possibilities curve: a graphical representation of the various combinations of maximum output that can be produced.

We can take the data from Table 1.1 and use it to graph what is called a **production possibilities curve**, which is a visual representation of the various outputs that can be produced. What appears in **Figure 1.2** is simply another way of presenting the data in Table 1.1.

FIGURE 1.2 Production Possibilities Curve I

This society's limited resources allow for the production of a maximum of 20 tonnes of wheat if no cars are produced, as represented by point *a*. Moving down the curve from point *a*, we find other combinations of fewer tonnes of wheat and more cars until we reach point *f*, which is 30 cars and no wheat. Point *u* indicates either the underemployment of resources, inefficiency in resource use, or the use of inappropriate technology. Point *x* is unobtainable.

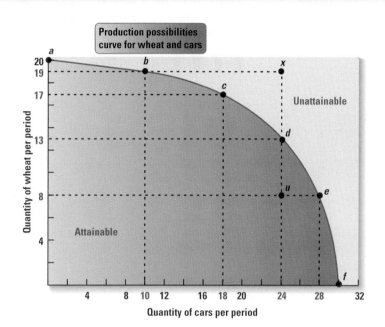

We should pause here and note that what is shown on the production possibilities graph are the various combinations of *outputs* that this economy is capable of producing. It does not show the *inputs* (the percentage of productive resources) that are necessary to produce those outputs.

Now, recall the three assumptions that lie behind our production possibilities curve:

> **full employment, the use of the best technology, and efficiency.**

If any one of these three assumptions does not hold, then the economy would be operating somewhere inside the production possibilities curve as illustrated by point *u*, 24 cars and 8 tonnes of wheat. On the other hand, point *x* represents an output of 24 cars and 19 tonnes of wheat, which, given this economy's current resources and technology, is unobtainable.

Next, let's address the actual shape of the curve. Why is it bowed out such that it is concave to the origin? We need to understand the implication of this particular shape. **Figure 1.3** will help.

EFFICIENCY MEANS GETTING THE MOST FOR THE LEAST

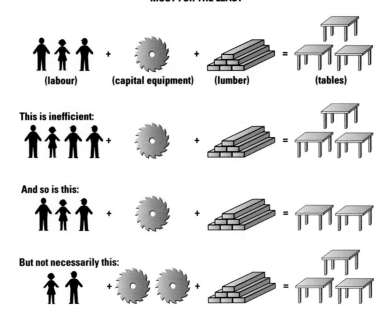

This is inefficient:

And so is this:

But not necessarily this:

Just a different technology.

FIGURE 1.3 Production Possibilities Curve II

At point *b*, 19 tonnes of wheat and 10 cars are being produced. If society decided that it wanted 8 more cars (point *c*), then 2 tonnes of wheat would have to be sacrificed. Thus, 1 more car would cost 0.25 tonnes of wheat. Moving from point *c* to *d* would increase car production by 6 (18 to 24) at a sacrifice of 4 tonnes of wheat (from 17 to 13). In this instance, one more car costs 0.67 tonnes of wheat. Moving from point *d* to *e* would increase car production by only 4 (from 24 to 28), while wheat production would drop by 5 (from 13 to 8). Thus, the cost of 1 more car rises to 1.25 tonnes of wheat.

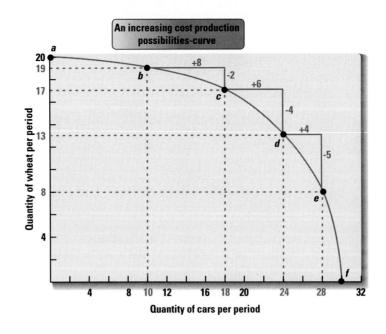

Assume that our hypothetical economy is currently producing 19 tonnes of wheat and 10 cars, as illustrated by point *b* on the production possibilities curve. Then let's assume that production decisions are made to reallocate 20 percent of the productive resources (labour, machines, materials) from wheat production to car production. This new output, *s* is illustrated by point *c*. Note that the opportunity cost of producing the additional 8 cars is *not* the additional 20 percent of resources that must be allocated to their production, *but* the decreased output of wheat that these resources could have produced. That is to say, the additional 8 cars could only be obtained by reducing the output of wheat from the original 19 tonnes to the new 17 tonnes. Thus, 8 more cars cost 2 tonnes of wheat. This can be restated as: 1 more car cost 0.25 tonnes of wheat (2 divided by 8). This seems clear enough, but we are not done.

Next, assume that society, still at point *c*, decides to produce even more cars, as illustrated by moving to point *db* (24 cars and 13 tonnes of wheat). This time an additional 20 percent of the resources produces only 6 more cars (18 to 24) at a cost of 4 units of wheat (17 to 13). This can be restated as: 0.67 tonnes of wheat for every additional car. This is considerably more than the previous cost of 0.25 units of wheat per car. Another shift of 20 percent of resources would move the economy from point *d* to e, with the result of an addition of only 4 more cars at a cost of 5 tonnes of wheat. Now, each additional car costs 1.25 (5/4) units of wheat.

law of increasing costs: as an economy's production level of any particular item increases, its *per unit* cost of production rises.

We have just identified what economists call the **law of increasing costs**. This law states that as the production of any single item increases, the per unit cost of producing additional units of that item will rise. Note that this law is developed in the context of on a whole economy and, as we will see in later chapters, need not apply to the situation of an individual firm.

Thus, you can see that as the total production of cars is increased, the rising per unit cost of cars gives the production possibilities curve its bowed-out shape.

But why does the per unit cost of cars increase—what is the reason behind the law of increasing costs? The answer is that not all resources are equally suitable for the production of different products. Our hypothetical society has a fixed amount of resources that are used to produce different combinations of both wheat and cars. However, some of these resources would be better suited to producing cars, whereas others would be better suited to producing wheat. An increase in the production of cars requires that some of the resources currently producing wheat would need to be reallocated to the production of cars. It is only reasonable to assume that those resources that are reallocated first are the ones that are relatively well suited to the production of cars, whereas while those resources not so suited to the production of cars would continue to produce wheat. After all this has taken place, if even *more* cars are to be produced, the only resources left to reallocate will be ones that are not very well suited for the production of cars. Therefore, a larger quantity of less well suited resources will have to be reallocated to obtain the desired increase in car production. This will increase the per unit cost of cars because a larger sacrifice of wheat production will be required.

It is not difficult to find examples of this law. Thirty years ago, when there were very few air pollution controls in effect, the costs of obtaining a 10 percent reduction in air pollution was relatively cheap. Today, when air pollution levels have been substantially reduced in many industries, an additional reduction of 10 percent would be much more costly because the most cost-effective reductions have already been made.

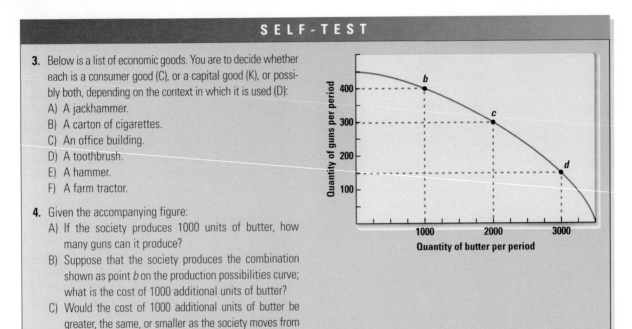

SELF-TEST

3. Below is a list of economic goods. You are to decide whether each is a consumer good (C), or a capital good (K), or possibly both, depending on the context in which it is used (D):
A) A jackhammer.
B) A carton of cigarettes.
C) An office building.
D) A toothbrush.
E) A hammer.
F) A farm tractor.

4. Given the accompanying figure:
A) If the society produces 1000 units of butter, how many guns can it produce?
B) Suppose that the society produces the combination shown as point *b* on the production possibilities curve; what is the cost of 1000 additional units of butter?
C) Would the cost of 1000 additional units of butter be greater, the same, or smaller as the society moves from point *c* to *d*, compared with a move from point *b* to *c*?

Consider another example. Assume that the infant mortality rate in a less-developed country is 55 out of every 1000 births. The reduction of this level by five (to 50 out of 1000), could been achieved relatively cheaply—say, with a smallpox vaccination campaign that would require only a small quantity of resources. However, once the rate dropped to, say, 25 out of 1000, then the resources required to gain an additional drop of five points, to 20 out of 1000, would probably be substantial and the costs involved would be much greater. This is the law of increasing costs.

Technological Change and Capital Accumulation

Earlier in the chapter we spoke of the important role that technology plays in economic performance. Technology is the application of human knowledge to lower the cost of producing goods and services.

To illustrate the effects of technological change, imagine a society that produces capital goods and services and consumer goods and services. **Consumer goods and services** are those products used by consumers to satisfy their wants and needs.

Let's start, in **Figure 1.4**, with the economy operating efficiently on the production possibilities curve PPI at point *a*. Now let's assume that a new technology becomes available that has application *only* in the consumer goods and services industry. This is represented by a shift outward in the curve, with the new production possibilities curve becoming PPII. There are three possible results. First, the same quantity of capital goods and services, but more consumer goods and services, can be produced as represented by *b*. Second, more of *both* goods can also be produced, as represented by point *c*. And third, this economy could now achieve an increase in the production of capital goods and services if the same number of consumer goods and services were produced (point *d*) *despite* the fact that this new technology could only be applied to the consumer goods and services industry. This emphasizes the important role of

consumer goods and services: products used by consumers to satisfy their wants and needs.

FIGURE 1.4 The Effect of Technological Change on the Production Possibilities Curve

Start at point *a*, which is a point of efficient production on PPI. An improvement in technology in the consumer goods and services industry shifts the production possibilities curve to PPII. This creates three possible results. First, the same quantity of capital goods and services, and more consumer goods and services, can now be produced as represented by point *b*. Alternatively, more of *both* consumer goods and services and capital goods and services can be produced, as represented by point *c*. Point *d* represents the third possible result, which is more capital goods and services and the same quantity of consumer goods and services, despite the fact that the technological change was in the consumer goods and services industry.

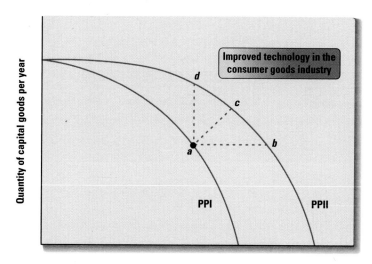

technological change. It widens the choices (there's that word again) available to society and is often seen in a positive light. Alas, technological change also carries costs, and this is another subject that will receive our attention later.

Now, look at Figure 1.4 and ask yourself the following question: Which of the three new possible combinations is preferable? If the choice had been between two consumer goods and services, such as wheat and cars, then we could not give a definitive answer to this question without knowing something about the country's wants and needs. But the choices illustrated in this figure are between capital goods and services and consumer goods and services, and choosing combination *b*—more capital goods and services—leads to significantly different effects than does choosing combination *d*.

This point is illustrated in **Figure 1.5**, in which we show two different economies. Atlantis places greater emphasis on the production of capital goods and services than does Mu. This can be seen by comparing point a_1 (40 units of capital goods and services) with point b_1 (20 units of capital goods and services). This emphasis on capital goods and services production also means a lower production of consumer goods and services (30 units in Atlantis, compared with 50 in Mu). The emphasis on capital goods and services production in Atlantis means that it will experience more economic growth in the future. This faster growth is illustrated by the production possibilities curve shifting to the right more in the case of Atlantis than in Mu. After the increase in production possibilities, Atlantis can continue producing 40 units of capital goods and services but now can produce 70 units of consumer goods and services (a_2). Mu, by contrast, can produce only 60 units of consumer goods and services while maintaining capital goods and services production at the original 20 units (a_2). All of this is a result of a different emphasis on the output choices by the two economies.

FIGURE 1.5 Different Growth Rates for Two Economies

We begin with Atlantis and Mu being the same size, as indicated by the same PPI curves. However, since Atlantis chooses to emphasize the production of capital goods and services (point a_1) while Mu emphasizes the production of consumer goods and services (point b_1), Atlantis will grow faster. The result of this faster growth is that, over time, PPII shifts out more in the case of Atlantis than it does in the case of Mu.

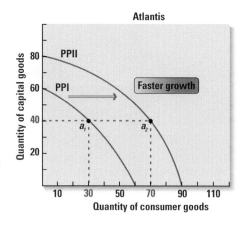

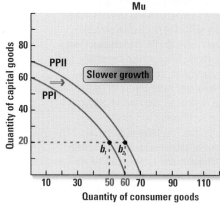

Source: Adapted from Statistics Canada, CANSIM Database, Series D768478 and D20556.

SELF-TEST

5. Assume that the economy of Finhorn faces the following production possibilities:

Quantities per Year

	A	B	C	D
Grain	50	40	25	0
Tools	0	4	8	12

A) Draw a production possibilities curve (PPI) with tools on the horizontal and grain on the vertical axis.

   Now assume new technology that can be used only in the tool industry is developed, which increases tool output by 50 percent.

B) Draw a new production possibilities (PPII) curve that reflects this new technology.

C) If Finhorn produced 12 units of tools per year, how many units of grain could be produced after introduction of the new technology?

A sage of some bygone age said that there is no such thing as a free lunch. We can now make some sense out of this idea. Producing more of anything—a lunch, for example, since it involves the use of scarce resources—necessarily means producing less of something else. The lunch might be provided free to the people who eat it, but from the point of view of the society as a whole, it took scarce resources to produce it and therefore is not free.

Macroeconomic Goals

The production possibilities model is very useful in highlighting a number of economic issues, including the costs of unemployment and the benefits of growth. But more importantly it graphically illustrates the important concepts of choice and cost. The dilemma facing policy makers in all governments is the same dilemma that faces all of us on a daily basis: how to satisfy conflicting goals. We know we cannot have everything in life, so we have to make choices. You have six hours available; you want to go for a walk, you want to visit friends, you want to study economics. What do you do? You could abandon two of your goals and wisely decide to study for the whole six hours. More probably, you might decide to divide up your time between the three activities. But do you allocate two hours to each activity or rank them in importance and spend more time on things you consider of greater importance? These are also the type of considerations that face policy makers who have to decide among a number of competing goals.

This raises the important question:

> **What would be a typical list of economic goals in a modern market economy like Canada?**

The first goal that we want to look at is the achievement of *full employment.* In order to evaluate how well the economy is able to achieve this goal, we have to define and quantify "full" employment. (Is it 0 percent unemployment or 2 percent of the labour force or 4 percent of the labour force...?) In addition, is the objective of society to ensure that everyone has a job, or only those who want a job? Furthermore, is it our goal to ensure that people get the jobs they want or simply that everyone gets *a* job, any job?

The second goal is that of stable prices. High rates of inflation can cause a great deal of damage to an economy and its people. But before we jump to the conclusion that a zero rate of inflation (no change in the overall price level) is desirable, remember that we are looking at things from a macroeconomic perspective. Thus, while higher prices may be looked at with alarm by buyers, they may be greatly welcomed by sellers. Perhaps some increase in the price level is desirable. But how much: 1, 3, or 5 percent per year? Furthermore, should the goal of the economy and its government be stable prices (zero inflation) or stable inflation, in which the price level increases by the same amount each year? As a result, there may well be considerable controversy over what is the "right" number.

In addition, goals are not set in a vacuum. What an economy is capable of achieving is affected by what it has achieved in the past. **Figure 1.6** presents an overview of Canada's unemployment–inflation performance over the past 60 years or so.

Some interesting features emerge from this graph. Looked at in broad terms, we can see that the 1930s was a period of high unemployment and low inflation (in fact, a period of deflation between 1929 and 1933). The decade of the 1930s was the period of the Great Depression. World War II brought about an economic recovery, which saw unemployment rates dipping below 5 percent for the first time in over a decade and inflation rates starting to creep up. The 1950s and 1960s were periods of low unemployment and generally low inflation rates, although prices did take a sharp turn upward during the Korean War in the early 1950s. The mid-1960s to the mid-1980s saw both unemployment and prices starting to rise, with an extra jump in unemployment rates during the recession of the early 1980s. Following this recession, unemployment along with inflation generally fell throughout the rest of the 1980s. The beginning of the 1990s saw Canada head into another recession, with unemployment rising to over 11 percent by 1992. These broad trends can also be seen in **Table 1.2**.

FIGURE 1.6 Unemployment and Inflation in Canada 1932–97

This figure shows time series data for Canada for the years 1932–97. The green line plots unemployment, with unemployment rates shown on the left axis. From a high of almost 20 percent in 1933, the unemployment rate hit a low of just over 1 percent in 1944. Thereafter it has gradually risen. The other line shows the annual inflation rates for the same period with the scale on the right axis. From a deflation rate of almost 10 percent in 1932, prices hit new highs following World War II and later continued upward throughout the 1960s and 1970s.

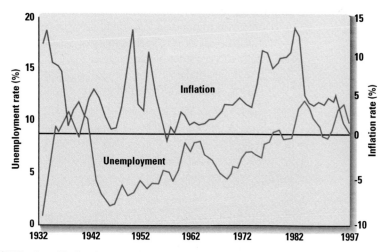

Source: Adapted from Statistics Canada, CANSIM Database, Matrices 3651 and 3685; and Series B3400.

TABLE 1.2 Unemployment and Inflation Rates: Averages per Decade

Years	Average Unemployment Rate (%)	Average Inflation Rate (%)
1926–39	10.0	−1.4
1940–49	3.1	+5.0
1950–59	4.2	+2.7
1960–69	5.1	+2.7
1970–79	6.7	+7.1
1980–89	9.3	+5.4
1990–97	10.0	+1.8

Source: Adapted from Statistics Canada, CANSIM Database, Series D768478 and D20556.

From the data in this table one might conclude that achieving zero inflation may be possible, but what about the goal of full employment? The lowest rate that Canada has ever achieved since 1926 was 1.2 percent, and this rate was achieved only in wartime conditions (in 1944). Since 1975, Canada's unemployment rate has never been below 6.9 percent. It would certainly appear that the goal of full employment is more elusive than that of zero inflation. This point is one we need to keep in mind as we proceed with the study of macroeconomics.

Before we take a look at other economic goals, one interesting aside needs to be mentioned. Many economists believe that attaining *both* low unemployment and low inflation rates concurrently is virtually impossible in a modern economy. They would argue that achieving one of these goals is possible only at the expense of the other. If this is true, Figure 1.6 should indicate that low levels of unemployment are associated with high levels of inflation and high unemployment with low inflation. A cursory glance at the two curves doesn't show an obvious relationship of this nature, although until the mid-1960s there were a number of periods when the two did seem to move in opposite directions. However, since 1967, if anything, the two curves seem to move together more or less in tandem. In other words, when inflation rates were high, so too were unemployment rates. All of this raises interesting questions that we will try to answer in later chapters.

Let us now turn our attention to the international aspects of the economy. As a whole, a nation cannot, in the long run, spend more abroad than it earns. The accounting of what it spends and earns abroad is called the *international balance of payments*. Maintaining a "viable" balance of payments in the long run then becomes our third goal. Again, most would agree that this goal is a legitimate one for an economy to try to achieve. However, it is often not enough for a country just to sell abroad as much as it buys. What types of things a country is selling can make a difference to a country's long-term welfare. For example, it is of some importance whether a country is selling manufactured and processed goods rather than selling off its raw materials, or whether it is selling goods and services rather than selling off its assets. Concerns about the balance of payments also involve the nation's *exchange rate*, and there can be, and often is, some controversy about what is the best exchange rate. Should the Canadian dollar, for instance, be high relative to the U.S. dollar? If this is the case, then our exports will be very expensive for foreigners while at the same time the effective price of imports will be very cheap for Canadians. Perhaps a low Canadian dollar is better? Then exports will be cheap but imports become more expensive. It is easy to see from this that there are both good and bad aspects of trying to achieve this particular economic goal. **Figure 1.7** illustrates the behaviour of the Canadian dollar and of the Canadian balance of trade (its total exports less its total imports of goods and services) in recent years.

FIGURE 1.7 Canada's Balance of Trade and the Value of the Canadian Dollar, 1972–97

The left scale shows an index of the value of the Canadian dollar in terms of the U.S. dollar. Until 1976, the Canadian dollar was at or above par with the U.S. dollar but declined until the mid-1980s. It continued to rise until 1991. Thereafter it steadily declined. The right scale shows the value of Canada's balance of trade, which apart from 1975 has been "favourable." This means that Canada consistently sells more goods and services abroad than it buys.

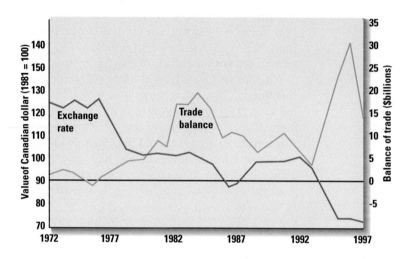

Source: Adapted from Statistics Canada, CANSIM Database, series D20463.

There is some controversy involved in any discussion of the goals of low unemployment, stable prices, and a viable balance of payments. Turning to the next four goals, we see that the controversy heats up considerably.

The next goal is that of achieving *economic growth*. Most people probably do accept growth, in some sense, as being desirable, but gone are the days when everyone blindly assumed that the more economic growth, the better. It does, after all, depend on what is growing! It is not enough these days (if it ever was) to assume that a higher output of goods and services means greater economic welfare. The fact that economic growth carries many forms of costs (for example, increased congestion, pollution, and other forms of environmental damage) has led to the increased questioning of growth as a legitimate goal. Nevertheless, let us look at Canada's economic growth over the last 60 years or so. Figure 1.8 shows the annual growth of real GDP. (We will look at this concept of real GDP in some detail in Chapter 3. For now think of it simply as the total volume of goods and services produced in a year.)

A few things stand out in Figure 1.8. The first is that although low (and negative) growth rates are correlated with high rates of unemployment, it is not necessarily a close correlation. In the early years of the Great Depression, when the Canadian economy was suffering unprecedented levels of high unemployment, the growth rate was in fact negative, as it was at the height of the recession in 1982. However, note that the growth rates from 1934 till the end of that decade were very high by modern standards, despite the fact that unemployment remained above 10 percent for the whole of the decade. In general terms, however, it is true to say that an economic boom means both a high growth rate and low unemployment, and a *recession* will almost always imply a period of high unemployment. (In fact, Statistics Canada defines the term "recession" as a fall in real GDP over two consecutive quarters.)

FIGURE 1.8 Canada's Growth Rate, 1932–97

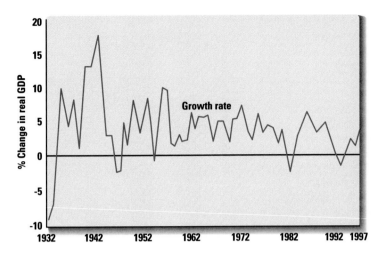

Canada's annual percentage growth rate in GDP for the years 1932–97.

Source: Adapted from Statistic Canada, CANSIM Database, Series D469409.

The other feature that Figure 1.8 demonstrates is that although the Canadian economy has grown almost every year since World War II (so much so that the real GDP in 1990 was over eight times as big as in 1946), the growth has been far from steady. Even so, it has been impressively smooth compared with the years prior to 1946. Many economists would argue that it is not just growth, but *stable* economic growth, that is important.

Next we turn to the achievement of an *equitable,* or *fair, distribution of income* as a possible goal. Most Canadians would probably agree that this is a valid goal in some limited sense—that, for example, no one in Canada should ever starve to death. On the other hand, to advocate that every Canadian should be provided with a certain minimum level of guaranteed income will bring forth considerable argument. So, in the end, most would agree that an equitable distribution of income is a legitimate goal if "equitable" is defined in the "right" way.

Our last two goals probably wouldn't have even made the list 20 years ago. The first of these involves the *national debt.* The definition of terms can be a problem in trying to nail down any of the above discussed goals, really come to the surface here. Most people agree that the national debt should not get too big. But just what is "too big"? And how far should the debt be reduced, if at all? In fact, is it really a problem anyway? Figure 1.9 charts the history of the national debt back to 1932. Since the curve would literally go off the graph if the figures were in actual dollars, and because it makes a more valid comparison, the graph shows the growth of the national debt in constant 1986 dollars.

FIGURE 1.9 Canadian National Debt and the Debt–GDP Ratio, 1932–97

The actual debt of the federal government (shown here in constant 1986 dollars) shows a slow rise between the 1930s and the early 1970s. Since then it has increased far faster. As a percentage of GDP, the trend shows a similar increase, with two prominent peaks in the 1930s and in World War II. Thereafter, there was a steady decline for 30 years, until it again started to rise in the mid-1970s.

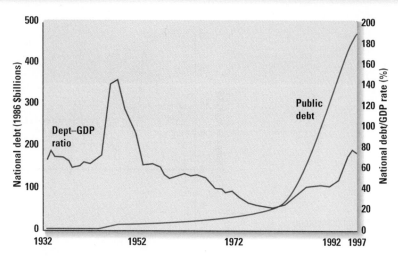

Source: Adapted from Statistic Canada, CANSIM Database, Series C23144.

The issue of the size of the debt has been a hot topic for much of the 1990s. We will discuss this issue at some length in Chapter 12.

Finally, we have the goal of a *livable environment*. Again, there is very little controversy about the need to be concerned about our environment, but just how to define specific objectives and limitations can generate a great deal of controversy. Most people see a conflict between the goals of economic growth and a clean environment. Protecting the environment may well cost jobs and production; at the same time, economic growth can result in the depletion of natural resources and the despoilation of the environment.

This book, and indeed the study of macroeconomics, is concerned with each of these goals and with the various different policies that have been advocated over the years (indeed over the centuries) in pursuit of them. However it is almost impossible to study an economy and specific goals in a piecemeal fashion. To fully understand the implications of fighting inflation, for example, we really do need to develop a model of the whole economy, because the price level and many other variables are interrelated.

Something you need to be aware of early in your study of macroeconomics is that although most economists are in agreement on the desirability of the goals we have looked at, they do disagree on which of these goals are more important and on what are the costs of achieving the goals. The root cause of these disagreements is the differing beliefs among economists as to exactly how a modern economy works. The often acrimonious debates have been interesting not only from a historical point of view but because they tend to bring critical aspects of economic theory into sharp relief. Let us take a look at some of the more important and interesting of these controversies by briefly comparing different "schools of thought."

Schools of Thought

Neoclassicism versus Keynesianism

Neoclassical economists were those economists writing in the early part of this century who felt themselves to be the intellectual heirs of the classical tradition laid down by writers like Adam Smith, David Ricardo, and Thomas Malthus one hundred years earlier. Like these earlier economists, the neoclassical economists were generally advocates of the philosophy of *laissez-faire* (or "leave it alone") and believed that economies worked best with a minimum of government interference. Some of these writers distrusted governments in general and were afraid that a government may not necessarily work in the interests of those it should help. Furthermore, they believed that government action is definitely unnecessary because markets work best when left alone. They felt that as long as governments restrict their involvement to a minimum, the market will ensure that the economy will be fully employed. In other words, they believed that a prolonged or major recession or depression is impossible.

Keynesians (adherents to the views of the British economist John Maynard Keynes, who published *The General Theory* in 1936) were diametrically opposed to the neoclassicists. As prima facie evidence that neoclassical theory was invalid, Keynes pointed to the mid-1930s, when the world was plunged into the deepest recession in history. Keynes himself did far more than just suggest that people should open their eyes to the misery surrounding them; he built a whole new model of the macroeconomy, which was vastly different from the neoclassical model. In his model, Keynes demonstrated that not only is full employment not a certainty, it is probably not even attainable—at least not without help from the government. In fact it is from Keynes that the idea came that governments are responsible for managing the economy and that economic failure also signifies government failure.

Keynesianism versus Monetarism

In the late 1950s and the 1960s a school of thought known as "monetarism," led by Milton Friedman at the University of Chicago, came into prominence. Monetarists felt that Keynesian theory had misled policy makers into believing that all (or at least many) of a country's economic woes could be cured by judicious mixtures of taxation and government spending (what is called "fiscal policy"). Monetarists believed that not only was such action misdirected but also that it was likely to be fairly ineffective. In addition, they felt that Keynesian theory tended to underestimate the importance of the money supply in an economy. Research led monetarists to conclude that not only is money a very powerful engine of change, but it can be so powerful that it is best not to leave it in the hands of policy makers. Instead, the supply of money should only change as a result of a change in overall economic activity and then only by a fixed and preannounced amount.

Demand-Siders versus Supply-Siders

In the late 1970s, just after the dust had settled on the monetarist–Keynesian debate, a group of economists started to question both schools of thought. As we mentioned, monetarists felt that changes in the money supply, that is, monetary policy, had a great effect on the overall spending levels in the economy, whereas fiscal policy did not. Keynesians, on the other hand, believed the reverse was true—fiscal policy greatly changed the level of spending, whereas monetary policy did not. This debate centred on spending and thus on *demand*. Not a word was said about supply. A new group, supply-siders, believed this to be a grievous error. They asked: how on earth can you make intelligent assumptions about how the economy operates without looking at the role played by producers, that is, *supply*?

Supply-siders were convinced that the only way to bring about lasting change in an economy was to affect the conditions of supply, in particular to improve the levels of productivity and capital investment. One of their more controversial themes was the belief that a reduction in the tax rates of businesses and individuals would greatly stimulate the economy. Keynesians also believed that a decrease in tax rates would stimulate the economy, but such stimulation comes through encouraging more spending. Supply-siders believed that tax cuts would have an even greater impact on levels of productivity because they would encourage people to work, save, and invest more.

Supply-siders also felt that the current choice of policy tools was far too limited. These tools were often far too imprecise to accomplish the often complex economic tasks required of governments in a modern economy. They felt that more emphasis should be put on such things as more generous depletion allowances, manpower training, more assistance given to disadvantaged groups in society, work-sharing schemes, and so on. Besides all this, supply-siders were very much in favour of downsizing government, particularly the bureaucracy of government, and reducing the amounts paid out in income support programs.

In addition, supply-siders were also inclined to the belief that in the long run the economy is self-regulating, as long as markets are reasonably competitive. Competition, incentives, and productivity thus became the catchwords of supply-siders.

So Who Is Right?

Many students, new to economics, become disappointed with the subject when they discover that economists often seem to disagree more than they agree on some very fundamental aspects of theory. These students would feel far more comfortable if there were an accepted body of doctrine in economics that provided definitive answers to economic problems. (After all, there are right and wrong answers on economics exams!) But the truth is that economists are forever and continually revising their ideas, and they continue to make mistakes. Besides, it is this aspect of the discipline that makes economics such an endlessly fascinating subject. The truth seldom turns out to be totally black or white. In terms of the major disagreements of this century, it's true to say that Keynesians and neoclassicists have learned from each other. Perhaps governments do need to be involved in trying to cure some of an economy's major ills. But perhaps, too, they may not be capable of curing everything and the market should be left to find its own solutions. Keynesians also began to recognize that perhaps money has a far more important role to play than they first believed, and monetarists likewise started to realize that fiscal policy can and does have an important role to play. Finally, trying to decide which is the more important ingredient in economics—demand or supply—is akin, as the famous economist Alfred Marshall suggested, to asking whether it is the top or the bottom blade of the scissors that actually does the cutting.

We have ranged over a wide number of issues in this chapter and have introduced a number of terms, some of which you may not be familiar with. It is not vital for you to understand everything all at once, and for that reason we have avoided giving too many precise definitions at this stage. The topics discussed here, after all, are the subject matter of the whole book, and we will be returning to them throughout. It is hoped, however, that you at least taste the flavour of the various issues and debates.

Since we have spent a good deal of time talking about Canada's economic performance in this chapter, it might be interesting to see how we are faring compared with other countries. Table 1.3 shows Canada's position relative to other countries in terms of a number of economic indicators. For each category, the top five countries are shown, along with five other nations, including Canada.

TABLE 1.3 Economic Performance of Selected Countries

GNP per Capita ($US) (128 countries)		GDP per Capita (equal purchasing power) (128 countries)		GNP per Capita Growth Rate (%) (128 countries)		Inflation Rate (%) (105 countries)		Income Received by Poorest 20% (92 countries)		Central Government Debt (% of GNP) (53 countries)		Unemployment Rate (%) (36 countries)	
1996		1996		1995–96		1990–96		1988–96		1995		1996	
1. Switzerland	$44 350	1. USA	28 020	1. Malawi	13.0	1. Japan	1.1	1. Slovak Rep.	11.9	1. Thailand	4.6	1. S. Korea	2.0
2. Japan	40 940	2. Singapore	26 910	2. Morocco	10.4	2. Panama	1.1	2. Belarus	11.1	2. South Korea	9.0	2. Singapore	3.0
3. Norway	34 510	3. Switzerland	26 340	3. China	8.9	3. Canada	1.8	3. Czech Rep.	10.5	3. Botswana	11.5	3. Czech Rep.	3.1
4. Denmark	32 100	4. Hong Kong	24 260	4. Ireland	8.7	4. Finland	1.8	4. Austria	10.4	4. Paraguay	12.8	4. Japan	3.4
5. Singapore	30 550	5. Japan	23 420	5. Gautemala	8.6	5. Saudi Arabia	1.8	5. Finland	10.0	5. Czech Rep.	15.5	5. Austria	4.1
6. Germany	28 870	10.France	21 510	48. Japan	3.6	17. USA	3.0	6. Norway	10.0	18. Germany	37.3	10. USA	5.4
8. USA	28 020	11.Canada	21 380	80. USA	1.4	18. UK	3.0	21. Germany	9.0	23. Japan	44.7	21. Germany	9.0
10. France	26 270	12.Germany	21 110	87. Germany	0.9	20. Germany	3.3	33. Canada	7.8	25. USA	51.3	23. Canada	9.7
17. UK	19 600	15.S. Korea	13 080	94. Canada	0.5	85. Iran	29.3	66. USA	4.8	41. Canada	74.6	26. Italy	12.0
18. Canada.	19 020	101. India	1580	121. Russia	-0.5	104. Brazil	643.9	84. Colombia	3.1	51. Belgium	127.9	36. Spain	21.9

Source: The World Bank, World Development Indicators 1998.

REVIEW

1. When was the last time Canada suffered double-digit inflation? When did it last experience deflation?
2. Since 1926, when did Canada experience major recessions and major booms?
3. What effect does the depreciation of the Canadian dollar have on our exports and imports?
4. List seven economic goals that might be considered when policy is being formulated.
5. What is meant by economic growth?
6. What does the term "laissez-faire" mean?
7. Contrast the attitudes of the neoclassical and the Keynesian schools of thought toward the role of government.
8. How did the monetarists change the focus of policy making?
9. How would supply-siders bring about lasting change in an economy?

Chapter Highlights

This chapter gives an overview of the discipline of economics and an introduction to the many facets of macroeconomics. After defining economics, we make the distinction between micro- and macoeconomics and look at the three fundamental questions of economics—what, how, and for whom—that every economy must somehow answer. Next is a discussion of cooperation, custom, command and competition as the four elements that blend together to coordinate our economic affairs. The chapter then discusses the methodology and the language of economics and introduces a simple representation of an economy in the form of a circular flow diagram.

The development of the production possibilities curve brings out the law of increasing costs and illustrates the cost of unemployment and the concept of economic growth.

The chapter then looks at how the Canadian economy has performed over the last half-century or so. The focus is on how well or how badly it has performed in terms of achieving seven economic goals. These goals are: full employment; stable prices (control of inflation); a viable balance of payments; economic growth; an equitable distribution of income; reduction or elimination of the national debt; and maintaining a livable environment.

The final section of the chapter looks at different schools of thought and briefly explains the points of debate.

New Glossary Terms

capital   2
consumer goods and services and services   16
enterprise   2
factors of production   2
interest   9
labour   2
land 2
law of increasing costs   15
macroeconomics   3
microeconomics   3
opportunity cost   5
production possibilities curve   13
profit   9
rent   9
wages   9

STUDY GUIDE

Study Tips

1. Since this is the first chapter, you should not be overly concerned if it seemed to contain so much new ter-minology that it feels overwhelming. Mastering the principles of economics requires that you first learn the language of economics, and the best way to do this is to use it over and over. Let this workbook help you do this. Conscientiously work through all of the questions before proceeding to the next chapter.

2. Opportunity cost is one of the most important concepts in economics. As a start, make sure that you understand the basic idea that cost can be measured not just in dollars and cents but also in what has to be given up as a result of making a particular decision.

3. This chapter introduces you to the use of graphs with the production possibilities curve. If you have any difficulty understanding graphs, practice with the simple PP graphs until you become more comfortable using them, because graphs are an integral part of economics.

4. For many of you, economics will be one of the more difficult courses that you will encounter in your undergraduate studies. Yet, it can be mastered, and doing so can be very rewarding. You will probably be much more successful if you work a little on economics several times a week, rather than have one long session a week. This way, you will gain mastery over the language more quickly through repetition and thereby gain confidence. You might consider buying a pack of 3" x 5" index cards and writing two or three definitions or simple ideas on each card. Carry several cards around with you so that you can glance at them several times a day. The authors found this technique helpful when (oh, so many years ago) they started to learn the discipline.

Key Problem

Table 1.4 contains the production possibilities data for capital goods and services and consumer goods and services in the economy of New Harmony.

TABLE 1.4	A	B	C	D	E
Capital goods	0	3	6	9	12
Consumer goods	30	27	21	12	0

a) Use the grid in **Figure 1.10** to draw the production possibilities curve for New Harmony, and label it PPI. Label each of the five output combinations with the letters *a* through *e*.

FIGURE 1.10

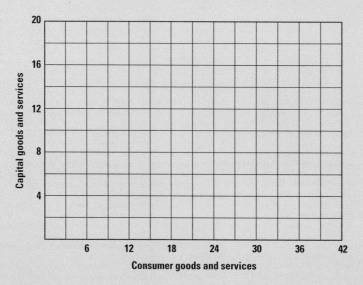

b) Assume that the people of New Harmony have decided to produce 12 units of capital goods and services. How many units of consumer goods and services could be produced?

Answer: _____ .

c) Assuming the economy is producing combination C, what would be the opportunity cost of 3 more units of capital goods and services?

Answer: _____ .

d) Assuming the economy is producing combination D, what would be the opportunity cost of 3 more units of capital goods and services?

Answer: _____ .

e) What law is illustrated by your answers to c) and d)?

Answer: _____ .

f) Fill in **Table 1.5** assuming that, 10 years later, the output potential of capital goods and services has increased 50 percent while the output potential for consumers goods has risen by 12 for each of combinations A through D.

TABLE 1.5

	V	W	X	Y	Z
Capital goods and services	____	____	____	____	____
Consumer goods and services	____	____	____	____	____

g) Using the data from this table, draw in PPII in Figure 1.10.

h) Given the new table in f), how many units of consumer goods and services could be produced if 9 units of capital goods and services were produced? Label it point *x* on Figure 1.10.

Answer: _____.

i) Given the new PPII on Figure 1.10, approximately how many units of capital goods and services could be produced if 12 units of consumer goods and services were produced? Label it point *y*.

Answer: _____.

j) Given PPII, is the combination of 13.5 units of capital goods and services and 24 units of consumer goods and services possible?

Answer: _____.

k) Given PPII, is the combination of 8 units of capital goods and services and 40 units of consumer goods and services possible?

Answer: _____.

l) Given PPII, what could you say about the economy of New Harmony if 8 units of capital goods and services and 30 units of consumer goods and services were being produced?

Answer: _____.

m) What are three possible reasons that would explain the shift from PPI to PPII?

Answer: _____.

More of the Same

Table 1.6 contains the production possibilities data for capital goods and services and consumer goods and services in the economy of Waldon.

TABLE 1.6

	A	B	C	D	E
Capital goods	0	2	4	6	8
Consumer goods	20	19	16	10	0

a) Draw a PPI for Waldon on Figure 1.11.

FIGURE 1.11

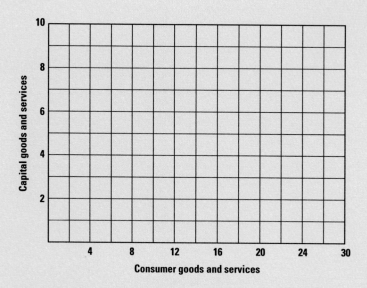

b) Assume that the people of Waldon have decided to produce 2 units of capital goods and services and 19 units of consumer goods and services, and indicate this combination with the letter *b* on the graph.

c) Assuming the economy is currently producing combination B, how many more units of consumer goods and services could be obtained if 2 less units of capital goods and services were produced?

d) Again starting from combination B, what would be the opportunity cost of 2 more units of capital goods and services?

e) What is the opportunity cost of the very first 2 units of capital goods and services? Of the last 2 units?

f) Make a table assuming that, 10 years later, the potential output of both capital and consumer goods and services increases by 25 percent.

g) Draw the data (from the table you constructed in f) above) on Figure 1.11 as PPII.

h) Given PPII, approximately how many units of consumer goods and services could be produced if 2 units of capital goods and services were produced?

i) Given PPII, approximately how many units of capital goods and services could be produce if 19 units of consumer goods and services were produced?

j) In this problem, the shift out of PPII was much less than it was for New Harmony in the Key Problem. Why would this be if we assume that technological change and any increase in the quantity of resources in the two economies were similar?

Translations

Assume that a piece of land can produce either 600 bushels of corn and no soybeans or 300 bushels of soybeans and no corn. You may further assume that this corn–beans ratio of 2:1 is constant.

On the grid in **Figure 1.12**, draw a production possibilities curve for this piece of land. Next, indicate with the letters *a* and *b* an increase in bean production of 50 bushels. Finally, illustrate with a triangle the cost of this additional 50 bushels of beans.

FIGURE 1.12

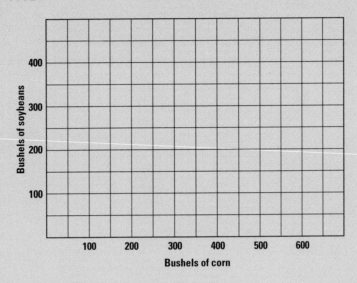

Are You Sure?

Indicate whether the following statements are true or false. If false, indicate why they are false.

1. An economy as a whole faces scarcity because of limited national income.

   T or **F**   If false: _____

   _____

2. The three fundamental questions in economics are what, how, and how many.

   T or **F**   If false: _____

   _____

3. Opportunity cost is the value of the next-best alternative that is given up as a result of making a particular choice.

   T or **F**   If false: _____

   _____

4. There are only three Cs that humankind has used to coordinate its economies: cooperation, custom, and competition.

   T or **F**   If false: _____

   _____

5. Wages, interest, rent, and profits are the four factors of production.

   T or **F**   If false: _____

   _____

6. A production possibility curve is a graphical representation of the various combinations of output that are wanted.

   T or **F**   If false: _____

   _____

7. Macroeconomics focuses on the outcomes of decisions by people and firms, whereas microeconomics is a study of how the major components of an economy interact.

   T or F   If false: _____

   _____

8. Technological improvement can be illustrated graphically by a rightward shift in the production possibilities curve.

   T or F   If false: _____

   _____

9. Tax policy, tariff policy, budget policy, monetary policy, and exchange rate policy are all examples of economic policies.

   T or F   If false: _____

   _____

10. Adam Smith, David Ricardo, Thomas Malthus, and John Maynard Keynes are the giants of the classical tradition.

    T or F   If false: _____

    _____

Choose the Best

11. The building blocks of a theory are:
    a) Concepts and mathematics.
    b) Concepts and ideas.

12. An economist's model comes in the form of:
    a) A physical representation of reality.
    b) Concepts, numbers, and equations.

13. A decision to produce more capital goods and services and fewer consumer goods and services now means:
    a) Less consumption of consumer goods and services now and in the future.
    b) Less consumption of consumer goods and services now, but more consumption in the future.

14. "Factors of production" is a term that can be used interchangeably with:
    a) Models.
    b) Consumer goods and services.
    c) Either productive resources or inputs.

15. What is the distinction between a positive and a normative statement?
    a) Positive statements are assertions that can be tested with data, whereas normative statements are based on a value system of beliefs.

    b) Normative statements are assertions that can be tested with data, whereas positive statements are based on a value system of beliefs.

16. Which of the following two goals are often paired?
    a) Unemployment and inflation.
    b) Economic growth and an equitable distribution of income.
    c) A cleaner environment and a viable balance of payments.

17. Which of the following is a macroeconomic topic?
    a) Inflation rates.
    b) The supply and demand of computers.
    c) Monopolies.

18. Which of the following is most valid with respect to macroeconomic goals?
    a) They tend to complement each other.
    b) They are always in conflict with each other.
    c) Some are complementary and some are in conflict.
    d) They are accepted as valid by everyone in society.

19. A simple model of the circular flow includes reference to all but one of the following. Which is the exception?
    a) Spending on exports and imports.
    b) Both physical and financial flows.
    c) The factors of production.
    d) Both the business and the household sectors.

20. Which of the following is true concerning Canada's annual economic growth rate (in real GDP terms)?
    a) Throughout the twentieth century, it has never been negative.
    b) It has never exceeded 7 percent.
    c) It has been positive for about the same number of years that it has been negative.
    d) It has been positive for many more years than it has been negative.

21. Which of the following is correct about inflation in North America?
    a) It has not occurred in the twentieth century.
    b) It was high in the years following the end of World Wars I and II and the Korean War.
    c) It occurred in the early part of the Great Depression of the 1930s.
    d) It peaked in the 1960s.

Figure 1.13 shows Mendork's production possibility curve for the only two goods that it produces—quirks and quarks. Refer to this figure to answer questions 22–27.

22. Refer to Figure 1.13 to answer this question. If this society chooses to produce 10 quirks, what is the maximum quantity of quarks it can produce?
    a) 500 quarks.
    b) 800 quarks.
    c) No quarks.
    d) 600 quarks.

23. Refer to Figure 1.13 to answer this question. What is the opportunity cost of producing 200 quarks?
    a) 10 quirks.
    b) 18 quirks.
    c) 2 quirks.
    d) The answer cannot be determined from the information given.

24. Refer to Figure 1.13 to answer this question. If Mendork's production is currently that indicated by point *a*, what is the (approximate) cost of producing one more quirk)?
    a) 100 quarks.
    b) 50 quarks.
    c) 25 quarks.
    d) 200 quarks.
    e) 1 more quark.

25. Refer to Figure 1.13 to answer this question. What is the opportunity cost of one more quark as output changes from point *b* To *a*?
    a) 0.04 quirks.
    b) 4 quirks.
    c) 400 quirks.
    d) 1 quirk.
    e) 0.4 quirks.

Table 1.7 lists areas of economic concern.

FIGURE 1.13

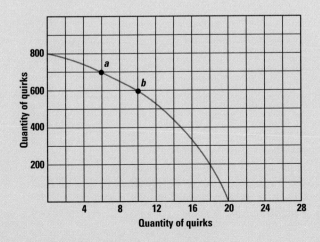

TABLE 1.7	
A	Unemployment in Nova Scotia
B	Interest rates
C	Wage levels in agriculture
D	Inflation rates
E	Government's farm-price supports
F	Monopoly practices in Canada

26. Refer to Table 1.7 to answer this question. Which of the table's concerns are macroeconomic questions?
    a) B, D, and F.
    b) A, B, and D.
    c) B, C, and D.
    d) B, C, and E.
    e) A, C, and D.

27. Neoclassical economists:
    a) Included Smith, Ricardo, and Malthus.
    b) Rejected the concept of laissez-faire.
    c) Were advocates of the concept of laissez-faire.
    d) Rejected the possibility of automatic full employment.
    e) Are the intellectual heirs to the Keynesian tradition.

28. Which of the following statements describes the law of increasing costs as it relates to the whole economy?
    a) As the quantity produced of any particular item decreases, its per unit cost of production rises.
    b) As the quantity produced of any particular item increases, its per unit cost of production rises.
    c) The prices of consumer goods and services always rise and never fall.

    d) If you wait to make a purchase, you will pay a higher price.
    e) The total cost of production rises as output goes up.

29. The monetarist school of thought:
    a) Stresses the importance of fiscal policy.
    b) Is the forerunner to Keynes.
    c) Is synonymous with supply-siders.
    d) Feels that Keynes overestimated the role of money.
    e) Feels that Keynes underestimated the role of money.

30. Which of the following is the best example of what supply-siders believe?
    a) The government should rely on fiscal policy over the long run.
    b) Economic policies should be directed at aggregate demand.
    c) Economic policy should emphasize the role of money.
    d) Economic policy should stress the role of productivity and capital investment.
    e) Economic policy should stress the role of exports and population growth.

Other Problems

31. Match the letters on the left with the numbers on the right. Place the correct letter in the blank.

a) capital good	1. cooperation, custom command, and competition
b) recession	2. the service of a brain surgeon
c) exchange rates	3. high unemployment
d) labour	4. a satellite
e) enterprise	5. land, labour, capital, and enterprise
f) factors of production	6. what, how, and for whom
g) ways of coordinating an economy	7. balance of payments
h) the fundamental questions in economics	8. the original marketing of a new power cell

32. Pacifica produces only two goods: bats and balls. Only labour is required in producing both goods, and the economy's labour force is fixed at 50 workers. Table 1.8 indicates the amounts of bats and balls that can be produced daily by fully utilizing the labour available.

TABLE 1.8

	A	B	C	D	E
Bats	400	350	250	150	0
Balls	0	150	250	275	300

a) On the grid in **Figure 1.14** draw the production possibilities curve for Pacifica, labelled PPI.

FIGURE 1.14

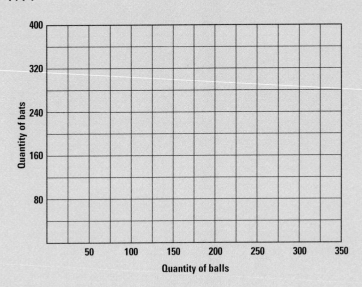

b) What is the opportunity cost of increasing the output of bats from 250 to 350 units a day?
Answer: _____.

c) What is the opportunity cost of increasing the output of balls from 150 to 250 units a day?
Answer: _____.

d) Suppose that a central planning office dictates an output of 250 bats and 300 balls per day. Is this output combination possible?
Answer: _____.

Table 1.9 shows the result of technological change in the ball industry.

TABLE 1.9

	A	B	C	D	E
Bats	400	350	250	150	0
Balls	0	200	325	375	400

e) Plot the new PP curve, labelled PPII. Is the central planning office's dictate in d) now possible?
Answer: _____.

33. Jennifer is planning how to spend a particularly rainy Sunday, and the choice is between watching video movies (each lasting 2 hours) or studying her economics textbook. She has 10 hours available to her. If she decides to study, she could read the following number of pages:

2 hours	80 pages
4 hours	130 pages
6 hours	160 pages
8 hours	175 pages
10 hours	180 pages

a) Given this information, draw Jennifer's production possibilities curve between movies watched and pages studied on the grid in **Figure 1.15**.

FIGURE 1.15

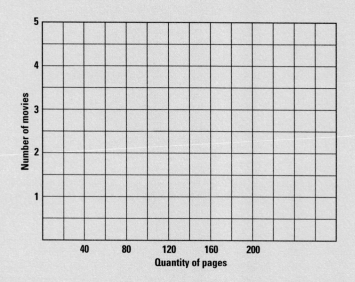

b) What happens to the opportunity cost of watching movies as more movies are watched?

c) Could Jennifer watch 3 movies and study 150 pages of her textbook?

d) If Jennifer has already watched 4 movies, what is the opportunity cost of watching the fifth movie?

UNANSWERED QUESTIONS

Short Essays

1. Identify the four factors of production, and give two examples of each.

2. What does the term "technology" mean, and how would you describe the effects of an increase in technology?

3. Why is economics sometimes described as the science of choice?

4. Comment on the following statement: "While society does have a choice about what types of goods to produce, it has no choice about the total quantity that can be produced."

5. Why do economists often disagree with one another?

6. Do you think studying for long periods is subject to increasing opportunity costs?

7. List and explain the three fundamental questions in economics.

8. Explain the distinction between macroeconomics and microeconomics.

9. What are the major differences between the neoclassical and the Keynesian schools of thought?

10. Explain the term "supply-siders."

11. List three possible economic goals. For each goal, identify a conflicting goal and a complementary goal, and explain your reasoning.

Analytical Questions

12. Following is a list of resources. Indicate whether each is land (N), labour (L), capital (K), or enterprise (E).
     a) Fishing grounds in the north Pacific.
     b) An irrigation ditch in Manitoba.
     c) The work done by Jim Plum, a labourer who helped to dig the irrigation ditch.
     d) The work done by Yves Gaton, a symphony conductor.
     e) A fish farm in Nova Scotia.
     f) A water reservoir.
     g) A golf course.
     h) The air we breathe.
     i) The efforts of the founder and primary innovator of a successful new software company.

13. Identify each of the following statements as positive or normative:
     a) The price of oil rose by over 10 percent last year.
     b) The price of oil will be lower this time next year.
     c) The government should try to reduce the price of oil.
     d) A decrease in taxes should help reduce the price of oil.
     e) The high price of oil in Canada is unacceptable.

14. Kant Skatte is a professional player in the National Hockey League. Because he loved the game so much, Kant dropped out of high school and worked very hard to develop his physical strength and overcome his limitations. Eventually he made it to the NHL. Estimate Kant's annual opportunity costs, in dollars, of continuing to play in the NHL.

15. Construct your own definition of economics.

16. Explain the analogy between the use of theory and the use of a map.

17. Can you think of three examples in which contemporary Canadian society uses the element of command to help coordinate production?

18. To what extent is the organization of the family based on the four Cs? Give examples of how each of the four Cs is used to assign household chores to its members. What blend of the four Cs do you think is preferable, and why?

19. Explain how a society based on custom and cooperation would answer the what, how, and for whom questions.

20. Comment on the following statement: "The 'for whom' question is the easiest of the three fundamental questions in economics to answer because it involves normative statements."

Numerical Questions

21. Ken has just graduated from secondary school. His uncle has offered him a full-time job, at $20 000 per year, at his home-improvement supply outlet. Ken, however, has his heart set on going to university for four years to get a degree in engineering, and, unfortunately, his uncle can't use him on a part-time basis. Tuition and books for the four years will cost Ken $14 000. What is Ken's opportunity cost of getting a degree?

22. Construct a simple circular flow model. Include two sectors, two physical flows, and two financial flows.

23. The graph in **Figure 1.16** is for the country of Leviathon.
    a) What could explain the shift from PPI to PPII?

FIGURE 1.16

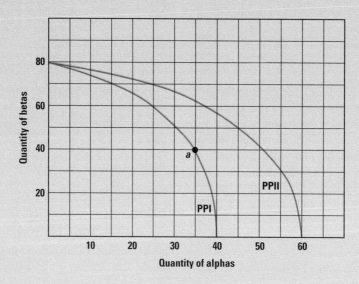

b) Given PPII, indicate with point *b*, the maximum quantity of alphas that can now be produced if 40 betas are produced.
c) Given PPII, indicate, with point *c*, the maximum quantity of betas that can now be produced if 35 alphas are produced.
d) Given point *a*, indicate, with point *d*, an increase in the production of both alphas and betas.

24. The data in **Table 1.10** below is for the small country of Xanadu. Assume that the economy is originally producing combination C and technological change occurs that enables it to produce 60 percent more capital goods.

TABLE 1.10

	A	B	C	D	E	F
Capital goods	0	25	40	50	55	58
Consumer goods	50	40	30	20	10	0

a) If the economy wants to continue with the same quantity of consumer goods and services, how many more capital goods can it now have as a result of the technological improvement?
b) If instead the economy wants to continue with the same quantity of capital goods, how many more consumer goods and services can it now have as a result of the technological improvement?
c) Suppose that the economy wishes to have an additional 30 percent more capital goods than before. How many more consumer goods and services can it have?

25. **Table 1.11** presents the production possibilities for tractors (in millions) and carrots (millions of tonnes) for the country of Risa.

TABLE 1.11

	A	B	C	D	E	F
Tractors	200	180	150	110	60	0
Carrots	0	100	180	240	290	330

a) Can this economy produce 130 tractors and 140 carrots?
b) Can this economy produce 165 tractors and 210 carrots?
c) What is the *total* cost of producing 110 tractors?
d) What is the *total* cost of producing 180 carrots?
e) If the economy is presently producing 60 tractors and 290 carrots, what is the *per unit* cost of producing an additional tractor?
f) In what sense (if any) could combination C be regarded as preferable to combination D?

26. Shangri-La produces only two goods: bats and balls. Each worker comes with a fixed quantity of material and capital, and the economy's labour force is fixed at 50 workers. **Table 1.12** indicates the amounts of bats and balls that can be produced daily with various quantities of labour.

TABLE 1.12

Number of Workers	Daily Production of Bats	Number of Workers	Daily Production of Balls
0	0	0	0
10	150	10	20
20	250	20	36
30	325	30	46
40	375	40	52
50	400	50	55

a) Draw a production possibilities curve for this economy, assuming that labour is fully employed.

b) What is the opportunity cost of increasing the output of bats from 325 to 375 units a day? What is the opportunity cost of increasing the output of balls from 46 to 52 units per day?

c) Suppose that a central planning office dictates an output of 250 bats and 55 balls per day. Is this output combination possible?

d) Now assume that new technology is introduced in the production of balls so that *each worker* can produce half a ball more per day. On the same graph, draw the new production possibilities curve. Is the central planning office's output goal in c) now possible?

 Web-Based Activities

1. Since the early 1990s, several economies of Eastern Europe have been embarking on a process of transforming state-controlled economies into market economies. The process is one in which the three fundamental questions of economics are being reapplied to these economies. Go to **http://www.worldbank.org/html/prddr/trans/WEB/trans.htm** and look at newsletters from 1990 and 1991. Identify the problems associated with transforming control economies into market economies. As you identify each problem you should classify it as a problem associated either with "What to Produce," "How to Produce," or "For whom to Produce."

2. Read the following speech, given by the Honourable Paul Martin, minister of finance, on October 14, 1998: **http://www.fin.gc.ca/update98/update98_e.pdf.** What are the macroeconomic goals currently being followed by the federal government? What do you think is the most important macroeconomic goal? Explain.

The Fundamentals of Demand and Supply

What's ahead... In this chapter we introduce the fundamental economic ideas of demand and supply. We explain the distinction between individual and market demand and look at the various reasons why consumers change their demand. Next, we examine things from the producers' point of view and explain what determines the amounts that they put on the market. We then explain how markets are able to reconcile the wishes of these two groups, by introducing the concept of equilibrium. Finally, we look at how the market price and the quantity traded adjust to various changes.

Have you ever wondered why the prices of some products, like computers or CD players, tend to fall over time while the prices of other products, such as cars or auto insurance, tend to rise? Or, perhaps, you wonder how the price of a house can fluctuate tens of thousands of dollars from year to year. Why does a bad orange harvest in Florida cause the price of apple juice made in Ontario to rise? And why do the sales of typewriters continue to fall, despite their lower prices? This chapter will give you insights into questions like these.

A ll students of economics, whether of micro- or macroeconomics, need to have a sound understanding of the basics of demand and supply, which are integral to any type of economic analysis. This chapter will examine briefly, but reasonably thoroughly, the way that demand and supply determine the price and quantity of products in a free market. We start with the idea of demand.

Demand

Individual Demand

demand: the quantities that consumers are willing and able to buy per period of time at various prices.

Economists use the term **demand** not in the sense of commanding or ordering but in the sense of wanting something. However, this want also involves the ability to buy. In other words, it refers to both the *desire and the ability* to purchase a good or service. This means that although I may well have a desire for a new top-of-the-line BMW, at current prices, I don't have the ability to buy one, and therefore my quantity demanded is zero.

Actually, demand means a bit more than this. It is a hypothetical construct that expresses this desire and ability to purchase, not at a single price, but over a range of feasible prices. Demand is also a flow concept, in that it measures quantities over a

demand schedule: a table showing the various quantities demanded per period of time at different prices.

period of time. This should be clear in **Table 2.1**, which shows the **demand schedule** for an enthusiastic beer drinker named Tomiko. What the demand schedule makes clear is the entire relationship between the price and the quantities that people wish to purchase. We need to, at this point, make clear an assumption that lies behind the presentation of all demand schedules:

> We are assuming that all other factors that might influence demand, such as income, do not change.

TABLE 2.1 Individual Demand

Number of Cases per Week	
Price per Case	**Quantity Demanded**
$12	6
13	5
14	4
15	3
16	2
17	1
18	0

Table 2.1 shows the amounts that Tomiko is willing and able to purchase at the various prices shown. Note that there is an *inverse* relationship between the price and quantity. This simply means that at higher prices Tomiko would not be either willing or able to buy as much as at lower prices. In other words, the higher the price, the lower the quantity demanded, and the lower the price, the higher the quantity

demanded. Another, though less obvious, statement of this law of demand is to say that in order to induce Tomiko to buy a higher quantity of beer, the price must be lower. This demand schedule is graphed in **Figure 2.1**.

FIGURE 2.1 Individual Demand Curve

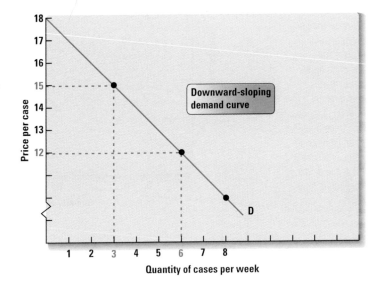

At a price of $12 per case, Tomiko is willing and able to buy 6 cases per week. At a higher price, $15 per case, the amount she is willing and able to buy falls to 3 cases. Thus, the higher the price, the lower the quantity demanded.

change in the quantity demanded: the change in the quantity that results from a price change. It results, graphically, in a movement along a demand curve.

In this figure, we see that a price of $15 results in a quantity demanded by Tomiko of 3 cases per week, while at a lower price of $12 she would be willing to buy 6 cases. The demand schedule therefore plots as a downward-sloping curve. An important point to note is that when we use the terms "demand" or "demand schedule" or "demand curve," we are referring to a whole array of different *prices and quantities.* You will remember that since price is part of what we call "demand," a change in the price cannot change the demand. Certainly it can affect the amounts we are willing to purchase, and this we refer to as **a change in the quantity demanded**. This is illustrated in **Figure 2.2**.

A change in the quantity that is the result of a price change is called a change in the quantity demanded. Graphically, as we move down the demand curve, the quantity demanded increases; as we move up the demand curve, the quantity demanded decreases.

How much beer would you demand at this price? Mohamed Al-Fayed, owner of London's Harrods Department store, drinks from a bottle of "Tutankhamun Ale," said to be the most expensive beer in the world at over $100 a bottle.

FIGURE 2.2 Changes in the Quantity Demanded

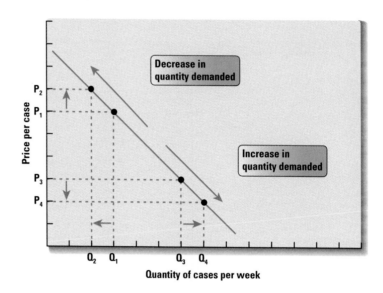

Whenever the price changes, there is a movement along the demand curve. An increase in the price from, say, P_1 to P_2, causes a decrease in the quantity demanded from Q_1 to Q_2. A decrease in the price from P_3 to P_4 leads to an increase in the quantity demanded from Q_3 to Q_4. Neither the demand nor the demand curve, however, changes.

Market Demand

market demand: the total demand for a product by all of its consumers.

Up to this point, we have focused on individual demand. Now we want to move to the **market demand** (or total demand). Conceptually, this is easy enough to derive. By summing every individual's demand for a product, we obtain the market demand. This is shown in **Table 2.2**.

TABLE 2.2 Deriving the Market Demand

	Number of Cases per Week				
Price per Case	Tomiko's Demand	Meridith's Demand	Abdi's Demand	Jan's Demand	Market Demand
$12	6	3	4	9	22
13	5	2	4	7	18
14	4	2	4	6	16
15	3	0	3	3	9
16	2	0	3	1	6
17	1	0	2	0	3
18	0	0	2	0	2

Let's say we know not only Tomiko's demand but also the demands of her three friends in a small four-person economy. The market demand then is the horizontal summation of individual demands, which simply means that to find the quantities demanded at $12 we add the quantities demanded by each individual, that is, 6 + 3 + 4 + 9 = 22. The same would be done for each price level. This particular market demand is graphed in **Figure 2.3**.

Note that, as with the individual demand curve, the market demand curve also slopes downward, indicating an inverse relationship between price and quantity demanded. This is because not only do people buy more as the price drops, but in addition more people buy. At a price of $18, only Abdi, in our example, would buy any beer. As the price drops to $16, not only would Abdi buy beer, but so too would Tomiko and Jan. The price would need to drop to $14 to induce Meridith to enter the market.

FIGURE 2.3 The Market Demand Curve

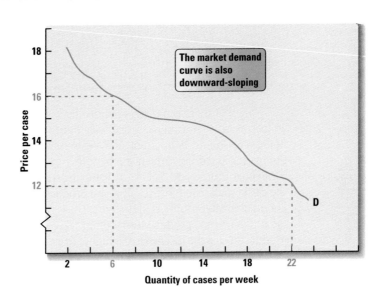

At a price of $12, the total or market quantity demanded equals 22 cases. As with individual demand, when the price increases to $16, quantity demanded will drop, in this case to 6. The reason for this inverse relationship between price and quantity demanded is because at a higher price, each individual generally buys less, and, in addition, there are fewer people who can afford to or are willing to buy any at all.

Finally, before we take a look at the supply side of things, note again that our demand schedule tells us only what people *might* buy; it tells us nothing about what they are actually buying, because to know this, we also need to know the actual price. And to find out what the actual price of beer is, we need to know .... yes, the supply.

Supply

Individual Supply

In many ways the formulation of supply is very similar to that of demand. Both measure hypothetical quantities at various prices, and both are flow concepts. However, we are now looking at things through the eyes of the producer rather than the consumer. We assume that the prime motive for the producer is to maximize profits. Certainly, as Adam Smith noted in *The Wealth of Nations*, few producers are in business to please consumers; nor of course, do consumers buy products to please producers. Both are motivated, instead, by self-interest.

supply: the quantities that producers are willing and able to sell per period of time at different prices.

supply schedule: a table showing the various quantities supplied per period of time at different prices.

The term **supply** refers to the quantities that suppliers are *willing and able* to make available to the market at various different prices. **Table 2.3** shows a hypothetical **supply schedule** for Bobby the brewer.

TABLE 2.3 Bobby's Supply

Number of Cases per Week	
Price per Case	Quantity Supplied
$12	2
13	3
14	4
15	5
16	6
17	7
18	8

Note that there is a *direct* relationship between the price and the quantity supplied, which means that a higher price will induce Bobby to produce more. Remember that Bobby's reason for being in business is to make as much profit as possible. Suppose that Bobby was asked how much she hypothetically would be prepared to supply if the beer could be sold at, say, $12 per case. Knowing what her costs are likely to be, she figures that she could make the most profit if she produced 2 cases. At a higher price, there is a likelihood of greater profits, and therefore she is willing to produce more. Also, as Bobby, and most other firms, produce more, often the cost per unit tends to rise, and therefore the producer needs the incentive of a higher price to increase production. For the time being, however, we can rely on the proposition that a higher price means higher profits and therefore will lead to higher quantities produced. This is illustrated in **Figure 2.4**.

Joining together the individual points from the supply schedule gives us the upward-sloping supply curve shown. Remember as with the term demand, *supply* does not refer to a single price and quantity, but to the whole array of hypothetical

FIGURE 2.4 Individual Supply Curve

At a low price of $12, the most profitable output for Bobby is 2 cases. If the price increased, she would be willing and able to produce more, since she would be able to make greater profits. At $18, for instance, the quantity she would produce increases to 8 cases.

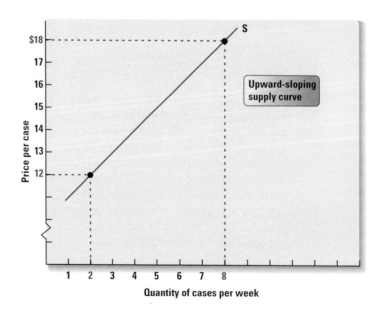

change in the quantity supplied: the change in the amounts that will be produced as a result of a price change. This is shown as a movement along a supply curve.

price and quantity combinations in the supply schedule and illustrated by the supply curve. Since price is only part of what we mean by the term supply, a change in the price level cannot change the supply. It does of course lead to a change in the quantity that a producer is willing and able to supply. Such a change in price is referred to as a **change in the quantity supplied**. These changes are shown in **Figure 2.5**.

An increase in the price will lead to:

> an *increase in the quantity supplied* and is illustrated as a movement up the supply curve.

Similarly, a decrease in the price will lead to:

> a *decrease in the quantity supplied*, which is illustrated as a movement down the supply curve.

FIGURE 2.5 Changes in the Quantity Supplied

If the price changes, it will lead to a movement along the supply curve. An increase in the price from, say, P_1 to P_2 will cause an increase in the quantity supplied from Q_1 to Q_2. A decrease in the price from P_3 to P_4 will lead to a decrease in the quantity supplied from Q_3 to Q_4. The supply curve itself, however, does not change.

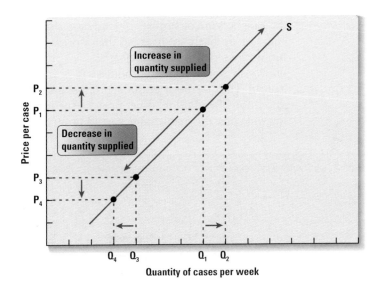

Market Supply

market supply: the total supply of a product offered by all producers.

Just as we did with the market demand, we could derive the **market supply** of a product by summing the supply of each and every individual supplier. A word of caution, however, is in order. We must make the necessary assumptions that the producers are all producing a similar product and that consumers have no preference as to which supplier or product they use. Given this, it is possible to add together the individual supplies to derive the market supply. In our example, suppose that Bobby the brewer has three other competing brewers of similar size and with similar costs. The market supply of beer in this market is shown in **Table 2.4**.

TABLE 2.4 Deriving the Market Supply

Price per Case	Number of Cases per Week		
	Bobby's Supply	Supply of Other Brewers	Market Supply
$12	2	6	8
13	3	9	12
14	4	12	16
15	5	15	20
16	6	18	24
17	7	21	28
18	8	24	32

The total quantities supplied by the three other brewers are equal to the quantities that Bobby would supply at each price, multiplied by three. The market supply, the fourth column, is the addition of every brewers' supply, that is, the second column plus the third column.

The market supply of beer is shown in **Figure 2.6**. The market supply curve is upward-sloping for the same reason the individual supply curve is upward-sloping: because higher prices imply higher profits and will therefore induce a greater quantity supplied. There is an additional reason. In the example we have used, we assumed that the suppliers are of similar size and have similar costs. In reality, that's unlikely; costs and size are likely to differ, so that a price that generates a profit for one firm may mean a loss for another. As the price of a product increases, however, some firms that previously were unable to produce will now find that they can successfully operate at a profit. Thus, as the price of the product increases, currently operating firms will produce more. In addition, other firms in the industry that were not previously producing will enter the market and start to produce.

FIGURE 2.6 The Market Supply

The market supply is the horizontal summation of each individual producer's supply curve. For instance, at a price of $15, Bobby would supply 5 cases; the other brewers combined would produce 15 cases. The market supply, at that price, therefore, is the total quantity supplied of 20 cases. To derive the market supply curve, we add the totals for each supplier at each price level.

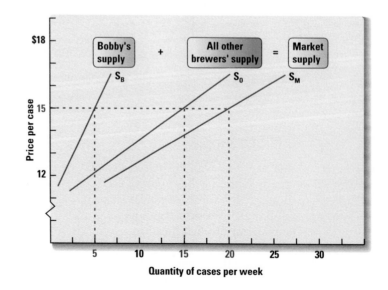

In summary, then:

> **A higher price, which acts as a deterrent to consumers' desire to buy more, is an incentive for suppliers to produce more.**

A lower price serves as an inducement to consumers to buy more but is a reason for suppliers to cut back their output.

We have established that the motives of consumers and producers are very divergent—the former wishes to obtain the lowest price possible; the latter wants to sell at the highest price. How can their wishes converge? How is trade possible in these circumstances? Well, if the question means, is it possible for *all* prospective consumers and suppliers to be satisfied, the answer must be no. If the question means, is it possible for *some* of these people to be satisfied, the answer will be, almost always, yes. Of course, this will require them in some sense to meet and get together. A market is a place that provides such an opportunity.

Market Equilibrium

Let us now see how the wishes of buyers and sellers coincide, by combining the market demand and supply for beer in **Table 2.5**.

TABLE 2.5 Market Supply and Demand

| | Number of Cases per Week | | |
Price per Case	Market Demand	Market Supply	Surplus(+)/Shortage(−)
$12	22	8	−14
13	18	12	− 6
14	16	16	0
15	9	20	+11
16	6	24	+18
17	3	28	+25
18	2	32	+30

equilibrium price: the price at which the quantity demanded equals the quantity supplied such that there is neither a surplus nor a shortage.

You can see from this table that there is only one price, $14, at which the wishes of consumers and producers coincide. Only when the price is $14 are the quantities demanded and supplied equal. This price level is referred to as the **equilibrium price**. Equilibrium, in general, means that there is a balance between opposing forces; here, those opposing forces are demand and supply. The word equilibrium also implies a condition of stability, so that if this stability is disturbed, there will be a tendency to return automatically to equilibrium. To understand this point, refer to Table 2.5 and notice that if the price were, say, $12, then the amount demanded of 22 would exceed the amount supplied of 8. At this price there is an excess demand, or more simply, a shortage of beer in the amount of 14 cases. This amount is shown in the last column and marked with a minus sign. In this situation there would be a lot of unhappy beer drinkers. Faced with the prospect of going beerless, many of them will be prepared to pay a higher price for their suds and will therefore bid the price up. As the price of beer starts to rise, the reaction of consumers and producers will differ.

Some beer drinkers will not be able to afford the higher prices, so the quantity demanded will drop. On the supply side of things, producers will be delighted with the higher price and will start to produce more, that is, the quantity supplied will increase. Both of these tendencies will combine to reduce the shortage as the price goes up. Eventually, when the price has reached the equilibrium price of $14, the shortage will have disappeared and the price will no longer increase. Part of the law of demand suggests, then, that:

Shortages cause prices to rise.

This is illustrated in **Figure 2.7**.

FIGURE 2.7 How the Market Reacts to a Shortage

At a price of $12, the quantity supplied of 8 is far below the quantity demanded of 22. The horizontal distance between the two shows the amount of the shortage, which is 14. As a result of the shortage, competition between consumers will force up the price. As the price increases, the quantity demanded will drop, but the quantity supplied will rise until these two equate at a quantity of 16.

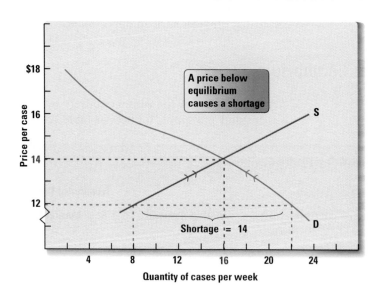

Now let's see, again using Table 2.5, what will happen if the price happens to be above equilibrium, at, say, $16 a case. At this price, the quantity demanded is 6 cases, and the quantity supplied is 24 cases. There is insufficient demand from the producers' point of view, or more simply, there is a surplus of 18 cases. This is shown in the last column of Table 2.5 as +18. This is not a stable situation, since firms cannot continue producing a product they cannot sell. They will be forced to lower the price in an effort to sell more. As the price starts to drop, two things happen concurrently. Consumers will be happy to consume more, or to use economic terms, there will be an increase in the quantity demanded. In **Figure 2.8**, note that as the price falls, the quantity demanded increases, and this increase is depicted as a movement down the demand curve. At the same time, faced with a falling price, producers will be forced to cut back production. This is what we have called a decrease in the quantity supplied. In the same figure, this is shown as a movement along (down) the supply curve. The net result of this will be the eventual elimination of the surplus as the price moves toward equilibrium. In other words:

Surpluses cause prices to fall.

FIGURE 2.8 How the Market Reacts to a Surplus

A price above equilibrium will produce a surplus. At $16, the quantity supplied of 24 exceeds the quantity demanded of 6. The horizontal distance of 18 represents the amount of the surplus. The surplus will result in producers dropping the price in an attempt to increase sales. As the price drops, the quantity demanded increases, while the quantity supplied falls.

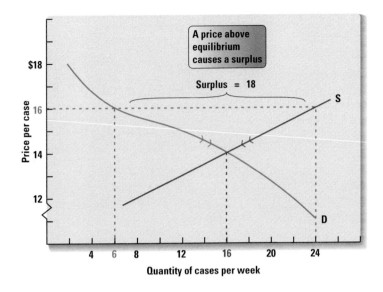

equilibrium quantity: the quantity that prevails at the equilibrium price.

Only if the price is $14 will there be no surplus or shortage and will the quantity supplied be equal to the quantity demanded. This is the equilibrium price. The quantity prevailing at the equilibrium price is known as the **equilibrium quantity**, and is, in this example, 16 cases.

SELF-TEST

1. Can a change in the price of a product lead to a change in the demand? Can it lead to a change in supply? Explain.
2. The following table shows the demand and supply of eggs (in hundreds of thousands per day).

Price	Demand	Supply	Surplus/ Shortage
$2.00	60	30	_____
2.25	58	33	_____
2.50	56	36	_____
2.75	54	39	_____
3.00	52	42	_____
3.25	50	45	_____
3.50	48	48	_____
3.75	46	51	_____
4.00	44	54	_____

A) What are the equilibrium price and equilibrium quantity?
B) Complete the surplus/shortage column. Using this column, explain why your answer in question A) must be correct.
C) What would be the surplus/shortage at a price of $2.50? What would happen to the price as a result?
D) What would be the surplus/shortage at a price of $4.00? What would happen to the price as a result?

REVIEW

1. Define and explain the difference between the terms *demand* and *quantity demanded*.
2. What is a *demand schedule*?
3. Explain how the market demand curve can be derived.
4. What is the distinction between the *supply* and the *quantity supplied*?
5. Why are producers willing to produce more at a higher price than at a lower one?
6. What does the term *market supply* mean?
7. What do the terms *equilibrium price* and *equilibrium quantity* mean?
8. Surpluses cause prices to increase; shortages cause them to fall. True or false?

Change in Demand

change in demand: a change in the quantities demanded at every price, caused by a change in the determinants of demand.

Recall from the definition of demand that this concept refers to the *relationship* between various prices and quantities. In other words, both price and quantity make up what is known as demand. Thus, a change in price causes a change in the quantity demanded. That said, we must now ask: what are the other determinants, besides the price, that would influence how much of any particular product consumers will buy? Another way of looking at this is to ask: once equilibrium price and quantity have been established, what might disturb that equilibrium? Well, one of these factors is a **change in demand**. **Table 2.6** shows such a change in the demand for beer.

TABLE 2.6 An Increase in Demand

Price per Case of Beer	Number of Cases per Week	
	Demand 1	Demand 2
$12	22	33
13	18	29
14	16	27
15	9	20
16	6	17
17	3	14
18	2	13

The original market demand, labelled Demand 1, is from Table 2.5, and was the demand that existed, let's say, last month. Demand 2 is the market demand for beer this month. There has been an increase in demand of 11 cases per week at each price. Or put another way, whatever the price, consumers are willing and able to consume an additional 11 cases. Thus, there has been an increase in the demand, as illustrated in **Figure 2.9**.

FIGURE 2.9 An Increase in Demand

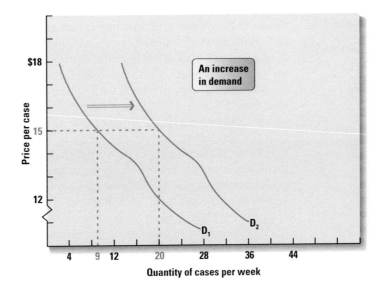

At each price, the quantities demanded have increased. In this example, the increase is by a constant amount of 11, thus producing a parallel shift in the demand curve; for example, at $17, the quantity demanded has risen from 3 to 14; at $15, the quantity demanded has increased from 9 to 20 (by 11).

An increase in demand, then, means an increase in the quantities demanded at each price, that is, a total increase in the demand schedule, which is illustrated by a rightward shift in the demand curve. Similarly, a decrease in demand means a reduction in the quantities demanded at each price, that is, a decrease in the demand schedule, and this is illustrated by a leftward shift in the demand curve.

Determinants of a Change in Demand

Having illustrated what an increase in demand looks like, we now need to look at the factors that could bring about such a change. One factor that affects consumers' willingness to purchase a product is their own particular *preferences*. An increase in demand as shown in Table 2.6 could simply have been caused by a change in consumer preferences: consumers now prefer more beer. There are a host of different things that could affect our preferences. Styles and fads change over time and are influenced by the weather, advertising, articles and reports in books and magazines, the opinions of friends, special events, and many other things.

The second factor affecting the demand for a product is the *income* of consumers. This will affect their ability to consume. Generally speaking, you would expect that an increase in income leads most people to increase their purchases of most products, and a decrease in income generally causes a drop in the demand; that is, there is a direct relationship between income and demand. Indeed, for most products that we buy this is true, and these products are called **normal** products. However, for so-called **inferior products** like low-quality hamburger meats, packets of macaroni and cheese, cheap toilet paper, and so on this may not be true. As income levels go up, the demand for these products goes down, and as incomes fall, our demand for these inferior products will rise.

A third important determinant of demand is the *prices of related products*. Products are related if a change in the price of one causes a change in the demand for the other. For instance, if the price of Pepsi were to increase, a number of Pepsi

normal products: products whose demand will increase as a result of an increase in income and will decrease as a result of a decrease in income.

inferior products: products whose demands will decrease as a result of an increase in income and will increase as a result of a decrease in income.

substitute products: any product whose demand varies directly with a change in the price of a similar product.

complementary products: products that tend to be purchased jointly and whose demands, therefore, are directly related.

drinkers might well switch over to Coke. There are, in fact, two ways in which products may be related. They may be related as substitutes, or they may be related as complements. **Substitute** (or **competitive**) **products** are products that are sufficiently similar in the eyes of most consumers that price becomes the main distinguishing feature. Pepsi and Coke, therefore, are substitute products, since an increase in the price of one will cause an increase in the demand for the other. The relationship between the price of a product and the demand for its substitute is, therefore, a direct one.

Complementary products tend to be purchased together, and their demands are interrelated. Skis and ski boots are complementary products, as are cameras and film, or beer and pretzels. If the price of one product increases, causing a decrease in the quantity demanded, then people will also purchase less of the complement.

A fourth determinant of demand is the *future expectations of consumers*. There are many ways that our feelings about the future influence our present behaviour. In particular, future expected prices and incomes can affect our present demand for a product, as does the prospect of a shortage. If consumers think that the price of their favourite beverage is likely to increase in the near future, they may well stock up in advance. Similarly, an anticipated pay increase may cause some people to spend more now as they adjust to their expected higher standard of living. Finally, the possibility of future shortages, caused, for instance, by the threat of an impending strike, often causes a rush to the stores by customers anxious to stock up.

These four determinants of demand—preferences, income, prices of related products, and future expectations—affect people's individual demand in varying degrees. If we shift our attention to the market demand, these four factors still apply. In addition, three other factors need to be mentioned in reference to market demand. The *size of the market population* will affect the demand for all products. An increase in the size of the population, for example, will lead to an increase in the demand for most products in varying amounts. In addition, a *change in the distribution of incomes* will lead to an increase in the demand for some products, and a decrease in the demand for others, even though the total income has not changed. The same will also be true for the *age composition of the population*. An aging population will increase the demand for

Canapress/Bill Becker

A Statistics Canada report released in 1996 showed that annual beer sales fell to 86.5 litres from 87.1 litres per person. The decline in beer drinking is probably due to the aging population, lifestyle changes, and taxes, said Howard Collins of the Brewers Association of Canada.

products that appeal to older people (Anne Murray CDs), and decrease the demand for those that appeal only to the young (Tragically Hip CDs).

In summary, the determinants of demand are:

- consumer preferences
- consumer incomes
- prices of related goods
- expectations of future prices, income, or availability
- population size, income, and age distribution

SELF-TEST

3. The following table shows the initial weekly demand (D_1) and the new demand (D_2) for packets of pretzels (a bar snack).

To explain the change in demand from D_1 to D_2, what might have happened to the price of a complementary product, like beer? Alternatively, what might have happened to the price of a substitute product, like nuts?

Price	Demand (D_1)	Demand (D_2)
$2.00	10 000	11 000
2.50	9 800	10 800
3.00	9 600	10 600
3.50	9 400	10 400
4.00	9 200	10 200

The Effects of an Increase in Demand

We have seen that the demand for any product is affected by many factors. A change in any of these factors will cause a change in demand, and, as we shall see, lead to a change in price and production levels. Let us first consider the effects of an *increase* in the demand for a product. This is illustrated in **Table 2.7**.

TABLE 2.7 The Effects on the Market of an Increase in Demand

	Number of Cases per Week		
Price per Case	Supply	Demand 1	Demand 2
$12	8	22	33
13	12	18	29
14	**16**	**16**	27
15	**20**	9	**20**
16	24	6	17
17	28	3	14
18	32	2	13

You can see that at the old demand (Demand 1) and supply, the equilibrium price was $14 and the quantity traded was 16 cases. Assume now that the demand for beer increases. Since consumers do not usually signal their intentions to producers in advance, producers are not aware that the demand has changed until they have evidence. The evidence will probably take the form of irate customers. At a price of $14 a case, the producers in total have produced 16 cases. At this price, the new demand is 27 cases. There is a shortage of 11 cases, and some customers are going to go home disappointed because there is not sufficient beer to satisfy all customers. The important question is: will these brewers now increase production to satisfy the higher demand? The surprising answer is no—at least not at the present price of $14. Brewers are not in the business of satisfying customers, they are in the business of making profits. As the dean of economics, Adam Smith, wrote over 200 years ago:

> It is not from the benevolence of the butcher, the brewer, or the baker that we expect our dinner but from regard to their own self-interest.[1]

You may object that unless firms are responsive to the demands of customers, they will soon go out of business. And you are right. But equally, a firm that is solely responsive to its customers, without regard to its own profits, will go out of business even faster. Look back at the supply schedule in Table 2.7. At a price of $14, the brewers said they are prepared to produce 16 cases. They are not prepared to produce 27 cases, the amount that consumers now want. Why is that? Because, presumably, they can make more profits producing 16 cases than they can producing 27 cases; otherwise they would have produced 27 in the first place. In fact, it may well be that if they produced 27 cases, they would end up making a loss. Does this mean therefore that the shortage of beer will persist? No, because we saw earlier, *shortages drive prices up* until the shortage disappears and the new demand is equal to the supply. This will occur at a price of $15 where the the quantity demanded and the quantity supplied are equal at the equilibrium quantity of 20. This adjustment process can be seen in **Figure 2.10**.

FIGURE 2.10 Adjustment to an Increase in Demand

The increase in demand from D_1 to D_2 creates an immediate shortage of 11. This will cause an increase in the price of beer. The increase affects both the producers, who will now increase the quantity supplied, and consumers, who will reduce the quantity demanded. Eventually, the price will reach a new equilibrium at $15 where the equilibrium quantity is 20, and there is no longer a shortage.

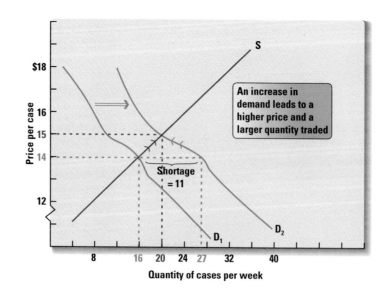

---

[1] Adam Smith, *Wealth of Nations* (Edwin Cannan Edition), pp. 26–27.

You can see in the graph that at the old price of $14, the new quantity demanded exceeds the quantity supplied. This shortage causes the price to rise. As it does so, notice that the quantity of beer that producers make also rises, that is, there will be an *increase in the quantity supplied*. Producers will produce more *not* because there is a shortage, but because the shortage causes a rise in price. Note also that the increase in price causes some customers to reduce their purchases of beer; that is, there is a *decrease in the quantity demanded*. The price of beer will continue to increase as long as there is a shortage and will stop as soon as the shortage disappears. This occurs when the price has increased to $15. At the new equilibrium price, the quantity demanded will again equal the quantity supplied but at a higher quantity traded of 20 cases. The increase in the demand therefore causes the price to increase and the quantity traded also to increase.

The Effects of a Decrease in Demand

Now let's see what happens when there is a *decrease* in demand. Remember that a decrease in demand cannot be caused by an increase in price but is caused by a change in any of the non-price determinants, such as

- a decrease in the preferences for the product
- a decrease in incomes if the product is a normal product, or an increase in incomes if the product is an inferior product
- a decrease in the price of a substitute product
- an increase in the price of a complementary product
- the expectation that future prices or incomes will be lower
- a decrease in the population or a change in its income or age distribution

A decrease in demand is illustrated in **Figure 2.11**. The initial equilibrium price is $14, and the quantity traded is 16. Assume that the demand now decreases to demand 2 in the table and D_2 on the graph. At a price of $14, producers will continue to produce 16 cases; yet consumers now wish to purchase only 10 cases. A surplus is immediately created in the market. Mounting unsold inventories and more intensive competition between suppliers will eventually push down the price. Notice in Figure 2.11 that as the price drops, the quantity supplied also starts to decrease and the quantity demanded begins to increase. Both of these factors will cause the surplus to disappear. The price will eventually drop to a new equilibrium of $13 where the demand and supply are equal at 12 cases. A decrease in demand will cause both the price and the quantity traded to fall.

FIGURE 2.11 Adjustment to a Decrease in Demand

The drop in demand from D_1 to D_2 will cause an immediate surplus of 6, since the quantity supplied remains at 16, but the quantity demanded drops to 10. This surplus will cause the price to fall, and, as it does, the quantity demanded will increase while the quantity supplied will fall. This process will continue until the surplus is eliminated. This occurs at a new equilibrium price of $13 and an equilibrium quantity of 12.

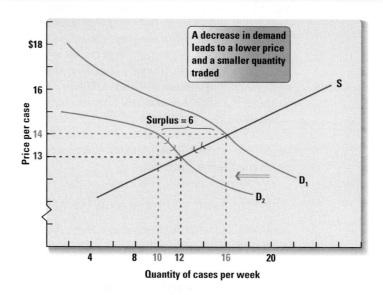

A decrease in demand leads to a lower price and a smaller quantity traded

Surplus = 6

Quantity of cases per week

SELF-TEST

4. What effect will the following changes have on the demand, the price, and the quantity traded of commercially brewed beer?

A) A new medical report praising the healthy effects of drinking beer (in moderation, of course).

B) A big decrease in the price of home-brewing kits.

C) A rapid increase in population growth.

D) Talk of a possible future strike of brewery workers.

E) The fear of a future recession.

Determinants of a Change in Supply

change in supply: a change in the quantities supplied at every price, caused by a change in the determinants of supply.

Let us again be clear about what we mean by supply: it is the relationship between the price of the product and the quantities that producers are willing and able to supply. Price is part of what economists call supply. What we now need to figure out is what could cause a **change in supply**. What factors will cause producers to offer a different quantity on the market, even though the price has not changed; that is, what will cause a change in supply? We begin with **Table 2.8,** where an *increase* in supply is illustrated.

TABLE 2.8 An Increase in Supply

	Number of Cases per Week	
Price per Case of Beer	Supply 1	Supply 2
$12	8	14
13	12	18
14	16	22
15	20	26
16	24	30
17	28	34
18	32	38

For reasons we will soon investigate, suppliers are now willing to supply an extra 6 cases of beer at every possible price. This is illustrated in **Figure 2.12**.

FIGURE 2.12 An Increase in Supply

An increase in supply causes the whole supply curve to shift right. (Be careful if you are tempted to describe it as a downward shift, because then you would be saying that as the supply goes up, the supply curve goes down, which could make things very confusing! Better to talk about a rightward shift.) This means that at each and every price, producers are now willing to produce more.

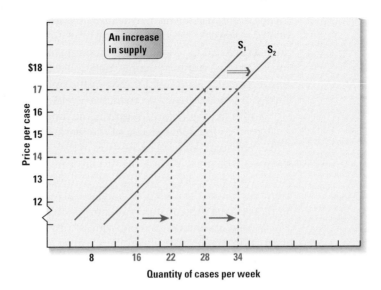

What could have happened in the brewers' world to make them wish to produce more, even though the price is unchanged? Since we are assuming that the prime motivation for the supplier is profit, then something must have happened to make brewing more profitable, and it is this that is inducing a higher supply. Profit is no more than the difference between revenue and cost, and since the price is unchanged, then something must have affected the cost of producing beer. The first factor that might have decreased costs is the price of productive resources. For the brewer this includes the price of yeast, hops, malt, and other ingredients, as well as the price that must be paid for the brewing vats and bottles, not to mention the price of labour, that is, wage levels. If any of these should drop in price, then the cost for the brewer will fall and her profits will rise. Under these circumstances, since she is now making a bigger profit on each case of beer, she will be very willing to produce more. A fall in the price of productive resources will lead to an increase in supply. Conversely, an increase in the price of resources will cause a decrease in supply.

A second major determinant of supply is the *business taxes* levied by the various levels of government. They are similar to the other costs of doing business, and a decrease in them (or an increase in a subsidy) will lead firms to make higher profits and encourage them, therefore, to increase the supply; an increase in business taxes, on the other hand, will cause a decrease in supply.

A third determinant of supply is the *technology* used in production. An improvement in technology means nothing more than an improvement in the method of production. This will enable a firm to produce more with the same quantity of resources (or for that matter, to produce the same output with fewer resources). An improvement in technology will not affect the actual price of the resources, but, because more can now be done with less, it will lead to a fall in the cost of production. This means that an improvement in technology will lead to an increase in the supply.

(Occasionally, however, the producer may be required to change to an inferior technology because of new government regulation outlawing the current methods.)

The price of related products also affects the supply, just as it affected the demand. But here we must be careful, since we are looking at things from a producer's point of view and not from a consumer's. In other words, what a producer regards as related will usually differ from a consumer's view of what is related. A fourth determinant of supply then is *the price of productively related products*. To a wheat farmer, for instance, the price of other grains like rye and barley will be of great interest, since the production of all grain crops are related in terms of production methods and equipment. A significant increase in the price of rye, for example, may well tempt the wheat farmer to grow rye in the future. In other words, an increase in the price of one product will cause a drop in the supply of products that are productively related. A decrease will have the opposite effect.

A fifth determinant of supply is *the future expectations of producers*. Again, this is analogous to the demand side of the market, but with a difference. While consumers will eagerly look forward to the drop in the price of products, producers view the same prospect with great anxiety. If a producer feels that the market is going to be depressed in the future and prices are likely to be lower, she may be inclined to increase production now before the anticipated collapse. Lower expected future prices, therefore, tend to increase the present supply of a product.

Finally, the market supply will also be affected by *the number of suppliers*. An increase in the number of suppliers will cause an increase in the market supply, while a decrease in the number of suppliers will reduce the overall market supply. In summary, the determinants of market supply are:

- prices of productive resources
- business taxes
- technology
- prices of productively related products
- future expectations of suppliers
- number of suppliers

The Effects of an Increase in Supply

In **Table 2.9** we see the effects of an increase in supply using our original supply and demand for beer, with the increase in supply from **Table 2.8**.

TABLE 2.9 The Effect on the Market of an Increase in Supply

Price per Case of Beer	Number of Cases per Week		
	Demand 1	**Supply 1**	**Supply 2**
$12	22	8	14
13	**18**	12	**18**
14	**16**	**16**	22
15	9	20	26
16	6	24	30
17	3	28	34
18	2	32	38

At the original demand (Demand 1) and supply (Supply 1), the equilibrium price was $14 per case and the quantity traded was 16 cases. Assume that the supply now increases to Supply 2. At the present price of $14, there will be an immediate surplus of 6 cases. Before we look at the implications of this surplus, we ought to address a couple of possible qualms that some students might have. The first is this: won't customers take up this excess of beer? It is easy to see that, at this price, consumers have already given their response: they want to buy 16 cases, not 22 cases, or any other number. In other words, consumers are buying beer to satisfy their own tastes, not to satisfy the brewers. A second question is this: why would producers produce 22 cases, knowing that the demand at this price is only 16 cases? The answer is, they don't know. Each producer knows the circumstances in her own brewery and knows that, until now, she has been able to sell everything she has produced. With the prospect of higher profits coming from, let's say, a decrease in costs, the brewer wants to produce more. If all producers do the same, there will be a surplus of beer. Figure 2.13 shows what will happen as a result of this surplus.

FIGURE 2.13 Adjustment to an Increase in Supply

The increase in the supply has the immediate effect of causing a surplus, since the demand has remained unchanged. In this figure, at a price of $14, the quantity supplied has increased from 16 to 22, causing a surplus of 6. This will cause the price to drop, and as it does, the quantity demanded increases and the quantity supplied decreases, until a new equilibrium is reached at a new equilibrium price of $13 and quantity of 18.

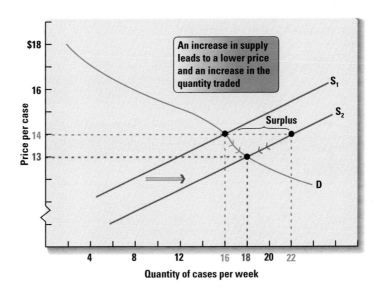

Faced with a surplus of beer, the market price will be forced down. As the price falls, the quantity demanded increases and the quantity supplied falls. Production increased initially, but because of the resulting drop in price, it is now dropping back. The price will continue to drop until it reaches $13. Table 2.9 shows that, at this price, the quantity demanded and the quantity supplied are now equal at 18 cases. The effect of the increase in supply, then, is a lower price and a higher quantity traded.

SELF-TEST

5. Suppose that the demand and supply for strawberries in a particular market are as follows (the quantities are in thousands of kilos per week):

Price	Demand	Supply 1	Supply 2
$4.00	140	60	_____
4.25	130	70	_____
4.50	120	80	_____
4.75	110	90	_____
5.00	100	100	_____
5.25	90	110	_____
5.50	80	120	_____

A) What are the present equilibrium price and equilibrium quantity? Graph the demand and supply curves, labelling them D_1 and S_1, and indicate equilibrium.

B) Suppose that the supply of strawberries were to increase by 50 percent. Show the new quantities in the Supply 2 column. What will be the new equilibrium price and quantity? Draw in S_2 on your graph, and indicate the new equilibrium.

6. What effect will the following changes have on the supply, price, and the quantity traded of wine?
   A) A bad harvest in the grape industry results in a big decrease in the supply of grapes.
   B) The number of wineries increases.
   C) The sales tax on wine increases.
   D) The introduction of a new fermentation method speeds up the time it takes for the wine to ferment.
   E) There is a big increase in wages for the workers in the wine industry.

Final Words

We leave it to the student to confirm that the effect of a decrease in supply will be to cause a shortage, which will eventually raise the price of the product. The net result will be a higher price *but* a lower quantity traded. To complete this introduction to demand and supply, let's use the following chart as a summary:

↑ Demand	→	shortage	→	↑ P	and ↑ Q traded
↓ Demand	→	surplus	→	↓ P	and ↓ Q traded
↑ Supply	→	surplus	→	↓ P	and ↑ Q traded
↓ Supply	→	shortage	→	↑ P	and ↓ Q traded

Note that when the demand changes, both the price and the quantity traded move in the same direction; when the supply changes, the quantity traded moves in the same direction, but the price moves in the opposite direction.

From this table you should confirm in your own mind that it is supply of and demand for a product that determines its price, and not the price that determines supply and demand. A change in any of the factors that affect demand or supply will therefore lead to a change in the price. The price of a product *cannot* change *unless* there is a change in either the demand or the supply. It follows therefore that you cannot really analyze any problem that starts: "What happens if the price increases (decreases)...?" The reason for this, as the above chart makes clear, is that an increase in the price of a product might be caused by either the demand increasing or by the supply decreasing. But in the case of an increase in the demand, the quantity traded also increases, whereas in the case of a decrease in the supply, the quantity traded falls. In the first case, we are talking about an expanding industry; in the second, we are looking at a declining industry.

To close this chapter, let's work through a simple example of how demand and supply works in practice.

Looking back over the past decade or so, what has happened to the prices of personal computers? Generally speaking, they have decreased, despite the effect of inflation. And what about the quantity of computers that are bought and sold now, compared with a decade ago? Definitely, it has increased. So, according to the previous chart, what could have produced this result in the marketplace? Well, there is only one thing that could lead to a decrease in price and an increase in the quantity traded, and that is an increase in supply. And what in the computer world over the past years could have caused an increase in supply? The answer must be an improvement in computer technology that has significantly reduced the costs of producing computers.

This completes our look at demand and supply. From now on, whenever you can, try to translate the economic events that you read about in newspaper articles into the language of demand and supply. You will often surprise yourself at how easy it is to do, and, more importantly, at how useful and revealing this exercise can be. In later chapters of the text, we shall use the tool of demand and supply analysis to examine, not the markets for individual products, as we did in this chapter, but the total market for all products.

SELF-TEST

7. Following are various changes that occur in different markets. Explain what will happen to the equilibrium price and quantity, and in each case state whether demand or supply is affected.

A) An increase in income on the market for an *inferior product*.

B) A decrease in the price of steel on the *automobile industry*.

C) A government subsidy given to operators of *day-care centres*.

D) A government subsidy given to parents who want their children to attend *day-care centres*.

E) A medical report suggesting that *wine* is very fattening.

F) A big decrease in the amount of Middle East oil exports on the *refined-oil market*.

G) An increase in the popularity of *antique furniture*.

H) An increase in the price of coffee on the *tea market*.

REVIEW

1. What are the four major determinants of individual demand?
2. Explain the difference between an *inferior* and a *normal* product.
3. What will happen to the price of a product if:
   a) the price of its substitute decreases?
   b) the price of its complement decreases?
4. Explain how future expectations can affect the behaviour of consumers.
5. What factors, aside from the determinants of individual demand, can affect the market demand?
6. Explain, step by step, how an increase in demand eventually affects both the price and the quantity traded.
7. Explain, step by step, how a decrease in demand eventually affects both the price and the quantity traded.
8. What are the six major determinants of the market supply?
9. Explain how the market adjusts to both an increase and a decrease in the supply of a product.
10. What can cause the price of a product to increase? What can cause it to decrease?

Chapter Highlights

The most important lesson to be learned from this chapter is that, in competitive markets, the prices and outputs produced are both determined by the forces of demand and supply. This means that the price of a product and the quantity produced will not change unless there has first been a change in either the demand for the product or in the supply of the product. The other lesson to learn is that it is people's ability and desire to purchase that constitutes the demand, whereas costs and productivity lie behind the supply.

The chapter begins by explaining that the demand for any product is not a single quantity, but a variety of various quantities that consumers would be willing and able to purchase at different prices. Similarly, the supply is the various quantities that producers would be willing and able to produce at different prices. It explains why consumers would tend to buy less at higher prices while, conversely, producers would be inclined to produce more. It then explains that equilibrium is a situation in which the quantity demanded and the quantity supplied are equal. It next shows that if the price is above equilibrium, the resulting surplus will eventually force the price back down, and if the price is below equilibrium, then a shortage will result that will push the price up toward equilibrium.

Next, the chapter explains how various factors can affect the demand and analyzes the effects of these changes. The major determinants of the demand are given as preferences, incomes, the prices of related products like substitutes and complements, future expectations, and the size of the population as well as its income and age distribution. We see that the result of an increased demand will be a higher price for the product and an increased quantity traded, whereas a decreased demand will result in both a lower price and quantity traded.

Finally, the chapter looks at the major factors that affect the supply of the product, including the prices of the resources, as well as changes in business taxes, technology, the price of productively related products, the future expectations of producers, and the number of producers. It concludes that an increase in supply also increases the quantity traded but causes the price to fall, whereas a decrease in supply has the opposite result.

New Glossary Terms

STUDY GUIDE

Study Tips

1. It is with this chapter that you will learn to appreciate the need for precision in the use of economic terms. For instance, the terms *demand* and *supply* have very clear definitions. Demand does *not* mean the amount a person wishes to buy or the amount she is buying. Demand is not a single quantity but a combination of different prices and quantities. Similarly, you cannot use the term supply synonymously with output, production, or quantity supplied. It is *not* a single quantity but, again, a range of different quantities and prices.

2. If you have understood the first point, then this next one should make sense. A change in price cannot affect the demand, since price is already part of what we mean by demand. That doesn't mean that a change in price doesn't affect consumers; generally, people change the amounts they purchase as a result of a price change, but this is what we call a change in the quantities demanded and *not* a change in demand. Similarly a change in price leaves the supply unaffected. But it definitely affects the *quantity supplied*. These points are illustrated in the way that the demand and supply curves are affected. A change in price causes no change in the demand or supply curves but results in a movement *along* the curves. Only changes in other determinants, besides price, will cause a shift in the curves.

3. There really is no alternative to learning the factors that do affect the demand and supply. Memorize the five determinants of market demand and the six determinants of market supply. Note that with the exception of expectations of future price changes, the factors that affect demand have no impact on supply, and vice versa. If possible, don't be too "cute" when trying to figure out the way in which various changes in determinants affect markets. It is possible to give a convoluted explanation why, for example, a change in the number of suppliers can affect preferences and, therefore, the demand of customers of that product. While remotely possible, the effect would be of minor significance. Instead, use common sense and focus on the main effects. Remember that usually a change in one determinant will affect *only* the demand or the supply, but seldom both.

4. Finally, the most important lesson you can get from this chapter is that the price of a product is determined by both demand and supply. Price is the effect and not the cause. This means that the price cannot change in a free market unless there has been a change in either the demand or the supply.

Key Problem

Table 2.10 shows the market for wool in Norseland (the quantities are in tonnes per year).

TABLE 2.10

Price ($)	100	200	300	400	500	600	700
Quantity demanded	10	9	8	7	6	5	4
Quantity supplied	1	3	5	7	9	11	13

a) Plot the demand and supply curves on **Figure 2.14**, and label them D_1 and S_1.

FIGURE 2.14

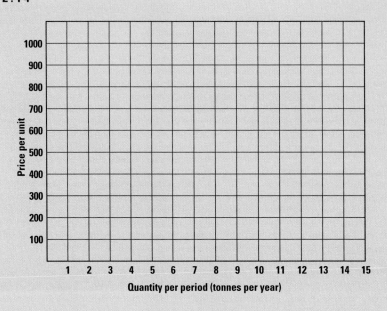

b) What are the values of equilibrium price and quantity? Mark the equilibrium as e_1 on Figure 2.14.

Equilibrium price: _____; equilibrium quantity: _____.

c) If the price of wool were $300, would there be a surplus or a shortage?

(Surplus/shortage) _____ of _____.

Indicate the amount of the surplus or shortage on Figure 2.14.

d) Suppose that the demand were to increase by 50 percent. Draw and label the new demand curve as D_2. What are the new values of equilibrium price and quantity? Mark the new equilibrium as e_2 on Figure 2.14.

Equilibrium price: _____; equilibrium quantity: _____.

e) Following the change in d), assume now that the supply decreases by 7 units. Draw and label the new supply curve as S_2. What are the new values of equilibrium price and quantity? Mark this new equilibrium as e_3.

Equilibrium price: _____; equilibrium quantity: _____.

More of the Same

Table 2.11 shows the market for olives Aegea (the quantities are in thousands of kilos per year).

TABLE 2.11

Price ($)	0	0.50	1.00	1.50	2.00	2.50	3.00	3.50	4.00
Quantity demanded	5.5	5	4.5	4	3.5	3	2.5	2	1.5
Quantity supplied	1	2	3	4	5	6	7	8	9

a) On a graph, plot the demand and supply curves, and label them D_1 and S_1.

b) What are the values of equilibrium price and quantity? Mark the equilibrium on the graph as e_1.

c) If the price of olives were $3.50, would there be a surplus or a shortage? How much? Mark the amount on the graph.

d) Suppose that the demand were to decrease by 3. Label the new demand curve D_2. What are the new values of equilibrium price and quantity? Mark the new equilibrium on the graph as e_2.

e) Following the change in d), assume now that the supply decreases by 50 percent. Label the new supply curve S_2. What are the new values of equilibrium price and quantity? Mark the new equilibrium on the graph as e_3.

Translations

Explain the possible cause and the effect of the movement from point a to point b in **Figure 2.15**.

FIGURE 2.15

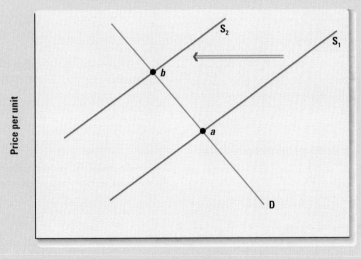

Answer: _____ .

Are You Sure?

Indicate whether the following statements are true or false. If false, indicate why they are false.

1. The term "demand" means the quantities that people would like to purchase at various prices.

   T or F   If false: _____

   _____

2. A change in the price of a product has no effect on the demand for that product.

   T or F   If false: _____

   _____

3. An increase in the price of a product leads to an increase in the supply.

   T or F   If false: _____

   _____

4. Equilibrium price implies that everyone who would like to purchase a product is able to.

   T or F   If false: _____

   _____

5. Surpluses drive prices up; shortages drive prices down.

   T or F   If false: _____

   _____

6. An increase in incomes will lead to a decrease in the demand for an inferior product.

   T or F   If false: _____

   _____

7. A decrease in the demand for a product will lead to a decrease in both the price and the quantity traded.

   T or F   If false: _____

   _____

8. An increase in business taxes causes the supply curve to shift left.

   T or F   If false: _____

   _____

9. An increase in the price of a product causes an increase in the demand for its substitute.

   T or F   If false: _____

   _____

10. A decrease in supply causes the price to fall and the quantity traded to increase.

    T or F   If false: _____

    _____

Choose the Best

11. What does the term "demand" refer to?
    a) The amounts that consumers are either willing or able to purchase at various prices.
    b) The amounts that consumers are both willing and able to purchase at various prices.

12. What will a surplus of a product lead to?
    a) A reduction in supply.
    b) A reduction in price.

13. What is the effect of a decrease in the price of a product?
    a) It will increase the quantity demanded.
    b) It will increase the demand.

14. How will a change in income affect the demand for an inferior product?
    a) The demand will increase if the income of consumers increases.
    b) The demand will increase if the income of consumers decreases.
    c) The demand is not affected by consumer incomes.

15. Which of the following could cause an increase in the supply of wheat?
    a) A decrease in the price of oats.
    b) An imposition of a sales tax on wheat.
    c) An increase in the price of fertilizer.

16. What is the effect of an increase in the price of coffee?
    a) It will lead to an increase in the demand for tea.
    b) It will lead to a decrease in the demand for tea.
    c) It will have no effect on the tea market.

17. What effect will an increase in the price of a product have on the demand for a complementary product?
    a) It will increase the demand.
    b) It will decrease the demand.
    c) It will not affect the demand.

18. Which of the following factors will shift the demand curve left?
    a) An increase in the price of a substitute product.
    b) A decrease in the price of a complementary product.
    c) An increase in income if the product is an inferior product.
    d) The expectation that the future price of the product will be higher.

19. What is the effect of an increase in the price of a productive resource?
    a) It will cause a decrease in the supply of the product.
    b) It will cause an increase in the supply of the product.
    c) It will cause a decrease in the demand for the product.
    d) It will cause an increase in the demand for the product.

20. What is the effect of a shortage?
    a) It will cause a decrease in the price, leading to an increase in the quantity supplied and a decrease in the quantity demanded.
    b) It will cause a decrease in the price, leading to a decrease in the quantity supplied and an increase in the quantity demanded.
    c) It will cause an increase in the price, leading to an increase in the quantity supplied and a decrease in the quantity demanded.
    d) It will cause an increase in the price, leading to a decrease in the quantity supplied and an increase in the quantity demanded.

21. In what way are Pepsi-Cola and Coca-Cola related?
    a) They are substitute products.
    b) They are complementary products.
    c) They are inferior products.
    d) They are unrelated products.

22. A rightward shift in the supply curve for a product could be caused by all *except one* of the following. Which is the exception?
    a) The expectation by suppliers that the future price of the product will be higher.
    b) A decrease in the price of a productive resource used in its manufacture.
    c) A decrease in the price of a productively related product.
    d) A technological improvement in manufacturing methods.

23. What is the effect of a decrease in the supply of a product?
    a) It will cause an increase in both the price and in the quantity traded.
    b) It will cause an increase in the price but a decrease in the quantity traded.
    c) It will cause a decrease in both the price and in the quantity traded.
    d) It will cause a decrease in the price but an increase in the quantity traded.

Table 2.12 depicts the market for mushrooms in Struland (in thousands of kilos per month).

TABLE 2.12

Price ($)	2.50	3.00	3.50	4.00	4.50	5.00	5.50	6.00
Quantity demanded	64	62	60	58	56	54	52	50
Quantity supplied	40	44	48	52	56	60	64	68

24. Refer to Table 2.12 to answer this question. What are the values of equilibrium price and quantity traded?
   a) $3 and 52.
   b) $3 and 62.
   c) $4 and 58.
   d) $4.50 and 56.
   e) They cannot be determined from the data.

25. Refer to Table 2.12 to answer this question. What will happen if the price of the product is $3?
   a) There would be a surplus of 18, which would lead to a decrease in price.
   b) There would be a shortage of 18, which would lead to an increase in price.
   c) There would be a shortage of 18, which would lead to a decrease in price.
   d) There would be a surplus of 18, which would lead to an increase in price.
   e) There would be neither a surplus nor a shortage.

26. How will the demand and supply of a product be affected if people expect the future price of a product to be higher than it is at present?
   a) It will cause an increase in demand but a decrease in supply.
   b) It will cause an increase in both the demand and supply.
   c) It will cause a decrease in both the demand and supply.
   d) It will cause an increase in supply but will have no effect on demand.
   e) It will cause an increase in supply but a decrease in demand.

27. In what way are products A and B related if an increase in the price of product A leads to a decrease in the demand for product B?
   a) Product A must be a productive resource used in the manufacture of product B.
   b) Product B must be a productive resource used in the manufacture of product A.
   c) The two products must be complements.
   d) The two products must be substitutes.
   e) The two products must be inferior products.

Use **Figure 2.16** to answer questions 18, 19, and 20.

FIGURE 2.16

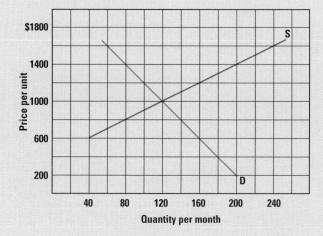

28. Refer to Figure 2.16 to answer this question. What will be the effect if the price is $1200?
   a) There would be a surplus of 30.
   b) There would be a shortage of 30.
   c) 160 would be purchased.
   d) There would be a surplus of 60.
   e) The price will increase.

29. Refer to Figure 2.16 to answer this question. If the quantity traded is 80, what does this mean?
   a) Purchasers would be willing to pay an additional $600 for this quantity.
   b) The price must be above equilibrium.
   c) There must be a surplus of 30.
   d) There must be a shortage of 30.
   e) There must be a surplus of 60.

30. Refer to Figure 2.16 to answer this question. Suppose that initially the market was in equilibrium and demand increased by 60. What will be the new equilibrium as a result?
a) A price of $1000 and quantity traded of 120.
b) A price of $1000 and quantity traded of 160.
c) A price of $1200 and quantity traded of 160.
d) A price of $1400 and quantity traded of 160.
e) A price of $1400 and quantity traded of 240.

Other Problems

31. In Karin, at a market price of $1 per kilo, there is a shortage of 60 kilos of avocados. For each 50-cent increase in the price, the quantity demanded drops by 5 kilos while the quantity supplied increases by 10 kilos. What will be the equilibrium price?

Equilibrium price: _____.

What will be the surplus or shortage at a price of $4.50?

(Surplus/shortage): _____ of _____ kilos.

32. Circle whichever of the following factors will lead to an increase in the market demand for cranberry juice (which is a normal good).
a) A drop in the price of cranberries.
b) A drop in the price of apple juice.
c) A drop in the price of cranberry juice.
d) A decrease in consumer incomes.
e) The expectation by consumers that the price of cranberry juice is likely to increase.
f) An improvement in the juicing process that lowers the costs of production of cranberry juice.

33. Circle whichever of the following factors will lead to a drop in the price of wine (a normal product that is regarded by consumers as a substitute for beer and a complement to cheese).
a) A drop in the price of grapes.
b) An increase in the price of beer.
c) A drop in the wage costs in the brewery industry.
d) A drop in the tax on wine but no change to beer taxes.
e) A drop in the tax on beer but no change to the wine tax.

34. Consider the effects of each of the events listed in **Table 2.13** on the market indicated. Indicate by placing a ($\uparrow$), ($\downarrow$), or (0) under the appropriate heading whether there will be an increase, decrease, or no change in demand (D), supply (S), equilibrium price (P), and quantity traded (Q):

TABLE 2.13

Market	Event	D	S	P	Q
a) Compact discs	A technological improvement reduces the cost of producing compact disc players.				
b) Butter	Medical evidence suggests that margarine causes migraines.				
c) Newspapers	Because of worldwide shortages, the price of pulp and paper increases dramatically.				
d) Generic toilet paper	Consumer incomes rise significantly.				
e) Video rentals	Movie theatres halve their admission prices.				
f) Beef	World price of lamb increases.				

UNANSWERED QUESTIONS

Short Essays

1. Explain, in terms of demand and supply analysis, why the price of maple syrup may be different in London, Ontario, than in London, England.

2. Explain some of the factors that might reduce the price of movie theatre admission.

3. Explain what could cause a surplus and what could cause a shortage in a competitive market. How does the market eliminate them?

4. Explain the difference between a decrease in supply and a decrease in the quantity supplied.

5. What is the difference between "scarcity" and "shortage"?

6. Does the term "quantity demanded" mean the same thing as "quantity purchased"? Explain.

Analytical Questions

7. Given the graph of the market for a product shown in **Figure 2.17**, explain each change in terms of a shift in the appropriate curve, or movement along a curve, and for each change give an example of what might have caused the change.

FIGURE 2.17

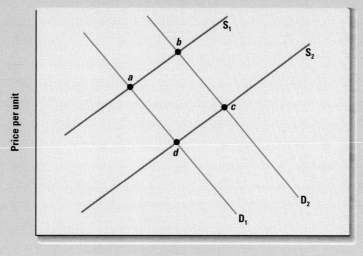

Quantity per period

a) From point *a* to point *b*.
b) From point *a* to point *d*.
c) From point *a* to point *c*.
d) From point *c* to point *d*.

8. "The price of houses rises when the demand increases. The demand for houses decreases when the price increases." Are both of these statements correct? Are they contradictory? Explain.

9. Consider the effects of each of the events listed in **Table 2.14** on the *market for beef* in Canada. Indicate by placing a (↑), (↓), or (0) under the appropriate heading whether there will be an increase, decrease, or no change in demand, supply, equilibrium price, and quantity traded.

TABLE 2.14

Event	Demand	Supply	Price	Quantity Traded
a) Medical research indicates that cholesterol in beef is a major cause of heart attack.				
b) Improved cattle feeds reduce the cost of beef production.				
c) Chicken sales are banned due to an outbreak of chicken cholera.				
d) The price of pork increases because the government removes its subsidy to pork producers.				
e) A reduction in income taxes causes the incomes of Canadian consumers to rise sharply.				
f) The price of cattle feed rises due to a drought.				

10. The two graphs in **Figure 2.18** show the markets for orange juice and for apple juice, which are initially in equilibrium.

FIGURE 2.18

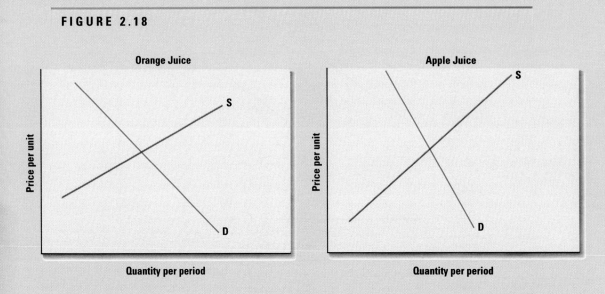

Show what will happen to the prices and quantities traded of both products if a severe frost in Florida were to seriously damage the orange crop.

Numerical Questions

11. **Table 2.15** shows the demand for and supply of packaged cookies.

TABLE 2.15

Price ($)	0	1	2	3	4	5	6	7	8	9	10
Demand	10	9	8	7	6	5	4	3	2	1	0
Supply	0	1	2	3	4	5	6	7	8	9	10
Shortage/Surplus	____	____	____	____	____	____	____	____	____	____	____

a) Complete the table, and then graph the demand and supply curves and label them D_1 and S_1. What is the equilibrium price and quantity?
b) Assume that the supply increases by 50 percent; that is, the quantity increases by 50 percent at every price. Draw and label the new supply curve, S_2. What is the new equilibrium price and quantity?
c) Assume *instead* that the supply increases by 2 units at every price. Draw and label the new supply curve S_3. What is the new equilibrium price and quantity?
d) Now assume that the demand increases by 2 units at every price. Draw and label the new demand curve D_2. What is the new equilibrium price and quantity (D_2/S_3)?

12. **Table 2.16** shows the demand for the upcoming concert to be given by the string quartet, Guns and Butter, at the new 3000-seat Saskatoon Auditorium.

TABLE 2.16

Price	Quantity Demanded
$10	8000
15	7000
20	6000
25	5000
30	4000
35	3000
40	2000
45	1000

a) Over what price range would there be a shortage of seats? Over what range would there be a surplus?

b) Suppose the promoters of the concert set the price at $25 per ticket. What will be the result?

c) In response to the great demand for the first concert, the promoters decide to add a second show open *only* to those who were unable to attend the first concert. What is the maximum price they could charge for this concert and still fill the auditorium?

13. **Figure 2.19** shows the market for the new Guns and Butter compact disc, "Live at the Saskatoon Auditorium."

   a) Suppose that the CD producers put the disc on sale for $8 each. How much will be the surplus or shortage? How many will be sold?

   b) What is the maximum price at which the quantity actually sold in a) could have been sold?

   c) If the CD producers had actually put the CD on the market at the price mentioned in b), what would have been the resulting surplus/shortage?

FIGURE 2.19

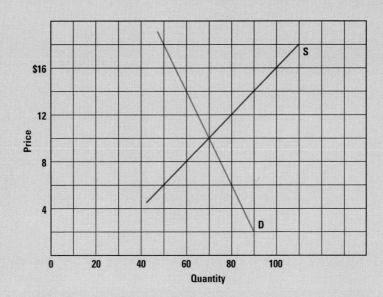

Web-Based Activities

1. Draw a demand curve for public transportation. Is your hypothetical good "inferior" or "normal"? Explain. (You can go to **http://www.tc.gc.ca/tfacts/StatFor/economy/economy70.htm** to help you find the answer to this question.) Now visit **http://www.tc.gc.ca/tfacts/StatFor/economy/economy64.htm** to determine what has happened to disposable personal income per person in your province. Draw what you predict would happen to your demand curve if everything else were held constant over the period 1961–96.

2. Go to **http://www.move.de/amm/cdmarket.htm.** In 1996, what was the equilibrium price and quantity in the CDs market in Canada, in the United States, in Japan, and in the United Kingdom? Why do you suppose the market equilibrium differs for CDs in these countries? What is the impact on the CD market if it becomes more costly or difficult to pirate (illegally copy) CDs?

Measuring National Income

What's ahead... What determines the level of an economy's national income, and how that income relates to real output, is at the heart of macroeconomics. In this chapter we begin the explanation of this determination by using the circular flow of income approach. We then introduce the method for measuring national income. Since we are just at the beginning of a long process, the introduction of many new terms here is unavoidable.

Suppose that you heard on the TV news that tax rates were being cut by the government. It is easy for you to see immediately how this would affect you and other members of your family. Although people quickly recognize how some new items affect them directly, they fail to even notice other news items, sometimes just as important. For example, suppose that you read in the newspaper that Canadians were saving much less this year than last, or that Canadian exports were higher this year than last, or that interest rates would likely remain unchanged for the foreseeable future. How would you react to these news items? Do you consider them as significant as the item on tax cuts? The fact is that they might be just as significant. This chapter will help to explain why.

In 1997, Canada's national income was $605 billion. What are the major determinants of a country's income? How is national income measured? How do decision makers in government and business influence the level of national income? How significant is international trade in determining this level? All these questions need reasonably well-thought-out answers. The first step in the process of finding these answers is to understand the way in which income flows in an economy. To do this, we will construct a simplified model of the economy.

Circular Flow of Income

Flow of Services

Imagine, to begin with, a simple economy with only two sectors: the household sector and the business sector. Clusters of individuals make up the household sector while businesses of various types and sizes, from small family-run proprietorships to large corporations, make up the business sector. Next, recall the definition of the factors of production. As mentioned in Chapter 1, the factors (think of them as production inputs, if that is helpful) are divided into four categories: land, labour, capital, and enterprise.

You may recall, also from Chapter 1, that economists consider land to be anything that is natural, such as minerals, all natural vegetation, natural harbours, supplies of water, and so on. The term labour is used in the broadest sense to describe a wide range of human endeavour, including that of a skilled surgeon, a construction labourer, or a symphony musician. Capital is defined as the physical plant, tools, and equipment used to help produce other goods or services. Note that in conventional language, capital is often equated with money. In economics, however, capital refers to things that are used to produce other goods. Money can be used to purchase capital goods, but it is not a factor of production. Finally, enterprise is the specialized human effort that organizes the other factors, innovates, and bears risks. These four factors of production are combined to produce the goods and services that individuals consume on a daily basis. In our private enterprise or market economy, the factors of production

Even a small business like a bicycle shop is made up of the factors of production: land, labour, capital, and enterprise.

are, ultimately, owned by individuals. Individuals control the sale of their own labour; individuals own land and mineral rights; and individuals own the shares of a corporation's assets or (for our purposes) capital.

We can now begin to build our model with a series of diagrams. The initial flow in Figure 3.1 represents the factor services flowing from the household sector to the business sector. Businesses use these factor services, which are provided by the household sector in order to produce goods and services. Figure 3.2 shows the upper-loop flow from the business sector to the household sector. This represents a flow of consumer goods and services from firms to households.

FIGURE 3.1 The Flow of Factors of Production

FIGURE 3.2 The Flow of Goods and Services

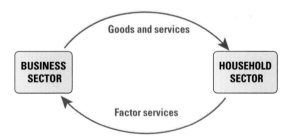

The Financial Flows

Next, let's turn to the financial flows that move in the opposite direction. The business sector must pay for the factor services they receive. This payment goes to the household sector and becomes income and is divided into specific categories. Remember that many of these terms differ from their conventional usage. Rent, for instance, is the income received from the use of the factor land, that is, the payment for the use of a natural resource, and is not simply the payment for the use of an apartment or other building. Wages means the income received for the use of the factor labour and includes commissions, tips, and all employee benefits. Interest means the income received for the use of the factor capital, which again differs from conventional use. Finally, by profits economists mean income that is left over after all the factors of production have been paid, and it can be thought of as a reward for enterprise. Thus, the basic lower-loop financial flow in **Figure 3.3** represents the flow of factor incomes (costs of production to the firm), wages (w), interest (i), rent (r), and profits (p) from the business sector to the household sector.

    Individuals in the household sector earn income by receiving payment for the factors they sell. And what do these same individuals do with their incomes? Primarily, they engage in **consumption**—paying for the consumer goods and services received from the business sector. This flow represents an expenditure for households but is an income (in the way of business receipts) for the firms. So, now we have two financial flows as shown in Figure 3.3.

consumption: the expenditure by households on goods and services.

FIGURE 3.3 The Financial Flows

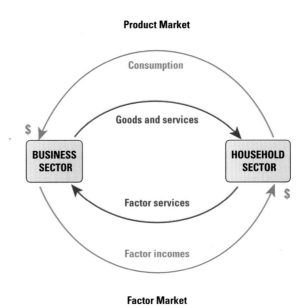

Product Market

Consumption

Goods and services

$

BUSINESS SECTOR

HOUSEHOLD SECTOR

Factor services

$

Factor incomes

Factor Market

This is the basic circular flow:

> **Households sell factor services to the business sector and earn incomes. With this income, they pay for the goods and services received from the business sector.**

    Many complications are on the way, but each can be handled easily if you keep this basic circular flow clear in your mind.

Francois Quesnay and the Circular Flow

The circular flow concept owes a big debt to Francois Quesnay (1694–1774), court physician to Louis XV and Madame de Pompadour of France and the founder a group of scholars called the Physiocrats, who were highly critical of the French government's interference in the economy. This interference had taken the form of a myriad of regulations and taxes. Quesnay published his *Tableau Economique* in 1758 to explain how income in an economy flows from one group in society to another. He believed that only nature was truly a creator of wealth by generating what he called a surplus each year. Humans, he believed, merely "transform" this surplus into various products. Further, this surplus eventually "flows" to the landowners (the king, the aristocracy, and the church), and therefore only this group should be subject to taxation. He advocated that all other taxes should be abolished, leaving only a single tax on "wealth." Not surprisingly, his views did not go down well in the circles of power.

product market: the market for consumer goods and services.

factor market: the market for the factors of production.

We have now also identified what economists call the **product market**, which is the buying and selling of goods and services (the upper loops); and the **factor market**, which is the buying and selling of the factors of production (the lower loops).

Also notice that each buy–sell transaction in either market is income to one sector and spending to the other. Thus:

> **National income is the *sum of all incomes* earned from economic transactions or the *sum of all spending*.**

The Flow of Income versus the Stock of Money

income: the earnings of factors of production expressed as an amount per period of time.

money: any medium of exchange that is widely accepted.

Before we move to some complications, there is a straightforward but very fundamental point that has to be understood. We are building a circular flow of **income** model, and it is important that we distinguish between the flow of income and the stock of **money**. An example will help. Imagine a simple economy made up of only three businesses: Bill owns and operates a bakery, Wick is the proprietor of a candle-making business, and Tammy has a tailor's shop. Within this economy there is only a single $10 bill, which is currently in the possession of Bill the baker. So we begin our story with three businesses (and three households), a stock of money equal to $10, and no income (yet). Let us assume that Wick has just produced some candles and that Bill the baker notices that his inventory of candles is getting low, so he goes to Wick and buys $10 worth of candles and pays cash. Wick, in receipt of $10, decides he needs to purchase a new pair of jeans, produced by Tammy the tailor, which just happen to cost $10. Tammy has spent all day producing these jeans and for her efforts receives $10 from Wick. After all this effort, Tammy requires sustenance and makes her way to Bill the baker to buy some freshly baked bread, which has a price of $10. Bill the baker receives the $10 bill for his efforts. Let us summarize today's activities in this mini-economy:

- Total production came to $30.
- Total spending came to $30; and total income is $30.
- All of this activity was financed by a single $10 bill.

Clearly the stock of money and the flow of income are not the same thing! To cement this simple point, think of a retired couple with a lot of money—$200 000 in a bank account—but relatively little income—$16 000 a year in interest. Compare this with the young double-income professional couple just starting out, with an annual household income of $90 000 but almost no money, since all the income is going to mortgage and car payments and the expenses of a fast-lane lifestyle. Again, the fundamental point—distinguishing between the flow of income and the stock of money—is important. In 1997, Canada's stock of money was approximately $73 billion. The flow of income during the same year was approximately $605 billion.

The First Set of Leakages and Injections: Savings and Investment

Our simple economy example above seemed to demonstrate that: the value a) of total production ($10 worth of candles, of bread, and of jeans); and b) of total expenditure (the purchase of each of these three items); and c) of total income (what Wick, Bill, and Tammy each receive) are equal. Does this equality always hold true, or is it merely a coincidence? We will answer this question soon, but for now you should realize that a good part of macroeconomics is concerned with looking at the link between production spending and incomes.

savings: the portion of income that is not spent on consumption.

Keeping all this in mind, let's now return to the circular flow and introduce the first complication by asking the question: what else do individuals in the household sector do with their income besides spend on consumption? The answer is: they save. This activity of **savings** (S) can be defined as income (Y) received but not spent on consumption (C).

$$S = Y - C$$

leakage: income received within the circular flow that does not flow directly back.

Savings thus becomes a **leakage** from the circular flow of income. This is shown in **Figure 3.4**.

FIGURE 3.4 The Savings Leakage

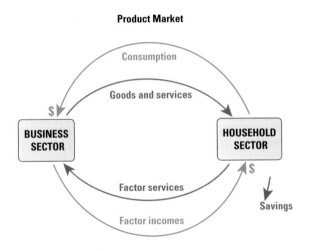

Product Market

Consumption

Goods and services

BUSINESS SECTOR

HOUSEHOLD SECTOR

Factor services

Savings

Factor incomes

Factor Market

Economists have developed a fairly standard set of abbreviations for often-used terminology. As you can see from the equation above, C stands for consumption, S for savings, and Y for income. (If you are wondering why I is not used for income, the answer is quite simple—it is used for investment.)

The reasons that people want to save can be quite varied: for retirement; for a major purchase in the future, such as a house, car, or holiday; for a child's future education; or quite simply, for a rainy day. The primary determinant of how much people are able to save is their level of income; that is:

$$S = f(Y)$$

The above equation is read as: savings is a function of income. If you wish, you can replace the word "function" with "depends on." The fact that savings depends primarily on income is a point we'll want to keep in mind later, when we discuss the effect of changes in interest rates.

It should also be noted that a business can also save by not paying out in dividends *all* of its after-tax profits. Nonetheless, our focus will be on savings by households. People can hold both current-period savings, which is a function of current-period income, and accumulated savings held over from a previous period's income. Current-period savings is thus a flow that comes from the current flow of income. Accumulated savings that is held over from the previous periods' income is, of course, a stock. This stock of savings changes as a result of the current flow and is part of people's **wealth**. Wealth includes not only savings, but also such things as rare paintings, vintage wines, antique cars, real estate, and many other assets. Both current-period and accumulated savings make up the portion of wealth that is held in the form of financial instruments, such as bonds, term deposits, accumulated savings accounts, chequing accounts, and so on. Another way of looking at it is that savings is that portion of wealth that we call **loanable funds**. Normally, these funds are deposits in various financial intermediaries, like banks, credit unions, and trust companies, and are available for loan.

Let us pull together the main points up to here:

- Savings is both a function of income and a leakage from the circular flow of income.
- The reasons people want to save are varied.
- Savings normally flow to financial intermediaries.

Let's therefore take our diagram one step further, as shown in **Figure 3.5**.

wealth: the sum of all valuable assets less liabilities.

loanable funds: the portion of wealth that is available for loan through financial intermediaries.

FIGURE 3.5 The Addition of Financial Intermediaries

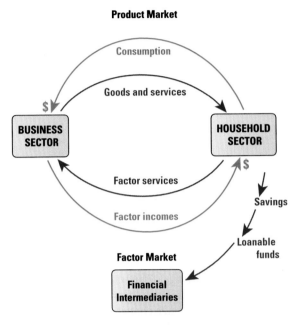

injection: any spending
flow that is not dependent
on the current level of
income.

investment: spending on
capital goods.

Next we want to add the first injection. An **injection** is any expenditure received by firms in the business sector that does not come from the household sector and is not, therefore, dependent on the current flow of income.

One form of injection is **investment** spending. Investment is defined as spending that results in a physical increase in plant or equipment. Another way of thinking of investment is spending that increases the economy's capital stock.

Why would a firm invest in new machinery or equipment, thereby expanding its production capacity? Quite simply, to make greater profit in the future.

You will notice that the definition of investment differs from the conventional use of the term. If you overheard someone say: "I invested in some General Corporation stock today," you would correctly understand him to mean that he had *bought* some General Corporation stock. Yet, he has technically misused the term "investment," at least from the economist's point of view! Let's get this sorted out. The person in our example was able to buy the stock through his broker only because someone else wanted to sell General Corporation stock. Someone sold the stock; someone bought it; brokers arranged the transactions and took a commission. From the point of view of the overall economy, what has changed? The answer is: very little. Somebody used to have stock and less money. The student used to have more money and no stock. Now the positions of the two have switched—that's all. Each is now holding some (past and current) savings in a different form, that is, their portfolios have changed, but the economy has not experienced any new investment. Investment is an increase in the economy's capacity to produce goods and services and is done by business for profit. Technically, what the person should have said is: "I *bought* some General Corporation stock today."

To re-emphasize:

> The reasons individuals save (for retirement, future purchase, and so on) differ from the reasons business invests. Savings (a leakage) and investment (an injection) are quite distinct actions.

Does this imply that there is no connection between savings and investment whatsoever? No, it doesn't mean that at all. Most of the time, investment by business is financed with borrowed funds, and it is the savings in the economy that provide the pool of funds that is available for loan. This pool is the loanable funds mentioned earlier. In short, the savings available in the economy, which become loanable funds, enable business investment to occur.

You may well ask: doesn't all savings become loanable funds? The answer is: most of it, but not all. Once again, savings is income received and not spent. If this savings is put into a bank, it does indeed become loanable funds, but if it ends up in the cookie jar or under the mattress, it does not add to the loanable funds available in the economy.

financial security: any claim on assets that usually takes the form of a bond or certificate of deposit or similar financial instrument.

Now we can finish things off. When households put their savings into financial intermediaries, they receive some sort of **financial security** in return, usually a certificate of deposit or a bond or equity stock. As a result, the households will receive interest payments or dividends in the future. These payments are an expense to the business that issues the financial instruments and income to the households that receive them. We will now add the investment injection to the circular flow of income diagram in **Figure 3.6**.

FIGURE 3.6 The Investment Injection

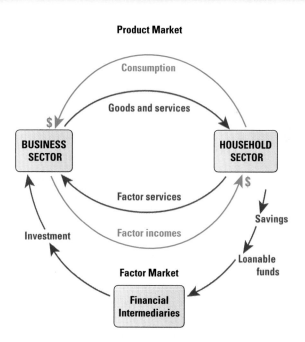

Let's now consider another aspect of this savings–investment link. Note that the mere existence of loanable funds is not sufficient to guarantee investment. For example, there were plenty of funds to borrow in the middle of the Great Depression of the 1930s, yet businesses simply were not borrowing much because of widespread pessimism about the economy's future.

Conversely, a country may suffer from a lack of loanable funds. This is the situation faced by some economically less developed countries today. Often, the total savings within these economies are so small that loanable funds are very limited. The result is that many viable investment projects never come to fruition because the funds necessary to finance them simply aren't available.

Even among the richer economies of the world, savings rates can vary a great deal. What we can conclude from these points is the abstract but fundamental point that in an economy without government or international trade:

> Savings is a *necessary but not sufficient* condition for investment.

ADDED DIMENSION

Investment in the Great Depression

Here are some actual data to illustrate the significant decrease in investment spending that occurred in Canada during the Great Depression:

As you can see, investment decreased by more than 85 percent between 1929 and 1933 and, in fact, didn't return to the 1929 level until the early 1940s.

Year	Investment ($ billions)
1929	1.41
1933	0.21
1937	0.76
1939	0.97

Source: Statistics Canada, National Income and expenditure Accounts, Catalogue 13-001.

The Second Set of Leakages and Injections: Imports and Exports

imports: goods and services that are bought from other countries and reflect a leakage from the circular flow of income.

exports: goods and services produced in one country and sold to another country.

Putting savings and investment aside for now, let's turn to the second pair of leakages–injections. First the leakage. Some of the goods and services that households buy, as well as some of the investment goods purchased by business, are goods and services imported from outside the domestic economy. Such expenditure does not flow back to the domestic economy but instead leaks out. We call this import spending, or just plain **imports** (IM). Although it is usually business that does the actual importing of goods, we will illustrate this leakage as coming from the household sector, reflecting the fact that the ultimate consumers of most products are individuals.

Conversely, the business sector receives payment for goods and services exported, and this payment is in addition to the consumption expenditure from (domestic) households. **Exports** (X) are, therefore, an injection into the circular flow of income. Note, then, that the value of exports does not depend on the level of income in this country, but on the level of income in the rest of the world. This is illustrated in **Figure 3.7.**

FIGURE 3.7 The Import Leakage and Export Injection

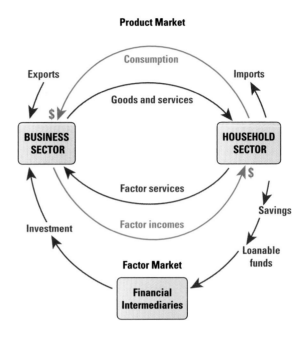

The Third Set of Leakages and Injections: Taxes and Government Spending

The third pair of leakages–injections that we need isn't so simply handled. First, we need to add another sector to our analysis—government. The government sector taxes both the household sector and the business sector, so that taxes (T) are the third leakage. Also, the government sector purchases goods and services from the business sector, so that government spending (G) on goods and services is the third injection. In addition, government also disburses what are called **transfer payments** (TP). These are defined as payments made for which no goods or services are given in exchange (at the time of the payment). Examples of transfer payments would be Employment Insurance payments, Canada Pension Plan payments, and subsidies to businesses.

We will treat all transfer payments as a flow from the government sector directly to individuals in the household sector.

The addition of the government sector is illustrated in **Figure 3.8**. (To avoid making the illustration too involved, we include only the financial flows to and from government; the real flow of goods and services is omitted.)

transfer payments: one-way transactions in which payment is made, but no good or service flows back in return.

FIGURE 3.8 The Addition of Government

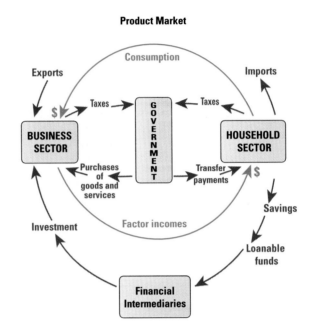

What you see in Figure 3.8 is an illustration of the basic circular flow of income with the three leakages:

- savings   (S)
- imports (IM)
- taxes   (T)

and the three injections:

- investments   (I)
- exports   (X)
- government   (G)

Equilibrium

equilibrium: a state of balance of equal forces resulting in no tendency to change.

We are now ready to take on the first of several views of **equilibrium** that we will encounter in our development of macro principles. The dictionary definition of this term is "a state of balance or equality between opposing forces." The opposing forces here are leakages on the one hand and injections on the other. If these two opposing forces are in balance, that is, if:

$$S + IM + T = I + X + G$$

then the level of income will remain *unchanged* and can be said to be in equilibrium. However, if leakages exceed injections, that is, if:

$$S + IM + T > I + X + G$$

then the level of income will *fall.* Conversely, if:

$$I + X + G > S + IM + T$$

then the income level will *rise.*

We could use an analogy here. Think of the income level as being the level of water in a bathtub. The injection could be thought of as the open tap that is adding water to the tub, and the leakage as the open drain resulting in water flowing out. The level of water in the tub (the level of income) rises, falls, or remains unchanged, according to the flow of the leakage compared to the injection. Thus, our first formal definition of **national income equilibrium** is:

national income equilibrium: that level of income where total leakages from the circular flow equal total injections.

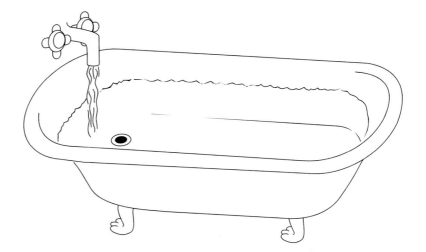

the level of income where the total of all three leakages equals the total of all three injections.

The second view of equilibrium is, in some respects, more fundamental, in that it introduces the concept of the value of production. How can we measure **value of production** (or the value of total output)? The answer is by summing the total receipts of all producers. This recognizes that the value of output is exactly the amount for which that output is sold. In other words, output has no measurable "value" until it is sold and, further, the output's value is equal to what it sells for. Thus:

value of production: the total receipts of all producers.

The value of production = total receipts of producers.

Our next step is to recognize that:

Total receipts of producers = total expenditures.

Does this guarantee that everything produced will always be sold? Isn't it possible that, in any given time period, producers might produce more than is bought? The answer to this question is yes, and if this happens producers' inventories will rise. As a result, firms will be forced to cut prices and, more significantly, cut production in the next period, which will cause layoffs and a reduction in income. (More about this later.)

aggregate expenditures:
total spending in the economy, divided into the four components: C, I, G, and $(X - IM)$.

Next, let's look at this equality again after substituting the term **aggregate expenditures**, which will be used a lot in the future for total expenditures. Aggregate expenditures is the total of all spending on consumption and investment, of government spending on goods and services, and of net exports. You are familiar with most of these terms from the circular flow of income discussion. Next, recall that the total receipts by producers will become income in the sense that what firms receive, they ultimately pay out in the form of wages, interest, rents, or profits. Therefore, when the economy is in equilibrium:

$$\text{Total income} = \text{aggregate expenditures}$$

It is this last equality that lies at the heart of the model of the economy we will be developing in later chapters. From the individual household point of view, total income will not be equal to total expenditures, for the reasons we have already discussed: part of all income goes to the government in the form of taxes, and some of that income is saved. However, if the incomes not spent by households (leakages) are instead spent by others (injections), then total income must be equal to aggregate expenditures, and the economy will be in equilibrium.

Once again, the fundamental point:

> **Equilibrium implies not only that total leakages equals total injections, but also that total income equals aggregate expenditures.**

SELF-TEST

1. If the economy is in disequilibrium because total income exceeds aggregate expenditure, what would be happening to inventories?

2. Does the term "consumption" refer to spending by households on domestically produced goods and services only? Does the term "investment" include the purchase of stocks and bonds?

REVIEW

1. What are the four *factors of production*?
2. What is the payment to each of the factors of production?
3. Distinguish between the *product market* and the *factor market*.
4. Define the term *loanable funds*.
5. Distinguish between *savings* and *investment*.
6. List the three leakages and the three injections.
7. What does the word *equilibrium* mean?
8. Describe two conceptual views of equilibrium.
9. Define the term *aggregate expenditure*.

Measuring National Income: Adding Up the Flows

The development of the circular flow of income model is complete. We now turn to the measurement of national income. Just as the circular flow diagram was helpful in conceptualizing equilibrium, it can also be helpful in recognizing that there are two different ways to measure income. The first is the *expenditures approach*. As the name implies, this approach adds up the four forms of expenditures, which, once again, are:

- C   consumption
- I   investment spending
- G   government spending on goods and services
- X   exports

and then subtracts spending on imports (IM).

In short, the basic expenditure—consumption—plus the three injections give us aggregate expenditures (AE). This gives us an equation you will become quite familiar with:

$$AE = C + I + G + (X - IM)$$

net exports: total exports minus total imports of goods and services which can be written as (X – IM) or as Xn.

Defining **net exports** (Xn) as X − IM, we could rewrite this as:

$$AE = C + I + G + Xn$$

The second conceptual approach to measuring national income—called the incomes approach—simply adds the four types of incomes that flow from the business sector to the household sector: wages, interest, rents, and profits.

Adding the total expenditures in the economy or adding the total incomes in the economy are both valid measurements of the value of production. When the economy is in equilibrium, these two sums will equal each other. So we have:

$$AE = C + I + G + Xn = \text{National Income} = w + i + r + \pi$$

Measuring National Income: The Mechanics

This section is filled with many terms that may seem a little tedious. Yet, every student of economics needs to have some understanding of how production is accounted for.

gross domestic product (GDP): the value of all final goods and services produced in an economy in a certain period.

The most-used economic statistic is **gross domestic product** (**GDP**), which is defined as the money value of all final goods and services produced in the whole economy within a given time period, such as a month, a quarter, or a year.[1]

national income (Y): total earnings of all the factors of production in a certain period.

For our purposes, the other significant statistic is **national income** (**Y**). (Government agencies use the symbol NI for national income, but we will use Y to be consistent with later chapters.) National income is defined as the total earnings of all factors of production within the economy in a given time period, such as a month, a quarter, or a year.

There are two different ways to look at the value of any particular thing produced. The first, and most straightforward, is in terms of the price it finally sells for, for example, $3 for a tube of toothpaste off the retailer's shelf. Thus, one view is that the $3 is

---

[1]All GDP figures and national income figures are adapted from Statistics Canada, Catalogue 30-001-X-PB.

its price and thus will equal the amount spent on acquiring it. The other view, equally valid, is that there is $3 worth of income to distribute to all those factors that went into the activity of getting that tube of toothpaste to the retailer's shelf. So the value of the toothpaste is the $3 of total income generated, which is paid to the various factors of production. In short:

> **The value of output is determined by the income generated in getting it into the hands of the consumer and is equal to the amount that consumers have paid for it.**

Conceptually then, *at equilibrium* GDP, the value of output must equal AE, which must equal Y.

$$GDP = AE = Y$$

Measuring GDP by the Expenditure Method

Let us next explain exactly what Statistics Canada includes in each item of expenditures. First, consumption includes spending on consumer goods and is subdivided into various components such as: consumer durables (for example, cars and household appliances); semidurables (clothes); nondurables (food and beverages); and consumer services (travel agents, hairdressers).

The next item, investment, is composed of spending on machinery and equipment, changes in the value of inventories, and spending on all construction (including residential construction). The term Ig used below refers to gross investment—that is, before any depreciation (to be discussed later in this chapter) is taken into account. Government spending is made up of the total spending on goods and services at all levels of government (including investment spending by government). It does not, however, include transfer payments or subsidies. Finally, net exports is the total value of all exports (whether of consumer goods, capital goods, or government services) less the total value of all imports. The actual figures (in $ billions) for Canada in 1997 were as follows:

C	Ig	G	Xn
505	149	187	+15

Summing these four figures gives us a GDP of $856 billion.

It is important to note that Statistics Canada is attempting to *measure* GDP, the value of production. If the economy is in equilibrium, GDP will equal aggregate expenditures. But what if the economy is not in equilibrium? For example, what happens if the total value of production exceeds aggregate expenditures? The result will be an increase in inventories (unsold goods) in the economy during that year. Conversely, if aggregate expenditures exceed the value of production, firms would find their inventories being depleted. Statistics Canada collects data on the change of inventories from one year to the next and can therefore quite easily calculate the value of production. For instance, suppose that the level of inventories in the economy at the beginning of the year is $100 billion. During the year total sales (equals aggregate expenditures) amounted to $500 billion, and the economy found itself with $120 billion in inventories at the end of the year. The value of total production during the year must therefore equal aggregate expenditure ($500 billion) plus or minus the change in the value of inventory. In this year, inventory changed by + $20 billion ($120 minus 100). Therefore, the value of production equals $520 billion. We can easily check that this is the correct answer:

Inventory at the beginning of the year:	$100 billion
Value of production:	$520 billion
Production available for sale:	$620 billion
Total sales (equals aggregate expenditures):	$500 billion
Inventory at the end of the year:	$120 billion

In summary, then,

> **value of production = aggregate expenditures plus or minus change in inventories**

This adjustment for inventories is considered as a form of investment by Statistics Canada and is what economists term unplanned investment.

gross national product (GNP): the total market value of all final goods and services produced by the citizens of a country regardless of the location of production.

Note that the GDP measures the value (at market prices) of all goods and services produced *in Canada* in a year. Many of the other statistics we will be developing are concerned with production and incomes *by Canadians*. The term given to this latter statistic is the **gross national product (GNP)**. To calculate this measure, we need to add investment income (and production) by Canadians abroad, and subtract investment income (and production) earned by foreigners in Canada as follows:

GDP at market prices	856
+/– net foreign investment income	–28
= GNP at market prices	828

SELF-TEST

3. Identify the items in the statements below (from the point of view of the Canadian economy) according to the following code.

C	consumption	*S*	savings
I	investment	IM	imports
G	government spending on		
	goods and services	T	taxes
N	not applicable	X	exports

A) A student gets her haircut from a self-employed hairdresser.

B) The hairdresser buys a pair of scissors from the Ace Beauty Supply Company.

C) Out of each day's revenue, the hairdresser puts $5 in her piggy bank.

D) Each time she has enough set aside, the hairdresser buys a share of GM stock.

E) GM expands its computer facilities in its head office.

F) American tourists go skiing in the Canadian Rockies.

G) Two Canadians go to Tokyo and stay at the Hilton Hotel.

H) Russia buys beef from Alberta beef-cattle producers.

I) The Province of Saskatchewan pays for the building of a new highway.

Measuring GDP by the Income Method

Now, we turn to the income approach to measuring GDP. Statistics Canada uses five major groupings of income. The first is wages and salaries, which includes all benefits received and are expressed as gross earnings before taxes or deductions. Next, gross profits are the earnings of corporations before any distribution of dividends or payment of taxes. Third is interest and investment incomes, which include business interest only and not interest on consumer loans or on loans to government (the latter is regarded as a form of transfer payment). Farmers' incomes is self-explanatory, though you might wonder why Statistics Canada has decided to single out farmers for special treatment. The reason is simply that it is difficult to know what portion of their total incomes is wages, what portion is profits, and what portion is from crop-retention. (Yes, eating your own crops doesn't go unnoticed by the government.) The fifth category, the clumsily titled net income of non-farm unincorporated business (hereafter, self-employed income), includes the incomes of all businesses, other than corporations (for example, self-proprietors and partners, and also includes some rent). The amounts for these categories in 1997 (again in $ billions) were as follows:

Wages	Gross Profits	Interest	Farmers' Income	Self-employed Income
446	80	47	2	58

net domestic income: incomes earned in Canada (equals the sum of wages, profits, interest, farm, and self-employed income).

Therefore, total income or, using Statistic Canada's official term, **net domestic income** = $633 billion.

This represents the total gross incomes in all forms received in Canada. As we did before, we need to make the same adjustment to find the total incomes received by Canadians, that is,

net domestic income	633
+/– net foreign investment income	–28
= national income (of Canadians)	605

Given what we learned about the circular flow of income earlier in this chapter, you may well be wondering why there is no separate category for rent. The absence of rent in the national income accounts is a practical problem rather than a conceptual one. Some profits are undoubtedly rent return, as are portions of farm income and even self-employed income. StatsCan, however, simply doesn't try to determine how much. Therefore, what was "wages, interest, rents, and profits" in the circular flow analysis is "wages, interest, profits, farm income, and self-employed income" in the national accounts.

Reconciling GNP and National Income

Perceptive readers might have noticed that the GNP (the expenditures approach) and national income (the incomes approach) totals don't agree! Didn't we say earlier that they are conceptually the same thing? Yes, they are, but in national income accounting not all the receipts (the same as aggregate expenditures) of firms are paid out in the form of incomes. First, firms set up a fund for the replacement of worn-out capital. This is termed *depreciation* (or capital consumption allowance) and is not available for distribution, either to employees or to shareholders. If we subtract the amount of depreciation from the GNP, we have another statistic called **net national product (NNP)**. Thus, for 1997:

net national product (NNP): gross national product less capital consumption (or depreciation).

GNP at market prices	828
– depreciation	110
= NNP at market prices	718

In addition to depreciation, there is another item of income that firms receive but do not pay out as income to anyone, and that is the amount of sales taxes (indirect taxes) that firms are required to collect on behalf of the government. If this amount (net of subsidies) is taken into account, we get:

NNP at market prices	718
− indirect taxes (net of subsidies)	113
= NNP at factor costs	605

Thus, after the two technical adjustments (depreciation and indirect taxes), the expenditures approach and the incomes approach do balance.

So now you know that there is a technical difference between GDP and Y, and that is important. Even more important, you also know that conceptually the two terms—GDP and Y—can be used interchangeably. We will do so throughout the text.

personal income: income paid to individuals before the deduction of personal income taxes.

Our next focus is on the term **personal income**, which can be thought of as people's gross income. Moving from national income to personal income in the national income accounting framework requires four adjustments (again we show the figures for 1997):

national income	605
− undistributed corporate profits	25
− corporate profit taxes	29
+ government transfer payments	182
− other income not paid out	9
= personal income	724

Let's explain the top two subtractions first. A corporation does one of three things with the profits it earns:

- pays taxes
- retains (saves) them
- pays dividends to its shareholders

Obviously, only the portion paid in dividends actually goes to individuals and thus becomes part of personal income. Therefore, the portion that goes to taxes and the portion that is saved is not part of personal income and thus must be subtracted from national income to get personal income.

Transfer payments (the very same ones talked about in the circular flow discussion earlier in this chapter) have to be added because they do become part of people's gross income, but are not part of national income since they have nothing to do with the payment to the factors of production. The last adjustment, other income not paid out, includes quite technical items such as transfers from non-residents, and government investment income not paid out.

To complete our national income accounting framework, we need one final adjustment.

personal income	724
− personal income taxes	200
= disposable income	524

disposable income: the personal after-tax income of people.

Disposable income can be thought of as people's take-home or net income and is the amount received after deduction of income tax (and other payroll deductions). This is what is at the disposal of the household for consumption spending and saving. In other words, disposable income is either consumed or saved. In 1997, consumption was 505 (it was the first item of expenditures) so personal savings must have been 19 (524 disposable income less 505 spent on consumption).

SELF-TEST

4. If gross profits are $62, corporation taxes are $15, and dividends are $26, then what is the value of undistributed corporation profits?

5. Given the following data for the country of Hemlock:

net foreign investment income	−10
national income	600
government spending on goods and services	175
indirect taxes	50
gross investment	60
consumption	420
depreciation	20

determine the value of Xn.

6. Given the following data for the country of Seymour:

personal income	589
undistributed corporate profits	42
corporate profit taxes	41
other income not paid out	52
government transfer payments	172

determine the value of national income.

Problems in Measuring GDP

Since many policy decisions are based on the level and growth of GDP (as we will see in later chapters), it is important for you to understand that there are some limitations in collecting and measuring the various statistics.

The real problem is in deciding what should and should not be measured. Let us spell out exactly what it is that we are trying to measure: the value of all final goods and services produced in economy in a year. By and large, this will mean the market value of all items produced, plus government-provided services (which are included at cost). However, we do not want to include the market value of everything that has been produced. For instance, we don't want to include both the value of tires produced and the finished value of the car of which they are a part; the inclusion of these intermediate goods would represent double-counting. As the definition suggests, we want to include the value of final goods only. Another obvious exclusion would be the sale and purchase of financial transactions like stocks and shares. Although they are market activities, they do not represent real production but merely the transfer of ownership between people. (The value of the services of the stockbroker who made this transfer would be included.) For a similar reason, public transfer payments (CPP, UIC, and so on) and private transfers (such as gifts and donations) are also excluded. Finally, because GDP is trying to measure current production only, second-hand sales would also be excluded since their value was included when they were first produced. In summary, economic transactions that are not included in the measurement of GDP are:

- the sale of intermediate goods
- sales that merely transfer ownership of assets
- both public and private transfer payments
- the sale of second-hand goods

An additional thought: since the value of a good or service is measured by the amount that the consumer actually pays for it, it is clear that sales taxes are included.

Canapress/Phill Snel

Squeegee labour would be considered part of the "underground economy." Although not illegal, the income is not reported to tax collectors and is therefore not part of GDP measurement.

For this reason, many people suggest that national income (and not GDP) is a better measure of an economy's performance since it excludes all indirect (sales) taxes.

Finally, we should mention a number of items that are excluded in the measurement of GDP even though they often do represent real productive effort. Some things are excluded because Statistics Canada does not hear of them. This includes all illegal activities and other activities that, though not illegal, are not reported to the tax collector (such as, hairdressing or child-minding at home). The presence of this "underground economy" means that the GDP may be seriously understated. Also excluded are productive services such as the value of the activities of a homemaker, do-it-yourself work, and voluntary work. They are excluded because, again, they are non-market activities. A non-market activity is, quite simply, any economic activity that does not involve a payment (or because the payment received is not reported to Revenue Canada). If this work were "paid for," then it would be included. This means of course that if one-half of the population were to do the housework of the other half and vice versa, and each paid the other, then the GDP would increase dramatically!

It means also that one must be very careful when making comparisons of GDP over a period of time. It is certainly true that the GDP of Canada has grown substantially over the years. But a part of the reason is that many of the services now provided commercially were once provided on a non-market voluntary basis. We now have commercial homemakers, day-care centres, interior decorators, gardeners, and so on, where once these services were mostly non-market activities. In summary, productive activities that are excluded from the measurement of GDP are:

- those that occur in the underground economy
- all non-market activities

SELF-TEST

7. Forty years ago, few households employed a housekeeper and almost no one had a nanny. In the 1990s, more and more households employed part-time housekeepers, and nannies were not that uncommon. What has this change in employment pattern done to GDP? Is more produced as a result of this change?

8. How could reported GDP remain constant yet real production rise?

1. Define *net exports*.
2. Define *GDP*.
3. Define *NNP*.
4. What is the conceptual relationship between *GDP* and *Y*?
5. Distinguish between the *expenditures approach* and the *income approach* to the measurement of GDP.
6. What is another name for *depreciation*?
7. In Canada today, which is normally larger: *national income* or *personal income*?
8. Define *disposable income*.
9. What type of transactions are *not* included in GDP figures?
10. Are all productive activities that are *not* included in the measurement of GDP illegal activities?

Chapter Highlights

The circular flow of income diagram is used in this chapter to help students conceptualize the workings of the economy on a macro level. There are several important relationships within it. These include the fact that the income flow (wages, interest, rents, and profits) is in response to the real flow of the factor services and the expenditures flow is in response to the real flow of goods and services. Savings, imports, and taxes are the three leakages from this flow, whereas investment, exports, and government spending on goods and services are the three injections. This chapter brings out the crucial distinction between savings and investment, while at the same time recognizing that the two are connected because savings creates loanable funds that are used to finance investment.

The important concept of equilibrium is introduced next, and it is concluded that equilibrium income occurs when total leakages equal total injections or, from a different perspective, when aggregate expenditures equals income.

The chapter then moves to national income accounting. Two approaches are used in the actual measurement of GDP. The first, the expenditures approach, is a summation of consumption spending by households, investment spending by business, government spending on goods and services, and net export spending. The incomes approach is a summation of the various types of income received by individuals. Next, the two approaches are reconciled and other important statistics like personal income and disposable income are defined and derived by using actual Canadian data. Finally, the problems involved in measuring GDP are discussed.

New Glossary Terms

STUDY GUIDE

Study Tips

1. The circular flow diagram gives a very effective overview of the workings of the whole economy. While you do need to learn the details of the complete diagram, try not to, in the process, lose sight of the basic relationships that are contained within it. For example, if the flow of consumption spending from the household sector to the business sector decreases, then one of the leakages, imports, savings, or taxes, must have increased.

2. There are 27 new terms introduced in this chapter. Those students who have studied microeconomics will recognize some of them. Those students who are taking macroeconomics as a first course will simply have to "bite the bullet" and learn each of these as quickly as possible. Remember our point from Chapter 1's "Study Tips" that the language of economics must be learned before the concepts can be understood. Learn several new terms a day rather than attempting all 27 in one sitting.

3. When working through the circular flow presentation, you should recognize that the position of the household sector on the right and the business sector on the left or the product market at the top and the factor market on the bottom is arbitrary; that is, each could be put the other way around. It is customary, however, to put real flows as the inner loop and financial flows as the outer.

4. Almost all students find the important distinction between money as a stock and income as a flow novel. A physical analogy may help. A lake is a stock in that the fixed amount of water, say 120 million litres, can be measured at any point in time. A river is a flow that can only be measured as a rate per unit of time, that is, 60 000 litres per minute.

5. There is no shortcut in learning the framework for national income accounting. It has to be memorized. You might try inventing your own "shorthand." For example, national income is equal to: **f**armers' income, **i**nterest, **g**ross profits, **s**elf-employed income, and wages. This could be remembered as figs + wages (or the wages of figs, or as: "He was so cheap he paid wages in figs").

6. Do not short-change the two-page discussion on equilibrium in the middle of the chapter. There is some conceptual abstraction here involving how we measure the value of production and expenditures that you need to understand.

Key Problem

Figure 3.9 is the circular flow diagram for the economy of Argos.

a) Place the following items appropriately on the diagram in Figure 3.9.

Rent	$100	Savings	$100
Wages	400	Government spending	280
Profits	60	Exports	100
Interest	80	Imports	80
Taxes (HH's only)	360	Investment	40
Transfer payments	120		

What are the values of the following?

b) The costs of production?

Answer: _____.

c) Total factor payments?

Answer: _____.

FIGURE 3.9

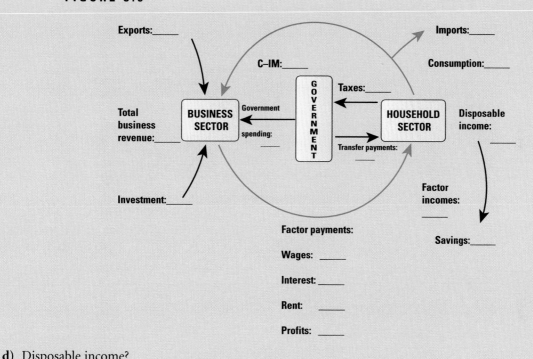

d) Disposable income?

Answer: _____.

e) Aggregate expenditures?

Answer: _____.

f) The total revenue of all businesses?

Answer: _____.

g) Total injections? Leakages? (*Hint*: Use net taxes, that is, taxes less transfer payments.)

Injections: _____; leakages _____.

h) The balance of trade (net exports)?

Answer: _____.

i) The government's budget surplus/deficit? (*Hint*: Use net taxes.)

Answer: _____.

More of the Same

Figure 3.10 is the circular flow diagram of the economy of Naxos.

a) Place the following items appropriately on the diagram in Figure 3.10.

FIGURE 3.10

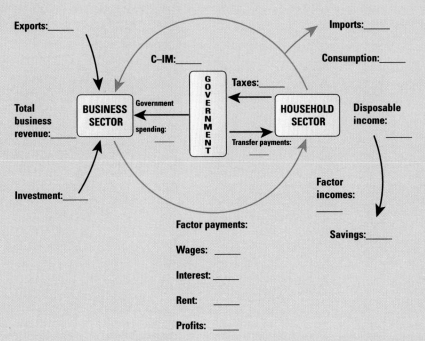

Rent	$150	Savings	$200
Wages	600	Government spending	420
Profits	90	Exports	150
Interest	120	Imports	120
Taxes (HH's only)	540	Investment	110
Transfer payments	180		

What are the values of the following?

b) The costs of production?

c) Total factor payment?

d) Disposable income?

e) Aggregate expenditures?

f) Total revenue of all business?

g) Total injections (and leakages)?

h) The balance of trade (net exports)?

i) The government's budget surplus/deficit?

You will find the national income accounting framework (**Table 3.1**) helpful in doing several of the problems below. You may want to make a few photocopies.

TABLE 3.1

Expenditures		Incomes	
Consumption	$	Wages	$
Gross Investment	$	Interest	$
Government Spending	$	Gross Profits	$
Net Exports	$ _____	Farmers' Income	$
		Self-employed Income	$ _____
Gross Domestic Product	$	**Net Domestic Income**	$
+/– Net Foreign I Income	$ _____	+/– Net Foreign I Income	$ _____
Gross National Product	$		
Less Depreciation	$ _____		
Net National Product	$		
Less Indirect Taxes	$ _____		
NNP at Factor Costs	$	**= National Income**	$
	Add Transfer Payments	$	
	Less Undistributed Profits	$	
	Less Corporate Profit Taxes	$	
	Less Other Inc. Not Paid	$ _____	
	Personal Income	$	
	Less Personal Income Taxes	$ _____	
	Disposable Income	$	
	Savings =	$	
	Consumption =	$	

Translations

Figure 3.11 depicts the economy of Hundred Acre Wood, in which there is no government, no foreign investment income, and no depreciation on capital stock.

What is Hundred Acre Wood's:

a) GDP?

b) National income?

c) Disposable income?

d) Total injections?

e) Total leakages?

FIGURE 3.11

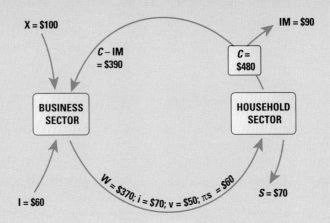

Are You Sure?

Indicate whether the following statements are true or false. If false, indicate why they are false.

1. Both the goods and services flow and the factors of production flow are money flows.

   T or F   If false: _____

   _____

2. Individuals in the household sector earn income by receiving payment for the goods and services that they sell.

   T or F   If false: _____

   _____

3. The amount of income in an economy is always equal to the amount of money in the economy.

   T or F   If false: _____

   _____

4. Savings is equal to consumption minus income.

   T or F   If false: _____

   _____

5. Transfer payments are a flow from the business sector to the government sector.

   T or F   If false: _____

   _____

6. At equilibrium, the total receipts of producers is a way of measuring the value of production.

   T or F   If false: _____

   _____

7. The two conceptual approaches used to measure GDP are the expenditures approach and the incomes approach.

   T or F   If false: _____

   _____

8. National income is the total earnings of all businesses.

   T or F   If false: _____

   _____

9. One definition of equilibrium income is the income at which total injections equals total leakages.

   T or F   If false: _____

   _____

10. National income may be a better measure of an economy's economic performance than GDP because it excludes sales taxes.

   T or F   If false: _____

   _____

Choose the Best

11. Identify the factors of production.
    a) Competition, cooperation, command, and custom.
    b) Land, labour, capital, and enterprise.

12. What are net exports?
    a) Exports less imports.
    b) Exports plus imports.

13. Which of the following is included by Statistics Canada in investment?
    a) An increase in business inventories from one year to the next.
    b) The purchase of any durable good, such as a car or a television.

14. Which of the following is regarded as real capital?
    a) A savings account.
    b) A share of Bank of Montreal stock.
    c) A dump truck.

15. Which of the following leads to an understatement of the official GDP figure?
    a) The exclusion of work done by homemakers.
    b) A decrease in the GST rate.
    c) Government spending on an oil-spill clean-up.

16. Which of the following will result in an increase in the stock of capital goods?
    a) If net investment is negative.
    b) If net investment is positive.
    c) If gross investment exceeds consumption.

17. What is the level of savings in an economy with no government and no international trade, if total factor payments are $600 and consumption spending is $480?
    a) –$120.
    b) $120.
    c) Cannot be determined from the information given.

18. Which of the following are considered activities that fall under the category of enterprise?
    a) Employing high-risk innovations.
    b) The organization and coordination of a business.
    c) The investigation and establishment of new markets.
    d) All of the above.

19. Which of the following is necessary for national income to be in equilibrium?
    a) $S + IM + T = I + X + G$.
    b) $S + IM + T = I + Xn + G$.
    c) $C + I + G - Xn = GNP$.
    d) $C + I + G + X = GDP$.

Refer to **Figure 3.12** to answer questions 21 to 23.

FIGURE 3.12

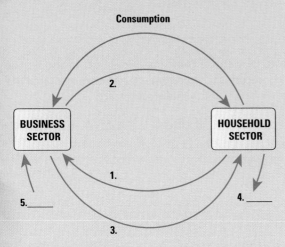

20. Refer to Figure 3.12 to answer this question. What is flow 1?
    a) Consumer goods and services.
    b) Factor services.
    c) Factor incomes.
    d) Investment.

21. Refer to Figure 3.12 to answer this question. What is flow 2?
    a) Consumer goods and services.
    b) Factor services.
    c) Factor incomes.
    d) Investment.

22. Refer to Figure 3.12 to answer this question. What is flow 3?
    a) Consumer goods and services.
    b) Factor services.
    c) Factor incomes.
    d) Investment.

23. Refer to Figure 3.12 to answer this question. What are flows 4 and 5 respectively?
    a) Exports and imports.
    b) Exports and taxes.
    c) Savings and investment.
    d) Investment and savings.

24. All *except one* of the following are factors of production. Which is the exception?
    a) Land.
    b) Labour.
    c) Capital.
    d) Money.
    e) Enterprise.

25. All *except one* of the following are examples of the factor, land. Which is the exception?
    a) Minerals.
    b) Natural harbours.
    c) Mortgages held on land.
    d) Supplies of fresh water.
    e) Fertile soil.

26. What does the simple circular flow show?
    a) That households are both buyers and sellers of products and resources.
    b) That businesses are sellers of resources and buyers of products.
    c) That households are buyers of products and sellers of resources.
    d) That businesses are sellers and households are buyers of both products and resources.
    e) That businesses both buy and sell products and resources, whereas households only buy.

27. All *except one* of the following are components of aggregate expenditures. Which is the exception?
    a) Investment.
    b) Government spending on goods and services.
    c) Transfer payments.
    d) Consumption.
    e) Exports.

28. What does the sum of national income, indirect taxes, and depreciation equal?
    a) Personal income.
    b) Disposable income.
    c) Gross domestic product.
    d) Gross national product.
    e) Net national product.

29. All *except one* of the following adjustments to national income are necessary to obtain personal income. Which is the exception?
    a) Subtract undistributed corporation profits.
    b) Subtract corporation taxes.
    c) Subtract indirect taxes.
    d) Subtract other income not paid out.
    e) Add government transfer payments.

30. What is the value of production?
   a) It always equals total expenditures.
   b) At equilibrium it is equal to the total receipts of producers.
   c) It equals $C + I + X$.
   d) It depends on the rate of savings.
   e) It is determined by inventory changes.

Other Problems

31. Using the data below for the country of Magnolia, fill in the blanks in the national income accounting framework in Table 3.1.

Disposable income	920
Dividends paid out by corporations	80
Imports	240
Investment (net)	80
Corporate profit taxes	60
Other income not paid out	20
Personal savings	120
Wages	530
Net exports	−40
Depreciation	120
Personal income taxes	160
Net foreign investment income	−20
Gross profits	180
Indirect taxes	220
Government transfer payments	200
Government spending on goods and services	400
Interest	160
Farmers' income	90

32. Answer the questions below using the following data for the country of Tameric. (All figures are in $ billions).

Wages	400
Personal income taxes	310
Farmers' income	12
Interest	38
Other earnings not paid out	9
Transfer payments	240
Gross corporate profits tax	40
Undistributed corporate profits	6
Self-employed income	30
Depreciation	60
Corporate profit taxes	20
Net foreign investment income	−20

What are the values of:
a) National income: _____ .
b) Personal income: _____ .
c) Disposable income: _____ .

33. Fill in the blanks in the data below for the country of Baobob.

C	_____
Ig	_____
G	340
Xn	20
GDP	800
Net foreign investment income	_____
GNP	780
Depreciation	70
NNP	_____
Indirect tax	_____
National income	550
Government transfer payments	210
Undistributed corporate profits	30
Corporate profit taxes	80
Other income not paid out	20
Personal Income	_____
Personal income tax	230
Disposable Income	_____
Personal savings	50

UNANSWERED QUESTIONS

Short Essays

1. Explain the difference between the term investment as used in economics and the conventional use of the word.

2. Explain the difference between the stock of money and the flow of income.

3. Not all savings becomes part of loanable funds. Why not?

4. Explain the concept of equilibrium in terms of injections and leakages.

5. Compare the expenditures approach of GDP measurement with the incomes approach.

Analytical Questions

6. Explain why government transfer payments are excluded from the measurement of GDP.

7. Which do you consider the best measure of performance of an economy: GDP, GNP, or NI? Why?

8. Do you think that the value of a homemaker's work should be included in the GDP? What would be the biggest difficulty in trying to include it?

9. While there is a technical difference between the level of national income and the level of GDP, they are conceptually the same. Explain.

10. Equilibrium occurs when the level of aggregate expenditures equals the value of total production, but not necessarily when the value of total production equals the level of income. Explain.

11. Suppose that automobile purchases were treated like housing purchases in national income accounts. How would that affect savings, consumption, investment, GDP, and DI? (*Hint*: This question is about reclassification and not about cause and effect.)

12. **a)** As part of its drive to replace welfare with "welwork," the government decides to reclassify all welfare recipients as government employees. The welfare benefits of $100 million become government wages. How does this change affect GDP, national income, and disposable income?
    b) Suppose that, in an attempt to reduce government spending even further, the government sets up a private corporation called Welwork Ltd. and the previous welfare recipients now become employees of this new corporation. The government stands ready to subsidize Welwork Ltd. with up to $100 million a year to cover its costs. Since Welwork Ltd. has no products to sell, the subsidy ends up being the full $100 million, which is paid to its employees. How does this change affect GDP, national income, and disposable income?

Numerical Questions

13. In **Figure 3.13**, replace each * with the appropriate term(s).

FIGURE 3.13

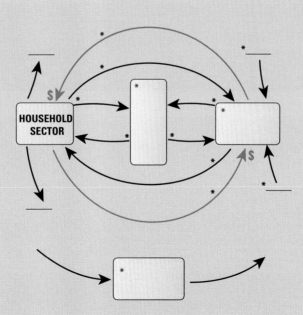

14. The following are *some* of the national income accounts for the economy of Willow Place (all figures are in $ billions).

Investment (net)	40
Wages	350
Net foreign investment income	−10
Imports	120
Gross corporate profits	90
Personal savings	60
Government transfer payments	100
Disposable income	460
Depreciation	60
Government spending on goods and services	200
Dividends paid out by corporations	40
Net exports	−20
Indirect taxes	110
Corporate profit taxes	30
Other income not paid out	10
Personal income tax	80

From this information, calculate the value of:
a) GDP.
b) Personal income.
c) Consumption.
d) National income.
e) GNP.

15. Answer the questions below using the following data for the country of Arbutus.

Rent	$50	Savings	$50
Wages	200	Government spending	90
Profit	30	Exports	60
Interest	40	Imports	40
Taxes (households)	180	Investment	60
Transfer payments	60		

What are the values of the following?
a) The costs of production
b) Total factor payments
c) Factor income
d) Total business receipts
e) Aggregate expenditures
f) Disposable income
g) Total injections (and total leakages)
h) Net exports
i) The government's budget surplus or deficit

16. You are given the following data for the country of Poplar.

Exports	30	Government spending	80
Consumption	150	Imports	40
Gross investment	70	Foreign investment income	10

a) What is the value of GDP?
b) What is the value of GNP?

17. Answer the following questions using the following information for the country of Dogwood (all figures are in $ billions).

Consumption	120
Government transfer payments	29
Farmers' income	5
Depreciation	20
Interest	10
Self-employed income	12
Exports	30
Gross corporate profits	34
Wages	113
Indirect taxes	21
Undistributed corporate profits	8
Personal savings	17
Imports	25
Personal income taxes	30
Corporate profit taxes	9
Government spending on goods and services	40
Investment (gross)	50
Other earnings not paid out	9
Net foreign investment income	−10

a) GDP
b) National income
c) Personal income
d) Disposable income

18. You are given the following data for the country of Yew.

Net Exports	−20	Consumption	200
Depreciation	30	Indirect taxes	50
Net investment	40	Government Spending	80
Foreign investment income	−10		

a) What is the value of GDP?
b) What is the value of GNP?
c) What is the value of national income?

Web-Based Activities

1. Draw a picture of the circular flow of income. Now, go to **http://www.statcan.ca/english/econoind/ gdpexp.htm** and fill in the dollar amounts for consumption, investment, government, and net exports in your diagram.

2. From the data found on the following pages, do leakages equal injections? Illustrate and explain. **http://www.statcan.ca/english/econoind/gdprev.htm**, **http://www.statcan.ca/english/econoind/ gdpexp.htm**, and **http://www.statcan.ca/english/econoind/indic.htm**.

Growth, Unemployment, and Inflation

What's ahead...This is a mostly descriptive chapter because its focus is on issues rather than on explaining specific principles or model building. We discuss the issues of growth, unemployment, and inflation. These are eternal issues, because it is a political reality that all governments have to, in some way, develop policies to address them. First, we describe how economic growth is measured and look at both the benefits and costs of growth. Next, we describe how unemployment and inflation are each measured, give a brief explanation of their causes, and discuss their costs.

In the second half of the twentieth century, market economies have shown a remarkable tendency to continuously grow over time. As an example, Canada's real GDP per capita more than tripled between the 1960 and 1995. Do we want economic growth to continue at the pace that it has? What lies behind the relatively high unemployment rates—particularly among young people—that have persisted in Canada over the last 20 years? Will you be able to avoid being an unemployment statistic during your working life? Does the rate of inflation really affect you personally in any way? These are questions that begin to take on more urgency as you approach the transition from student to active participant in the labour force with career aspirations. This chapter will help you think more about these issues.

There are three macroeconomy issues that seem to be eternal, in the sense that one or the other, or sometimes a combination of them, seems always to be headlines in the media. The first is the issue of economic growth—is the economy growing fast enough, or maybe too fast? The second is unemployment—what can be done to lower this rate in Canada, or why is this rate lower in other countries? The third issue is inflation—what are the costs of containing it, and are these costs too high? We will look at these three issues one at a time.

Economic Growth

economic growth: an increase in an economy's real GDP per capita or an increase in the economy's capacity to produce.

The discussion in Chapter 1 about growth as an economic goal established that growth has both positive and negative aspects. Before we discuss this in more depth, we need to define **economic growth**. The standard definition is an increase in an economy's real GDP. Often, this is extended to include an increase in real GDP per capita, which is real GDP divided by total population. This recognizes the fact that the population as a whole will not experience the benefits of growth unless real GDP grows faster than population.

Another valid view of economic growth is an expansion in the economy's *capacity* to produce goods and services. Graphically, you could think of this concept of growth as an outward shift in the production possibilities curve. This view is helpful because it emphasizes the fact that growth can only be sustained if it is the result of an increase in a country's potential to produce.

Measuring Growth

nominal GDP: the value of GDP in terms of prices prevailing at the time of measurement.

real GDP: the value of GDP measured in terms of prices prevailing in a given base year.

You will recall that Statistics Canada measures the GDP of Canada by taking the market value of all final goods and services produced in the country in a year. It's possible, then, for GDP to increase from one year to the next simply because market prices rose. The economy may not have, in fact, produced more. Thus, we need to make the important distinction between **nominal GDP** and **real GDP**. To see if an economy is growing, we need to know if it did actually produce more goods and services. In other words, we need to extract the effect of rising prices. If we think of real GDP as the physical quantity of goods and services produced and of nominal GDP as the market value of those goods and services, then the relation between the two can be summed up as:

$$\textbf{Nominal GDP} = \textbf{Real GDP} \times \textbf{Price Level}$$

Thus, to be able to compute real GDP we need to know the price level, that is, the *average* price of all products. We do this by using a price index, which assigns a weighted-average price for all goods and services in a particular year, called the base year, and gives this average a value of 100. The values assigned to each subsequent year will rise in proportion to any rise in the average price that occurs. For instance, let's make year 1 the base year and assume that the price index, for the following six years, is as shown in **Table 4.1**.

TABLE 4.1 A Hypothetical Price Index

Year 1	100
Year 2	105
Year 3	112
Year 4	120
Year 5	125
Year 6	128

In essence, the average "price" (measured in points rather than dollars) of the bundle of goods and services that people bought in year 1 was 100 and rose by 5 points in year 2. This gives an inflation rate of :

$$5 \div 100 \times 100 = 5\%$$

Similarly, the inflation rate in year 3 is:

$$7 \div 105 \times 100 = 6.6\%$$

Verify for yourself that the inflation rate for year 4 is 7.1%.

GDP deflator: a price index based on a representative bundle of GDP goods and services.

There are, in fact, several different types of price indexes. The one we use for GDP is called the GDP deflator. Let's use it to calculate Canada's real GDP by using actual nominal GDP and GDP deflator data. We will select 1992 as the base year. **Table 4.2** shows the results.

TABLE 4.2 Canada's Real GDP, 1992–97

Year	Nominal GDP (billions)	GDP Deflator	Real GDP (billions)
1992	$690	100.0	$690
1993	725	101.3	716
1994	762	102.4	744
1995	799	105.1	760
1996	820	106.5	770
1997	855	107.1	798

Source: Adapted from Statistics Canada, CANSIM Database, Matrices 6547 and 6544.

In 1993, nominal GDP rose by $35 billion from the previous year. This represents an increase of:

$$35 \div 690 \times 100 = 5.1\%$$

However, between the same two years, prices rose by 1.3% (101.3 − 100 in the GDP deflator column). To extract the effect of inflation, we want to find out what the 1992 nominal GDP of $725 is worth in terms of 1992 prices. We can rearrange our nominal GDP formula, mentioned above, to give us the following:

$$\text{Real GDP} = \text{Nominal GDP/GDP Deflator} \times 100$$

The real GDP for 1993 is therefore:

$$\$725 \div 101.3 \times 100 = \$716$$

In real terms, GDP rose from $690 billion to $716 billion, which is an increase of $26 billion divided by the base of $690 billion times 100, or 3.8%. The rest of Table 4.2 was calculated in the same way. You can now see that while nominal GDP rose by $165 billion, or 24 percent, between 1992 and 1997, in real terms the actual increase was only $108 billion, or 15.7 percent.

One further adjustment is necessary. While we have made allowance for the fact that inflation increases the GDP figures, we may want to also consider the fact that real GDP may have risen solely because population has increased. If that were the case, then the average person would not be any better off. To calculate real GDP per capita (per head), we simply divide real GDP by the population, as is done in **Table 4.3**.

TABLE 4.3 Canada's Real GDP per Capita, 1992–97

Year	Real GDP (billions)	Population (millions)	Real GDP per Capita	Annual Growth Rate (%)
1992	$690	28.4	$24 295	—
1993	716	28.9	24 775	2.0
1994	744	29.3	25 392	2.5
1995	760	29.6	25 676	1.1
1996	770	30.0	25 667	0.0
1997	798	30.3	26 337	2.6

The calculations made in this table are quite simple. Take the year 1993 as an example. Canada's actual real GDP was $716 billion, and its population was 28.9 million. If we divide the population into the real GDP, we get per capita real GDP of $24 775, which is $480 more than in 1992. That is, in 1993 real GDP rose by an average of $480 over the 1992 figure for every man, woman, and child in Canada. The 2 percent growth rate was calculated by taking this $480 increase and dividing by the 1992 real GDP figure of $24 295 and then multiplying by 100. Note that over the whole six-year period, Canada's real GDP per capita rose by $2042—an increase of 8.4 percent, or approximately 1.7 percent per year.

SELF-TEST

1. Fill in the blanks (to one decimal place) in the following table of Etruria's GDP statistics:

	1996	1997	1998
Nominal GDP ($billion)	443	_____	507
Real GDP ($billion)	374	389	_____
GDP deflator (1986 = 100)	_____	122	126
Population (millions)	26.1	26.4	27
Real GDP per capita	_____	_____	_____

To appreciate the benefits of economic growth, it is both sobering and instructive to ask, from time to time, what would our condition in life most likely have been if we had lived just 300 or 400 years ago? For almost all of us, the answer would probably have meant eking out a subsistence existence in a potato field somewhere in Europe or a rice paddy in Asia. By contrast, all of us today have an incredible wealth of material well-being—from central heating and clean water to cheap air travel and VCRs.

All this is the more visible benefit of economic growth. Not so apparent, but just as important, is the fact that economic growth enables society to better meet the social needs of its population. An economy that has just experienced 20 years of robust growth can provide more freeways, seats in colleges and universities, exercise rooms in community centres, and state-of-the-art medical care. In sum, all of us have far more opportunities and are far richer materially than our ancestors were, thanks to economic growth.

Despite all of this, students are often unimpressed with the concern that economists show over growth rates. What difference does it make, many wonder, if the annual growth rate of an economy is only 3 percent rather than 4 percent? Considering that Canada's GDP was, in 1997, $855 billion (in current prices), a 1 percent difference in growth translates into $8.5 billion. If we divide the $8.5 billion by the approximately 10 million families in Canada, we get $850. Could your family use an extra $850 per year *every year* from now on? As you can see, even small differences in the growth rate can be significant over time.

ADDED DIMENSION

Asian Tigers

The effects of a high growth rate, especially in an economy that starts off with a relatively low per capita GDP, can be very dramatic, even over a short period. Let's take a hypothetical example of a developing Asian nation in the 1980s whose per capita income starts at only one-half of that of a typical developed nation. Let's assume a growth rate in the Asian "tiger" of 8 percent (*below* the actual rates experienced by some of the fast-growing Asian economies in the 1980s, by the way). We will assume a growth rate of 1 percent in the developed economy. You can see what would be the results, in only twelve years, in **Table 4.4**.

With the higher growth rate, in just over a decade, the tiger has not only caught up with the developed nation but surpassed it! And all of this is a result of growth rates that aren't that wildly different—8 percent compared with 1 percent. Thus you can see the power of high growth rates.

TABLE 4.4 The Effect of Different Growth Rates on Real GDP per Capita

Year	Asian Tiger: Real GDP per Capita	Developed Economy: Real GDP per Capita
1986	$7 500	$15 000
1987	8 100	15 150
1988	8 748	15 300
1989	9 448	15 455
1990	10 203	15 610
1991	11 020	15 765
1992	11 902	15 923
1993	12 854	16 082
1994	13 882	16 243
1995	14 993	16 405
1996	16 192	16 570
1997	17 487	16 736

Table 4.5 illustrates a fact that seems to come as a surprise to many Canadians. Canada's growth in real GDP has been good over the last 30 years. For example, it was among the highest of the G-8 nations (Canada, United States, Britain, France, Germany, Italy, Japan, and Russia) in terms of real GDP between 1980 and 1993. The real GDP per capita figures are much lower, however, reflecting Canada's relatively rapid population growth. The table below shows the growth rates of real GDP and of real GDP per capita in the (then) G-7 countries.

TABLE 4.5 Growth rates of Real GDP and Real GDP Per Capita

Country	Real GDP 1980–93 (%)	Real GDP per Capita 1980–93 (%)
Japan	4.0	3.4
Canada	2.6	1.4
Italy	2.2	2.1
France	2.1	1.6
Germany	2.6	2.1
United States	2.7	1.7
United Kingdom	2.5	2.3

Source: Statistics Canada, *World Development Report*, 1995.

Sources of Economic Growth

Now that we have a clear idea of what growth is and how to measure it, let's ask the question: what makes economies grow? Economists have traditionally identified four fundamental sources of economic growth. We will discuss each of these in turn.

There is a growing consensus among economists that the *quality of an economy's labour resources* is the prime source of economic growth. A highly educated population results in a labour force that is both mobile and adaptable. As the world moves into the twenty-first century, these traits of mobility and adaptability are becoming more and more important. We are witnessing a shift in the paradigm (that is, the fundamental pattern) of what is important for an economy to be successful.

Between 100 and 200 years ago, today's successful economies shifted internally from an emphasis on agriculture to one on manufacturing. Tomorrow's successful economies are already in the process of a shift from a manufacturing base to an information–communications base, in which the whole world is "the market." The areas in which new jobs are being created is changing—in fact, the definition and nature of work is also experiencing a paradigm shift. Gone are the days when a high school graduate could step into a job at the local mill and earn, for a lifetime, an above-average income. Young people today will probably change careers three or four times in their work life, and training and education, both formal and self-taught, will be essential. Thus, the need to educate and not just train young people becomes increasingly important. And what of the older workers who have been laid off from the mills, which are now moving to other parts of the world? Here, we see the need for some form of retraining and encouragement to relocate. The old words to describe a high-quality labour force might have been "hard-working and dedicated." The new words are likely to be "smart, mobile, and adaptable."

What we are driving at in this discussion is a very important concept that economists call productivity. **Labour productivity** is the output per unit of labour input during a specific time period. As an example, assume that 100 workers produce 6000 tonnes of paper in a week. Here, labour productivity would be 60 tonnes per unit of labour or per worker. If, in three years, that figure rises from 60 to 70 tonnes per worker, there has been an increase in labour productivity. To a large extent, economic growth is about just such increases in productivity. But as the nature of work changes, just what is regarded as productive and what isn't also changes. Within the already industrialized countries of the world, output per unit of the mill worker is becoming

labour productivity: a measure of the amount of output produced per unit of labour input (per unit of time).

Canapress/Ryan Remiorz

Chief executive James Nininger and chief economist Jim Frank from the Conference Board of Canada discuss the economic outlook of Canada on October 15, 1998. The report called for increased productivity if Canadians were to maintain their standard of living.

human capital: the accumulated skills and knowledge of human beings.

less important, compared with the creativity of computer programmers, product designers, and organizational managers. All this brings a whole new meaning to the term "labour quality." This last point emphasizes the importance of what economists call **human capital**, which is defined as the accumulated skills and knowledge of human beings. An economy with a government that encourages human capital investment with well-funded and innovative education and training efforts, combined with a population that embraces the desire to improve its accumulated skills and knowledge, will be an economy with bright growth prospects.

A second fundamental source of economic growth is the amount of physical capital available within the economy. A worker with a mechanical backhoe will move more earth in a day's work than could a worker with a hand shovel in a week. Thus, an economy with a *higher capital–labour ratio* will be an economy with higher labour productivity.

Increasing the amount of capital stock in an economy is a direct result of more investment spending, which can be defined as a physical increase in the economy's plant and equipment. Canada has one of the highest capital–labour ratios in the world, and this, along with our rich endowment of natural resources, has resulted in relatively high labour productivity in past years. However, again, things are now changing so fast that we cannot continue to rely on huge machines or natural resources to provide us with continued economic growth.

The third source of economic growth is *technological change.* Here, we are referring not just to more machines (capital) but better machines, not just to finding more natural resources but finding and extracting them more efficiently. Technological change often involves better machines and equipment and always involves better methods of production, better ways of organizing work, and better ways of solving problems—in short, becoming more productive. A society that fosters and embraces technological change will soon be far ahead of one that does not. To some extent, this involves the attitudes of people as much as it does the brainpower that a society has at its disposal. Technological change can also be stimulated by spending, in both the public and the private sectors, on research and development—something that the Japanese have done more than any other society.

Finally, we need to mention that the amount and quality of an economy's *natural resources* can be a source of growth. Canada is richly endowed in this area, and that does make growth easier. This was particularly true in the early development of this country, in which beavers, fish, lumber, grains, and minerals played a significant role in growth. But we should not assume that a rich endowment of natural resources by itself ensures economic growth—think of Brazil with a rich endowment and a poor growth record. Nor should we assume that a poor endowment means no growth—witness Japan, which has practically no natural resources but a fantastic growth record.

In summary, the sources of economic growth for an economy are:

- the quality of its labour resources
- the amount of capital available
- the rate of technological change
- the amount and quality of its natural resources

What causes economic growth is a fascinating topic that can extend to almost all aspects of economics. We have given you just a bare outline of what is involved. We hope that it is enough to leave you with a sense of its importance.

ADDED DIMENSION

Robinson Crusoe and Economic Growth

Let's assume that Robinson Crusoe, the celebrated fictional castaway, is troubled by the prospects of making it on his own for an indefinite period of time on his new-found, uninhabited island. He obviously needs to catch a lot of fish to do more than just survive. He has a crude fishing pole and has been catching the odd fish recently, but he wonders if there isn't a better way to catch more and thus improve his standard of living. Perhaps there is another location on the island, where the fish are more plentiful, bigger, and easier to catch. But spending time looking for another place would leave less time for his current fishing efforts. Alternatively, he could stay where he is and hope that his fishing skills improve with experience and persistence (he curses the day he chose a course in Chinese cooking rather than a fishing class at night school). Finally, there is the possibility of fashioning a crude net or even building a boat, but, again, either of these activities would take time from actual fishing. He has three choices in trying to improve his economic well-being:

- increase the resources available to him (find a better fishing spot)
- improve his productivity (become a better fisher through experience)
- increase his capital (a net or a boat rather than just a pole)

Each of these choices requires that he sacrifice time and the fish that would be caught during this time (consumption), but in return promises a richer harvest of fish in the future. In effect, every economy faces the same choices and sacrifices, because economic growth involves more effort, less leisure, and less *present* consumption. The rewards, however, can be great and continue to pay off long into the future.

SELF-TEST

2. Given the following information:

Year	Output	Labour Input
1997	12 600 tonnes	1000 units
1999	13 860 tonnes	1050 units

calculate labour productivity (to one decimal place) per unit in both years. Approximately what percentage increase in labour productivity has occurred?

Economic Growth and the Business Cycle

Economic growth is seldom smooth and steady. For example, **Table 4.6** shows the annual growth in real GDP for Canada from 1988 to 1997.

TABLE 4.6 Canada's Rate of Growth in Real GDP

Year	Growth Rate (%)
1988	5.0
1989	2.4
1990	− 0.2
1991	−1.8
1992	0.6
1993	2.2
1994	3.9
1995	2.2
1996	1.3
1997	3.7

Source: Adapted from Statistics Canada, CANSIM Database, Matrices 6547 and 6544.

The average annual rate of growth for this 10-year period is 1.9 percent. As you can see from the data, however, the actual growth rate was nowhere near a steady 1.9 percent *each* year. This is true for most periods and most economies. In any 10-year period, some years will have high growth rates, say 5 or 6 percent, while other years will have rates below average or negative. While the *average* long-run growth *rate* is positive for most economies, the year-to-year fluctuations can be quite unstable. In short, all economies experience **business cycles.** What is meant by this term is that every economy goes through expansionary and contractionary phases in the rate at which real GDP changes. **Figure 4.1** illustrates this point using Canadian data. On the horizontal axis we have time, starting with 1988, while on the vertical axis we have the growth rate (in real GDP).

business cycle: the expansionary and contractionary phases in the growth rate of real GDP.

FIGURE 4.1 The Business Cycle

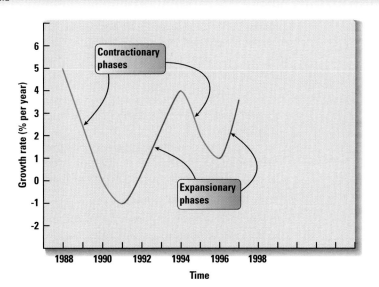

The rate of growth in real GDP reflects two contractionary phases (in red) and two expansionary phases (in blue). The average annual growth rate for the 10-year period is 1.9 percent.

You can see that the growth rate declined in the first three years of this period (1989–91). We call this a contractionary phase. The growth rate then rose in the next three years (1992–94), an expansionary phase. Next, we have another contractionary phase, this time of two years (1995 and 1996). Finally, the growth rate again rose in 1997, which signalled the beginning of another expansionary phase. These expansionary and contractionary phases in the growth of real GDP form the business cycle—what goes up comes down, and vice versa. Just what causes these expansions and contractions in an economy is at the very heart of macroeconomics, and we will, hopefully, be in a very much better position to try to answer this question by the end of this book. For now, we can just briefly mention that expansions can be triggered by such things as an increase in exports or investment spending, or, perhaps, an increase in consumer confidence, which leads to a rise in consumer spending. Contractions involve these same factors working in reverse—a fall in Canadian exports, lower business investment spending, or a decrease in consumer spending.

Growth and Economic Welfare?

We have put a good deal of emphasis on economic growth because it seems to be a necessary prerequisite for the welfare of a country's citizens. But we do need to add a word of caution to this discussion. "More" doesn't always mean "better." It is true that economic growth is seen by many as an indicator of the comparative "wellness" of an economy. After all, most people would feel that we are all better off if our economy grows, since most people view growth in a positive way. Although there is some truth in this proposition, we should realize that GDP figures are *not designed to measure welfare*; they simply measure market activity of produced goods and services. In this context, we cannot simply assume that higher GDP is necessarily better. Because of the problems of inclusions and exclusions in the measurement of GDP that we discussed in the previous chapter, it is possible for measured GDP to grow year after year, even though we are not actually producing any more. Conversely, the reported GDP may be constant, whereas in reality production is actually increasing.

There are other problems with equating the level of GDP with the well-being of a population. GDP figures give no indication of the quality of goods produced, nor do they tell us what types of goods are being produced: a gun and an economics textbook are rated equally if they are priced the same. Nor can we assume that anyone is better off if population grows faster than GDP. For this reason, as we saw, it is better to express GDP in terms of GDP per capita. Finally, the social and environmental costs of growth may well exceed the benefits. Simply producing more and more each year may not be a desirable goal if it means more pollution, more garbage dumps, more stress, and more crime. In summary, higher GDP doesn't necessarily mean that citizens are better off, because:

- higher GDP may be the result of including the value of some services that were previously excluded
- the quality or desirability of the goods produced is ignored
- per capita GDP will fall if population growth exceeds the growth of GDP
- the social and environmental costs of higher GDP are ignored

In trying to better address the question of how to measure a society's well-being, the United Nations compiles a list of the more desirable countries to live in. Things like the level of pollution, crime rates, and the availability of health care, as well as the level of GDP, are considered. Canada has consistently ranked high on this list.

In conclusion, we need to recognize that the way that GDP gets measured should prevent us from automatically equating the value of an economy's GDP with the well-being of its population.

REVIEW

1. Define *economic growth*.
2. What are some benefits of economic growth?
3. Is a 3 percent growth in GDP significantly different from a 4 percent growth rate?
4. List the four fundamental sources of economic growth.
5. Define the term *labour productivity*.
6. How is *per capita GDP* calculated?
7. What is the *business cycle*?
8. Why might economic growth not mean an increase in economic welfare?

Unemployment

unemployment: the situation in which persons 15 years old and over are actively seeking work but do not have employment.

Unemployment, as a concept, applies to any factor market since, if the economy is not producing at full capacity, then some of the factors of production must be idle—or unemployed (assuming efficient methods of production). For our purposes, however, we will focus only on the labour market. **Unemployment** can be defined as the number of persons 15 years of age and older who are not in gainful employment but who are actively seeking employment. First, we will examine three types of unemployment: frictional, structural, and cyclical.

Frictional Unemployment

frictional unemployment: that part of total unemployment caused by the fact that it takes time for people to find their first job or to move between jobs.

In a free society, where employees have the right to quit a job and employers have the right to dismiss their employees, **frictional unemployment** is inevitable. This is simply a reflection of the fact that seldom does anyone who leaves, is laid off, or dismissed from a job on, say, Friday, start a new job on the following Monday. In more general terms, unemployment and unfilled job vacancies can exist simultaneously because it takes time to match the vacant jobs with the people seeking employment.

Canapress/John Lehmann

Unemployment can affect all ages.

In addition to this matching process, there are other aspects to frictional unemployment. The first involves the growing phenomenon of people searching for the right job rather than for just any job. A growing percentage of households have more than one wage earner. Thus, if one partner earns a good income, the unemployed partner can take longer in the job-search process to increase the chances of finding job satisfaction. Prolonging the job search would, of course, result in the level of frictional unemployment rising.

Furthermore, many feel that Canada has, by world standards, generous employment insurance benefits that allow for people, in some circumstances, to accept periodic layoffs without actually searching energetically for other work. Examples would be a racetrack employee in the winter or a contract college instructor in the summer. Some economists call this phenomenon insurance-induced unemployment.

Finally, we should mention that there is a continuous inflow of new people into the labour market. This includes students who leave school and begin looking for a job as well as homemakers who enter (or re-enter) the labour market after their children are older. These people often do not find work immediately and are, therefore, frictionally unemployed until they do.

Frictional unemployment is a part of a modern market economy. It will never be eliminated and, in fact, we don't want to try to eliminate it. We need to recognize that it takes time to match people and jobs, and that some people take extra time in searching for the right job. In addition, there are some on layoff who are not actively searching for alternative employment. We can therefore conclude that frictional unemployment in Canada is a significant portion of the official unemployment rate reported monthly in the popular press.

Structural Unemployment

structural unemployment: the part of total unemployment that results from structural changes in an economy's industries.

Next, we want to examine **structural unemployment**. Some have called this "long-term frictional," but such a description doesn't capture the sense of the major shifts that take place in the economy that result in structural unemployment. A natural spin-off of a dynamic, growing economy is the fact that new industries are continually emerging and entering the expansionary stage—think of computer software, underwater submersibles, and cardboard packaging for the fast-food industry. Meanwhile, others are "sunset" industries, which have experienced declining employment for years—the East Coast fishery, for example. Some industries might even suddenly die, as was the case with the slide rule, carbon paper, and typewriter industries.

Those individuals in the sunset industries may require both a geographical and an occupational move in order to transfer into one of the newly created jobs in the growth industries. Whether retraining is required or not, this undoubtedly takes some time. In short, continuous structural changes within the economy lead to a certain amount of structural unemployment being always present. In addition, some economic observers argue that the forces of globalization in the world today have increased the rate at which businesses, and even whole industries, leave Canada in order to set up in some other, lower-wage, country. To the extent that this is true, structural unemployment becomes a bigger problem.

Cyclical Unemployment

We earlier established there are fluctuations in the economy called business cycles. These fluctuations are reflected in changes in employment and unemployment. A

full employment: the situation in which there is only frictional and structural unemployment, that is, where cyclical unemployment is zero.

cyclical unemployment: unemployment that occurs as a result of the recessionary phase of the business cycle.

natural rate of unemployment: the unemployment rate at full employment.

complete cycle consists of an expansion followed by a recession or contraction and then, once again, a recovery or expansion. This sequence of change is recurrent, but not regular in length or duration.

When the business cycle is at its expansionary peak, the economy would likely be at what is called **full employment**. Another way of looking at this is to realize that "full employment" refers to the situation in which any unemployment in the economy is a result of only frictional and structural causes. In other words, full employment is the situation of no **cyclical unemployment**.

It is from this idea that economists get the **natural rate of unemployment**. This exists when there is only frictional and structural unemployment and no cyclical unemployment. When an economy is in a recession, the total amount of unemployment is greater than the sum of frictional and structural unemployment and is therefore above the natural rate.

Thus we could say that full employment exists when the economy is experiencing *only* the natural rate of unemployment. This natural rate is considered to be the lowest unemployment rate an economy can achieve without triggering inflation. This means that it is possible to achieve a lower rate of unemployment, but only at the cost of higher prices. In addition, the natural rate of unemployment can vary from country to country and from time to time within the same country, as social and economic conditions change. For example, Japan, where the practice of changing jobs frequently is thought to show a lack of loyalty (loyalty is a highly regarded virtue), is likely to have a much lower natural rate of unemployment than is found in North America, where people frequently change jobs. As another example, some economists argue that Canada's natural rate of unemployment increased in the 1970s following an overhaul of the unemployment insurance plan that increased coverage and benefits, as well as an increase in two-income families. Today, it appears that Canada's natural rate of unemployment is about 6 to 8 percent.

Despite unemployment, job vacancies will still exist. The reason why these jobs have not been filled is that the people who want work may be located in the wrong region of the country or may not have the right skills or experience. These concepts are illustrated in **Figure 4.2**.

FIGURE 4.2 Job Vacancies and Unemployment

The jv = u line is also a 45° line coming out of the origin. The number of job vacancies in the economy and the number of unemployed people would be equal at any point on the 45° line.

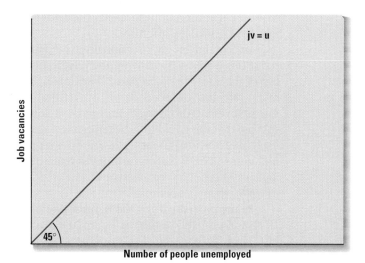

On the vertical axis is the number of job vacancies in the economy. On the horizontal axis is the number of people unemployed. At any point on the 45° (jv = u) line, the number of job vacancies and the number of people unemployed would be equal. This idea is developed further in **Figure 4.3**.

FIGURE 4.3 The Natural Rate of Unemployment

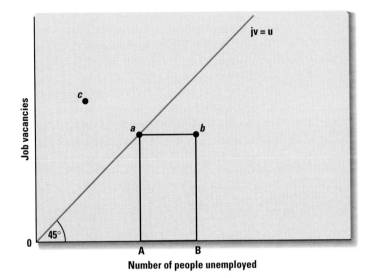

At point *a* the number of job vacancies in the economy equals the number of people unemployed, and thus unemployment is at its natural rate. As we move to point *b* we find unemployment exceeding job vacancies. Thus, cyclical unemployment is present.

Point *a* represents a situation of no cyclical unemployment in that the number of job vacancies and the number of unemployed are equal. This is our definition of full employment, in which the level of unemployment, OA, would be the natural level of unemployment. Point *b*, on the other hand, illustrates a situation in which unemployment exceeds the number of job vacancies and the distance AB represents the level of cyclical unemployment. At point *a* there are enough jobs available, but either the jobs are not suitable for the job seekers, or the job seekers are not suitable for the jobs. At point *b*, on the other hand, there is not only this mismatch, but also the situation of insufficient jobs to go around. The challenge of government policy, therefore, is both to ensure that the labour force has the right type of skills and to help create sufficient jobs for a growing work force.

An economy might occasionally experience a situation like that indicated by point *c*, but this would only be temporary. Here, because of very strong demand, the number of job vacancies, compared with unemployment, is so large that the unemployment rate has dropped below its natural rate due to frictional and structural unemployment dropping temporarily below normal levels. Again, however, it is stressed that this could only be temporary, since such a low rate of unemployment will likely generate inflationary pressure on both prices and wage rates. The effect of such inflation will likely be a return of the unemployment rate to its natural level (or even higher). Many observers felt that this was the situation that existed in the United States in 1998, when its unemployment rate fell to a very low 4.4 percent.

As mentioned earlier, the natural rate of unemployment in Canada in the mid 1990s was probably as high as 7 or even 8 percent. If so, it was surely higher than it was just 25 or 30 years ago. There are three possible explanations for this increase in the natural rate of unemployment. First, changes in employment insurance (EI) legislation in the early 1970s significantly increased benefits. Second, a longer job-search time is being taken by job seekers, who are now more affluent than they used to be and therefore can afford to extend the time spent looking for a satisfying job. Third, an increase in the female participation rate has contributed to a rapid increase in the number of people looking for employment. If these explanations are correct, the recent reductions in EI coverage and benefits and the levelling out of the female participation rate may well result in a decrease in the natural rate of unemployment in Canada in the first few years of the millennium. In summary, the natural rate of unemployment could change if:

- employment insurance benefits change
- the average job search time changes
- labour-force participation rates change

SELF-TEST

3. Categorize each of the following set of circumstances as frictional, structural, or cyclical unemployment.
A) Sanjit, a pulp-mill worker, is laid off because the mill's inventories are at an all-time high.
B) Five weeks ago, Alison left a job she didn't like and is still looking for another job.

C) Ian was a fisher on the East Coast but sold his boat after years of hard work with little return. He hasn't been employed now for almost a year.

Measuring Unemployment

To get us started on the actual measurement of Canada's unemployment rate, we turn to **Table 4.7** for some 1997 data.

TABLE 4.7 Population and Employment, Canada, 1997 (millions)

Total population	30.3
Labour-force population	23.6
Labour force	15.4
Employed	14.0
Unemployed	1.4

Source: Adapted from Statistics Canada, CANSIM Database, Matrices 3472-3482.

labour-force population: the total population in a country, excluding those under 15 years of age, inmates of institutions, those in the armed forces, and residents of Indian reserves or the territories.

labour force: members of the labour-force population, either employed or unemployed.

The term **labour-force population** is defined as the country's total population, excluding.

- those under 15 years of age;
- those living in the three territories or on Indian reserves;
- full-time members of institutions, including those in the armed forces.

As can be seen in the table, 6.7 million (30.3 minus 23.6) people fell into one of these three categories. Next, Statistics Canada takes all those in the labour-force population and subtracts those considered to be "not in the labour force." The result gives us the category entitled the **labour force**. Those not in the labour force include retired people, those who are financially independent, and those who choose not to participate in the labour market for reasons such as devoting full attention to child rearing. As can be seen in Table 4.7, those in the category called the labour force totalled 15.4 million while those not in the labour force totalled 8.2 million (23.6 – 15.4).

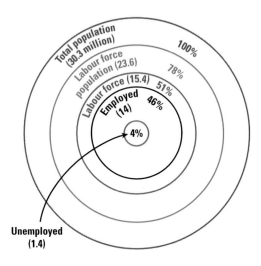

The actual mechanics of computing this data involves a random survey of 58 000 Canadian households done each month. Questions are asked of each member 15 years of age and older in each household. The questions used to determine if an individual is in the labour force are as follows:

1. Is he or she currently gainfully employed for at least one hour per week, or self-employed?
2. Is he or she temporarily not employed due to illness, vacation, or industrial dispute?
3. Is he or she laid off (within the last 26 weeks) but expecting to be recalled?
4. Is he or she not employed but starting a new job within 30 days?
5. Is he or she not employed, nor laid off, but actively seeking employment?

If none of the above five categories apply, then that person is categorized as not in the labour force.

Having identified those who are in the labour force, the next distinction is between those who have gainful employment of at least one hour per week—those who are **employed** (categories 1 and 2)—and those who are **unemployed** (categories 3, 4, and 5), since they do not currently hold paid employment. It is important to note that the fact that a person does not have a job does not mean that he or she is unemployed. To be unemployed, the person must be available for work and actively seeking employment.

Out of these various categories come two important rates: first, the **participation rate**, which is the percentage of the labour-force population who are in the labour force. **Table 4.8** shows this rate as a total for both genders for the last several years. The second is the **unemployment rate**, which is the percentage of the labour force actually unemployed—Table 4.8 gives us Canada's unemployment rate for 15 recent years.

employed: those who are in the labour force and hold paid employment.

unemployed: those who are in the labour force and are actively seeking employment, but do not hold paid employment.

participation rate: the percentage of those in the labour-force population who are actually in the labour force.

unemployment rate: the percentage of those in the labour force who do not hold paid employment.

TABLE 4.8 Labour-Force Participation Rates, Canada, 1983–97

Year	Total (%)	Male (%)	Female (%)
1983	64.4	76.7	52.6
1984	64.8	76.6	53.6
1985	65.3	76.6	54.6
1986	65.7	76.6	55.3
1987	66.2	76.6	56.4
1988	66.7	76.6	57.4
1989	67.0	76.7	57.9
1990	67.3	76.3	58.7
1991	66.7	75.1	58.5
1992	65.9	74.0	58.0
1993	65.5	73.5	57.9
1994	65.3	73.5	57.6
1995	64.8	72.5	57.4
1996	64.9	72.4	57.6
1997	64.8	72.5	57.4

Source: Adapted from Statistics Canada, CANSIM Database, Matrices 3472-3482.

Throughout this period, the female participation rate in Canada rose while the male rate fell by approximately the same percentage. This is one of the most rapid changes of any society in the world. A direct result of this is that Canada's overall labour force (labour supply) grew quickly as well. Consequently, for the unemployment rate to remain constant, the rate of new-job creation in the economy would also have had to expand rapidly.

TABLE 4.9 Unemployment Rates, Canada, 1983–97

Year	Total (%)
1983	11.9
1984	11.3
1985	10.5
1986	9.6
1987	8.9
1988	7.8
1989	7.5
1990	8.1
1991	10.3
1992	11.3
1993	11.2
1994	10.4
1995	9.5
1996	9.7
1997	9.2

Source: Adapted from Statistics Canada, CANSIM Database, Matrices 3472-3482.

Table 4.9 illustrates an important feature of the business cycle. The unemployment rate rises in periods of recession (1991–94) and falls in periods of expansion, such as occurred in l984–88 or 1994–97. Also, it is quite clear that the fluctuation is not between zero and say, 4 or 5 percent, but instead is between a low of about 7–7.5 percent up to 11–12 percent and back down.

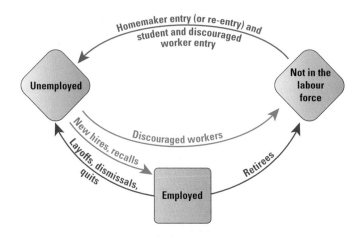

ADDED DIMENSION

Economic Growth and Recessions

A recession is defined by StatsCan as a decline in real GDP in two consecutive quarters. A drop in real GDP, one would think, will lead to layoffs in the economy and therefore a rise in unemployment. However, the average person would more likely define a recession as an increase in the unemployment rate rather than a change in the growth rate. Are these two perspectives the same thing?

Although it is true that a negative or low growth rate is usually associated with high unemployment and that a high growth rate implies low unemployment rates, this relationship is not exact. For example, in the early years of the Great Depression of the 1930s, the Canadian economy experienced negative growth rates and high unemployment. In consecutive years from 1930 to 1933, the Canadian economy experienced an annual decline in real GDP of 8.5 percent. At the same time, the average annual unemployment was 12.1 percent. From 1934 onwards the unemployment rate remained at an annual average of rate of 12.3 percent, despite the fact that the economy actually experienced positive growth in real GDP at an average annual rate of 7.1 percent. That is, an economy in the recovery stage of a recession (and it was a very slow recovery in the 1930s) can expect to record positive growth rates. Thus, while there may be some truth in regarding negative growth as heralding a recession, it would be a mistake to assume that positive growth rates always mean an economic boom.

The figures in Table 4.9, as well as those often reported in the media, are actually what StatsCan calls "seasonally adjusted" unemployment rates. What this means is that increases and decreases in the unemployment rate that are *purely* the result of seasonal influences are removed. The rationale behind all this is that the seasonally adjusted rate is a better indicator of the economy's current performance than is an unadjusted rate, which would always rise in the winter and fall in the summer.

Criticism of the Official Rate

There are four grounds on which one could criticize the official unemployment rate, despite the fact that the interview and statistical techniques used to measure them are quite legitimate. The first two criticisms discussed below cause the official rate to be *understated*.

First, it should be realized that a person who responds that she worked only part time (and it may be as little as one hour a week) in the applicable time period will be classified as employed. If this part-time status is, in fact, involuntary, then some real unemployment is being masked.

discouraged worker: an individual who wants work but is no longer actively seeking it because of the conviction that no opportunities exist.

The second point involves what critics refer to as the **discouraged worker** phenomenon. According to the official definitions used by StatsCan, a person who is not actively seeking work is not in the labour force and thus would not be counted as unemployed. Yet, some argue, many individuals have become so discouraged in their attempts to secure employment that they have stopped looking. To exclude these discouraged workers is to understate the magnitude of the unemployment problem.

The third common criticism of unemployment statistics is one that may cause the official rate to be overstated. When people who are collecting EI or welfare payments are asked if they are actively seeking work, the response is very likely to be "yes." Yet, at least some of these individuals are not involuntarily unemployed but are, instead, simply waiting for benefits to expire (or their claim to be challenged) before returning to active participation in the job market.

The fourth cause of unreliability is due to the fact that there is a whole group in the underground economy who are working in illegal occupations and, for obvious reasons, are going to declare themselves unemployed. The same may well be true for people with legal jobs who are not declaring their incomes. They too would probably declare themselves unemployed.

We will make no attempt to judge whether reasons one and two, which tip the scale one way, outweigh reasons three and four, which tip it the other way. What is probably more important to note is that measuring the unemployment rate *consistently* is crucial if we are to make sense out of time comparisons. Measured consistently, the official rate allows valid conclusions about the economy's performance in one year compared with that in another, and that's useful. In summary, the reported unemployment rates can be:

- understated because all part-timers are included as full-timers
- understated because they exclude discouraged workers
- overstated because of false information from some EI recipients
- overstated because of false information from those working in the underground economy

The Costs of Unemployment

How serious a problem is unemployment? Should we really be concerned with it? Certainly, there are some obvious personal economic costs associated with unemployment. In addition, there are serious social costs that can affect all of us. The true costs of unemployment cannot be measured simply in terms of EI or welfare payments going to the unemployed. In a sense, you might regard them as costs for the taxpayer, but obviously, from the recipient's point of view, they definitely represent a benefit. Overall, to an economist they are not true economic costs at all, but merely transfer payments. The true economic costs come from the fact that unemployment in an economy means that the quantity of goods and services being produced is less than it could be. (Like time, this lost production is gone forever.) There is an empirical relationship in economics known as **Okun's law**, which observes that for every 1 percent of cyclical unemployment, the economy's level of GDP falls 2.5 percent short of its potential.

Okun's law allows us to quantify the economic costs of unemployment. For example, in 1997 the unemployment rate was 9.2 percent (see Table 4.9). If one assumes 7 percent as the natural rate of unemployment, then Canada was experiencing cyclical unemployment of 2.2 percent. Two and one-half times 2.2 percent, or 5.5 percent, gives us the approximate level of what we could call the **GDP gap**—the difference between potential GDP and actual GDP. Given that the GDP in 1997 was $855 billion (actual GDP), we can conclude that it would have been approximately 5.5 percent higher ($47 billion) at $902 billion (potential GDP) if we had had full employment. Hence the cost due to lost production because of unemployment in that year was $47 billion—a significant amount.

As important as these dollar amounts are, the social costs to the individual and to society can represent an even greater waste. Cyclical unemployment of 4.2 percent translates into approximately 615 000 people being involuntarily unemployed. In those 615 000 stories, one would find a lot of bitterness, disappointment, anger, loss of self-esteem, and a sense of failure. Such feelings are not a recipe for social harmony. Alcoholism, accidents, claims on the health-care system, violence, and crime will all rise as a result.

Whether we try to categorize these costs as social, psychological, economic, or political, the fact remains that by whatever measure, unemployment is expensive.

Okun's law: the observation that for every 1 percent of cyclical unemployment an economy's GDP would be 2.5 percent below its potential.

GDP gap: the difference between potential GDP and actual GDP.

SELF-TEST

6. Given a natural rate of unemployment of 8 percent, an actual rate of 10 percent, and actual GDP of $800 billion, calculate potential GDP.

REVIEW

1. Distinguish between *frictional* and *structural unemployment*.
2. Describe a *business cycle*.
3. Define the *natural rate of unemployment*.
4. Define *cyclical unemployment*.
5. Define the terms *employed, unemployed* and the *labour force*.
6. How are the *participation rate* and the *unemployment rate* measured?
7. What has been the general trend of the *participation rate* over the past 20 years?
8. If the business cycle is in an expansionary phase, what will be happening to the *unemployment rate*?
9. Define *Okun's law*.
10. What is meant by *GDP gap*?

Inflation

inflation: a persistent rise in the general level of prices.

Let's now turn to inflation. Public-opinion polls consistently show that people consider inflation, or the threat of inflation, to be a major problem facing society. In fact, people's concern about inflation usually ranks above their concern about unemployment. The reason for this is probably the simple fact that while unemployment in the economy touches only the unemployed and others close to them, inflation touches everyone daily. For our purposes, **inflation** can be defined as an increase in the general level of prices that is sustained over a period of time in an economy.

Measurement of Inflation

consumer price index: an index of the changes in the prices of goods and services based on the cost of those same items in a base period.

The measurement of inflation with which most people are familiar uses the monthly **consumer price index** (CPI). StatsCan derives this index by defining a representative basket of goods and services and then collecting prices, monthly, on each item. The basket reflects the spending habits of a household of four, and the prices are weighted to reflect a typical consumption pattern.

The cost of this basket is then converted to an index, based upon a chosen (base) year. Currently, StatsCan uses 1992 as the base year. That is to say, the prices of the defined basket that prevailed in 1992 are given the value 100. The CPI for the next five years is shown in **Table 4.10**.

TABLE 4.10 Consumer Price Index, 1992—97

1992	100.0
1993	101.8
1994	102.0
1995	104.2
1996	105.9
1997	107.6

Source: Adapted from Statistics Canada, CANSIM Database, Matrix 9957.

Thus, Canada's CPI grew by 7.6 percent in this five-year period.

In addition to the CPI, which is of interest to the media and the general public, StatsCan also constructs other indexes that are of interest to more specialized groups of people, such as wholesalers and farmers. Probably the most specialized of these groups is economists, who are particularly interested in the GDP deflator that we used earlier. We have seen that this deflator is like a price index of GDP goods and services and includes not only consumer goods, but also capital goods and government goods and services.

The Rule of 70—A Helpful Tool

The "rule of 70" is useful in estimating the time it will take for a figure to double in value given a certain percentage growth rate. The formula is:

$$\text{Number of years to double} = \frac{70}{\%\ \text{growth rate}}$$

For example, if inflation is 5 percent per year, the CPI will double in:

$$\frac{70}{5} = 14\ \text{years}$$

Or, $1000 in a savings account earning 10 percent will double in:

$$\frac{70}{10} = 7\ \text{years}$$

The Costs of Inflation

Like unemployment, inflation involves some very heavy costs. Economists often categorize such costs as the *redistributive* effects on the one hand and *output* effects on the other. We will analyze each of these, starting with the redistributive effects. To do this we need to distinguish between a person's **nominal income**—the actual amount printed on the paycheque—and his or her **real income,** which is the purchasing power of the paycheque's amount. If, one year from now, your take-home pay—nominal income—is 8 percent higher and prices have increased by 5 percent during the year, would you be any better or worse off? The answer is that your real income has increased by 3 percent and you would be better off.

This can be expressed in terms of an equation:

$$\text{Real income} = \frac{\text{nominal income}}{\text{price level}}$$

or in terms of percentage change:

% change in real income = % change in nominal income − the inflation rate

With this definition in hand we can go on to say that the inflationary effects on the real income of different groups is quite uneven. The classic contrast is between an elderly couple living primarily on a private pension and a yuppie couple who are both in sales and receive, as income, a percentage of total sales volume. The real income of the elderly couple is eroded annually by inflation—in fact, between the years 1972 and 1981, for example, it was cut in half! Meanwhile it is quite possible that the yuppie couple gained from inflation because their sales volume grew faster than the overall rate of inflation. In short, inflation can be unfair in that it at times hurts the economically weak and often leaves the strong unaffected or, perhaps, even benefits them. In general, those whose nominal income increases less than the rate of inflation will suffer because their real income decreases.

nominal income: the present dollar-value of a person's income.

real income: the purchasing power of income, that is, nominal income divided by the price level.

Inflation can also redistribute wealth, particularly if the inflation rate was unexpected. The easiest way to see this is to imagine yourself borrowing $1000 today, assuming a current inflation rate of, say, 5 percent. This means that what costs you $1000 today will cost you $1050 a year from now. Anyone lending you $1000 now will definitely want to ensure they get the equivalent amount back. But in addition, they will want to earn a return on the money they lend, if for no other reason than the risk that is involved. Let's say that they want to earn a real return of 7 percent. They would therefore charge you 5% (to cover current inflation) + 7% = 12%. That is:

$$\text{Nominal interest rate} = \text{real interest rate} + \text{inflation rate}$$

or

real interest rate: the rate of interest measured in constant dollars.

$$\textbf{Real interest rate} = \text{nominal interest rate} - \text{inflation rate}$$

So, let's say that you agree to the nominal rate of 12 percent and therefore the repayment of $1120 in a year's time. If the actual inflation rate turns out to be 5 percent, then your friend will receive in real terms exactly what he expected to receive. But what would happen if the actual inflation rate turned out to be 10 percent? You will still pay back $1120 to your friend. But how much is this worth to him in purchasing power compared with the $1000 he lent to you a year ago? The answer is only approximately $1020, because of the increase in prices. He earned, in real terms, therefore, only $20 on $1000, or 2 percent. In other words:

$$\text{Real interest rate} = \text{nominal rate (12\%)} - \text{the inflation rate (10\%)} = 2\%$$

This clearly hurts the lender of the $1000 while you are not hurt and, in fact, if your real income rises because of the higher inflation, then you, the borrower, will actually gain. In general, an unexpected rise in inflation hurts lenders and can benefit borrowers, with the result being an unpredictable redistribution of wealth. On the other hand, an unexpected drop in the inflation rate will hurt borrowers and help lenders.

While these redistribution costs hurt some people, they help others. On the other hand, inflation can have another cost that really does hurt everyone. These are what are termed the output costs.

Let's start this discussion by pointing out that long-term investment is an uncertain business at the best of times. Consider the example of a company that anticipates it will have to spend $10 million to produce and market a new product. The financial viability of such a decision depends on many variables—from expected sales to production costs and many more. If estimating these unknowns also requires that uncertain inflation rates—which will affect both revenue and production costs—must be factored in, then the risks may become just too large to accept, and as a result the company may shelve the launching of the new product. All the investment spending and new hiring that would have otherwise gone ahead is foregone.

The key phrase in the above paragraph is "unknown inflation rate." Any rate—zero, 10 percent, 20 percent—is not a problem in the sense that we are discussing, as long as it remains unchanged and therefore predictable. It's the *uncertainty* associated with inflation that generates concern, making investment decision-makers nervous. If such hesitancy reduces the amount of investment in the economy, then the rate of economic growth slows and total output will be lower than it would have been. Such is the output cost of inflation.

ADDED DIMENSION

Galloping Inflation

Some unfortunate countries in the twentieth century have experienced the ravages of extreme rates of inflation that economists term galloping or hyper-inflation. The experience of Germany following World War I is both instructive and well documented. As a result of the Versailles Peace Treaty at the end of the war, Germany was presented, by the victorious nations, with a staggering reparations bill of 132 billion gold marks, which was an estimate of the war damage "caused" by Germany. Although the German government was (kindly?) allowed to pay this reparation in annual installments, the amount was far in excess of what it could reasonably raise through taxation or by borrowing. It therefore resorted to a method used by despotic kings, emperors, and corrupt governments throughout history—it simply printed more money in order to pay its bills. The result of "too much money chasing too few goods" was that prices rose by 5470 percent in 1922 alone. In 1923, things got even worse and prices rose an astonishing 1 300 000 000 000 times! One egg cost 600 000 marks, butter cost 1.5 million marks, and a pound of meat cost 2 million marks. (If you put a dollar sign in front of these figures you will sense the seriousness of the situation.)

Prices rose so rapidly at one point that waiters changed the amount charged for menu items throughout the meal. Workers demanded to be paid daily, and then, later, twice a day. And immediately upon being paid, people would rush to buy almost anything that was available for sale—especially non-perishable goods. Eventually, money was literally not worth the paper it was printed on. It was used by housewives to light the fire in stoves or by children to make building blocks. At this point, the economy collapsed and unemployment and violence rose quickly. All of this led to one of the darkest chapters in human history—the rise of Hitler and the Nazi Party.

Causes of Inflation: Two Classifications

In a very real sense, the entire study of macroeconomic principles is necessary to understand what causes inflation. Nevertheless, it is useful to briefly identify two classifications of causes at this point.

demand–pull inflation:
inflation that occurs when total demand for goods and services exceeds the economy's capacity to produce those goods.

The first is referred to by economists as **demand–pull inflation**, which occurs when the total demand for goods and services in the whole economy exceeds its capacity to produce those same goods. That is to say, people are trying to buy more goods and services than the economy is capable of producing, even at full employment. This excessive demand will pull up prices and cause demand–pull inflation.

You may well ask at this point: but don't we also experience inflation at times when unemployment is high and, thus, when there is no demand–pull inflation? The answer is yes, and thus we have the second classification of inflation called **cost–push inflation**. This occurs on the supply side of the economy, whereas demand–pull inflation is a demand-side phenomenon. Cost–push inflation has three variations.

cost–push inflation:
inflation caused by an increase in the costs of production or in profit levels, with the effect being on the supply side.

The first of these is *wage–push inflation*. For example, if a union succeeds at the bargaining table in pushing the nominal wage rate up more than any recent increase in labour productivity would justify, then the employer's real cost will rise. If we assume that this increase was not simply a catch-up in response to inflation from some other cause, then we have the makings of further inflation. If the employer who agreed to the increased nominal wage did so thinking that by increasing the price of the products she sells she can recoup the increased costs, and if the employer has sufficient market power, then we have a completed picture of wage–push inflation–increased wages pushing up costs, which push up prices. Needless to say, the impact of one union and one employer probably isn't noticeable, but if the above scenario is typical of a general pattern, then the impact will become very apparent.

The second variation of cost–push inflation, called *profit–push inflation*, can occur if firms have enough market power to enhance profits by simply increasing the prices of what is sold. This is more likely to occur in industries in which competition is weak and aggregate demand is strong.

The name of the third variation, *import–push inflation*, is almost self-explanatory. The classic example here is the OPEC oil price increases of the 1970s, which affected every economy in the world, particularly those that imported a significant percentage of the oil they consumed. Here, the cost of imported oil triggered price increases in all industries that were heavily dependent on oil. This had a snowballing effect throughout the economy.

What this brief little glimpse does for us at this point is emphasize that the cause of inflation can be either a demand-side or a supply-side phenomenon. We will go much deeper into this distinction in a later chapter.

SELF-TEST

7. A) If you borrowed a sum of money for one year at a nominal rate of interest of 11 percent and during that same year the inflation rate was 4 percent, what real rate of interest do you pay?

B) Assume that you retire with a pension fixed at $12 000 per year and that, in each of the two years following retirement, the inflation rate is 5 percent. At the end of those two years, what will be the amount of your real income?

C) Assume that wages have increased by 6 percent over the last year and that labour productivity and all other costs of production are unchanged. If labour costs are 70 percent of total costs, by how much have total costs risen?

REVIEW

1. Define *inflation*.
2. Distinguish between *nominal* and *real GDP*.
3. What is the *GDP deflator*?
4. What is the *rule of 70*?
5. Distinguish between *nominal* and *real income*.
6. Distinguish between the *nominal* and the *real interest rate*.
7. Give an example of the *distributional* effect of inflation.
8. What causes the *output* effects of inflation?
9. What is *demand–pull inflation*?
10. What is *cost–push inflation*?

Chapter Highlights

This is a mostly descriptive chapter that focuses on three macroeconomic issues that receive a great deal of attention from economists—growth, unemployment, and inflation. The chapter begins with a discussion of economic growth, which is defined as an increase in the economy's capacity to produce. The major sources of growth are then identified. These are: a) the quality of the economy's labour resources; b) the amount of capital available; c) the rate of technological change; and d) the amount and quality of its natural resources. Next, the chapter looks at the question of whether the growth in GDP can be considered a valid measure of an economy's well-being. The chapter then turns to a discussion of unemployment, which is first defined, and then three categories are identified: frictional, structural, and cyclical. Full employment is defined as the absence of cyclical unemployment. The frictional and structural unemployment that exists when cyclical unemployment is zero determines the natural rate of unemployment.

Next, the measurement of unemployment is examined; the important categories are the labour force, employed, and unemployed. StatsCan releases figures on each of these categories monthly. The monthly unemployment rate is the most-used reference in identifying the stage of the business cycle that the economy is currently experiencing.

Next, the chapter examines the cost of unemployment as it affects individuals, the society as a whole and the level of output. The distinction between actual and potential GDP is made, and Okun's law is introduced as a method of measuring this gap.

Finally, inflation is defined, and its measurement, using the concept of a price index, is examined. The costs of inflation involve the redistribution of income and the potential loss of output. Next is a brief explanation of the causes of inflation, which are categorized as demand–pull and cost–push.

New Glossary Terms

STUDY GUIDE

Study Tips

1. The material covered in this chapter contains very little theory; the chapter could be described as descriptive or institutional. This does not mean that it is unimportant, but it probably does mean that you don't need to study it quite as much as some of the other chapters.

2. In a very real sense, growth, unemployment, and inflation are subjects of the entire course that we call macroeconomics. This chapter is meant to be an introduction to these topics and not the final word. Therefore, you should not be concerned at this point if you are still unclear about questions like what is the cause of unemployment and what are the solutions to inflation. We still have a long way to go.

3. The concept of full employment and the definition of the natural rate of unemployment both play an important role in later chapters. Make sure that you understand that full employment does not mean zero unemployment.

4. Statistics Canada releases unemployment and inflation rates around the middle of each month. Often, upon their release, the media coverage is extensive. You might start listening and looking for this coverage and thus become a little more tuned in to the significance of what you are studying.

5. Many students have a tendency to assume that a person who is not working is, therefore, unemployed. You should recognize that many people who are not working are doing so either because they don't have to work (for example, they have accumulated enough money to live happily without a regular source of employment income) or because they choose to not work (such as a parent who chooses to stay home with young children). In short, people are unemployed only if they are actively seeking, but do not have, paid employment.

Key Problem I

The data in **Table 4.11** can be used to calculate a price index that we will use to convert nominal GDP figures into real GDP values. The first column lists six product categories. The second is an average annual weighting of each product bought by an average family in the distant country of Harappa and provides an indication of the importance of each product in the index. Columns 3, 5, and 7 list the price for each product in the years 1996, 1997, and 1998. Column 4 is the total amount spent on all goods in 1996 and is obtained by multiplying columns 2 and 3. The base year is 1996.

a) Complete columns 6 and 8 in the table.

TABLE 4.11

(1)	(2)	(3)	(4) 1996 Total Amount	(5)	(6) 1997 Total Amount	(7)	(8) 1998 Total Amount
Type of Product	Quantity	1996 Price	Spent	1997 Price	Spent	1998 Price	Spent
Food	10	$160	$ 1 600	$165	$_____	$175	$_____
Autos plus gas, etc.	16	290	4 640	301	_____	307	_____
Insurance	12	80	960	88	_____	99	_____
Computers	8	110	880	102	_____	104	_____
Housing	30	420	12 600	415	_____	424	_____
G Services	24	360	8 640	380	_____	391	_____
Annual Totals			29 320		_____		_____

b) What is the value of the price index in 1996?

Answer: _____ .

c) What is the value of the price index for 1997 and 1998?

1997: _____ ; 1998: _____ .

d) What is the annual rate of inflation for 1997 and 1998?

1997: _____ ; 1998: _____ .

e) Using the price indexes calculated above, complete **Table 4.12** (to the nearest whole number).

TABLE 4.12

Year	Nominal GDP (in $ billions)	Price Index	Real GDP
1996	708	_____	_____
1997	741	_____	_____
1998	768	_____	_____

f) What was the rate of growth in real GDP in 1997 and 1998?

1997: _____ ; 1998: _____ .

Assume that the population of Harappa in each of the three years was as follows:

1996   26 640 000
1997   26 902 000
1998   27 212 000

g) What was the real GDP per capita in Harappa in each of the three years (to the nearest dollar)?

1996: _____ ; 1997: _____ ; 1998: _____ .

h) What is the growth rate of real GDP per capita in

1997: _____ ; 1998: _____ .

More of the Same

Table 4.13 is set up in the same way as the table in Key Problem I. The data is for the nearby country of Mohenjo-daro. The base year is 1996.

a) Complete columns 4, 6, and 8 in the table below.

TABLE 4.13

(1)	(2)	(3)	(4) 1996 Total Amount Spent	(5)	(6) 1997 Total Amount Spent	(7)	(8) 1998 Total Amount Spent
Type of Product	Quantity	1996 Price		1997 Price		1998 Price	
Food	12	$110	$_____	$165	$_____	$175	$_____
Autos plus gas, etc.	14	320	_____	301	_____	307	_____
Insurance	10	104	_____	88	_____	99	_____
Computers	10	190	_____	102	_____	104	_____
Housing	32	462	_____	415	_____	424	_____
G Services	22	380	_____	380	_____	391	_____
Annual Totals			_____		_____		_____

b) What is the value of the price index for 1996?

c) What is the price index for 1997 and 1998 (to one decimal place)?

d) What is the annual rate of inflation for 1997 and 1998?

e) Using the price indexes calculated above, complete **Table 4.14** (to the nearest whole number).

TABLE 4.14

Year	Nominal GDP ($ billions)	Price Index	Real GDP
1996	610	_____	_____
1997	688	_____	_____
1998	744	_____	_____

f) What was the rate of growth in real GDP in 1997 and 1998 (to one decimal place)?

Assume that the population of Mohenjo-daro, in each of the three years, was as follows:

1996   22 260 000
1997   22 320 000
1998   22 500 000

g) What was the real GDP per capita in Mohenjo-daro in each of the three years (to the nearest dollar)?

h) What is the growth rate of real GDP per capita in:

1997: _____ ; 1998: _____ .

Key Problem II

Following are some facts and information about the country of Lamancha, a very beautiful and interesting land in the sixth dimension of the second parallel universe.

Lamancha uses the same population and labour force definitions as Canada does.

20 percent of Lamancha's population is 15 years old and under, or lives either on Native reserves or in its territories, or are full-time members of an institution such as a prison or hospital.

Both Lamancha's total population and its labour-force population, in all age categories, are exactly 50 percent male and 50 percent female. The male participation rate is 85 percent, while the female rate is 75 percent.

Last month's statistics reported that 48 million Lamanchians were working part-time and 96 million held full-time employment.

Recent studies have shown that frictional unemployment is 4 percent and structural unemployment is 2 percent and there is no reason to assume that these figures have changed.

Lamancha's GDP is $60 trillion.

a) With help from the information above, fill in **Table 4.15**.

TABLE 4.15

Total population	250 million
Labour-force population	_____
Labour force	_____
Employed	_____
Unemployed	_____
Discouraged workers	20 million

b) What is the unemployment rate in Lamancha?

Answer: _____ .

c) How many Lamanchians are cyclically unemployed?

Answer: _____ .

d) What is the size of Lamancha's GDP gap?

Answer: _____ .

e) If half of the discouraged workers joined the labour force and total employment did not change, what would be the new unemployment rate?

Answer: _____ .

More of the Same

Following are some facts and information about the country of Avalon, a rather dull and boring land stuck in a worm hole somewhere in the Alpha quadrant.

Avalon uses the same population and labour force definitions as Canada does.

20 percent of Avalon's population is 15 years of age and under, or lives either on Native reserves or in its territories, or are full-time members of an institution such as a school or hospital.

Both of Avalon's total population and its labour force population is exactly 50 percent male and 50 percent female. The male participation rate is 75 percent, and the female rate is 85 percent.

Recent studies have shown that frictional unemployment is 6 percent and structural unemployment is 4 percent.

Avalon's GDP is $30 trillion.

a) With help from the information above, fill in **Table 4.16**.

TABLE 4.16

Total population	125 million
Labour-force population	_____
Labour force	_____
Employed	64 million
Unemployed	_____
Discouraged workers	4 million

b) What is the unemployment rate in Avalon?

c) How many Avalonians are cyclically unemployed?

d) What is the size of Avalon's GDP gap?

e) If all of the discouraged workers joined the labour force and total employment did not change, what would be the new unemployment rate?

Translations

Look over the data that is presented in Table 4.9 of the chapter and put into words what you consider to be the highlights of this information. Do the same for the data in Table 4.5. In your answer, mention how you think the information in these two tables might be related.

_____

_____

Are You Sure?

Indicate whether the following statements are true or false. If false, indicate why they are false.

1. Frictional unemployment is likely to be greatest in sunset industries.

   T or F   If false: _____

   _____

2. The natural rate of unemployment is the unemployment rate at full employment.

   T or F   If false: _____

   _____

3. If the number of job vacancies in an economy is equal to the number of people unemployed, then cyclical unemployment is zero.

   T or F   If false: _____

   _____

4. Both male and female participation rates in Canada have been steadily rising for the past 20 years.

   T or F   If false: _____

   _____

5. The higher the rate of inflation, the lower the redistribution effect of inflation.

   T or F   If false: _____

   _____

6. Cost–push inflation is caused by the total demand for goods and services exceeding the economy's capacity to produce those goods.

   T or F   If false: _____

   _____

7. The real interest rate is equal to the nominal interest rate plus the expected inflation rate.

   T or F   If false: _____

   _____

8. Labour productivity is a measure of the amount of output produced per unit of labour input.

   T or F   If false: _____

   _____

9. If the annual inflation rate is 7 percent, then the price level will double in ten years.

   T or F   If false: _____

   _____

10. An increase in the quality of goods produced would increase the well-being of people, but this will not be captured in real GDP figures.

    T or F   If false: _____

    _____

Choose the Best

11. What is the real rate of interest if the nominal rate of interest is 10 percent and the rate of inflation is 4 percent?
    a) 6 percent.
    b) 14 percent.

12. Which of the following is a variation of cost–push inflation?
    a) Import–push inflation.
    b) Demand–deficient inflation.

13. What can be said about Canada's GDP growth rate between the years 1980 and 1993?
    a) It was among the highest of the G-7 countries.
    b) It was the lowest of the G-7 countries.

14. Suppose that in a particular economy there are 2 million part-time workers, 10 million full-time workers, and 4 million unemployed. What would be the effect on the unemployment rate if all the part-time workers were to become full-time workers?
    a) It would decrease.
    b) It would increase.
    c) It would remain unchanged.

15. What is the type of unemployment that is associated with recessions?
    a) Structural.
    b) Cyclical.
    c) Frictional.

16. Which of the following does inflation affect?
    a) Both the level and the distribution of income.
    b) The distribution but not the level of income.
    c) The level but not the distribution of income.

17. How is real GDP calculated?
    a) By dividing nominal GDP by the GDP deflator and multiplying by 100.
    b) By multiplying nominal GDP by the GDP deflator and dividing by 100.
    c) By multiplying nominal GDP by the CPI and dividing by 100.

18. According to the official StatsCan definition, what is the minimum amount of time a person must have worked in the previous week in order to be counted as employed?
    a) 5 hours.
    b) 36 hours.
    c) 40 hours.
    d) 60 minutes.

19. What would be the effect of 100 000 unemployed people becoming discouraged workers?
    a) The unemployment rate would remain unchanged, and the size of the labour force would decline.

    b) Both the unemployment rate and the size of the labour force would decline.
    c) The unemployment rate would decline, and the size of the labour force would remain unchanged.
    d) Both the unemployment rate and the size of the labour force would rise.

20. Which of the following statements is correct if we apply the "rule of 70" to a known rate of inflation?
    a) We would be able to calculate the corresponding rate of unemployment.
    b) We could determine when the value of a real asset will approach zero.
    c) We could calculate the number of years it will take for the price level to double.
    d) We could calculate the size of the GDP gap.

21. Which of the following statements supports the contention that larger real GDP per capita figures may not mean a better life for the population?
    a) Work such as house cleaning, which used to be entirely a non-market activity, is becoming more and more a market activity.
    b) Higher production has negative side-effects, such as more pollution.
    c) In the measurement of GDP, no distinction is made as to the type of goods produced.
    d) All of the above.

22. Which is a valid description of economic growth?
    a) It is an increase in an economy's real GDP.
    b) It is an increase in an economy's capacity to produce goods and services.
    c) It can be represented by a shift out in the production possibilities curve.
    d) All of the above.

23. How is real income calculated?
    a) By dividing the price level by nominal income.
    b) By dividing nominal income by a price index and multiplying the result by 100.
    c) By multiplying nominal income by the rate of inflation.
    d) By adding the rate of inflation to the rate of increase in nominal income.

24. When is the Canadian economy considered to be at full employment?
    a) When 12 percent of the labour force is unemployed.
    b) When 90 percent of the total population is employed.
    c) When 90 percent of the labour force is employed.
    d) When approximately 6 to 8 percent of the labour force is unemployed.
    e) When everyone who wants a job has one.

25. Which of the following statements concerning the natural rate of unemployment is correct?
    a) It is made up of both frictional and structural unemployment.
    b) It is the rate of unemployment at full employment.
    c) It is when the total number of job vacancies equals the number of people unemployed.
    d) It is probably about 6% to 8% in Canada today.
    e) All of the above.

26. What is the cause of cyclical unemployment?
    a) The recessionary phase of the business cycle.
    b) The declining importance of goods production and the growing importance of service production in our economy.
    c) The normal dynamics of a free-market economy.
    d) Technological change.
    e) The changing nature of demand from one product to another.

27. What does Okun's law refer to?
    a) The relationship between job vacancies and unemployment.
    b) The seemingly constant ratio between those in the labour force and the total population.
    c) The relationship between the level of cyclical unemployment and the difference between potential and actual GDP.

    d) The difference between an economy's potential and actual GDP level.
    e) The time it takes a number to double given a certain percentage growth rate.

28. All of the following statements, *except one*, are correct concerning unanticipated increases in inflation. Which is the exception?
    a) It redistributes wealth and income in unpredictable ways.
    b) It increases the real value of savings.
    c) It decreases the purchasing power of money.
    d) It benefits debtors at the expense of creditors.
    e) It affects some individuals much more than others.

29. All of the following, *except one*, has contributed to Canada's relatively high rate of economic growth. Which is the exception?
    a) A high capital–labour ratio.
    b) A rich endowment of natural resources.
    c) High expenditures on research and development over many years.
    d) High investment spending on new capital goods.
    e) Technological improvements.

30. All of the following, *except one*, are correct statements about labour productivity. Which is the exception?
    a) It is an important determinant of economic growth.
    b) It is a measure of the amount of output produced per unit of labour input.
    c) It is an integral part of labour quality.
    d) It is the basis for measuring economic growth.
    e) It increases as the capital–labour ratio rises.

Other Problems

31. Answer the following questions using the graph in Figure 4.4.

FIGURE 4.4

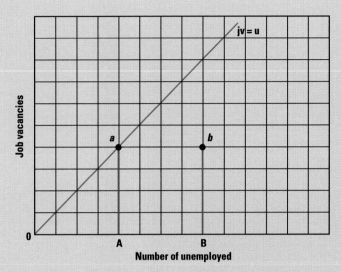

a) If the economy is currently at point *a*, what is true about the number of job vacancies and the number of unemployed?
Answer: _____

b) What does your answer in a) suggest about cyclical unemployment?
Answer: _____

Suppose that the economy is at point *b*.

c) What can you say about the number of job vacancies and the number of unemployed?
Answer: _____

d) What distance on the graph measures the natural level of unemployment?
Answer: _____

e) What distance on the graph measures cyclical unemployment?
Answer: _____

32. Answer the following questions using Table 4.17.

TABLE 4.17

	Year 1	Year 2
Labour-force population	20.0	20.0
Labour force	13.2	13.6
Employed	12.2	____
Unemployed	____	1.2

a) What is the rate of unemployment in years 1 and 2?
Year 1: _____ ; year 2: _____ .

b) How do you explain your answer in a) in light of the fact that total employment in year 2 is higher than it was in year 1? (Make reference to both discouraged workers and participation rates in your answer.)
Answer: _____
_____

33. Fill in the blanks in **Table 4.18**.

TABLE 4.18

	1996	1997	1998
Nominal GDP	672	____	708
Real GDP	600	620	____
GDP deflator (1993 = 100)	____	115	118

34. Answer the following questions using the information in **Table 4.19**.

TABLE 4.19

Year	Real GDP per Capita
1	100
2	80
3	100

a) What is this economy's growth rate between years 1 and 2?
Answer: _____

b) What is this economy's growth rate between years 2 and 3?
Answer: _____

c) Given your answers to a) and b), what was the average annual growth rate for the same two time periods? Is your answer consistent with the fact that real GDP in year 3 is the same as year 1?
Answer: _____

UNANSWERED QUESTIONS

Short Essays

1. List and describe four sources of economic growth. Which of the four do you think will be the most important source for Canada in the twenty-first century?

2. Explain some of the costs of economic growth.

3. Explain how unemployment is costly to those who experience it, to others in society, and to the economy as a whole.

4. Explain how Canada's official unemployment rate could actually understate the amount of unemployment. Then explain how it could overstate it.

5. Describe two types of inflation. Do you think it is possible for both types to occur at the same time?

Analytical Questions

6. Can you think of two consequences of a rise in the economy's capital–labour ratio?

7. "There is nothing bad about inflation if everyone knows what future rates will be." Explain how this statement might be defensible.

8. Suppose that an economy were to experience zero economic growth, but the amount of cyclical unemployment dropped by 2 percent. Comment on the change in the GDP gap.

9. Suppose that an economy were to experience 5 percent economic growth but the amount of cyclical unemployment remained the same. Comment on the change in the GDP gap.

10. "The unemployment rate has not been below 7 percent for the last 15 years. This, surely, is a failure of government policy." Do you agree?

11. In this chapter, we mentioned some of the criticisms of the definition of unemployed and employed. Can you devise a definition that overcomes the problem of including part-time workers and excluding discouraged workers?

12. Explain how an increase in unemployment might suggest an improvement in economic conditions. Could a decrease in unemployment ever imply that economic conditions are worsening?

Numerical Questions

13. Given the information in **Table 4.20**.

TABLE 4.20

Labour-force population	500
Number of people in full-time employment	160
Number of people in part-time employment	65
Number of people unemployed	25
Number of discouraged workers	15
CPI	140

a) What is the unemployment rate?
b) What is the participation rate?
c) How much inflation has occurred since the base year?

14. The following table shows national data for the economy of Darian (to the nearest whole number).

	1996	1997	1998
Nominal GDP (in billions)	$480	$520	_____
GDP deflator (1991=100)	_____	125	128
Real GDP	$400	_____	_____
Population (in millions)	_____	20.2	21
Real GDP per capita	$20 000	_____	$21 429

a) Fill in the blanks in the table.
b) What is the inflation rate in 1997?
c) What is the growth rate in 1998?

15. The inflation rate unexpectedly rises from 2 to 5 percent. What would be the effect on the following individuals?
    a) Nigel, who borrowed $20 000 last year, repayable over three years, to buy a new boat.
    b) Lars, who is an elderly man living on a fixed company pension.
    c) Yoko, who keeps her savings in a credit union that pays a fixed 4 percent on customers' deposits.
    d) Joan, who is an assembly-line worker whose employment is covered by a two-year union contract. The contract calls for an annual wage increase of 5 percent.
    e) Robert, who owns shares in the company for which Joan works.

16. Given the information in Table 4.21:

TABLE 4.21

Year	Output per Year	Labour Input
1996	80	5
1997	88	5
1998	97	5

Calculate labour productivity for each year. What is the percentage increase in productivity for 1997 and 1998?

17. Suppose that Ingrid's income in year 1 was $40 000. Over the next five years her income increases by 5 percent per year. At the same time, the economy experiences an inflation rate of 3 percent per year. At the end of five years, what will be Ingrid's real income—what is her income in terms of the prices in year 1?

18. Suppose that on January 1 the government creates 100 000 new jobs. Only those people currently without employment may apply for these jobs. The advertisement attracts 300 000 applicants, half of whom would not normally be looking for work in January.
    a) Has the labour force in January changed from what it otherwise would have been without the new jobs?
    b) Suppose that without the new jobs, the labour force would have been 10 million and the unemployment rate 7 percent. What will be the unemployment rate for January before the jobs are filled?
    c) What will be the unemployment rate after the jobs have been filled?

 ## Web-Based Activities

1. Economists have spent a great deal of time researching the costs and benefits of inflation. Skim over http://www.bank-banque-canada.ca/pub/publications/techreports/tr83.pdf and summarize what the author believes are the costs and benefits of inflation.

2. Canada's unemployment rate has persistently been higher than that of the United States. Go to http://www.csls.ca/new/cpp.html and read the article written by W. Craig Riddell and Andrew Sharpe. Explain why our unemployment rate is so much higher than the American rate.

Aggregate Expenditures

What's ahead...In this chapter we present the expenditures model of national income determination. You will see that the basic tenet of this model is that the level of national income depends on the level of spending in the economy. The discussion of the model, which is done in tabular, graphical, and algebraic forms, will increase your awareness of how the various parts of the economy are interrelated. It is important that you understand the concept of equilibrium first presented early in this chapter and then discussed in detail later. Understanding the concept of equilibrium is the key to your understanding of how national income is determined.

You are probably aware that Canada is one of the best countries in the world in which to live. One reason for this is this country's relatively high level of national income, which, of course, means a high level of per capita income. But have you wondered what determines this level of national income? And why does it grow quickly at times and not at all at other times? What role does consumer spending play in all this? And what about business investment and exports? This chapter will help you answer questions like these.

The circular flow model in Chapter 3 gave us an overview of the macroeconomy by highlighting the interrelationship between four elements of spending—consumption, investment, exports, and government—and three leakages: savings, imports, and taxes. This same circular flow model also revealed a fundamental aspect of how an economy works. The production of goods and services (GDP) generates income (national income). In fact, income can be generated *only* from real production, and the value of that production (at whatever level that it might be) is the amount of income generated as a result. It is important for you to remember that:

> **GDP and national income (Y) are conceptually the same thing—two sides of the same coin, and thus always equal to each other.**

National income ends up in the hands of individuals. And what do people do with this income? Well, they spend it on the consumption of both domestically produced goods and services and on imports, and they pay taxes with some of it and save some of it. Thus we have our three leakages and the first of the four components of aggregate expenditures—consumption. Taxes paid are the source of the government's spending on goods and services, and savings are the source of investment spending. Add exports, which originate from outside the economy, and we have all four components of spending, or aggregate expenditures.

The central question of this chapter is: do aggregate expenditures always equal national income? The clear and simple answer is no. Is it possible for aggregate expenditures to equal national income? Yes it is, and this is the condition economists call expenditure equilibrium. But it is *only* at equilibrium that aggregate expenditures equal national income. And, as we shall see, when these two are not equal the economy will change as incomes rise or fall, and when income rises or falls all the other components will change as well. This is one of the conclusions of John Maynard Keynes, who published his *General Theory* in 1936. The expenditures model presented in this chapter is in many ways a brief summary of some of the essential ideas of the *General Theory*.

The Expenditures Model

Let us start our investigation with **Table 5.1**, which shows data for the hypothetical country of Karinia (all figures are in billions of Karinian dollars), and then explore, one by one, each of the relationships between the various components in the table. We will be using national income throughout this discussion, but keep in mind that we could have just as easily used the term GDP.

TABLE 5.1 National Income and Aggregate Expenditures

Y	T	Yd	C	S	I	G	X	IM	X_N	AE (C+I+X_n+G)
$0	40	−40	100	−140	200	400	200	100	100	800
200	80	120	220	−100	200	400	200	120	80	900
400	120	280	340	−60	200	400	200	140	60	1000
600	160	440	460	−20	200	400	200	160	40	1100
800	200	600	580	20	200	400	200	180	20	1200
1000	240	760	700	60	200	400	200	220	0	1300
1200	280	920	820	100	200	400	200	220	−20	1400
1400	320	1080	940	140	200	400	200	240	−40	1500
1600	360	1240	1060	180	200	400	200	260	−60	1600
1800	400	1400	1180	220	200	400	200	280	−80	1700
2000	440	1560	1300	260	200	400	200	300	−100	1800

The levels of expenditures shown in the shaded columns indicate what the level of spending *would be* at various levels of national income. You can see right away that the first column (national income) and the last column (aggregate expenditures) are quite different. At low incomes, for instance, aggregate expenditures exceed national income, whereas at high incomes it is the other way around. Furthermore, the table suggests that even if national income in Karinia were zero, aggregate expenditures are not zero.

autonomous spending: the portion of total spending that is independent of the level of income.

We have a term for spending that does not depend on the level of income: **autonomous spending** (autonomous simply means "independent of") Spending that occurs when income is zero is autonomous. You will notice in Table 5.1 that we have autonomous consumption spending of $100, autonomous investment spending of $200, autonomous government spending of $400, and autonomous net exports of $100. This gives us a total of $800 in autonomous aggregate expenditures.

Next, notice how national income and aggregate expenditures are directly related. Clearly the two increase and decrease together. Furthermore, this relationship is constant in that for every $200 increase in national income, aggregate expenditures increase by $100. This illustrates the point that higher incomes *induce* higher levels of spending. In other words, some spending is autonomous spending and some is **induced spending**.

induced spending: the portion of spending that depends on the level of income.

Now, you may well ask how any economy could experience any spending at all if income were zero. Or how is it possible for the country to spend more than it earns in income? The answer is that people or the businesses or the government (or all three) must be borrowing. And who would they be borrowing from? From anyone who has built up a fund of past savings, which includes lenders in their own country and lenders from outside the economy. In short, the source of autonomous spending is past savings, and it really doesn't matter who or where those past savings come from.

On the other hand, the source of induced spending is current income. Again, this is seen by the fact that aggregate expenditures increase as income increases. The relationship between changes in income and the corresponding changes in spending is termed the **marginal propensity to expend** (MPE). The term propensity is similar to the concept of demand and includes the idea of both willingness and ability to spend. The formula for the MPE is:

marginal propensity to expend: the ratio of the change in expenditures that results from a change in income.

$$\text{MPE} = \frac{\Delta \text{ aggregate expenditures}}{\Delta \text{ national income}}$$

Given the data in Table 5.1, the value of the MPE in Karinia is 100/200, or 0.5. What this means is that every *additional* dollar of income earned in Karinia results in an *additional* 50 cents of induced spending. If you are wondering what happens to the other 50 cents, the answer is that it "leaks" into taxes or savings or imports. The amount of each extra dollar not spent on domestic products is referred to as the **marginal leakage rate** (MLR). Thus,

marginal leakage rate: the ratio of change in leakages that results from a change in income.

$$\text{MLR} = \frac{\Delta \text{ total leakages}}{\Delta \text{ national income}}$$

Since all income is either spent or is part of a leakage, we know that:

$$\text{MLR} = (1 - \text{MPE})$$

Before we go any further, you should note that incomes equal aggregate expenditures in Karinia only at *one* income level. This occurs at $1600 and is referred to as **expenditure equilibrium**. Again, we ask the question: does this mean that the economy of Karinia will always be at this income level of $1600? Again, the answer is no, not necessarily. But, as we shall soon see, there are forces at work that will drive the economy toward equilibrium.

expenditure equilibrium: the income at which the value of production and aggregate expenditures are equal.

We will return to this idea of equilibrium soon, but first we need to take a closer look at the various categories of expenditure and leakages. Let's take each element of Table 5.1 (which is duplicated in your Answer Key for easy reference) in turn, beginning with the tax function.

The Tax Function and Disposable Income

Notice in Karinia that taxes are $40 even when income is zero. This is the level of autonomous taxes. There are several examples of autonomous taxes, including highway tolls, user fees, property taxes, and so on. These taxes are not dependent on the level of income. However, the majority of the Karinian government's tax revenue comes from induced taxes. These are taxes whose amount depends on, or are related to, income levels. Examples would be personal income taxes, corporate taxes, and sales taxes. Some of the tax revenue that goes to the government is given back in the form of transfer payments. These payments take the form of unemployment insurance, pensions, and welfare payments. If we subtract transfer payments from tax revenues, we have what are termed **net tax revenues**. In other words,

net tax revenues: total tax revenue received by government less transfer payments.

net tax revenues (NTR) = tax revenue − (government) transfer payments

marginal tax rate: the ratio of the change in taxation as a result of a change in income.

For simplicity, we will mostly use the word "tax" rather than "net tax revenue." However, remember that tax always means that it is net of transfer payments. Notice in Table 5.1 that taxes increase by a constant $40 for every $200 increase in income levels. The **marginal tax rate** is therefore equal to 40/200, or 20 percent (0.2).

We can deal with the third column very quickly. It shows the disposable income of Karinian householders. Disposable income is simply national income minus tax (net tax revenues), or:

$$Yd = Y - T$$

Disposable income increases with national income but at a slower rate: for every $200 increase in national income, disposable income increases by $160, reflecting the tax bite.

The Consumption Function

autonomous consumption: the portion of consumer spending that is independent of the level of income.

induced consumption: the portion of consumer spending that is dependent on the level of income.

marginal propensity to consume: the ratio of the change in consumption to the corresponding change in disposable income (MPC) or national income (MPC*).

Consumption spending is the first of the four components of aggregate expenditures, and, as you can see in the shaded column in Table 5.1, it rises as disposable income rises. This indicates a direct relationship between disposable income and consumption spending, just as we saw between national income and taxes. Again, as with the tax function, there is both an autonomous and an induced aspect to consumption spending. The level of **autonomous consumption** in Karinia is currently $100, since that is the level of consumption when income is zero. **Induced consumption** is reflected in the fact that consumption rises by $120 for every increase of $160 in disposable income.

The **marginal propensity to consume** (MPC) defines the *relationship* between changes in disposable income and the corresponding change in consumption. Thus:

$$\text{marginal propensity to consume} = \frac{\Delta \text{ consumption}}{\Delta \text{ income}}$$

$$\text{or MPC} = \frac{\Delta C}{\Delta Y}$$

Here, the MPC out of disposable income is 120/160, or 0.75. We could also measure the MPC for changes in national income, which would be 120/200, or 0.6.

These days, it seems the majority of household spending takes place in a mall.

marginal propensity to save: the ratio of the change in savings to the corresponding change in disposable income (MPS) or national income (MPS*).

Generally, the MPC is calculated from disposable income, and we will use the abbreviation MPC when doing this. Occasionally, we will need to measure the MPC out of national income, in which case we will use MPC*. The MPC has a constant value of 0.75, which means that Karinian citizens spend 75 cents in every dollar of disposable income earned.

The Savings Function

We now come to the second leakage, savings (taxes was the first). Savings is defined quite simply as that portion of disposable income (Yd) which is not consumed. This is indicated by:

$$S = Yd - C$$

$$\text{or } Yd = C + S$$

Table 5.1 shows us that when disposable income is, say, $1080, consumption equals $940. Savings is therefore the difference of $140. Notice that at low levels of disposable income, savings are negative. This is called dissaving. In other words, even when income is zero, dissavings is $140. This is because at zero income, Karinians still pay $40 in autonomous taxes and $100 in autonomous consumption. Doing this is possible only by borrowing. This means that Karinians must make use of their accumulated past savings, and the total amount of these accumulated savings will therefore fall. This is what is meant by dissaving. At incomes above $800, saving is positive, and Karinians are therefore adding to their accumulated savings.

The **marginal propensity to save** (MPS) defines the *relationship* between a change in disposable income and a corresponding change in savings. The formula for the MPS is:

$$MPS = \frac{\Delta \text{ Savings}}{\Delta \text{ Disposable Income}}$$

Note that savings increase at a constant rate, just as consumption did. For every $160 increase in disposable income, savings increase by $40. Therefore, the value of the marginal propensity to save currently in Karinia is 40/160, or 0.25. (Analogously to the MPC, we could also calculate the value of the MPS out of national income [MPS*], which would give us a value of 40/200, or 0.2.)

If you think about it, we already know that the MPS has a value of 0.25. Why? Well, since consumers spend 0.75 of every dollar on consumption, they must be saving the remainder. This means that:

$$MPC + MPS = 1$$

The Investment Function

Again, looking at Table 5.1, our model regards investment spending as wholly autonomous in the amount of $200. That is to say, there is no direct relationship between investment spending and income levels. It is possible to argue that there is a natural link between the level of national income and the level of investment spending, since an increase in national income *may* increase corporate profits, which in turn *may* encourage firms to invest more. But, in reality, the link between them is, at best, weak. In our model, therefore, we will regard investment spending as entirely autonomous. This does also have the advantage also of keeping things as simple as possible.

Do not get the impression that "autonomous" means unchanging. Certainly, the amount of investment spending can change from year to year. There are many factors that can cause this to happen, and we will look at some of these factors a little later.

The Government Spending Function

As with investment spending, government spending is also treated as wholly autonomous. Now, you might object to this and believe that the amount that a government is able to spend is, in turn, determined by the amount of tax and other revenue it receives. Since this tax revenue is dependent on national income, wouldn't this mean that the amounts the government spends are also dependent on the level of national income? While there is some truth in this, it would in fact be a gross simplification. In fact, governments can and do spend whatever they feel is necessary, irrespective of the tax revenues they receive. Therefore, we will regard government spending as autonomous for the time being. In doing this, there is again the advantage of simplicity. We will return to this point later.

Exports, Imports, and the Net Export Function

Table 5.1 indicates that exports, just like government spending on goods and services, are solely autonomous. That is to say, Karinia's exports have nothing to do with its own income but everything to do with the income levels of the countries that buy Karinian exports. We have assumed exports to be an autonomous $200, but, again, you should realize that this level can change from one period to the next.

marginal propensity to import: the ratio of the change in imports that results from a change in national income.

Imports are a different story. As we saw earlier, an increase in Karinian disposable income will cause an increase in consumption spending. But that spending will not be just on domestically produced goods and services; some of it will be on imports. There is a wrinkle here though, since some imports will be made by Karinian business firms on resources and capital goods. Therefore, the level of imports is directly related to the level of *national* income rather than *disposable* income. The relationship between imports and the level of national income is known as the **marginal propensity to import** (MPM). Formally, this is:

$$MPM = \frac{\Delta \text{ Imports (IM)}}{\Delta \text{ Income (Y)}}$$

For Karinia, the value of the MPM is currently 0.10, since for every $200 increase in national income, imports increase by 20, that is, 20/200 = 0.10.

You will notice that there is an autonomous component to imports also, since the level of imports is $100 when national income is zero. Presumably, since Karinia does not possess certain products and resources, it will need to import them from abroad, regardless of its income level. That is to say, import spending is both autonomous (the $100) and induced (the MPM), just as was the case when we looked at the consumption function.

SELF-TEST

1. What exactly does it mean to suggest that some amount of imports may be autonomous? Explain the phrase and give examples to illustrate your answer.

Let's turn now to net exports, which is, quite simply, the difference between exports and imports. It is also referred to as the balance of trade, and this balance might be positive or negative. Notice in Table 5.1 that net exports are positive and highest when national income is lowest. This is a result of autonomous exports being a constant $200, whereas imports are mainly induced and thus rise as national income rises. In fact, at income levels above $1000, imports have risen sufficiently so as to exceed exports. As a result, net exports become negative. This means that as Karinia enjoys a higher national income, it also starts to see a reduction in its trade surplus and then an increase in its trade deficit. This is illustrated in **Figure 5.1**.

We see in Figure 5.1 that since exports are an autonomous $200, the export function is a horizontal line at that level. Since imports are partly autonomous, the import function starts at $100. However, it is also related to incomes so that the import function rises from that point. The slope of the import function is equal to the value of the MPM, which, you recall, has a value of 0.10 in Karinia.

FIGURE 5.1 The Net Export Function

Imports increase as income levels increase, so that the import function is upward-sloping. On the other hand, exports are autonomous of income levels, and therefore its function is a horizontal line. At low income levels, exports exceed imports, which results in a trade surplus; that is, net exports are positive. At higher income levels, however, imports exceed exports, which implies a trade deficit; that is, net exports are negative. At income level of $1000, there is trade balance of zero.

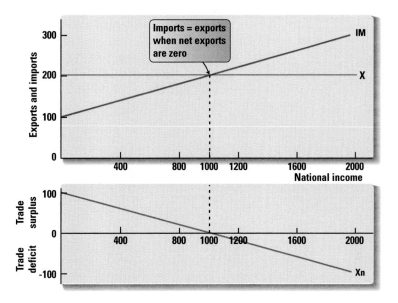

Figure 5.1 also shows that the net export function begins at a surplus of $100 because this is the amount of the difference between autonomous exports and autonomous imports. As national income rises, imports also rise. However, exports do not change with income levels, so that *net* exports (or the trade surplus) declines. At a national income level of $1000, exports are equal to imports, which means that net exports are zero; that is, there is a zero balance of trade. This is indicated by the net export function crossing the horizontal line.

In bringing our discussion of Table 5.1 to a close, you are reminded that if we add the four components of spending, C + I + G + Xn (the shaded columns), we get aggregate expenditures. It is the interplay between aggregate expenditures and national income to which we now turn.

SELF-TEST

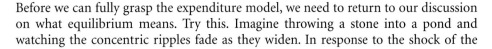

2. If $IM_o = 40$, $X_o = 200$, and MPM = 1/5, what is Xn at Y = 650?

Expenditure Equilibrium

Before we can fully grasp the expenditure model, we need to return to our discussion on what equilibrium means. Try this. Imagine throwing a stone into a pond and watching the concentric ripples fade as they widen. In response to the shock of the stone striking the water's surface, that same surface immediately begins returning to normal or to a smooth state—returning to equilibrium. Thus, equilibrium can be thought of as a state of rest, or a state of normalcy, which can, from time to time, be disrupted by various shocks. It also suggests, as we shall see, a state of equality and balance between opposing forces.

Expenditure equilibrium occurs in our model at $1600, since this is where national income equals aggregate expenditures. To clearly understand *why* that is so, we have extracted the appropriate columns from our earlier table and added an additional one to create **Table 5.2**.

TABLE 5.2 National Income and Aggregate Expenditures

Y	AE (C+I+Xn+G)	Unplanned Investment
$0	800	−800
200	900	−700
400	1000	−600
600	1100	−500
800	1200	−400
1000	1300	−300
1200	1400	−200
1400	1500	−100
1600	1600	0
1800	1700	+100
2000	1800	+200

Recall that the level of national income always equals the value of production. However, these two may or may not equal aggregate expenditures. In fact, you can see that for levels of income less than $1600, aggregate expenditures are greater than the value of production. This means that at these income levels there would be shortages, since people want to buy more goods and services than are currently being produced. The last column, unplanned investment, could also have been labelled shortages (−)/surpluses (+). **Unplanned investment**, therefore, is simply the difference between the value of production and the level of spending. At incomes greater than $1600, aggregate expenditures are less than production, which would cause surpluses, as is shown in the last column. Another way of looking at equilibrium income is that:

unplanned investment: the amount of *unintended* investment by firms in the way of a build-up or run-down of inventories; that is, the difference between production (Y) and aggregate expenditures (AE).

> **Equilibrium income is that level of income (and production) at which there is neither a surplus nor a shortage of goods.**

Let's make sure that we understand this last point. Suppose that the level of income was $1200. Here, aggregate expenditures are $1400. So where is this additional $200 of goods and services coming from? The answer is that since spending in the economy is greater than current levels of production, firms will be depleting their levels of inventory. After all, they are not going to refuse to fill orders. On the other hand, there is a definite shortage of products. This situation cannot last. In the next period, firms will increase the level of production in order to replenish those inventories and to meet the higher demand for products. The result will be a higher level of production, and if production rises, so too will national income. How high will production and income rise? Table 5.2 has already provided us the answer: it will eventually increase to the point where there are no shortages, and that will be at the $1600 level of national income.

Now let us look at the opposite scenario. Suppose that the level of GDP and national income in Karinia happened to be above the equilibrium level, say at $2000. In this case Table 5.2 tells us that aggregate expenditures, at $1800, are lower than the national income of $2000. Firms are producing, in total, more products than people are buying. The result is a surplus of goods and services produced. Firms will find that they have an unwanted build-up of inventories. You can imagine that in the next period, producers are not likely to produce another $2000 worth of goods. Instead, their response will be to produce less. This process will continue with production and incomes both falling until the economy is at the equilibrium level of national income of $1600.

We have uncovered something significant here:

> **Production and income will adjust to the level of aggregate expenditures in the economy.**

According to our expenditures model, production, and thus income (and employment), adjust to the level of aggregate expenditures in the economy.

There is another way of looking at the concept of equilibrium. If you think back to Chapter 3, the circular flow model defined expenditure equilibrium as a situation in which total injections and total leakages are equal. Let us see if this is the case in Karinia. In **Table 5.3**, we have brought forward the appropriate information (from Table 5.1) and have added subtotals for total leakages and injections.

TABLE 5.3 National Income and Aggregate Expenditures

Y	T	S	IM	Total Leakages	I	G	X	Total Injections	AE (C+I+Xn+G)
$0	40	−140	100	0	200	400	200	800	800
200	80	−100	120	100	200	400	200	800	900
400	120	−60	140	200	200	400	200	800	1000
600	160	−20	160	300	200	400	200	800	1100
800	200	20	180	400	200	400	200	800	1310
1000	240	60	200	500	200	400	200	800	1300
1200	280	100	220	600	200	400	200	800	1400
1400	320	140	240	700	200	400	200	800	1500
1600	360	180	260	**800**	200	400	200	**800**	**1600**
1800	400	220	280	900	200	400	200	800	1700
2000	440	260	300	1000	200	400	200	800	1800

As we pointed out earlier, the three injections—investment spending, government spending, and exports—are all autonomous. The reason that the injections in the circular flow model are autonomous is the same reason they are autonomous in the expenditures model: they do not depend on the level of Karinia's national income. The total for these three autonomous expenditures is $800 and remains constant. On the other hand, each of the three leakages—taxes, savings, and imports—are (mainly) induced, and therefore the total value of leakages depends on the level of income. Total leakages increase as the levels of national income increase. Thus, there is only one level of income where total injections and leakages are equal, and that is at $1600. This is expenditure equilibrium, and at this level, both injections and leakages are equal. Below $1600, injections exceed leakages, which will serve to increase national income. Above $1600, leakages exceed injections, which will serve to reduce national income. In summary, expenditure equilibrium implies all three of the following:

- the national income level at which the value of production and aggregate expenditures are equal
- the national income level at which there is neither a surplus nor a shortage of production
- the national income level at which total injections equal total leakages.

We now turn to a graphical presentation of the expenditure model.

SELF-TEST

3. If injections exceed leakages, is there a surplus or shortage? Which is greater, Y or AE?

The Expenditures Model Graphically

Let us begin our graphical analysis by looking at **Figure 5.2**. You may recall that consumption spending has both an autonomous component and an induced component. In Karinia, autonomous consumption spending is $100, and this is where the consumption function (line) starts. The slope of the consumption function, C, is equal to MPC* and reflects the fact that consumption increases $120 for every $200 rise in national income; that is, MPC* has a value of 0.6. Both the marginal propensity to consume (MPC) and the marginal tax rate (MTR) lie behind the relationship between an increase in national income and the resulting increase in induced consumption spending. The bigger the MPC or the smaller the MTR, the bigger the MPC* and the greater the amount of every extra dollar of income that is spent on consumption. This implies a steeper consumption function.

Next, you'll remember that the value of autonomous net exports is $100, so this function begins at this level on the vertical axis. For every $200 rise in national income, imports *increase* by $20, and therefore net exports *decrease* by $20, and this gives us the slope of X_n. Thus, it is the marginal propensity to import (MPM) which lies behind the slope of the X_n function. The larger the value of the MPM, the steeper the (downward) slope of X_n.

FIGURE 5.2 Aggregate Expenditures

Both investment and government spending are wholly autonomous and therefore plot as straight lines parallel to the horizontal axis. The consumption function is upward-sloping and the net export function is downward-sloping, but the consumption function increases faster than the net export function decreases. The result is an upward-sloping AE function that has a slope of 0.5.

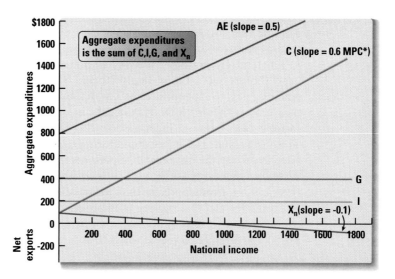

Government spending on goods and services is entirely autonomous at $400, so its function begins at this level and is parallel to the national income axis. Similarly, investment spending is treated in exactly the same way. It starts at the $200 level and is also parallel to the national income axis. Summing up the values of autonomous expenditures gives us a total value of $800, and this is where the aggregate expenditures (AE) function begins. The slope of the AE function is the value of the MPE, which, we earlier determined, is 0.5.

Having derived the AE curve, let us show expenditures equilibrium in **Figure 5.3**.

FIGURE 5.3 Expenditures Equilibrium

Autonomous aggregate expenditures are $800. The slope of the aggregate expenditures function is 0.5, so that expenditures increase by $100 for each increase of $200 in national income. When income reaches $1600, aggregate expenditures will have increased by $800 and will now equal income. This is expenditure equilibrium and is graphically indicated by the AE function crossing the 45° line.

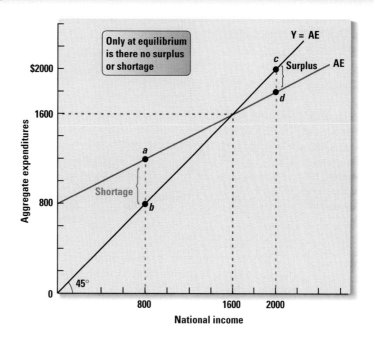

Here we introduce a 45° line, which enables us to easily locate expenditure equilibrium. Any point on the 45° line indicates that what is being measured on the horizontal axis and what is being measured on the vertical axis are equal. (Of course, this assumes that the scale of the two axes is the same; that is, zero to $200 of national income and zero to $200 of aggregate expenditures is the same *distance* on each axis.) In short, the 45° line is the locus of all points where national income equals aggregate expenditures and is accordingly labeled Y = AE. Expenditure equilibrium occurs where aggregate expenditures equals national income, and this is where the AE function crosses the 45° line. This occurs in our model at the $1600 level of national income. Notice that at incomes below $1600, the AE function is above the 45° line. This means that aggregate expenditures exceed national income. Any gap between the two curves, say the distance *ab*, represents the amount of shortage (unplanned disinvestment) that exists at that income level (the shortage equals $500 at the $800 level in this case). At incomes greater than $1600, the AE function is below the 45° line, which illustrates the fact that income (and production) exceeds aggregate expenditures, thus resulting in a surplus (unplanned investment). For example, at an income level of $2000, the distance *cd* (equal to $200) is the amount of the surplus.

We have just seen that we can also express expenditure equilibrium in terms of the equality between total injections and leakages. Using the data from Table 5.3, this is shown graphically in **Figure 5.4**.

FIGURE 5.4 Injections–Leakages Equilibrium

Here we plot some of the data from Table 5.3. Total injections are an autonomous $800 and plot as a straight line parallel to the horizontal axis. Each of the leakages (and thus total leakages) increases with the level of national income. The slope of the leakages function is 0.5. Expenditure equilibrium occurs when total injections and leakages are equal. This occurs where the two curves cross at an income level of $1600.

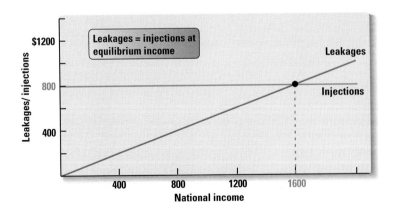

Just to remind you, total injections are autonomous, and therefore this function plots as a straight line parallel to the horizontal axis at a value of $800. If you glance back at Table 5.3 you will see that at income zero, total leakages equal $0 (T = +40, S = −140, and IM = +100). The total leakages function therefore starts from the origin.

This function is upward-sloping, with its slope equal to the value of marginal leakage rate (MLR), which in our model has a value of 0.5. That is to say, for every $200 increase in national income, total leakages increase by $100. Not surprisingly, the total leakages function crosses the total injections function at $1600, which is the value of expenditure equilibrium.

REVIEW

1. What is meant by *autonomous spending*?
2. What is *induced spending*?
3. What is the *marginal propensity to expend*?
4. Write out the *MPE* in equation form.
5. Define *net tax revenues*.
6. How are people able to save at a *zero level of income*?
7. Explain the *marginal propensity to import*.
8. What happens to the value of *net exports* as *national income* increases? Why?
9. What is the value of *unplanned investment* at *expenditure equilibrium*?
10. What is meant by the term *expenditure equilibrium*? What are the three equivalent ways of expressing it?

The Expenditures Model Algebraically

It is very helpful in economics to be quadlingual! The most important language is always verbal: if you can express economic ideas clearly and comprehensively in words, you don't really need another language. Often, however, this is difficult, and very occasionally, next to impossible. In these cases you need to resort to math. Data contained in tables of number sometimes will work. As you just saw, often graphs will do the trick. Occasionally, algebra is the simplest and clearest approach. This is the case with the expenditures model. Even if you can understand the model using the other three "languages" (words, tables, graphs), algebra is very effective and often provides additional insights. Try not to be daunted by the algebra: it's not as bad as it looks on first appearance!

We first need to understand how to derive an algebraic expression for a straight line. (Our expenditure model only deals with straight-line functions.) It takes the form of:

(1) $Y = \alpha + \beta X$

where α is a constant and β (it is called the coefficient of Y) shows how much the value of Y changes when X changes. (In the language of our expenditures model, α is the autonomous value and β is the marginal rate of change.) Since the sign of β is +, this means that there is a direct relationship between X and Y so that when X increases, Y also increases. Let us use this general equation to work out some of the particular equations for the expenditures model. For instance, let us work out the value of the tax function using Karinia's data from Table 5.1. We know that autonomous tax (T_0) is 40 and the marginal tax rate is 0.2. Therefore, the tax function is:

(2) $T = 40 + 0.2Y$

To derive a function for the next variable, disposable income (Yd), we just need to note that Yd = Y − T. Since we have just derived an expression for T, we know the expression for Yd is:

$$Yd = Y − (40 + 0.2Y) \quad \text{which rewritten is:}$$

$$Yd = Y − 40 − 0.2Y \quad \text{therefore}$$

(3) $Yd = 0.8Y −40$

Next, we can derive an algebraic expression for the consumption function, relating consumption to disposable income. First we have a slight obstacle to overcome. We need to know first the value of autonomous consumption, that is, the value of consumption when disposable income is zero. Unfortunately, the first row in Table 5.1 tells us the value of consumption when disposable income is −40, rather than zero. However, we do know that the value of the MPC is 0.75. So, if disposable income goes from −40 to 0, then consumption increases by 0.75 × 40, or 30. At disposable income of zero then, consumption is 100 + 30, or 130. The consumption function therefore is:

(4) $C = 130 + 0.75\,Yd$

Our next step is to relate consumption to national income rather than disposable income. We can do this by replacing the term Yd in equation (4) with the expression for Yd in equation (3) above, i.e:

$$C = 130 + 0.75\,(0.8Y − 40) \qquad = 130 + 0.6Y − 30; \text{ or}$$

(5) $C = 100 + 0.6Y$

(Alternatively, we could have derived this consumption function directly by simply relating consumption to national income in Table 5.1. However, the step-by-step approach that we used here is often more revealing.)

SELF-TEST

5. If t = 0.20; T_0 = 100; and C = 80 + 0.7Yd, write out an expression relating consumption to income, that is, C as a function of Y.

We can now move to the expression for savings by noting that savings is the portion of *disposable* income that is not consumed, that is, S = Yd − C, or

$$S = Yd − (100 + 0.6Y)$$

If we substitute our expression for Yd from equation (3), we have

$$S = (0.8Y − 40) − (100 + 0.6Y) \qquad = 0.8Y − 40 − 100 − 0.6Y \text{ or}$$

(6) $S = −140 + 0.2Y$

The other equations are relatively straightforward. The next three columns in Table 5.1 are injections and all are autonomous:

(7) $I = 200$ \qquad (8) $G = 400$ \qquad (9) $X = 200$

Finally, imports are partly autonomous (IM_0) at a value of $100 and partly induced. Since the MPM is 0.1, the equation for imports is:

(10) $IM = 100 + 0.1Y$

Since our last element of aggregate expenditures is net exports, or exports minus imports, its equation is:

(11) $Xn = 200 - (100 + 0.1Y) = 100 - 0.1Y$

That's all the hard work! Now it's a straightforward job of deriving an algebraic expression for aggregate expenditures. We know that aggregate expenditures are the sum of consumption, investment, government spending, and net exports. Thus,

$$C = 100 + 0.6Y \qquad \text{(equation 5)}$$

$$I = 200 \qquad \text{(equation 7)}$$

$$G = 400 \qquad \text{(equation 8)}$$

$$\underline{Xn = 100 - 0.1Y \qquad \text{(equation 11)}}$$

(12) $AE = 800 + 0.5Y$

Although we have now derived an algebraic expression for the AE function, we could have saved a lot of time and trouble by deriving it directly from Table 5.1 (or as repeated in Table 5.2). You can see immediately that autonomous AE equals 800 and the value of the MPE is 0.5. However, we spent some time deriving it from its components so that you will have some idea of the ingredients and therefore a better understanding of the effects of changing any one of them.

Now that we have an algebraic expression for aggregate expenditures, it's a fairly simple job to find out the value of expenditure equilibrium. To do this we simply make AE and national income equal and then find what value it gives us for expenditure equilibrium. Thus, let

$$Y = AE = 800 + 0.5Y$$

Gathering up the Y-terms on the left side gives us:

$$Y - 0.5Y = 800$$

$$0.5Y = 800$$

$$Y = 1600$$

Once we have figured out the value of expenditures equilibrium, it is always a good idea to get into the habit of checking the answer. We can do this by laying out a *balancing row*. This is a row of variables for which we compute their values at equilibrium, enabling us to check for accuracy.

Y	T	Yd	C	S	I	G	X	IM	Xn	AE
	$(40+0.2Y)$	$(Y-T)$	$(130+0.75Yd)$					$(100+0.1Y)$	$(X-IM)$	
1600	360	1240	1060	180	200	400	200	260	-60	1600

After calculating the figures for the balancing row, the sum of the elements of aggregate expenditures $(C + I + G + Xn)$ should add up to 1600, the value of national income. If you have made a mistake, this row simply will not balance.

Autonomous and Induced Spending Once Again

We have spent some time with this expenditure model. Hopefully, you can now appreciate how interrelated these variables are and how important spending is in determining the level of national income. Since a rise or fall in national income will also mean a rise or fall in total employment, the expenditures model is also a model that indicates the level of employment, and unemployment, in the economy. In fact, Keynes regarded the role of expenditures in an economy as pivotal in determining income and employment. Thus, it is important for us to understand what can causes expenditures to *change* and what the effect of these changes will be.

We now know that some spending is induced by income. Therefore, aggregate expenditures will increase if the level of national income increases. This happens because a higher income will induce more consumption spending. This is illustrated in **Figure 5.5A**, which shows how an increase in aggregate expenditures, from $1600 to $1700, is the *result* of an increase in the level of income from $1600 to $1800. That is, aggregate expenditures rises because income rises.

FIGURE 5.5 An Increase in Spending and an Increase in the Level of Spending

Figure 5.5A illustrates how a $200 increase in national income can increase aggregate expenditures by $100. This is an increase in induced expenditures, causing a movement along the AE curve. Figure 5.5B shows a similar increase in aggregate expenditures of $100. However, this is caused by an increase in autonomous expenditures, causing a shift in the AE function from AE_1 to AE_2.

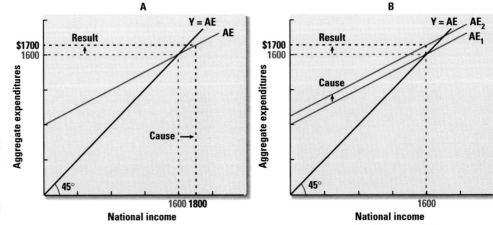

In contrast, **Figure 5.5B** shows a quite different source of change, reflecting the fact that some expenditures are autonomous. Here, aggregate expenditures have also increased from $1600 to $1700 *at the same* $1600 level of national income. This increase in aggregate expenditures must be the result of a change in something other than the level of national income. In fact, what this reflects is the result of a change in autonomous expenditures.

In graphical terms, a change in national income will produce a movement *along* the AE curve, whereas a change in autonomous expenditures will cause a *shift* in the AE curve. What causes these shifts is an aspect we need to examine.

Changes in Autonomous Expenditures

We have just seen that a change in autonomous spending will, graphically, shift the aggregate expenditures function and this will lead to a new equilibrium level of national income. Let us now look at what will cause autonomous expenditures to change. Recall that all four sectors of spending can be affected by autonomous changes, some partially, and some wholly. Let us take each in turn and see what factors might affect each of them.

A Change in Autonomous Consumption

wealth effect: the effect of a change in wealth on consumption spending (a direct relationship between the two).

First, let's look at what will cause a change in autonomous consumption. Economists know that the wealth held by people can influence consumption spending. This is called the **wealth effect**. To use a micro-level example, imagine a middle-aged professional computer programmer driving home from work, reflecting how well her life seems to be unfolding—good job, kids well on their way to growing up, spouse working at something he likes, and a mortgage that is now quite manageable. She then hears the day's closing stock quotations, which prompt her to do quick calculations after dinner on the current value of the $5000 she put into stocks a couple of years back. She is pleasantly surprised to realize that the stock is now worth over $8000—at least on paper. Her thought is to surprise the family with a proposal for a spontaneous holiday, or perhaps announce that the hot tub they had been discussing will indeed be purchased. The point is that the rise in wealth might well lead to increased consumption, even though income is unchanged.

Stockholders' wealth went up on this particular day.

TSE	Dow	London	FPX Gth.	C$
+48.33	-36.05	+113.00	+4.87	-0.09
5822.66	7897.20	5103.30	1320.37	US65.38¢
ME	**S&P 500**	**Tokyo**	**FPX Bal.**	**Gold**
+21.81	+5.91	+192.51	+3.38	-1.00
3000.42	1029.80	13789.81	1330.07	US$287.50
VSE	**Nasdaq**	**Hong Kong**	**FPX Inc.**	**Crude oil**
-3.94	+17.37	+203.28	+3.16	+0.18
397.17	1697.80	7373.51	1320.51	US$15.67

Source: *The Financial Post*, September 21, 1998.

Second, the level of consumption depends on the price level. A change in the price level will cause consumption spending to change. The reason for this may seem obvious. However, it is not simply a case of higher prices causing spending to drop because people can afford less and lower prices causing them to spend more because they can afford to. (We will see in some detail in later chapters why this simple view is not valid.) The proper explanation has to do with the real value of assets. Suppose, for instance, that both prices *and* your own money income were to increase by 10 percent, so that your real income remained constant. Would this change have any real effect on your consumption? Well, even though your real income is unchanged, there is one portion of your wealth that is affected by the price increase, and that is the value of your financial assets. Your wealth now has a lower purchasing power and has, in fact, declined in value. Under these conditions you may well cut your consumption and save more to replenish your real wealth. Similarly, a drop in prices will increase the real value of your wealth and lead to an increase in consumption. The effect of a change in the price level on the level of real wealth, and therefore on consumption, is known as the **real-balances effect**.

real-balances effect: the effect that a change in the value of real balances has on consumption spending (the value of real balances is affected by changing price levels).

Third, most households today possess a number of durable goods, ranging from kitchen appliances to VCRs, from autos to furniture. These things get replaced for two reasons. First, people get tired of them and can afford to replace them. Such action is obviously dependent on income. Second, durables get replaced simply because they wear out and must be replaced regardless (within reason) of the current state of the householder's income flow. When the water heater quits, most of us just shrug, mumble that we will have to manage somehow and arrange for a replacement. Thus, as the stock of consumer durables gets older, the likelihood of increased consumption spending grows as the need for replacement increases.

Finally, at any given time there is a prevailing mood among an economy's consumers concerning the future state of the economy, particularly in the area of job availability, salary and wage rate trends, and changes in expected future prices. If this mood changes from, say, pessimistic to optimistic, then an autonomous increase in consumption spending is very likely to occur as well. In short, a change in consumer expectations can cause an autonomous change in consumption spending. In summary, the major determinants of autonomous consumption spending are:

- changes in wealth (wealth effect)
- changes in the price level (real balances effect)
- changes in the age of consumer durables
- changes in consumer expectations

SELF-TEST

7. Explain how each of the following affects the level of consumption and savings:
A) A sharp decrease in stock prices.
B) Rising fears of political uncertainty concerning the possible break-up of the country.
C) A dramatic decrease in the prices of most consumer goods.
D) A decrease in income tax rates.
E) A significant increase in the Goods and Services Tax.

Are Interest Rates Important?

You may have noticed a possible important omission from this list of the major determinants of consumption: interest rates. It is certainly true that increases in interest rates may cause some people to think twice before taking out consumer loans or buying a new car. (Remember that new house purchases are regarded—at least by StatsCan—as a form of investment and will, as we shall see in the next section, definitely be affected by changes in interest rates.) Then why are most economists reluctant to include interest rates as a determinant? The reason is, because research on the topic is inconclusive.

It could well be that for some people higher interest rates mean that they cut down on consumer loans and instead start saving more because of the higher return they can now expect. But other people may see the higher interest rates as a reason to cut back on their monthly savings, since they can now earn as much as they did before, given the higher interest rates.

Keynes himself felt that interest rates are not important determinants of consumption and savings. Most of us, he felt, are creatures of habit, and it is a fairly painful exercise to readjust our spending patterns, which of course is what we would have to do if we adjusted our level of savings each time there was a change in interest rates. Income levels, and the other factors we have mentioned, are far more significant when it comes to figuring out our spending levels.

A Change in Investment

You will recall that our model regards investment spending as totally autonomous of income. So what does determine the level of investment spending in the economy? For most businesses most of the time, investment spending is financed with borrowed money. That is, corporations don't just write a cheque for several million dollars to refit some of their production equipment. Instead, they borrow the money from a bank, or perhaps from some other financial intermediary via a bond issue. Given this, it is important to recognize the impact of an interest-rate change on the total interest cost of borrowing. As an example, look at the difference in interest costs when $10 million is borrowed at 10 percent for a 20-year period and when it is borrowed at 12 percent:

$$\$10 \text{ million @ } 10\% \text{ for 20 years} = \$20 \text{ million}$$

$$\$10 \text{ million @ } 12\% \text{ for 20 years} = \$24 \text{ million}$$

It is clear that a particular investment possibility may be judged to be "worth it" at, say, 10 percent interest but not at 12 percent because of an additional $4 million that must be paid in interest and is an added cost to the firm making the investment.

In short, whether an investment project appears profitable or not depends on the interest costs of the money that must be borrowed to finance it. Note also that even if the investment is self-financed by a company, the rate of interest is still a determining factor in deciding whether or not to invest, since the alternative to investing is simply to leave the money in some form of savings certificate or in a savings account and earn a guaranteed return.

In all of this it is important to realize, as we mentioned in Chapter 4, that the real, not the nominal, rate of interest is the important determinant of investment spending. A firm that must pay a nominal rate of interest of 10 percent per annum over the next three years will be less inclined to borrow if it believes the rate of inflation is going to be 2 percent per annum over that period (so making the real rate of interest it has to pay equal to 8 percent) rather than if it believes that inflation will be 7 percent (which would make the real rate equal to only 3 percent).

Besides the interest rate, the initial price that must be paid for the equipment or a building has a clear impact on whether that purchase will be profitable or not. Similarly, the maintenance and operating costs involved over the life of the new machine, equipment, or building must also be considered in calculating potential profitability.

Sometimes new investment must be undertaken simply because equipment has worn out or a building is in a serious state of disrepair. Thus, as the age of an economy's capital stock increases, this sort of thing occurs with greater frequency, and investment spending is higher than it would otherwise have been. In addition, investment spending may well increase when businesspeople turns optimistic about the future and decrease as pessimism sets in. These psychological factors have an important bearing on investment decisions. Finally, business taxes and/or bureaucracy or "red-tape requirements" add to costs and thus have an impact on the potential profitability of any proposed investment project. If red tape was cut and business taxes lowered, one would also expect that investment spending would increase.

In summary, the major determinants of investment spending are:

- interest rates
- purchase price, maintenance, and operating costs
- the age of capital goods
- business expectations
- business taxes and government policies

SELF-TEST

8. Explain how each of the following affects the level of investment:
   A) A sharp increase in the world price of oil.
   B) A decline in interest rates.
   C) Rising fears of political uncertainty concerning the possible break-up of the country.
   D) The prospect of a big increase in corporate taxes over the next few years.
   E) An increase in the level of savings in the country.

A Change in Government Spending

Although our model assumes that the amount spent on goods and services by government is autonomous, this spending component can change at any time as a result of government policy. We asked earlier whether the amount of government spending is determined by tax revenues, which in turn are partly determined by the level of national income. The truth is that the amount that a government spends on the purchase of goods and services in any one period has little, if any, relation to the current level of national income. In the short run, the level of government spending is not constrained by the level of tax and other revenues. Governments can and often do spend in excess of revenues. In addition, other factors play their part in determining the government's spending policies. These factors include the level of interest rates, social and cultural standards, voters' expectations, budget philosophies, and political considerations. Government spending therefore can change for many reasons.

A Change in Autonomous Net Exports

We have established that exports are wholly autonomous, whereas imports are partially autonomous and partly induced by national income. If you recall, there are two major factors affecting net exports. First, net exports will be affected by the level of prices in the country compared with prices abroad. If the prices of goods and services were to fall in Karinia, then foreigners would be more likely to buy Karinian exports and Karinians would be less likely to buy as many foreign imports. Second, the value of a country's currency in relation to foreign currencies will also affect net exports. A decrease in the Karinian dollar (in terms of foreign currencies) has the same effect as a decrease in the price of Karinian goods and services. Finally, Karinian exports (but not imports) are affected by the level of national income in the countries that import Karinian products. A change in any of these three factors will cause a change in net exports. In summary, they are:

- comparative price levels
- the value of the exchange rate
- income levels abroad

The Multiplier

As you can now see, many factors influence the level of autonomous spending in a country, and we need to be able to work out the effect of these changes. For instance, let's start with the assumption that businesses in Karinia become more optimistic about the future. As a result they decide to increase their spending on new investment projects. Instead of spending $200 billion on investment, as they did last year, let's suppose their investment spending increases to $300 billion. Karinian businesses place additional orders for new construction, equipment, computers, and other capital projects. This will, of course, increase production by $100 billion above that of the previous year and thus boost national income by a similar amount. But is that the end of the story? Is it simply the case that an extra $100 billion in spending translates into $100 billion of extra income? The answer is, in fact, no. As we shall soon see, income will increase by more than $100 billion. **Figure 5.6** will help to provide an explanation.

FIGURE 5.6 The Multiplier

The increase in autonomous spending of $100 has an immediate effect of increasing aggregate expenditures by $100. This results in a shortage. This will lead to an increase in production and, thus, income. The economy will eventually move to a new equilibrium, where the new AE function (AE$_2$) crosses the Y = AE curve. As a result, income will increase by a total of $200, twice as much as the initial increase in spending.

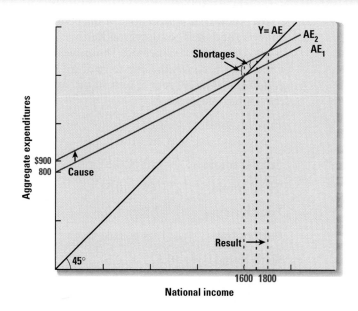

The increase in investment spending increases aggregate expenditures by $100 at every level of national income so that there is a parallel shift up in the AE function from AE_1 to AE_2. After the shift, there would be a shortage of goods and services of $100 at the original level of income of $1600. The result of the shortage is that production will increase. Even if national income rises by $100 (the same amount as the increase in spending) to $1700, there would still be a shortage of goods and services, since at this income level AE_2 is still above the $Y = AE$ line. The new equilibrium, in fact, occurs at the $1800 level of national income. In other words, national income will increase by *twice* the amount of the increase in aggregate expenditures. The reason for this phenomenon is termed the **multiplier**, and it is one of the more intriguing aspects of macroeconomics. Let us work through a simple example of the multiplier at work.

The Multiplier Derived

Suppose that a new bicycle plant was built in a small community in Central Karinia. The cost of the investment is $10 million. The immediate effect of this increase in spending is a rise in income for the contractors, suppliers, and their employees, who set up the plant. But this is not the end of the story. Presumably, these income recipients will do something with their extra income: they will spend it, or at least part of it. In other words:

> **An increase in investment will lead to an increase in income, which will in turn lead to an increase in consumption.**

But by how much will consumption in Karinia increase? The answer depends on the value of the marginal propensity to expend. Recall that in Karinia, the MPE is equal to 0.5. That is to say, consumption will not initially increase by the full $10 million because the government will take away taxes, some will be saved, and some of it will be spent on goods and services made elsewhere. In fact, we know that 50 percent leaks out, since the marginal leakage rate (MLR) in Karinia is 0.5. This means that spending on goods and services produced in Karinia will initially increase by $5 million.

We know that this $5 million in spending becomes additional income for other producers and their employees in Karinia. And what will this second group of people do with this additional income? The answer: spend 50 percent of it. This second round of spending becomes income for a third group of people; 50 percent of this third round of income is spent ... and so on. Arithmetically we would have the following series of income increases:

Initial round		$10 million
and assuming that the MPE is 0.5		
Second round	(10×0.5)	5.00
Third round	(5×0.5)	2.50
Fourth round	(2.5×0.5)	1.25
Fifth round	(1.25×0.5)	0.625
Sixth round	(0.625×0.5)	0.3125
Total		$20 million

Therefore, given an MPE of 0.5, a $10 million rise in autonomous investment will generate a $20 million rise in income. Another view of exactly the same phenomenon is that the eventual increase in income is twice the original increase in autonomous spending. This is what is meant by the **multiplier**. In terms of an equation the multiplier is equal to:

multiplier: the effect on income of a change in autonomous expenditures.

$$\text{Multiplier} = \frac{\Delta \text{ income}}{\Delta \text{ autonomous expenditures}}$$

This is a very important conclusion. It says that if autonomous spending in Karinia could be increased by $1 million, it would increase incomes and production by $2 million, which would lead, accordingly, to a decrease in unemployment.

On the surface, this seems to provide a dramatic solution to a recession and a simple formula for growth. We just need to encourage people to spend more! We will do more with this idea later in the chapter. It is important for you to be able to calculate the multiplier. The formula is:

$$\text{Multiplier} = \frac{1}{(1 - \text{MPE})} \text{ or } \frac{1}{\text{MLR}}$$

Since Karinia's MPE is 0.5, the MLR also equals 0.5. Karinia's multiplier therefore comes to:

$$\text{Multiplier} = \frac{1}{(1-0.5)} \text{ or } \frac{1}{(0.5)} = 2$$

Suppose that the MPE in Karinia were to increase to 0.6. That means that each round of extra income creates a greater amount of additional spending and less would go into leakages. Consequently, the MLR would be lower and have a value of 0.4. The result is a bigger multiplier. Its value is: 1/0.4, or 2.5. This leads us to the conclusion that:

A country with a high MPE will have a bigger multiplier than will a country with a small MPE.

It is helpful to note that the MPC* tells us how much of each additional dollar of earned income (GDP) is spent on goods and services. Therefore, MPC*—MPM tells us how much is spent on *Canadian* goods and services.

SELF-TEST

9. What is the value of the multiplier in the case of the following values of the MPE?   A) 0.75; B) 0.9; C) 1; D) 0.5; E) 0.

You can now see why Keynesians place such emphasis on the role of spending in the economy. It's their belief that a little spending goes a long way.

With a little arithmetic, let us confirm that the value of Karinia's multiplier is in fact equal to 2. Looking again at Table 5.1, we can see that of every $200 increase in national income, 20 percent goes in taxes (the MTR is 0.2), 20 percent of national income is saved (the MPS* is 0.2), and imports increase by 10 percent (the MPM is 0.1). The sum of these percentages is 50 percent, which gives us a marginal leakage rate of 50 percent, or 0.5. The multiplier therefore has a value of 2. In general, the value of the value of the multiplier is equal to:

$$\frac{1}{(\text{MPS}^* + \text{MTR} + \text{MPM})} = \frac{1}{\text{MLR}}$$

10. Suppose that the MPS* is 0.2, the MTR is 0.15, and the MPM is 0.05. What is the MLR, the MPE, and the value of the multiplier?

Finally, let us examine the effects of the changes brought about by the multiplier. Let's look in a bit more detail at the effects of Karinian businesses increasing their investment spending from $200 billion to $300 billion. We have already seen the effects graphically in Figure 5.6. We know that with a multiplier of 2 in Karinia that national income will increase by $200. Let us confirm that the new level of equilibrium income in Karinia is indeed $1800 and, also, see how this affects the other parts of the economy:

Y	T	Yd	C	S	I	G	X	IM	X_N	AE (C+I+X_n+G)
1600	360	1240	1060	180	200	400	200	260	−60	1600
1800	400	1400	1180	220	**300**	400	200	280	−80	1800

You can see that the additional $100 of investment spending leads to an increase in aggregate expenditures of $200. But why did it increase by this amount? The reason is that the extra income also increased consumption, which went up by $120 (from $1060 to $1180).

However, $20 of this extra consumption went on foreign products (imports rose from $260 to $280). Therefore, spending on Karinian-made consumer products rose by $100 which with the additional $100 spending on investment products makes up the extra $200 of aggregate expenditures.

The other changes that occurred were in the other two leakages: taxes went up by $40 and savings also went up by $40. If we add these amounts to the extra $20 in imports, we can see that total leakages went up by $100. Therefore, the increase in investment of $100 not only increased the equilibrium level of income, but in doing so, induced additional leakages of $100.

The Multiplier Algebraically

To derive an equation for the multiplier, all we need to do is write our algebraic equations in a general form, rather than using actual numbers. For instance, we can rewrite equation (2), the tax function, as:

(2A) $T = T_0 + tY$

(The little $_0$ after T signifies that this variable is autonomous)
Equation (3) then becomes:

(3A) $Yd = Y - (T_0 + tY) \qquad = Y - T_0 - tY$

Equation 4 in general form is:

(4A) $C = a_0 + bYd$

where a_0 is autonomous consumption and b is the MPC (out of disposable income). If we replace Yd in equation (4A) with equation (3A) we get:

(6A) $C = a_0 + b(Y - T_0 - tY) \qquad = a_0 + bY - bT_0 - btY$

The only other equation we need to rewrite is equation (12) for the net export function:

(12A) $Xn = (X_0 - IM_0) - mY$

(where X_0 and IM_0 are autonomous exports and imports respectively, and m is the marginal propensity to import.)

The four elements of expenditures in general form, you will recall, can be written and summed as follows:

$$C = a_0 + bY - bT_0 - btY$$

$$I = I_0$$

$$G = G_0$$

$$Xn = (X_0 - IM_0) - mY$$

$$\overline{}$$

$$AE = (a_0 + I_0 + G_0 + X_0 - IM_0 - bT_0) + bY - btY - mY$$

or $$AE = (a_0 + I_0 + G_0 + X_0 - IM_0 - bT_0) + (b - bt - m)Y$$

This last equation is often referred to as the reduced form equation. It looks fairly horrendous at first. However, it's not nearly as daunting as it looks. The first big bracket is the total of all the autonomous expenditures. The bracket in front of Y (the coefficient of Y) is the value of the marginal propensity to expend (MPE) and is equal to $(b - bt - m)$. The marginal leakage rate (MLR) is therefore $(1 - MPE)$ or $(1 - b + bt + m)$. The multiplier then is $1/(MLR)$ or:

$$1/(1 - b + bt + m)$$

Since $(1 - b)$ is the MPS, the denominator includes the three marginal leakages, the MPS, the MTR, and the MPM. We therefore have two equivalent formulations for the multiplier: either, as we saw before, $1/(MPS^* + MTR + MPM)$ or the one derived here $1/(MPS + bMTR + MPM)$. You can use either. Note that the bigger the value of these leakages, the smaller the value of the multiplier. This reduced-form equation also tells us that:

> **If any element of autonomous expenditures ($a_0 + I_0 + G_0 + X_0 - IM_0 - bT_0$) changes, then equilibrium income will change by a multiplied amount.**

SELF-TEST

11. Suppose the MPC is 0.8, the MTR is 0.2, and MPM is 0.04. What is the value of MPE, the MLR, and the multiplier?

A Summing Up

The level of national income is determined by the level of aggregate expenditures. An *increase* in any of the following will cause the level of income to *increase*:

- autonomous consumption
- investment
- exports
- government spending

The size of the increase is determined by the value of the multiplier.

Of course, a decrease in any of the above items will cause a multiple decrease in income. Furthermore, an *increase* in either of the following will cause a *decrease* in national income:

- autonomous taxes
- autonomous imports

Finally, the value of the multiplier will *increase* if any of the following were to *decrease*:

- marginal propensity to save
- marginal tax rate
- marginal propensity to import

And the multiplier will decrease if any of the preceding were to increase.

Does Equilibrium National Income Mean Full Employment?

The above summary brings out the essence of the expenditures model. National income depends on the level of autonomous spending, and if this spending changes, then income will change by some multiplied amount. That is to say, a small increase can have a significant effect on raising the level of income.

By now you should also realize that this model demonstrates that the macroeconomy is always driving national income to its equilibrium level. And what is the importance of equilibrium national income? Is it a desirable level of income? Is it a goal worth attaining? The answer unfortunately is: not necessarily. Simply because an economy is at an expenditure equilibrium tells us nothing about how well it is performing. This means that the economy could well be at equilibrium but still have 25 percent of its labour force unemployed. All we know is that at equilibrium, all that is produced in total is being purchased. But that total could be below what the economy is capable of producing and could result in high levels of unemployment. The economy could well find itself in a low-level trap: the economy is at equilibrium, but that equilibrium is well below the full-employment level. This is the message of Keynesian economics: though competitive markets have a natural tendency to move toward equilibrium, they do not necessarily have the same tendency to move toward full employment. In fact, according to Keynes, the only way to move toward full employment is by achieving the right level of aggregate expenditures.

A Look at the Keynesian Revolution

What happened to the industrial economies of the world in the Great Depression of the 1930s is that they all got stuck in low-level traps: national incomes that fell alarmingly in the early years of the decade and showed no signs of ever recovering. Once this occurs, the only way back to recovery is for spending to increase. But this was much easier said then done in the 1930s. Let's do more with this idea.

Getting consumers to spend more requires people to increase their autonomous spending on consumption goods, that is, to spend more even when they have not experienced a rise in income. In the 1930s, unemployed people without steady incomes simply were not able to do this. Households headed by someone who was still employed could, but wouldn't, because most were terrified that tomorrow or next week, or next month, it would be they themselves who would be laid off. In short, frightened people spend as little as possible. As the decade wore on, little occurred that might have changed this fear.

You might well ask, at this point: couldn't government have lowered taxes to raise consumption spending? The answer is yes, and it would have helped. Such an option was not, however, as clear-cut then as it appears to us now, simply because, for the average income earner, taxes were already very low—there just wasn't much to cut! More importantly, most governments were wedded to the idea of balancing their budgets, and seeing their own taxes revenues decline dramatically as the depression worsened would have caused them to reject any suggestion of cutting tax rates. An increase in autonomous investment spending would have done the trick, but there was little prospect of this occurring, given that a large proportion of the existing stock was underemployed or just plain unemployed. In short, who was going to build new factories when many existing ones were idle?

Well, what about export spending? Wouldn't an increase in exports mean an increase in spending? The answer, in the abstract, is yes. However, with the outbreak of the Great Depression and the collapse of the world's gold standard, international trade also collapsed as each individual nation tried, fruitlessly, to protect domestic jobs with higher and higher tariffs (taxes) on imports.

The conclusion we are approaching here is that there was very little prospect of consumption spending, investment, or exports rising. If this was valid, then the only way out of the Great Depression was to increase the only other component of aggregate expenditure—government spending on goods and services.

Paradoxically, it appeared that governments needed to spend their way out of the Great Depression. This idea of spending our way to prosperity was (and to a lesser extent) still is a difficult concept for most to accept. In the 1930s it ran counter to prevailing ideology of laissez-faire, which implied that a government was supposed to remain small and in the background and, above all, to balance its budget annually. The depression had caused tax revenue to fall, and thus the only appropriate response, according to the thinking of the day, was for government to cut spending, not increase it.

SELF-TEST

12. Explain how a government could spend more in the face reduced tax revenues. In other words, where would it obtain the funds?

ADDED DIMENSION

John Maynard Keynes

John Maynard Keynes (1883–1946) (the pronunciation rhymes with "rains") was an extraordinary man who in 1936 published a revolutionary work titled *The General Theory of Employment, Interest and Money*. Keynes was a man of many colours—not only was he an economist but also a mathematician, philosopher, civil servant, corporate executive, editor, sponsor of the arts, and a gambler. He exhibited a true "love of life" in all of these pursuits. The *General Theory* will certainly live as a classic in economics and is, despite its age, quite relevant today as a starting point in a serious student's study of macroeconomics. Like most classics, it revolutionized the way economists understood the workings of the economy, particularly in the area of the causes and cures of unemployment.

Let's review some basic tenets of Keynesian economics as contained in our expenditure model:

- Equilibrium income is not synonymous with full employment. The economy might be in equilibrium, and therefore stable and unchanging, and yet be suffering mass unemployment. Worse still, this depression might last indefinitely. There is nothing in the workings of the economy that would automatically push the country to full employment.
- The level of equilibrium income depends on the level of aggregate expenditure, which consists of the four spending components.
- Equilibrium income below full-employment income, if it occurred, would reflect a lack of sufficient aggregate expenditure.
- The only way to raise such an equilibrium income level to the full-employment income level would be to raise aggregate expenditure.
- Government action could affect the government-spending-on-goods-and-services component of aggregate expenditure but, seemingly, could not affect the other three components, except through tax changes.

Therefore, our tentative conclusion above seems valid: the only way out of the Great Depression was for governments of the day to *increase* their spending. This was, however, a very big order. Most economists were reluctant to embrace the new "Keynesian" perspective. A revolution in macroeconomic thinking was needed to overcome such reluctance.

Similarly, the prevailing ideology among politicians and the general public needed to be turned a full 180 degrees. Everyone knew, so went the prevailing thinking, that in tough times like the 1930s, governments had to "tighten their belts" and make do with less. Yet, the Keynesian view was the exact opposite—spend more, and quickly. Keynes himself lobbied for his new ideology and was somewhat successful with the Roosevelt government in the United States. Federal government spending there did go up in 1934 and 1935, and national income did rise. But then spending was cut back soon after Roosevelt was re-elected in 1936, and any hope of a full recovery was extinguished.

All of this changed radically with the outbreak of World War II. Government spending for the war effort rose dramatically and rapidly. The expenditures model of Keynes would predict, given such an increase in aggregate expenditures, a prompt return to full-employment equilibrium. This is exactly what happened.

The Keynesian perspective seemed validated, and more and more people within the economics profession began calling themselves "Keynesians." Equally significant, the public mood changed, and with the end of World War II, governments around the world passed legislation that we could roughly tag "Full Employment Acts." In these pieces of legislation, governments committed themselves, at least in principle, to pursuing economic policies that would result in full employment. For our purposes, the significant point here is that it was recognized that government policy could be used to achieve the goal of full employment and, further, that governments had some *responsibility* in this matter. Laissez-faire economics was dead. The Keynesian revolution was complete. At least for the time being.

REVIEW

1. What four factors will cause a change in *autonomous consumption*?
2. What five factors will cause a change in *autonomous investment*?
3. What three factors will cause a change in the *net export function*?
4. Define the *multiplier* and write it out in the form of a ratio.
5. What can cause a change in the *value* of the multiplier?
6. What will happen to national income if *exports* fall? If *autonomous taxes* increase?
7. What is the difference between *equilibrium income* and *full-employment equilibrium*?
8. Why was it necessary for a government to spend its way out of the Great Depression of the 1930s?

Chapter Highlights

Most students will find this a challenging chapter because of the complexity of its content. However, it is a very important step in your mastering of macroeconomic principles and coming to a better understanding of how the macroeconomy works.

The chapter begins by presenting the complete expenditures model in tabular form (Table 5.1, which you will find duplicated in your Answer Key). It is here that the important distinction between autonomous spending, which is independent of income, and induced spending, which depends on the level of income, is emphasized. Related to this distinction are the concepts of the marginal propensity to expend (MPE) and the marginal leakage rate (MLR), which are then discussed.

The chapter then proceeds by discussing each column in Table 5.1. We point out that taxes have both an autonomous and an induced component and that national income minus taxes $(Y - T)$ gives us disposable income (Yd). Similarly, consumption also has autonomous and induced components. Induced consumption is indicated by the size of the marginal propensity to consume, which, it is pointed out, can be calculated by using disposable income (MPC) or national income (MPC*). Next, savings is dealt with in exactly the same way. It has an autonomous component and an induced component, which is indicated by either MPS or MPS*.

Brief mention is then made of investment and government spending, which are both entirely autonomous. The chapter then moves on to discuss international trade, treating exports as entirely autonomous, whereas imports have, again, both an autonomous and an induced component, which is indicated by the marginal propensity to imports (MPM). Subtracting imports from exports gives us net exports, Xn.

Having identified the elements of spending, C, I, G, and Xn, we can then determine aggregate expenditures (AE) by simply adding them together.

Next, we discuss the concept of income equilibrium, which occurs when $Y = AE$. A level of national income that is not equal to aggregate expenditures results in unplanned investment being either negative (which means business inventories are falling) or positive (rising inventories).

After completing the discussion of Table 5.1, we then introduce the basic 45° graph and present the model graphically, using the same hypothetical figures.

Following this, the model is then presented in a third way—algebraically. The power of this approach is quite evident to those who work through it, although doing so is not essential to an overall understanding of the model.

Having presented the model in tabular, graphical, and then algebraic forms, the chapter proceeds to discuss what could cause *changes* in any one of the four spending elements, which are, again, C, I, G and Xn.

Next, the concept of the multiplier is introduced by pointing out that any change in autonomous spending results in a multiplied change in national income. This important concept is explained verbally, illustrated graphically, and derived algebraically (optional).

Finally, the chapter explains that equilibrium income does not necessarily imply full employment, which is at the heart of the Keynesian revolution, discussed in the closing pages.

New Glossary Terms

STUDY GUIDE

Study Tips

1. It is essential for you to be clear about the distinction between autonomous spending, which does *not* depend on the level of income, and induced spending, which does.

2. Be careful when you draw your diagrams that the vertical and horizontal axes are drawn to the same scale. If they are not, your 45° line will not be a 45° line, and your graph will be misleading. In this section of the course, it is important that you construct reasonably big, accurate graphs. It's worth the extra effort.

3. Another aspect of graphing deserves mention. The vertical axis in math is often referred to as the Y-axis, and the horizontal is called the X-axis. This might occasionally be confusing, since economists use the letter Y to stand for income. In macroeconomics, income (or Y) is placed on the X-axis!

4. Probably the area of this chapter that causes most confusion for the student is the distinction between national income (GDP) and disposable income. If it helps, think back to Chapter 3 and remember all the additions and subtractions that had to be made to GDP to arrive at a figure for disposable income. In this model, all of those adjustments have been lumped together into a single heading: tax. Again, remember from GDP accounting that the amounts people consume and save are determined by *disposable* income and not by *national* income.

5. Some students have difficulty appreciating the fact that Y stands for not just the concept of income, but also the *value* of income. When the letter Y occurs in an equation like $Y = 100 + 0.6Y$, for instance, the Y is short for 1Y.

6. Be careful in your derivation of disposable income that taxes are deducted and not added to income. For example, if autonomous taxes are $100 and induced taxes are 20 percent of income, then total taxes are $(100 + 0.2Y)$. This whole term is *subtracted* from national income to give disposable income:

$$Yd \quad = \quad Y - \quad (100 + 0.2Y)$$

(disposable income)   (national income)   (taxes)

When you remove the brackets from the tax function, the plus sign becomes a minus:

$$Yd = Y - 100 - 0.2Y$$

Key Problem

Table 5.4 shows some of the expenditure amounts in the economy of Arkinia.

TABLE 5.4

Y	T	Yd	C	S	I	G	X	IM	X_N	AE (C+I+X_n+G)
$0	___	___	___	___	60	150	50	___	___	___
100	___	50	___	−10	___	___	___	___	30	___
200	75	___	___	___	___	___	___	___	___	___
300	___	___	180	___	___	___	___	40	___	___
400	125	___	___	35	___	___	___	___	___	___
500	___	___	300	___	___	___	___	60	___	___
600	___	425	___	___	___	___	___	___	___	___
700	___	___	420	___	___	___	___	___	___	___
800	___	575	___	95	___	___	___	___	−40	___

The MPC, the MTR and the MPM are all constant as are the values of the three injections.

a) Complete Table 5.4, and in **Figure 5.7** graph a 45° line and the aggregate expenditure function, labelled AE_1. Identify expenditure equilibrium.

FIGURE 5.7

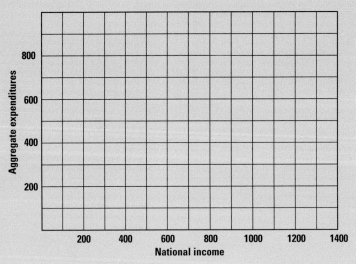

b) What is the value of equilibrium national income?

National income: $_____.

c) What is the value of total injections and total leakages at equilibrium?

Total injections: _____ ; total leakages: _____.

d) What is the value of the MPE in Arkinia?

MPE: _____.

e) What is the value of the multiplier in Arkinia?

Multiplier: _____.

f) Suppose that exports from Arkinia were to increase by $150. Draw the new aggregate expenditure function on Figure 5.7 and label it AE_2. Identify the new expenditure equilibrium.

g) What is the value of the new equilibrium national income, and at equilibrium, what is the value of net exports?

National income: _____ ; net exports: _____.

More of the Same

Table 5.5 shows some of the expenditure amounts in the economy of Nakarini. The MPC, the MTR, and the MPM are all constant, as are the values of the three injections.

TABLE 5.5

Y	T	Yd	C	S	I	G	X	IM	X_N	AE (C+I+X_n+G)
$0	___	___	___	___	135	320	150	___	___	___
200	___	100	___	−35	___	___	___	___	110	___
400	140	___	___	___	___	___	___	___	___	___
600	___	___	375	___	___	___	___	80	___	___
800	220	___	___	85	___	___	___	___	___	___
1000	___	___	615	___	___	___	___	120	___	___
1200	___	900	___	___	___	___	___	___	___	___
1400	___	___	855	___	___	___	___	___	___	___
1600	___	1220	___	245	___	___	___	___	−30	___

a) Complete Table 5.5, and in **Figure 5.8** graph a 45° line and the aggregate expenditure function, labelled AE_1. Identify expenditure equilibrium.

FIGURE 5.8

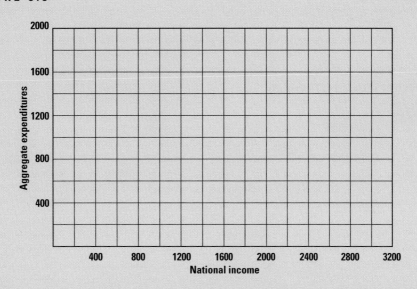

b) What is the value of equilibrium national income?

National income: $_____.

c) What is the value of total injections and total leakages at equilibrium?

Total injections: _____ ; total leakages: _____.

d) What is the value of the MPE in Nakarini?

MPE: _____.

e) What is the value of the multiplier in Nakarini?

Multiplier: _____.

f) Suppose that government spending from Nakarini were to decrease by $200. Draw the new aggregate expenditure function on Figure 5.8, and label it AE_2. Identify the new expenditure equilibrium.

g) What is the value of the new equilibrium national income, and at equilibrium, what is the value of net exports?

National income: _____ ; net exports: _____.

Translations

The following data provide information on Akinira's economy in a particular year. Explain which variables depend on others. Is the economy in equilibrium, and what has happened to the country's level of inventories in this particular year? Also comment on what implications this might have for the following year's GDP.

GDP ($=Y$) = $500; savings = $120; planned investment spending = $100; government spending = $200; taxes = $180 and the balance of trade = +70.

_____

_____

Are You Sure?

Indicate whether the following statements are true or false. If false, indicate why they are false.

1. Autonomous spending depends on the level of income, whereas induced spending does not.

T or F   If false: _____

_____

2. Equilibrium income occurs where the value of production is equal to aggregate expenditures.

T or F   If false: _____

_____

3. Induced taxes do not change with income, but autonomous taxes do.

T or F   If false: _____

_____

4. It is possible for the economy to be in equilibrium but not at full employment.

T or F   If false: _____

_____

5. The real-balances effect refers to the effect that a change in interest rates has on the real value of wealth.

   T or F   If false: _____

   _____

6. A decrease in the interest rate will cause an increase in investment spending.

   T or F   If false: _____

   _____

7. The value of the multiplier is equal to the reciprocal of the marginal leakage rate.

   T or F   If false: _____

   _____

8. Growth in an economy's GDP (if not caused by a change in exports) results in a larger trade deficit or in a reduction of a previous trade surplus.

   T or F   If false: _____

   _____

9. If taxes increase, disposable income will fall but consumption will remain the same.

   T or F   If false: _____

   _____

10. If the marginal tax rate increases, then the marginal propensity to expend will be smaller and the marginal leakage rate will be larger.

    T or F   If false: _____

    _____

Choose the Best

11. If the MPE is equal to 0.4, what is the value of the MLR?
    a) 0.6.
    b) 2.5.

12. If the MPE is equal to 0.4, what is the value of the multiplier?
    a) 1.67.
    b) 2.5.

13. What does the multiplier effect indicate?
    a) That a small increase in total income will generate a large change in aggregate expenditures.
    b) That a change in autonomous expenditures will cause income to change by a larger amount.

14. If X is an autonomous $90 and the MPM is 0.2, what is the value of Xn at an income of $500?
    a) +$10.
    b) −$10.
    c) +$90.

15. What does the marginal propensity to expend mean?
    a) It is the fraction of income that is not spent.
    b) It is the ratio of change in income that results from a change in expenditures.
    c) It is the ratio of change in expenditures that results from a change in income.

16. What does the multiplier effect mean?
    a) That a small change in autonomous expenditures usually leads to bigger changes in investment.
    b) That a small change in autonomous expenditures can cause income to change by a larger amount.
    c) That a small decline in the MPC can lead to a big change in income.

17. What is the effect of a decrease in government spending?
    a) It leads to an even larger increase in equilibrium income.
    b) It leads to an even larger decrease in equilibrium income.

c) It leads to a smaller increase in equilibrium income.

d) It leads to a smaller decrease in equilibrium income.

18. What effect does an increase in exports have?
   a) It leads to an even larger increase in equilibrium income.
   b) It leads to an even larger decrease in equilibrium income.
   c) It leads to a smaller increase in equilibrium income.
   d) It leads to a smaller decrease in equilibrium income.

19. What is the effect of a decrease in the MTR?
   a) The MLR will increase and the multiplier will increase.
   b) The MLR will decrease and the multiplier will increase.
   c) The MLR will increase and the multiplier will decrease.
   d) The MLR will decrease and the multiplier will decrease.

20. What is the most important determinant of the level of consumption?
   a) The level of prices.
   b) Consumer expectations.
   c) The stock of wealth.
   d) The level of income.

21. What circumstance will lead to a smaller multiplier?
   a) If the MPS becomes bigger.
   b) If the MPC becomes bigger.
   c) If the MPM becomes smaller.
   d) If the MLR becomes smaller.

22. All *except one* of the following statements concerning the equilibrium level of GDP are correct. Which is incorrect?
   a) There will be no tendency for firms to increase or decrease production.
   b) The economy is operating at full employment.
   c) Unplanned investment in inventories will not occur.
   d) Leakages equal injections.
   e) Aggregate expenditures equal GDP.

23. What does the real-balances effect refer to?
   a) The effect that a change in savings has on the real rate of interest.
   b) The level of income where it is exactly equal to the level of consumption.
   c) The effect that a change in interest rates has on the real value of savings.
   d) The effect that a change in the price level has on the real value of wealth.
   e) The effect of a change in consumption on the real value of wealth.

Refer to **Figure 5.9** to answer questions 24 and 25.

FIGURE 5.9

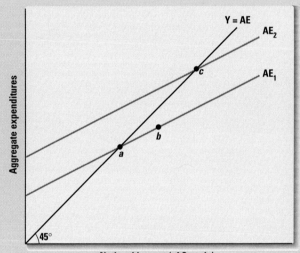

National income (of Canada)

24. Refer to Figure 5.9 to answer this question. What could cause a change from *a* to *b*?
   a) An increase in national income in the United States.
   b) An increase in government spending.
   c) A decrease in interest rates.
   d) An increase in Canadian national income.
   e) A decrease in autonomous taxes.

25. Refer to Figure 5.9 to answer this question. All of the following *except one* could cause a change from *a* to *c*. Which is the exception?
   a) An increase in Canadian income.
   b) A decrease in interest rates.
   c) A decrease in the Canadian exchange rate.
   d) A decrease in autonomous taxes.
   e) An increase in U.S. national income.

Refer to **Table 5.6** to answer questions 26 and 27.

TABLE 5.6

Y	T	Yd	C
100	40	60	50
200	60	140	90
300	80	220	130
400	100	300	170
500	120	380	210

26. Refer to Table 5.6 to answer this question. What is the algebraic expression for disposable income?
a) $Yd = -20 + 0.8Y$.
b) $Yd = -20 + (Y + 0.2Y)$.
c) $Yd = 20 + 0.8(Y - 20 - 0.2Y)$.
d) $Yd = 60 + 0.8(Y - 20 - 0.2Y)$.

27. Refer to Table 5.6 to answer this question. What is the algebraic expression for the consumption function?
a) $C = 20 + 0.5Yd$.
b) $C = 20 + 0.4Yd$.
c) $C = 50 + 0.4Yd$.
d) $C = 10 + 0.4Yd$.

Answer questions 28–30 on the basis of the parameters for an economy shown in **Table 5.7**. (All figures are in $ billion.)

TABLE 5.7

$a_0 = 80$	$b = 0.80$
$I_0 = 500$	$t = 0.25$
$G_0 = 1{,}200$	$m = 0.20$
$X_0 = 800$	
$T_0 = 100$	
$IM_0 = 100$	

28. Refer to Table 5.7 to answer this question. What is the value of the multiplier in this economy?
a) 1.
b) 1.54.
c) 1.67.
d) 2.
e) 5.

29. Refer to Table 5.7 to answer this question. What is the value of equilibrium income in this economy?
a) $3840.
b) $3967.
c) $4000.
d) $4133.
e) $5000.

30. Refer to Table 5.7 to answer this question. At equilibrium, what is the balance of trade?
a) A surplus of $100.
b) A deficit of $100.
c) A surplus of $300.
d) A deficit of $300.
e) A zero balance of trade.

Other Problems

31. The data in **Table 5.8** is for the economy of Anariki.

TABLE 5.8

Y	AE	Unplanned Investment
$1600	_____	−$400
1800	_____	−300
2000	_____	−200
2200	_____	−100
2400	_____	0
2600	_____	+100
2800	_____	+200

a) Fill in the AE column.

b) What is the value of equilibrium income?
   Equilibrium income: $_____.

c) At income $2000, will inventories be increasing or decreasing?

   _____.

d) If planned investment increases by $200, what will be the value of the new equilibrium income?
   Equilibrium income: $_____.

32. Irkania's aggregate expenditures function is shown in **Figure 5.10**.

FIGURE 5.10

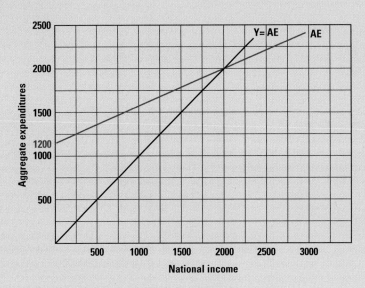

a) What is the value of MPE and the multiplier in Irkania?
   MPE: _____; multiplier: _____.

b) What is the value of equilibrium income?
   Equilibrium income: $_____.

c) If investment in Irkania were to increase by $360, what would be the new level of equilibrium income?
   Equilibrium income: $_____.

33. Complete **Table 5.9**'s balancing row for the economy of Kaniria, which is in equilibrium:

TABLE 5.9

Y	T	Yd	C	S	I	G	X	IM	Xn	AE
			110	80	180			80	10	800

34. Given the information in **Table 5.10** for the economy of Rinakia:

TABLE 5.10

$C = 60 + 0.6Yd$ $IM = 0.15Y$
$T = 40 + 0.25Y$ $X_0 = 44$
$I_0 = 90$ $G_0 = 110$

    a) What is the value of equilibrium income?
       Equilibrium income $_____.
    b) At equilibrium, what is the value of T and of C?
       T: $_____; C: $_____.
    c) What is the value of the multiplier?
       Multiplier : _____.

35. The partial data in **Table 5.11** are for the economy of Arinaka. Planned investment, government spending, and all taxes are autonomous. Furthermore, you may assume that the MPC, MPS, and MPM are constant.

TABLE 5.11

Y	T	Yd	C	S	Planned Investment	G	Xn	AE	Unplanned Investment
$400	$40	___	$320	$40	$60	$50	+ $10	___	___
450	___	___	45	___	___	___	−5	___	___
500	___	___	___	___	___	___	___	___	___
550	___	___	___	___	___	___	___	___	___

    a) Fill in the blanks in Table 5.11.
    b) What is the value of equilibrium income?
    _____

    c) If planned investment decreases by 20, what is the new value of equilibrium income?
    _____

UNANSWERED QUESTIONS

Short Essays

1. What determines the level of consumption in an economy? In answering, distinguish between autonomous consumption and induced consumption.

2. What is meant by the *net export function*? Why do net exports decrease when an economy's income increases?

3. Explain what is meant by *macroeconomic equilibrium*. What are the three ways of looking at it?

4. Explain the concept of the *multiplier*. On what factors does the size of the multiplier depend?

5. Explain why Keynes put such emphasis on spending as the key to curing a depression.

6. Why did Keynes feel that only the government is capable of increasing the level of spending in the economy during a recession?

Analytical Questions

7. Canadians save a lot, are taxed a lot, and buy a lot of imported goods. What effect does this have on the size of the Canadian multiplier? Explain.

8. Do you think that giving people a tax break to encourage them to save more (through RRSPs and so on) is beneficial to the economy?

9. Sometimes spending increases because income increases, and sometimes spending increases without a change in income. Explain.

10. Since exports imply that products are leaving the country, while imports involve products coming into the country, wouldn't our economic welfare be enhanced by a trade deficit?

11. If, initially, injections were equal to leakages and injections were to increase, this would cause an increase in leakages until the two are again equal. Explain what this means and which leakages are affected.

Numerical Questions

12. You are given the following data for the economy of Ranikia:

    $MPC^* = 0.765$ $(MPC = 0.9)$ $X_0 = \$120$

    $MTR = 0.15$ $IM = \$40$

    $MPM = 0.165$

    The economy is in equilibrium at $Y = \$800$.
    a) What is the value of Xn?
    b) What is the value of the multiplier?

    Suppose that X_0 now increases to \$200.
    c) What is the new value of equilibrium Y?
    d) What is the new value of Xn?

13. Table 5.12 shows partial data for the economy of Nikaria. Fill in the blanks in the balancing row.

TABLE 5.12

Y	T	Yd	C	S	I	G	X	IM	Xn	AE
___	___	480	___	___	110	300	90	105	___	800

What assumption is necessary for you to fill in the blanks?

14. Figure 5.11 shows the aggregate expenditure function for the economy of Arianki.

FIGURE 5.11

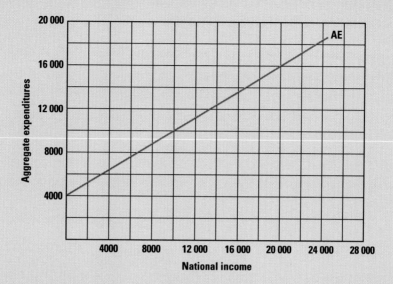

a) What is the value of equilibrium income in Arianki?

b) What is the value of the multiplier?

c) If government spending were to increase by 4000, what would be the new value of equilibrium income?

d) If, instead, autonomous imports were to increase by 2000, what would be the new value of equilibrium income?

15. Figure 5.12 shows the economy of Kinaria.

FIGURE 5.12

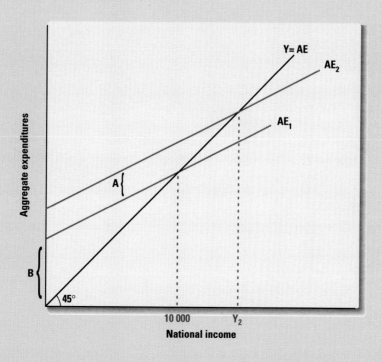

a) If the value of A is 3000 and the multiplier is 2, what is the value of Y_2?
b) If the value of Y_2 is 14 000 and the value of A is 2000, what is the value of the multiplier?
c) If the value of the multiplier is 4, what is the value of B?

16. Given **Table 5.13**'s information for the economy of Airkina:

TABLE 5.13

$C = 50 + 0.8Yd$	$IM = 0.2Y$
$T = 80 + 0.25Y$	$X_0 = 84$
$I_0 = 70$	$G_0 = 160$

a) Calculate equilibrium income.
b) Set up a balancing row to verify your calculations.
c) If investment increased by 15, what would the new equilibrium income be?

17. **Table 5.14** shows the parameters for the economy of Irakian.

TABLE 5.14

$a_0 = 100$	$b = 3/4\ (0.75)$
$I_0 = 150$	$t = 1/3\ (0.33)$
$G_0 = 350$	$m = 1/10\ (0.1)$
$X_0 = 100$	
$T_0 = 80$	
$IM_0 = 10$	

a) What is the value of equilibrium income?
b) If X were to decrease by 30, what would the new equilibrium value of Xn be?
c) Given the equilibrium income level in a), if full-employment income is $900, what change in G_0 is necessary to move the economy to this level?

 ## Web-Based Activities

1. Read **http://strategis.ic.gc.ca/SSI/ra/mei1098e.pdf.** What happened to the marginal propensity to save over the period 1996-98? How does the change in the saving rate affect the aggregate expenditure function? Now, look at the average household debt-to-income ratio. Is there cause for concern? (How might household behavior change in the future?)

2. Read the article found at **http://www.infoexport.gc.ca/viewdocument-e.asp?continent=Europe& country=52&name=ovrw** and answer the following questions:
    a) What countries accounted for Canada's export growth between 1985 and 1996?
    b) Does Canada have a trade surplus (X>IM) or a trade deficit (IM>X) with the European union? Illustrate how an increase in a trade deficit (surplus) affects the aggregate expenditure diagram.
    c) What are our primary exports to Europe? What are the primary imports from Europe?

Aggregate Demand and Supply

What's ahead... This is a pivotal chapter in which we extend the expenditures model of the last chapter by introducing the price level as well as other factors that affect production. In later chapters we will use this model extensively to examine various economic policies and problems. We look separately at how aggregate demand and aggregate supply are determined and then explain the factors that cause them to change and how this will affect the economy. Finally, through the eyes of two opposing schools of thoughts, we look at the question of whether the economy is self-adjusting or needs the active intervention of government.

Which of the following acts do you think will improve economic conditions more: you buy a new CD player for $300, or you increase your work productivity effort by 20 percent? Aside from your obvious objection that neither act will have much impact on the whole economy, you probably would opt for the second one, since it seems to involve real production. After all, if we all became 20 percent more productive at our work, then the economy would surely be more wealthy than if people simply bought more things. Surprisingly, in the short run, the two acts will have about the same effect on the economy. In the longer run, however, a sustained productivity increase will make for a healthier economy.

The last chapter went into some detail in building a model of the economy. This model has a definite Keynesian perspective and does a reasonably good job of explaining the workings of the economy under certain circumstances. It has been a major influence on the thinking of most economists and policy makers since World War II, and to a certain extent still is. However, in recent years the theory has been challenged, not because it is wrong, but because its scope is too restricted. Thus, this chapter presents not so much an alternative model of the economy as an extension and elaboration of the expenditures model we have so far developed.

One major criticism of the expenditures model of the previous chapter is that the price level, if it is mentioned at all, plays an almost insignificant role. It is not that Keynes ignored prices in writing his *General Theory*, but simply that in the context of the time in which it was written, the problem of inflation was of minor concern when compared with the very real hardship caused by high levels of unemployment.

The relevance of Keynes's model was increasingly questioned from the 1960s on, when prices started to increase year after year, causing great concern among policy makers and the general public. It was suggested that what Keynes had produced was a "depression theory" that was of decreasing relevance in the prosperous postwar world, a world in which other economic problems needed to be addressed. It has been suggested that, if anything, modern citizens are suffering from the "poverty of affluence."

Another, and allied, criticism of the Keynesian model is that it places total emphasis on spending and spenders. According to Keynes, the lack of spending causes recessions and government spending holds the cure. Very seldom is mention made of the other side of the equation: the supply of goods and services. Keynesian theory is very much a theory of demand. Therefore, it has been asked, how can it fully explain the complete workings of the economy, unless the supply side of things becomes an active ingredient in the recipe?

Thus, in this chapter, we will extend the expenditures model to include explicit mention of the price level, and we will introduce the concept of aggregate supply, which will go a long way toward giving us a model that is better able to explain today's economy.

Aggregate Demand

aggregate demand: the aggregate quantity of goods and services demanded by all buyers at various different price levels.

Aggregate demand means the same thing as the amount of aggregate expenditures *at various price levels*. This simply means that we are trying to find the quantity of aggregate expenditures at a price level of say, P_1, P_2, P_3, and so on. **Figure 6.1** shows how we can derive an aggregate demand curve directly from the expenditures equilibrium diagram.

FIGURE 6.1 Derivation of the Aggregate Demand Curve

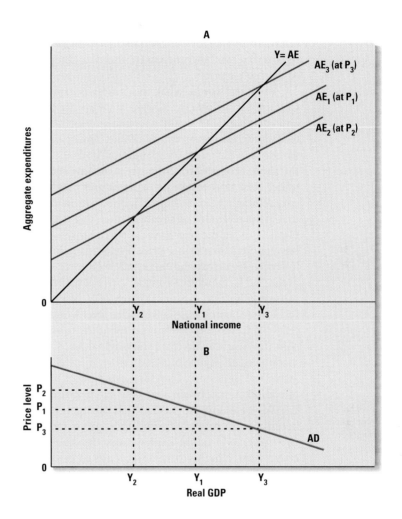

AE_1 in Figure 6.1A shows the total amount of spending at the present price level, say P_1. Given this level of aggregate expenditures, equilibrium would be at real income level Y_1. In Figure 6.1B, therefore, we show a price level of P_1 and income level Y_1. If the price level were to increase to P_2, then aggregate expenditures would be at the lower level AE_2. This would produce a lower income level Y_2. Therefore, in Figure 6.1B, a higher price level P_2 is paired with a lower income level Y_2. Likewise, if the price level were to decrease to P_3, then aggregate expenditures would increase to AE_3 producing a higher income level Y_3. This means that in Figure 6.1B, a lower price P_3 is matched with a higher income level Y_3. Joining these points together produces a downward-sloping aggregate demand curve.

Figure 6.1A shows the familiar Y = AE diagram, in which expenditure equilibrium is identified as Y_1 when aggregate expenditures are AE_1. This spending is done at some average price level. Let's call this present price level P_1 and show in Figure 6.1B that when the price level is P_1, equilibrium real GDP is at Y_1. You should note that we have made a change in the way we label the horizontal axes on these two figures. When we use aggregate expenditures on the Keynesian 45° graph, the horizontal axis is labelled national income. When we use the aggregate demand–aggregate supply graph, we label the horizontal axis real GDP. Of course, real GDP and real national income are conceptually the same, but this change is to help you keep the two models distinct.

Now we want to figure out the effect on aggregate expenditures if the price level happens to be higher. To most people, whether or not they have studied economics, one possible explanation seems fairly straightforward: if the price level goes up, people will simply buy less. But we need to understand why this is so. We learned in microeconomics that one of the reasons for this is that people would substitute other products for the now more expensive ones. But since we are looking here at the average price level of *all* goods and services, there are no substitutes for *all goods*. The other reason that we remember from microeconomics is that with higher prices, people simply cannot afford as much. However, this explanation is equally invalid because higher prices also means that total incomes must also rise, since someone must be receiving the benefit of the higher prices.

In other words, what this graph is trying to explain is the level of *real* GDP. Certainly, if the price level were to go up, the measured value of nominal expenditures and *nominal* GDP would increase proportionately. However, the values of both *real* GDP and real consumption would remain unchanged. Therefore, what we need to work out is the effect on spending if both the price level and nominal incomes rise by the same proportion, so that real income remains the same. You might suggest that under these circumstances, expenditures may well remain unchanged. However, as you may remember from Chapter 5, one portion of wealth is affected by a price change, and that is the real value of savings, which will decline as the price level rises. This, you will recall, is called the *real-balances effect*. Lower real wealth will cause people to cut down on spending. So a higher price level leads to lower real wealth, lower consumption, and lower aggregate expenditures and, therefore, will produce a lower level of real GDP. In Figure 6.1A, therefore, a higher price level will shift the AE_1 curve down to AE_2 and cause equilibrium income to drop to Y_2. In Figure 6.1B, a higher price level P_2 will lead to a lower income Y_2. A lower price level will produce the opposite results: it will cause real balances and consumption spending to increase. A lower price level will therefore shift the AE curve up from the original AE_1 to AE_3. This leads to a higher equilibrium income Y_3. In Figure 6.1B, therefore, a lower price level (P_3) means a higher income level (Y_3). In essence, therefore, every point on the aggregate demand curve is a point of equilibrium between aggregate expenditures and national income.

We have now established that the aggregate demand curve is downward-sloping because consumption expenditures are inversely related to the price level. There are two other additional explanations for the downward-sloping aggregate demand curve. First, a higher price level tends to push up interest rates, which in turn causes a reduction in investment spending and, therefore, aggregate expenditures. This is known as the **interest-rate effect**. Second, higher Canadian prices make our exports less attractive while at the same time making imports more appealing to Canadians. This is called the **foreign-trade effect**. We will examine both of these effects in detail in later chapters. So, in addition to lower levels of consumption, higher prices cause a drop in investment spending and in net exports. Lower prices will, of course, have the opposite effect. In summary, the aggregate demand curve is downward-sloping because of the:

- real-balances effect
- interest-rate effect
- foreign-trade effect

interest-rate effect: the effect that a change in prices, and therefore interest rates, has upon investment; for example, higher prices cause higher interest rates, which leads to lower investment.

foreign-trade effect: the effect that a change in prices has upon exports and imports.

SELF-TEST

1. Explain how a drop in the price level could affect consumption, investment, and net exports.

Aggregate Supply

aggregate supply: the aggregate quantity of goods and services produced by all sellers at various price levels.

Aggregate demand refers to *spending* by all four sectors of the economy: consumers, firms, government, and the international sector. **Aggregate supply**, on the other hand, refers to the *production* of goods and services in the economy. It relates the quantity of goods and services that producers would be willing to produce at various prices. When considering aggregate supply, it is important to distinguish between the short run and the long run.

The short run for the producer is a period of time in which wages and the prices of other resources remain constant. The majority of firms, particularly the big ones, tend to enter into contracts with their employees and with their suppliers so that, for most firms, factor prices (factor costs to the firms) are fixed in the short run.

short-run aggregate supply: the quantity of goods and services produced at various price levels assuming that factor prices remain constant.

Given this, how would firms react to a change in prices? Since factor prices remain fixed, a higher price for the goods or services they sell will mean higher profits and will induce firms to produce more. On the other hand, lower prices will cause firms to cut back on production. Higher prices, then, are associated with higher levels of production (GDP) and lower prices with lower GDP. The **short-run aggregate supply** curve, therefore, is upward-sloping, as shown in **Figure 6.2**.

FIGURE 6.2 Short-Run Aggregate Supply Curve

The upward-sloping short-run aggregate supply curve (labelled SAS) shows that, with factor prices (wage levels, and so on) constant, a higher price level will induce higher levels of production because of the prospects of higher profits; a lower price level will lead to lower profits and therefore lower levels of production.

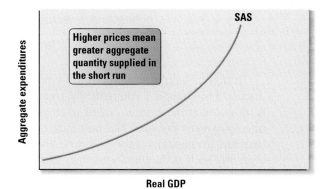

long-run aggregate supply: the aggregate quantity of goods and services produced after all prices and wages have adjusted; that is, the full-employment level of real GDP.

real wage: nominal wage divided by the price level; that is, the amount of goods and services that can be bought from a given nominal wage.

The **long-run aggregate supply**, in contrast, shows the quantity of goods and services that would be produced at various price levels assuming that wage rates and all other factor prices have adjusted to changing conditions. In the long run, firms will no longer enjoy the short-run advantage of higher profits that results from factor costs remaining constant as prices increase. In the long run, we assume that wage levels and other costs will also adjust accordingly.

This means that in the long run, the **real-wage** rate is constant. Under these circumstances, how much would the firm, and in total the whole economy, produce at various price levels? The answer presumably is: the quantity that will generate the greatest total profit, that is, at capacity or full-employment output. If both the prices of their products and all other factor costs were to increase or decrease by the same amount, say, 10 percent, how much would the average firm want to produce? The answer again is capacity or full-employment output. In other words:

> **The long-run aggregate supply is not affected by changes in the price level.**

We can therefore plot it as a vertical line at the full-employment level of real GDP, Y_{FE}, as shown in **Figure 6.3**.

FIGURE 6.3 Long-Run Aggregate Supply Curve

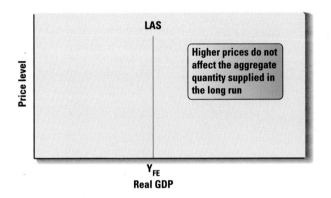

The long-run aggregate supply curve (labelled LAS) shows the level of real GDP at full employment (marked Y_{FE}). This level of real GDP does not depend on the price level; that is, the LAS is vertical.

It may be helpful to think of full-employment real GDP as potential real GDP, as discussed in Chapter 4. Alternatively, you could think of it as the level of real GDP that is produced at the natural rate of unemployment, with only frictional and structural unemployment present. The potential or full-employment level of real GDP (and therefore the position of the LAS curve) is determined by real productive factors in the economy, such as the size and skill level of the labour force, the amount of capital, and the level of technology. Also, since full employment is defined to include structural and frictional unemployment, the full-employment level of real GDP depends on factors that affect the amount of both frictional and structural unemployment. We will come back to this in a moment.

> **Capacity real GDP, potential real GDP, and full-employment real GDP all mean the same thing.**

The conclusion to this is that you can think of the long-run supply as representing the normal sustainable level of maximum output produced in the economy. This being so, neither a change in the nominal wage level nor one in the price level will affect it.

Macroeconomic Equilibrium

macroeconomic equilibrium: a situation in which the quantity of real GDP demanded equals the quantity of real GDP supplied.

Macroeconomic equilibrium exists when the quantity of aggregate demand equals the quantity of short-run aggregate supply. Only at one price level will the total that people want to buy equal the total that is produced. This is illustrated in **Figure 6.4A**, where P_1 and Y_1 are the equilibrium values for the price level and real GDP.

FIGURE 6.4 Macroeconomic Equilibrium

Equilibrium exists where the aggregate demand and the short-run aggregate supply curves intersect. This determines the equilibrium price level P_1 and the equilibrium real GDP level Y_1, as seen in Figure 6.4A. In Figure 6.4B, P_2 is a price level above equilibrium, and there is a surplus of goods and services because quantity supplied exceeds the quantity demanded. In this circumstance, firms will be forced to cut prices. At prices below equilibrium, as seen by P_3 in Figure 6.4C, there would be a shortage, because quantity demanded exceeds quantity supplied, which will force the price level up.

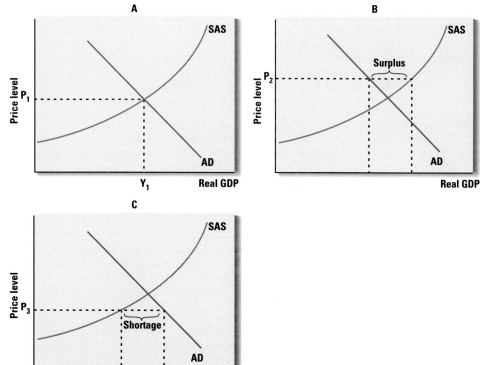

Only at price level P_1 are the quantity demanded and quantity supplied equal. It is possible that the price level, temporarily, may not be at equilibrium, but if this is the case it is an unstable situation. This is illustrated in **Figure 6.4B**, where the price level is above equilibrium at P_2. At this higher price level there is a surplus of goods and services, because the quantity supplied exceeds the quantity demanded. To rid themselves of such surpluses, firms will be forced to cut prices and will continue to do so until the price level is back to equilibrium. In contrast, a lower price level of P_3, as seen in Figure 6.4C, would result in a shortage of goods and services, and prices would be pushed up until the economy is back at equilibrium, with neither surpluses nor shortages.

SELF-TEST

2. Following are the aggregate demand and supply schedules for the economy of Tagara:

A) What is the equilibrium level of prices and real GDP?
B) If the price level were 95, would there be a shortage or surplus? How much? What if the price level was 115?

Price Index	Aggregate Demand	Aggregate Supply
85	$1250	$825
90	1200	950
95	1150	1025
100	1100	1100
105	1050	1150
110	1000	1190
115	950	1220
120	900	1240

In Chapter 5, we saw that there's no guarantee that equilibrium also means that the economy is operating at capacity with full employment. In fact, equilibrium could exist at any level of real GDP, as **Figure 6.5A, B**, and **C** illustrates.

This figure shows three possible positions for an economy. In 6.5A, the economy is in equilibrium because the quantity of aggregate demand is equal to the quantity of short-run aggregate supply. In addition, this economy is also at full employment, which means that this intersection occurs at a point *on* the long-run aggregate supply curve. In 6.5B, the economy is suffering a **recessionary gap** because, while it too is in equilibrium (the AD curve intersects the SAS curve at the present level of real GDP, Y_1), this equilibrium is below the full-employment level of real GDP, Y_{FE}. In other words, the intersection is not a point on the LAS curve. A recessionary gap implies that some of the factors of production are unemployed. For most people, therefore, recession and unemployment are synonymous. Keynes felt that this was the type of situation in which many economies found themselves in the 1930s. They were in a sense caught in a low-level trap. Unemployment was high and production was low, but there was no incentive for firms to produce more because they were just selling what they produced. Despite this recessionary gap, the economy is stable because there is no tendency, and no incentive, to change. Obviously, closing a recessionary gap involves raising the level of aggregate demand.

Figure 6.5C shows the opposite situation. Here again the economy is in equilibrium at a real GDP level of Y_2, but the equilibrium occurs above the full employment level of real GDP. This is the situation of an **inflationary gap**. People are trying to buy

recessionary gap: the difference between actual real GDP and potential real GDP when the economy is producing below its potential.

inflationary gap: the difference between actual real GDP and potential real GDP when the economy is temporarily producing an output above full employment.

more goods and services than the economy can produce. The level of aggregate demand, indicated by Y_2, exceeds the level of full employment output. The result is a situation that could be termed "too much spending chasing too few goods" but is often erroneously described as "too much money chasing too few goods." We, however, know that money is a stock and spending is a flow, and we must be careful how we state things. Certainly, in such a situation, prices and wages will start to increase, but it may not have anything to do with the amount of money in the economy. What is certainly true is that the amount of spending is in excess of the economy's present ability to produce goods. Such a situation is going to result in buyers bidding up prices in an effort to secure what they want and firms being forced to pay higher wages to attract labour, which is in high demand. Such price increases are, of course, inflationary, and the gap between Y_2 and Y_{FE} is the inflationary gap. This situation is not stable, since the economy simply cannot continue to produce a level of real GDP above its full-employment level on a sustained basis. In summary, equilibrium in the macroeconomy might:

- occur at full employment
- result in a recessionary gap
- result in an inflationary gap

What we need to do now is look at how these various situations come about and what will happen as a result. In other words, we need to look at the dynamics of the model.

FIGURE 6.5 Equilibrium and Full Employment

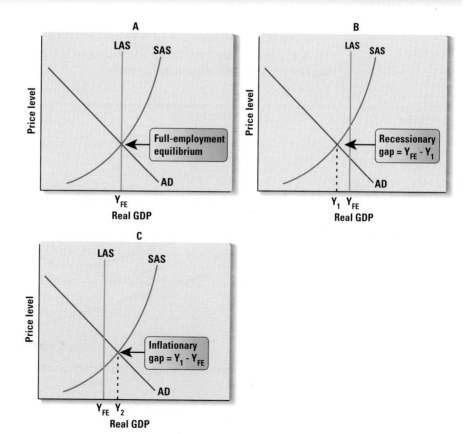

Figure 6.5A shows an economy in equilibrium, and this equilibrium is also at full employment. In other words, the AD and SAS curves intersect at full employment (indicated by the position of the LAS curve). Figure 6.5B shows equilibrium occurring below full employment; that is, there is a recessionary gap. In Figure 6.5C, equilibrium occurs above full employment; that is, there is an inflationary gap.

Determinants of Aggregate Demand

Let us now consider the factors that will cause aggregate demand to change, and, therefore, the aggregate demand curve to shift. Remember that the aggregate demand is simply the amount of aggregate expenditure at various price levels. Anything, therefore, that affects aggregate *expenditure* and its components will also affect aggregate *demand*. In other words, the determinants of consumption, investment, government spending, and net exports are also the determinants of aggregate demand. As we saw in Chapter 5, the list of possible determinants includes such things as wealth, the age of consumer durables, future expectations, interest rates, capital costs, exchange rates, foreign income levels, and so on. The only two items that should *not* be on this list are the level of real GDP and the price level. (These are the variables on the axes, and if either of these changes, it would not change the aggregate demand curve itself but would merely change the position *on* it.)

SELF-TEST

3. Which of the following factors will lead to an increase or decrease in aggregate demand (and a shift in the AD curve)?

A) A decrease in stock market prices.

B) An increase in the price level.

C) An increase in real GDP.

D) An increase in interest rates.

E) A decrease in government spending.

F) An increase in foreign incomes.

G) A drop in the price of capital goods.

H) A decrease in the price level.

If any of the determinants of aggregate demand were to change, it would mean that at any given price level buyers are willing to buy more or less goods and services than before. This is illustrated in **Figure 6.6**.

FIGURE 6.6 Shifts in the Aggregate Demand Curve

When the level of aggregate demand increases, the aggregate demand curve shifts to the right, from AD$_1$ to AD$_2$. This means that at every price level, the quantity of goods and services demanded has increased. In contrast, a decrease in aggregate demand will shift the AD curve to the left, in this case from AD$_1$ to AD$_3$.

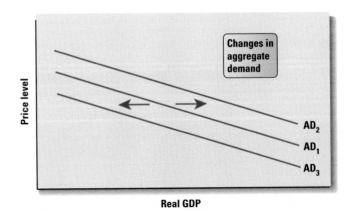

An increase in the level of aggregate demand is illustrated by a rightward shift in the aggregate demand curve, from AD_1 to AD_2. Such an increase could have been caused by, say, an increase in foreign incomes, which led to a higher demand for exports. This shift occurs despite the fact that the price level has remained the same. An example of something that could cause a decrease in aggregate demand (a leftward shift from AD_1 to AD_3 in Figure 6.6) might be, say, an increase in interest rates, which leads to a decline in investment spending.

In addition to the various determinants of aggregate demand that we have mentioned, there are other determinants of importance, since they are under the control of policy makers. These are known as fiscal and monetary tools. The former include changes in government spending and taxation; the latter include changes in the money supply. We will be looking at these tools in some detail in Chapters 11 and 12. However, for now, note that an increase in government spending or a decrease in taxation will increase aggregate demand and cause a rightward shift in the AD curve. The same effect would result from an increase in the money supply. In summary, the determinents of aggregate demand are:

Consumption
- wealth
- age of consumer durables
- consumer expectations

Investment
- interest rates
- purchase price, maintenance and operating costs
- age of capital goods
- business expectations and government policies

Net Exports
- value of exchange rate
- income levels abroad
- price of competitive (foreign) goods

Government Spending and Tax Rates

Money Supply

Determinants of Aggregate Supply

Let's first investigate the long-run aggregate supply and try to work out what could cause it to change. It is important to realize that the position of the long-run aggregate supply curve is at the full-employment level of real GDP. Full-employment real GDP is the amount of real goods and services that an economy is capable of producing at capacity. Essentially, what an economy is capable of producing in any one year is determined by the quantity and quality of its resources and the type of technology it is using. A country's potential real GDP will increase, therefore, if there is an increase in:

- the size of its labour force
- the productivity (or the skill level) of the labour force
- the size of its capital stock
- technology

Generally speaking, a country's productive potential, and therefore its long-run aggregate supply, increases year by year; the change, however, is usually gradual.

What about the short-run aggregate supply—what factors will cause it to change? In essence, the factors that affect the long-run aggregate supply also affect the short-run supply. This is because anything that changes productivity also affects the profitability of firms, and this, in turn, will affect the short-run supply. If productivity increases, for example, it means that, at the given price level, firms will be making greater profits and will therefore produce more. This implies an increase in aggregate supply, which is reflected in a rightward shift in *both* the long-run and the short-run aggregate supply curve. Bear in mind that those factors that change aggregate supply affect an economy's *ability* to produce in the long, and short, run. This does not necessarily mean that the amount actually produced is affected. For instance, an increase in the size of the labour force will affect the economy's ability to produce, but that does not guarantee that the economy will necessarily produce more. We need to emphasize that the following factors affect *both* the long-run aggregate supply and the short-run aggregate supply: a change in the quantity or quality of productive resources, a change in technology, or a change in productivity. Graphically, a change in any of these factors will cause the two curves to shift by an equal amount, as shown in **Figure 6.7**.

FIGURE 6.7 An Increase in Aggregate Supply

An increase in the size or the quality of the labour force or in the amount of capital stock or an improvement in technology shifts both the long- and short-run aggregate supply curves, LAS_1 and SAS_1, to the right by an equal distance. The new short-run supply curve SAS_2 intersects the new long-run supply curve LAS_2 at the same price level, P_1.

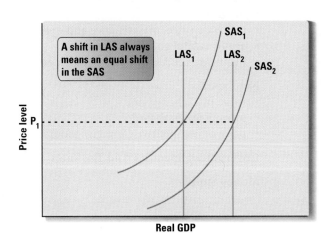

Figure 6.7 demonstrates that any factor that shifts the long-run supply curve will also shift the short-run supply curve. An increase in the long-run supply curve from LAS_1 to LAS_2, caused perhaps by an improved technology, will shift the short-run supply curve by an equal amount horizontally, from SAS_1 to SAS_2.

4. Suppose the long-run aggregate supply for the country of Taymar has a value of $1100 and the short-run aggregate supply is as follows:

Price Index	Aggregate Supply
85	$825
90	950
95	1025
100	1100
105	1150
110	1190
115	1220
120	1240

A) Plot the long- and short-run aggregate supply curves.

B) Assume that the aggregate supply changed by $100 as a result of increased productivity. Plot the new curves.

There is one additional consideration, and this affects the short-run aggregate supply only: it is changes in *factor prices*. Under this heading we would include such things as a change in wage rates, resource prices, or business taxes. Each of these would affect the profitability of firms. An increase in wage rates, assuming the price level remains the same, will mean lower profits for the firm and will lead to a cutback in production. This will lead to a decrease in aggregate supply and a leftward shift in the short-run aggregate supply curve. A decrease in these costs would, on the other hand, increase profitability and production and cause the short-run supply to increase, which would be reflected in a rightward shift in the curve. Let us emphasize, however, that:

A change in factor prices will have no effect on the long-run aggregate supply.

This is because a change in factor prices will not in any real sense lead to an increase in an economy's productive capability.

A change in factor prices is shown in **Figure 6.8**. This figure shows the effect of, say, a significant reduction in the prices of imported inputs. This will cause a drop in production costs in Canada and will encourage firms to produce more at the present price level. This implies a rightward shift in the short-run aggregate supply curve from SAS_1 to SAS_2. Once again, since a change in factor costs has no effect on the productive capacity of the economy, there is no shift in the long-run aggregate supply curve LAS.

FIGURE 6.8 Change in Factor Prices

A decrease in factor prices, such as lower prices of imported oil, for instance, will lower the costs of production and therefore shift the short-run aggregate supply curve from SAS_1 to SAS_2 while leaving the long-run aggregate supply curve (LAS) unaffected.

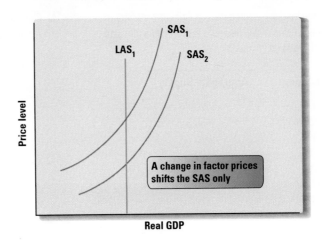

Before we examine the effects of changes in aggregate demand and supply on the economy, it might be useful to remind ourselves of the determinants of both short-run and long-run aggregate supply.

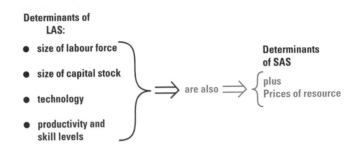

Determinants of LAS:

- size of labour force
- size of capital stock
- technology
- productivity and skill levels

are also ⟹ **Determinants of SAS**

plus
Prices of resource

SELF-TEST

5. What effect will the following changes have on either the short-run or the long-run aggregate supply or both?
   A) A big reduction in payroll taxes.
   B) An increase in the price of imported crude oil.
   C) The imposition of stringent pollution standards on all oil-burning engines.
   D) An increase in the number of immigrants entering Canada.
   E) The discovery of extensive oil deposits in northern Canada.
   F) A substantial increase in wage settlements.
   G) The introduction of a microchip that reduces computer processing time by 80 percent.

REVIEW

1. What are thought to be the shortcomings of the Keynesian model?
2. What does the term *aggregate demand* mean?
3. What are the three reasons for the downward slope of the aggregate demand curve?
4. What do the terms *aggregate supply*, *short-run aggregate supply*, and *long-run aggregate supply* mean?
5. What is the *real wage*? Is the real wage constant on the short-run aggregate supply curve? On the long-run aggregate supply curve?
6. What does *macroeconomic equilibrium* mean?
7. What are the determinants of aggregate demand?
8. What are the determinants of long-run aggregate supply?
9. What are the determinants of short-run aggregate supply?

Determinants of Real GDP and the Price Level

It's now time to put this model to work and see how it explains various changes in the economy. It is clear that changes in the aggregate demand, short-run aggregate supply, and the long-run aggregate supply can all bring about changes in the price level and in real GDP, so let us take each one in turn.

A Change in Aggregate Demand

Suppose that both firms and consumers become more optimistic about future economic conditions in Canada and as a result start to loosen their purse strings and buy more. The effect of this will be an increase in aggregate demand, as shown in **Figure 6.9**.

FIGURE 6.9 An Increase in Aggregate Demand

Assume that the economy was originally at price level P_1 and real GDP level Y_1. A widespread expectation of future improvements will lead to an increase in the level of aggregate demand, shown as a shift in the aggregate demand curve from AD_1 to AD_2. The effect of this will be to push up prices to P_2 and real GDP to Y_2.

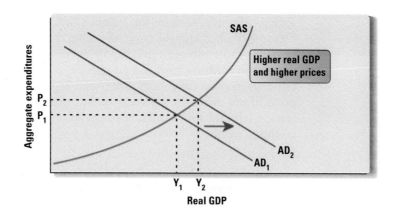

An increase in aggregate demand from AD_1 to AD_2 in Figure 6.9 will lead to higher prices (the price level increases from P_1 to P_2), and a higher level of real GDP (real GDP increases from Y_1 to Y_2). You should recall from our discussion in the previous chapter that the existence of the multiplier means that the increase in aggregate demand (AD_1 to AD_2) is greater than the initial increase in expenditures. Other factors that could bring about an increase in the level of aggregate demand include a decrease in interest rates, a decrease in the value of the Canadian dollar, an increase in foreign incomes, a decrease in taxes, or an increase in government spending or in the money supply. A decrease in aggregate demand would have the opposite effect.

SELF-TEST

6. The following table shows the aggregate demand and short-run aggregate supply schedules for the economy of Zee:

Aggregate Demand	Price Index	Aggregate Supply
$2000	85	$1650
1950	90	1670
1900	95	1700
1850	100	1740
1800	105	1800
1750	110	1890
1700	115	2000
1650	120	2200

A) What are the equilibrium values of price and real GDP?

B) Assume that aggregate demand decreases by $200 at every price level. What will be the new equilibrium values of price and real GDP?

A Change in Short-Run Aggregate Supply

As we have seen, a number of factors influence short-run aggregate supply, but we want to focus on factor prices since, as mentioned, they do not affect the long-run aggregate supply. Assume for instance that the price of imported oil were to fall. Figure 6.10 illustrates the effect of such a change. When there is a decrease in factor costs, the short-run aggregate supply curve will shift to the right, and the result is a decrease in the price level and an increase in real GDP. Other factors that might also cause an increase only in the short-run aggregate supply include a decrease in the prices of raw materials, a decrease in the money wage levels, or a decrease in business taxes. A leftward shift would, of course, produce the opposite result. We can generalize this to say that:

Any change in the price of any of the factors of production will shift the short-run aggregate supply curve.

What impact would a decrease in the price of imported oil have on the short-run aggregate supply?

FIGURE 6.10 An Increase in Short-Run Aggregate Supply

A decrease in the price of imported oil will improve profitability, causing the aggregate supply curve to shift to the right from SAS$_1$ to SAS$_2$. This change will cause the price level to drop from P$_1$ to P$_2$ and the level of real GDP to increase from Y$_1$ to Y$_2$.

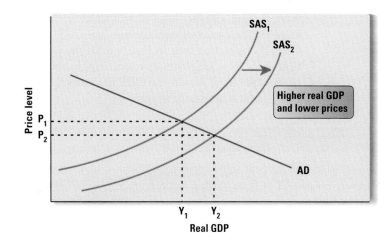

A Change in Long-Run Aggregate Supply

This is the trickiest of the three changes we are considering, because anything that changes the long-run aggregate supply also affects the short-run aggregate supply. Assume for instance that the labour-force participation rate increases, which effectively means that the size of the labour force increases. Let us examine the effect of such a change on an economy. (We assume that the economy is initially at full-employment real GDP). We know that in this case both the short- and long-run aggregate supplies will increase simultaneously, as illustrated in **Figure 6.11**.

FIGURE 6.11 An Increase in Long-Run Aggregate Supply

An increase in the size of the labour force will shift both the short-run and the long-run aggregate supply curves to the right. The former curve shifts from SAS$_1$ to SAS$_2$, the latter from LAS$_1$ to LAS$_2$. This change causes a reduction of the price level from P$_1$ to P$_2$ and an increase in real GDP from Y$_1$ to Y$_2$. One other significant result is that the economy, which was initially at full employment, is now experiencing a recessionary gap; that is, the economy is at Y$_2$, which is below the new full-employment real GDP, Y$_3$.

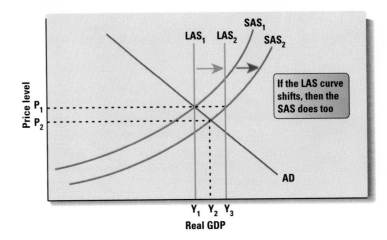

As a result of the increase in the size of the labour force, both supply curves shift to the right by an equal amount. The new equilibrium is where the AD$_1$ and the SAS$_2$ curves intersect, which is at real GDP level Y$_2$. The result of the change is a lower price level, P$_2$, and a higher level of real GDP, Y$_2$. Note that a recessionary gap now exists, since the new level of equilibrium real GDP is below the new level of potential real GDP, Y$_3$. As can be seen in Figure 6.11, the potential real GDP is shown by the position of the new long-run aggregate supply curve, LAS$_2$, which is now greater than the new output level. Actual real GDP has grown, but potential real GDP has grown more, resulting in a recessionary gap.

SELF-TEST

7. Explain why, when both the short- and long-run aggregate supplies increase, the economy is left in a recessionary gap situation.

8. The long-run aggregate supply for the economy of Ithica is $1500. The aggregate demand and short-run aggregate supply schedules are shown below:

Price Index	Aggregate Demand	Aggregate Supply
$ 85	1750	1180
90	1700	1200
95	1650	1240
100	1600	1300
105	1550	1380
110	1500	1500
115	1450	1630
120	1400	1800

A) What are the equilibrium values of price and real GDP? What type of equilibrium is this?

B) Assume that an increase in productivity increases aggregate supply by $300. What will be the new equilibrium values of price and real GDP? Is there now a recessionary or inflationary gap? How much is the gap?

Is the Economy Self-Adjusting?

We have now seen what happens when there is a shift in (a) aggregate demand, (b) the short-run aggregate supply, or (c) the long-run aggregate supply. In doing this, we have seen that the economy may experience a recessionary gap as a result. In this regard, was Keynes correct in his belief that the economy is doomed to remain in this situation unless it is bailed out by government intervention, or, on the contrary, is the economy capable of curing itself? The answer to this depends on how well or how quickly wages and prices adjust to the situation. If they do adjust quickly—if they are totally flexible—an economy is likely to move to a full-employment situation very rapidly. At the other extreme, which is what Keynes believed, if prices and wages do not change at all in the short run, then a recessionary (or, for that matter an inflationary) gap is likely to last indefinitely. The view of most economists these days is that neither extreme view is valid. Although prices and wages are often inflexible in the short run, eventually they do adjust to the changing conditions of the economy. That is why, in our analysis so far, we have distinguished between the short and long run. Let us explain exactly how this adjustment process works. Assume, as in **Figure 6.12**, that the economy finds itself in a recessionary-gap situation, with actual real GDP below full-employment real GDP.

FIGURE 6.12 Adjustment from a Recessionary Gap

Initially, the economy is at price level P_1 and real GDP level Y_1, below the full-employment level Y_{FE}. This situation will put downward pressure on wages. As wages fall, the short-run aggregate supply curve shifts to the right until it is at SAS_2. The net result will be a lower price level, P_2, and a full-employment real GDP, Y_{FE}.

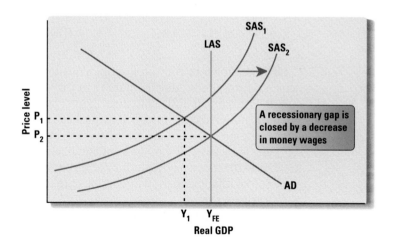

The economy is currently in equilibrium at real GDP level Y_1, where aggregate demand, AD, is equal to the short-run aggregate supply, SAS_1. However, the full-employment level of real GDP is at Y_{FE}. In this recessionary gap situation, unemployment is above its natural rate. Firms find it easy to hire labour, and workers find it difficult to get jobs. Eventually, nominal wage levels will be forced down. Remember that SAS_1 is based on a particular unchanging level of nominal wages; that is, the wage rate is constant along the short-run aggregate supply. If the nominal wage level drops, this means that the short-run aggregate supply curve will shift rightward. As this happens, firms hire more workers, production (real GDP) increases from Y_1 to Y_{FE} and the price level falls from P_1 to P_2. The process continues, with the SAS shifting rightward until the economy is in equilibrium at Y_{FE}, where the new short-run aggregate supply, SAS_2, is equal to the aggregate demand. This new equilibrium is at full employment.

Let's turn to the opposite situation and work out how the economy adjusts to an inflationary-gap situation. Assume that the economy finds itself in equilibrium at real GDP level Y_3 in **Figure 6.13**.

FIGURE 6.13 Adjustment from an Inflationary Gap

The economy is initially at equilibrium, with AD equal to SAS_3 at real GDP level Y_3. This is not a stable situation. With real GDP above its full-employment level, the unemployment rate is below the natural rate. The high demand for labour will push up nominal wage rates, causing short-run aggregate supply to decrease and pushing the SAS curve back to SAS_2. The new equilibrium level of real GDP is now lower and the price level is higher than initially—price increases from P_3 to P_1.

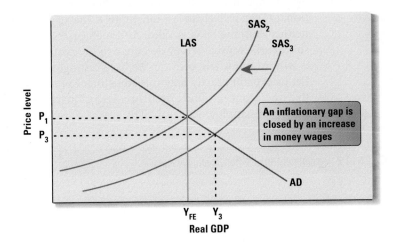

The economy is above full employment, which means that, faced with a high demand, firms are producing more than they would consider their normal capacity output. Firms find it difficult to hire labour, and workers find it easy to get jobs. In this situation, nominal wage rates will be pushed up. This will cause the short-run aggregate supply curve to shift left, pushing the price level up and real GDP down until the economy is back at full-employment equilibrium, with aggregate demand, AD, equal to the new short-run aggregate supply curve, SAS_2.

In all of this analysis you might object that in the modern world, while price and wage levels do seem to increase year by year, they very seldom decrease. And yet this model suggests that this is exactly what happens when there is a surplus of production or labour. The problem here is not so much a defect of the model, but the limitation of picturing changes in terms of a two-dimensional graph. In reality, all economies are in a perpetual state of flux, with both the aggregate demand and supply constantly changing. If we could, it would be better to depict *rates of change* rather than actual changes, but then the analysis becomes unnecessarily complicated. In actuality, rather than the nominal wage level dropping, it rises but at a slower pace than does the price level.

This completes our discussion of the aggregate demand-supply model, which is the model that we will use to look at various issues in later chapters. However, it may be helpful in understanding this model to highlight in a bit more detail the disagreement between the two major schools of thought regarding the flexibility of prices and wages, which we have touched on in this chapter.

Keynesians versus the Neoclassical School

The opposing camps, if you remember from Chapter 1, were the neoclassical school and the Keynesians. Although the heat has died down a little since the sometimes acrimonious debates between the two that raged in the decades following the publication of Keynes's *General Theory* in 1936, occasional flare-ups still break out. The neoclassicists generally believed that the marketplace was competitive and efficient and would adjust rapidly whenever there was a general shortage or surplus. By adjustment, they meant that prices and wages would move up or down quickly and easily to ensure full employment. In terms of our graphs, they would have made no distinction between the short-run and long-run aggregate supply curves since, as we have said, changes would occur so rapidly there would be no time lag in the adjustment process. In addition, the economy would always remain at full employment. This is illustrated in **Figure 6.14**.

FIGURE 6.14 Neoclassical Aggregate Demand–Supply

According to the neoclassical school, there is no distinction between the long and short run, and therefore there is only a single aggregate supply curve that is vertical. This means that the price level has no effect on the quantity supplied. The aggregate supply curve will always be at the full-employment level of real GDP, labelled Y_{FE}. Changes in aggregate demand, therefore, have no effect upon real GDP and affect *only* the price level. In fact, the only thing that can affect the price level is a change in aggregate demand. An increase in aggregate demand from AD_1 to AD_2, for instance, will increase the price level from P_1 to P_2 but will leave real GDP unaffected at Y_{FE}.

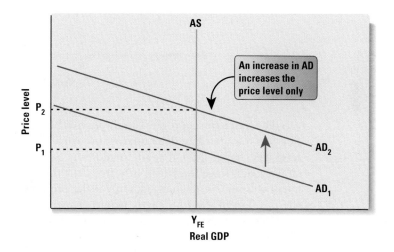

The aggregate supply curve is a vertical straight line at the full-employment level of real GDP, Y_{FE}. The position of the curve is determined by such real variables as factor endowment and technology; that is, it is a long-run aggregate supply curve. However, since the neoclassical economists made no distinction between the short and long run, there is really only one aggregate supply curve. The neoclassicists saw the aggregate demand curve as the normal downward-sloping demand curve. (To most neoclassical economists, the only factor that could really affect aggregate demand was the money supply.) In addition, a change in aggregate demand would leave real GDP unaffected but would most definitely cause a change in the price level. Furthermore, it is the only thing that could produce such a change. This means that neoclassical economists believed that demand–pull was the only cause of inflation. Moreover, they felt that the economy can only grow if there is a growth in the factors of production or an improvement in technology. Of course, in their model, a major depression or recession is impossible.

In contrast, Keynesian economists believed that the marketplace is not very competitive because of the existence of big corporations and unions. They felt that prices and wages are, as a result, inflexible. Changes in aggregate demand, therefore, have little impact on the price level. This is shown in **Figure 6.15**.

FIGURE 6.15 The Keynesian View of Aggregate Demand–Supply

The short-run aggregate supply curve, according to Keynesians, is horizontal at the prevailing price level. Changes in aggregate demand, therefore, have no effect on the price level but do cause changes in real GDP. An increase in aggregate demand from AD_1 to AD_2 will cause an increase in real GDP from Y_1 to Y_2 but leave the price level unchanged at P_1.

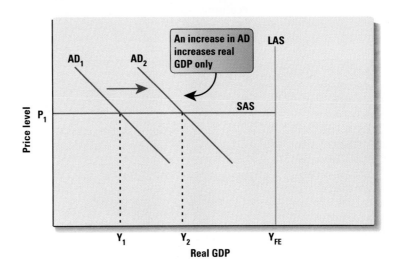

The short-run aggregate supply curve is horizontal at the prevailing price level, P_1. Shifts in the aggregate demand can and will lead to changes in real GDP, but the price level will change little, if at all. In addition, Keynesians believe that if there is a recessionary gap, wage levels will not drop and therefore the short-run aggregate supply curve will remain unchanged. Only if the economy is at full employment, shown by the position of the LAS curve, would changes in aggregate demand affect the price level. However, without government intervention, there is nothing to guarantee that the economy will ever be at full employment.

SELF-TEST

9. Explain what will happen to nominal GDP and real GDP if there is an increase in aggregate demand according to:

A) Keynesians (if the economy is below full employment);
B) Neoclassicists.

Shape of the Short-Run Aggregate Supply Curve

From the above discussion you can see that what a good deal (but by no means all) of the Keynesian–neoclassical controversy boiled down to was disagreement about the shape of the short-run aggregate supply curve. Was it flat, which would mean inflexible prices, as Keynes believed? Or was it vertical, and synonymous with the long-run aggregate supply curve, which would imply perfectly flexible prices, as the neoclassicists suggested? Now that the dust has largely settled, most economists nowadays would answer with an unequivocal: "It all depends!" What we mean is this: whether prices change quickly or not at all depends on the situation of the economy. If the economy is in the middle of a major recession, then probably prices will not change greatly in response to a change in demand, since firms do not need much of an inducement to persuade them to produce more. In a recession, firms will be operating below capacity, there will be idle equipment and machines, and a large portion of the labour force will be unemployed. An increase in production under these circumstances can be effected reasonably cheaply, since firms can employ the best workers and machines. In other words, the short-run aggregate supply curve is fairly flat. But what happens as the economy starts to recover and moves toward full employment? Now productivity per worker will fall as firms are forced to hire less-efficient operatives and make use of older and less-efficient machines. Because of this, unit costs of production start to rise as firms, and the economy, move closer to full employment, which means, in turn, that extra output can only be produced at higher prices. This is consistent with the law of increasing costs that was introduced in Chapter 1. The closer we move toward full employment, therefore, the steeper will be the short-run aggregate supply curve. In fact, some economists see the short-run aggregate supply curve eventually becoming vertical as the economy reaches the physical capacity of the economy. This can be seen in **Figure 6.16**.

FIGURE 6.16 Shape of the Aggregate Supply Curve

The short-run aggregate supply curve is fairly flat in the area around real GDP level $Y_1 - Y_2$. Real GDP in this area is well below its full-employment level. An increase in aggregate demand, from AD_1 to AD_2, has little effect on the price level, but real GDP increases significantly from Y_1 to Y_2. In contrast, the same increase in aggregate demand at higher levels of real GDP, say from AD_3 to AD_4, will have less impact on real GDP than it does on the price level.

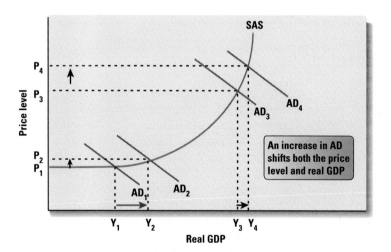

In Figure 6.16 we can see that the short-run aggregate supply curve is fairly flat at low levels of real GDP and becomes steeper as it approaches full-employment GDP. Therefore, if the economy is at low levels of real GDP, an increase in aggregate demand (from AD_1 to AD_2) has only a small effect on the price level but a big impact on real GDP. If the same increase in demand occurred near full employment (from AD_3 to AD_4), then real GDP would only increase a small amount, from Y_3 to Y_4, but there would be a big increase in the price level, from P_3 to P_4.

ADDED DIMENSION

Is the SAS Becoming Flatter?

A recent report in *The Economist* magazine suggests that there is growing opinion that the shape of the short-run aggregate supply curve is becoming flatter as the economy approaches full employment. If true, this would be good news indeed, because it would mean that there would be less inflationary pressure as the full-employment level of output was approached. The main reason for this optimism involves the globalization of the world's economies. The increased competition that results from globalization is thought to severely restrain the ability of companies to raise prices. As a result, there is a growing recognition by business that they must generate profit by boosting efficiencies rather than prices.

We will be returning to, and elaborating on, some of these basic themes later on, but this completes our look at the aggregate demand–supply model.

REVIEW

1. **What effect will a decrease in aggregate demand have on price and real GDP?**
2. **What effect will a decrease in short-run aggregate supply have on price and real GDP?**
3. **What effect will a decrease in long-run aggregate supply have on price and real GDP? Will the change produce a recessionary or inflationary gap?**
4. **How does the economy adjust if there is a recessionary gap? If there is an inflationary gap?**
5. **What is the shape of the aggregate supply curve, according to neoclassicists? According to Keynesians?**
6. **What effect does a decrease in aggregate demand have on price and real GDP at low levels of GDP? At close to full-employment GDP?**

Chapter Highlights

This chapter begins by explaining that the expenditures model we developed in Chapter 5 needs to be extended to include changes in the price level and production. It begins this task by first introducing the concept of aggregate demand and then showing how the aggregate demand curve can be derived from the aggregate expenditures of the previous chapter. The three reasons for the downward slope of the aggregate demand curve are then explained. The idea of aggregate supply is less straightforward, since it is necessary to distinguish between the short run and the long run. The short run is defined as the period in which factor prices are constant; if they should change, then so does the short-run aggregate supply. The long run is explained as the period of time during which nominal wages and other costs can fully adjust so that the real wage is constant. The more straightforward idea of the long-run aggregate supply being synonymous with full-employment or capacity real GDP is explained.

After explaining that macroeconomic equilibrium implies equality between aggregate demand and short-run aggregate supply, the chapter discusses the important point that equilibrium does not necessarily mean full employment. This is made easier to understand with the help of Figure 6.5.

The first part of the chapter closes by explaining and showing graphically what could cause changes in aggregate demand, short-run aggregate supply, and long-run aggregate supply.

The material so far, despite its apparent complexity on first exposure, is really just an introduction to the last part of the chapter, which seeks to explain the crucial question of what determines the level of real GDP and the price level. It does this by explaining the effects of various changes, starting with a change in aggregate demand. Next, a change in short-run aggregate supply is investigated before looking at the much trickier change in long-run aggregate supply. This last change is more difficult, since any change in long-run aggregate supply also changes short-run aggregate supply.

Next, the chapter looks at a more controversial aspect of the model: the ability or inability of the economy to adjust to situations in which the economy is not operating at full employment. It explains that a recessionary gap is eventually cured because it causes a drop in nominal wages, which results in an increase in the short-run aggregate supply and an increase in real GDP until the economy is at full employment. Similarly, an inflationary gap leads to an increase in nominal wages and a drop in short-run aggregate supply.

Finally, the chapter wraps up by contrasting the views of the neoclassicists and Keynesians and explains that a good part of their disagreement centred on the shape of the aggregate supply curve, with Keynesians believing it to be quite flat, which implies inflexible prices and wages, whereas neoclassical economists regarded the aggregate supply curve to be vertical at the full-employment level of real GDP, which implies totally flexible wages and prices.

The chapter makes a final point that the current view is that the short-run aggregate supply curve is an amalgam of both curves: flat at lower levels of real GDP, getting progressively steeper as full employment is approached.

New Glossary Terms

aggregate demand   198
aggregate supply   201
foreign-trade effect   200
inflationary gap   204
interest-rate effect   200
long-run aggregate supply   201
macroeconomic equilibrium   203
real wage   201
recessionary gap   204
short-run aggregate supply   201

STUDY GUIDE

Study Tips

1. The most difficult part of this chapter for students to master is the distinction between the short-run and the long-run aggregate supply curves and what can cause them to shift. You must first be clear what the terms "short run" and "long run" mean. As in microeconomics, they do not necessarily correspond to periods of time. Think about what a supply curve means. It doesn't refer to the amounts that firms are actually producing *now* but hypothetically what they would produce under certain circumstances. In particular, the short-run aggregate supply is based on what firms are *willing and able* to produce at various prices if nominal wages and other resources prices don't change. On the other hand, the long-run supply curve has nothing to do with willingness but is tied totally to an economy's ability to produce. It's rather like a production possibilities curve, which shows physical amounts a country is capable of producing. It tells you nothing about what a country is actually producing. Nor does it tell you how long it will take to get there nor, for that matter, if it ever will. The long run is an indicator of potential and not a measurement of time.

2. Try to make sure that you understand this distinction between the long and short run, because it will greatly help you in figuring out which curves move and why. The short-run aggregate supply has everything to do with profitability, and anything that affects profitability will affect it. The long-run aggregate supply, on the other hand, has everything to do with productivity, and anything that affects productivity will affect it. Imagine, in other words, that there is a $ sign above the short-run supply curve. Now given this, anything that affects productivity, such as technology, quality, and quantity of productive resources, will also impact on profitability. You can, therefore, never shift the long-run supply curve without also shifting the short-run aggregate supply curve. The reverse, however, is not true. For instance, a change in nominal wages, in business taxes, or in the price of imported resources will definitely affect profitability and therefore the short-run aggregate supply. They do not, however, affect a country's productive potential; that is, the long-run aggregate supply remains unchanged.

3. A number of students will have difficulty at times disentangling those things that affect the demand side of things and those that affect the supply. As in microeconomics, it's a good idea not to get too "cute" by thinking of ways in which a change in one thing can have an impact on other factors, however remote they may be. By some esoteric reasoning it's possible to link pretty well all factors in life; in economics it is better to stick to the more obvious. Learn the table of determinants in Chapter 6, and remember that these factors affect only the demand or the supply, and not both. Only one major factor can affect both aggregate demand and supply, and that is business taxes. But that story can wait until a later chapter.

Key Problem

Table 6.1 shows Chunderland's aggregate demand and short-run aggregate supply.

TABLE 6.1

Price	Aggregate Quantity Supplied	Aggregate Quantity Demanded
$65	$20	$240
66	40	236
67	60	232
68	80	228
70	100	220
72	132	212
75	160	200
80	180	180
85	200	160
90	220	140
95	230	120
100	240	100
105	248	80
110	250	60

a) Assume that the economy of Chunderland is at full-employment equilibrium. Draw the aggregate demand, short-run aggregate supply, and long-run aggregate supply on **Figure 6.17** and label them AD_1, SAS_1, and LAS_1.

FIGURE 6.17

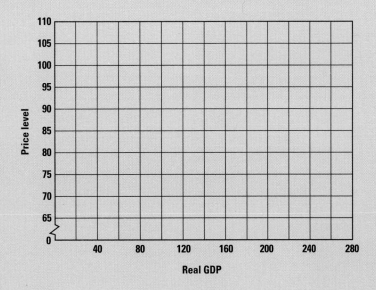

b) What are the equilibrium values of the price level and real GDP?

Equilibrium price: _____ ; equilibrium real GDP: $_____.

c) Suppose that the aggregate demand in Chunderland were to increase by 80 at every price level. Show the new aggregate demand on your graph, and label it AD_2. What is the amount of *change* in the price level and in the level of real GDP? Is there a recessionary gap or inflationary gap?

Change in price level: _____ ; change in real GDP: $_____ ;

recessionary or inflationary gap: _____ .

d) Suppose *instead* that the aggregate demand in Chunderland had *decreased* by 80 at every price level. Show the new aggregate demand on your graph, and label it AD_3. What is the amount of *change* in the price level and in the level of real GDP? Is there a recessionary gap or inflationary gap?

Change in price level: _____ ; change in real GDP: $_____ ;

recessionary or inflationary gap: _____ .

e) Compare the increase in c) to the decrease in d). Briefly explain the difference.

_____

f) Using the original data in Table 6.1, suppose the economy was at full-employment equilibrium when the nominal wage level in Chunderland dropped. The result is a change in aggregate supply of 40 at every price level. Show the new aggregate supply on your graph; label it SAS_2. What is the new equilibrium price level and level of real GDP? Is there a recessionary gap or inflationary gap?

Price level: _____ ; real GDP: $_____ ;

recessionary or inflationary gap: _____ .

g) Suppose in f) that the change in aggregate supply had been caused by a technological improvement in Chunderland's important manufacturing sector. Explain how your answer in f) might have been different.

_____

More of the Same

Thunderland's economy is apt to be a bit volatile. Its aggregate demand and short-run aggregate supply are shown in **Table 6.2**.

TABLE 6.2

Price	Aggregate Quantity Supplied	Aggregate Quantity Demanded
$60	$150	—
60	200	—
60	250	$500
80	350	450
100	400	400
110	430	350
120	450	300
130	470	250
140	480	200
150	490	150

a) Assuming that Thunderland's full-employment level of real GDP is $450, draw the aggregate demand, short-run aggregate supply, and long-run aggregate supply in **Figure 6.18** and label them AD_1, SAS_1, and LAS_1.

FIGURE 6.18

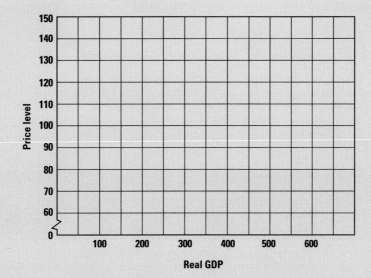

b) What are the equilibrium values of the price level and real GDP? Is there a recessionary or inflationary gap?

c) Suppose that the aggregate demand in Thunderland were to increase by 250 at every price level. Show the new aggregate demand on your graph, and label it AD_2. What is the amount of *change* in the price level and in the level of real GDP? Is there a recessionary gap or inflationary gap?

d) Suppose *instead* that the aggregate demand in Thunderland *decreases* by 250 at every price level. Show the new aggregate demand on your graph and label it AD_3. What is the amount of *change* in the price level and in the level of real GDP? Is there a recessionary gap or inflationary gap?

e) Compare the increase in c) and the decrease in d). Briefly explain the difference.

f) Returning to the original data in Table 6.2, suppose that the economy was at equilibrium and the nominal wage level in Thunderland increased. The result was a change in aggregate supply of 150 at every price level. Show the new aggregate supply on your graph, and label it SAS_2. What is the new equilibrium price level and level of real GDP? Is there a recessionary gap or inflationary gap?

g) Suppose that the change in aggregate supply in f) had been caused by mass emigration from the country. Explain how your answer in f) might have been different.

Translations

Blunderland's economy is depicted in Figure 6.19. The present price level is P_1. Explain in words its present situation and what is likely to occur in the short and long run.

FIGURE 6.19

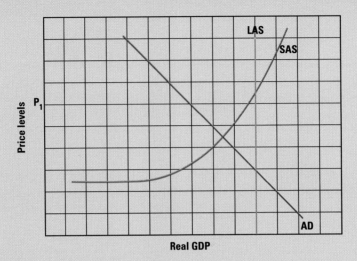

_____

_____

Are You Sure?

Indicate whether the following statements are true or false. If false, indicate why they are false.

1. Aggregate demand is the aggregate quantity of goods and services demanded by all buyers at various different price levels.

   T or F   If false: _____

   _____

2. The foreign-trade effect is the effect that a change in exports and imports has on the price level.

   T or F   If false: _____

   _____

3. The short-run aggregate supply curve is upward-sloping, whereas the long-run aggregate supply curve is vertical.

   T or F   If false: _____

   _____

4. Macroeconomic equilibrium occurs where the aggregate demand is equal to the long-run supply.

   T or F   If false: _____

   _____

5. A change in resource prices will shift both the long-run and short-run aggregate supply curves.

   T or F   If false: _____

   _____

6. An increase in the long-run aggregate supply has no effect on macroeconomic equilibrium.

   T or F   If false: _____

   _____

7. An increase in aggregate demand will cause an increase in both real GDP and the price level.

   T or **F**   If false: _____

   _____

8. An increase in wage rates will cause an increase in both real GDP and the price level.

   T or **F**   If false: _____

   _____

9. According to Keynes, the short-run aggregate supply curve is vertical.

   T or **F**   If false: _____

   _____

10. According to neoclassicists, an increase in aggregate demand will have no effect upon real GDP but will cause the price level to increase.

    T or **F**   If false: _____

    _____

Choose the Best

11. Why is the aggregate demand curve downward-sloping?
    a) Because production costs decline as real GDP increases.
    b) Because at lower prices aggregate expenditures are higher.

12. Why is the SAS curve upward-sloping?
    a) Because firms will produce more if prices are higher, despite no increase in profits.
    b) Because firms will experience higher profits at higher prices and will therefore produce more.

13. What is the slope of the aggregate supply curve, according to neoclassical economists?
    a) Vertical, because prices tend to be inflexible.
    b) Vertical at the capacity level of output in the economy.

14. Which of the following will cause the aggregate demand curve to shift to the right?
    a) A decrease in the money supply.
    b) A decrease in the interest rate.
    c) An increase in the exchange rate.

15. When does macroeconomic equilibrium occur?
    a) When short-run aggregate supply equals long-run aggregate supply.
    b) When the aggregate demand is equal to short-run aggregate supply.

    c) When the aggregate demand is equal to long-run aggregate supply.

16. What could cause the level of real GDP to rise but the price level to fall?
    a) A rightward shift in the aggregate demand curve.
    b) A leftward shift in the aggregate demand curve.
    c) A rightward shift in the short-run aggregate supply curve.

17. What can cause a shift in the long-run aggregate supply curve?
    a) An increase in nominal wage rates.
    b) A decrease in taxes.
    c) The introduction of an important technological change.

18. What effect will an increase in the Canadian price level have on trade?
    a) It will increase the volume of both Canadian exports and imports.
    b) It will decrease the volume of both Canadian exports and imports.
    c) It will increase the volume of Canadian exports but decrease the volume of imports.
    d) It will decrease the volume of Canadian exports but increase the volume of imports.

19. What is the slope of the LAS curve?
    a) Horizontal.
    b) Upward-sloping.
    c) Vertical.
    d) The same slope as the SAS curve.

20. What is the effect of an increase in the incomes of a country's major international trading partners?
    a) The aggregate demand curve will shift to the right.
    b) The aggregate demand curve will shift to the left.
    c) The aggregate supply curve will shift to the right.
    d) The aggregate supply curve will shift to the left.

Table 6.3 shows the aggregate demand and supply schedules for the economy of Adana.

TABLE 6.3

Aggregate Quantity Demanded	Price Index	Aggregate Quantity Supplied
$800	100	$550
750	105	650
700	110	700
650	115	740
600	120	770

21. Refer to Table 6.3 to answer this question. What are the implications if the price level is 100?
    a) The price level is above equilibrium.
    b) There is a shortage of real output of $250.
    c) There is a surplus of real output of $250.
    d) There is a surplus of real output of $150.

22. Refer to Table 6.3 to answer this question. If the aggregate quantity demanded falls by $100 at every price level, what will be the new equilibrium price level and real output, respectively?
    a) 100 and $550.
    b) 105 and $650.
    c) 110 and $650.
    d) 115 and $500.

23. Refer to Table 6.3 to answer this question. At what level of real output will full-employment occur in this economy?
    a) $600.
    b) $650.
    c) $700.
    d) Cannot be determined from the information.

Refer to **Figure 6.20** to answer questions 14 and 15.

FIGURE 6.20

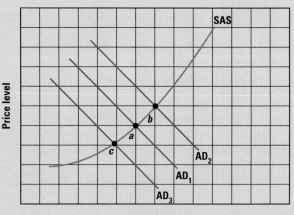

24. Refer to Figure 6.20 to answer this question. All of the following *except one* would cause a movement from *a* to *b*. Which one would not cause such a movement?
    a) A fall in the price level.
    b) An increase in wealth holdings.
    c) An increase in government spending.
    d) A decrease in the interest rate.
    e) An increase in foreign incomes.

25. Refer to Figure 6.20 to answer this question. Which of the following could cause a movement from point *a* to point *c*?
    a) An increase in the price level.
    b) An increase in wealth holdings.
    c) An increase in government spending.
    d) An increase in the interest rate.
    e) An increase in foreign incomes.

26. What does the real-balances effect mean?
    a) A higher price level will lead to an increase in the rate of interest, thereby causing a decrease in consumption.

b) A lower price level will lead to an increase in the rate of interest, thereby causing a decrease in consumption.

c) A higher price will increase the real value of financial assets, thereby causing an increase in consumption.

d) A higher price will decrease the real value of financial assets, thereby causing an increase in consumption.

e) A higher price will decrease the real value of financial assets, thereby causing a decrease in consumption.

Refer to **Figure 6.21** to answer question 17.

FIGURE 6.21

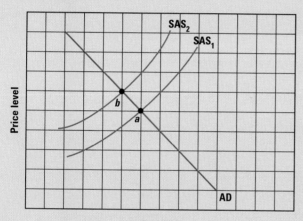

Real GDP

27. Refer to Figure 6.21 to answer this question. What could cause a movement from point *a* to point *b*?
   a) An increase in government spending.
   b) A decrease in labour productivity.
   c) The discovery of new oil fields.
   d) A decrease in business taxes.
   e) A decrease in the prevailing nominal wage.

28. What effect will a decrease in aggregate demand have if the economy is in a recession?
   a) The price level will drop a great deal, but real GDP will fall only a little.
   b) The price level will drop a little, but real GDP will fall a great deal.
   c) The price level will drop a little, but real GDP will increase a great deal.
   d) The price level will drop a little, and real GDP will increase a little.

e) Both the price level and real GDP will fall about the same amount.

Refer to **Figure 6.22** to answer questions 19 and 20.

FIGURE 6.22

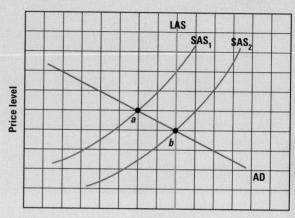

Real GDP

29. Refer to Figure 6.22 to answer this question. Which of the following statements is true if the economy is at point *a*?
   a) Firms will find it hard to hire labour, and people will find it easy to find jobs.
   b) Wages will eventually be forced down.
   c) An inflationary gap exists.
   d) Unemployment is at its natural rate.
   e) The achievement of full employment must await a decrease in aggregate demand.

30. Refer to Figure 6.22 to answer this question. If the economy was initially at point *a*, then what would a movement to point *b* suggest?
   a) The movement could be the result of an increase in aggregate demand.
   b) The movement could be the result of a decrease in prices.
   c) The movement could be the result of a decrease in wages.
   d) It is a movement from one full-employment level of real GDP to another.
   e) The movement could be the result of expansionary monetary policy.

Other Problems

31. Underland's economy is depicted in **Figure 6.23**.

    a) What are the equilibrium values of the price and real GDP levels? Is the country experiencing a recessionary or inflationary gap?

FIGURE 6.23

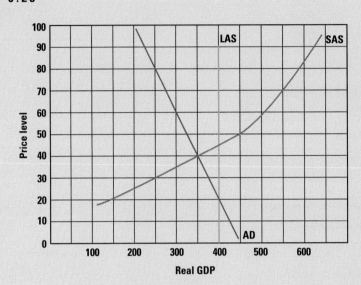

Price level: _____ ; real GDP: $_____ ;

recessionary or inflationary gap: _____ .

    b) If the price level in Underland's is 50, is there a shortage or surplus of goods and services? How much?

    (Surplus/shortage) _____ of $_____ .

    c) If the price level in Underland's is 30, is there a shortage or surplus of goods and services? How much?

    (Surplus/shortage) _____ of $_____ .

    d) Suppose that the economy of Underland is in equilibrium. In order for it to get to full employment, how much must aggregate demand increase, and what effect will this have on the price level? Show the change on your graph.

    Increase in aggregate demand: $_____ ; new price level: _____ .

    e) Alternatively, in order to get to full employment, how much must aggregate supply increase, and what effect will this have on the price level? Show the change on your graph.

    Increase in aggregate supply: $_____ ; new price level: _____ .

32. **Table 6.4** shows aggregate expenditures at four different price levels for the economy of Hormaz.

TABLE 6.4

At price = 95					At price = 100					At price = 105					At price = 110				
Y	C	I	G	Xn	Y	C	I	G	Xn	Y	C	I	G	Xn	Y	C	I	G	Xn
$400	$330	$80	$130	+20	$400	$310	$70	$130	+10	$400	$290	$60	$130	$0	$400	$270	$50	$130	−10
500	410	80	130	0	500	390	70	130	−10	500	370	60	130	−20	500	350	50	130	−30
600	490	80	130	−20	600	470	70	130	−30	600	450	60	130	−40	600	430	50	130	−50
700	570	80	130	−40	700	550	70	130	−50	700	530	60	130	−60	700	510	50	130	−70
800	650	80	130	−60	800	630	70	130	−70	800	610	60	130	−80	800	590	50	130	−90

a) From this information, construct and plot the corresponding aggregate demand curve in Figure 6.24. (*Hint*: You need to find expenditure equilibriums for each price level.)

FIGURE 6.24

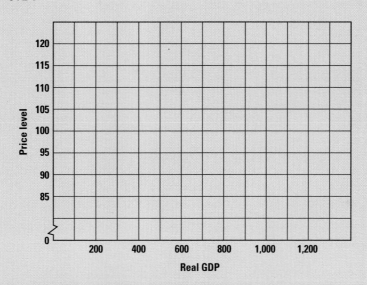

The short-run aggregate supply for Hormaz is shown in Table 6.5.

TABLE 6.5

Price Level	Aggregate Supply
$ 95	$400
100	500
105	600
110	700

b) Plot the SAS curve on Figure 6.24.

c) What is the equilibrium level of price and real GDP?
Equilibrium price: $_____ ; equilibrium real GDP $_____.

d) If the long-run aggregate supply is $500, plot the LAS curve on Figure 6.24.

e) Is there a recessionary or inflationary gap? How much?
Recessionary or inflationary gap: _____ of $_____.

33. Sunderland's aggregate expenditure curve is shown in Figure 6.25.

FIGURE 6.25

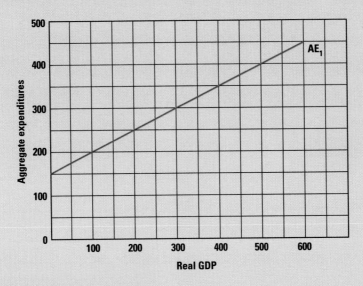

The present price index in Sunderland is 100.

a) Locate and label equilibrium as e_1.

b) For every 10-point change in the price index, aggregate expenditures changes by $50. In Figure 6.25, draw in aggregate expenditure curves for price levels of 90, 110, and 120, and label them AE_2, AE_3, and AE_4. Label each of the equilibriums as e_2, e_3, and e_4.

c) In Figure 6.26, show the four expenditure equilibriums you have derived at the appropriate price levels.

FIGURE 6.26

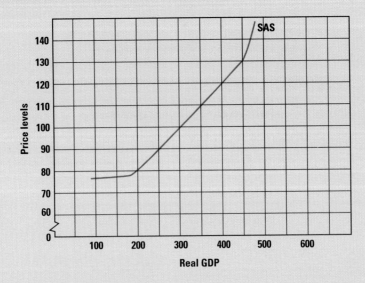

d) What is the level of equilibrium real GDP and the price level? If full-employment real GDP is $350, is there a recessionary or inflationary gap? How much?

Equilibrium real GDP: $_____ ; price level: _____ ;

recessionary or inflationary gap: _____ of $ _____ .

34. Suppose that the economy of Punderland in Figure 6.27 is at full employment equilibrium and the present nominal wage rate is $910 per week.

FIGURE 6.27

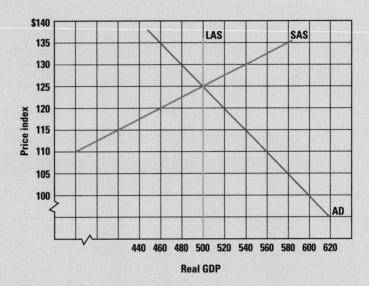

a) What is the real wage rate (in base year prices)?

b) Suppose that aggregate demand increases by $60. At the new equilibrium real GDP level, what will be the value of the real wage rate?

c) As a result of the change in prices in a), suppose that nominal wages increase, causing aggregate supply to change by $120. At the new equilibrium, what will be the value of real wages?

d) At the new equilibrium in b), what is the value of nominal wages?

UNANSWERED QUESTIONS

Short Essays

1. What are the three factors that cause the aggregate demand curve to be downward-sloping? Explain each factor.

2. Name and explain five different factors that can cause a change in aggregate demand. Explain the direction of change in each case.

3. Why is the short-run aggregate supply curve upward-sloping? What things change and what things remain constant when comparing different points on the aggregate supply curve?

4. Differentiate between the factors that change the long-run and the short-run aggregate supply.

5. How did the different views of the aggregate supply curve affect the way that neoclassical and Keynesian economists viewed the macroeconomy?

Analytical Questions

6. Is the nominal wage constant along the short-run aggregate supply curve? Is it constant along the long-run aggregate supply curve? Is the real wage constant along both curves?

7. Explain how each of the following factors will affect aggregate demand and short- and long-run aggregate supply in Canada, and what effect this will have on the price and real GDP levels:
    a) An increase in government spending.
    b) An increase in labour productivity.
    c) A decline in the real GDP of the United States.
    d) An increase in the money supply.
    e) A big rise in nominal wage rates.
    f) A big cut in the price of imported oil.

8. Explain why an increase in aggregate demand might have no effect on the price level. Explain why an increase in aggregate demand might have no effect on real GDP.

9. Why does an increase in long-run aggregate supply leave the economy in a recessionary gap?

10. Use aggregate demand–supply diagrams to illustrate the following events in Canadian economic history:
    a) at the beginning of the Great Depression of the 1930s, prices, production, and employment all decreased dramatically.
    b) in the mid-1970s, as a result of a high increase in the price of oil coming from OPEC countries, both prices and unemployment increased.

11. Assume that the economy is originally at full-employment equilibrium. Show diagramatically two major causes of inflation. What could cause each to happen?

12. Explain how an economy eventually recovers from a recessionary gap. How does it recover from an inflationary gap?

Numerical Questions

13. Suppose that the economy of Tabuk is initially in full-employment equilibrium. Diagrammatically, illustrate the effects of the following changes on the price level, the level of real GDP and on the type of equilibrium produced:
    a) An increase in foreign incomes.
    b) An increase in immigration.
    c) An increase in wage levels.

14. Table 6.6 shows the aggregate demand for the economy of Mandu.

TABLE 6.6

Price Level	Aggregate Demand
97	$1150
98	1100
99	1050
100	1000
101	950
102	900
103	850
104	800

Table 6.7 below shows two aggregate supplies for the same economy.

TABLE 6.7

Price Level	Aggregate Supply (1)	Price Level	Aggregate Supply (2)
97	$1000	100	$850
98	1000	100	900
99	1000	100	950
100	1000	100	1000
101	1000	100	1050
102	1000	100	1100
103	1000	100	1150
104	1000	100	1200

a) Which of the two aggregate supply schedules, (1) or (2), is the neoclassical aggregate supply? Which is the Keynesian aggregate supply? According to each, what would be the equilibrium levels of price and real GDP?

b) Assume that the aggregate demand increased by $100. What would be the new equilibrium values of price and real GDP, according to neoclassicists? According to Keynesians?

15. Assume that the long-run supply of the economy of Arion is $1000 and that the aggregate demand and the short-run aggregate supply are as shown in **Table 6.8**.

TABLE 6.8

Aggregate Demand	Price Level	Aggregate Supply
$1080	96	$880
1060	97	940
1040	98	965
1020	99	985
1000	100	1000
980	101	1015
960	102	1025
940	103	1033
920	104	1040
900	105	1045

a) What is the value of equilibrium real GDP and the price level? Is there a recessionary or inflationary gap?

b) If firms become more optimistic and aggregate demand increases by $65, what will be the new values of equilibrium real GDP and the price level? Is there a recessionary or inflationary gap? What is the size of the gap?

16. Given the values of long- and short-run aggregate supply and the aggregate demand for the economy of Arion shown in Table 6.8, if the prices of imported resources increase and the short-run aggregate supply decreases by $120, what will be the new values of equilibrium real GDP and the price level? Is there a recessionary or inflationary gap? What is the size of the gap?

17. Given the values of long- and short-run aggregate supply and the aggregate demand for the economy of Arion shown in Table 6.8, if productivity rates increase, causing the long-run aggregate supply to increase by $120, what will be the new values of equilibrium real GDP and the price level? Is there a recessionary or inflationary gap? What is the size of the gap?

 Web-Based Activities

1. For each of the articles found below, illustrate and explain how the event described in the article will affect the aggregate demand–supply model. Be sure to explain what happens to the price level and the level of real GDP.
   a) http://cnnfn.com/hotstories/economy/9807/28/confidence/index.htm
   b) http://cnnfn.com/hotstories/economy/9810/21/ifo_survey/
   c) http://cnnfn.com/hotstories/washun/9811/10/sanctions/
   d) http://cnnfn.com/hotstories/economy/wires/9811/06/canada_wg/index.htm

2. In this chapter you learned that when the economy is at full employment, the economy is operating at capacity. Read **http://strategis.ic.gc.ca/SSG/ra00111e.html** and answer the following questions:
   a) Is Canada currently operating above or below capacity? Is there a relationship between unemployment and capacity utilization? Explain.
   b) Illustrate and explain how a fall in aggregate demand will decrease capacity utilization and create a recessionary gap.

Money and Banking

W**hat's ahead...**In this chapter we look at the definition and functions of money. We look at its origins at and how the concept of money has changed over the centuries. We then briefly examine the development of banks and explore the process through which the banking system is able to create money.

You and four friends decide to go out for a fancy meal to celebrate another successful year at college. When the bill arrives, you split into five shares. Frederick pays by cheque. Sian pays by credit card. Althea digs deep into her pocket and comes up with 20 loonies. Bosie gives an IOU to the manager (a friend of his). Finding that you have none of the above means, you have to pay by "volunteering" to wash up (for yourself and 200 other diners). You all paid in different ways. But who used money? Some of you? All of you? So what does constitute money in our modern economy?

Money has been called humanity's greatest invention and its greatest curse. People fret for it, and they sweat for it. For some it's the root of all evil and for others it is the source of all joy. Economists, however, being less fanciful and poetic, refer to it merely as a medium of exchange. The reason economists don't wax quite so lyrical when they discuss money is that they regard it as merely one form of holding wealth. After all, it is possible to be extremely wealthy but literally have no money. In fact, there is a problem with wealth holding in the form of money, because money generally doesn't accumulate. That is, you cannot earn a return from money alone. This is not the case with other forms of wealth, such as stocks and bonds, real estate, or a term deposit in a bank. The other reason why economists remain unemotional on the topic of money is because they do not focus on the effect of money on the individual (in that respect, most economists revere money as much as the next person), but on the role of money in the whole economy.

A group of young students in Toronto take turns playing the "My Money" game. The former stockbroker who designed the game for the Bank of Montreal hopes it will help children learn to invest wisely once they get some genuine green.

As for this latter aspect, economists over the centuries have had differing views. Adam Smith suggested that money was merely a veil that often conceals the phenomena of real production that lies behind it. He used the analogy of money being like a river that helps to bring goods to the market but does not affect the actual volume of goods. Today, we know that money can have a determining influence over the "real" variables, such as production and employment. For example, we saw in the previous chapter that an increase in the money supply can result in an increase in real GDP. It is these and other aspects of money that we will be looking at in these two chapters on money. We'll conclude these opening remarks by mentioning one obvious aspect of money: it has an important role in determining prices.

SELF-TEST

1. What do you think Adam Smith might have meant by the phrase, "Money is a veil"?

As the market economy was emerging in the sixteenth and seventeenth centuries, many people had personal experience of how the amount of money (and, more specifically, changes in the amount of money) in a society could affect prices. The huge influx of gold from the new colonies into Europe produced a persistent and pernicious increase in prices in most European countries. Gold meant money, and if the amount of money quickly increases while the volume of production changes slowly, then you get the makings of what we previously called demand–pull inflation. This is sometimes characterized as too much money chasing too few goods. In the same vein, consider one of the possibly apocryphal stories coming out of World War II, which relates a devious scheme by the Germans to disrupt the Allied war effort. This plan involved the dispatch of bombers over Britain, equipped not with bombs but with millions of counterfeit pound notes. These were to be scattered all over British towns and cities. The effects would have been obvious. The British people, as the heirs to this sudden windfall, would do the predictable: they would spend it. Thus the demand for the limited quantity of consumer goods would rise dramatically, and since production could not increase immediately, the only effect would be the bidding up of prices. Britain would have been faced with the same devastating phenomenon that the Germans themselves had experienced in the early 1920s: hyper- or galloping inflation. This story is used to illustrate that there is a very strong link between changes in the supply of money and the level of prices. More on this later.

The Functions and Characteristics of Money

medium of exchange:
something that is accepted
as payment for goods and
services.

So far we have discussed some aspects of money without actually defining it. Let's continue to skirt around the definition for now by asking the question: what is money good for? Well, of course the answer is: to spend. In fact, it has been suggested that money imparts value only in parting. The first, and prime, function of money is that it acts as a **medium of exchange**. Without money, people would be forced to barter goods and services directly. However, barter requires what is called a coincidence of wants. This simply means that if I am to trade with you, you must have what I want, and I must have what you want. If this is not the case, then we must try to find a third, fourth, or fifth party to act as intermediaries. All of this would mean that to obtain the hundreds of goods and services that the average person consumes, he or she would spend far more time in exchanging than in producing.

ADDED DIMENSION

Money Increases Wealth

A society possessing no money would be very simple and materially very poor. Since exchange would be difficult and time-consuming, almost everybody would be forced to produce most of the necessities of survival for themselves. Few could earn a livelihood by specializing in producing just one product and then trading it for other products. This lack of specialization, along with the high cost of exchange, would ensure an existence in which a minimal quantity of goods and services were exchanged.

The use of money reduces the wasted effort associated with barter as long as people will readily accept money as a medium of exchange. Money, as we will see, can be almost anything, but its most important characteristic is that it should be widely acceptable. In addition, if we are going to carry it around with us, it should be reasonably portable.

store of wealth: the function of money that allows people to hold and accumulate wealth.

Money, however, is not just used for exchange. Some of us like to keep it. In other words, money can be used as a **store of wealth**. This is its second function. As we mentioned, wealth can be stored in other forms, but these other forms are not as convenient as money. If it is to act as a store of wealth, money should obviously possess other desirable characteristics. Besides portability, it should also be reasonably durable and of such a nature that people are willing to hold it.

unit of account: the function of money that allows us to determine easily the relative value of goods.

Finally, money is used as a **unit of account** (or measure of value). Think of the problems in trying to value a commodity in a moneyless community. Assume, for instance, that a suit of clothes is worth 10 flagons of beer, that a flagon of beer is worth 2 loaves of bread, and that you need 100 loaves of bread to buy a table—how many suits of clothes does it take to buy a table? The answer is 5 suits, but the answer doesn't come quickly.

In summary, the functions of money are:

- a medium of exchange
- a store of value
- a unit of account

SELF-TEST

2. Given the clothes–table question above, how many suits of clothes would it cost to buy a table if a flagon of beer were worth only one loaf of bread?

In a money-using society, each product and service can be valued in terms of a single commodity: money. If we measure everything in money terms, that is, in dollar-and-cents prices, we might ask the question: what is money itself worth? The answer must be in relative terms: what we can get in exchange for it. And what we can get is determined by prices: the lower the price, the more we can obtain, and therefore the higher the value of money. The *value of money* is therefore inversely related to the price level. If prices were to increase, then the value of a unit of money would decrease.

While anything can be, and most things have been, used as money, some things are definitely better than others. For instance, let us imagine a (particularly silly) society that hit upon the idea of using stones as a form of money. Well, certainly stones are durable, portable, divisible (big stones and little stones), and easily recognized, which are characteristics that all money needs. The trouble is that without very much trouble at all, everybody would think they had become fabulously rich overnight. It would make sense, therefore, that money should also have the characteristic of being reasonably scarce. On the other hand, it should not be so scarce and limited in supply that it couldn't be increased as trade and circumstances dictate. In short, money needs to be:

- acceptable
- durable
- portable
- divisible
- easily recognized
- relatively scarce

Different Kinds of Money

commodity money: a type of money that can also function, and is useful, as a commodity.

When such things as beads, whales' teeth, salt, or shells are used as money, they have intrinsic value in themselves as well as having value as money. This type of money is called **commodity money**. Even today, in situations like jails and prisoner-of-war camps, where people have no access to the outside community, things such as cigarettes or playing cards act as forms of commodity money.

One particularly important commodity that has been used as money over the ages is gold (and, less often, other precious metals). Gold certainly fits the bill in terms of portability, durability, and scarcity. However, there is one serious drawback: precious metals don't come in standardized units: the metal needs to be weighed out each time a transaction is made. To overcome this problem, since the dawn of civilization metals have been produced in the standardized form of coins of specific size and weight. The trouble with *coins* made of gold is that they are open to abuse. Gold is a particularly soft metal, so that in earlier times it was possible for some people to make money out of money. They did this by such practices as sweating the currency (shaking the coins up in a bag so as to produce a residue of gold dust in the bottom) or by clipping the currency (shaving a thin sliver from the outside of unmilled coins). Perhaps the worst offenders were the sovereigns whose portrait on the coins was supposedly a mark of trust and integrity. An important event like a coronation or royal wedding was the occasion for the sovereign to call in the old coin and replace it with newly minted coins. However, in the process of melting down the old coins, a base metal like lead was often added to the vat of gold. Over time, the currency became more and more debased, so that it became worth only its own weight in lead.

In addition, gold has another serious defect as a form of money: it is very heavy. Because of this, and because of the dangers of carrying about large sums of money, people in Europe in the Middle Ages started to deposit their money in the goldsmith's vault. In return for making a deposit (for which they were required to pay a fee), they received a certificate from the goldsmith acknowledging the deposit. In time, these certificates were considered as reliable as gold and could be easily transferred from one person to another as a form of payment. In other words, *paper money* was introduced. (It is interesting to note that paper currency appeared in China even earlier). With the formation of commercial banks in the early eighteenth century, many of the functions of the goldsmiths were taken over by these banks—including that of issuing paper money. Since 1935 in Canada, the only bank with the power to issue bank notes is the Bank of Canada. As we will see later, Canada's central bank no longer acts as a commercial bank, as it once did, but now acts solely as an agent of the government.

As the commercial banks became more prominent, so too did bank notes become more acceptable. But just as people, in earlier times, were wary of carrying large sums of gold and coins, they also preferred to deposit their bank notes in the banks. Thus, the nineteenth century saw the development of the last form of modern money: *chequebook money*. In return for depositing notes and coins with the bank, the customer could now receive a chequebook from the bank. A cheque is nothing more than a standardized form of instruction by a customer to the bank, telling it to transfer a sum of money from the customer's account to the person specified on the cheque. Generally speaking, this order from one of its customers presents the bank with no great problem. The average bank certainly has enough cash. However, banks do not act simply as big safety deposit boxes, guarding your money until you require it. This means that if all of the bank's customers were to descend en masse demanding their money, any bank in the modern banking world would find itself acutely embarrassed. It simply wouldn't have that

Many transfers that were once carried out using cheques are now completed using electronic banking machines.

amount of cash on hand. So what happened to the cash that you and all the other customers deposited in the past? The answer is that the bank lent it out. Banks only keep a small fraction of the amounts of cash that have been deposited, and thus they may be prone to a run on the bank. So how did such a state of affairs come to be? Before answering this question, let's summarize the different kinds of money:

- commodity money
- gold and other precious metals
- coins
- paper money
- chequebook money

ADDED DIMENSION

The Cashless Society

Cash has a number of advantages, including the fact that the transactions costs of using it are nearly zero. If I want to pay off a debt or buy something, I just hand over the cash. I don't need to register the transfer, and the seller need not record that she received the cash from me. Also, in the case of cash, possession implies ownership. But this is also one of its great disadvantages. Cash is easy to steal and it is difficult to recover once gone. For this reason, many people look forward to the day when we can dispense with cash.

Well, the day has already arrived. In many cities around the world, experiments with using "electronic money" are taking place. Small plastic cards embedded with computer chips have been introduced that will record the value of each transaction and the remaining balance on the card. For instance, you could buy a $30 card (say, from a bank) that enables you to spend up to that amount using only your card.

You could use the card to pay for items like transit fares, parking meters, telephone calls, and so on.

Besides the obvious convenience of carrying one small card rather than many coins and bills, the overall savings from the use of electronic money could be considerable, since it cuts down on the handling, safekeeping, and depositing of traditional cash. However, there are potential drawbacks to this new form of cash. What would happen, for instance, if the company that issued the card went out of business? Who is going to honour the card then? Furthermore, there are many people in society who would be concerned about leaving an electronic trail of their purchases. This includes not only members of the underworld, but also ordinary consumers who may not want merchants and card issuers to obtain detailed information about their spending habits.

Fractional Reserve Banking

Now let's go back to the goldsmiths. Goldsmiths discovered, very early on in the game, that most of the time the gold and coins sitting in the vaults did just that: they sat there. Most unproductively! Certainly, customers came in from time to time to withdraw some of their cash, but that same cash usually got redeposited with the goldsmith rather soon. Certainly money was turning over. But the goldsmiths realized that on any one day of the week, about as much gold was deposited as was withdrawn.

So what would be the harm in the goldsmiths lending out the gold that wasn't needed? Unless all of the customers arrived on the doorstep at the same time—a very remote possibility—there would be no harm done. So, lend it they did. In fact, the goldsmiths also learned that when they started offering loans, most people didn't particularly want to receive gold but preferred to receive one of the goldsmiths' certificates of deposit. The goldsmiths could simply make loans by giving customers a piece of paper. Thus was born the very basis of modern banking: the **fractional reserve system**. In a similar manner, with the rise of commercial banking, bankers discovered that they too only needed to keep a small fraction of their customers' deposits in the form of cash reserves. Today, banks in Canada keep only a very small percentage of their customers' deposits in the form of cash. As long as people don't hoard it, any cash that any one bank issues to its customers generally finds its way back to another bank, that is, back into the banking system. So the average bank is safe as long as its depositors do not all demand their cash on the same day. The fact that modern banks operate on a fractional reserve basis has important implications for the monetary system and for monetary policy, as we shall see later.

fractional reserve system: a banking system whereby banks keep only a small fraction of their total deposits on reserve in the form of cash.

And at Last a Definition

money: anything that is widely accepted as a medium of exchange and therefore can be used to buy goods or to settle debts.

M1: currency in circulation plus demand deposits.

The following definition of **money** encompasses the vital elements: money is any item that is widely accepted as a medium of exchange and is used to buy goods and services and to settle debts.

In the next chapter we will see that changes in the amount of money in an economy can have significant consequences. It is of some importance therefore that economists and policy makers are able to define clearly what constitutes money in a modern economy. Let us start with the simplest, most basic definition, called the **M1** definition, which includes currency in circulation (coins and paper bank notes) plus demand deposits in the chequing accounts of all commercial banks. The word "demand" in demand deposits refers to the fact that depositors can demand their deposits in cash at any time.

The amount of M1 money (in $ billions) in Canada in February 1998 was:

$$M1 = \text{currency} \quad \text{plus} \quad \text{demand deposits}$$
$$76 = 29 \quad\quad + \quad\quad 47$$
$$(38\%) \quad\quad\quad (62\%)$$

Some have suggested, however, that this definition is not sufficiently broad. They argue that if chequing accounts are included as money, then why not also include savings accounts and other types of notice deposits? Notice deposits, as the name suggests, requires the depositor to give notice to the bank before making a withdrawal. Surely, these accounts, in practice, are no different from chequing accounts, since

M2: M1 plus all notice and personal term deposits.

banks seldom enforce the requirement of giving notice before withdrawal. So, we have a wider definition of money, called **M2**, which includes all of M1 plus all notice deposits (savings accounts on deposit for an undefined length of time) and what are called personal term deposits, which are on deposit for a specific term such as six months. The amounts in 1998 were:

$$M2 = M1 \quad \text{plus} \quad \text{notice deposits and personal term deposits}$$
$$289 = 76 \quad + \quad 213$$
$$(26\%) \quad\quad (74\%)$$

M3: M2 plus non-personal term deposits known as certificates of deposits.

Finally, an even broader measurement, **M3**, includes M2 but adds to it term deposits of businesses (known as certificates of deposit), which are easily convertible into chequable deposits. The M3 measurement, then, includes all of M2 plus certificates of deposit. Again, for 1998, the amounts were:

$$M3 = M2 \quad + \quad \text{certificates of deposit}$$
$$402 = 289 \quad + \quad 113$$
$$(72\%) \quad\quad (28\%)$$

Money Supply in Canada as of February 1998 (in billions)

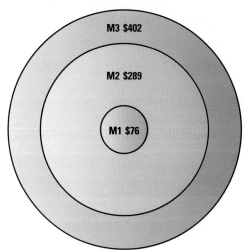

For reasons of expediency we will confine our discussion and analysis of money to the simplest definition, M1: currency in circulation plus demand deposits (chequing accounts). This helps to keep things simple and recognizes the essential characteristic of money: the direct and immediate control over goods and services.

What Is Not Money?

Not all currency issued by the Bank of Canada is included as money, but only the portion that is in circulation. In other words, the currency in the vaults or tills of banks is not included in any definition of money.

The reason for this is that when you or I deposit currency in a bank, the balance of our bank account increases, and since the amount of deposits in our accounts is part of the money supply, it would be double-counting to count both the increase in our accounts and the increase in the bank's tills. In other words, when people deposit currency in a bank, the amount of currency *in circulation* goes down, and the amount in deposit accounts goes up. You should note that:

> **A new bank deposit changes the composition of the money supply but does not change its total.**

Another exclusion from the money supply is gold. (Try paying for your designer jeans with a bar of gold.) Similarly, such financial securities as stocks and bonds are also excluded. So too is peoples' available credit on their credit cards. That is, credit cards, as well as the more recent debit cards, are merely a means of accessing money but are not money in themselves. You might argue that in many instances credit cards are more acceptable than personal cheques, and that's true. However, credit cards merely represent a loan that you have negotiated with a finance company. More importantly, you cannot pay off a debt with a credit card. Certainly you can obtain cash with a credit card, but that's the clue: you can use a credit card to get money; it is not itself money. The final exclusion from the modern definition of money is chequing accounts at **near-banks**. These near-banks include credit unions, trust companies, and mortgage and loan associations. In other words, all of our three alternative definitions of money—M1, M2, M3—refer to accounts only at commercial banks. Canada's central bank, the Bank of Canada, exercises a degree of control over the commercial banks but has a lesser degree of power over near-banks (also termed non-bank financial intermediaries). The central bank prefers to count as money only that which it can control directly; hence the exclusion of accounts at near-banks. Nonetheless, the Bank of Canada does also measure what it calls M2+, which includes demand and notice deposits at near-banks.

The term *chartered banks* includes the five major banks in Canada (all of which received a charter under the Bank Act) and a few dozen much smaller banks.

near-banks: financial institutions, like credit unions or trust companies, which share many of the functions of commercial banks but are not defined as banks under the Bank Act (they are also known as non-bank financial intermediaries).

ADDED DIMENSION

Canada's Big Banks

The five largest chartered banks in Canada, in order of size, are: Royal Bank, Bank of Montreal, Canadian Imperial Bank of Commerce, Bank of Nova Scotia, and Toronto Dominion Bank. Credit unions, which are regulated provincially, are major players in British Columbia and Quebec, where they are called *caisses populaires*.

Recently, the world has seen a trend of mergers of large banks. It appears, however, that this trend will not include Canada, since the attempted merger of the Bank of Montreal and the Royal Bank of Canada was blocked by the federal government.

A Word on Modern Banks

spread: the difference between the rate of interest a bank charges borrowers and the rate it pays savers.

Banks, like other corporations, are in business to make profits. Their major source of profits comes from using any excess deposits productively by lending them out. Their profit comes from the **spread**, the difference between the interest rate a bank charges to borrowers and the interest rate it pays to depositors. There's not much difference in the spread among Canada's major banks. The total profits of a bank come more from the total volume of its transactions rather than from a difference in the spread. Like any other business, banks do not like to carry excess inventories. In the case of banks, their inventory is money. They do not earn a return on idle money balances. They will always try to ensure that the amount of reserves they retain is kept to a minimum, consistent with security. Until recently, the Bank Act laid down exactly how much commercial banks had to keep in reserves. Such a required reserve ratio is no longer applicable, but banks still hold reserves. What we will call the **target reserve ratio** is the proportion of demand deposits that a bank wants to hold in the form of cash. These target reserves provide a small degree of security for the bank's customers. However, the main security for depositors comes from insurance. All banks are required by law to take out insurance on customers' deposits. The deposits are insured with the Canada Deposit Insurance Corporation up to a maximum of $60 000 per depositor per bank.

The Canadian banking system is remarkably secure. (There have been only two bank failures in all of this century, although both were within the last 20 years.) What economists call a branch banking system accounts for this stability. This is a system dominated by a few very large banks, each of which is large and has many branches operating across the entire country. For example, Canada's big five banks each have several hundred branches coast to coast. The sheer size and geographical diversity of this type of structure minimizes the possibility of bank failure.

Contrast this with a unit banking system, which, though currently in transition, is still the basic system in the United States. This system is made up of thousands of relatively small banks that either have only one branch or multiple branches that are confined to a single state. Such a system is less secure. For example, the First National Bank of Dalton (Nebraska) is small compared with the average branch of any one of Canada's big five banks. Furthermore, most of the loans by First National would be to local wheat farmers for equipment, seed, and so on. If a bad hailstorm wipes out the local wheat crop and most of the farmers go bankrupt, then the bank may face the same fate.

target reserve ratio: the portion of deposits that a bank wants to hold in cash.

Chances are that your bank branch doesn't look like this. Canada's five major banks have several hundred branches across the country.

Does this mean that the Canadian banking system is superior? From a security sense, yes. But the source of this security is a system dominated by only five big banks, and this means that competition within the system is weak. There are several consequences of this lack of competition. First, the merely irritable: long line-ups for routine transactions, short operating hours (closed on Saturdays and Sundays), and the inability of customers to deal face-to-face with the decision makers. More significantly, the spread in the Canadian banking system is, historically, wider than that in the American system. Finally, there is the issue of the banks' loan policies. From time to time throughout history, one can find references to a reccurring complaint by small businesses in Canada: large banks don't recognize the unique circumstances of a small business, and they don't make loans to unproven companies or ideas. Although one can understand the position of the large banks on this issue, it is also obvious that the whole economy does, from time to time, fail to benefit from the potential success of a new business or product because of the lack of loans needed to get started. In summary, the Canadian branch banking system is very secure and stable, but it is also uncompetitive and, therefore, very conservative.

Some of this may be changing. Foreign banks are now allowed to operate in Canada, although there are constraints on their size. This should, at least to some extent, increase competition in this industry.

ADDED DIMENSION

Financial Markets

The financial market consists of different types of financial institutions. All of these institutions have one thing in common: they are intermediaries and act as agents between people and firms who have funds available for loan and others who want to borrow those funds. Canadian banks are the biggest borrowers and lenders. Other institutions came into existence because banks were originally forbidden to provide certain types of loans. Mortgage companies specialized in giving long-term loans (mortgages) for people wishing to purchase real estate like houses or apartments. Trust companies looked after pensions and trust accounts of both firms and individuals. Credit unions (*caisses populaires* in Quebec) sprang up because many small firms were unable to obtain loans from the banks.

The financial market can be divided into the money market and the capital market. Money markets usually deal in loans of less than three years, whereas capital markets are for longer-term loans. Long-term loans take the form of bonds, which are nothing more than a type of IOU. Suppose that you are a big firm interesting in obtaining funds to fiance a major expansion. You could, of course, apply for a loan from one of the various financial institutions. But why bother? Why not cut out the agent and go directly to the public? Consequently, many corporations, as well as the federal, provincial, and municipal governments, sell bonds directly to the public. These bonds are for a fixed term and also pay a fixed rate of interest. Generally speaking, shorter-term bonds pay a lower interest rate than do longer-term bonds. As well, bonds issued by governments and larger corporations pay a lower interest rate than do those of smaller or newer firms.

The capital market deals not only in bonds but also in stocks. A corporation could issue either bonds or stocks, and both bring new funds into the firm. These instuments are easily negotiable, which means holders can freely sell them in the market. The main differences between these two financial instuments is that the holder of a bond is a creditor of the corporation, whereas the holder of stock (the shareholder) is a part-owner of the firm. If the corporation is successful, the shareholder will share in that success and get part of the porfits, in the form of dividends, but may get no return at all if the firm struggles. The bondholder, on the other hand, will simply receive a fixed amount of interest, regardless of the performance of the firm.

REVIEW

1. **What are the three functions of money?**
2. **What will happen to the value of money if the general price level rises?**
3. **Historically, how did those in power debase the money supply?**
4. **What are the historical origins of a modern banking system?**
5. **Distinguish between *M1*, *M2*, and *M3*.**
6. **Define the term *target reserve ratio*.**
7. **Define the term *spread*.**
8. **What is the role of the Canada Deposit Insurance Corporation?**

The Creation of Money by the Banks

We now know that money includes demand deposits as well as currency. The only institution that can actually create currency is the Bank of Canada. The public can decide what fraction of this currency is held outside the banks and what fraction it deposits with banks and other financial institutions. However, it is the banks, given the amount of currency they hold, who can decide how much they wish to hold as reserves and how much they want to lend.

To understand how just a small amount of reserves can support a multiple amount of loans and deposits, we need first to understand a few very basic accounting terms.

Assets, Liabilities, and Balance Sheets

assets: the part of a company's balance sheet that represents what it owns or what is owed to it.

liabilities: the part of a company's balance sheet that represents what it owes.

net worth: the total assets less total liabilities of a company—also called equity.

Actually, all we need to understand are the basic features of a balance sheet. (The profit and loss statement is of no concern here.) A balance sheet presents the financial condition of an institution at a particular moment in time. On one side, we list all the assets, and on the other side, the liabilities. The **assets** represent what a company owns or what others owe it. **Liabilities** represent what a company owes to others. The difference between the two is the **net worth** of the company, otherwise known as the equity. The equity is the book value of the company to its shareholders. (The company's market value may be more or less than its book value.) The following is a simplified balance sheet of the Saymor Bank Limited:

Balance Sheet of Saymor Bank Ltd. as at December 31, 1995

Assets		Liabilities and Equity	
Reserves	$ 10 000	Demand deposits	$100 000
Loans to customers	60 000	Shareholders' equity	20 000
Securities	30 000		
Fixed assets	20 000		
	$120 000		$120 000

The assets are all listed in terms of liquidity (closeness to cash), with the most liquid at the top. Remember that reserves are the currency held by the bank. Loans to customers represent one of the income-earning assets of the bank and are their most important and most lucrative assets. Securities are stocks (gilt-edged) or bonds (usually government bonds and treasury bills). Fixed assets include the buildings, equipment, and furniture of the bank. The major liability, and the only one shown here, is demand deposits, which represents the total amount of depositors' accounts owed by the bank to its customers. (We will ignore notice or savings deposits.) The equity figure shows that the book value of this bank is $20 000 (in $ million, of course).

Let's practise a few simple transactions to familiarize you with bookkeeping entries. Standard accounting procedures require that every transaction involves two entries. In addition, after making any entries, the balance sheet should remain in balance. (The totals may change, but the assets should still equal liabilities plus equity.)

Transaction 1: Fred, a customer of the bank, deposits $200 cash in the bank. The reserves of the bank would therefore increase by $200. The other entry? Fred's bank balance will increase by $200. (An asset for Fred, of course, but a liability for the bank since it now owes Fred $200 more.) So demand deposits increase by $200. In sum, both assets and liabilities have increased.

Transaction 2: Penny withdraws $500 cash from her account. This is straightforward, since it is just the reverse of transaction 1. The bank's reserves are reduced by $500 and the demand deposits go down by $500. So, both assets and liabilities are reduced accordingly.

Transaction 3: The bank buys some securities for $200 cash. In this case, reserves decrease by $200 and securities increase by $200. Therefore, one asset decreases, another increases; the net effect on total assets is zero.

Transaction 4: The bank sells $50 worth of securities to Han, one of its own customers, and receives a cheque from Han. Slightly trickier? Note that no cash changed hands, so reserves should stay the same. But the bank has fewer securities, since it has sold some. Thus, securities are reduced by $50. And the other entry? Well, Han's bank account has been reduced, since he has just written a cheque on it. Therefore, the bank owes Han $50 less. This reduces demand deposits by $50. In this case the assets are reduced, and so are the liabilities.

SELF-TEST

3. Give the necessary bookkeeping entries for each set of circumstances below.
   A) The bank sells $500 worth of securities for cash to Fadia, who is not a customer.

   B) The bank sells $500 worth of securities and is given a cheque by Volpe, who is a customer.

The Money Multiplier

That's enough bookkeeping for the present. Now, what we want to figure out are the implications for a bank and for the banking system when a bank holds more than its targeted reserves. Let's start off the analysis by assuming that the Saymor Bank and all other banks are just meeting their target reserves of 10 percent. Remember that this means that each bank wants to hold a minimum of 10 percent of its demand deposits in the form of cash reserves. For instance, assume that Saymor starts from this position:

> ### Balance Sheet of Saymor Bank Ltd.
> ### as at December 31, 1998
>
> | Assets | | Liabilities and Equity | |
> |---|---|---|---|
> | Reserves | $ 10 000 | Demand deposits | $100 000 |
> | Loans | 60 000 | Shareholders' equity | 20 000 |
> | Securities | 30 000 | | |
> | Fixed assets | 20 000 | | |
> | | $120 000 | | $120 000 |

Now, assume that Tom, rummaging about under his bed one morning, comes across $1000 in currency. Not knowing what to do with it, he decides to deposit it in the bank. The bank credits the $1000 to his account. Its reserves now equal $11 000, and its demand deposits are $101 000. The bank now finds that it has excess reserves, since it wants to hold only 10% × $101 000, or $10 100. It is over-reserved to the tune of $900. Or, look at it another way: of the $1000 that Tom deposited, the bank aims to keep only 10 percent in the form of cash reserves and therefore has $900 more than it considers necessary to hold. As we mentioned before, banks do not like to have such idle cash; they want to earn some return on it. They will be very happy to lend it out. Now let's assume Wing Kee happens to come into the bank the next day in need of a $900 loan. The loan is happily granted, and he walks out with $900, and within ten minutes purchases a used Volkswagen from the New Star Car Company. A New Star employee deposits this money in the J.M.K. Bank. This bank, prior to the deposit by New Star, had no reserves in excess of its targeted amount. After the deposit, the following accounts at J.M.K. Bank will be affected:

> Reserves   +$900   Demand deposits   +$900

excess reserves: reserves in excess of what the bank wants to hold as its target reserves.

J.M.K. also wants to keep 10 percent of the increased demand deposits, that is, 10% × $900, or $90. It therefore has $810 **excess reserves**. It too is anxious to lend it out. Now let's assume that Sue is in need of $810 to pay off a debt to her friend Sarbjit and manages to negotiate an $810 loan from J.M.K. She immediately pays Sarbjit. Sarbjit, not wanting to keep too much cash on the premises, deposits the money at his bank, the M.P.C. Bank. After the deposit, the balance sheet of the M.P.C. Bank changes as follows:

> Reserves   +$810   Demand deposits   +$810

M.P.C. Bank now finds itself with excess reserves (over its targeted amount). It wants to keep back only 10 percent of the $810, or $81, as cash reserves. Therefore, it has $810 minus $81, or $729 in excess reserves. Let's assume that this amount is lent out. Regardless of whom it is lent to, and regardless of how the cash is spent (assuming that recipients of the money deposit it back into a bank), sooner or later one of the banks in the banking system will find itself again with excess reserves and be ready and able to lend. The banking *system* seems unable to get rid of this cash. A bank lends it out, but each time it returns to some other bank. However, each time it returns, the bank decides to retain 10 percent of that new deposit in additional reserves. Let's follow the trail resulting from Tom's initial deposit of $1000:

Reserves	Loans	Deposits
+1000		+1000 (Tom)
	+900 (to Wing Kee)	+ 900 (New Star)
	+810 (to Sue)	+ 810 (Sarbjit)
	+729	+729
	. . .	. . .
	. . .	. . .
	. . .	. . .

You can see that both the loans and deposits columns above follow a geometric pattern. What we are interested in finding out is the total of the deposits column. Why would we be interested in this figure? Because *it is money*. Think back to the definition of money (M1): currency in circulation plus demand deposits. The banks' cash reserves are not part of the money supply, but the total amount in peoples' chequing accounts certainly is. This means that:

Each time that a bank issues a loan it creates money.

We will do more with this idea in a moment.

So what will be the total of all demand deposits that result from Tom's initial deposit of $1000? The answer is $1000 + 900 + 810 + 729 + ... It's reasonably easy to solve if you remember the formula for summing a geometric progression. But let's tackle the problem from a different perspective by looking at part of the balance sheet of the *entire banking system*. Assume it looked like the following prior to Tom's deposit:

Reserves	$100 000	Demand deposits	$1 000 000
Loans	900 000		

Staying with our assumption that banks want to keep a 10 percent reserve ratio, the banking system illustrated above is neither over- nor underreserved. If the target reserves must equal 10 percent of deposits, it means that demand deposits will equal ten times the amount of reserves. Now Tom deposits $1000 in one of the banks, so that reserves equal $101 000. Demand deposits can rise to a maximum of 10 × $101 000, or $1 010 000. As a result of the lending process we described, the new combined balance sheet would look like this:

Reserves	$101 000	Demand deposits	$1 010 000
Loans	$909 000		

money multiplier: the increase in total deposits that would occur in the whole banking system as a result of a new deposit in a single bank.

In other words, if the target reserve ratio is 10 percent, a new deposit of $X will lead to an increase in total deposits throughout the *whole* banking system of ten times $X. As you probably recognize, what we have here is another multiplier; this time, the **money multiplier,** which is determined in the following way:

$$\text{Money Multiplier} = \frac{\Delta \text{ in deposits}}{\Delta \text{ in reserves}}$$

or

$$\text{Money Multiplier} = \frac{1}{\text{Target Reserve Ratio}}$$

In our example, the target reserve ratio is 10 percent, or 0.1, so the money multiplier is 1/ 0.1, or 10. If the target reserve ratio was 5 percent, or 0.05, it would mean that banks want to keep a smaller amount of reserves and therefore would have more to lend out. In this case, the money multiplier would be 1/0.05, or 20.

The principle of the money multiplier is based on the fact that banks only keep a small fraction of deposits in the form of cash reserves. Excess reserves allow banks to increase loans and therefore increase deposits by a multiple of the excess reserves. The money multiplier shows what will happen in the whole banking system over a period of time.

SELF-TEST

4. What will be the increase in total deposits in the whole banking system of a new deposit of $2000 into the XYZ bank in each of the following circumstances?

A) a target reserve ratio of 20 percent;
B) a target reserve ratio of 5 percent.

Be careful not to confuse the effect of the money multiplier working through the *whole* banking system with the circumstances facing a single bank. Simply because a *single* bank happens to find itself with excess reserves does not mean that it could increase loans by a multiple of those excess reserves. For instance, look at the following circumstances for the Saymor Bank:

Reserves $100   Demand deposits $1000

The target reserve ratio is 10 percent. Someone now deposits cash of $50. Excess reserves would then equal $45, and this is all Saymor wants to lend. It could not lend out $450, since the bank would be in a very embarrassing situation if the borrower immediately asked for cash. In short:

A single bank has to tread carefully and limit its loans to the amount of its excess reserves.

SELF-TEST

5. The J.M.K. Bank has demand deposits of $60 000 and reserves of $6000. By how much can it increase its loans if:
A) the target reserve ratio is 8 percent?
B) the target reserve ratio is 5 percent?

C) Assume the same $60 000 and $6000 applied to the entire banking system. What are your new answers to A) and B)?

Can Banks Ever Be Short of Reserves?

bank rate: the rate of interest that the Bank of Canada charges a commercial bank for a loan.

It can certainly happen that at the end of a day's business, a bank might find that it has less reserves than it targeted. In that case what can it do? It would need to borrow. The Bank of Canada will lend money to a commercial bank, but the bank must pay interest equal to the **bank rate** to the Bank of Canada. However, since the bank rate is regarded by the banks as a penalty rate (since they can borrow from the public at a much lower rate), banks will try to ensure that they pay off any loans from the Bank of Canada as quickly as possible. As a result, such loans tend to be very short-term.

The Money Multiplier Also Works in Reverse

Are there other consequences if a single bank—Saymor, for instance—finds itself underreserved? Well, after receiving a loan from the Bank of Canada, Saymor will have to increase its reserves in some more permanent way. While it is not difficult for a single bank to increase its reserves, doing so will be at the expense of some other bank's reserves. Let's explain this by assuming that Saymor calls in an outstanding loan that was made earlier to the New Star Car Company. New Star will be forced to quickly sell off some of its inventory. The buyers involved in this selloff will be reducing their deposits in other banks as they pay for their purchases. This will result in other banks finding themselves underreserved and thus forced to call in some of their loans. Soon, we will find the total loans in the whole banking system decreasing and, as a result, deposits also being reduced by an amount determined by the money multiplier. Look at the following combined balance sheet of a banking system:

Reserves	$ 95	Demand deposits	$1000
Loans	905		

If the target reserve ratio is 10 percent, the banking system is underreserved in the amount of $5. How can the whole banking system produce another $5 worth of reserves? It cannot. What will happen is that the banking system, over a period of time, will be forced to call in outstanding loans. In this case, the money multiplier is 10, so the banks in total will have to call in $10 \times \$5$, or $50, to get their reserves back in line with the deposits. After this contraction, the balance sheet will look like this:

Reserves	$ 95	Demand deposits	$950
Loans	855		

We emphasize that banks can neither create nor destroy *currency*. What they can do is create or destroy loans and demand deposits, and this is what they do whenever they are over- or underreserved. It is in this sense that we mean that banks can create and destroy *money* (demand deposits). However, as we will see in the next chapter, it is the Bank of Canada that ultimately controls the money supply by determining the amount of currency held by the commercial banks.

Some Final Complications

Some additional complications need mentioning. So far we have assumed that all bank loans were taken in the form of cash. Obviously, this is a simplification. What usually happens when you negotiate a loan from a bank is that neither you, the customer, nor the bank actually deals in cash. Usually, upon obtaining a loan, the bank will set up an account for you and give you immediate credit in the amount of that loan. Now, whether you actually draw out cash or instead write a cheque is up to you. The bank doesn't know in advance if the amount of the loan will actually be withdrawn in cash or not. If you were to write a cheque payable to a friend who is also a customer of the same bank, all that is involved is a bookkeeping entry decreasing the amount in your account and increasing the amount in your friend's. No cash would leave the bank, and the bank could keep issuing loans until reserves actually left the bank (say, as a result of a cheque being paid to the customer of another bank). In this case, we say that the cheque has *cleared against* the bank. None of these complications, however, affect the principle of money creation that we described in this chapter.

There are certain instances, however, when this money multiplier effect will be diminished. For instance, if a bank were to increase its target reserves, obviously it would be lending out less, and the money multiplier would be reduced. However, in modern banking circles, banks are likely to keep their targets as low as is safely possible, since they earn no return on idle cash. It is also possible that recipients of bank loans may want to keep a portion of the loan in the form of cash. This, too, would reduce the size of the money multiplier. Finally, it should be noted that in a recession, banks often find it difficult to give loans, because many people simply do not want to go further into debt when times are tough. This would also reduce the size of the multiplier.

REVIEW

1. What is represented by a list of a company's *assets*?
2. What is represented by a list of a company's *liabilities*?
3. Define the *money multiplier*.
4. What is the *bank rate*?
5. What does it mean for a bank to be *overreserved*?
6. Can a single bank create money?
7. Can the banking system create currency?

Chapter Highlights

This chapter represents a significant change in direction. It moves beyond the focus on national income and its determination and begins to lay the groundwork for a thorough discussion of policy. An essential part of this groundwork is a discussion of money, the banking system, and the process of demand–deposit creation.

After a brief description of the functions of money, the chapter uses a historical approach to bring out several points about our current banking system, as well as the nature and role of money. Among these points are (a) the link between money and the price level (b) the need for money to be scarce and the need to prevent anyone from debasing it (c) the fact that paper currency, banks as we know them, and a central bank are all fairly modern institutions, and (d) the important role that fractional reserve banking plays.

Next comes the definition and measurement of money, as well as a discussion of what money is not. The most significant aspect of this discussion is that most of the economy's money supply is made up of demand deposits in the commercial banks. That is, the money an individual has in a chequing account is just as much money as the currency that she might carry in her pocket. Further, this demand–deposit money is, in total, larger than the total of coin and paper currency.

It is for this reason that the next logical step in the chapter is a discussion of how the banking system creates demand deposits. This is done by following a series of sequential loans and deposits through the banking system, using various bank balance sheets for illustration. The importance of the target reserve ratio is emphasized in this discussion. Finally, the chapter looks at the significance of the money multiplier and explains why even a small change in cash reserves cause big changes in the amount of loans and deposits.

New Glossary Terms

STUDY GUIDE

Study Tips

1. Many students have a lot of trouble with the material in this chapter. For a long time, we had difficulty in understanding this, because the concepts involved are not complicated. We have now come to believe that the source of the difficulty is, yet again, the mistake of equating money with income. The chapter is about how the banking system can create money. Students who (consciously or unconsciously) confuse this with creating income seem to "freeze up" at this prospect and never really understand much that follows. Only by combining resources in production can we create wealth and real income. On the other hand, a banking system is quite capable of creating more money, even though no more real income has been created. Obviously, if this is done in excess, prices will be driven up because more money will be chasing the same quantity of goods. There really isn't anything mysterious going on here. Don't let yourself get spooked into thinking that there is.

2. When working with the many balance statements in this chapter, remember that the key entry is the amount of demand deposits. This is the bank's (or the system's) primary liability, and reserves must be large enough to cover expected net withdrawals (new withdrawals less new deposits in the future). The target reserve ratio is always a percentage of demand deposits.

3. Students sometimes have difficulty in understanding what might happen if a bank becomes underreserved. The bank might be able to get a loan and thus increase its reserves by the amount that it borrows; that is easy to comprehend. Not quite so easy is the idea that the only other way out of being underreserved is for the bank to decrease its demand deposits. The way a bank does this is to call in loans that it has previously made. A bank cannot call in, say, a fixed-term mortgage that it made to you (or your parents) a year or two ago. However, many loans to businesses are what are called demand loans and are subject to being called in "on demand" if necessary.

Key Problem

Table 7.1 is the current balance sheet for the Maple Leafs Bank. Answer the following questions assuming that the bank's target reserve ratio is 5 percent.

TABLE 7.1

Maple Leafs Bank
Balance Sheet, as of the Current Date

Assets		Liabilities/Equity	
Reserves	$ 100 000	Demand deposits	$1 000 000
Loans	650 000	Shareholders' equity	250 000
Securities	300 000		
Fixed assets	200 000		
	1 250 000		1 250 000

---

a) Is this bank over- or underreserved, and what is the amount?

Answer: _____

b) Suppose that a loan, in the amount of the excess reserves found in a), is made to Sat Mundin. What effect does this transaction have on the bank's balance sheet?

Answer: _____

c) Suppose that Sat immediately spends all of his loan by writing a cheque to his psychologist, Freda Freud, who deposits it in her bank account, which happens to also be at the Maple Leafs Bank. What effect do these transactions have on the bank's balance sheet?

Answer: _____

d) Now, is the Maple Leafs Bank over- or underreserved? If so, by how much?

Reserved? _____ ; amount? _____ .

e) Suppose the bank now makes another loan for the amount of your answer in d), which then clears against the Maple Leafs Bank. How much excess reserves does the bank now have?

Answer: _____

f) Fill in the blanks in the balance sheet in **Table 7.2** after taking into account all the transactions in a) through e).

TABLE 7.2

Maple Leafs Bank
Balance Sheet after Many Transactions

Assets		Liabilities/Equity	
Reserves	_____	Demand deposits	_____
Loans	_____	Shareholders' equity	_____
Securities	_____		
Fixed assets	_____		
Totals	_____		_____

Suppose that the balance sheet for the whole banking system just happens to be exactly ten times that of the Maple Leafs Bank's statement in Table 7.1. The balance sheet for the whole system is presented in **Table 7.3**. You can assume that each of the other banks also has a target reserve ratio of 5 percent.

TABLE 7.3

Whole Banking System
Balance Sheet

Assets		Liabilities/Equity	
Reserves	$1 000 000	Demand deposits	$10 000 000
Loans	6 500 000	Shareholders' equity	2 500 000
Securities	3 000 000		
Fixed Assets	2 000 000		
	$12 500 000		$12 500 000

g) What is the maximum potential increase in the money supply if all the banks were fully loaned up?

Answer: _____

h) Suppose all ten banks changed their target reserve ratio to 4 percent. What is the maximum potential increase in the money supply resulting if again all the banks were fully loaned up?

Answer: _____

i) Finally, returning to the balance sheet in Table 7.3, what would be the consequence of the economy's central bank imposing a 12.5 percent required reserve ratio on all banks? What amount of loans must be called in?

Answer: _____

More of the Same

Table 7.4 shows the current balance sheet for the Canadiens Bank. Answer the questions below assuming that the bank's target reserve ratio is 10 percent.

TABLE 7.4

Canadiens Bank
Balance Sheet as of Current Date

Assets		Liabilities/Equity	
Reserves	$120 000	Demand deposits	$900 000
Loans	680 000	Shareholders' equity	500 000
Securities	250 000		
Fixed assets	350 000		
	$1 400 000		$1 400 000

a) Is this bank over- or underreserved, and what is the amount?

b) Suppose that a loan, in the amount of the excess reserves found in a), is made to Lessier Lark. What effect does this transaction have on the bank's balance sheet?

c) Suppose that Lessier immediately spends all of his loan by writing a cheque to his astrologer, Misty Starship, who deposits it in her account at the Canadiens Bank. What effect do these transactions have on the bank's balance sheet?

d) Is the Canadiens Bank now over- or underreserved? If so, by how much?

e) Suppose the bank makes a loan for the amount in your answer in d), which then clears against the Canadiens Bank. How much excess reserves does the bank now have?

f) Fill in the blanks in the balance sheet in Table 7.5 after taking into account all of the transactions in a) through e).

TABLE 7.5

Canadiens Bank
Balance Sheet after Many Transactions

Assets		Liabilities/Equity	
Reserves	_____	Demand deposits	_____
Loans	_____	Shareholders' equity	_____
Securities	_____		
Fixed assets	_____		
Totals	_____		_____

Suppose that there are a total of nine other banks in the economy and that the balance sheet for the whole banking system is presented in **Table 7.6**. You can assume that each of the other banks also has a target reserve ratio of 10 percent.

TABLE 7.6

Whole Banking System
Balance Sheet

Assets		Liabilities/Equity	
Reserves	$1 200 000	Demand deposits	$9 000 000
Loans	6 800 000	Shareholders' equity	5 000 000
Securities	2 500 000		
Fixed assets	3 500 000		
Totals	14 000 000		14 000 000

g) What is the maximum potential increase in the money supply resulting from the banks becoming fully loaned up?

h) If all ten banks changed their target reserve ratio to 5 percent, what is the maximum potential increase in the money supply resulting from banks becoming fully loaned up?

i) What would be the consequence of the economy's central bank imposing a 15 percent required reserve ratio on all banks? What amount of loans must be called in?

Translations

Rearrange in correct position the items in the balance sheet shown in **Table 7.7** Change one figure only to reflect the bank achieving a 10 percent target reserve ratio.

TABLE 7.7

Balance Sheet of Cunucks Bank Ltd.
December 31, 1998

Assets		Liabilities/Equity	
Reserves	$100 000	Demand deposits	$500 000
Loans	330 000	Securities	120 000
Shareholders' equity	80 000		
Fixed assets	80 000		

Are You Sure?

Indicate whether the following statements are true or false. If false, indicate why they are false.

1. Money acts as a medium of exchange, a store of wealth, and a unit of account.

   T or F   If false: _____

   _____

2. Individuals in a society that had no medium of exchange would be forced to barter all goods and services directly.

   T or F   If false: _____

   _____

3. The most important characteristic of money is that it be portable.

   T or F   If false: _____

   _____

4. Canada's largest commercial bank is the Bank of Canada.

   T or F   If false: _____

   _____

5. M1 is defined as currency in circulation plus notice deposits in commercial banks.

   T or F   If false: _____

   _____

6. The target reserve ratio is that portion of a bank's deposits that it wishes to loan out.

   T or F   If false: _____

   _____

7. The spread is the difference between the interest rate that a bank pays to borrowers and the interest rate it charges depositors.

   T or F   If false: _____

   _____

8. A bank will try to lend out all of its excess reserves.

   T or F   If false: _____

   _____

9. The bank rate is the rate of interest that the Bank of Canada charges a commercial bank for a loan.

   T or F   If false: _____

   _____

10. If some of the recipients of bank loans keep a portion of the loan in the form of cash, the money expansion process would expand.

   T or F   If false: _____

   _____

Choose the Best

11. What is the basis of the modern banking system?
    a) Fractional reserves.
    b) Commodity money.

12. What is the value of the money multiplier?
    a) 1 divided by the targeted reserve ratio.
    b) The reciprocal of the MPC.

13. What kind of banking system does Canada have?
    a) A unit banking system.
    b) A branch banking system.

14. If you were working out the cost of attending school next year, which function of money would you be using?
    a) A medium of exchange.
    b) A unit of account.
    c) A store of wealth.

15. If you wrote out a cheque to make a purchase of textbooks, which function of money would you be using?
    a) A medium of exchange.
    b) A unit of account.
    c) A store of wealth.

16. What is the spread?
    a) The difference between a bank's actual reserves and its target reserves.
    b) The interest rate difference between what a bank charges borrowers and what it pays savers.
    c) The difference between a bank's demand deposits and its total loans to customers.

17. Why is the banking system able to increase loans and demand deposits by a multiple of its excess reserves?
    a) Because reserves lost by one bank are gained by another.
    b) Because the MPC of borrowers is positive.
    c) Because one person's debt becomes another person's income.

18. What is the definition of M1?
    a) Currency in circulation only.

b) Currency in circulation plus demand deposits and savings accounts.
c) Currency in circulation plus demand deposits and Canada Savings Bonds.
d) Currency in circulation plus demand deposits.

19. Which of the following statements about the value of money is correct?
    a) It varies inversely with the price level.
    b) It varies directly with the interest rate.
    c) It varies directly with the price level.
    d) It varies directly with the quantity of money.

20. Which of the following are assets to a bank?
    a) Demand deposits, equity, and reserves.
    b) Reserves, loans to customers, and securities.
    c) Reserves, property, and equity.
    d) Equity, property, and demand deposits.

21. Historically, why were goldsmiths able to create money?
    a) Because consumers and merchants preferred to use gold rather than currency for transactions.
    b) Because they always kept 100 percent reserves.
    c) Because only a few of their customers would redeem their notes for gold at any one time.
    d) Because they held the right to print money.

22. Suppose that the Canucks Bank has excess reserves of $6000 and demand deposits of $100 000. If its targeted reserve ratio is 10 percent, what is the size of the bank's actual reserves?
    a) $4000.
    b) $16 000.
    c) $10 000.
    d) $14 000.

23. Suppose that Adam Ricardo deposits $1000 of cash into the Penguins Bank. On the same day, David Smith negotiates a loan for $4000. By how much has the money supply changed?
    a) It has increased by $3000.
    b) It has decreased by $3000.

c) It has increased by $4000.
d) It has increased by $5000.

24. All of the following *except one* are characteristics that money should possess. Which is the exception?
   a) It should have general acceptability.
   b) It should be divisible.
   c) It should be convertible into gold or other precious metals.
   d) It should be portable.
   e) It should be durable.

25. The currency held by banks is considered to be part of what definition of money?
   a) M1.
   b) M2.
   c) M3
   d) Part of all three—M1, M2, and M3.
   e) Not part of any definition of money.

26. All of the following statements *except one* are correct. Which is the exception?
   a) A bank's total reserves are equal to its excess reserves plus its target reserves.
   b) A bank's assets plus its net worth equals it liabilities.
   c) When a bank makes a loan, it creates demand deposits.
   d) A single bank can safely lend out only an amount up to the value of its excess reserves.
   e) If a bank transaction decreases the value of one of its assets, then either some other asset must increase in value or one of its liabilities must decrease in value.

27. If Guy and Laraine both have chequing accounts at the same bank and Guy writes a cheque for $1000, payable to Laraine, what will happen to the bank's accounts?
   a) They will not be affected.
   b) Assets and liabilities will both decrease by $1000.

c) Liabilities will decline and the bank's equity will increase by $1000.
d) Reserves and demand deposits will both decrease by $1000.
e) Demand deposits will increase and loans to customers will decrease by $1000.

28. Which of the following statements is correct if a bank is holding excess reserves?
   a) It is in a position to make additional loans.
   b) Its reserves exceed its loans.
   c) It is making above-normal profits.
   d) Its actual reserves are less than its targeted reserves.
   e) Its loans to customers exceed its required loans.

29. Suppose that the Just Right Coffee company negotiates a $100 000 loan from the Blackhawks Bank and takes $40 000 in the form of cash, leaving the remainder in its account. What has happened to the supply of money?
   a) It has increased by $100 000.
   b) It has decreased by $100 000.
   c) It has increased by $40 000.
   d) It has increased by $60 000.
   e) It has not changed.

30. Suppose that a banking system has $10 000 000 in demand deposits and actual reserves of $1 200 000. Given a 10 percent targeted reserve ratio for all banks, what is the maximum possible expansion of the money supply?
   a) $2 200 000.
   b) $115 000.
   c) $200 000.
   d) $12 000 000.
   e) $2 000 000.

Other Problems

31. **Table 7.8** is the balance sheet for the Oilers Bank, which has a target reserve ratio of 5 percent.

TABLE 7.8

Oilers Bank
Balance Sheet as of Current Date

Assets		Liabilities/Equity	
Reserves	$ 6 000	Demand deposits	$80 000
Loans	68 000	Shareholders' equity	20 000
Securities	17 000		
Fixed assets	9 000		
Totals	$100 000		$100 000

a) By how much is the Oilers Bank over- or underreserved?

Answer: _____

b) If the bank makes a loan equal to the excess reserves and the borrower writes a cheque (for the full amount of the loan) to another customer of the bank, who then deposits it, what will be the new amount of excess reserves?

Answer: _____

c) If, instead, the cheque written by the borrower is cleared against the Oilers Bank (the cheque was written to a customer of another bank), what will be the amount of excess reserves?

Answer: _____

32. **Table 7.9** is the balance sheet for all banks combined in the banking system. All banks have a target reserve ratio of 8 percent.

TABLE 7.9

Whole Banking System
Balance Sheet

Assets		Liabilities/Equity	
Reserves	$ 78 000	Demand deposits	$900 000
Loans	720 000	Shareholders' equity	100 000
Securities	102 000		
Fixed assets	100 000		
Totals	$1 000 000		$1 000 000

a) What is the amount of excess reserves?

Answer: _____

b) What is the maximum amount that loans and deposits can be increased?

Answer: _____

c) If the system becomes fully loaned up, by how much will the money supply have increased?

Answer: _____

33. Answer the questions below from the data in **Table 7.10**. (All figures are in $ billions.)

TABLE 7.10

Total currency issued by the Bank of Canada	$ 20
Total personal savings deposits	192
Total demand deposits	23
Deposits of the federal government at the Bank of Canada	2
Currency held by commercial banks	2
Government bonds owned by public	100
Non-personal fixed-term deposits (certificates of deposit)	46

a) What is the total currency in circulation?

Answer: _____

b) How much larger is M1 than total currency in circulation?

Answer: _____

c) How much larger is M2 than M1?

Answer: _____

d) How much larger is M3 than M2?

Answer: _____

34. Fill in the blanks in the balance sheet of the Flames Bank in **Table 7.11**, assuming that the value of fixed assets is the same as Shareholders' Equity and that the bank is fully loaned up. You may assume that the targeted reserve ratio is 5 percent.

TABLE 7.11

Flames Bank
Balance Sheet

Assets		Liabilities/Equity	
Reserves	$_____	Demand Deposits	$100 000
Loans	_____	Shareholders' Equity	_____
Securities	10 000		
Fixed Assets	_____		_____
Totals			$120 000

UNANSWERED QUESTIONS

Short Essays

1. Describe the characteristics of a society that does not use money.

2. Explain how goldsmiths acted as storage agents.

3. What are the three functions of money? Do you think one is more important than the others, and, if so, which one?

4. Compare a unit banking system with a branch banking system and explain whether you think one is better than the other.

5. What is meant by fractional reserve banking, and why does it form the basis of modern banking?

Analytical Questions

6. What would happen if all depositors were to demand their cash back from the banks at the same time? What security do depositors have against this possibility?

7. Many people believe that the ability to buy goods with credit cards makes such cards "money." Explain why a credit card is *not* money. Do you think debit cards are money?

8. The Bank of Canada used to *require* that banks hold reserves of approximately 10 percent. Now there is no such requirement. Has this affected the money multiplier?

9. In which of the following circumstances has the money supply changed?
   a) Mario deposits $1000 at his bank.
   b) Mario withdraws $1000 from his bank.
   c) Mario lends Luigi $1000.
   d) The bank lends Mario $1000.
   e) Mario lends the bank $1000.

10. Why can't a single bank increase its loans by a multiple of its excess reserves? Can you imagine a situation in which it could?

11. Many students think that the government (or the Bank of Canada) still has a pile of gold somewhere that "backs" our money. Since this is not true, what does back Canadian money?

12. The central bank of Muldovia has issued $100 000 in Muldovian dollars. What is the size of the Muldovian money supply if:
    a) Muldovians have deposited none of the currency in its banks?
    b) Muldovians have deposited all of the currency in its banks, and the banks have a 100 percent target reserve ratio?
    c) Muldovians have deposited 50 percent of the currency in its banks, and the banks have a 100 percent target reserve ratio?
    d) Muldovians have deposited 50 percent of the currency in its banks, and the banks have a 10 percent target reserve ratio and are fully loaned up?

13. Can a country have too much money? Can it have too little? What is the right amont of money for a country?

Numerical Questions

14. If a monopoly bank has a target reserve ratio of 10 percent and it is holding $2000 in excess reserves, by how much can it increase its loans? What is your answer if the target reserve ratio is 1 percent?

15. Table 7.12 is the balance sheet for the Senators Bank. The target reserve ratio is 10 percent.
    a) What is the size of the bank's excess reserves?
    b) Change the balance sheet to show the effect of the bank loaning out all of its excess reserves.

TABLE 7.12

**Senators Bank
Balance Sheet**

Assets		Liabilities	
Reserves	$ 60 000	Deposits	$400 000
Securities	80 000	Shareholders' equity	60 000
Loans	260 000		
Fixed assets	60 000		
Totals	$460 000		$460 000

c) Now change the balance sheet to show the effect of a cheque for the amount of the loan in b) clearing against the bank.
d) Suppose that the target reserve ratio is 20 percent. What is its reserve situation, and what action will it take?

16. Table 7.13 is the combined balance sheet for all the banks in a banking system. Each bank has a target reserve ratio of 5 percent.

TABLE 7.13

Whole Banking System
Balance Sheet

Assets		Liabilities	
Reserves	$80	Deposit	$800
Securities	30	Shareholders' equity	40
Loans	690		
Fixed assets	40		
Totals	$840		$840

a) Write out a new balance sheet that reflects the complete effect of all excess reserves being loaned out.
b) What is the maximum possible increase in the money supply?
c) Given Table 7.13, if the target reserve ratio changes to 12.5 percent, what quantity of loans will the system be forced to call in? Write in the figures that show this process completed.

17. Table 7.14 is the balance sheet for all the banks combined in the banking system.

TABLE 7.14

Whole Banking System
Balance Sheet

Assets		Liabilities/Equity	
Reserves	$900 000	Demand deposits	$900 000
Loans	—		
Securities	50 000	Shareholders' equity	100 000
Fixed assets	50 000		
Totals	$1 000 000		$1 000 000

a) Which of the above figures is part of the money supply?
b) If all banks maintain 100 percent reserves, what happens to the money supply if $1000 cash is deposited into one of the banks in the system?
c) If none of the banks maintain reserves, what happens to the money supply if $1000 cash is deposited into one of the banks in the system?

18. Given the following:

Fixed assets	$180 000
Customers' deposits	$800 000
Reserves	$50 000
Loans to customers	$500 000
Securities	$170 000

a) Arrange the data in the form of a balance sheet.
b) What is the value of equity for this bank?
c) If the bank has a 5 percent target reserve ratio, what is the value of excess reserves?

Web-Based Activities

1. Go to **http://www.bank-banque-canada.ca/pdf/qgreys.pdf** and look at how M2 and M2+ have changed over the last 10 years. Which aggregate grew faster? What might account for the different rates of growth in the money aggregates. Which component of M2+ grew fastest?

2. How will the transition from a paper-based monetary system to an electronic payments system affect the process of money creation? Go to **http://www.cato.org/pubs/books/money/tableof.htm** and read the introduction written by J. Dorn to answer this question. Do you think that electronic money will be beneficial to the economy? Why or why not?

The Money Market

What's ahead...This chapter has two main objectives: to explain how interest rates are determined, and to show how changes in the money supply can bring about important changes in the economy. To begin with, we explain how the money supply is determined and then we examine the factors that influence the demand for money. Equilibrium in the money market occurs at an interest rate at which the quantity demanded and quantity supplied of money are equal. We then look at how this equilibrium can be disturbed and at how the money market reacts to such disturbances. Finally, we look at two contrasting views of the way that changes in the supply of money can produce real changes in the market.

How much money do you have at the moment? Remember, this includes coin and currency in your pocket, and at home, plus the current balance in your checking account. Is it $20? $200? $1000? Does your holding of money vary from week to week or month to month, or is it some constant amount? What is the minimum you hold? What is the maximum you would hold before you started to look for something to "do with" your money? Have you thought about what determines the amount of money that you hold? Even people with the same level of income sometimes hold quite different amounts of money. Why is that? These are the questions, and their implications, that we look at in this chapter.

Few people would dispute the usefulness of money to both individuals and society. In fact, most economists consider it one of the fundamental elements of a wealthy society, even though they do not consider money itself to be a form of wealth for a nation. However, as we shall see, economists do most definitely disagree on the role of money in producing real change in the economy. In order to see just how money can affect things like production and employment, we need to understand the workings of the money market. To begin with, we look at the supply side of the money market.

The Supply of Money

For simplicity's sake we will use the narrow definition of the money supply, M1, in our discussion. The supply of money, if you remember, is composed of currency in circulation and the total of all demand deposits at chartered banks. The Bank of Canada can determine exactly how much currency is issued, but it is the public that decides what portion of this it wishes to keep in circulation (in our pockets, in the tills of shops, in office safes, and so on) and what portion is deposited with banks. The portion that is deposited constitutes the banks' reserves, which in turn will determine the amount of loans and demand deposits they are able to support. We will leave until Chapter 12 the discussion of the way in which the Bank of Canada is able to affect the amount of money in the economy. The important point we wish to make at this stage is that, to all intents and purposes:

> **The supply of money is determined by the Bank of Canada, which, can and does change the supply as it sees fit.**

Let us now look at the other side of the equation: the demand for money.

Courtesy of the Bank of Canada.

The Bank of Canada building in Ottawa.

The Demand for Money

Before you start thinking that the average person's demand for money is unlimited, bear in mind that money is a stock and is only one form of wealth. The average person's demand for *income* might well be unlimited, but we are speaking about (the stock of) money. Like any other form of wealth, money has certain advantages and disadvantages. Except in times of high inflation, money holds its value reasonably well, unlike such things as land or stocks and bonds, whose value can vary greatly. From this point of view it involves less risk. Balanced against that is the fact that holding money does not produce a return, whereas most other forms of wealth can provide a source of income. In general, the safer the "investment," the lower the return; the greater the risk, the higher the return. So why bother holding money at all; why not, on receipt of income, immediately transfer it into some sort of financial investment? The reason is obvious: we need to keep a portion of our wealth in the form of a chequing account or as currency simply because other forms of wealth are unacceptable as a means of payment. It is certainly true that over the years, the introduction of credit cards, debit cards, and chequing–savings accounts has meant that we need only keep a smaller proportion of our wealth in the form of money; nevertheless most of our transactions still require that we pay for them with money. One reason to hold money, therefore, is what economists call the **transactions demand for money**. And what is it that determines this transactions demand? The answer is the value of transactions we make. And what determines the value of our transactions? The level of our income. The higher the income level of an individual, the more she will spend, and the higher will be the transactions demand for money. This is similarly true for the whole economy. The higher the level of GDP, the higher will be the transactions demand for money. Note here that we are speaking of nominal GDP. This means that a higher demand for money can come about either because real GDP increases and/or because prices increase. The major determinants of the transactions demand for money, then, are the level of real income and the level of prices; a change in either can cause a change in the transactions demand for money.

transactions demand for money: the desire of people to hold money as a medium of exchange, that is, to effect transactions.

Another way of looking at the transactions demand is that it is related to money functioning as a medium of exchange. But, as we have already noted, money is often used as a store of wealth. Under what circumstances will it be a popular form of wealth holding? Presumably, when other forms of wealth holding are not attractive. If for instance, the return on stocks and bonds was a piddling 1 percent, and the value of real estate was declining, then most people would start to regard money as a very secure "investment." When the return on other assets is low, therefore, people's demand for money tends to be high. This motive for holding money is termed the **asset demand for money**. On the other hand, when the average return on other types of financial investment is high, people will tend to economize on their money balances and try to ensure that they keep as little as possible beyond their transactions needs. In general, the best indicator of the return on financial investment is the rate of interest. Rates of return tend to move in concert with the rate of interest. There is, therefore, an *inverse* relationship between rates of interest and the asset demand for money. When interest rates are high, asset demand is low; when rates are low, asset demand is high. This idea is illustrated in **Figure 8.1**.

asset demand for money: the desire by people to use money as a store of wealth, that is, to hold money as an asset.

FIGURE 8.1 Transactions, Asset, and Total Demand for Money

Graph A shows the transactions demand for money, which, since it is unrelated to the rate of interest, plots as a vertical straight line. This means that irrespective of the rate of interest, the transactions demand will be equal to Q_{MT}. Graph B shows the asset demand for money, which is inversely related to the interest rate and therefore plots as a downward-sloping curve. This means that when the rate of interest is high, the quantity of money demanded for asset purposes will be low, and low interest rates are associated with a high asset demand. The final graph, C, shows the total demand for money, which is obtained by summing the first two graphs horizontally (Q_{MT} + Q_{MA1} = Q_{M1}; Q_{MT} + Q_{MA2} = Q_{M2}, etc.).

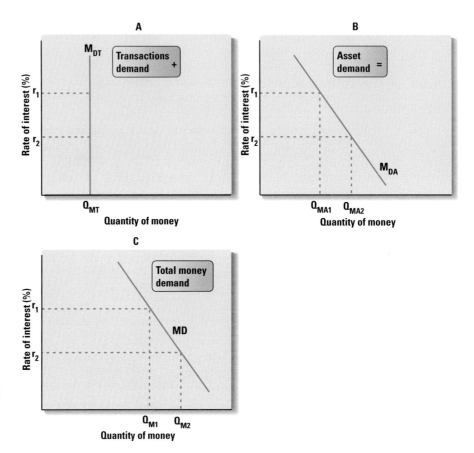

Figure 8.1A simply states that the transactions demand for money is unrelated to the rate of interest. We need a certain amount of money, Q_{MT}, irrespective of how high or low is the rate of interest. Of course, this demand would increase with a rise in real incomes or prices and decrease with a fall in either.

Figure 8.1B shows the inverse relationship between the asset demand for money and the rate of interest. At interest rate r_1, the asset demand will be relatively low at Q_{MA1}. At this high rate of interest, people will economize as much as possible in their holdings of money; they will try to put any excess cash into some form of income-earning asset. At interest rate r_2, on the other hand, the asset demand at Q_{MA2} is high. At this low rate of interest, people are fairly indifferent about holding other financial investments and would just as soon hold on to money.

Figure 8.1C shows the total demand for money, which is simply the addition of the transactions and asset demands. (The two curves are just summed together horizontally.) It shows that when the rate of interest is at r_1, the total demand for money is Q_{M1}. This total is composed of an amount Q_{MT}, the amount of money required for transactions, and Q_{MA1}, the amount of idle money or asset demand. When the rate of interest is r_2, the total demand for money is Q_{M2}, composed of transactions demand Q_{MT} and asset demand Q_{MA2}.

What we have, then, is that people will hold enough money to finance their daily transactions, but will often possess an additional amount of "idle balances," which is what we have called the asset demand. There is controversy among economists regarding such idle balances. Keynes, for example, gave other explanations of why people might rationally hold such additional balances of money. He suggested it is perfectly rational to hold idle balances in situations where holding bonds is risky. This might happen if bond prices were high (and interest rates low) because many people might feel that there is a great chance that prices might soon fall and bondholders suffer a loss as a result. (Keynes called this the speculative motive for holding money.) Besides offering this explanation, Keynes felt that many people might hold cash as a form of security, or insurance, for the future (what he termed the precautionary motive). Even allowing for the fact that the value of money erodes through inflation, many people may still want to hold on to money because of its immediate accessibility in an emergency. In summary, the demand for money in the economy is determined by:

- the level of transactions (real GDP)
- the average value of transactions(the price level)
- the rate of interest

Equilibrium in the Money Market

We have now looked at both the supply of money and the demand for money in an economy. Hopefully, you know what's coming next. To find out under what circumstances the public will be happy to hold the amount of money that the Bank of Canada has supplied, we need to put the two together. **Figure 8.2** does this.

FIGURE 8.2 Surplus and Shortage of Money

This figure illustrates the fact that at interest rates above equilibrium (such as at r_2), the quantity of money supplied exceeds the quantity demanded — there is a surplus. People will rid themselves of this surplus by buying bonds, which will increase the price of bonds, thus reducing the interest rate. Conversely, at interest rates below equilibrium (such as at r_3), there will be a shortage, causing people to sell off bonds in order to obtain more money. The effect of this will be to push down bond prices, thus causing an increase in the rate of interest. Only at equilibrium interest rate r_1 will people be happy to hold the amount of money that is supplied by the Bank of Canada.

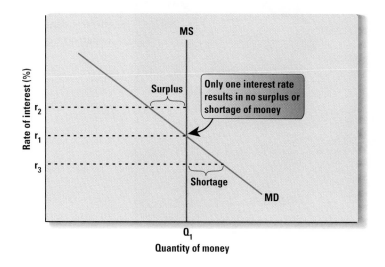

The supply of money, as mentioned before, is determined by the Bank of Canada, and we will regard it as independent of the rate of interest. It is simply a fixed autonomous amount equal to Q_1. The demand for money curve is merely a repeat of Figure 8.1C. The graph shows that only at interest rate r_1 will the quantities supplied and demanded of money be equal. At interest r_1, then, we have equilibrium in the money market. But what will happen if the money market is not in equilibrium? For instance, what will happen if the interest rate happens to be above the equilibrium, at say, r_2? At this rate of interest, there is obviously a surplus of money; that is, the quantity supplied exceeds the quantity demanded. The quantity demanded is lower because at higher rates of interest, people are going to reduce their money holdings; they will want to keep their money balances to a minimum and will want to buy other financial instruments such as bonds. Or put it another way: at a rate of interest above equilibrium, such as r_2, people simply do not want to hold the quantity of money available. One use of these excess funds would be to buy bonds or other financial instruments. This increase in the demand for bonds bids up the price of bonds, which effectively reduces the rate of interest being earned. For example, suppose you owned a $100 bond that paid you a fixed $10 interest each year (a 10 percent yield, or return, on your investment). If you now had to pay $110 for that bond, you would only be earning a return of 9.1 percent ($10/$110 $\times$ 100). In short:

> **The higher the price of bonds, the lower is the rate of return.**

All newly issued bonds will offer no more than the same return as existing bonds. In our example, they would offer a return of $9.10 on a new $100 bond; that is, the rate of interest offered would be 9.1 percent.

This means that the higher the price of bonds, the lower will be the yields (rates of return). In effect, this will mean a lower rate of interest. In other words, like the demand and supply for any product, a surplus tends to cause prices to fall (and the rate of interest is the price of money). On the other hand, a shortage will cause the price (the interest rate) to increase. Perhaps this will become clearer when we look at what happens if the demand or supply of money changes. **Figure 8.3** shows the effect of an expansion of the money supply.

Canapress/Tom Hanson

A pressman stacks some of the new Canada Premium Bonds as they come off the presses at the Canada Bank Note Company in Ottawa.

FIGURE 8.3 A Shift in the Supply of Money

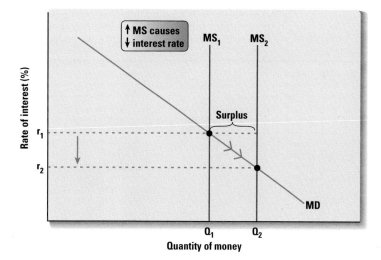

An increase in the supply of money from MS_1 to MS_2 will initially cause a surplus of money at the prevailing interest rate r_1. People will want to rid themselves of the surplus by buying bonds, thus causing bond prices to rise and the interest rate to fall to r_2.

Suppose the money supply increases, which is illustrated by a rightward shift in the money supply curve from MS_1 to MS_2. Given the present interest rate, an increase in the supply of money will lead to an immediate surplus. People simply do not wish to hold this extra quantity supplied at this rate of interest. What they will do is get rid of any surplus by buying stocks, bonds, or other types of income-earning assets. This increase in the demand for bonds will cause bond prices to increase and, therefore, the rate of interest to fall, in Figure 8.3, from r_1 to r_2. Only when the rate of interest has fallen to r_2 will people be happy to hold the additional supply. In summary:

> **An increase in the supply of money will cause interest rates to fall; a decrease in the supply of money will cause interest rates to rise.**

From this, one can appreciate that it is impossible for the Bank of Canada to change the money supply without also affecting interest rates.

SELF-TEST

1. Assume that the money demand for a particular economy is as follows (all money figures in $ billions):

Rate of Interest (%)	Asset Demand ($)	Transactions Demand ($)	Total Demand ($)
12	50	80	_____
11	55	80	_____
10	60	80	_____
9	65	80	_____
8	70	80	_____
7	75	80	_____
6	80	80	_____

Complete the table and answer these questions:
A) If the money supply equals $150, what must the equilibrium interest rate be?
B) If the money supply equals $140, what must the equilibrium interest rate be?
C) If the rate of interest is 11 percent and the money supply is $150, what are the implications?

Let's now look at the effect of a change in the demand for money on the rate of interest. Assume, for instance, that the demand for money increased because nominal incomes increased. At higher incomes, the value of transactions will increase and people will want to hold higher money balances. **Figure 8.4** shows the effect of an increase in the demand for money.

FIGURE 8.4 An Increase in the Demand for Money

The total demand for money will change if nominal GDP changes. A higher price level or a higher income will shift the demand for money curve to the right. Such an increase will initially cause a shortage of money, causing people to sell some of their bonds. As a result, bond prices will drop, which means that interest rates will rise (from r_1 to r_2 in this figure). A decrease in the demand for money, on the other hand, will cause interest rates to fall.

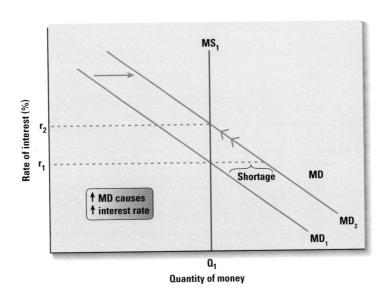

Here we see that the money demand curve has shifted right from MD_1 to MD_2 as a result of an increase in either real income or the price level. At interest rate r_1, this increased demand will produce a shortage of money. (After all, we cannot assume that the Bank of Canada will automatically increase the supply of money just because the demand increases.) To obtain this extra money, people will be forced to sell off some of their income-earning investments. (For instance, they may have to transfer money from a savings account to a chequing account or sell off bonds or other financial instruments.) The effect of this action will be to increase the supply of these types of instruments as people cash them in. This causes their price to fall and the rate of interest to rise, as it does in Figure 8.4, from r_1 to r_2. Similarly, a decrease in the demand of money will cause interest rates to fall. In summary:

> **An increase in the demand for money causes interest rates to rise; a decrease in the demand for money will cause interest rates to fall.**

SELF-TEST

2. Assume you are given the following asset demand for an economy:

Interest Rate (%)	Asset Demand ($ billions)
12	50
11	55
10	60
9	65
8	70
7	75
6	80

You are also told that the transaction demand for money is equal to 10 percent of nominal GDP.

A) If the level of GDP in this economy is $800 and the supply of money is $150, what must the equilibrium interest rate be?

B) If the level of GDP rose to $900, what would be the equilibrium rate of interest?

This whole discussion (in fact, this whole book) has spoken of *the* interest rate as if there were one single rate. In fact, what we have in any economy is an interest-rate structure made up of many rates: the rate paid by banks on savings accounts, the rate charged by banks for loans of different types (mortgages or personal loans or credit card charges), as well as the bank rate, which we will look at in more detail in Chapter 12. For convenience, however, we will continue to speak of "the interest rate," and the reader can use the context of the discussion to determine whether it would be for saving or for borrowing.

ADDED DIMENSION

Gold and Wealth

One of the reasons that Adam Smith's *The Wealth of Nations* became the seminal work in economics is because it attempted to look beyond the economic fears and aspirations of the individual and shift the focus to a study of the whole economy. The title of Smith's opus is, after all, *The Wealth of Nations*, not *The Wealth of People*. It would have been a very simple task for Smith to have defined what constitutes wealth as far as the individual is concerned. What is far less obvious and far more interesting is to figure out what comprises the wealth of nations.

At first glance, it would seem that this is made up of the total wealth of all the individuals plus any assets that are held in common. However, there was major disagreement as to whether or not money should be included as a form of wealth. Although gold could certainly be used as an international medium of exchange, did it mean that the more gold a country had, the richer it was? What if a country's stock of gold were to increase appreciably—would the country be any richer? Well, by and large, people in possession of the gold are able to buy more foreign goods. However, they probably want to buy more domestic goods too. Since there is no reason for the amount of goods produced to change, the only thing that is likely to happen is an increase in prices. What will happen eventually is that prices increase in line with the amount of gold. The net result is that people are no better off than they were before.

What Smith tried to do in his book was to redirect people's views regarding wealth. Being wealthy for Smith meant that a nation was able to produce and had produced an abundance of goods and services—not that it merely owned a stock of pretty pieces of metal like gold. Gold is not wealth in the same way that labour and capital goods are forms of wealth. The latter are regenerative, in that they can re-create themselves; gold, in contrast, is totally sterile.

How Changes in the Money Market Affect the Economy

So far we have been concerned with the mechanics of how changes in the money supply and demand affect interest rates. But by itself this is of no great interest (if you'll forgive the pun). We need to go one step further and show how this change in interest rates can bring about other changes in the economy.

A Change in the Price Level

transmission process: the Keynesian view of how changes in money affect (transmit to) the real variables in the economy.

As we shall discover, the money market and the product market are intrinsically linked: changes in the one will bring about changes in the other. For instance, let's work through the effects of a change in the price level. In working through this **transmission process**, we will see that the interest rate is the link between the two markets. You may recall from Chapter 6 that one of the reasons why aggregate quantity demanded increases when the price level decreases is because it causes the level of investment spending in the economy to increase. We called this the interest-rate effect, and it is one of the causes of the downward slope of the aggregate demand curve. Let us work through this process, illustrated in **Figure 8.5**.

Suppose for instance that the price level drops, caused perhaps by an increase in aggregate supply, as shown in Figure 8.5D. This drop in price means that we would be able to finance the same number of transactions as before, but with less money. The demand for money therefore falls. This is shown in Figure 8.5A.

The decrease in the demand for money from MD_1 to MD_2 causes a drop in the rate of interest from r_1 to r_2. We saw in Chapter 5 that the type of spending most affected by changes in the interest rate is investment. A higher rate of interest will cause firms to reduce the amount of real investment, whereas a lower rate of interest will cause firms to invest more. Thus, there is an inverse relationship between the two.

FIGURE 8.5 Equilibrium in the Money and Product Markets

This figure shows the effect of a decrease in the price level in both the money market and the product market. In 8.5A we see that the money demand curve shifts back from MD_1 to MD_2, resulting in a decrease in the interest rate from r_1 to r_2. Figure B shows how this lower interest rate will lead to an increase in investment spending from I_1 to I_2. In C we see the effect of the higher investment spending on aggregate expenditures, AE_1 to AE_2, and on real GDP, Y_1 to Y_2. Figure D shows that the effect of this decrease in the price level, from P_1 to P_2, is an increase in real GDP, from Y_1 to Y_2.

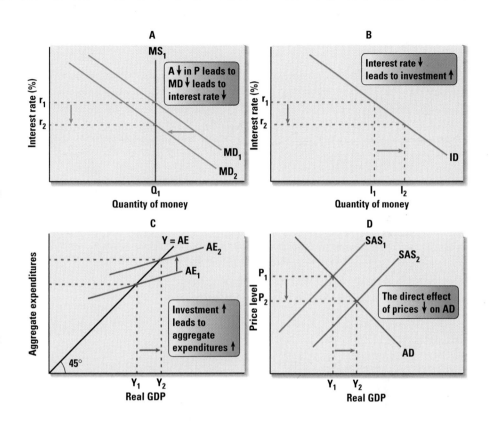

This relationship is referred to as the **investment demand** and is illustrated in Figure 8.5B. The fall in the rate of interest from r_1 to r_2 will reduce the cost of borrowing for firms, which will be encouraged to increase investment spending from I_1 to I_2.

Figure 8.5C is the $Y = AE$ diagram of Chapter 5. Since investment is part of aggregate expenditure, the increase in investment will increase aggregate expenditure from AE_1 to AE_2, resulting in real GDP increasing from Y_1 to Y_2. You will recall that real GDP will increase by a multiple of the change in investment.

investment demand: the inverse relationship between investment spending and interest rates.

Finally, Figure 8.5D illustrates that the decrease in the price level results in a movement down the AD curve, with income increasing from Y_1 to Y_2.

In summary:

> **A lower price level causes a lower demand for money, reducing the interest rate and increasing both investment and real GDP.**

Changes in the Money Supply: The Keynesian View

Figure 8.6 illustrates how the transmission process explains the effect of a direct change in the money supply.

FIGURE 8.6 The Effects of an Increase in the Money Supply

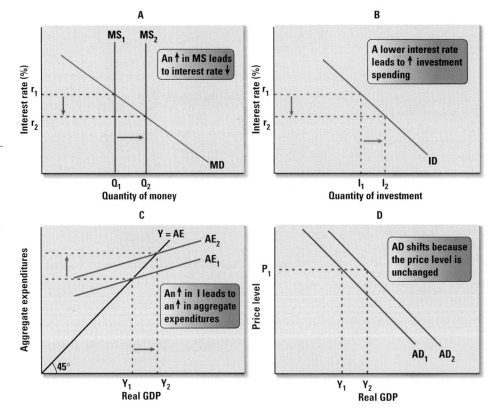

Figure A illustrates an increase in the money supply, MS₁ to MS₂, which results in a decrese in the interest rate from r₁ to r₂. B shows the that this decrease in the interest rate increases the level of investment spending from I₁ to I₂. Since investment spending is part of aggregate expenditures, C shows the shift from AE₁ to AE₂ and the resulting increase in real GDP from Y₁ to Y₂. Finally, D shows the effect on the aggregate demand curve as it shifts from AD₁ to AD₂.

In Figure 8.6A we start with the money market in equilibrium. The increase in the supply of money from MS_1 to MS_2 will cause a reduction in the interest rate from r_1 to r_2. This lower interest rate will increase investment spending from I_1 to I_2 in Figure 8.6B. The higher investment spending will increase aggregate expenditures, causing the AE curve to increase from AE_1 to AE_2, thus increasing real GDP from Y_1 to Y_2, as shown in 8.6C. Finally, the increased aggregate expenditure is reflected in the shift in the aggregate demand curve in Figure 8.6D. Since the price level has remained unchanged, the increase in the money supply will *shift* the AD curve from AD_1 to AD_2.

SELF-TEST

3. What would be the effect on the level of investment and real income if the money supply were reduced?

4. Many retail stores are now introducing the debit card system as a possible form of payment. If this becomes widely popular, what do you think will be the effect on the rate of interest, investment, and real income in the economy?

5. Suppose that the economy depicted below is a closed, private (no government) economy:

Rate of Interest	Money Demand	Rate of Interest	Investment	GDP	Savings
12%	$ 60	12%	$ 60	$300	$ 60
11	70	11	65	350	70
10	80	10	70	400	80
9	90	9	75	450	90
8	100	8	80	500	100
7	110	7	85	550	110
6	120	6	90	600	120
5	130	5	95	650	130
4	140	4	100	700	140

Assume that the money supply has been set at $100.

A) If the interest rate is 10 percent, would there be a surplus or shortage of money? How much?

B) What are the values of the equilibrium interest rate and level of GDP?

C) If the money supply was reduced to $80, what would the new equilibrium levels of interest and GDP be?

D) If the full-employment level of GDP is $500, what must the level of the money supply be to produce this?

6. If the price level increases, what effect will this have on interest rates, investment, and the aggregate quantity demanded?

You can appreciate from our analysis that the transmission process, according to Keynesians, is fairly indirect and subtle. Also, as we will see in a later chapter, Keynesians felt that the effect of a change in the money supply on the economy may not be very powerful. In contrast, monetarists feel that the effect of changes in the money market are far more direct and certainly more powerful. Let's take a look at this view.

Money Market Changes	transmit into		Product Market Changes
If P ↓ : ⟹ MD ↓ ⟹ r ↓	⟹	I ↑ ⟹ ↑ AE	or ↑ AD movement along the curve
If MS ↑ : ⟹ r ↓	⟹	I ↑ ⟹ ↑ AE	or ↑ AD shift in the curve

The Monetarist View

monetarism: an economic school of thought that believes that cyclical fluctuations of GDP and inflation are usually caused by changes in the money supply.

Monetarism refers to a school of thought popularized by the economist Milton Friedman. From the monetarist perspective, GDP determination can be summarized in a single equation referred to as the **equation of exchange**:

$$MV = PQ$$

The M is the supply of money that we have been discussing in this chapter. The V refers to the **velocity of money** (also called "velocity of circulation") and needs some explanation. If, for example, the GDP in a given year was $800 billion and the supply of money was $80 billion, the velocity would be ten. What this means is that every loonie, every $5 bill, and every $10 bill and so on changes hands, from person to person, ten times during the year. The velocity of money, therefore, is the rate at which the money supply turns over in generating income.

equation of exchange: a formula that states that the quantity of money times the velocity of money is equal to nominal GDP (price times real GDP).

The Q refers to the quantity of goods and services sold (real GDP), whereas the P is a composite (or index) of their prices.

Given this equation of exchange, we can see that:

$$M \times V$$

velocity of money (or circulation): the number of times per year that the average unit of currency is spent (or turns over) buying final goods or services.

is equal to nominal GDP.

We learned in Chapter 3, that the value of all goods sold is also the value of income generated by those transactions. Therefore:

$$(\text{nominal}) \ GDP = P \times Q \ (\text{real GDP})$$

It therefore follows that MV equals PQ, in that they both equal nominal GDP. In short, the two terms equal each other *by definition*.

ADDED DIMENSION

Milton Friedman: Mr. Monetarist

The 1976 Nobel Prize winner in economics, Milton Friedman, has had an enormous influence on modern economic thinking. As a lifetime professor at the University of Chicago, he is most famous for his work in the field of monetary policy. However, he has been influential in many other areas too, including his seminal work on the consumption function, the role of expectations, the idea of a negative income tax, and the concept of the natural rate of unemployment. Also, he has gained fame outside economics as a journalist for *Newsweek*, in a television documentary series, and as adviser to then presidential candidates Barry Goldwater and Richard Nixon. His book *Capitalism and Freedom* is an elegant presentation of his laissez faire views.

ADDED DIMENSION

The Velocity of Money

The velocity of money is often used to describe the number of times that money is actually used each year. If this is the case, the money would be used to finance all sorts of expenditures, including stock market transactions, second-hand sales, and all those other transactions that we do not include in GDP. Defining V this way results in the equation of exchange being

$$MV = PT$$

where V relates to the number of times money is used to finance *all transactions* and T is the number of transactions (not just those on GDP items).

We are more interested in looking at the effect of money changes on GDP rather than its effects on all transactions in an economy during a year. However, it is only a short step from one formulation to the other, since the level of GDP is usually closely related to the total of all transactions that take place.

In terms of what is the actual size of V in Canada, it very much depends on which definition of money is used. This is because the actual velocity cannot be directly measured but is obtained by dividing nominal GDP (P x Q) by the size of the money supply (M). If we use the narrow (M1) definition, empirical data shows that the value of V has increased steadily from approximately 7.5 in the early 1960s to over 17 in the early 1990s. Using the broader (M2) definition of money yields a value of V, which has remained a fairly constant 3 over the last 30 years.

Now that this basic equation has been established, we can explore some of its implications. For example, monetarists believe that one can treat V (the velocity of money) as a constant. Thus:

$$M\overline{V} \equiv PQ$$

(The line above V indicates that the term is a constant; the triple equality symbol means that this is an identity rather than just an equality.)

If this is true, then it immediately establishes the fact that any change in M will have an impact on the right side of the equation: on prices or on the quantity of goods, which, combined, we just saw, is the same thing as real GDP. That is, if M were to rise by 10 percent, then either the price level or quantity of goods and services produced, or a combination of the two, would also rise by the same 10 percent.

If we were to assume that the economy is currently at full-employment output, then Q would not be able to rise (at least not permanently), and any increase in M would have a direct and proportional impact on P—the price level. That is, if both V and Q are constant, then increases in M translate into inflation—pure and simple. Thus the phrase: "inflation is a monetary phenomenon."

We should also point out that monetarists believe that V is constant because they feel that individuals only demand money for transactions purposes; that is, there is no asset demand for money. For monetarists, it is irrational for anybody to hold "idle balances" of money for any purpose. They point out that there are a whole variety of financial instruments (bonds, term deposits, and so on) that are as safe and convenient as money but also provide the individual with an income. Therefore, if people find themselves with excess cash balances—because, for example, of a recent increase in the supply of money—they will divest themselves of these excess balances by purchasing either financial instruments or goods and services rather than hold those balances.

According to the monetarist position, an increase in the money supply would cause a big drop in interest rates and an increase in investment spending. It will also cause an increase in consumption on major consumer goods such as autos as people try to rid themselves of what they see as excess cash balances. If the economy was experiencing a recessionary gap, then this additional demand will raise the *real* GDP. If, however, the economy is already at full-employment equilibrium, then the increase will directly raise only *nominal* GDP by pushing up prices.

This is a different view of the demand for money and of the causes of inflation than the Keynesian view. It does bring the role of money more to centre stage, which can be helpful in our attempt to better understand inflation. As an example of this latter point, consider this true story, which is now more than 30 years old. This macroeconomics course was being taught by one of the authors in the soon-to-be-independent country of Malawi (south-central Africa). In the class was the nation's designated minister of finance, who, one day, stated that the people of Malawi were poor (which was quite true then and continues to be so today) because they didn't "have enough money." The answer to this poverty, it seemed to him, was for the new government, once it took power, to increase the supply of money by some significant amount—say, double it.

You will undoubtedly see the fallacy in this argument. This very small, very under-developed economy would not be able to significantly increase the output of goods and services simply as a result of doubling the money supply. It is also unlikely that the average Malawian would hold cash as an asset. Much more likely, any increase in the supply of money would be quickly spent.

So what would the end result of a doubling of the money supply be in these circumstances? You're right—a doubling of prices! The fastest, easiest way of explaining this end result is with the equation of exchange:

$$MV = PQ$$

In sum, monetarists argue that "money does count" when it comes to understanding macroeconomic phenomena.

To wrap things up, let's point out that both the Keynesians and monetarists agree that changes in the supply of money do have an effect on spending and therefore on aggregate demand. However, they disagree on how, such changes come about and the extent to which interest rates are affected. Similarly, they agree that changes in the demand for money influence spending but, again, disagree on exactly how these changes manifest themselves.

SELF-TEST

7. A) If M is $100, P is $2, and Q is 500, what is the value of the velocity of money?

B) Given the same parameters, if the velocity of money stays constant, and assuming the economy is at full employment, what will be the level of P if M increases to $120?

Chapter Highlights

The main purpose of this chapter is to show how changes in the money supply and demand have an important impact on the "real" variables in the economy, like investment and GDP.

The first significant concept is that, like other prices, the economy's interest rates are determined by the forces of supply and demand for money. It is noted that the supply is largely under the control of the Bank of Canada. Demand is discussed in some detail, and the main determinants of the demand for money are examined. Here the chapter notes that people often hold money as well as holding some other types of asset, such as bonds. The end of the section explains what is meant by the idea that people might have "too much" money.

After distinguishing between the transactions and asset demand for money, the chapter then brings together money supply and money demand, thereby identifying the equilibrium interest rate. From here it is a short step to the Keynesian view that for any given rate of interest there is one, and only one, level of equilibrium income. Next, the link between money and aggregate demand is explained. It discusses what is meant by the interest rate effect and how this effect helps to explain why the aggregate demand curve is downward-sloping. Finally, it shows how a change in the money supply shifts the aggregate demand curve and brings about changes in both the price level and real GDP.

The monetarist view, in contrast, sees changes in the money supply having a much more direct impact on real income, because monetarists deny the existence of the asset demand for money. They feel that changes in the quantity of money have a very direct impact on spending.

New Glossary Terms

asset demand for money   271
equation of exchange   282
investment demand   279
monetarism   282
transactions demand for money   271
transmission process   278
velocity of money   282

STUDY GUIDE

Study Tips

1. Once again, as in other chapters, it is very important not confuse the concepts of money and income. Money is a commodity, and like all commodities there are substitutes for it and there is a price attached to its ownership. The price of money, as we point out in this chapter, is the rate of interest. When we talk about the demand for the stock of money, we are not thinking of the flow of income. So try to think of money as something that can be bought and sold like any other commodity.

2. Perhaps you can get a good handle on the idea of what drives the transactions demand for money by realizing how it changes over the years. Thirty-five years ago, when one of the authors was still at school, he needed only $100 in cash to make normal day-to-day purchases for the whole month. These days, he finds himself having to take out twice that amount just to last through a single week. Although he is somewhat richer, the main reason for his increased demand for money is the increase in prices of goods and services that has occurred over the years. Inflation, by itself, will cause the demand for money to increase, though it will also increase, of course, as both individuals and countries get richer in real terms.

3. Don't at this stage be overly concerned about how the Bank of Canada controls the money supply and how it is able to increase or decrease it. This will come in Chapter 12. For now, just concentrate on the effects of such changes.

4. The relationship between interest rates and bond prices is not particularly complicated. Allowing for differences in risks and terms, the rates of return (the interest rate) on various bonds tend to be very similar. Let's say you earn $5 a year on a bond that sells for $50. This is the same return (10 percent) as earning $2 on a bond selling for $20. What if it were possible to earn $5 on some other bond worth $20? Now, that is a return of 25 percent a year. Everyone would be clamouring to purchase these bonds. And what would happen to their price? It would increase and continue to increase until the return is the same as on all other similar securities. When it got to a price of $50, it is no more or less attractive than other bonds. As the price of a bond rises, the interest earned by the bond holder declines.

Key Problem

The economy of Everton is closed to international trade and has no government involvement. The supply of money is $90 (in billions), the transactions demand is equal to 20 percent of GDP. The asset demand is shown in **Table 8.1**.

TABLE 8.1

Rate of Interest	Asset Demand
6%	$80
7	70
8	60
9	50
10	40
11	30
12	20
13	10

Table 8.2 shows Everton's investment demand.

TABLE 8.2

Rate of Interest	Investment Spending
6%	$80
7	75
8	70
9	65
10	60
11	55
12	50
13	45

Finally, **Table 8.3** shows the savings function for Everton.

TABLE 8.3

GDP	Savings
$100	$45
150	50
200	55
250	60
300	65
350	70
400	75
450	80

a) If Everton's GDP is $350 and its interest rate is 11 percent, will there be a surplus or shortage of money? Will there be a surplus or shortage of goods and services?

Surplus/shortage: _____ of $_____ of money.

Surplus/shortage: _____ of $_____ of goods and services.

b) What must be the values of GDP and interest rate in Everton if both its product and money markets are going to be in equilibrium?

GDP: $_____ and interest rate: _____ %.

c) What is the total demand for money at equilibrium?

Total demand for money: $_____ .

d) What will happen to the equilibrium values of money and GDP if the money supply is increased to $110?

GDP: $_____ and interest rate: _____ %.

e) In summary, what effects does an increase in the money supply have on the following variables? (Indicate with ↑ for increase and ↓ for decrease.)

Interest rate: _____ ; investment _____ ; GDP: _____ .

More of the Same

The economy of Ajax is closed to international trade and has no government involvement. The supply of money is $50 (in billions), the transactions demand is equal to 10 percent of GDP. The asset demand is shown in **Table 8.4**.

TABLE 8.4

Rate of Interest	Asset Demand
3%	$28
4	26
5	24
6	22
7	20
8	18
9	16

Table 8.5 shows Ajax's investment demand.

TABLE 8.5

Rate of Interest	Investment Spending
3%	$82
4	78
5	74
6	70
7	66
8	62
9	58

Finally, **Table 8. 6** shows the savings function for Ajax.

TABLE 8.6

GDP	Savings
$220	$58
240	62
260	66
280	70
300	74
320	78
340	82
360	86
380	90

a) If Ajax's GDP is $300 and its interest rate is 9 percent, will there be a surplus or shortage of money? Will there be a surplus or shortage of goods and services?

b) If Ajax's GDP is $260 and its interest rate is 4 percent, will there be a surplus or shortage of money? Will there be a surplus or shortage of goods and services?

c) What must be the values of GDP and the interest rate in Ajax if both its product and money markets are in equilibrium?

d) What will happen to the equilibrium values of the interest rate and GDP if the money supply is decreased to $42?

e) What is the effect of a decrease in the money supply on the interest rate, investment, and GDP?

Translations

The money demand for the economy of Notlob is shown in **Figure 8.7**. As the money supply is increased (several different times), explain how the shape of the money demand curve affects the results.

FIGURE 8.7

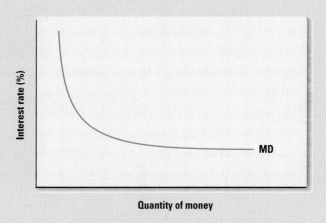

Quantity of money

_____

_____

Are You Sure?

Indicate whether the following statements are true or false. If false, indicate why they are false.

1. The transactions demand for money is determined by how much money people need.

    T or **F**   If false: _____

    _____

2. The quantity of asset demand for money that people wish to hold increases as the rate of interest falls.

    T or **F**   If false: _____

    _____

3. The interest rate is determined by savings and investment.

   T or F   If false: _____

   _____

4. An interest rate above equilibrium will lead to a surplus of money.

   T or F   If false: _____

   _____

5. If there is a shortage of money in the economy, the Bank of Canada will increase the amount supplied.

   T or F   If false: _____

   _____

6. An increase in real GDP will cause an increase in interest rates.

   T or F   If false: _____

   _____

7. The Keynesian transmission process refers to the way in which changes in interest rates affect the demand for bonds and their prices.

   T or F   If false: _____

   _____

8. An increase in the money supply, according to Keynes, will cause investment and real GDP to increase.

   T or F   If false: _____

   _____

9. The velocity of money refers to the number of times a particular product is bought and sold in the period of a year.

   T or F   If false: _____

   _____

10. The equation of exchange is: $MV = PQ$.

    T or F   If false: _____

    _____

Choose the Best

11. The supply of money is determined by:
    a) The Bank of Canada.
    b) The interest rate.

12. The demand for money is:
    a) The same as the demand for income.
    b) Made up of the transactions demand and asset demand.

13. What is the effect of an increase in the money supply?
    a) It will lower the interest rate.
    b) It will increase the interest rate.

14. The transactions demand is most closely related with which function of money?
    a) Unit of account.
    b) Medium of exchange.
    c) Store of wealth.

15. The quantity of asset money demanded:
    a) Varies directly with nominal GDP.
    b) Varies indirectly with nominal GDP.
    c) Varies indirectly with the interest rate.

16. In which of the following cases would the quantity of money demanded be the greatest?
    a) When the nominal GDP is $200 billion and the interest rate is 6 percent.

b) When the nominal GDP is $100 billion and the interest rate is 6 percent.
c) When the nominal GDP is $100 billion and the interest rate is 8 percent.

17. What can cause the demand for money curve to shift to the left?
a) If nominal GDP increases.
b) If the interest rate increases.
c) If the price level decreases.

Table 8.7 contains data relating to the money market.

TABLE 8.7

Rate of Interest (%)	Asset Demand for Money ($)	Transactions Demand for Money ($)	Total Demand for Money ($)
4	100	70	_____
5	90	70	_____
6	80	70	_____
7	70	70	_____
8	60	70	_____

18. Refer to Table 8.7 to answer this question. If the supply of money is $150, what is the value of the equilibrium interest rate?
a) 4 percent.
b) 5 percent.
c) 6 percent.
d) 7 percent.

19. Refer to Table 8.7 to answer this question. What are the implications if the current supply of money is $160 and the interest rate is 7 percent?
a) The interest rate will fall.
b) The interest rate will rise.
c) The asset demand will fall.
d) The transactions demand will fall.

20. How does the interest rate effect help explain why the aggregate demand curve is downward-sloping?
a) Because it suggests that a lower price level causes a higher interest rate and therefore a lower level of aggregate expenditures.
b) Because it suggests that a lower interest rate causes a higher price level and therefore a lower level of aggregate expenditures.
c) Because it suggests that a lower price level causes a lower interest rate and therefore a higher level of aggregate expenditures.
d) Because it suggests that a lower interest rate causes a lower price level and therefore a higher level of aggregate expenditures.

21. What is the effect of an increase in the money supply?
a) It causes the aggregate demand curve to shift right.
b) It causes the aggregate demand curve to shift left.
c) It causes a movement down the aggregate demand curve.
d) It causes a movement up the aggregate demand curve.

22. In the equation MV = PQ, what does the Q stand for?
a) The quantity of goods and services sold.
b) The quantity of investment.
c) The quantity of money in circulation.
d) The quantity of aggregate demand.

23. Suppose that in a particular economy, M = 200, P = 2, Q = 500, and V = 5. What is the value of nominal GDP?
a) 200.
b) 400.
c) 500.
d) 1000.

Refer to **Figure 8.8** to answer questions 24, 25, and 26.

FIGURE 8.8

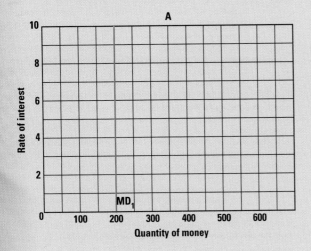

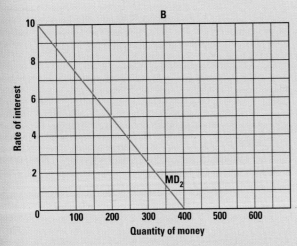

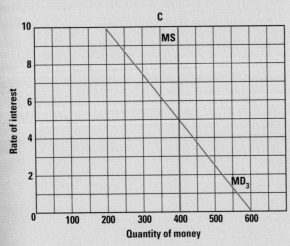

24. Refer to Figure 8.8. How would people react if the interest rate was 3 percent?
    a) They would sell bonds, which would cause bond prices to fall and the interest rate to rise.
    b) They would buy bonds, which would cause bond prices to fall and the interest rate to rise.
    c) They would sell bonds, which would cause bond prices to rise and the interest rate to rise.
    d) They would buy bonds, which would cause bond prices to rise but have an uncertain effect on the interest rate.

25. In Figure 8.8, what does curve MD_2 represent?
    a) The asset demand for money.
    b) The transactions demand for money.
    c) The investment demand.
    d) The stock of money.
    e) The total demand for money.

26. Refer to Figure 8.8 to answer this question. Suppose that the economy is in equilibrium and each dollar held for transaction purposes is spent, on average, five times per year. What can we infer from this?
    a) That nominal GDP is $1000.
    b) That real GDP is $1200.
    c) That the money supply is $1000.
    d) That nominal GDP is $400.
    e) None of the above can be inferred.

27. According to the Keynesian transmission process, what will be the effect of an increase in the money supply?
    a) An increase in the interest rate, an increase in investment spending, and an increase in GDP.
    b) An increase in the interest rate, an increase in investment spending, and a decrease in GDP.
    c) An increase in the interest rate, a decrease in investment spending, and a decrease in GDP.
    d) A decrease in the interest rate, an increase in investment spending, and an increase in GDP.
    e) A decrease in the interest rate, a decrease in investment spending, and a decrease in GDP.

Refer to **Figure 8.9** to answer questions 28, 29, and 30.

FIGURE 8.9

A

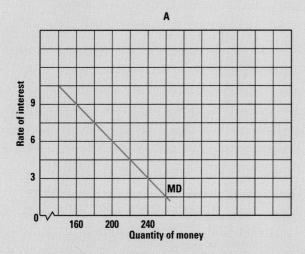

B

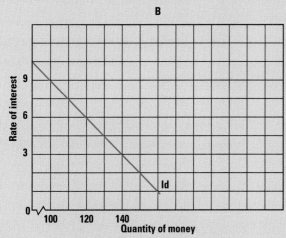

C

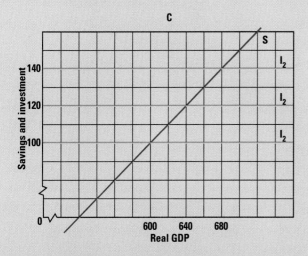

28. Refer to Figure 8.9 to answer this question. What will be the effect of an increase in the supply of money from 160 to 200?
    a) An increase of 1 percentage point in the interest rate.
    b) A decrease in the transactions demand for money.
    c) A decrease of 40 in investment spending.
    d) A decrease in aggregate expenditures.
    e) An increase of 40 in real GDP.

29. Refer to Figure 8.9 to answer this question. What is the value of the multiplier?
    a) 1.
    b) 2.
    c) 20.
    d) 40.
    e) Cannot be determined from this information.

30. Refer to Figure 8.9 to answer this question. Suppose that the equilibrium interest rate is 6 percent. What fraction of real GDP does the transactions demand represent?
    a) 6 percent.
    b) 10 percent.
    c) 12.5 percent.
    d) 20 percent.
    e) Cannot be determined from this information.

Other Problems

31. The economy of Albion is closed to international trade and has no government intervention. In addition, its transactions demand for money remains constant, whatever the level of GDP. Its economy is depicted in the graphs in **Figure 8.10** (all money figures are in billions.)

   a) If the money supply is equal to $50, what is the level of equilibrium GDP?

   Equilibrium GDP: $_____.

FIGURE 8.10

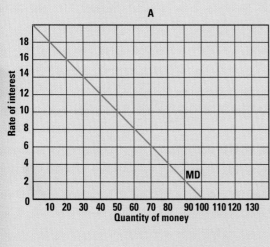

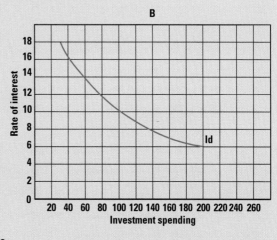

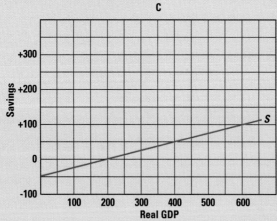

   b) Suppose instead that the money supply is $25. What is the level of equilibrium GDP?

   GDP: $_____.

   c) Suppose the full-employment level of GDP is $520. What should the money supply be to produce this level of GDP? What is the level of investment spending?

   Money supply: $_____ ; investment: $_____.

32. Show, in the series of diagrams **Figure 8.11**A–D, how an increase in the money supply from the present MS_1 to a higher level MS_2 will affect investment, real GDP, and the price level. Carefully label each new curve and each new equilibrium point.

FIGURE 8.11

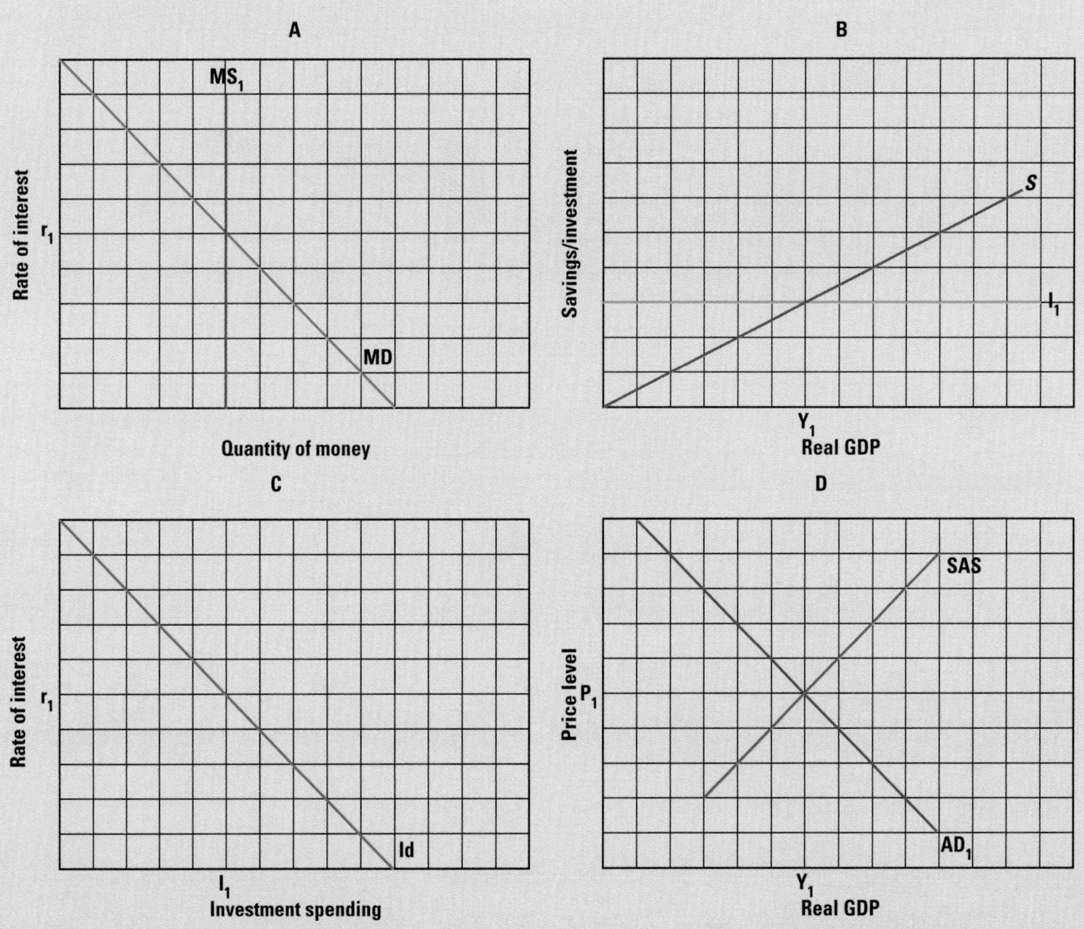

A — Rate of interest / Quantity of money; MS_1, r_1, MD

B — Savings/investment / Real GDP; S, I_1, Y_1

C — Rate of interest / Investment spending; r_1, Id, I_1

D — Price level / Real GDP; SAS, P_1, AD_1, Y_1

Summarize the changes to the following in terms of ↑ (increase) or ↓ (decrease):

Interest rate: _____ ; real GDP : _____ ; price level: _____.

33. Show, in the series of diagrams **Figure 8.12** A–D, how an increase in the price level will impact on investment and real GDP. Carefully label each new curve and each new equilibrium point.
Summarize in terms of ↑ (increase) or ↓ (decrease) what happened to the following:

Interest rate: _____ ; real GDP : _____.

FIGURE 8.12

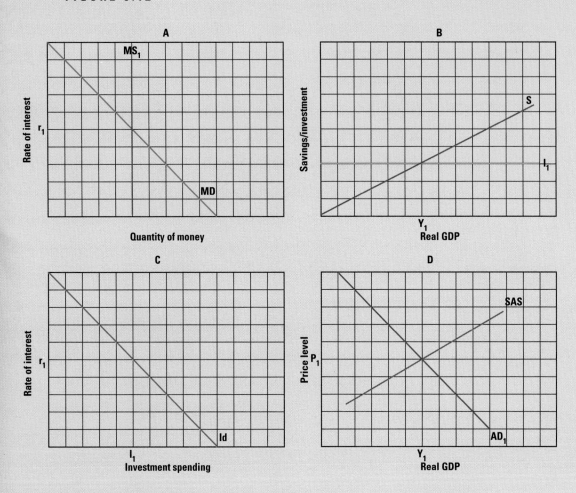

34. In the country of Juventus, the money supply is equal to 40 (billion), the velocity of circulation is 5, and real GDP is 100 (billion).

a) What is the price level in Juventus, and what is the value of its nominal GDP?

Price level: _____ ; nominal GDP: _____.

b) If the money supply were to increase by 20 percent, what would be the new values of the price level and nominal GDP, assuming that V and real GDP remain constant?

Price level: _____ ; nominal GDP: _____.

c) What does this suggest about the connection between the money supply and the price level?

_____

UNANSWERED QUESTIONS

Short Essays

1. Explain what factors would cause the interest rate to rise.

2. What could cause a shortage of money? How is this shortage eliminated?

3. Explain the relationship between the interest rate and the asset demand for money.

4. Explain how a change in the price level can affect interest rates and aggregate demand.

5. Explain how a change in the money supply affects aggregate demand.

6. Explain the equation of exchange and how a change in the money supply can affect the economy.

Analytical Questions

7. Explain why (or why not) each of the following will cause an increase in the transactions demand for money: a) an increase in the price level; b) an increase in real income; c) an increase in nominal income; d) an increase in both the price level and nominal income by the same percentage.

8. What would happen to the aggregate demand curve if both prices and money income increased by the same proportion?

9. What happens to the level of equilibrium income if the investment demand curve and demand for money curve shift right, at the same time?

10. The story about the Malawian student in the chapter made it clear that if the money supply is increased too quickly, severe inflation can result. So why increase it at all?

11. In the the mid-1990s, interest rates dropped to levels not seen in the previous 25 years. What would Keynesians expect the asset demand for money to be at this point? What would monetarists expect?

12. Using the equation of exchange, explain what could cause an increase in the demand for money, according to monetarists.

13. In what ways, if any, will the increased use of credit and debit cards have an impact on the demand for money? Will they affect the supply of money?

Numerical Questions

14. Suppose that in a particular economy, M = 50, P = 1, Q = 500, and V = 10. What is the value of nominal GDP? Assuming that V is constant and real GDP increases by 10 percent, what must happen to the money supply in order to keep prices stable?

15. Given the parameters in question 14 and assuming that V is stable, draw an aggregate demand curve, labelled AD_1, with prices of 0.8, 0.9, 1, 1.1, and, 1.2. Now draw AD_2, AD_3, and AD_4 on the basis of a 10 percent increase, a 20 percent increase, and a 30 percent decrease in the money supply respectively.

16. Table 8.8 shows actual data for the Canadian economy for the period 1993–97 (all money figures in $ billion). For each year, calculate the velocity of money. (Hint: You may need to rearrange the equation of exchange and divide by 100.)

TABLE 8.8

Year	M1	Price Level (1992 = 100)	Real GDP (GDP at 1992 price level)
1993	48.3	101.2	716
1994	54.2	102.4	744
1995	57.1	105.1	760
1996	63.1	106.6	770
1997	73.5	107.1	798

What happened to the value of the velocity of money over the five years?

17. The economy of Boca is closed to international trade and has no government intervention. In addition, its transactions demand for money remains constant, whatever the level of GDP. The supply of money is $60. Its economy is depicted in Figure 8.13 (all money figures are in billions).

FIGURE 8.13

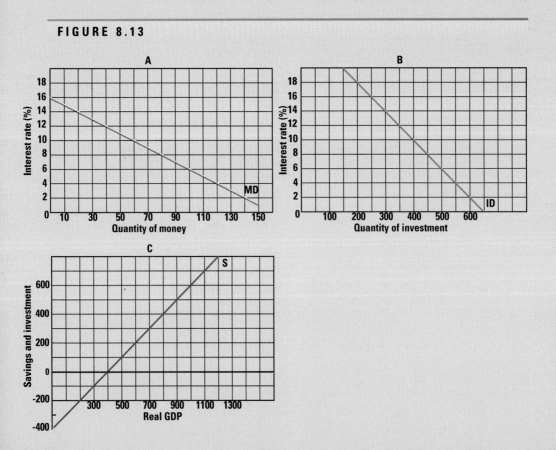

a) What is the equilibrium interest rate and level of GDP in Boca?

b) Suppose that the interest rate is 6 percent and GDP is 700. Is there a surplus or a shortage of money? How much? Is there a surplus or shortage of goods and services? How much?

18. Suppose that the economy of Celtic, depicted in **Table 8.9**, is a closed, private (no government) economy. In addition, there is no transactions demand for money in Celtic.

TABLE 8.9

Rate of Interest	Money Demand	Rate of Interest	Investment	GDP	Savings
12%	$ 60	12%	$ 60	$300	$ 60
11	70	11	65	350	70
10	80	10	70	400	80
9	90	9	75	450	90
8	100	8	80	500	100
7	110	7	85	550	110
6	120	6	90	600	120
5	130	5	95	650	130
4	140	4	100	700	140

Assume that the money supply has been set at $100.

a) If the interest rate is 10 percent, would there be a surplus or shortage of money? Of how much?

b) If the interest rate is 10 percent, and GDP is $500, would there be a surplus or shortage of goods and services? Of how much?

c) What are the equilibrium values of GDP and interest rate?

d) If the money supply was reduced to $80, what would be the new equilibrium values of GDP and interest rate?

e) If the full-employment level of GDP is $500, what must be the level of the money supply to produce this?

19. The economy of Aston has the data shown in **Table 8.10**.

TABLE 8.10

Rate of Interest	Total Money Demand	Investment Demand
10%	$200	$10
9	250	15
8	300	20
7	350	25
6	400	30

a) If the money supply in Aston is equal to $300 and the transactions demand does not vary with income levels, what is the equilibrium interest rate?

b) Given your answer to a), what will be the level of investment in the economy? Next consider the savings function for Aston in **Table 8.11**.

TABLE 8.11

GDP	Saving
$600	$10
650	20
700	30
750	40

c) Assuming there is no government intervention in Aston, which is a closed economy, what will be the level of equilibrium GDP?

d) If the money supply decreases to $200, what will be the new equilibrium interest rate and GDP?

e) Assume that the full-employment level of GDP in Aston is $700. What supply of money is necessary to achieve this?

 Web-Based Activities

1. Go to **http://www.bank-banque-canada.ca/english/spherm.htm.** According to this speech, how do changes in the money market impact the economy?

2. Read **http://www.cato.org/pubs/books/money/money15.htm** and answer the following questions. How will financial innovation affect the demand for money? Given the impact on money demand, how will these changes in the money market affect the economy? Explain.

International Trade

What's ahead...We start by looking at the reasons why individuals and countries trade with each other, and discover that the reason in both cases is differences in endowment: some are endowed with attributes not available to others but often lack things possessed by others. These differences lead to the cost advantages over others that some producers enjoy and is at the heart of Ricardo's theory of comparative advantage, which we investigate in the first part of the chapter. We then look at the concept of the terms of trade and show how this determines who gets what share of the increased production that results from trade. The chapter then looks at some of the arguments against free trade and ends with an investigation of how and why trade has often been restricted and impeded.

Have you looked at the little tag on your jeans lately? Were they made in Canada? What about your camera? Your fishing rod? Your tennis racket? Your CD player? Does it concern you that they all might well have been made abroad? It probably won't come as a surprise to you that Canada imports approximately a quarter of all its products. Is this good for the country? Surely it would be in Canada's interest to produce its own goods. Or would it? This chapter looks at the question of whether Canada is better or worse off as a result of international trade.

P eople have traded in one form or another since the dawn of time, and most of the great powers in history have also been famous traders: the Phoenicians and the Greeks; medieval Venice and Elizabethan England; the early American colonies and modern Japan. It seems obvious that great benefits are obtained from trading, but there has always been the underlying suspicion that someone also loses as a result. For many, a great trading nation is one that consistently, and through shrewd practice, always manages to come out on top during trade negotiations. This "beggar thy neighbour" attitude was the cause of no great concern for writers immediately preceding Adam Smith, who thought it was part of the natural state of affairs that there are always winners and losers in trade. It was the job of policy-makers, they felt, to ensure that their own country was always on the winning side.

It took the mind of Adam Smith, however, to see that whenever two people enter into a voluntary agreement to trade, both parties must gain as a result. If you trade a textbook in exchange for your friend's new Guns 'n Butter CD, you obviously want that CD more than the textbook, and your friend must want the textbook more than the CD. Trade is to the advantage of both of you, otherwise it would not take place. When we look at international trade between nations, all we are doing is simply looking at this single transaction multiplied a billionfold. It is not really nations who trade, but individual people and firms who buy from other foreign individuals and firms. In many ways the reason you trade with a friend is the same reason you buy products from a Toronto brewery or Winnipeg car dealer or Tokyo fishing rod manufacturer: you hope to gain something as a result, and what you give up in return (usually money) is of less value to you than the thing you obtain in return.

All of which raises the question of why you personally (or a whole nation for that matter) would want to buy something rather than make it at home. In other words, why are people not self-sufficient? Why do they not produce everything that they personally consume? Well, Adam Smith had an answer for this (as for most things):

> It is the maxim of every prudent master of a family, never to make at home what it will cost him more to make than to buy.[1]

There, in essence, is the main argument for trade: why make something yourself if you can buy it cheaper elsewhere? If it takes Akio three hours to make a certain product but he can buy it elsewhere from the income he gets from one hour's work in his regular job, then why would he bother? It would pay him to do his own job for three hours; he could afford to buy three units of the product. An additional consideration is the fact that there are many things that Akio is incapable of making (actually, most things), or that he could make only after extensive training and with the help of very expensive equipment.

Specialization and Trade

Specialization is the cornerstone of trade. As we have seen in earlier chapters, big advantages can be gained from specialization. From an individual's point of view, each of us is better suited to one thing than to another. Rather than trying to grow all our own food, make our own clothes, brew our own beer, and so on, it makes more sense to specialize in our chosen occupation and with the proceeds to obtain things that

---

[1] Adam Smith, *Wealth of Nations* (Edwin Cannan edition, 1877), p. 354.

other people can make better and cheaper. Similarly, firms will be far more productive if they specialize in the production process, that is, make use of the division of labour. As we shall see in this chapter, there are also great benefits to be enjoyed by countries that specialize rather than try to be self-sufficient.

It follows that the result of more specialization is more trading. Specialization and trade go hand in hand. Modern nations, firms, and individuals have become increasingly specialized, and with this has come a huge increase in the volume of trade, domestically and internationally. But is there a limit to specialization? From a technical point of view, Smith thought not; but he did believe that specialization would be limited by the size of the market. The smaller the market, the less output and therefore the less opportunity or need for extensive specialization. The bigger the size of the market, the more specialization that can take place and the lower will be the cost of producing goods. The prime driving force behind the expansion of markets is that it enables firms to produce in higher volumes and at a lower cost. All things being equal (including demand), it is the cost of production and therefore the price of the product that induces trade. If you can produce a product cheaper than I can, then it will make no sense for me to try to produce it myself. And why are you able to produce certain products cheaper than I can? The answer presumably is that you possess certain advantages over me. Let us look at these advantages.

ADDED DIMENSION

Canada, the Great Trader

Canada is certainly one of the world's great trading nations, at least in relative terms. In 1997, for example, Canada exported $343 billion worth of goods and services and imported $327 billion from abroad. Since the GDP of the country in that year was $855 billion, exports and imports represented nearly 40 percent of this amount. Only a few countries, such as Germany and the Netherlands, trade a larger fraction. The United States and Japan, in comparison, trade only about 10 percent of their GDPs (though, of course, in actual dollars this represents a lot more). In terms of Canada's trading partners, the United States is far more dominant than all other countries combined (buying approximately 80 percent of our exports). In fact, Canada sells three times as much to the United States as it does to all other countries combined and buys approximately 76 percent of all its merchandise from that country.

Factor Endowment

One person has an advantage in production over others if he or she is endowed with certain natural or acquired skills or has more or better equipment or other resources. Just as there are many explanations of why some people are better gardeners or truck drivers or hockey players than others, so too it is with countries. A country will have a great advantage in producing and trading pineapples, for instance, if it possesses the right type of soil and climate. But the same country may well be at a disadvantage in growing coniferous trees. Another country has an advantage in producing electronic equipment if it has the right capital, the technical expertise, and a well-educated labour force. It may not, however, be able to compete with other countries in raising sheep. All people are different. Although some are graced with certain advantages over others, they are often handicapped in other areas. So too with countries; they are well endowed in certain areas, they are impoverished in others. Japan has a well-educated and motivated work force, possesses great technical expertise, and is highly capitalized, yet it is very poorly provided with arable land and possesses very few mineral resources.

It is often suggested that the prime reason a country trades is in order to buy resources that it does not naturally possess. Although there is some truth in this, it often obscures the main motivation. Canada, for instance, is not endowed with a warm and sunny climate throughout the year and is unable to produce bananas commercially. However, through the use of geodesic domes with artificial light and heating, it could grow its own bananas, but the cost would be enormous. The reason it does not grow bananas is not because it cannot, but because it is cheaper to buy them from countries that possess the necessary resources at lower cost. Most countries, then, can often overcome a resource deficiency by using different methods or other resources, but it would not make sense if this production method results in more expensive products than those obtainable from abroad.

Theory of Absolute Advantage

A country will tend to gravitate to producing in those areas where, because of its own factor endowments, it possesses a cost advantage over other producing countries: Canada produces wheat, lumber and minerals; Colombia produces coffee; Malaysia produces rubber; Japan produces electronic equipment, and so on. This is no more or less than what Adam Smith proposed when he put forward his *theory of absolute advantage.* Nations, like firms and individuals, should specialize in producing goods and services for which they have an advantage, and they should trade with other countries for goods and services in which they do not enjoy an advantage. Let us work through a simple example of this theory. We will concentrate on just two countries and suppose that they produce just two products. We will assume that the average cost of producing each product remains constant. In addition, to begin with, we will further assume that each country is self-sufficient and that no trade is taking place. **Table 9.1** shows the productivity per worker (average product) of producing wheat and beans in Canada and Mexico.

TABLE 9.1 Output per Worker by Country and Industry

	NUMBER OF BUSHELS PER DAY	
	Wheat	**Beans**
Canada	3	2
Mexico	1	4

We can see at a glance in Table 9.1 that Canada is more productive than Mexico at producing wheat, whereas Mexico is more productive than Canada at producing beans. Let us examine the possibility of gains if both countries were to specialize— Canada in wheat and Mexico in beans. Since the table shows output per worker, let's move a single worker in Canada out of the bean industry and over to the wheat industry. In Mexico, the transfer is in the opposite direction: one worker goes from the wheat industry to the bean industry. Table 9.1 has already shown us what each country will gain and what it will lose. Canada would gain an additional 3 bushels of wheat, since that is the average productivity in that industry, but lose 2 bushels of beans. In Mexico, the gain would be 4 bushels of beans at a loss of 1 bushel of wheat. (To keep things simple here, we are assuming that the average and marginal products are equal; that is, each worker in Canada, for instance, produces three bushels of wheat regardless of the number of workers employed.) The movement of workers is summarized in **Table 9.2.**

TABLE 9.2 Gain/Loss of Output

	NUMBER OF BUSHELS PER DAY	
	Wheat	**Beans**
Canada	+3	−2
Mexico	−1	+4
Total	+2	+2

It is possible, then, with just the transfer of one worker in each country, for there to be a net increase in the production of both products. These are what are known as the *gains from trade.* Strictly speaking, they are the gains from specialization. It would seem to be the case from this example that if more workers were to shift industries in this manner, then the gain would be commensurately higher. Presumably, the greater the specialization, the bigger the gains. Note that if a country is not to end up consuming just a single product, it will be forced to trade.

SELF-TEST

1. Suppose that the productivity per worker in the beer and wine industries of Freedonia and Libraland are as follows:

	Output in Hundreds of Litres	
	Beer	**Wine**
Freedonia	4	1
Libraland	3	4

A) Which country should specialize in which product?
B) Suppose that a single worker in each country is transferred from the less- to the more-productive industry. What will the total gains from specialization be?

Theory of Comparative Advantage

The eminent economist David Ricardo, following in the footsteps of Adam Smith, agreed in principle with his mentor and added a subtle but important refinement to Smith's theory of trade. To see the effect of his modification, let's change our example to that of theoretical trade between the United States and the Philippines, but keep the same two products, wheat and beans. The output per worker in each country is shown in **Table 9.3.**

TABLE 9.3 Output per Worker by Country and Industry

	NUMBER OF BUSHELS PER DAY	
	Wheat	**Beans**
United States	6	4
Philippines	1	2

If we compare the United States' productivity in wheat, you can see from the table that it is six times as great as that of the Philippines; similarly, the United States is twice as productive as the Philippines in producing beans. If we were to follow Smith's dictum, then presumably the United States should produce both products itself. After all, how can it possibly be of any advantage to that country to trade with the Philippines, since it could produce both products cheaper? The heart of Ricardo's idea is that it is not *absolute* but **comparative advantage** that provides the mutual gains from trade. Let us see exactly what this means, through an example.

Suppose you happened to be the absolutely best lawyer in town. Not only that, but you are also its greatest secretary. Given this, why would you bother to hire a secretary to do your clerical work, since you are faster and, by all measurement, more efficient than anyone you could possibly hire? The answer is that you would still hire a secretary because you couldn't afford not to. The reason for this is that you are so productive. Your high productivity is both a blessing and a curse. It is a blessing because you earn a great deal as a lawyer; it is a curse because you sacrifice a great deal in not being a secretary. In other words, your opportunity cost of being a lawyer is the lost salary of not being a secretary. Your opportunity cost of being a secretary is your lost earnings as a lawyer. But because you can earn *comparatively* more as a lawyer than as a secretary, you would be advised to concentrate on that career and hire someone (admittedly less productive than yourself) to act as your secretary.

What Ricardo did with his idea of comparative advantage was, in a sense, to direct attention away from making comparisons between countries and instead focus attention on the comparison between products. In Table 9.3, for instance, what is the cost for the United States of producing wheat? One way to answer this would be to express it in dollars and cents. Knowing that the value of money varies over time and that it is often misleading to translate one currency into another, Ricardo was at pains to express costs in more fundamental terms. One way of doing this would be to express costs in terms of the number of hours it takes to produce something. For instance, if in our example the average worker in the United States can produce 4 bushels of beans in an average 8-hour day, then the cost of 1 bushel of beans would be 8/4, or 2 hours. In contrast, the cost of one bushel of beans in the Philippines would be 8/2, or 4 hours. So, it is twice as expensive in the Philippines. However, a better and more illuminating way of measuring costs is in terms of opportunity costs. This is the method Ricardo chose.

You will remember that the opportunity cost of producing one thing can be measured in terms of another thing that has to be sacrificed in order to get it. As far as the United States and the Philippines are concerned, the cost of producing more wheat is the sacrifice of beans, and the cost of increased bean production is the loss of wheat. Let us work out these costs for each country. The cost of employing a worker in the wheat industry is what that worker could have produced in the bean industry, assuming that the country is fully employed. In other words, for every 6 bushels of wheat that an American worker produces, the country sacrifices 4 bushels of beans. In per unit

comparative advantage: the advantage that comes from producing something at a lower opportunity cost than others are able to do.

terms, since 6 bushels of wheat costs 4 bushels of beans, then 1 wheat costs 4/6 or 0.67 beans. Likewise, since the production of 4 bushels of beans costs 6 bushels of wheat, then 1 bean costs 6/4 or 1.5 wheat. In the Philippines, the cost of 1 wheat is 2 beans and the cost of 1 bean equals 1/2 wheat. Let us summarize these figures in **Table 9.4.**

TABLE 9.4 Opportunity Costs of Production

	COST OF PRODUCING ONE UNIT	
	Wheat	**Beans**
United States	0.67 beans	1.5 wheat
Philippines	2 beans	0.5 wheat

Hopefully, you can now understand the significance of comparative costs. Whether you measure the costs in hours or dollars, beans are very cheap to produce in the United States. But in comparative terms they are very *expensive*. Why is that? Because to produce beans, the United States has to make a big sacrifice in the product in which it is even more productive: wheat. Similarly, although beans in absolute terms are very expensive in the Philippines, in comparative terms they are cheap, since to produce them the Philippines doesn't have to make much sacrifice in wheat production because productivity in the wheat industry is so low.

In this example then, as Table 9.4 suggests, the United States should specialize in producing the product in which it has the comparative advantage, wheat; and the Philippines should specialize in beans, where it has the comparative advantage.

Let us extract some further insights by showing the production possibilities of the two countries on the assumption that the size of the labour force in the United States is 100 million, that of the Philippines is 80 million, and that unit costs are constant. Their respective production possibilities are shown in **Table 9.5.**

TABLE 9.5 Production Possibilities

	UNITED STATES: OUTPUT (millions of bushels per day)				
	A	B	C	D	E
Wheat	600	450	300	150	0
Beans	0	100	200	300	400

	PHILIPPINES: OUTPUT (millions of bushels per day)				
	A	B	C	D	E
Wheat	80	60	40	20	0
Beans	0	40	80	120	160

Suppose that initially the countries are self-sufficient and that both are producing combinations B. Before specialization and trade, therefore, their joint totals are as shown in **Table 9.6.**

TABLE 9.6 Output before Specialization and Trade

	TOTAL OUTPUT (millions of bushels per day)	
	Wheat	**Beans**
United States	450	100
Philippines	60	40
Total	510	140

If the two countries now specialize, the U.S. producing wheat and the Philippines producing beans, their output levels would be as shown in **Table 9.7**.

TABLE 9.7 Output after Specialization and Trade

	TOTAL OUTPUT (millions of bushels per day)	
	Wheat	**Beans**
United States	600	0
Philippines	0	160
Total	600	160

You can see by comparing the before and after positions that production of both products is now higher. **Table 9.8** outlines the gains from trade.

TABLE 9.8 Gains from Specialization and Trade

TOTAL OUTPUT (millions of bushels per day)	
Wheat	**Beans**
+90	+20

Before we try to figure out which country will get what portion of this increased production, let us look at the production possibilities graphically. **Figure 9.1** shows the production possibilities of each country on the same graph.

As we saw in Chapter 1, the slope of the production curve measures the cost of production. In Figure 9.1 this is the cost of beans measured in wheat. The slope of the U.S. production possibilities curve is 3/2, reflecting the fact that beans are relatively expensive at 1.5 wheat per unit of beans. The Philippines' production possibilities curve, in contrast, is much flatter. Its slope is 1/2, which means, as we have seen, that the cost of beans is only 0.5 wheat per unit of beans.

FIGURE 9.1 U.S. and Philippines' Production Possibilities Curves

The slope of the production possibilities curve measures the average cost of production of the product shown on the horizontal axis, beans. In this figure, the slope of the U.S. production possibilities curve is equal to 3/2 (wheat production drops by 3 for every increase of 2 beans); that is, the cost of 1 bean in the U.S. is $1\frac{1}{2}$ wheat. In contrast, the cost of beans in the Philippines is cheap because it sacrifices only $\frac{1}{2}$ wheat for each 1 bean produced; that is, the slope of the Philippines' production possibilities curve is $\frac{1}{2}$.

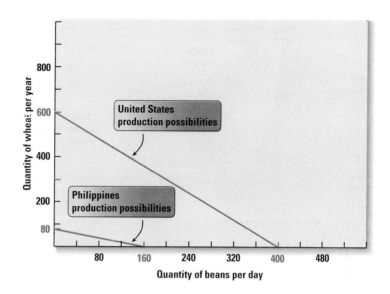

---

2. Suppose that the labour force in Freedonia is 10 million, of whom 6 million are producing apples, one of the two crops it produces; the other is pears. In contrast, Libraland's labour force is 16 million, half of whom are producing apples, and the rest, pears. The labour productivity in the two countries is as follows:

	Output per Worker (bushels per day)	
	Apples	**Pears**
Freedonia	5	2
Libraland	1	3

Assuming constant costs, draw the production possibilities curves of the two countries on the same graph. Mark on it the present production combinations and the quantities that each would produce, were they to specialize according to their absolute advantages.

Thus, we can conclude that

> **As long as there are differences in comparative costs between countries, regardless of the differences in absolute costs, there is a basis for mutually beneficial trade.**

What these examples show is that it is possible for both countries to gain from trade, but the remaining questions are: Will they? How will the increased production be shared? Will it be shared equally, or will one country receive more than the other? Discussion of the terms of trade will help answer these questions.

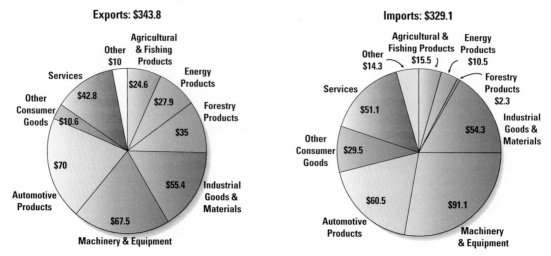

Canada's Exports and Imports, 1997 (billions)

Exports: $343.8

Imports: $329.1

Source: Compiled from Statistics Canada, CANSIM Matrix 3651

Terms of Trade

terms of trade: the average price of a country's exports compared with the price of its imports.

The **terms of trade** refers to the price at which a country sells its exports compared with the price at which it buys its imports. In reality, the price of any product is determined by a whole host of factors that we collectively gather under the headings of demand or supply. If the worldwide demand for softwood lumber were to increase, for example, it would increase the average price of Canadian exports, with the result that the terms of trade would be said to have moved in Canada's favour. The result would be the same if Canadian prices remain the same but the price of imports drops. In either case, the sale of our exports would enable us to purchase more imports. On the other hand, the terms of trade would shift against Canada if Canadian export prices dropped and/or the price of imported goods rose.

In our previous United States–Philippines example, the simple answer as to which country gains most from trade is that it all depends upon the terms of trade. But let us look at what would be acceptable prices from the two countries' point of view. Remember that the United States is the wheat producer and exporter. A glance back at Table 9.4 shows that it costs the U.S. 0.67 beans to produce 1 unit of wheat. What price would it be willing to sell its wheat for? Presumably for as high a price as it can get, but certainly not for less than 0.67 beans. What about the Philippines: how much would it be willing to pay for wheat? Remember, Table 9.4 tells us that the Philippines can itself produce 1 unit of wheat at a cost of 2 beans each. It certainly would not pay any higher than this price and would be happy to buy it for less. You can see that as long as the price is above the U.S. minimum and below the Philippines' maximum, both countries would be willing to trade. In other words, trade is possible if the price of one unit of wheat is anywhere between 0.67 and 2 units of beans. We could have just as easily expressed things in terms of beans, and a glance back at Table 9.4 shows that feasible terms of trade would be anywhere between 0.5 wheat to 1.5 wheat for 1 bushel of beans. Where the actual terms of trade end up will depend on the strength of demand in the two countries for these products.

Let us choose one particular rate among the many possible terms of trade and work out the consequences. Suppose, for instance, that the terms end up at one bushel of wheat for one bushel of beans. Suppose further that the Philippines is quite happy consuming the 40 million bushels of beans that it was producing before it decided to specialize, as shown in Table 9.5. However, it is now producing beans only and will have therefore $160 - 40 =$ 120 million bushels of beans available for export, which it sells to the United States at a rate of 1 bean for 1 wheat. It will receive back 120 million bushels of wheat and will finish up with 40 million bushels of beans and 120 million bushels of wheat. Because of trade, it will have gained an additional 60 million bushels of wheat, compared with its self-sufficient totals shown in combination B of Table 9.5. The United States will also gain. It was the sole producer of wheat, and of the total of 600 million bushels produced, it has sold 120 million bushels to the Philippines in exchange for 120 million bushels of beans. It will end up with 480 million bushels of wheat and 120 million bushels of beans, which is 30 million bushels of wheat and 20 million bushels of beans more than when it was producing both products as shown in combination B. All the numbers above can be a bit overwhelming, so let's summarize what we have just done in the graphic below. Recall that we are assuming that the Philippines consumes the same 40 million bushels of beans before and after trade.

PHILIPPINES

		Before Trade	After Trade
	Beans produced	40	160
	Beans exported	0	−120
Beans consumed		**40**	**40**
	Wheat produced	60	0
	Wheat imported	0	+120
Wheat consumed		**60**	**120**

Gain = 60 Wheat

UNITED STATES

		Before Trade	After Trade
	Beans produced	100	0
	Beans imported	0	+120
Beans consumed		**100**	**120**
	Wheat produced	450	600
	Wheat exported	0	−120
Wheat consumed		**450**	**480**

Gain = 20 Beans and 30 Wheat

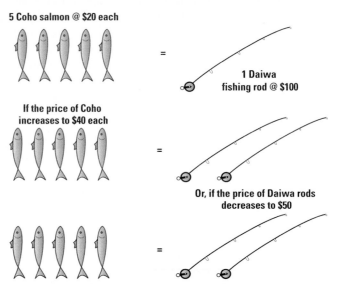

Terms of Trade

5 Coho salmon @ $20 each

=

1 Daiwa
fishing rod @ $100

If the price of Coho
increases to $40 each

=

Or, if the price of Daiwa rods
decreases to $50

=

In either case, the terms of trade has moved in Canada's favour;
that is, Canada now gets more for the same.

SELF-TEST

3. Suppose that the average productivity in Freedonia and Libraland is as follows:

	Output per Worker (bushels per day)	
	Apples	**Pears**
Freedonia	6	3
Libraland	3	2

Assuming the two countries wish to trade, would terms of trade of 1 pear = 2.5 apples be feasible? What about 1 pear = 1 apple? 1 pear = 1.75 apples?

Terms of Trade and Gains from Trade, Graphically

Let us now look at each country's trading picture separately. **Figure 9.2** shows the production possibilities curve for the United States. Before it decided to trade, this was also its consumption possibilities curve, since it could obviously not consume more than it produced. The slope of the curve is 1.5, which is the cost of 1 bean (that is, it equals 1.5 wheat). The curve to the right is its trading possibilities curve, which shows how much the United States could obtain through a combination of specializing its production and trading. Note that the slope of the trading possibilities curve is equal to 1. This is the terms of trade of 1 wheat for 1 bean, which the United States can now obtain from the Philippines. You can see from this graph that the United States, at one extreme, could produce the same maximum quantity of 600 million bushels of wheat as before and keep all of it. However, before trade, the maximum amount of beans available was 400. Now, if it wished, the United States could produce 600 million bushels of wheat and trade *all* of it, and receive in exchange 600 million bushels of beans. More likely, of course, it will opt to have a combination of both products, such as 480 million bushels of wheat and 120 million bushels of beans as in our numerical example above.

FIGURE 9.2 U.S. Production and Trading Possibilities Curves

The slope of the production possibilities curve shows the cost of producing beans in the United States and is equal to 1.5 wheat per bean. The slope of the trading possibilities curve shows the cost of buying beans internationally; that is, it is the terms of trade and equals 1 wheat per bean. The previous maximum obtainable quantity of beans was 400 million bushels, when the United States was self-sufficient. Its new maximum, as a result of trading, is now 600 million bushels because it could produce, if it wished, a maximum amount of 600 million bushels of wheat and trade this output for 600 million bushels of beans.

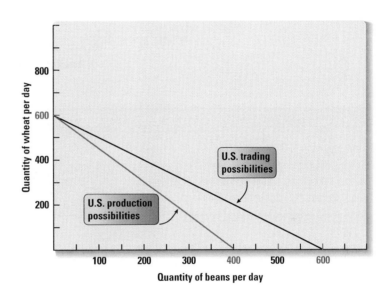

Figure 9.3 shows the position from the Philippines' point of view. The inside curve is its production (and therefore its consumption) possibilities curve, representing the maximum of both products that can be produced when the country is self-sufficient. The slope of the curve represents the cost of 1 bushel of beans and is equal to 0.5 bushels of wheat. The outer curve is the trading possibilities curve based on the terms of trade: 1 bean = 1 wheat. You can see that trading allows the Philippines also to enjoy increased consumption. After specialization, the maximum amount of beans remains unchanged at 160 million bushels. However, the maximum amount of wheat has increased from 80 (if produced in the Philippines) to 160 (by trading away all its 160 million bushels of beans for this quantity of wheat).

FIGURE 9.3 Philippines' Production and Trading Possibilities Curves

The Philippines specializes in the production of beans, and its trading possibilities curve lies to the right of the production possibilities curve. In other words, irrespective of whether it trades or not, the cost of beans remains the same; the cost of wheat, however, is now lower as a result of trade, since it can now obtain wheat at a cost of 1 bean per 1 wheat, whereas producing its own wheat costs 2 beans per 1 wheat.

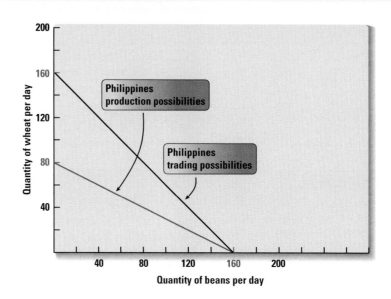

SELF-TEST

4. From the data contained in Figure 9.2 and Table 9.5, how many beans can the United States obtain if it is self-sufficient and is producing 450 million bushels of wheat? If, instead, it specializes in wheat production and can trade at terms of 1 wheat = 1 bean, how many beans could it have to accompany its 450 million bushels of wheat? What if the terms were 1 wheat = 2 beans?

The Benefits of Free Trade and Some Important Qualifications

Ricardo's theory of comparative advantage, which we have been looking at, is very important because it clearly highlights the major benefits of trade. Free and unrestricted trade allows nations and individuals the opportunity to sell in world markets, and this will, as a result, enable them to specialize in the products in which they enjoy an advantage over others. The result will be that products will be produced and sold at a *lower price* and in higher volumes, which translates into *higher incomes* and standards of living for all. In addition, the *variety of products* available when the world becomes one big market would presumably increase. A final benefit of free trade is the fact that it is more difficult to be a world monopolist than it is to be a monopolist in the home market. In other words, it is often suggested that free trade *increases competition*. In summary, free trade has the following advantages:

- lower prices
- higher incomes
- a greater variety of products
- increased competition

Canapress/Moe Doiron

Canada's minister for international trade, Art Eggleton, shakes hands with Israel's minister of industry and trade, Natan Sharansky, after the signing of the Canada–Israel Free Trade Agreement in 1996.

These are indeed powerful arguments in favour of free trade, but before we leave the topic let us look at some of the qualifications that need to be introduced. First, free trade is never free, because there will always be transport, insurance, and other freight charges, which must be added to the cost of production and which will usually reduce the trading advantage of foreign sellers. (However, in a country as extensive as Canada, it is often cheaper to transport products to American states bordering the country than it is to transport them from one end of the country to the other.) In addition, selling in a foreign country is always going to be more difficult (and usually, therefore, more expensive) than selling in the domestic market because of the differences in language, culture, taxation, regulations, and so on. Besides cost differences, the analysis we have presented so far has assumed constant costs. This leads to the result in our examples that countries should specialize in, perhaps, a single product and produce that product to a maximum. However, as we learned in Chapter 1, if any country tries to concentrate on a single product, its production is subject to the law of increasing costs. This means that one country only enjoys a cost advantage over others *up to a point*. As it tries to push production levels higher, its cost will start to increase so that it no longer enjoys a competitive advantage. This is the reason why few countries specialize entirely and why many countries both produce *and* import the same product. The presence of increasing costs will also lessen the advantages that one country enjoys over another in trade.

Even allowing for these cautions, it is still true that there are a number of benefits to be obtained from trade. This leads us to ask: why then does free trade tend to be the exception rather than the rule throughout history? Why does the question of free trade still divide countries and lead to such acrimonious debate? To understand part of the reason, let us look at the consequences of trying to restrict trade.

ADDED DIMENSION

Trade Organizations and Treaties of the World

Several international organizations exist today. The more important ones include the following.

WTO

The World Trade Organization (WTO) was established on January 1, 1995, and consists of more than 100 nations. It was formerly known as GATT (General Agreement on Tariffs and Trade) and is devoted to liberalizing world trade by reducing tariffs and quotas between nations. WTO regularly issues publications that document every aspect of its activities. Its secretariat is in Geneva.

OECD

The Organization for Economic and Cooperative Development (OECD) grew out of the Marshall Plan, which was designed to aid war-ravaged Europe at the end of World War II. This Paris-based intergovernmental organization's main purpose is to provide its 29 members with a forum in which governments can compare their experiences, discuss the problems they share, and seek solutions that can then be applied in their own national contexts. Each member is committed to the principles of the market economy and pluralistic democracy.

NAFTA

The North American Free Trade Agreement (NAFTA) is an agreement between Canada, the United States, and Mexico, implemented in 1989, whereby barriers to trade between the countries would be phased out over a 10-year period. In addition, it promotes fair competition and increased investment and provides protection of intellectual property rights. An important aspect of the treaty is a final and binding dispute-resolution mechanism that can be triggered by any one of the parties.

EU

The European Union (EU) currently has 15 member countries and grew out of the former European Economic Community,

which was established in 1957. By 1993 it had evolved into a true common market, within which there is free movement of goods and service, capital, and labour. It is moving toward greater monetary union with the establishment of the euro currency in 1999 and, some believe, eventual political union.

G8

This group of eight nations consists of Canada, the United States, Japan, the United Kingdom, France, Germany, Italy, and, recently, Russia. It represents (along with China and Spain) the ten largest economies in the world. The heads of state of these eight countries hold summits in which the world's pressing economic, political, and social issues are discussed. Often a summit meeting is followed by the release of a position paper on policy objectives that each has agreed to pursue.

APEC

The Asia-Pacific Economic Cooperation (APEC) was formed in 1989 and includes Canada among its 18 members. Its goal is to advance Asia-Pacific economic dynamism and sense of community by encouraging the region's economic growth and development; encouraging the flow of goods and services, capital, and technology; and encouraging the reduction of barriers to trade in goods and services in a manner consistent with WTO principles.

MAI

The Multilateral Agreement on Investment (MAI) was a failed attempt by the OECD to negotiate a new agreement that would do for investment what had already been achieved for trade in goods and services: create a set of global rules that would liberalize international investment, ensure fairness, and replace a patchwork of over 1600 bilateral investment agreements. Many believe that the WTO will make a similar effort in the near future.

Trade Restrictions

Let us set up a scenario in which, initially, we have two self-sufficient countries, France and Germany, each producing wine. The demand and supply conditions in the two countries are very different, of course, with both the demand and supply being greater in France than in Germany, as is shown in **Table 9.9**.

TABLE 9.9 The Market for Wine in France and Germany (millions of litres per month)

	FRANCE			GERMANY	
Price ($ per litre)	Demand	Supply	Price ($ per litre)	Demand	Supply
3	24	13	3	12	2
4	19	14	4	11	3
5	**15**	**15**	5	10	4
6	12	16	6	9	5
7	10	17	7	8	6
8	9	18	**8**	**7**	**7**

The equilibrium price in France is $5 per litre and the equilibrium quantity is 15. In Germany, the equilibrium price and quantities are $8 and 7 respectively. These are shown in **Figure 9.4**.

FIGURE 9.4 Demand and Supply of Wine in France and Germany

In France, the demand and supply of wine are both higher than in Germany. The consequence is a greater quantity of wine traded in France: 15 million litres, compared with 7 million in Germany. The price of wine, however, is lower in France than in Germany.

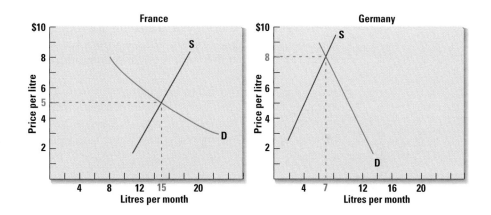

Now suppose that the two countries decide to engage in free trade. To keep things simple, let's assume there are no transport costs. If free trade is now introduced, what will be the price of wine in the two countries? Well, we know that at $5 per litre, the French winemakers were making a profit, so they should have no difficulty in competing with the German producers and presumably could easily undercut the German price of $8. Since we've assumed there are no transport costs, the price in the two countries should be the same. To find this price, all we need to do is look at the combined market of France and Germany. In other words, we need simply to add the demands and supplies of the two countries, as shown in **Table 9.10**.

TABLE 9.10 Deriving the Total Market Demand and Supply of Wine for France and Germany (in millions of litres per month)

	FRANCE		GERMANY		TOTAL MARKET	
Price ($ per litre)	Demand	Supply	Demand	Supply	Demand	Supply
3	24	13	12	2	36	15
4	19	14	11	3	30	17
5	15	15	10	4	25	19
6	12	16	9	5	**21**	**21**
7	10	17	8	6	18	23
8	9	18	7	7	16	25

The total market demand is obtained by adding together the French demand and the German demand at each price. For instance, at $3 per litre, the quantity demanded in France is 24 and in Germany it is 12, giving a total for the two countries of 36. Similarly, the quantity supplied at $3 is 13 in France and 2 in Germany, giving a total market supply of 15. This is done for all prices. The new market price (let's call it the world price) then, will be $6 per litre, and at that price a total of 21 million litres will be produced and sold.

Now let us look at the effect in each market. French winemakers are delighted at the situation because they are getting a higher price now that free trade has opened up a new market in Germany and their volume of business is higher. French winemakers are now producing 16 million litres, up from the 15 million litres produced before trade. Note also that in France the quantities produced (16) exceeds the demand from French consumers (12). What happens to the surplus of 4 million litres? The answer is that it is being exported to Germany. And what is the situation in that country? Well certainly, German consumers are delighted, because the new world price of $6 is lower than the previous domestic price of $8. But we can imagine that the German wine-makers are far from happy. The new lower world price has caused a number of producers to cut back production, and presumably some producers are forced out of

business. At the world price of $6, German producers are only producing 5 million litres, below the German demand of 9 million litres. How is this shortage going to be made up? Answer: from the import of French wine. This simply means that the French export of 4 million litres equals the German import of 4 million litres. These points are illustrated in **Figure 9.5**.

FIGURE 9.5 Demand and Supply of Wine in France and Germany with Free Trade

The new world price of wine is above the previous French price but below the previous German price. The result is a surplus of wine in France of 4 million litres but a shortage in Germany of 4 million litres.

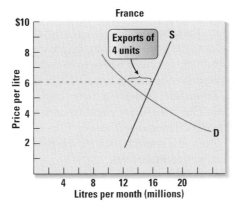

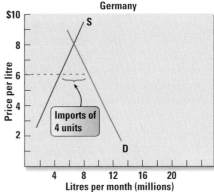

SELF-TEST

5. In Table 9.10, if the demand for wine in Germany increased by 5 (million litres) at every price, how much wine would now be produced in Germany, and how much would be imported from France?

So who are the losers and who are the gainers as a result of markets being opened up? The answer in our example is that both German wine consumers and French wine producers gain and French wine consumers and German wine producers lose. Free trade has cost French consumers $1 a litre, and it has cost German winemakers $2 per litre. Previously these winemakers were selling 7 million litres at $8 per litre, for a total revenue of $56 million. Now, they are selling only 5 million litres for $6 per litre, for a total revenue of $30 million. In total, then, these producers, of whom there may be fewer than 100, have collectively lost $26 million in revenue. It is easy to see why these producers may not be in favour of free trade! In fact, it would pay them to lobby their own parliament and to launch publicity campaigns in an attempt to keep out "cheap" French wines. As long as their efforts do not cost more than $26 million, they will be ahead of the game.

It is easy to see why powerful lobby and special interest groups have been very vocal throughout history in trying to persuade parliament and the public that it is in the country's interest to ban or curtail foreign imports. This **protectionism** can take many forms, which we need to look at.

protectionism: the economic policy of protecting domestic producers by restricting the importation of foreign products.

Imposition of Quotas

quota: a limit imposed on the production or sale of a product.

The most obvious restriction of imports is to ban them either entirely or partially, and this is exactly what is meant by a **quota**. A quota can take a variety of forms, ranging from a total restriction to a maximum limit being placed on each individual foreign exporter, or perhaps the requirement that each foreign exporter reduces its exports by a percentage of the previous year's sales. The essence of a quota is to reduce or restrict the importation of certain products. And what will be the effect of such restriction? Suppose in our wine example that German winemakers were successful in their efforts to keep out French wines, and the German government imposed a total ban on French wines. At the current price of $6 per litre, there will be an immediate shortage in Germany. The result of the shortage is to push up the price of wine. It will continue to rise, encouraging increased German production until the price returns to the pre–free-trade price of $8. In France, the immediate effect of the German quota will be to cause a surplus of French wine, which will depress the price of French wine until it too is back at the pre-trade price of $5 per litre.

Let's move on from our France/Germany example and look at trade from the Canadian perspective. The price of wine and of most products traded internationally is determined by the world's demand and supply. That is to say, for any one small country the world price is a given; the country's action will have little impact on the world price. This situation is illustrated in **Figure 9.6**.

FIGURE 9.6 The Effects of a Quota

Initially the Canadian demand and supply is D_d and S_d and the world price is Pw. The quantity demanded in Canada equals *c*, of which Canadian producers would produce *a* and foreign producers would export *ac* to Canada. A quota of *ab* would raise the price to P_q. As a result, domestic production will increase, and imports would drop to the amount of the quota.

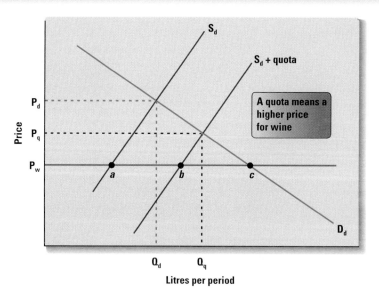

Figure 9.6 shows the domestic demand (D_d) and supply (S_d) of wine in Canada. P_d is the domestic price and Q_d is domestic production. Suppose that the world price is P_w and that Canada now freely allows imports into the country. At the world price of P_w, the amount produced by domestic Canadian producers is *a* and the amount demanded is *c*. Since Canadian consumers want to purchase more than Canadian producers are willing to produce, the difference of *ac* represents the amount of imports. Now suppose that the Canadian government yields to pressure from Canadian wine producers and imposes a quota of *ab* on imported wine. In effect, the total supply is equal to the domestic supply plus the amount of the quota. This is represented by the

new supply curve, S_d plus quota. Since the total available has now been reduced, the price will increase to P_q and the quantity will fall to Q_q.

From this, it can be seen that the losers will be Canadian consumers (who are paying a higher price and are having less quantity and variety of wines) and foreign winemakers whose exports are being restricted. The winners will be Canadian winemakers, who are producing more wine and receiving a higher price.

The Imposition of a Tariff

tariff: a tax (or duty) levied on imports.

A second way of restricting imports is by the use of a **tariff**, which is a tax on imports. It is a more frequently chosen method than quotas, because governments can derive considerable revenue from tariffs. The effects of a tariff are much the same as those of a quota because, in both cases, the price of the product will increase. With a quota, however, the domestic producers get the whole benefit of the higher price, whereas with a tariff, the benefit is shared between the domestic producers and the government. An additional benefit of a tariff over a quota is that a quota tends to treat foreign producers indiscriminately because each and every producer is treated in the same way, whereas with a tariff only the more efficient producers will continue to export, since only they will be able to continue to make a profit. A tariff discriminates against the less efficient producers, and therefore, from an efficiency point of view, it is superior to a quota. These points are illustrated in **Figure 9.7**.

In Figure 9.7, suppose again that we are describing the Canadian wine market. At the world price of P_w, Canadian producers are supplying a and Canadian consumers are buying b. The difference ab is the amount of imported wine. Suppose that the Canadian government imposes a tariff of t per unit. The price in Canada will rise to P_t. Note that at the higher price, Canadian producers, who will receive the whole price P_t, will increase production to Q_f. Canadian consumers will reduce consumption to Q_g. In addition, imports will fall to $Q_g - Q_f$. The result is very similar to what we saw in the analysis of quotas. Again, it is Canadian consumers and foreign producers who lose out, and Canadian producers who gain.

FIGURE 9.7 The Effects of the Imposition of a Tariff

The imposition of a tariff, t, will increase the price of wine in Canada to P_t from P_w. As a result, Canadian production will increase to Q_f and imports will drop to $Q_g - Q_f$. The tax revenue to the government is equal to t times the quantity of imports, $Q_g - Q_f$, the shaded area.

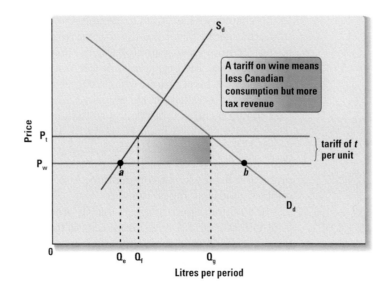

A tariff on wine means less Canadian consumption but more tax revenue

The other gainer in this scenario will be the Canadian government, which will receive tax revenue equal to the shaded rectangle in **Figure 9.7**.

Other Trade Restrictions

exchange controls: restrictions imposed by a government limiting the amount of foreign currencies that can be obtained.

Besides the two popular protectionist measures of tariffs and quotas, a number of other available methods deserve mention. **Exchange controls** are similar to quotas, but instead of a restriction being placed on the importation of a good, the restriction is placed on the availability of foreign currencies (that is, foreign exchange). The effect is the same because, since foreigners wish to be paid in their own currencies, if an importer is unable to get his hands on the appropriate currency, he will not be able to buy the foreign goods. The controls might be across-the-board restrictions or restrictions on particular currencies or on particular products or industries. The effect in all cases will be to increase the domestic price of the products affected, which will be to the benefit of the domestic producer at the expense of the domestic consumer. Another more subtle but often equally effective way of cutting imports is by way of *restrictions and regulations*. A government might make trade so difficult or time-consuming for the importer that the amount of trade is significantly reduced. For instance, the customs department of a particular country might tie the importer up with red tape by requiring that all imports must be accompanied by 10 different forms (all in triplicate) obtainable from 10 different government departments. Or perhaps the product must comply to certain very unrealistic standards of safety, or packaging, or hygiene standards that are not required for domestically produced items.

voluntary export restriction (VER): an agreement by an exporting country to restrict the amount of its exports to another country.

A more recent type of trade restriction is known as **voluntary export restrictions (VERs)**. Rather than imposing, say, tariffs and quotas, the importing country requests that the exporting country itself voluntarily restrict the amount being exported. In this way, the exporting country is given the power to administer the quotas, which will also prevent the importing country from receiving tariff revenue on the imports. Since the restrictions are voluntary, the exporting country does not have to comply. However, since the importing country has other weapons at its disposal, then...

Free Trade and Protectionism

In this chapter we have tried to avoid making an outright declaration in favour of free trade, though the flavour of the chapter would suggest that there are many benefits to be derived from trade, and probably the majority of economists feel that the freer the trade, the better. But even a notable free-trader like the astute Adam Smith recognized that there may be occasions when a degree of protectionism in the way of tariffs and quotas might be called for. He suggested, for instance, that a country's strategic industries should be offered protection so that, for instance, the country does not become dependent on foreign manufacturers for the production of military hardware. The problem with this *strategic industry argument*, however, is that most industries would claim that they are of "strategic importance" to a nation and therefore deserve similar protection from foreign competition. Also, the idea of hindering the production of military goods has appeal to many.

In addition, Smith suggests that in order for there to be a level playing field for both domestic and foreign producers, if the produce of domestic industry is being taxed, then foreign imports should be taxed by a similar amount. He also felt that if a foreign country is placing tariffs and quotas on your country's exports, then you should do likewise to its exports, but not, it should be noted, just for retaliation, but to help the foreign country to recognize the folly of its actions and to persuade it to restore free trade. Finally, Smith was prescient enough to realize that if a country has had a long history of protectionism, then the sudden arrival of free trade is likely to cause dramatic shifts of labour and capital away from industries that can no longer compete to those industries that find themselves growing. This dislocation may cause a great deal of suffering in the short term, so Smith felt that a wise government would introduce free trade gradually and would try to mitigate the suffering. This caveat is of particular importance in terms of the North American Free Trade Agreement discussions. Although many feel that there will be great long-term benefits for all the participating countries, it is equally certain that in the short term a great deal of suffering will be experienced by those industries, firms, and individuals who, through no fault of their own, find themselves unable to compete. Some type of government assistance may be needed to help in the adjustment process.

In addition, it ought to be mentioned that some economists feel that certain "infant" industries should be given a helping hand by the government until they are sufficiently mature to compete with foreign competition. This *infant industry* argument is strongest when the government feels that undue reliance on the exportation of a few staple products would leave the country in a vulnerable position if a future change in demand or technology were to occur. In order to diversify the economy and develop other industries, many feel that these "infants" should be sheltered from competition. However, the trouble is, these infant industries often never grow up! In addition, even if there are persuasive arguments in favour of protecting or assisting certain industries, it may be better for the government to give this aid in the form of direct subsidies rather than by interfering with normal trading patterns through the imposition of tariffs and quotas.

A final argument against free trade is the *cultural identity* argument. This one is difficult to dismiss solely on economic grounds. Many commentators feel that free trade brings with it mass production and standardization, which may harm the importing country's sense of individuality and cultural identity. As a result, some are totally against free trade while others feel that it should not extend into areas like communications, health, and education. They firmly believe that a country's radio and television stations, its newspapers and magazines, its educational institutions and hospitals, should not be foreign-owned or -controlled. In summary, three arguments against free trade are:

- the strategic industry argument
- the infant industry argument
- the cultural identity argument

REVIEW

1. What is meant by *terms of trade*? Explain how the terms of trade can change.
2. In general, what could cause the terms of trade to move in Canada's favour?
3. What does the slope of the production possibilities curve indicate? What does the slope of the trading possibilities curve indicate?
4. Give three major advantages of free trade.
5. What does *protectionism* mean? Mention five ways in which governments control trade.
6. Who is helped and who is hurt by the imposition of quotas and tariffs?
7. Explain three arguments against free trade.

Chapter Highlights

The chapter begins by addressing the fundamental question of why countries wish to trade with each other. It answers this question by explaining that countries trade for the same reason that individuals trade: because it is to their advantage to do so. The advantage is the result of differences between people and between countries. The key to explaining trade is that countries tend to specialize in producing products in which they have an advantage because of differences in factor endowment.

The chapter then goes on to give a theoretical explanation of why it is to the advantage of all countries to specialize. It looks first at Adam Smith's theory of absolute advantage, which simply suggests that a nation should specialize in what it does best because it will be able to produce in greater quantities and at lower costs than other nations. Next, it introduces Ricardo's very important refinement of Smith's idea: the theory of comparative advantage. It explains why it is to the advantage of all countries to trade. It shows why this is so even for a country that can produce all products cheaper than any other can. It shows, by way of production possibilities, why differences in comparative costs of production lie at the heart of trade.

The next section explains how the gains from trade are distributed between nations and explains the concept of the terms of trade, which measures the relative price of a country's exports compared with the price of its imports.

The first part of the chapter concludes by summarizing the main benefits to be derived from trade: that products will be produced in higher volumes and at lower costs; that trade will lead to a greater number of products being available; and that trade helps to promote competition.

The second half of the chapter begins by looking at the reasons why many countries prefer to protect their own domestic industries by restricting foreign imports. It explains why domestic producers gain and domestic consumers and foreign producers lose as a result. It shows that protectionism leads to higher prices and a decrease in the volumes produced.

The chapter ends by examining the five ways by which trade is restricted. It looks at the first two methods—quotas and tariffs—in some detail and explains, using graphs, how they operate and what are the results. It then describes the other three methods—exchange controls, restrictions, and regulations and voluntary export restrictions—before concluding with three arguments that have been used to support protectionism.

New Glossary Terms

comparative advantage   306
exchange controls   322
protectionism   319
quota   320
tariff   321
terms of trade   310
voluntary export restriction (VER)   322

STUDY GUIDE

Study Tips

1. The argument for free trade is based on Ricardo's theory of comparative advantage. It is important that you fully understand the basic idea of opportunity costs that lies behind this theory. A good way to test yourself is to make up your own figures for a two-country, two-product world, draw the corresponding production possibilities curves, and work out which country has an advantage in which product and why.

2. Some students have difficulty understanding that if we are dealing with only two products and if a country has a comparative advantage at producing one product it must, by definition, have a comparative *disadvantage* in the other product.

3. To get an understanding of the terms of trade, again try to make up some numbers for yourself and plot them on a production possibilities diagram. For instance, start off with a country that could produce 30 units of wool or 20 computers and has an advantage in wool production. If it could trade at 1 wool = 1/2 computer, what combinations could it have? Try 1 wool = 1 computer, 1 wool = 2, 3, 5 computers and so on. Draw each resulting trading possibilities curve. Note that both the trading and production possibilities curves reflect opportunity costs. The former case shows what must be given up in trading; the latter case shows what must be given up in production.

4. To understand the idea behind world markets, note, as in Figure 9.5, that what one country is exporting, another country must be importing. This means that if one country produces a trade surplus, then the other country must be experiencing a trade deficit. In the exporting country, the world price must be higher than the domestic price. In the importing country, the world price must be lower than the domestic price.

5. You will get a good grip on the effects of tariffs and quotas by drawing a simple demand and supply curve and noting, first, the effect of a price set above market equilibrium (which is what a tariff produces) and second, a quantity below market equilibrium (which is what a quota produces). This approach suggests that the effect of both tariffs and quotas is to produce higher prices and lower quantities.

Key Problem I

Suppose that Peaceland and Prosperity have the output figures shown in **Table 9.11**.

TABLE 9.11

Country	AVERAGE PRODUCT PER WORKER	
	Wheat	Wine
Peaceland	4 bushels	2 barrels
Prosperity	4 bushels	3 barrels

Assuming that costs and productivity remain constant:

a) What is the opportunity cost of producing 1 bushel of wheat in Peaceland? _____

b) What is the opportunity cost of producing 1 barrel of wine in Peaceland? _____

CHAPTER 9

c) What is the opportunity cost of producing 1 bushel of wheat in Prosperity? _____

d) What is the opportunity cost of producing 1 barrel of wine in Prosperity? _____

e) In what product does Peaceland have a comparative advantage? _____

f) In what product does Prosperity have a comparative advantage? _____

Suppose that the labour force in Peaceland is 10 million, and it is 20 million in Prosperity.

g) Fill in the missing production possibilities data for both countries in **Table 9.12**.

TABLE 9.12

PEACELAND'S PRODUCTION POSSIBILITIES (millions of units)

	A	B	C	D	E
Wheat	40	30	20	10	0
Wine	___	___	___	___	___

PROSPERITY'S PRODUCTION POSSIBILITIES (millions of units)

	A	B	C	D	E
Wheat	___	___	___	___	___
Wine	0	15	30	45	60

Suppose that both countries are presently producing combination D.

h) Show the joint totals below:

Total output in millions of units:

	Wheat	Wine
Peaceland	___	___
Prosperity	___	___
Total: both countries	___	___

Now suppose that each country specializes in the product in which it has a comparative advantage.

i) Show the new totals below:

Total output in millions of units:

	Wheat	Wine
Peaceland	___	___
Prosperity	___	___
Total: both countries	___	___

j) As a result, the joint gain from trade is equal to:

_____ wheat   _____ wine.

Suppose that the two countries establish the terms of trade at 1 wine =1.5 wheat, and Prosperity decides to export 15 wine to Peaceland.

k) As a result the two countries will gain as follows:

Gains for each country in millions of units:		
	Wheat	**Wine**
Peaceland	_____	_____
Prosperity	_____	_____
Total: both countries	_____	_____

More of the Same

Suppose that Hopeland and Faithland have the output figures contained in **Table 9.13**, shown in terms of productivity per worker.

TABLE 9.13		
	AVERAGE PRODUCT PER WORKER	
Country	**Wheat**	**Wine**
Hopeland	3 Bushels	1 barrels
Faithland	1 Bushels	2 barrels

Assuming that the costs and productivity remain constant:

a) What is the opportunity cost of producing wheat and wine in Hopeland and Faithland?

b) In which product does each country have a comparative advantage?

Suppose that the labour force in Hopeland is 20 million, and it is 10 million in Faithland.

c) Show the production possibilities data for both countries in a table.

Assume that both countries are now producing 5 million wine.

d) What are their present joint output totals?

Now suppose that each country specializes in the product in which it has a comparative advantage.

e) What will be the new output totals, and what will be the gains from trade?

Suppose that the two countries establish the terms of trade at 1 wine = 2 wheat, and Hopeland decides to trade 15 wheat to Faithland.

f) What will be the consumption totals for the two countries?

Key Problem II

Table **9.14** shows the market for wool in Australia, which is closed to trade.

TABLE 9.14

Price per Tonne ($)	Domestic Demand	Domestic Supply
1700	145	45
1800	140	60
1900	135	75
2000	130	90
2100	125	105
2200	120	120
2300	115	135
2400	110	150

a) What is the present equilibrium price and domestic production?

Price: _____;   domestic production: _____.

b) Suppose that Australia now opens to free trade and the world price of wool is $2000. How much wool will Australia produce domestically, and how much will it import?

Domestic production: _____;   imports: _____.

c) Assume that the Australian government, under pressure from the Australian wool industry, decides to impose an import quota of 20 tonnes. What will be the new price, and how much will the Australian industry produce?

Price: _____;   domestic production: _____.

d) Now suppose that the Australian government, wishing to benefit from the trade restriction, decides to replace the import quota with a tariff. If it wishes to maintain domestic production at the same level as with a quota, what should be the amount of the tariff and how much tariff revenue will it receive?

Tariff: $_____;   tariff revenue: $_____.

Translations

Latalia has a labour force of 12 million, one third of whom work in the wool industry, the remainder being employed in rice farming. The labour productivity in the wool industry is 40 kilos per worker per year, and in rice farming it is 100 kilos per worker per year. Latalia has discovered that the international terms of trade are 2 kilos of rice per kilo of wool. It is happy with its current consumption of rice but would like to obtain more wool.

FIGURE 9.8

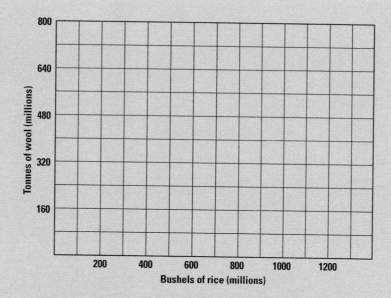

Assuming constant per unit costs, on the graph in **Figure 9.8**, draw a production and a trading possibilities curve for Latalia. Explain what product it should specialize in and show the gains, if any, it could receive from trade.

Explanation:

_____

_____

Are You Sure?

Indicate whether the following statements are true or false. If false, indicate why they are false.

1. A country has a comparative advantage over another only if it is able to produce all products more cheaply.

   T or F   If false: _____

   _____

2. David Ricardo first introduced the theory of comparative advantage.

   T or F   If false: _____

   _____

3. If a country chooses to specialize its production, it will want to engage in trade.

   T or F   If false: _____

   _____

4. If a country is able to produce all products more cheaply than any other country can, then there is no advantage in trade.

   T or F   If false: _____

   _____

5. The terms of trade relate to the laws and conditions that govern trade.

   T or F   If false: _____

   _____

6. If the price of both a country's exports and its imports decrease, then the terms of trade will move in its favour.

   T or F   If false: _____

   _____

7. If a country's trading possibilities curve lies to the right of its production possibilities curve, there are no gains from trade.

   T or F   If false: _____

   _____

8. Protectionism is the economic policy of protecting domestic producers by restricting the exportation of products.

   T or F   If false: _____

   _____

9. A tariff is a tax on exports; a quota is a tax on imports.

   T or F   If false: _____

   _____

10. Domestic producers gain and domestic consumers lose as a result of the imposition of tariffs or quotas.

   T or F   If false: _____

   _____

Choose the Best

11. To what does the term "gains from trade" refer?
    a) The surplus of exports over imports.
    b) The increase in output resulting from international trade.

12. What is a tariff?
    a) It is a tax imposed on an import.
    b) It is a tax imposed on an export.

13. Who was the originator of the theory of absolute advantage?
    a) Adam Smith.
    b) David Ricardo.

14. What is the definition of "the terms of trade"?
    a) It is the average price of a country's imports divided by the average price of its exports.
    b) It is the average price of a country's exports divided by the average price of its imports.
    c) They are the rules and regulations governing international trade.

15. What does it mean if the opportunity costs differ between two countries?
    a) Then comparative costs must be the same.
    b) There can be no gains from trade.
    c) It is possible for both countries to gain from specialization and trade.

16. On what basis are the gains from trade divided between countries?
   a) According to the terms of trade.
   b) According to international trade agreements.
   c) According to the quantity of resources possessed by each.

17. Under what circumstances will there be no opportunity for mutually advantageous trade between two countries?
   a) When the terms of trade are the same.
   b) When comparative costs are the same.
   c) When comparative costs are different.

18. Suppose that originally the average price of Happy Island's exports was 180, and the average price of its imports was 120. Now, the price of its exports drops to 160, and the price of its imports drops to 100. What effect will this have on Happy Island's terms of trade?
   a) There will be no change in the terms of trade.
   b) The terms of trade have moved in Happy Island's favour.
   c) The terms of trade have moved against Happy Island.

19. Suppose that the cost of producing 1 unit of wine in Happy Island is 2 units of rice and in Silly Island, 1 wine costs 4 rice. What does this mean for the two countries?
   a) Happy Island should specialize in and export rice to Silly Island.
   b) Happy Island should specialize in and export wine to Silly Island.
   c) Happy Island should specialize in rice but export wine to Silly Island.
   d) Happy Island should specialize in wine but export rice to Silly Island.

20. Suppose that the cost of producing 1 unit of wine in Happy Island is 2 units of rice; in Silly Island 1 wine costs 4 rice. What might be possible terms of trade between the two countries?
   a) 1 rice = 3/8 wine.
   b) 1 rice = 3 wine.
   c) 1 rice = 6 wine.
   d) 1 wine = 1 rice.

21. All the following, *except one*, are forms of protectionism. Which is the exception?
   a) Import subsidies.
   b) Tariffs.
   c) Exchange controls.
   d) Quotas.

Figure 9.9 shows the market for cloth in Smith Island. Refer to it to answer questions 22, 23, and 24.

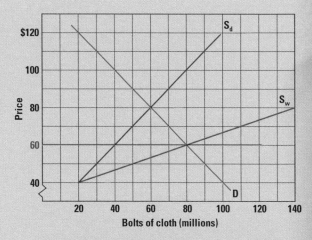

FIGURE 9.9

22. Refer to Figure 9.9 to answer this question. At the world price how much is Smith Island trading?
   a) It is importing 30 units.
   b) It is importing 40 units.
   c) It is exporting 30 units.
   d) It is exporting 40 units.

23. Refer to Figure 9.9 to answer this question. If Smith Island introduced an import quota of 20, what would be the new price in Smith Island?
   a) $55.
   b) $60.
   c) $70.
   d) $90.

24. Refer to Figure 9.9 to answer this question. If Smith Island introduced a tariff of $10 on cloth, how much would be imported?
   a) 0 units.
   b) 10 units.
   c) 20 units.
   d) 40 units.

25. What is the difference between a tariff and a quota?
  a) A tariff causes an increase in the price, whereas a quota does not affect the price.
  b) Both a tariff and a quota will affect the price, but a tariff has no effect on the quantity, whereas a quota will lead to a reduction.
  c) Both a tariff and a quota will affect the price, but a tariff has no effect on the quantity, whereas a quota will lead to an increase.
  d) A quota affects all foreign producers equally, whereas a tariff does not.
  e) A tariff affects all foreign producers equally, whereas a quota does not.

Refer to **Figure 9.10** to answer questions 26, 27, 28, and 29.

FIGURE 9.10

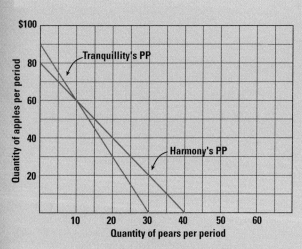

Quantity of apples per period / Quantity of pears per period

26. Refer to Figure 9.10 to answer this question. What is the opportunity cost of producing 1 apple in Harmony and in Tranquillity?
  a) 2 pears in Harmony and 3 pears in Tranquillity.
  b) 1/2 pear in Harmony and 1/3 pear in Tranquillity.
  c) 2 pears in Harmony and 1/3 pear in Tranquillity.
  d) 1/2 pear in Harmony and 3 pears in Tranquillity.
  e) 3 pears in Harmony and 2 pears in Tranquillity.

27. Refer to Figure 9.10 to answer this question. What do the comparative opportunity costs in the two countries suggest?
  a) That there are no advantages to be gained from trade.
  b) That Harmony should specialize in apples but export pears.
  c) That Tranquillity should specialize in apples but export pears.
  d) That Harmony should specialize in pears but export apples.
  e) That Harmony should specialize in pears and Tranquillity should specialize in apples.

28. Refer to Figure 9.10 to answer this question. Suppose that both Harmony and Tranquillity are producing 20 pears; what will be the total gains from trade for the two countries?
  a) 20 apples and 0 pears.
  b) 30 apples and 10 pears.
  c) 20 apples and 10 pears.
  d) 20 apples and 30 pears.
  e) 0 apples and 20 pears.

29. Refer to Figure 9.10 to answer this question. What could be possible terms of trade between the two countries?
  a) 1 apple = 0.25 pears.
  b) 1 apple = 2.5 pears.
  c) 1 apple = 3 pears.
  d) 1 pear = 0.5 apples.
  e) 1 pear = 2.5 apple.

Table 9.15 shows the output of kumquats per month. Refer to this table to answer question 30.

TABLE 9.15

Price ($ per kilo)	SMITHLAND Demand	Supply	IMPORTS INTO SMITHLAND Supply
3	100	40	30
4	90	50	40
5	80	60	50
6	70	70	60

30. Refer to Table 9.15 to answer this question. What is the world (free trade) price, and what quantity of this product is being consumed domestically?

a) $4 and 50 kilos consumed.
b) $4 and 90 kilos consumed.
c) $5 and 80 kilos consumed.
d) $6 and 70 kilos consumed.
e) $6 and 130 kilos consumed.

Other Problems

31. The following shows the maximum output levels for Here and There:

	Cloth		Computers
Here	100	or	50
There	60	or	120

a) What is the cost of a unit of cloth and a computer in Here?

1 unit of cloth: _____; 1 computer: _____.

b) What is the cost of a unit of cloth and a unit of computers in There?

1 unit of cloth: _____; 1 computer: _____.

c) In what product does each country have a comparative advantage?

Here: _____; There: _____.

d) What would be feasible terms of trade between the two countries?

1 unit of cloth: _____; 1 computer: _____.

32. **Table 9.16** shows the production possibilities for Canada and Japan. Prior to specialization and trade, Canada is producing combination D, and Japan is producing combination B.

TABLE 9.16

CANADA'S PRODUCTION POSSIBILITIES

Product	A	B	C	D	E	F
Compact disc players	10	8	6	4	2	0
Wheat	0	4	8	12	16	20

JAPAN'S PRODUCTION POSSIBILITIES

Product	A	B	C	D	E	F
Compact disc players	30	24	18	12	6	0
Wheat	0	6	12	18	24	30

a) On the graph (**Figure 9.11**), draw the production possibilities curve for each country, and mark their present output positions.

b) Suppose that the two countries specialize and trade on the basis of 1 CD player = 1.5 wheat. Draw the corresponding trading possibilities curves.

FIGURE 9.11

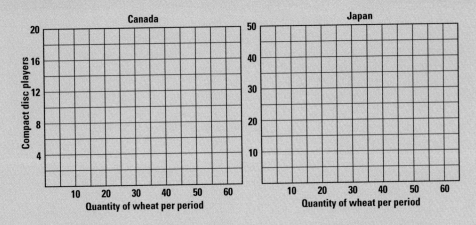

33. The following incomplete table (**Table 9.17**) shows the productivity levels of producing beer and sardines in Canada and Mexico.

TABLE 9.17

Production per Worker (average product)	Beer	Sardines
Canada	6	4
Mexico	3	?

In order for there to be no advantage to be gained from trade, what does the Mexican productivity per worker in the sardine industry need to be?

34. Suppose the Canadian demand for and the Japanese supply of cars to Canada is shown in **Table 9.18** (quantities in thousands).

TABLE 9.18

Price ($)	Quantity Demanded	Quantity Supplied (before tariff)	Quantity Supplied (after tariff)
$12 000	180	60	_____
13 000	160	80	_____
14 000	140	100	_____
15 000	120	120	_____
16 000	100	140	_____
17 000	80	160	_____
18 000	60	180	_____
19 000	40	200	_____

a) The present equilibrium price is $_____ and quantity is

_____ (thousand).

b) Suppose that the Canadian government imposes a $2000 per car tariff on imported Japanese cars. Show the new supply in the last column above. The new equilibrium price is:

$_____ and quantity is _____ (thousand).

c) The total revenue received by the government will be $_____.

d) Assume, instead, that the government imposes an import quota of 100 000 cars. The new equilibrium price is $_____ and quantity is _____ (thousand).

e) The total revenue received by the government will be $_____.

UNANSWERED QUESTIONS

Short Essays

1. Explain the difference between Adam Smith's and David Ricardo's theories of trade.

2. Explain what is meant by comparative costs and why there are no advantages to trade if nations have identical comparative costs.

3. Explain Adam Smith's dictum that the division of labour is limited by the extent of the market.

4. What are "terms of trade," and how can they be measured for nations that generally trade in more than two products?

5. Explain the main advantages of free trade.

6. Discuss the main arguments against free trade.

7. What are the main methods used by governments to protect domestic industries? Which do you think are the more successful methods?

8. Who gets helped and who gets hurt by the imposition of a tariff?

9. In what way are a tariff and a quota similar, and in what way are they different? Which is preferable, and why?

Analytical Questions

10. Why do some countries enjoy a cost advantage over others in the production of certain products? To what extent do these advantages remain constant? How may they disappear over time?

11. In what way is a direct subsidy from the government preferable to a tariff or quota as a way of assisting an infant industry?

12. What circumstances would make a country an exporter of a product? What would make it an importer?

13. If comparative cost is the basis for trade, why are Third World countries, which have very low wage rates, not the world's greatest trading nations?

14. If Third World countries are unable to compete in world markets, why are so many North American corporations locating plants in these countries?

15. The analysis in this chapter suggests that if a country produces only two products, and if it has a comparative advantage in one, it must have a comparative disadvantage in the other. How is this affected if a country produces three, or four, or a thousand products?

16. To what extent are the conclusions of the theory of comparative advantage affected if unit costs increase, rather than remain constant, as output increases?

Numerical Questions

17. The graph in **Figure 9.12** shows the domestic supply of and demand for mangos in India.

FIGURE 9.12

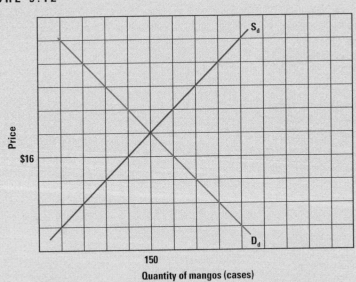

Quantity of mangos (cases)

The world price is $16 a case and India has free trade.
a) Will India export or import mangos?
b) What quantity will domestic producers supply?
c) What quantity will India export or import?
d) What will be the price in India?

18. **Table 9.19** shows the (hypothetical) annual demand and supply of cellular phones in Canada (in tens of thousands annually), where D is the quantity demanded by Canadian consumers, S_C is the quantity supplied by Canadian manufacturers, and S_J is the quantity supplied to the Canadian market by Japanese manufacturers.

TABLE 9.19

Price	D	S_C	S_J
$200	28	4	0
300	26	6	2
400	24	8	4
500	22	10	6
600	20	12	8
700	18	14	10
800	16	16	12
1000	14	18	14

a) Add a final column showing the total quantity supplied in the Canadian market, labelled S_T. Graph D, S_C, and S_T.

b) If Japanese imports were totally banned, what would be the price and quantity of cellular phones in Canada?

c) If Canada was open to Japanese imports, what would be the price and quantity of cellular phones in Canada as a result?

d) Suppose that the Canadian government were to impose a quota on Japanese imports limiting them to 4 (tens of thousands) per year. What would be the price and quantity of cellular phones in Canada now?

e) To produce the same result as in d), alternatively what amount of tariff would the Canadian government have to impose on Japanese imports?

19. The graph in **Figure 9.13** shows the domestic demand and supply of apples in Canada.

FIGURE 9.13

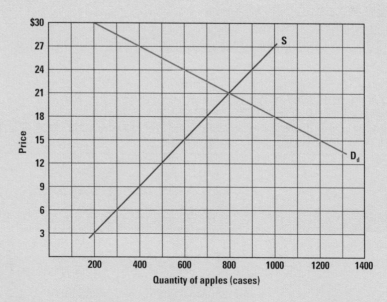

The world price is $15 per case and Canada is open to free trade.

a) How many cases per period will Canada import from abroad?

Suppose the government wishes to reduce imports by 300 cases per period.
b) What import quota should it impose, and what will be the effect on the price?
c) Alternatively, what tariff should the government impose, and what will be the total revenue from the tariff?

20. **Figure 9.14** shows the production possibilities for the countries of Kinell and Kenrick.
a) What are the costs for the two products in each country?
b) What products should they each specialize in and export?

FIGURE 9.14

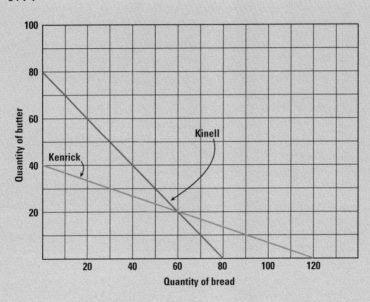

c) Suppose that terms of trade are established at 1 unit of butter = 2 units of bread. Show the trading possibilities curve for each country.
d) Assuming that each country is happy consuming the same quantity of its specialized product as it did before trade, show the amount of the imported product now available to it.

21. **Table 9.20** shows the production possibilities curves for Concordia and Harmonia.

TABLE 9.20

CONCORDIA'S PRODUCTION POSSIBILITIES

Product	A	B	C	D	E
Pork	4	3	2	1	0
Beans	0	5	10	15	20

HARMONIA'S PRODUCTION POSSIBILITIES

Product	A	B	C	D	E
Pork	8	6	4	2	0
Beans	0	6	12	18	24

a) What are the costs of the two products in each country?
b) What products should each country specialize in and export?
c) If, prior to specialization and trade, Concordia produced combination C and Harmonia produced combination B, what would be the total gains from trade for the two countries?
d) What would be feasible terms of trade between the two countries?

22. Given the production possibilities in question 21, suppose that before trading Concordia experienced a doubling of productivity in the pork industry but continued to produce 15 units of beans. From this initial position, answer the following questions:
a) What are the costs of the two products in each country?
b) What products should each country specialize in and export?
c) If, prior to specialization and trade, Concordia produced combination D and Harmonia produced combination B, what would be the total gains from trade for the two countries?
d) What would be feasible terms of trade between the two countries?

23. Suppose three countries have the productivity figures shown in **Table 9.21**.

TABLE 9.21

Productivity per Worker	Wheat	Beans
Alpha	1	2
Beta	4	2
Gamma	2	2

Show the calculations used to arrive at the answers to the following questions.
a) Which country can produce wheat comparatively more cheaply? Which country can produce beans comparatively more cheaply?
b) Suppose that the international terms of trade were 1 wheat = 3/4 beans. Which countries would export wheat? Which countries would import wheat?
c) Suppose instead that the international terms of trade were 1 wheat = $1\frac{1}{2}$ beans. Which countries would export wheat? Which countries would import wheat?

Web-Based Activities

1. Is free trade a good idea? What are the arguments for and against free trade? Read the following articles and summarize the case for and against free trade: **http://www.fraserinstitute.ca/pps/11/econ_case.html** and People's Global Action Manifesto at **http://www.agp.org/agp/en/index.html**

2. With the Canada–U.S. Free Trade agreement (FTA) in 1986 and NAFTA in 1989, Canada started to remove some of its barriers to trade. However, several barriers to trade still exist. What are they? Read **http://www.tradecompass.com/library/books/com_guide/CANADA06.html** and list all of the areas in which the Canadian federal and provincial governments restrict trade.

Exchange Rates and the Balance of Payments

What's ahead...This chapter begins by giving a definition of the exchange rate and explains the meaning of an appreciation or depreciation in exchange rates. We then examine the causes of such changes and look at the different effects under a flexible exchange-rate system and under a fixed exchange-rate system. We see how each system interacts differently with the domestic economy. Finally, we explain exactly how international transactions are recorded in a country's balance of payments.

Have you ever travelled abroad? If so, wasn't part of the excitement of a new country finding and purchasing goods and services that were really "cheap" by Canadian standards? Did you try to spend Canadian dollars? Did you have difficulty in calculating the exchange rate? Did this exchange rate change while you were in the foreign country? What caused it to change? On the other hand, didn't you find some things that were really "out of line" in terms of the prices that you are used to? So why are there such differences in prices around the world? This chapter will help clear up questions like these.

S uppose that a resident of Alberta buys a product that was made in Quebec. This involves an economic exchange that we all understand. The product is moved west and the money payment flows east, and that is that. But now suppose that the same Alberta resident buys a product that was made in Japan. How is this exchange any different? In one sense there is no difference, in that the product goes one way and the payment the other. But in another sense it is different—here, two currencies are involved. The Alberta resident will want to pay in Canadian dollars, and the Japanese seller will want to be paid in yen. This means that an exchange between the two currencies will have to occur as the one currency will be exchanged for the other. This exchange will involve at least one bank. As well, import and export regulations and procedures are also involved. Thus, international trade is more complicated than domestic trade, and the most obvious complication is the exchange rate itself. Let's now go to a discussion of exchange rates.

Exchange Rates

For most people, an exchange rate is an enigma, yet it is nothing more than the comparative value of one currency in terms of another. It is, if you like, the relative price of a currency. Until comparatively recently, it was possible to state the value of a currency in terms of an international medium of exchange: gold. When countries were on the gold standard, each currency could be valued in terms of a comparative amount of gold. Today, however, if you want to know how much a Canadian dollar is worth, it can be expressed only in terms of how many American dollars, British pounds, Swiss francs, or some other currency it can buy.

Before we look at the determinants of exchange rates, let's make sure that you are able to easily convert one currency into another. For instance, if the Canadian dollar is worth, let's say, 0.70 American dollars, then how much is an American dollar worth in Canada? The answer is $1.43 (not $1.30). If you're not sure why, then ask yourself, what is the value of an American dollar if a Canadian dollar is worth $0.50 American—$1.50? $2? The answer is $2 Canadian. Both the $0.50 and $2 are **exchange rates**: Canadian for American, and American for Canadian. In general, to convert one currency into another we simply take the reciprocal:

exchange rate: the rate at which one currency is exchanged for another.

Most banks and exchange bureaus post the exchange rates on display boards so that they are readily accessible to travellers.

$$1 \text{ Canadian dollar} = \frac{1}{1 \text{ unit of foreign currency}}$$

or

$$1 \text{ unit of foreign currency} = \frac{1}{1 \text{ Canadian dollar}}$$

If a Canadian dollar is worth 5 Mexican pesos, then 1 Mexican peso is worth 1/5, or $0.20 Canadian. If a Canadian dollar is worth 0.50 British pounds, then a British pound would be worth 1/0.50, or $2 Canadian. And if the Canadian dollar is worth 0.70 American dollars, then an American dollar is worth 1/0.70, or 1.43 Canadian dollars.

SELF-TEST

1. A) Assume that a French franc is worth 0.20 Canadian dollars. How much is a Canadian dollar worth in francs?

B) Assume one Canadian dollar equals 70 Japanese yen. How much is a yen worth in Canadian dollars?

---

currency appreciation: the rise in the exchange rate of one currency for another.

currency depreciation: the fall in the exchange rate of one currency for another.

Exchange rates fluctuate, sometimes rising and sometimes falling. Such an increase or decrease is always in terms of another currency. For example, assume that instead of 1 British pound equalling $2 Canadian, it now equals $4 Canadian. How much is the Canadian dollar worth now? The answer is 0.25 pounds. In other words, when one currency **appreciates** in terms of another, the other currency automatically **depreciates** in value. This is not a case of cause and effect; it's simply true by definition.

ADDED DIMENSION

Strong Currencies

The international value of a currency is, unfortunately, regarded by some people (even, at times, by some economists) as an indicator of a country's economic strength and prestige on the international stage. Thus, when the Canadian dollar appreciates in value, it is sometimes described as a "stronger" dollar. Exchange rates are nothing more than the price (in terms of some other currency) of a currency, and how can one possibly talk of strong or weak prices? If this made any sense, we could certainly say that the price of beer is getting much stronger in Canada. Exchange rates appreciate and depreciate. They do not get stronger or weaker.

---

flexible exchange rate: a currency exchange rate determined by the market forces of supply and demand and not interfered with by government action.

fixed exchange rate: a currency exchange rate pegged by government and therefore prevented from rising or falling.

purchasing power parity theory: a theory suggesting that exchange rates will change so as to equate the purchasing power of each currency.

Two of the questions we need to answer in this chapter are: what determines the value of any given currency, and what are the causes of changes in this value? The exchange rate is simply the relative price of a currency, and that price may be determined by either the interaction of demand and supply in the marketplace, or it may be determined by government decree. In the first case, we are looking at **flexible** (or floating) **exchange rates**; in the second, at **fixed** (or pegged) **exchange rates**. We will look at each in turn.

Before we get into a detailed analysis of currency value determination, we should mention an old economic theory known as the **purchasing power parity theory** of exchange rates. This theory suggests that in the long run, exchange rates will change so as to equate the purchasing power of each country's currency. This means, for instance, that a pint of beer should have the same price in every country. (You will have to use a different currency in each, of course.) It also means that a thousand

Canadian dollars should have the same spending power in Canada as the equivalent number of French francs in France, or Japanese yen in Japan.

On the surface, this seems difficult to accept. Most international jetsetters (and anybody who shops south of the border) realize that some countries are relatively cheap for Canadians and one can have a reasonably good time for very little (in parts of Africa and Asia and in most Latin American countries, for example), whereas other countries are prohibitively expensive for the average Canadian (such as Japan, Scandinavian countries, and Switzerland). So why on earth would anyone suggest that, over time, the cost of living in various countries should become comparable?

In answering this question, we'll work through a model in which we assume that transport costs are negligible and that each country produces products that are identical to those from other countries. For instance, suppose that France produces and sells coal at 1000 French francs a tonne; Canada also produces and sells coal for $200 a tonne. Further, suppose that the exchange rate is $1 Canadian = 5 French francs. The price of coal, therefore, is the same in both countries. Now, what would happen if the price of coal in Canada were to rise to $250 a tonne? If the exchange rate remained the same, everybody would buy their coal in France. But of course, the exchange rate would not remain the same. People would be demanding French francs in order to buy French coal. The French franc would appreciate (as would, in all likelihood, the price of French coal). But how much would it appreciate? Well, as long as there was a difference in prices, it would pay some enterprising company to buy coal in France, where it is cheap, and sell it in Canada, where it is expensive.

Assuming that the price of coal in France remains at 1000 francs a tonne, then the French franc will appreciate until the prices in Canada and France are the same; that is, until $250 is equal to 1000 francs. In other words, the French franc will appreciate until 1 Canadian dollar is worth only 4 francs instead of 5 francs.

Once again, the purchasing power parity theory says that if the same product is sold at different prices in different countries, it would be worthwhile buying it where it is cheap and selling it where it is expensive. But this action, by itself, will cause the exchange rates to change until there is no longer any difference in the relative prices.

Yet, prices are not the same worldwide—why? First, if the price of a haircut was only half the price in New Orleans that it was in Edmonton, we would not really expect a mass exodus of Edmontonians heading down to Louisiana to get their locks shorn. In other words, certain goods and services are not transportable, and therefore differences in the prices of these things may well persist over time between countries. Second, if transport and other shipping costs are taken into account, then again price differences might continue. Third, tariffs and quotas limit and increase the costs of trade and lead to price differences between countries. Fourth, products are not identical. Some people do prefer, say, Japanese cars over North American cars. Fifth, and finally, exchange rates don't equate the purchasing power among countries because they are also greatly affected by the sale and purchase of financial assets. The five factors that explain differences in purchasing power between countries are:

- the fact that many services, such as haircuts, are not traded internationally
- the existence of transportation and insurance costs
- the existence of tariffs and other trade restrictions
- the expression of particular preferences by consumers
- the effect on the value of currencies of trade in financial assets

Despite all these reservations, many economists still hold, however, that in the long run there is a tendency for exchange rates to move toward equalizing the purchasing power of currencies. Whether or not this is true, we still need to explain day-to-day and year-to-year fluctuations in exchange rates.

Flexible Exchange Rates and the Demand for the Canadian Dollar

In the absence of government involvement, exchange rates are determined by the interplay of demand and supply in a free market. However, even when governments don't actually peg exchange rates, they still often feel it necessary to intervene in international exchange markets so as to influence the value of currencies. They become, therefore, active players in the game of buying and selling currencies. For the time being, however, we will ignore such involvement and concentrate on the determination of exchange rates entirely by market forces.

Apart from Canadians, who else wants to obtain Canadian dollars? The first and most obvious group are foreigners who want to obtain Canadian goods and services. The demand for Canadian exports, such as forest products and automobiles, therefore creates a demand for the Canadian dollar. Note, however, that some services can only be enjoyed in Canada. We are thinking here of restaurant, hotel, and other tourist services required by foreigners travelling in Canada. Tourism in Canada, therefore, represents a (significant) Canadian export. Conversely, spending by Canadians on imported goods or by travel abroad represents a Canadian import.

A second demand for the Canadian dollar involves foreigners who want to purchase Canadian investments. These investments might include the purchase of Canadian real estate or real assets, which we call **direct investment**, or it might include the purchase by foreigners of Canadian shares or bonds, which we call **portfolio investment**. In either case, a demand for the Canadian dollar with which to purchase these investments is created.

direct investment: the purchase of real assets.

portfolio investment: the purchase of shares or bonds representing less than 50 percent ownership.

This brings us to the third group of people who demand Canadian dollars: Canadians who receive income from abroad. This includes, for instance, people who have previously bought foreign investments. These people will be earning returns on these investments, which will be paid to them in foreign currencies. As Canadians, of

Canapress/Chuck Stoody

Railway trains carrying grain for export are constantly on the move at the United Grain Growers elevator in Vancouver.

course, they do not have much use for foreign currencies, and they will want to convert these currencies into Canadian dollars.

A fourth group who want to buy Canadian dollars are speculators. Speculators who deal in foreign exchange are no different from other types of speculators. They hope to buy when the price is low and sell later when the price is high. Speculators buying Canadian dollars are therefore hoping for an appreciation of the Canadian dollar some time in the future, when they will then sell. There is another group of currency dealers who also buy and sell Canadian dollars, but for a different reason. They buy Canadian dollars (or any other currency) whenever they see a difference in quoted exchange rates on different international exchanges. For instance, let's say that the Canadian dollar is quoted at $0.715 U.S. on the Zurich exchange but is being quoted at $0.718 on the Tokyo exchange. Then it would pay someone to buy Canadian dollars in Switzerland (where they are cheap) and sell them in Japan (where they are relatively more expensive). This is known as **arbitrage**. Notice that, unlike speculators, those engaged in arbitrage are not concerned with the future value of the Canadian dollar and are not holding them to sell at some later date; they are selling immediately.

arbitrage: the process of buying a commodity in one market, where the price is low, and immediately selling it in a second market where the price is higher.

To sum up, those who have a demand for the Canadian dollar are:

- foreigners who want to buy Canadian exports or who travel in Canada
- foreigners who want to purchase Canadian investments
- Canadians who receive income from abroad
- currency speculators

Finally, as noted above, governments also sometimes buy and sell currencies, but more on this later.

Now, remember what we mean by the demand for a currency. It's no different from the demand for any other product or service; that is, it is defined as the quantities that people are willing and able to buy at various prices. As you would expect, the demand curve for the Canadian dollar is downward-sloping, as shown in **Figure 10.1**.

FIGURE 10.1 The Demand for the Canadian Dollar

The demand curve for the Canadian dollar is downward-sloping, reflecting the inverse relationship between the price of the currency and the quantity demanded. At P_1 the quantity demanded is Q_1.

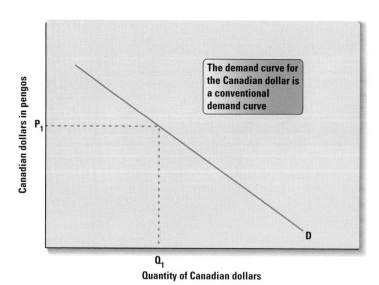

The demand curve for the Canadian dollar is a conventional demand curve

Note that on the vertical axis we need to express the price of the Canadian dollar in terms of another currency since, if you think about it, it would be a bit silly to express the price of the Canadian dollar in Canadian dollars, because then it would always equal one.

> **A Canadian dollar is always worth one dollar in Canada. It always was and always will be.**

Whatever currency you choose to express it in, other than the Canadian dollar, is of no importance. On our graph, we have used the pengo, the currency of the mythical and fascinating country of Pengoland. The demand curve is of course downward-sloping, which implies that at a higher exchange rate the quantity of Canadian dollars demanded will be low; at a low exchange rate, the quantity demanded will be high. Now let's figure out why that should be so. Remember that the demand for the Canadian dollar comes, by and large, from foreigners buying our goods, services, and investments, that is, from Canadian exports in the broad sense.

Let's start off by assuming that the Canadian dollar is worth 1 pengo and that one of our major exports to Pengoland is smoked salmon, which is priced at $100 a box in Canada and therefore sells for 100 pengos in Pengoland. Now, what would happen if the value of the Canadian dollar were to appreciate so that $1 Canadian is now equal to 2 pengos? (Note that as the Canadian dollar appreciates, the pengo depreciates; it is now worth only 50 cents). The effect of such an appreciation is summarized in **Table 10.1**.

ADDED DIMENSION

The Effective Exchange Rate

There is no single commodity whose value remains constant and against which all currencies can be measured. This means the Canadian dollar might well be *depreciating* against one currency, such as the U.S. dollar, but at the same time *appreciating* against all other currencies. It is possible, however, to work out an average of what is happening to the Canadian dollar. This is what is referred to as the effective exchange rate. The effective exchange rate compares the value of the Canadian dollar in terms of the average value of all currencies of countries with which Canada trades. It is a weighted average, which means that the value of the U.S. dollar, for instance, would carry more weight than, say, the Swiss franc in calculating its value, since Canada does much more trade with the United States than it does with Switzerland. The effective exchange rate is also based on an index value of 100, assigned in the base year. Following are figures for the effective Canadian exchange rate over sixteen years.

1981	100
1985	92.05
1990	99.27
1992	94.99
1994	83.69
1996	83.66
1997	83.65

Source: Bank of Canada, *Quarterly Review*, Spring 1998.

TABLE 10.1

Price of One Canadian Dollar	Price in Canada of a Box of Salmon	Price in Penogoland of a Box of Salmon
1 pengo	$100	100 pengos
2 pengos	$100	200 pengos

Despite the fact that the price of smoked salmon in Canada remains unchanged, its effective price has increased as far as the Pengolians are concerned. Whereas before they paid 100 pengos, now they will have to pay 200 pengos for the same box. One would expect therefore that they would buy less smoked salmon. In other words, when the Canadian dollar appreciates, the effective price of Canadian exports increases, and total exports are likely to decline.

You can see why, therefore, a high Canadian dollar is likely to be unpopular among Canadian exporters and in the high-export provinces of Canada. For example, even a small increase in the Canadian dollar can have big implications in terms of sales, profits, and employment in the B.C. lumber industry and is looked on with alarm. Not only that, but a higher Canadian dollar means that the effective price of Canadian financial investments will also be higher for foreigners, so that foreign investment is likely to decrease.

The depreciation of the Canadian dollar, on the other hand, has the opposite effect. Assume, for instance that, starting from $1 Canadian = 1 pengo, the Canadian dollar were to fall to $1 Canadian = 0.5 pengo. (The pengo now equals $2 Canadian; that is, it has appreciated). The same box of Canadian smoked salmon that used to cost the Pengolians 100 pengos can now be obtained for a mere 50 pengos. This will then cause exports of smoked salmon to increase. In general, therefore, when the Canadian dollar depreciates, the effective price of Canadian exports decreases, and total exports are likely to increase. Exporters will prefer a low Canadian dollar to a high Canadian dollar, since this makes Canadian products more competitive abroad.

We can summarize these results as follows:

> **When the Canadian dollar depreciates, the effective price of Canadian exports decreases and total exports are likely to rise.**

and

> **When the Canadian dollar appreciates, the effective price of Canadian exports increases and total exports are likely to fall.**

SELF-TEST

2. Given the events described below, indicate whether the demand for the Canadian dollar would appreciate, depreciate, or not change:

A) Canadian exports rise.

B) Toronto hosts the world to Expo 2002.

C) IBM, ITT, and the provincial government announce the construction of a $2 billion data processing and informational transferral complex in Halifax.

D) Immigration from the Maritime provinces to Ontario increases appreciably.

The Supply of Canadian Dollars

Let's now take a look at the other side of the coin, the supply of Canadian dollars on the world market, and examine who exactly provides this supply. Most people would probably answer: the government or the Bank of Canada. Well, under certain circumstances that may be true, as we shall see later. However, in a free market system it's not really necessary for these institutions to supply Canadian dollars to foreigners, since through trade, dollars will be made available automatically on the world's money market. How does this come about? It is from the simple fact that if we Canadians wish to purchase foreign currencies, then we will use Canadian dollars to make these purchases. Thus, in obtaining foreign currencies, we must automatically supply Canadian dollars. In general, therefore, the supply of Canadian dollars comes from our demand for foreign currencies. This relationship between the supply of and demand for currencies is important enough to emphasize:

Quantity demanded of foreign currencies	**=**	**Quantity supplied of Canadian dollars**
Quantity demanded of Canadian dollars	**=**	**Quantity supplied of foreign currencies**

The supply of Canadian dollars is graphed in **Figure 10.2**.

FIGURE 10.2 The Supply of the Canadian Dollar

The supply of the Canadian dollar is upward-sloping, reflecting the direct relationship between the price of the currency and the quantity supplied. At price P_1 the quantity supplied is Q_1.

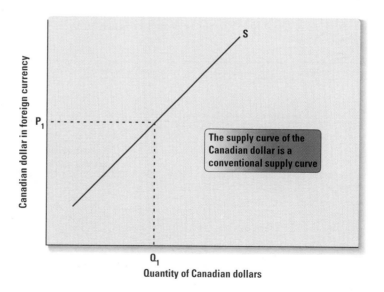

The supply curve of the Canadian dollar is a conventional supply curve

Why is the supply curve upward-sloping? It is for the usual reason, that an increase in the price (of a currency) will lead to an increase in the quantity supplied. Or, put another way, an appreciation of the Canadian dollar will lead to an increase in imports. Let's make sure that we understand this. Suppose that a Japanese car carries a price tag of 1 400 000 yen and that the exchange rate between the yen and the Canadian dollar is 80 yen for one Canadian dollar. A Canadian auto dealer would then sell this auto for $18 000 (1 400 000/80). (For simplicity, we are ignoring the dealer's mark-up, tariffs, transport costs, insurance, and so on.) Now, assume that the Canadian dollar appreciates so that one Canadian dollar buys 100 yen. Then, the auto dealer would have to sell the auto for $14 400. The dealer would sell more units of this auto at $14 400 than at $18 000. This increase in imports will increase the quantity of Canadian dollars supplied on the world market. We can summarize these results, as follows:

> **When the Canadian dollar appreciates, the effective price of Canadian imports decreases and total imports are likely to rise.**

Additionally,

> **When the Canadian dollar depreciates, the effective price of Canadian imports increases and total imports are likely to fall.**

From a Canadian importer's point of view, a high Canadian dollar is much preferred. This is also true from the average consumer's point of view: a high Canadian dollar makes foreign products much cheaper, and as a result one would expect more Canadians to do cross-border shopping.

Equilibrium in Foreign-Exchange Markets

We now need to put together the supply and demand curves to obtain an equilibrium exchange rate, as is done in **Figure 10.3**.

FIGURE 10.3 The Demand for and Supply of the Canadian Dollar

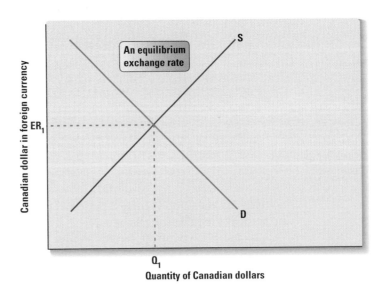

The intersection of the demand and supply curves yields the equilibrium exchange rate: ER_1. At ER_1 the quantity of dollars demanded and the quantity supplied are equal.

Note that at the equilibrium exchange rate, ER_1, the quantity demanded for the Canadian dollar is equal to the quantity supplied. The demand comes from foreigners (Canadian exports) and the supply comes from Canadians (Canadian imports). Can foreigners always get their hands on sufficient Canadian dollars to purchase Canadian goods? Certainly. It does not require any assistance from the Canadian government or from the Bank of Canada. With truly flexible exchange rates, sufficient Canadian dollars are made available by Canadians themselves, who automatically supply dollars when purchasing foreign currencies. Note also that at equilibrium, not only is the quantity supplied and the quantity demanded of Canadian dollars equal, but the quantities demanded and supplied of foreign currencies in Canada will also be equal. Remember that foreign currencies are made available to Canadians whenever a foreigner purchases Canadian products or investments, and at equilibrium such foreign currencies will just be sufficient to satisfy the demand by Canadians for these currencies.

ADDED DIMENSION

Real Exchange Rates

How would you feel about emigrating to the fictitious country of Albioni, where the average monthly salary is 20 000 albions? Before you could decide, you would probably want to know, among many other things, what are 20 000 albions worth? Suppose that you learned that 1 Albion equalled 1 Canadian dollar, would that help you decide? If you still cannot make up your mind, perhaps some more data would be helpful. An average meal in Albioni will cost you 200 albions per person, a pair of socks cost 20 albions, and a new car will cost you 200 000 albions. Now, a rational decision is easier to make. In other words, in order to compare the values of currencies we need to know not only the exchange rate but *also* the average price level in each country. This is what the real exchange rate measures. In terms of a formula, it is:

$$\text{real exchange rate} = \frac{\text{price level in Canada}}{\text{price level in other country}} \times \text{nominal exchange rate}$$

where the nominal exchange rate is simply the value of the Canadian dollar, in the sense that we have been talking about throughout this chapter. As an example, suppose that a brand-new Toyota costs 1 400 000 yen in Japan and that an equivalent Ford car in Canada costs $20 000. If the exchange rate was equal to 70 yen per Canadian dollar, then you can see that the two cars have equivalent value, for example,

$$\text{real exchange rate} = \frac{20\ 000}{1\ 400\ 000} \times 70 = 1$$

The real exchange rate, therefore, measures the comparative purchasing power of a currency. The formula tells you, for instance, that the value of Canada's real exchange rate will increase if either the nominal exchange rate or the Canadian price level increases or if the Japanese price level falls. Now suppose that the price of a new Ford dropped to $15 000. The value of the real exchange rate would change to

$$\text{real exchange rate} = \frac{15\ 000}{1\ 400\ 000} \times 70 = 0.75$$

In other words, a Canadian Ford owner is now poorer than a Japanese Toyota owner, since, if he sold his car and converted it into yen (obtaining 15 000 × 70 or 1 050 000 yen), he could only afford to buy 3/4 of a Toyota. The Toyota owner, on the other hand, could now buy 4/3 Fords. Given this, you can imagine that Japanese buyers will be flocking to buy Canadian Fords, which have become a real bargain. The result of this increased demand (for both Fords and for the Canadian dollar) is that both of them will increase. Can you figure out how far they will increase? The answer is, when the real exchange rate is again equal to 1. This the reason why economists suggest that there is a long-run tendency for the purchasing power of all currencies to move toward par.

Changes in Demand and Supply

Since the value of a currency is determined by the interplay of supply and demand, it follows that any change in supply or demand will change its value. We now focus on what could cause a change in demand or supply and how such a change will affect a currency's value. Let's start on the demand side. What could cause people to demand more Canadian dollars, even though there has been no change in the currency's value? Well, the first and most straightforward reason would be a rise in incomes in the countries that buy Canadian goods. It seems reasonable to suggest that if *foreign incomes* increase, then the demand for all available products, including Canadian ones, will increase. Let's trace through the effects on **Figure 10.4**.

The initial demand curve is D_1. The increase in foreign income and the resulting increase in the demand for Canadian exports will increase the demand for Canadian dollars. This is illustrated by the shift in the demand curve to D_2. The increase in demand creates a shortage of Canadian dollars, which results in the exchange rate rising from ER_1 to ER_2. At this higher exchange rate, we obtain a new equilibrium. This higher exchange rate means that the attractiveness of Canadian exports is reduced because they are effectively more expensive. However, the volume of trade has still increased, *despite* the higher Canadian dollar. Note that imports and exports have increased. Why have imports increased? Remember that the higher exchange rate, ER_2, makes imports cheaper and therefore more are bought. In other words, an increase in the demand for Canadian goods and services will increase Canadian exports, *despite* the appreciation of the Canadian dollar, and will increase Canadian imports *because* of the appreciation.

FIGURE 10.4 An Increase in the Demand for a Currency

A rightward shift in the demand for the Canadian dollar will cause the equilibrium exchange rate to rise from ER_1 to ER_2 and the equilibrium quantity to increase from Q_1 to Q_2.

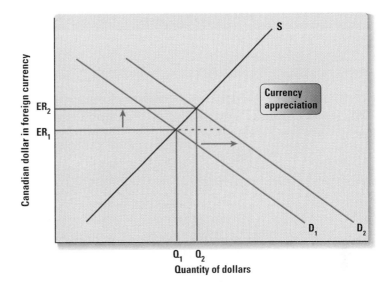

Other things besides an increase in foreign income will cause a change in the demand for Canadian dollars. For example, the *price of Canadian products that are traded* abroad will also have an impact on demand. A decrease in the price of these goods will cause the worldwide demand for such products to increase. It must be added, however, that it's not the absolute level of prices of traded goods that is important, but rather the relative level compared with that of other countries. An increase in the prices of foreign goods that compete with Canadian exports will have the same effect on the demand for Canadian exports as would the decrease in Canadian prices.

A third factor affecting the demand for a currency is the view foreigners hold toward Canadian goods—in short, *foreigners' tastes*. For example, if tastes shifted away from wood-frame houses towards metal-frame houses, this may well decrease Canada's lumber exports.

A final factor affecting the demand for Canadian dollars is *interest rates*. When foreigners are deciding whether or not to put money into Canada, they will look at a number of factors, but the rate of interest that they can obtain is certainly one of the most important. Traditionally, rates of interest in Canada have been kept above those in the United State for the express reason of encouraging the inflow of American money and to discourage the outflow of Canadian dollars to the United States. Obviously, the higher the rate of interest, the higher will be the level of foreign currency flow into Canada. This will mean a higher demand for Canadian dollars. As with prices, it's not the absolute level of interest rates that is important, but the difference between Canadian rates and those in other countries. The demand for the Canadian dollar would therefore increase with a drop in interest rates abroad. In summary, the demand for the Canadian dollar is determined by:

- the level of foreign incomes
- the price of Canadian products
- foreigners' tastes
- comparative interest rates

SELF-TEST

4. Assuming flexible exchange rates, draw a graph that illustrates a decrease in the demand for the Canadian dollar. On the graph, identify the effect of the decreased demand on the exchange rate and the quantity of dollars bought and sold. Next, list four reasons why such a decrease might occur.

ADDED DIMENSION

Foreign Investment and Interest-Rate Parity

The amount of international funds looking for a good (profitable) home is enormous. International investors are constantly seeking opportunities where they can earn the highest returns on their funds. It is estimated that $40 billion is traded every day in foreign-exchange markets. (In contrast, the demand for Canadian dollars to buy Canadian products is less than $1 billion per day.)

An investor buying foreign financial assets can earn a return from both the interest and from an appreciation in the value of the currency in which it is denominated. For instance, suppose I buy a French bond that has a value of 5000 francs and pays annual interest of 8 percent per annum. If the exchange rate is 5 French francs to the dollar, it will cost me $1000. At the end of the year, I receive 5400 francs. Now suppose that during the year the franc has appreciated to 4.5 francs to the dollar. Converting my francs back into dollars gives me $1200. I have therefore earned $200, or 20 percent on my original $1000. I earned 8 percent in interest and 12 percent from the appreciation of the franc.

This also means that if the currency I hold drops in value, the interest earned is wiped out by the loss on exchange.

Foreign investors therefore are concerned not only with interest to be earned but also with what might happen to the value of the foreign currency. This is the reason why there are often big differences in interest rates around the world.

Ask yourself this: if Canadians can earn only 5 percent interest in Canada but can earn 20 percent in Mexico, why wouldn't all the funds flow out of Canada and into Mexico? The answer is that in order to earn that 20 percent per year, you have to convert your dollars into pesos and leave it in pesos for a whole year. But many are fearful that during the year the value of the peso might fall against the dollar. How much does the average investor think it will fall? Presumably by 15 percent. Why this amount? Because they will earn a certain 20 percent on their funds but expect to lose 15 percent on the depreciation of the peso, netting them 5 percent—the same amount they can earn in Canada. In other words, if you take into consideration both the interest earned and the gain or loss on the foreign currency, the rate of return you can earn is more or less equal around the world. This is often referred to as *interest-rate parity*, though perhaps it would be better to refer to it as rate of return parity.

We now need to recognize that any change in the demand for the Canadian dollar will have effects on the domestic economy. If the demand for the Canadian dollar has increased because Canadian exports have increased, aggregate demand will also have increased. Whether this increase in exports is because of higher foreign incomes, lower Canadian prices, or a change in tastes in favour of Canadian goods doesn't matter. The higher exports mean greater aggregate demand. This is illustrated in **Figure 10.5**.

FIGURE 10.5 The Effect of an Increase of Exports on Aggregate Demand

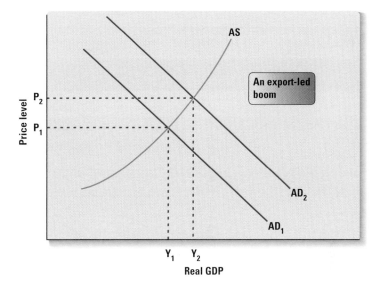

An increase in Canadian exports increases aggregate demand, as illustrated by the shift from AD$_1$ to AD$_2$. This results in a rise in both the price level and in GDP.

An increase in Canadian exports does indeed raise the value of the dollar (and also imports), but it also raises Canadian GDP (assuming that the increase in exports is greater than the increase in imports, which is almost always the case). This process is often given the name of an export-led boom. Foreigners buy more Canadian goods and this raises aggregate demand within Canada, creating new jobs, raising GDP and, finally, the price level.

You should also note that we can see here that this export-led boom may have the effect of reducing the size of the Canadian multiplier. This is because the boom will, as we just mentioned, likely increase the prices of Canadian products and, further, will raise the value of the Canadian exchange rate. Both of these effects will tend to dampen down the initial rise in exports.

A very important point in all this discussion is that the exchange rate does not move in isolation from the domestic economy. What happens on the international market very much affects what happens internally. This fact has always been true, but it is becoming increasingly pertinent as the world's economies become more integrated. This is a theme that we will return to in Chapter 14.

SELF-TEST

5. Assume that the demand for Canadian exports decreases. What would be the effect on:
A) The value of the Canadian dollar?

B) The level of aggregate demand?
C) The level of GDP?
D) The price level?

Let us now work through a situation that affects Canadians' demand for imported goods. Assume that Canada were to remove the tariffs on Mexican products coming into Canada. To the Canadian consumer this lowers the price of Mexican products, and we would expect the quantity demanded of such goods by Canadians to increase. This means that the Canadian demand for the Mexican peso increases, and this, in turn, implies that Canadians will be supplying more Canadian dollars on the world market. This last point is illustrated in **Figure 10.6**.

FIGURE 10.6 An Increase in the Supply of Canadian Dollars

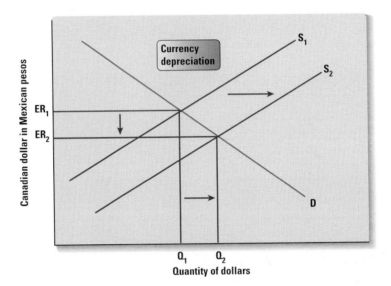

An increase in the supply of Canadian dollars is represented by the shift from S_1 to S_2. As a result of this increase, the value of the Canadian dollar decreases and the quantity of Canadian dollars bought and sold increases.

As Canadians demand more imports from Mexico and thus more pesos, the supply curve of Canadian dollars shifts outward from S_1 to S_2. This will cause the exchange rate to drop to a lower level at ER_2. The removal of tariffs on Mexican imports therefore will tend to lead to a depreciation of the Canadian dollar and, on the other side of the coin, an appreciation of the peso.

In other words, Mexican exports to Canada will increase *despite* the higher peso. In addition, Mexican imports of Canadian products will increase *because* of the higher peso. The total value of trade will therefore increase.

The intellectual appeal of market-determined flexible exchange rates is strong among most economists today. If the supply of, or the demand for, a currency changes for any one of a variety of reasons, the exchange rate itself changes and the economy adjusts automatically without any need for government policy and with a minimum of disruption to the domestic economy. Perhaps the best way to really understand all this is to now move to a discussion of fixed exchange rates and then to compare the two systems.

The Falling Loonie

In the last six months of 1998, the Canadian dollar fell from approximately 70 cents U.S. to record lows in the 63 to 66 cent range. Some political–economic commentators saw this as evidence that the Canadian economy was in serious decline. Others claimed that this was proof that the polices of the federal government had failed. In fact, the three main reasons for this fall were much less dramatic and much more global.

Courtesy Cam Cardow

First, demand for the U.S. dollar had been incredibly high, which had pushed up its value against almost all other currencies in the world, most notably the Japanese yen, but also the Canadian dollar. The reason for this was not complicated. Imagine that you live in Asia and that you are sitting on a large sum of cash. This could be because you sold your real estate holdings in Thailand before the crash in prices in 1997, or perhaps you sold out of the Asian stock markets before they crashed. You were painfully aware that if the currency you were holding depreciated, you would be less wealthy. So what did you do? You bought the currency that was least likely to decrease in value in the near future. And the markets at the time were telling the world that the U.S. dollar was that currency. So up went the demand for the American dollar, which increased its value, and down came the values of most other currencies.

Second was the fact that Canadian interest rates were at that time below those in the United States. Although this was historically unusual, it had been to the benefit of the Canadian economy in terms of stimulating growth and creating jobs. However, a lower rate of interest was not good news for those who held savings in Canadian dollars. Now, once again, ask yourself: if you held Canadian dollars and sensed that the value of the Canadian dollar was about to fall by 10 percent or so, and you also knew that U.S. rates on savings accounts paid higher interest, what might you do? You got it! Sell your Canadian dollars and buy U.S. dollars, and find a U.S. bank or Treasury Bill to park your money in. The supply of Canadian dollars on the world's currency markets went up (you just sold them), which pushed the price of the Canadian dollar down. Furthermore, the demand for U.S. dollars also went up (you just bought them), and this pushed the value of the U.S. dollar up, which, we know from above, meant that the value of the Canadian dollar was reduced.

Third, the general price trend for natural resources was down for most of the 1990s. In fact, some commodity price indices are showing the real prices (the price corrected for inflation) of oil, copper, zinc, nickel, and so on are now the lowest that they have ever been, including in the depths of the Great Depression. This is good news for those industries that use these commodities in production, but bad news for the firms, and the countries, that sell these commodities. And, of course, Canada is one of those countries. This has also put downward pressure on the value of the Canadian dollar.

Fixed Exchange Rates

Fixed exchange rates have been the rule rather than the exception over the centuries. Until as recently as the early 1970s, most governments throughout the world were persuaded that they needed to exercise control over the value of their own currency and not leave it open to the vagaries of international dealing. At that time, the Canadian dollar was fixed at $0.925 U.S. Let's look at some of the reasons for this belief.

It is suggested that, by its very nature, international trading is fraught with problems and uncertainties. If, as a Canadian company, you want to trade with a firm in Japan or Germany or any other country, you need to understand the different commercial laws and government regulations, the language and culture, the customs and history, and a host of other factors. What you do not need is the addition of another problem: fluctuating exchange rates. After all, if you have spent a good deal of time and money negotiating a contract with some foreign firm, you do not want to run the risk of seeing all your profit wiped out by an unforeseen shift in exchange rates.

Fixed exchange rates do add a degree of certainty to international trade. Without this security, many feel that the volume of international trade would be considerably less. Remember that, if flexible exchange rates change, both exports and imports are immediately affected. This means that employment and profits in the firms within these sectors can take rather abrupt swings up or down. An appreciation of the exchange rate, for instance, will lead to a decline in exports and an expansion of imports. This will be good news for those firms that do the importing, but it will involve layoffs, the cancellation of contracts, and the postponement of investment plans for export industries. The import industries, on the other hand, will be gearing up for the higher volumes by hiring additional staff, buying new equipment, and expanding capacity. What happens now if the exchange rate starts to depreciate? Everything will be thrown into reverse, with the export industries now booming but the import industries suffering. Thus, it is argued, flexible exchange rates can lead to a great deal of domestic disruption and make long-term planning very difficult. A corollary of this is the fact that flexible exchange rates can be affected by the actions of a small group of speculators. Why, it is asked, should the fortunes of many firms and the livelihood of many people be in the hands of a few people who are out for private gain and cannot be made accountable for their actions?

Finally, it should be mentioned that in people's minds there is a great deal of national prestige tied up in exchange rates. They are often fixed at rates that do not reflect economic reality. Many people want to feel that their nation has a "strong" currency, despite the fact that, as we have mentioned, appreciating and depreciating currencies are neither good nor bad. Yet, many people in Canada feel that since we have only a "66 cent" dollar, the Canadian dollar is weaker than the American dollar. They do not seem to realize that we are dealing with two different countries and two separate currencies, and there is no reason why, except through coincidence, they should be at par. Hardly anyone would suggest that the Canadian dollar should be at par with the pound sterling or the German mark or the Japanese yen, yet the comparison of the Canadian dollar with the American dollar still persists. In summary, the arguments in favour of fixed exchange rates are that:

- they add a degree of certainty to international trade
- they prevent instability in the export and import industries
- they discourage currency speculation
- they appeal to people who tend to equate the exchange rate with national prestige

Such are the arguments for a fixed exchange rate. Let us now go deeper into how such a system would function. Assume that initially the government of Canada fixed the exchange rate. This means that anyone buying or selling Canadian dollars could only do so at the official rate decreed by the government. Let's begin with the rate fixed at the equilibrium market rate. Suppose that later, however, an increase in the demand for Canadian exports and thus the Canadian dollar occurs. The situation is illustrated in **Figure 10.7.**

FIGURE 10.7 An Increase in Currency Demand under Fixed Exchange Rates

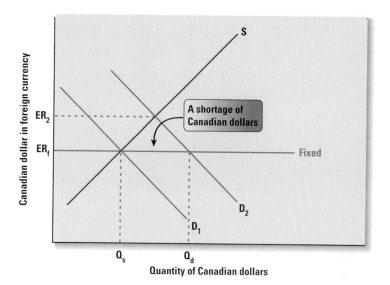

An increase in the demand for the Canadian dollar does not lead to an appreciation of the Canadian dollar under a fixed-exchange-rate system. The result, therefore, is a shortage of Canadian dollars on the world market and an undervalued dollar.

Given a fixed exchange rate, an increase in the demand for the Canadian dollar results in the dollar being undervalued, compared with what a free-market value would be (the market rate ER_2 is above the fixed rate, ER_f, in this case). Foreigners see Canadian goods as very attractive buys. At the fixed rate of ER_f, the quantity demanded (Q_d) of Canadian dollars exceeds the quantity supplied (Q_s). Since the government has fixed the exchange rate, it must ensure, for normal trading to continue, that enough Canadian dollars are made available. In other words, the Bank of Canada will have to supply this shortage by expanding the money supply. This strong demand for Canadian exports and the continual increase in money supply by the Bank of Canada will eventually be inflationary. Once this inflation occurs for a long enough time, the price of Canadian goods will rise until the demand for them declines. This decline in the demand for Canadian goods will decrease the demand for the Canadian dollar and equilibrium will eventually be restored. However, this adjustment process could be very long and painful.

Let's look now at the second scenario, which is in many people's view more serious for an economy and, for that reason, requires us to go into greater detail. Again, suppose that the Canadian government fixes the value of the Canadian dollar at ER_f. This time, however, the demand for the dollar drops, as shown in **Figure 10.8**.

The exchange rate is now above what would be the free-market equilibrium rate (the market rate ER_2 is below the fixed rate, ER_f), and thus there is a surplus of Canadian dollars on the world market. Let's think out what is happening. Before the change in demand, the quantity of dollars foreigners wanted to buy was equal to the quantity supplied of dollars on the market. Then the demand for the dollar dropped. Since foreigners are now buying fewer Canadian goods and services and therefore buying fewer Canadian dollars, the amount of foreign currencies available for Canadians to buy is reduced. Thus, this situation can be seen as either one of a surplus of Canadian dollars on the world market or as a shortage of foreign currencies in Canada. Whichever way you look at it, the fixed exchange rate ER_f is overvalued. So, what happens next?

FIGURE 10.8 A Decrease in Currency Demand under Fixed Exchange Rates

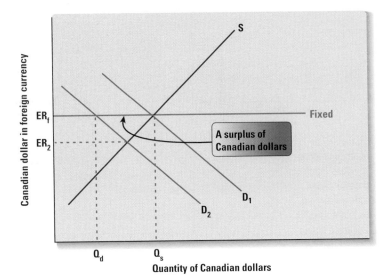

A decrease in the demand for the Canadian dollar does not lead to a lower Canadian dollar under a fixed-exchange-rate system. The result is a surplus of Canadian dollars on the world market and an overvalued dollar.

In instituting fixed exchange rates, the government must take responsibility for any surplus or shortage of currencies. Faced with an insufficient supply of foreign currencies from normal trading, the government, through the Bank of Canada, has got to make good the deficiency. One of the major assets of the Bank of Canada, apart from government bonds, is reserves of gold and foreign currencies. (At the end of March 1998, for instance, these stood at approximately $22 billion U.S., of which $19 billion was in U.S. dollars.) These official international reserves, or at least as much as necessary, have to be made available to Canadians. So, along with an overvalued fixed exchange rate, as in Figure 10.8, comes the depletion of the central bank's foreign reserves. This draining of foreign-currency reserves cannot continue indefinitely, and the government will, as a result, be forced to take some kind of action. There are few options open, and none of them is attractive.

One possible tactic to stem the demand for foreign currencies would be to introduce quotas or tariffs. However, introducing such trade policies to try to reduce the amount of imports would violate international trade agreements and probably result in retaliation against Canadian exports. Direct **subsidies** to increase Canadian exports could, again, be in violation of trade agreements and would be expensive for the government.

A policy of introducing foreign-exchange controls has been used by some governments in the past. Here, instead of directly restricting imports, the government restricts the amount of foreign currencies available to Canadians. In other words, it rations the relatively scarce foreign currencies by saying: this is the amount of currency being made available by foreigners buying our goods and services, and this amount only can be obtained by Canadians. What this does, in effect, is restrict the amount of imports. These foreign-exchange controls can take many forms, including quotas on foreign currencies available for foreign travel, placing currency quotas on importing companies or industries, or giving preference to certain imports over others. The problem with foreign-exchange controls is that they distort trade and production, favour some importers over others, and restrict consumer choice.

subsidy: a payment by government for the purpose of increasing some particular activity or increasing the output of a particular good.

Another alternative would be for the Canadian government to convince countries that are big exporters to Canada to agree to voluntary export restrictions. This would restrict imports to Canada. This is not often an easy option to exercise but has been achieved by a few countries recently.

There is only one other policy option for a government facing an overvalued fixed exchange rate. Since imports are a function of income, a reduction in imports could be achieved by reducing income. This involves reducing aggregate demand through specific policies that we will discuss in the next two chapters. In short, the adjustment mechanism for an overvalued exchange rate may be the deliberate creation of a recession. In summary, a government can defend an overvalued exchange rate in four ways:

- introducing quotas or tariffs
- introducing foreign-exchange controls
- negotiating voluntary export restrictions
- creating a recession at home

devaluation: the re-fixing by government of an exchange rate at a lower level.

A government that finds it politically impossible to impose any of the above policies, or that finds that those policies fail after being tried, will be forced to **devalue** its currency, that is, re-fix the exchange rate at a lower level.

Devaluation of a currency has serious political ramifications. It is often interpeted as a failure of a government to control its own destiny and, from that point of view, may lead to a loss of confidence generally in a government's economic policies. Furthermore, once even the possibility of a devaluation is recognized by the market, international currency dealers will ask only "when" and not "if." This lack of confidence by itself may make devaluation an inevitability, because dealers will not want to hold the currency when there is the possibility that it may be devalued. Their actions, in selling off the currency that is under siege, then become a self-fulfilling prophecy.

In sum, the adjustment mechanism for an under- or overvalued fixed exchange rate is very painful and throws the economy into either an inflationary situation or into recession. For this reason, most economists favour the flexible exchange-rate system. In fact, fixed exchange rates have been rare in the past 20 years. However, truly flexible rates are almost as rare. Instead, most countries operate a system of managed exchange rates, or a **dirty float**. This means that the degree to which a currency is allowed to float (or fluctuate) is managed by the central bank in order to stabilize the exchange rate. In Canada's case, then, the Bank of Canada buys and sells foreign currencies to keep the value of the dollar within what it perceives to be permissible limits. In order to prevent the depreciation of the dollar, the government sells foreign reserves and buys dollars so as to hold up the demand for the dollar. To prevent an appreciation of the dollar, the government will do the opposite and sell dollars in exchange for foreign currency. This hybrid of the fixed and flexible exchange-rate systems will probably be the continued choice of governments for the foreseeable future.

dirty float: an exchange rate that is not officially fixed by government but is managed by the central bank's ongoing intervention in the market.

SELF-TEST

6. Assume that the demand for the Canadian dollar increases. Describe the adjustment mechanism to this change, given: A) flexible exchange rates; and B) fixed exchange rates.

The Balance of Payments

balance of payments: an accounting of a country's international transactions that involves the payment and receipts of foreign currencies.

current account: a subcategory of the balance of payments that shows the income or expenditures related to exports and imports.

capital account: a subcategory of the balance of payments that reflects changes in ownership of assets associated with foreign investment.

Just like any other balance sheet, the **balance of payments** (or, more correctly, the international balance of payments) should always balance. But it is important to know where the dollars went and how they went. The balance sheet is divided up into three main sections: the **current account**, the **capital account**, and the official settlements account. In a sense, the balance of payments is a misnomer, since it is more like an income statement than a balance sheet. What it shows are the various categories of international buying and selling that involve the Canadian dollar during a year. **Table 10.2** is a simplified balance of payments for Canada for 1997.

TABLE 10.2 Canada's Balance of Payments 1997 ($ billions)

Current Account		
Export of goods and services	+343	
Import of goods and services	−327	
= Balance of trade		+16
Investment income from abroad	+30	
Investment income paid abroad	−59	
Net investment income		−29
Transfers (net)		+1
= Current Account balance		−12
Capital Account		
Foreign investment in Canada	+72	
less Canadian investment abroad	−52	
= Capital Account balance		+20
Total balance (Current Account and Capital Account)		+8
Official Settlements Account		
Change in Canadian dollars (change in foreign reserves)		−8
Total Balance (Current Account + Capital Account + Official Settlements Account)		0

Source: Adapted from Statistics Canada, CANSIM Database, Matrix 2360.

balance of trade: the value of a country's exports of goods and services less the value of its imports.

In a sense, the current account shows income and expenditures from international trading. The first two lines, exports and imports of goods and services, are self-explanatory. The difference between the two represents the **balance of trade** (what we called "net exports" in earlier chapters). Recall that imports create a supply of Canadian dollars; exports create a demand. However, when looking at the balance of payments, it is often more illuminating to look at the corresponding flows of foreign currencies. In other words, imports create a demand by Canadians for foreign currencies and exports produce a supply of foreign currencies. Traditionally, Canada has had a *positive* balance of trade. This means that trade in goods and services usually produces a net inflow of foreign currencies to Canada. In 1997, this inflow amounts to $16 billion.

The next line, investment income from abroad, includes the total amount of interest and dividends that Canadians received in this particular year from their previous foreign investments. This income produces an inflow of foreign currency into Canada.

Investment income paid abroad represents an outflow of foreign currencies. Since, in the past, foreigners have invested more in Canada than Canadians have invested abroad, the income going abroad far exceeds the income flowing into Canada.

The last line in the current account, transfers, includes gifts and other remittances (pensions, for example) as well as foreign aid. In our example, more transfers came to Canada than went abroad.

The balance on the current account equals -12, which means that $12 billion more in foreign reserves left Canada than came into Canada. Again, this shows the typical position for Canada. In most years, the current account has had a negative balance, despite the normally positive balance of trade.

The capital account shows the changes in international investment holdings during the year. Foreigners purchased $20 billion more in the way of stocks, bonds (portfolio investment), and purchases of companies (direct investment) than Canadians purchased abroad during the year.

Don't be confused by the negative sign of $8 billion in the change in Canadian dollars (foreign reserves). Although it is a minus, it does represent an increase in foreign reserves. The current account shows that from trading and transfers, imports exceeded exports by $12 billion. This means that Canadians were buying more foreign currencies than were being made available from exports. However, the capital account shows a positive balance of $20 billion, which means that there was a net inflow of foreign currencies to Canada. From private international transactions, there was an overall favourable balance of payments and therefore a net inflow of foreign currencies to the tune of $8 billion. A surplus of $8 billion implies that the quantity demanded for Canadian dollars exceeded the quantity supplied, and this shortage of dollars was made good by the Bank of Canada. In other words, there was a negative outflow of Canadian dollars but an inflow of foreign currencies.

If all of this sounds confusing, bear in mind that since the balance of payments includes both private and government currency dealings, it will always balance. If there is a deficit, the government will make up the shortage of foreign currencies; if there is a surplus, the government will make up the shortage of Canadian dollars. Only with complete, instantaneous flexible exchange rates will there be no government intervention and there will never be a balance of payments deficit or surplus.

SELF-TEST

7. Fill in the blanks in the hypothetical balance of payments statement below:

Canada's Balance of Payments for 2002

Current Account

Export of goods and services	+164	
Import of goods and services	___	
= Balance of trade		+2
Investment income from abroad	+8	
Investment income paid abroad	___	
Net investment income		−15
Transfers (net)	___	
= Current Account balance		−17

Capital Account

Foreign investment in Canada less Canadian investment abroad	+18	
= Capital Account balance		+18
Total balance (Current Account and Capital Account)		___

Official Settlements Account

Change in Canadian dollars	___
Total balance (Current Account + Capital Account + Official Settlements Account)	___

Let us now raise a new question. Since, with flexible exchange rates, the balance of payments automatically balances, can balance of payments problems ever arise? The answer is yes, because it really does make a difference what a country is importing and what it is exporting. Canada can earn foreign currencies by exporting goods or services or by selling assets. Exporting goods and services does not lead to any future obligations on the part of anyone in Canada. However, selling off Canadian assets obligates some Canadians to pay out future income to foreigners and, in a sense, represents a drain on our foreign reserves in the future.

It is important that we clear up one particular myth relating to these flows. It is often suggested that Canada needs to encourage the inflow of foreign investment because we need this inflow to pay off the deficit that Canada invariably has on its current account. Perhaps you've figured out why this is a myth. The reason why Canada generally has a deficit on the current account is because of the amount of investment income that has to be paid abroad. And the reason this is so high is the big amount of foreign investment in the past. If we express this in terms of the individual, it might make more sense. Picture a student who defends her excessive borrowing every year by pointing out that she needs to borrow because her expenditures always seem to exceed her income, so she is left with no choice. But the reason why her expenses are so high is because she's having to pay such huge interest payments on her previous loans. In a similar fashion, many people suggest that if Canada were to cut down its dependence on foreign investment, it would not have current account problems in the future.

REVIEW

1. If foreign incomes rise, what is likely to happen to the demand for Canadian exports?
2. If the price of Canadian goods rises, what is likely to happen to the demand for Canadian exports?
3. If Canadian interest rates rise, what is likely to happen to the demand for the Canadian dollar?
4. Define *tariff*.
5. What does it mean to devalue a currency?
6. What is a *subsidy*?
7. Define a *dirty float*.
8. Distinguish between the *balance of payments* and the *balance of trade*.
9. Distinguish between the *current account* and the *capital account*.

Chapter Highlights

This chapter begins with a discussion of the exchange rate and explains what is meant by an appreciation or depreciation of a currency.

The chapter then asks: what causes a change in a currency's exchange rate? In a flexible exchange rate system, the interaction of the supply of and demand for a currency yields an equilibrium and thus determines the exchange rate. By pursuing this approach in more depth, we find that there are four specific purposes for which people want to buy the Canadian dollar. These are: to buy Canadian exports; to make foreign investments in Canada; to exchange foreign income received by Canadians into dollars; and for speculation or arbitrage. These same four factors operating in reverse explain what lies behind the supply of the Canadian dollar on the world market.

After the mechanism for flexible exchange-rate equilibrium is established, the chapter stresses that a higher or lower exchange-rate is not good or bad *per se*. Some will benefit from any exchange-rate change, while others will be hurt. For instance, a higher Canadian dollar hurts Canadian exporters but helps importers, whereas a lower Canadian dollar has the opposite effect.

Next, the chapter asks what would cause a change in the demand for the Canadian dollar. Here, the level of foreign incomes, relative price levels, relative interest rates, and tastes all play a role. Again, the same four factors operate on the supply side, except that it is domestic income that is relevant.

Shifting focus, the chapter argues that the advantage of the fixed exchange-rate system is its stability. The disadvantage is its very awkward adjustment mechanisms in the face of economic changes. An undervalued fixed rate is inflationary; an overvalued one may lead to the need to depress the economy in order to reduce income and thus imports.

The chapter ends with a discussion of the balance of payments, which is nothing more than an accounting system for tracking the inflow of foreign currency to Canada and the outflow of Canadian dollars from the country.

New Glossary Terms

arbitrage   346
balance of payments   362
balance of trade   362
capital account   362
currency appreciation   343
currency depreciation   343
current account   362
devaluation   361
direct investment   345
dirty float   361
exchange rate   342
fixed exchange rate   343
flexible exchange rate   343
portfolio investment   345
purchasing power parity theory   343
subsidy   360

STUDY GUIDE

Study Tips

1. A lot of this chapter is about the idea of price being determined by supply and demand, something that students have little difficulty in accepting. The price we are focusing on is that of currencies, and (given a flexible exchange rate system) a currency's price (exchange rate) is determined by the supply and demand for that currency. Just keep thinking of currencies as commodities, and don't get hung up on the fact that they are also monies. You will find there is nothing unduly mysterious or difficult about the topic.

2. The value of any currency always has to be expressed in terms of another currency. The question, "What is the price of the Canadian dollar?" makes no sense. "What is the price of the Canadian dollar in yen?" is a sensible question.

3. It is quite important for you to keep in mind that (flexible exchange) rates are determined by the supply and demand for a currency, and *not* the other way around. Thus any question that starts with "if the exchange rate changes" has to be handled carefully, because one needs to know what caused the exchange rate to change in the first place.

Key Problem

The country of Tara, whose currency is the dollar, has a flexible exchange-rate system while the country of Nog, whose currency is the yen, has a fixed exchange-rate system. For many years, the economy of Tara has done well through the mining and export of solarium, which has recreational and medicinal uses. The country of Nog, on the other hand, has rich agricultural land, and its economy has also prospered over the years through the export of food products. The graph in **Figure 10.9** shows the international market for Tara's dollar.

FIGURE 10.9

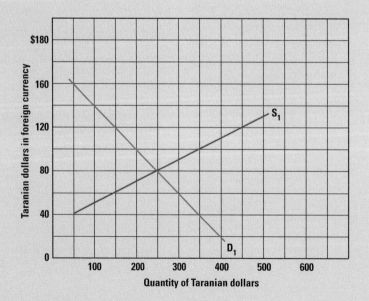

a) Now, suppose there is a discovery in Tara of vast quantities of a new variety of solarium that proves to be even more in demand throughout the world than the original. On Figure 10.9, draw in the result of Tara's good fortune. Label the appropriate new curve with the number 2, and indicate a new equilibrium with an exchange rate of 100 and the quantity of dollars traded at 350.

b) By how much has the value of dollars traded increased or decreased?

Answer: _____

c) As a result of this change, what has happened to imports?

Answer: _____

The people of Nog (Noggians?) are particularly fond of the new type of solarium, and imports of the product have increased significantly despite its rather high price.

d) On the graph in **Figure 10.10**, draw in the new supply curve (S_2) that reflects an increase in supply of yen of 50. Also indicate a fixed exchange rate for the yen of 250.

FIGURE 10.10

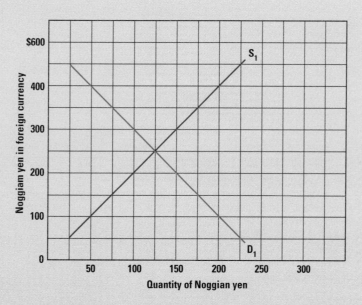

e) Is the yen now over- or undervalued?

Answer: _____

f) Given Nog's fixed exchange rate, how large is the surplus of Yen?

Answer: _____

g) What, if any, action must be taken by the central bank of Nog, given your answer in f)?

Answer: _____

h) Before the foreign-currency reserves of the central bank of Nog have completely run out, what options are left for the country in dealing with its overvalued currency? Your answer should not include devaluation of the yen, an option that has been ruled out by the government of Nog.

Answer: _____

More of the Same

Two of the more interesting countries (of many) in the world of Mohenjo-Daro are Tyre and Sidon. Tyre, whose currency is the lira, has a flexible exchange-rate system, whereas Sidon, whose currency is the rupee, has a fixed exchange-rate system. The country of Sidon is filled with enterprising individuals who have just developed a new energy source that is more efficient and cheaper than anything else available. Exports of this new technology are starting to boom. Tyre, who is also active in international trade, has proven to be one of the largest customers of Sidon's new energy technology. The graph in **Figure 10.11** shows the international market for the Sidon rupee. The fixed exchange rate for the Sidon rupee is 150.

FIGURE 10.11

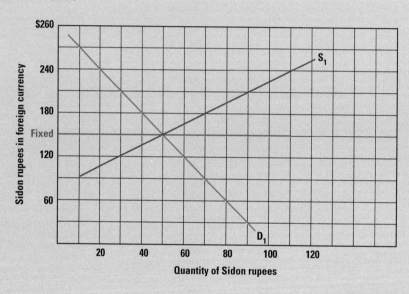

a) On Figure 10.11, illustrate the results of Sidon's booming exports by shifting the appropriate curve by 30. Label the new curve with the number 2.

b) Is the rupee now over- or undervalued?

c) Given the fixed exchange rate of 150, how large is the shortage of rupees?

d) What are the implications to the central bank of Sidon of your answer in c)?

e) If the situation in d) continues for a few years, what do you think will be the implications for the country of Sidon?

f) On **Figure 10.12**, indicate the effects of imports increasing the amount of currency by 80 in the country of Tyre.

FIGURE 10.12

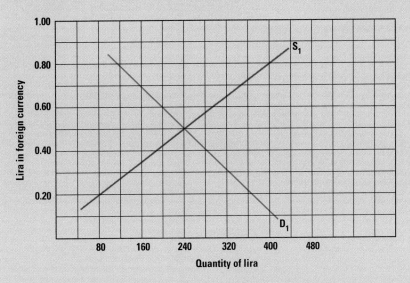

g) By how much has the lira's exchange rate appreciated or depreciated?

h) What do you think has happened to the level of Tyre's exports and imports, and why?

Translations

FIGURE 10.13

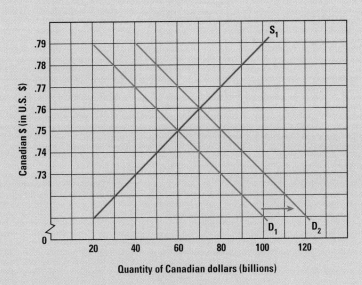

Explain in words the graph in **Figure 10.13**. Make reference in your answer to the possible causes of the shift from D_1 to D_2 and what might happen to exports and imports as a result.

Are You Sure?

Indicate whether the following statements are true or false. If false, indicate why they are false.

1. If a Panamanian balboa is worth 0.20 Canadian dollars, then a Canadian dollar is worth 4 balboas.

    T or **F**   If false: _____

    _____

2. The purchasing power parity theory suggests that exchange rates adjust so as to equate the purchasing power of each currency.

    T or **F**   If false: _____

    _____

3. A major source of demand for the Canadian dollar in the international money markets is the desire by foreigners to buy Canadian exports.

    T or **F**   If false: _____

    _____

4. A resident in Canada receiving a British pension will have a demand for the British pound.

    T or **F**   If false: _____

    _____

5. An increase in Canadian interest rates will lead to an appreciation of the Canadian dollar.

    T or **F**   If false: _____

    _____

6. When the Canadian dollar depreciates, the effective price of Canadian exports increases and, as a result, total exports are likely to fall.

    T or **F**   If false: _____

    _____

7. If the Canadian dollar appreciates, cross-border shopping by Canadians will increase.

    T or **F**   If false: _____

    _____

8. If Canada were on a fixed exchange-rate system, an increase in the demand for the Canadian dollar would result in the dollar being undervalued.

    T or **F**   If false: _____

    _____

9. A fixed exchange rate above the market value will lead to an outflow of foreign currencies.

    T or **F**   If false: _____

    _____

10. An increase in imports will have a negative effect on the current account balance.

    T or **F**   If false: _____

    _____

Choose the Best

11. What is the value of the Deutschmark in terms of francs if a French importer can buy 8 marks for 10 francs?
    a) 1.25.
    b) 0.8.

12. If the Canadian dollar appreciates in value against the Mexican peso, what happens to the value of the Mexican peso against the dollar?

    a) It appreciates.
    b) It might appreciate or depreciate.

13. An American who receives interest on the Canadian savings bond she holds will be be demanding what currency?
    a) Canadian dollars.
    b) U.S. dollars.

14. What will be the result of a change in exchange rates if fewer pesos are needed to buy a Canadian dollar?
    a) Canadians will buy more Mexican goods and services.
    b) Mexicans will buy fewer Canadian goods and services.
    c) Canadians will buy fewer Mexican goods and services.

15. What does arbitrage mean?
    a) The cost of shipping and insuring exported goods.
    b) The buying of a currency at one price and its immediate sale at another price.
    c) The cost of holding goods whose price is expected to increase in the future.

16. Assuming a flexible exchange-rate system, what would happen to the value of the Canadian dollar and the Mexican peso if Canadian interest rates increase while Mexican rates remain the same?
    a) The price of dollars in terms of the peso would increase.
    b) The price of pesos in terms of dollars would increase.
    c) The peso in terms of dollars would appreciate.

17. If Canada and the United Kingdom are both on flexible exchange-rate systems, what would happen if the United Kingdom experiences rapid inflation, compared with steady prices in Canada?
    a) The Canadian dollar will depreciate.
    b) The British pound will depreciate.
    c) The British pound will appreciate.

18. Which of the following would result from of an increase in Canada's GDP?
    a) Canadian exports would rise.
    b) Both Canadian exports and imports would rise.
    c) Canadian exports would rise, but imports would decrease.
    d) Canadian imports would rise.

19. Which of the following statements is true about the supply curve for the Canadian dollar?
    a) It is downward-sloping because a lower price for the dollar means Canadian goods are cheaper to foreigners.
    b) It is downward-sloping because a higher price for the dollar means Canadian goods are cheaper to foreigners.

c) It is upward-sloping because a lower price for the dollar means foreign goods are cheaper to Canadians.
d) It is upward-sloping because a higher price for the dollar means foreign goods are cheaper to Canadians.

20. What does it mean for a country that is on a fixed exchange-rate system to have a balance of payments surplus?
    a) The quantity supplied of its currency on the international money market will exceed the quantity demanded.
    b) The exchange rate is overvalued.
    c) There is an inflow of foreign currencies into the country.
    d) The balance of payments surplus is matched by a balance of trade deficit.

Table 10.3 contains hypothetical data for Canada's balance of payments accounts for a particular year. (Figures are in $ billions.)

TABLE 10.3

Exports of goods and services	$150
Imports of goods and services	145
Investment income received from abroad	10
Investment income paid abroad	30
Net transfers	−5
Foreign investment in Canada	200
Canadian investment abroad	190

21. Refer to Table 10.3 to answer this question. What is Canada's balance of trade?
    a) A surplus of $150 billion.
    b) A surplus of $5 billion.
    c) A deficit of $15 billion.
    d) A deficit of $10 billion.

22. Refer to Table 10.3 to answer this question. What is Canada's current account balance?
    a) A surplus of $10 billion.
    b) A surplus of $15 billion.
    c) A deficit of $10 billion.
    d) A deficit of $20 billion.

23. Refer to Table 10.3 to answer this question. What is Canada's capital account balance?
    a) A deficit of $10 billion.
    b) A surplus of $10 billion.
    c) A surplus of $5 billion.
    d) A surplus of $30 billion.

24. All of the following groups *except one* demand Canadian dollars. Which is the exception?
    a) An American tourist visiting Canada.
    b) Canadians who received dividends from American corporations.
    c) Texans who purchase Alberta beef.
    d) Americans who receive interest on their holdings of Canadian savings bonds.
    e) International speculators who think that the Canadian dollar will soon appreciate.

25. Which of the following would increase the supply of Canadian dollars on the international money market?
    a) Canadians travelling abroad.
    b) An American corporation investing in Canada.
    c) A Canadian resident receiving interest payments on a foreign bond.
    d) A Canadian exporter selling products abroad.
    e) A retired American, living on Vancouver Island, receiving a pension cheque from U.S. Social Security.

Use **Figure 10.14** to answer the next question.

FIGURE 10.14

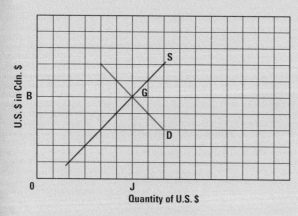

26. Refer to the graph in Figure 10.14 to answer this question. If the demand is D, what is the value of the U.S. dollar if a flexible exchange-rate system is in effect?
    a) OJ Canadian dollars for one U.S. dollar.
    b) OB Canadian dollars for one U.S. dollar.
    c) 1/OB dollars for one Canadian dollar.
    d) OJ U.S. dollars for one Canadian dollar.
    e) OB U.S. dollars for one Canadian dollar.

27. Assuming a fixed exchange-rate system, which of the following would contribute to a Canadian balance of payments deficit?
    a) Brian Adams and Anne Murray team up for a giant outdoor concert in Shanghai.
    b) The number of Indian tourists visiting Canada increases significantly.
    c) The United States increases its tariff on Canadian softwood lumber.
    d) A wealthy Taiwanese builds a mansion in Calgary.
    e) Honda builds a new assembly plant outside Montreal.

28. If a country is suffering perennial balance of payments deficits, all *except one* of the following will help solve the problem. Which is the exception?
    a) The introduction of quotas on imported goods.
    b) An increase in interest rates.
    c) The introduction of exchange controls.
    d) The reduction in tariffs on imported goods.
    e) An increase in subsidies to exporting industries.

29. What does a managed (or dirty) float mean?
    a) That a country's currency is fixed to the price of gold.
    b) That a country's currency is fixed to the value of the U.S. dollar.
    c) That a country's balance of payments is persistently in deficit.
    d) That the country's central bank fixes the value of its currency.
    e) That a country's central bank buys and sells currencies in order to smooth out short-run fluctuations in its own currency.

30. Assuming flexible exchange rates, which of the following would result in an increase in a country's exchange rate?
    a) The purchase by the central bank of its own currency.
    b) The purchase by the central bank of foreign currencies.
    c) The sale by the central bank of its own currencies.
    d) The central bank decreasing the country's interest rates.
    e) The government imposing an export tax.

Other Problems

31. Fill in the blanks below:
    a) If one Canadian dollar equals 0.75 U.S. dollars, then one U.S. dollar equals _____ Canadian dollars.
    b) If one Canadian dollar equals 150 yen, then one yen equals _____ Canadian dollars.
    c) If one German mark equals 0.60 Canadian dollars, then one Canadian dollar equals ___ German marks.

32. Following are some hypothetical data concerning exchange rates and the price of a Big Mac in the summer of 1998. The Asian currencies are expressed in **Table 10.4** in Canadian dollars.

TABLE 10.4

Location	Big Mac Price	Exchange Rate
Montreal	2.80 Canadian dollars	—
Tokyo	280 yen	$1 = 90 yen
Singapore	3.00 Singapore dollars	$1 = 1.12 Sgp.
Hong Kong	10.20 Hong Kong dollars	$1 = 5.25 H.K.

The theory of purchasing power parity would predict that long-term exchange rates would find an equilibrium, with the result that a Big Mac would cost the same in all countries.

a) Calculate exactly what the value of the Canadian dollar would be in terms of each of the other currencies in order for the price of a Big Mac to be the same in each of the three Asian countries as it is in Montreal.
   Value of Canadian $ in yen: _____ ;
   Value of Canadian $ in Singapore $: _____ ;
   Value of Canadian $ in Hong Kong $: _____ .

b) Given your calculations in a) above, would you say that the three Asian exchange rates were undervalued or overvalued in terms of the PPP theory?
   Yen: _____ ;
   Sgp. $ _____ ;
   H.K. $ _____ .

c) Given your answer in b) above, would you expect Asian exports to Canada would continue to grow or begin to decrease?

   Answer: _____

33. Which of the following items will show up in the current account of Canada's balance of payments and which in the capital account?
    a) An Iranian couple living in Canada sends money to Iran to support their parents.
    b) An Australian buys a cattle ranch in Alberta.
    c) An American corporation receives a cheque for interest on a Canadian savings bond.
    d) A tour group from Japan takes a vacation in the Canadian Rockies.
    e) The Canadian government sends foreign aid to Kosovo.

34. Arrange the following data into the form of a balance of payments for Etruria (all figures are in $ billions)

Foreign investment in Etruria	90
Transfers (net)	+4
Investment income from abroad	11
Imports of goods and services	153
Exports of goods and services	157
Etruria investment abroad	68
Investment income paid abroad	29

a) What is the value of the balance of trade?

_____.

b) What is the value of the balance on the current account?

_____.

c) What is the value of the balance on the capital account?

_____.

d) Is there a balance of payments surplus or deficit? How much?

_____. _____.

UNANSWERED QUESTIONS

Short Essays

1. Explain how flexible exchange rates will ensure a balance in the balance of payments.

2. Explain what lies behind the demand for the Canadian dollar. What lies behind its supply?

3. Explain the relationship between a country's balance of payments and its central bank's holdings of foreign currencies.

4. Explain why a country with a fixed exchange rate loses control over its money supply as an effective policy tool.

5. What are the pros and cons of a fixed exchange-rate system?

6. Explain how a fixed exchange-rate system may lead to painful adjustments in the domestic economy if there is a change in the demand for its currency.

Analytical Questions

7. A country that experiences a capital account surplus for many years will, eventually, experience many years of current account deficits. Explain.

8. Refer to the following list and explain who will be buying Canadian dollars and who will be selling.
   a) A Canadian businesswoman visiting Japan.
   b) A Russian tourist visiting Cape Breton.
   c) An American corporation building a branch plant in Saskatoon.
   d) A Canadian student living in Rome who receives a Canadian scholarship.
   e) A Honda dealer in Hamilton.
   f) A German currency speculator who feels that the Deutsche mark will depreciate against the Canadian dollar.

9. An increase in the demand for Canadian products will cause the Canadian dollar to appreciate. Yet an appreciation of the dollar causes the demand for Canadian products to fall. How can you reconcile these two statements?

10. Refer to the following list and identify who would be hurt and who would benefit from an appreciation of the Canadian dollar.

a) An Italian father spending the summer with his daughter in Toronto.
b) A Canadian research scientist living in Washington, D.C., who is paid a monthly salary in Canadian dollars by his Ottawa employer.
c) An English retired couple who major source of income is from a U.K. pension.
d) A Quebec manufacturer of light rapid transit systems sold around the world.
e) A Nova Scotia couple who are thinking of buying a winter home in Florida.

11. What effect will the following events have on the value of the Canadian dollar versus that of the Mexican peso?
a) Canadian interest rates rise significantly above Mexican rates.
b) An especially bad winter causes tens of thousands of Canadians to escape to the Mexican Riviera.
c) The Mexican government drastically reduces the tariff on imports of softwood lumber from Canada.
d) The Mexican economy experiences big growth in its national income.
e) Pemex, the Mexican oil giant, makes a huge investment in Canadian Arctic oil exploration.

12. Assume that the demand for the Canadian dollar increases because of a rising GDP level in the United States. What would you predict will happen to the value of the Canadian exchange rate, the unemployment rate in Canada, and the price of Japanese automobiles in Canada?

Numerical Questions

13. Graphically illustrate the effect of a decrease in exports on aggregate demand. Indicate the direction that you think GDP and prices will move.

14. The graph in **Figure 10.15** illustrates hypothetical supply and demand curves for the Canadian dollar. Use the graph to answer the questions below.
a) What is the dollar volume of exchange, given D_1 and S_1?
b) If you increase the demand for the dollar by 20 (draw in D_2), what would be the dollar volume of exchange if the exchange rate is fixed?
c) What is the dollar volume of exchange if the exchange rate is flexible?

FIGURE 10.15

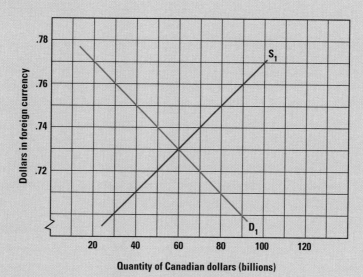

15. Given the following hypothetical data for the Canadian economy:

Export of goods and services	$180
Foreign investment in Canada less Canadian investment abroad	5
Investment income from abroad	18
Imports of goods and services	173
Change in foreign reserves	−4
Investment income paid abroad	36
Transfers	+10

Calculate:
a) balance of trade;
b) current account balance;
c) total balance (of both current and capital accounts). Is there a surplus or a deficit?

16. Set up a graph indicating equilibrium for a flexible Canadian dollar (label the axes).
   a) Show the effect of 18 months of wage settlement trends in Canada exceeding those in the United States. (Think about whether it would affect both curves or just one.)
   b) As a result of the change in a), what will be the effect on the level of foreign investment in Canada?

17. Karen operates a small foreign-currency exchange business. She begins each day with five boxes of cash. Each box contains 10 000 units of Canadian currency and 10 000 units of another currency. **Table 10.5** shows Karen's holdings of each currency at the end of a day's business.

TABLE 10.5			
French francs	16 000	and	$ 8 800 Cdn.
Japanese yen	7 000	and	10 050 Cdn.
U.S. dollars	6 400	and	15 000 Cdn.
U.K. pounds	14 000	and	1 200 Cdn.
Italian lira	9 370 000	and	2 200 Cdn.

What is the value of the Canadian dollar in terms of each of the five currencies?

Web-Based Activities

1. What to do about the Canadian dollar? Read the three articles found at **http://www.bmo.com/economic/special/bocdol.htm**, **http://www.cdhowe.org/pdf/buckaug.pdf** and **http://www.cdhowe.org/pdf/kbkool-2.pdf**. What was the cause of this depreciation? What could have been done to reverse the trend in the exchange rate? Is propping up the value of the dollar good for the economy? Why or why not?

2. Go to **http://www.oag-bvg.gc.ca/domino/reports.nsf/html/9509ce.html** and find the section entitled "Current Account, Balance of Payments and the Sustainability of Public Finances." What impact does the level of government debt and deficits have on the balance of payments?

Fiscal Policy

What's ahead... This chapter focuses on fiscal policy, which is one of the more important economic policies used by the government. We begin by defining several important terms, including net tax revenue, budget deficits, surpluses, and the national debt, and then exploring what can cause each of these to change. We then proceed to examine two distinct approaches to the use of fiscal policy: counter-cyclical fiscal policy and balanced-budget fiscal policy. We explain the assumptions that lie behind each approach as well as exploring criticisms of each. Then, a compromise between these approaches, the cyclically balanced-budget fiscal policy, is explained and briefly explored. The chapter ends with a discussion of the national debt.

Did you happen to see the digital national debt "clock" that was put on display at shopping centres around the country a few years ago? If so, you probably wondered about the national debt and might even have become a little concerned about its apparently huge size. Is the national debt a big problem facing younger Canadians today? How is this debt tied into the government's policies? Does solving the debt "problem" mean higher taxes? This chapter will address these questions.

I t is a truism that governments have to spend, and, therefore, they have to tax. So, what should be the government's attitude toward its own spending and taxation? How small or large should this spending and taxation be? Should the two be equal? Does the condition of the economy have anything to do with the answers to these questions? For example, when the economy is in the middle of a recession with high unemployment, what should be the attitude of government? Should the government decrease its own spending, increase it, or change nothing? Alternatively, should we expect it to cut taxes, to increase taxes, or to change nothing? These are the types of questions we will be looking at in this chapter. But first we need to define some terms.

Fiscal Policy, Budget Balances, and Government Debt

fiscal policy: the government's approach toward its own spending and taxation.

Fiscal policy refers to the government's approach toward its own spending and taxation. When the minister of finance "brings down" the budget in Parliament each spring, he reveals the government's fiscal policy for the coming year. This annual budget contains estimates of the government's revenues and expenditures. The sources of revenue include personal and corporate income taxes, the GST, excise taxes on specific goods (such as gasoline, tobacco, and alcohol), tariff revenue, and other miscellaneous revenue such as lottery proceeds.

The other half of the budget deals with spending projections. Budget day is headline news, and TV screens across the country are filled with political comments about how good or bad the new budget is.

You may recall from Chapter 3 that government spending includes only spending by government on goods and services and does not include transfers such as employment insurance, pension plan, and welfare payments. We now need to define **net tax revenue**, which is tax revenue received by government less transfer payments. The government's budget balance is defined as the difference between net tax revenues and government spending; that is,

net tax revenue: total tax revenue received by government less transfer payments.

$$\text{budget balance} = \text{NTR minus G}$$

Prime Minister Jean Chrétien and Finance Minister Paul Martin acknowledge a standing ovation from the Liberal caucus for the federal budget.

budget deficit:
government spending on
goods and services in
excess of net tax revenues.

budget surplus: net tax
revenue in excess of
government spending on
goods and services.

national debt: the sum of
the federal government's
budget deficits less
surpluses.

A positive balance means a **budget surplus**, since net tax revenue would be greater than spending on goods and services. Conversely, a negative balance means a **budget deficit**, since net tax revenues would be lower than government spending. It is important to note that government tax revenues, spending, and the deficit (or surplus) are all flows, because they occur over a period of time. If we were to add up all the deficit flows over the years and then subtract the sum of all the surpluses over the same time period, we would get the **national debt**. The national debt, or, as it is sometimes called, the public debt, is a stock concept because it is a total outstanding at any particular point in time and is the summation of the flows of all deficits and surpluses.

ADDED DIMENSION

Federal Spending and Revenues

To get a handle on the size of federal spending and tax revenues, the following table shows the amounts in Canada for the last few years. (The figures are in billions of dollars.)

		1995–96	1996–97
Total Revenues		142.9	153.7
Of which,	income taxes	81.7	87.5
	consumption taxes	30.1	32.0
	other revenues	31.1	34.2
Less Transfer Payments		100.7	93.5
Of which,	social services	54.0	48.3
	interest on public debt	46.7	45.2
Net Tax Revenues		42.2	60.2
Government Spending		74.7	73.7
Budget Deficit		−32.5	−13.5
Deficit		(32.5)	(13.5)

Source: Adapted from Statistics Canada, CANSIM database, matrix 3315.

Changes in the Economy and Government Revenues

It is important to emphasize the fact that changes in the economy can have an impact on government revenues. An example of this can be seen by glancing at the federal government's $32.5 billion deficit in the budget year 1995–96. The size of the deficit dropped significantly to $13.5 billion in the very next budget year. This was not because tax rates changed or because government spending was much different, but primarily because continued economic growth in the economy raised government revenues. In general, net tax revenues are directly related to the level of GDP. In addition, you may recall that we treat government spending on goods and services as autonomous of the level of real GDP. We put revenue and spending together in **Figure 11.1**.

FIGURE 11.1 Government Deficits and Surpluses

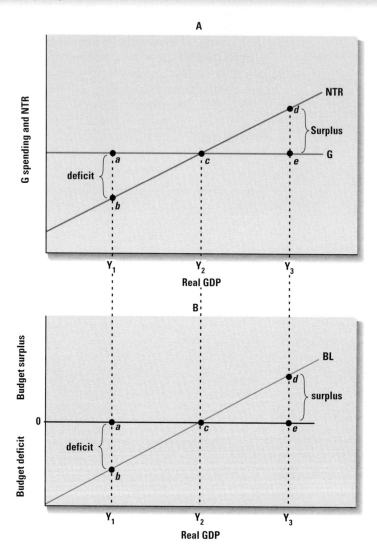

At real GDP level Y_2, government spending and net tax revenues are equal and, therefore, there is a balanced budget as illustrated by point c in Figure 11.1A. In 11.1B, a balanced budget is also indicated by point c, which is where the budget line, BL, crosses the zero axis. At real GDP level Y_3, net tax revenues exceed government spending and, therefore, there is a budget surplus indicated by de in either graph. Conversely, at real GDP level Y_1, there is a budget deficit of ab.

Since the government's tax revenue is greater and transfer payments are lower at higher levels of real GDP, net tax revenue (NTR) rises as the level of real GDP rises. We will assume that when GDP is zero, tax revenues and transfers are also zero, so that the NTR line begins at the origin and rises as GDP rises, as illustrated in Figure 11.1A. The horizontal line G reflects the autonomous nature of government spending. At a GDP level of Y_1, NTR is less than the level of government spending and there would be a budget deficit equal to ab. At a GDP level of Y_3, NTR exceeds G and there would be a budget surplus equal to de. When GDP is at a level indicated by Y_2, there would be neither a budget surplus or deficit, as illustrated by point c. The effect of different levels of GDP on the budget is shown explicitly in Figure 11.1B, with the budget line, BL, showing the same deficit, ab, at GDP level Y_1 and the same surplus, cd, at GDP level Y_3. Point c on either figure is the situation of a **balanced budget**.

Continuing with Figure 11.1, note that there are two things besides the level of GDP that will affect the government's budget and therefore the position of the budget

balanced budget: the equality of net tax revenues and government spending on goods and services.

line: a change in either the amounts of government spending or net tax revenues. An increase in government spending, for instance, will increase the amount of the budget deficit (or reduce the surplus) at every level of GDP and result in the budget line shifting down. An increase in tax rates (and thus the level of net tax revenues), on the other hand, will imply a reduced deficit (or increased surplus) at every level of GDP. This would be illustrated by an upward shift in the budget line. The essential point is that:

> **The state of the government's budget depends on the level of GDP in the economy as well as on tax rates and its own spending**

Table 11.1 shows the figures for the federal government's budget deficits, surpluses, and the accumulated national debt for some selected years over the last half century.

TABLE 11.1 Budget Surpluses/Deficits and the National Debt (current $ billion)

Year	Budget Surplus	Budget Deficit	National Debt
1940		0.1	5.1
1954		0.4	14.2
1960		0.6	16.8
1969	0.1		34.8
1973		1.9	29.7
1983		23.9	138.6
1992		34.5	424.8
1993		41.0	466.2
1994		42.0	508.2
1995		37.5	545.7
1996		28.6	574.3
1997		8.9	583.2

Source: Adapted from Statistics Canada, CANSIM database, matrix 3315, and *National Income and Expenditure Accounts*, catalogue no. 13-001.

SELF-TEST

1. Assume that current net tax revenues are $200 billion, government spending on goods and services is $180 billion, and the national debt at the beginning of the period was one half the size of current net tax revenues. What is the size of the national debt at the end of the period?

A question that often springs to people's minds at this point is: how is the government's budget deficit financed? There is no mystery to the answer: it is financed by borrowing. For example, when an individual buys a savings bond, she is, in effect, lending the government some of her savings so that it can finance a deficit. Such borrowing is done through the sale of government of Canada bonds and treasury bills to the public. The government can also borrow from the Bank of Canada. In this case, the government would issue bonds and sell them to the Bank of Canada, which would increase the amount that the government had on deposit with it. The government would then write cheques that would clear through the banking system and ultimately get debited against that same account with the Bank of Canada. The effect of this is pretty well the same as the government printing money to pay its bills: it leads to an increase in the money supply. This method of borrowing, known as **monetizing the debt**, is not used to a great extent in Canada today but has been frequently used by desperate governments in the past to finance wars or otherwise to help a country survive extreme economic conditions.

monetizing the debt: the action by government of borrowing from the central bank to finance increased spending.

We now want to address one of the more important questions posed at the beginning of this chapter. What, if anything, should the government do when the economy faces unemployment, or for that matter inflation? There are two distinct schools of thought on this issue. On the one hand we have economists and policy makers, interventionists, who believe that the government needs to deliberately intervene in the economy and overspend, or underspend, from time to time in order to help the economy achieve the goals of full employment and stable prices. On the other hand there are those, the non-interventionists, who believe that these goals can be achieved only if there is no government intervention. Let's now look at each of these schools of thought in some detail.

Counter-Cyclical Fiscal Policy

The interventionists start with the premise that the modern market economy is unstable and thus prone to periods of unacceptably high levels of unemployment or inflation. Thus they advocate the use of **counter-cyclical fiscal policy,** a policy used by governments in many countries around the world since World War II. The main purpose of counter-cyclical fiscal policy is to close recessionary and inflationary gaps; that is, figuratively speaking, to lean against the prevailing winds. If, for example, aggregate demand is weak and a recessionary gap exists, policy should be used to deliberately stimulate demand with higher spending or lower taxes. On the other hand, if aggregate demand is so strong that an inflationary gap exists, then policy should be used to dampen down demand through cuts in government spending or increases in taxes. The recessionary gap situation is illustrated in **Figure 11.2**.

counter-cyclical fiscal policy: deliberate adjustments in the level of government spending and taxation in order to close recessionary or inflationary gaps.

FIGURE 11.2 Counter-Cyclical Fiscal Policy with a Recessionary Gap

A recessionary gap exists if the current level of GDP is below the full employment level as illustrated by $Y_{FE} - Y_1$. Counter-cyclical fiscal policy is aimed at increasing the level of aggregate demand by either increasing government spending or decreasing taxes. It shifts up the aggregate demand curve from AD_1 to AD_2 and closes the recessionary gap.

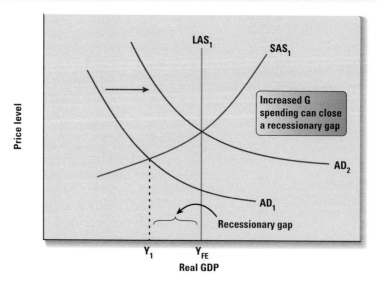

Given the current short-run aggregate supply curve, SAS$_1$, and the aggregate demand curve AD$_1$, equilibrium GDP is Y$_1$. Since this level of GDP is below the full-employment level of GDP, Y$_{FE}$, we have a recessionary gap of Y$_{FE}$ − Y$_1$. Counter-cyclical fiscal policy would call for either increased government spending or decreased taxes. This would increase aggregate demand, as indicated by the shift from AD$_1$ to AD$_2$. If such a policy was crafted well, aggregate demand would increase just enough to eliminate the recessionary gap by moving the economy to Y$_{FE}$.

The recessionary gap situation illustrated in Figure 11.2 is representative of most industrial economies, including Canada, in the 1930s. There was a debate among economists at the time, and there still is today, about the economy's ability to correct itself. This is a theme we will return to later in the chapter. It was in this atmosphere that John Maynard Keynes, rejecting any idea that the economy might self-adjust, originated the idea of counter-cyclical fiscal policy. He reasoned that, given the conditions of the Great Depression, consumers were not going to increase their spending because they were fearful of the uncertain future. Similarly, business was unlikely to increase investment spending because there was so much idle plant and equipment in the economy. World trade had collapsed, so any hope of increased exports seemed unlikely. Thus, if aggregate demand was to increase, it had to come from increased government spending. The laissez-faire governments of the industrial world were skeptical of this idea because it seemed to say that a nation could "spend its way to prosperity." Thus, Keynes's analysis was ignored and the Great Depression lingered on until huge military spending at the outbreak of World War II increased aggregate demand sufficiently that the depression came to an end.

Next, let's assume the economy is experiencing an inflationary gap. Here the appropriate counter-cyclical fiscal policy would be to decrease government spending or increase taxes in order to reduce the level of aggregate demand. This is illustrated in **Figure 11.3**.

FIGURE 11.3 Counter-Cyclical Fiscal Policy with an Inflationary Gap

If the economy is experiencing an inflationary gap such as Y$_1$ − Y$_{FE}$, then the appropriate counter-cyclical fiscal policy aimed at closing the gap is to lower the level of aggregate demand by either reducing government spending or increasing taxes. This is illustrated by a downward shift in the aggregate demand from AD$_1$ to AD$_2$.

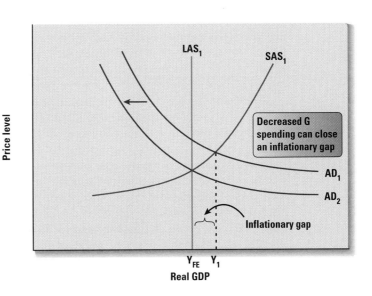

An inflationary gap is present because the equilibrium level of GDP, Y_1, is above the full employment level, Y_{FE}. Closing the gap requires a lower level of aggregate demand, as illustrated by the shift from AD_1 to AD_2. This could be accomplished by the government reducing its spending or increasing taxes.

In summary, counter-cyclical fiscal policy means that:

- When aggregate demand is low and the economy is experiencing a recessionary gap, governments should spend and tax in a way that *increases* aggregate demand.
- When aggregate demand is high and an inflationary gap is present, governments should spend and tax in a way that *reduces* the level of aggregate demand.

In this way, government policy would be helping to stabilize the economy and take some of the sting out of the fluctuations in the business cycle.

SELF-TEST

2. In the following cases, indicate the direction toward which the aggregate demand curve will shift (right or left).
A) Taxes increase.
B) Government spending on goods and services decreases.

C) Counter-cyclical fiscal policy is used to close a recessionary gap.
D) Counter-cyclical fiscal policy is used to close an inflationary gap.

Criticisms of Counter-Cyclical Fiscal Policy

Counter-cyclical fiscal policy has been used by many governments since World War II. However, in recent years it has come under a good deal of criticism. There are three potential problems associated with the use of counter-cyclical fiscal policy that we are going to look at.

The first involves the fact that interventionists see the essence of counter-cyclical fiscal policy as that of fine-tuning the economy. This is done by adjusting government spending or taxation by just the right amounts to achieve a level of aggregate demand sufficient to bring about full-employment GDP. Critics, however, argue that, in practice, the use of counter-cyclical fiscal policy is like fine-tuning with a sledgehammer. Even if just the right amount of adjustment can be determined, counter-cyclical fiscal policy takes time to implement and is slow to take effect. Furthermore, the economy often suffers from an overdose of spending when the policy does take full effect.

For example, consider a government that has just determined that the economy is in need of a $4 billion spending stimulant. This government cannot simply increase spending by $4 billion without first identifying how it is going to spend the money and then getting parliamentary approval for its fiscal plans. The next problem is that a number of procedures are necessary before the actual spending can begin, the most significant of which is putting out contracts for bids by various firms in the private sector. All of this takes time, and since major projects, such as a new port facility, may last a number of years, the full effect of the increased spending may be a long way down the road; by which time the need for such spending may no longer exist.

The second potential problem with counter-cyclical fiscal policy is the argument that it is, quite simply, ineffective. Critics argue that the effect of increased government spending to try to close a recessionary gap may prove to be much less potent than expected, for two distinct reasons. The first is that any increase in government spending that is not financed through taxation may be inflationary. Suppose, for instance, that the government uses counter-cyclical fiscal policy to get an economy out of a recession. The result will be an increase in aggregate demand, as shown in **Figure 11.4**.

FIGURE 11.4 The Effect of Counter-Cyclical Fiscal Policy on the Price Level

If the economy is experiencing a recessionary gap, counter-cyclical fiscal policy will increase the level of aggregate demand. This is illustrated by the shift from AD_1 to AD_2. The recessionary gap closes as real GDP increases from Y_1 to Y_{FE}. However, the price level will also increase from P_1 to P_2.

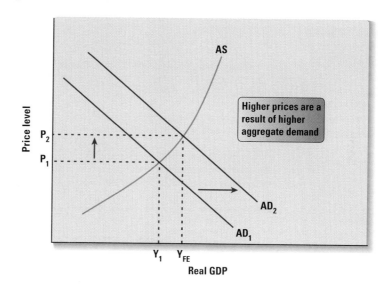

An increase in government spending (or a reduction in taxes) would shift the aggregate demand curve to the right from AD_1 to AD_2. Clearly, the level of GDP increases from Y_1 to Y_{FE}. Unfortunately, the price level also rises, in this case from P_1 to P_2. Counter-cyclical fiscal policy therefore is inflationary, and the rate of inflation depends on how close the economy is to full employment. As you may recall from Chapter 6, as we approach the full-employment level of GDP, the rise in prices accelerates. This inflation results in less consumption spending by Canadians. In addition, Canadian goods and services become less attractive to foreigners, and, therefore, Canadian exports fall. This loss of international competitiveness has serious consequences for an economy like Canada's that relies so much on exports.

The second reason why counter-cyclical fiscal policy may be ineffective is because of what is termed the **crowding-out effect**. As we just saw, counter-cyclical fiscal policy used to close a recessionary gap will increase the level of GDP. But as the level of GDP rises, so too will the money demand, as we learned in Chapter 8. The increase in demand for money will tend to push up interest rates, and this increase in interest rates will tend to reduce, or crowd out, the level of private investment spending. This is illustrated in **Figure 11.5**.

crowding-out effect: the idea that government borrowing to finance a deficit crowds out private investment because it causes interest rates to rise.

FIGURE 11.5 The Effect of Counter-Cyclical Fiscal Policy on Money Demand

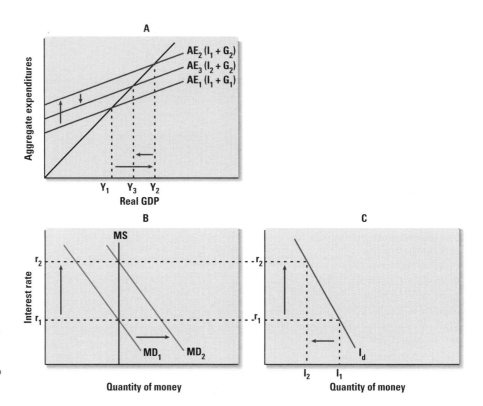

Counter-cyclical fiscal policy implies an increase in aggregate expenditures, shown as a shift from AE_1 to AE_2. As a result, real GDP increase from Y_1 to Y_2 in Figure 11.5A. This higher level of real GDP results in an increase in money demand and, thus, higher interest rates, as seen in Figure 11.5B. The higher interest rate reduces the level of investment spending, as seen in Figure 11.5C. The lower investment spending in turn pushes the AE line back down to AE_3 in Figure 11.5A and thereby reduces real GDP to Y_3.

In Figure 11.5A we see that counter-cyclical fiscal policy, and the resulting rise in aggregate expenditures, results in the shift from AE_1 to AE_2. If we could ignore the effect on the money market, then real GDP would increase from Y_1 to Y_2. However, the increase in real GDP will increase the transactions demand for money, and therefore the money demand curve will shift out from MD_1 to MD_2, as seen in Figure 11.5B. This, in turn, increases the interest rate from r_1 to r_2. This higher interest rate reduces investment spending, as illustrated in Figure 11.5C, where investment falls from I_1 to I_2. This then reduces aggregate expenditures so that the AE curve decreases from AE_2 to AE_3 back in Figure 11.5A. In summary, the increase in government spending pushes up aggregate expenditures and real GDP, but the subsequent decrease in investment spending causes both to fall back down.

ADDED DIMENSION

The Crowding-Out Effect

There is controversy over the existence of the crowding-out effect. The following extract is from an article in *The Economist* magazine of January 25, 1992:

"The Reagan years were not kind to those who contended that budget deficits were bad because they hogged, or 'crowded out', savings that would otherwise have flowed into productive investment. The notion seemed eminently commonsensical, yet no academic was able to prove it. Though budget deficits grew in seven of President Reagan's eight years, long-term interest rates fell, reducing the nominal cost of capital for investment. And the economy soared.

"So it was with a certain *Schadenfreude* that proponents of the crowding-out theory greeted George Bush's willingness after 1989 to see the annual deficits put Mr. Reagan's ones to shame. Here, at last, would be proof of crowding-out. Record fiscal deficits would drag down an economy that, finding the cost of borrowing too high, would be unable to invest in its own recovery.

"There is a flaw in this simple model, and it is called the rest of the world. Foreigners provided lots of capital for the Reagan boom, and are still doing so. Only if they stopped— i.e., if the external current-account deficit disappeared— might American interest rates have to jump."

We have just seen that counter-cyclical fiscal policy might push up interest rates and weaken the effect of fiscal policy through the crowding-out of private investment spending. There is another possible effect of higher interest rates that we need to consider. In an open economy with flexible exchange rates, such as in Canada, the higher interest rates will pull money into the country as foreign money-fund managers buy Canadian dollars in order to make deposits in Canadian financial institutions. The effect of this inflow of foreign currencies is that the demand for the Canadian dollar will rise and the Canadian dollar will appreciate. As we know from Chapter 10, the higher exchange rate will reduce the level of Canadian exports (just as higher Canadian prices did) and increase Canadian imports.

The net effect of all this is that counter-cyclical fiscal policy may crowd out net exports. Thus we have two possible aspects to this crowding-out effect—on investment spending and on net exports—both of which combine to weaken the effectiveness of fiscal policy.

In summary, the effectiveness of counter-cyclical fiscal policy to close a recessionary gap may be reduced because:

- it increases the price level and reduces consumption spending and exports
- it increases interest rates, which crowds out investment spending, and it increases the exchange rate, which crowds out net exports.

As you can see, the use of fiscal policy has a number of possible undesirable side-effects, which leaves it open to criticism.

SELF-TEST

3. What effect will counter-cyclical fiscal policy aimed at closing a inflationary gap have on interest rates, the exchange rate, net exports, and prices?

There is another way to look at the possible ineffectiveness of counter-cyclical fiscal policy. You will recall from Chapter 5 that an increase in government spending will increase the level of national income by an amount determined by the multiplier.

However, we have just seen that some of this increase in government spending is off-set by a decrease in consumption spending because of higher prices and a decrease in investment spending because of higher interest rates and a decrease in exports because of a higher exchange rate. The result of this is that the size of the multiplier is reduced.

The third, and some believe the most serious, problem with counter-cyclical fiscal policy is that it completely ignores the effect on the government's budget. Over the last half century Canada's counter-cyclical fiscal policy has been aimed mainly at attempting to close recessionary gaps. Such policy involves either higher levels of government spending or lower levels of taxation. Either of these will have a deficit-inducing effect on the current budget. The result will be an increase in the size of an already-existing budget deficit or a decrease in the size of an already-existing budget surplus. This is best illustrated with **Figure 11.6**.

FIGURE 11.6 Effect of Counter-Cyclical Fiscal Policy on Budget Deficits

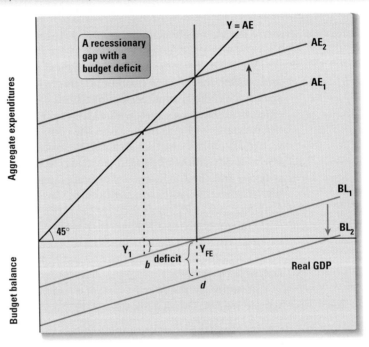

Suppose the economy is originally at GDP level Y_1 with a budget deficit of Y_1b. Counter-cyclical fiscal policy aimed at increasing aggregate demand from AE_1 to AE_2 will also shift the budget line down from BL_1 to BL_2. The result is a larger budget deficit.

Suppose that the current level of GDP in Figure 11.6 is Y_1. This means that the economy is experiencing a recessionary gap equal to the distance between full employment level of GDP, Y_{FE}, and the current level Y_1. In addition, at GDP level Y_1, the government has a budget deficit of Y_1b. If counter-cyclical fiscal policy is used to try to close the recessionary gap by increasing the level of aggregate expenditures from AE_1 to AE_2, then the budget line will shift down from BL_1 to BL_2. This would result in the economy moving to full-employment equilibrium at Y_{FE}, but this would result in an even larger deficit of $Y_{FE}d$.

If the deficit-inducing effects occur often and are allowed to accumulate over a period of time, the size of the government's national debt will grow substantially. This then requires that the government spend a larger percentage of its total spending on servicing that debt, leaving only a smaller percentage for conventional spending on things like health care and security.

In summary, the three criticisms of counter-cyclical fiscal policy are that it

- is effective but subject to serious time lags
- is ineffective because it may be inflationary, crowds out private spending, and thus reduces the size of the multiplier
- can cause serious budget deficits

Balanced-Budget Fiscal Policy

balanced-budget fiscal policy: the belief that a government's budget should be balanced in each budget period.

Some politicians and political commentators, and even a few economists, alarmed at the effect of counter-cyclical fiscal policy on the size of budget deficits, argue that the government should balance its spending and taxation revenues in each budget period. This is known as a **balanced-budget fiscal policy**. Advocates of a balanced-budget fiscal policy use three observations to support their position. The first is that as non-interventionists they see counter-cyclical fiscal policy as a very interventionist policy that is just as likely to do the economy harm as it is to help it. For example, they would argue that while unemployment insurance expenditures might help an immediate problem, they will adversely affect people's incentives and warp their sense of responsibility, which, in the long run, is quite harmful. In addition, they consider the three criticisms of counter-cyclical fiscal policy that we just discussed as a serious indictment of that approach and see the balanced-budget approach as the only alternative.

automatic stabilizers: government policies and programs that automatically change with the state of the economy so as to stabilize the economy.

Second, advocates of a balanced-budget fiscal policy approach believe that because of **automatic stabilizers**, the modern economy has enough built-in safeguards to ensure that it avoids extremes of high inflation or unemployment. Automatic stabilizers are government programs that ensure that spending remains relatively stable even in times of rapid economic change. For instance, as we have seen, when an economy enters a recession, because of the progressive nature of taxes, disposable incomes don't fall by as much as GDP. In addition, the amount paid out in unemployment benefits and welfare assistance increases, which buoys up disposable income and therefore consumption spending.

Automatic stabilizers also come into force when the economy is booming and in danger of "over-heating." In this case, the higher levels of GDP generate proportionately higher taxes, and, at the same time, the amounts paid out for unemployment benefits and welfare are also reduced. These both have the effect of dampening-down expenditures.

The third point used in support of a balanced-budget fiscal policy is by far the most significant. As mentioned earlier, non-interventionists believe that if either a recessionary or an inflationary gap exists (temporarily), then the economy is capable of returning to full-employment equilibrium by itself through a self-adjustment process, unaided by interventionist polices of any kind. We have touched on this self-adjustment process in Chapter 6, and we will examine it in depth in Chapter 13. For now we need only point out that if the self-adjustment process is effective, as the non-interventionists believe, then fiscal policy should be as neutral in its effects on the economy as is possible. The non-interventionists see such neutrality achieved through the use of a balanced-budget fiscal policy.

In summary, the arguments in support of a balanced-budget fiscal policy are that:

- the non-interventionist approach emphasizes incentives
- the economy has effective automatic stabilizers
- the economy is capable of returning to full-employment equilibrium through a self-adjustment process

Criticisms of Balanced-Budget Fiscal Policy

We now need to examine the economic effects of a government actually following a balanced-budget fiscal policy. In doing so we will find that the effects are significant and, in fact, not at all neutral.

Suppose that the economy is at full-employment equilibrium and, further, that the government's budget is balanced. Next, suppose that exports take a nosedive as a result of economic turmoil somewhere else in the world. This will reduce the level of aggregate expenditures, which will, in turn, reduce the level of equilibrium GDP, resulting in a recessionary gap. At the same time, the lower level of GDP leads to reduced tax revenues for the government, which will result in a budget deficit. **Figure 11.7** illustrates what can happen when a government pursues a balanced-budget fiscal policy under these conditions.

FIGURE 11.7 Reduced Government Spending and the Deficit

An attempt to eliminate the budget deficit that exists at Y_1 would call for a reduction in government spending or an increase in taxes. Thus, the budget line shifts up from BL_1 to BL_2, and the budget deficit appears to be eliminated. However, this action reduces aggregate expenditures from AE_1 to AE_2, which causes the level of equilibrium GDP to decrease to Y_2 and at this lower level of GDP, there is still a budget deficit of Y_2b.

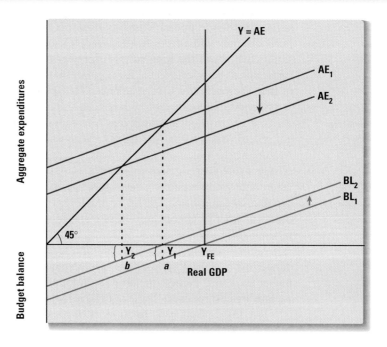

Here we see that, after the fall in GDP, the economy is at Y_1 and experiencing both a recessionary gap ($Y_{FE} - Y_1$) and a budget deficit (Y_1a) which occurred as a result of the lower GDP. If a balanced-budget fiscal policy is followed, the existence of a budget deficit would require that the government either reduce its spending or raise taxes in order to eliminate the deficit. The result will be a shift down in the aggregate expenditures curve from AE_1 to AE_2 and a shift up in the budget line up from BL_1 to BL_2. Since BL_2 intersects the horizontal axis at Y_1, it appears initially that the budget is now balanced. However, at Y_1, the economy is no longer in equilibrium. The drop in aggregate expenditures will cause GDP to drop by a multiple of the decrease in aggregate expenditures. At the lower equilibrium level of Y_2, NTR will be smaller, with the result that the budget deficit (Y_2b) will persist (although it is now smaller).

What we have just seen is that if the economy is experiencing a recessionary gap and a budget deficit, then the pursuit of a balanced-budget fiscal policy will be

pro-cyclical: action by the government that tends to push the economy in the same direction it is leaning in.

pro-cyclical. To understand this, note that a recession implies that there is unemployment in the economy. If the government takes action to try to eliminate the budget deficit, rather than the unemployment, then the level of unemployment will rise, since the level of GDP falls. In short, the business cycle has created a given level of unemployment and the government's fiscal policy, which was aimed at reducing the deficit, resulted in even *higher* unemployment.

Would a balanced-budget fiscal policy result in the same pro-cyclical tendencies if the economy was experiencing an inflationary gap? The answer to this depends on the state of the budget associated with the gap. Recall that an inflationary gap is a result of high aggregate demand, which generates a level of income that is temporarily higher than the full-employment level of GDP.

Let's assume that this high GDP level generates sufficient tax revenue for the government to be running a budget surplus. Strict adherence to a balanced-budget fiscal policy would then necessitate that either taxes be lowered or spending increased to eliminate the budget surplus. Such fiscal policy action would *raise* aggregate demand and, thus, the level of GDP. This would intensify the inflationary gap, and we again see the pro-cyclical nature of a balanced-budget fiscal policy in this situation.

Let's review what we have here. A balanced-budget fiscal policy will likely be pro-cyclical in circumstances in which the economy is experiencing a recessionary gap, since the low levels of income will generate low levels of tax revenue, which create budget deficits. Similarly, such a policy will be pro-cyclical when the economy is experiencing an inflationary gap. If the inflationary gap comes with a budget surplus, then balancing the budget will again be pro-cyclical.

The Arithmetic of a Balanced Budget

Let's now examine another aspect of the pro-cyclical nature of the balanced-budget philosophy in more detail. Let's again assume that the budget is balanced and that the economy is at full-employment equilibrium. Next, assume that a new government, which promised lower government spending, is elected. This new government is intent on carrying out its promise of cuts in spending. However, in consideration of the already balanced budget and given the fact that the economy is at full employment, they also announce that taxes will be reduced by a similar amount. Since government spending and taxes are to be cut by the same amount, won't the level of GDP be unaffected? That is to say, isn't it true that what the government takes out of the economy in the form of reduced spending is exactly offset by what it puts back into the economy in the form of reduced taxes? It comes as a surprise to most people that the answer to this question is no.

Suppose that the economy is at a full-employment equilibrium of $1000, government spending is $200, and taxes, which for simplicity we assume are entirely autonomous, are also $200. Furthermore, suppose that the value of the multiplier is equal to 2 and the MPC is 0.8. As we know, a reduction in government spending will definitely reduce aggregate expenditure and, therefore, the level of GDP. Suppose government spending is cut by $40. With a multiplier of 2, this will reduce GDP by $80. Next, we know that the corresponding cut in taxes will increase aggregate expenditures and the level of the GDP. But how much will GDP increase? Will it increase by the same $80?

Well, a cut in taxes of $40 will immediately raise disposable income by the same $40. Does this mean that consumers will spend all of this additional disposable income? The answer is no, since, with an MPC of 0.80, we know that the increase in spending will only be 0.8 x $40, or $32 (the other $8 will be saved). This additional $32 in spending, not the whole $40 cut in taxes, is the amount that gets multiplied. Schematically, therefore:

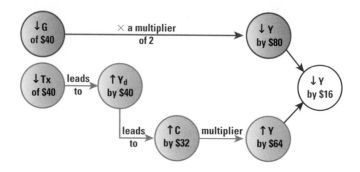

The cut in government spending reduces the level of GDP by $80, whereas the cut in taxes increases it by only $64. The net result is a drop in GDP of $16. In short:

> **A policy of decreasing both government spending and taxes by the same amount results in a lower real GDP and higher unemployment.**

We end this discussion of the two contrasting approaches to fiscal policy by noting that the essence of a counter-cyclical fiscal policy, which is aimed at the level of GDP and unemployment, is to use fiscal policy to address recessionary and inflationary gaps that might exist in the *economy*. In simple terms, it attempts to balance the economy, not the government's budget. By contrast, the essence of the balanced-budget fiscal policy, which is aimed at the government's budget, is to use fiscal policy to balance that *budget*, not the economy.

SELF-TEST

4. Assume that the economy is in a recession and that the government is experiencing a budget deficit. If fiscal policy is used to try to eliminate the deficit, what will happen to:
A) unemployment?
B) GDP?
C) NTR?
D) the deficit?

Next, assume the same conditions, but this time fiscal policy is used to try to reduce unemployment. How will your four answers above change?

5. Given the following data, and assuming all taxes are autonomous:

$$a_0 = 20 \qquad MPS = 0.25$$
$$I_0 = 50 \qquad MPM = 0.25$$
$$G_0 = 80$$
$$X_0 = 60$$
$$T_0 = 80$$

calculate equilibrium income. Next, assume that the government increases both its spending and autonomous taxes by 20. Calculate the new equilibrium income. Is this action by government neutral, or does it have some impact on the economy?

It is now clear that the issues regarding the use of fiscal policy to address recessionary gaps, inflationary gaps, and the question of the budget deficit are more complex than one would first imagine. It is true that some people object to counter-cyclical fiscal policy because such an approach ignores the issue of budget deficits and the associated level of the national debt. On the other hand, the balanced-budget fiscal policy has the potential problem of exacerbating the economy's situation because of its pro-cyclical tendencies. Is there another approach that could be used? In fact, the answer is yes. We now turn to a discussion of it.

Cyclically Balanced-Budget Fiscal Policy

Without overstating the obvious, one could ask, what is so sacred about a year? Why not balance the budget each week, or each month, or, for that matter, each day? A week or a month simply wouldn't be practical, because the government's flow of income and expenditures is not regular, so some weeks or months would have high deficits (surpluses), while others would have high surpluses (deficits). Given this, and given the fact that a government's budget also depends on the level of GDP in the economy, some economists suggest that governments should indeed try to balance the budget, but not on an annual basis but instead *over the life of the business cycle.* Here the use of fiscal policy to smooth out the business cycle would be viewed from a longer perspective than just each budget period. In these circumstances, the national debt might rise quickly at times, as the government uses its fiscal policy to close a recessionary gap. On the other hand, the debt would decline when fiscal policy is used to close an inflationary gap. This longer-view approach would continue to use fiscal policy to lean against the prevailing winds while addressing the concerns of many people about the size of the national debt.

cyclically balanced-budget fiscal policy: the use of counter-cyclical fiscal policy to balance the budget over the life of the business cycle.

In a sense, this policy is a compromise of the two approaches discussed above and is known as a **cyclically balanced-budget fiscal policy**. The exact definition of this term is the use of counter-cyclical fiscal policy with the aim of balancing the budget over the life of the business cycle. Such a policy would require governments to spend more (or tax less) at some times but also to spend less (or tax more) at other times.

There are two potential problems with this cyclically balanced-budget fiscal policy. The first is that there is no guarantee that the size and length of the recessionary gap, when the government is running a budget deficit, will be exactly offset by the size and length of the inflationary gap when the government is running a budget surplus. As a result, the end of the business cycle may still show a net budget deficit. Second is the political problem that most governments find it easier to increase spending in bad times than to decrease it in good times. In short, pursuing a cyclically balanced-budget fiscal policy would take a remarkable amount of discipline on the part of the government. In addition, most business cycles are longer than the term of office of any government. This invites the existing government to leave the problem of balancing the budget to the succeeding government.

REVIEW

1. Define *fiscal policy.*
2. What is meant by *monetizing the debt?*
3. Explain the difference between a *budget deficit* and the *national debt.*
4. What is counter-cyclical fiscal policy aimed at achieving? What are three criticims of it?
5. What is a balanced-budget fiscal policy aimed at achieving? What are three criticisms of it?
6. Why will an equal decrease in both government spending and taxes not have a neutral effect on the economy?
7. What is meant by a *cyclically balanced-budget fiscal policy?*

Fiscal Policy and the National Debt

The size of the national debt is a topic that has received a great deal of attention lately. The use of counter-cyclical fiscal policy usually leads to growth in the debt, and, thus, its use has created a lot of debate. Let's examine all this more closely by asking just what is wrong with a government running a long series of budget deficits and therefore a growing national debt.

First, let us establish to whom this debt is owed. Any Canadian individual, corporation, or bank who buys a Canada Savings Bond, a treasury bill, or other type of government bond is lending money to the government. The payment of interest and the redemption of the bond is the responsibility of the government. In this sense, it can be regarded as a debt that we Canadians owe to ourselves. One of the major problems with the debt is that the "we" and the "ourselves" in the last sentence do not refer to the same groups. We, the taxpayers, are responsible for paying off the interest and principle to ourselves, the bondholders. But while all bondholders are taxpayers, not all taxpayers are bondholders. And therein lies one of the problems: as the size of the debt increases, and with it the interest payments, increasing amounts must be raised in taxes, which will then get transferred to bondholders. Since it is normally the comparatively wealthy who hold the majority of bonds, while taxes are paid by rich and poor alike, the payment of interest on the national debt could represent a major redistribution of income.

For another angle on this redistributional aspect, let's assume the debt is entirely internal and that in response to public pressure it was decided to repay all of the debt of approximately $583 billion (as of 1997). How could this be done? The most straightforward answer is for the government to raise 583 billion additional dollars through increased taxes, of which all Canadians would pay some small part. What then would Ottawa do with this incredible rush of additional revenue? Turn around and send it back to those Canadians who hold Canada Savings Bonds and those institutions holding the other bonds. The net effect: all Canadians pay $583 billion in additional taxes, and some Canadians receive $583 billion in bond repayments. Why bother, many might argue? Why not leave it where it was in the first place?

Up to about 10 years ago, the above discussion may have ended at this point. Alas, the world is no longer so simple. In 1997, approximately one quarter of the national debt was held by foreigners. External debt is not just owed to ourselves, since a portion

Canapress/Jeff McIntosh

of the interest payments now require a transfer of Canadian real output to the outside world. The reason for this is easy to comprehend. Interest payments to a foreigner lead to an outflow of foreign currency, and the only way to earn that currency is to first sell real goods or services abroad. The amount of the national debt held by foreigners grew from less than $1 billion in 1975 to approximately $150 billion in 1997. While it is true that the Canadian economy benefited from this inflow at the time that it occurred, the needed outflow to pay interest on it must now be a consideration in the debate as to the seriousness of the debt.

Let's now turn to an examination of some statistics. Public discussion of the national debt often runs to hyperbole, and we hear mention of a "staggering" debt of "enormous" proportions as a result of "crippling" deficits. Dollar amounts in billions are certainly enormous from an individual's perspective, but one seldom hears the size of Canada's GDP described as staggering. We need therefore to put things in perspective. Just how big is our national debt? It might help if we look at it over a period of time. **Table 11.2** shows some figures for selected years.

TABLE 11.2 Total Debt (nominal $ billion)

1926	1940	1946	1967	1991	1997
2.4	5.2	16.0	22.0	347.9	651.2

Source: Adapted from Statistics Canada, CANSIM database, matrix 3199.

It certainly seems a "staggering" increase. But since the population of Canada has increased appreciably during this century, it might be better to show the figures in terms of per capita debt, as in **Table 11.3**.

TABLE 11.3 Per Capita Debt (nominal $)

1926	1940	1946	1967	1991	1997
263	453	1301	1100	12 770	21 500

Source: Adapted from Statistics Canada, CANSIM database, matrix 3199.

It still looks like a fairly staggering increase. But we need to make one further adjustment to allow for the effects of inflation over the years. So let's show the total debt, but this time in constant 1992 dollars, as in **Table 11.4**.

TABLE 11.4 Total Debt ($1992, billions)

1926	1940	1946	1967	1991	1997
22.2	55.9	144.3	103.5	358.1	608.0

Source: Adapted from Statistics Canada, CANSIM database, matrix 3199.

Finally, let's combine both factors in **Table 11.5** to give us figures in terms of constant dollars per capita.

TABLE 11.5 Per Capita Debt (in $1992)

1926	1940	1946	1967	1991	1997
2361	4920	11 731	5175	13 165	20 066

Source: Adapted from Statistics Canada, CANSIM database, matrix 3199.

This puts things in perspective. In real terms, the per capita debt doubled in the fourteen years leading up to World War II, it went up almost one and a half times during the war, declined to less than half by 1967, but almost quadrupled in the next 30 years.

These figures show clearly that one of the major causes of the growth of Canada's debt was the financing of World War II. During a major war, few nations are able to finance their military expenditures through taxation alone. They are often left with little choice but to borrow, and the majority of this borrowing is from the nation's own citizens. Most would feel this is a legitimate reason to increase the debt and might also agree that there are other legitimate reasons for the increased debt—for example, deficit financing to prevent or escape from a recession or the financing of necessary infrastructure such as bridges and airports. The third explanation for the increased Canadian debt, especially since the early 1970s, has been the increase in the size of income-support programs. Here, controversy about whether this is a good reason for the debt to increase heats up; some have suggested that these programs are too generous in comparison with those of other countries.

Finally, it should be noted that the very high interest rates between the mid-1970s and the 1990s have compounded the size of the debt. (As we saw, some economists suggest that the reason interest rates were so high in the first place was because of borrowing by governments, that is, the crowding-out effect. Complicated world, isn't it?) Leaving the statistics behind, let's examine some of the problems associated with the debt.

Well, we've already mentioned three of them. First, we have seen how borrowing by the government may well crowd out private investment and leave the economy with a smaller capital stock in the future. However, some would point out that this is a cost only if one assumes that private capital investment (say, another shopping mall) is superior to public capital investment (a hospital). It obviously depends on what investment is crowded out.

The second potential problem (as we just saw) involves the size of the foreign portion of the debt. Private financial agencies give ratings for government bonds sold around the world, as an aid to their clients for investing. The lower the rating given a particular government's bonds, the higher the interest payments that must be paid. In early 1995, there was a *perception* that Canada's national debt was too large. The result was a lower bond rating, and the outflow of interest payments on the foreign-held debt increased.

Third, we noted that payment of interest on the debt represents a big redistribution of income.

As a fourth point, the big interest payments also mean, from the government's point of view, that each year it has to earmark several tens of billions of dollars to be paid in interest before it can even start to consider other spending claims. This obviously curtails its ability to satisfy other demands in the economy. (The annual total interest payments in the 1990s are approximately $40 billion, which is higher than the annual deficits during the period.) A conundrum: if the government didn't have to pay these interest charges, then it could balance the budget. But because it didn't balance the budget in the past, it has to pay these interest charges.

A final criticism is that deficit spending by the government may be one of the major contributory causes of inflation. As we saw when we looked at inflationary gaps, if an economy experiences an increase in aggregate demand when it is at, or close to, full employment, the only thing that can change is the price level. By definition, full employment means working at capacity, so higher levels of production cannot be sustained indefinitely. Whether high deficits cause inflation or not depends, therefore, on the level of income of the economy. Deficit financing in a recession is one thing, but for governments to continue running up deficits when an economy is close to full employment is altogether a horse of a different colour. In summary, the problems with the national debt are:

- the potential crowding out of private investment spending and net exports
- the interest payments that must be paid on the foreign-held debt
- the income redistribution effects of large interest payments
- the reduced ability of government to meet the needs of its citizens
- the potential inflationary effects

Let's now take a brief look at what are sometimes seen as problems of the debt but really aren't.

One of these bogus arguments seeks to draw an analogy between a household or a business and the operations of the federal government. It suggests that just like an individual or a business, if revenue falls short of expenses for a long enough period of time, then bankruptcy will follow. This just isn't a legitimate concern when applied to a federal government, which has unlimited powers of taxation and borrowing and direct control over the nation's supply of money. Therefore, a federal government cannot go broke as a result of *internal* borrowing. The government of Germany went broke following World War I, but this was a result of external debt imposed on it by the victors in war. A particular city might go broke in the sense of defaulting on interest payments on the bonds it sold to borrow money, if urban decay and high taxes drive many higher-income taxpayers and businesses out of the city. The same might be said, although this would be stretching it, of a particular province or state, but not about a country as large, and as desirable to live in, as Canada.

Another argument suggests that a big national debt means that we are encumbering future generations, who will eventually have to pay it. It is true that our children and grandchildren will inherit a larger debt and the interest charges associated with it. However, it is also true that future generations will inherit the Canadian-held portion of the assets (bonds) represented by that debt. That is, if our descendants have to pay extra taxes to service a larger debt, they also, as a generation, will get those same taxes back as the interest payments are made to whoever holds those bonds.

One final point on this whole issue of the national debt is the fact that one never hears mention of the size of the government's assets. It is true that the federal government is in debt to the tune of hundreds of billions of dollars. But it also true that the government owns assets—airports, military hardware, land, buildings, and so on—that also total several hundred billion dollars more. Is the debt too large relative to the assets owned? Surprisingly, we know of no one who has addressed this question. However, we do have figures that relate Canada's debt in terms of its ability to repay. A glance back at Figure 1.9 in Chapter 1 reveals that Canada's debt–GDP ratio was highest at the end of World War II, then steadily fell to approximately 25 percent in the 1960s and has since risen to approximately 76 percent in 1997.

A Wrap-up and a Plea for Common Sense

A national debt that is internally held, is in the 40–50 percent range of GDP, and whose interest payments are in the 6–8 percent range of the government's annual budget is nothing to worry about. It is unfortunate that, in the last 15 years, Canada's national debt has grown to be over 75 percent of GDP, with interest payments now over 20 percent of the budget. In addition, we now have the foreign-held factor mentioned above. It would, however, be a mistake to overreact and impose rigid rules or laws on government policy in an attempt to bring the debt under control. Doing so would only rob the federal government of its counter-cyclical fiscal policy options. Instead it is important for government and the public to understand that curing any economic problem will often come at the expense of causing other problems. Deficits can be reduced but perhaps only at the cost of jobs and real economic growth. Decisions on issues like this are fundamental and should be made carefully.

SELF-TEST

6. Under what circumstances could it be said that the government's running a deficit is completely inappropriate?

REVIEW

1. Define *cyclically balanced-budget* fiscal policy.
2. Explain how the *crowding-out effect* might affect private investment spending.
3. Explain how the *crowding-out effect* might affect exports.
4. Explain how paying off the national debt would redistribute income.
5. To whom does the federal government owe most of its debt?
6. Why is it practically impossible for a country like Canada to go bankrupt?

Chapter Highlights

All national governments have fiscal policy of some kind. This chapter focuses on the two distinct approaches that can be used in setting fiscal policy.

We begin the chapter by defining net tax revenue and emphasizing that the state of the government's budget depends on government spending, the marginal tax rate, and the level of GDP. We then look at counter-cyclical fiscal policy, which sees the role of fiscal policy as deliberate intervention in the economy to "lean against the economic winds" and thereby to close recessionary or inflationary gaps. Next, the problems of inflation and the crowding-out effect associated with counter-cyclical fiscal policy are discussed. An alternative approach is a balanced-budget fiscal policy, which views the primary goal of fiscal policy as that of balancing the government's budget each budget year. This leads to a discussion of why this policy might result in fiscal policy being pro-cyclical rather than counter-cyclical. This last point is emphasized through the example of a government that cuts government spending and taxes by an equal amount, which we discover causes a drop in national income.

We then look at a possible compromise approach: a cyclically balanced-budget fiscal policy. The main idea here is to use counter-cyclical fiscal policy in the short run but with an eye to balancing the budget over the life of the business cycle. Finally, we explore the topic of the national debt and try to sort out the potential real problems from those that are simply misunderstandings.

New Glossary Terms

automatic stabilizers   389
balanced budget   380
balanced-budget fiscal policy   389
budget deficit   379
budget surplus   379
counter-cyclical fiscal policy   382
crowding-out effect   385
cyclically balanced-budget philosophy   393
fiscal policy   378
monetizing the debt   382
national debt   379
net tax revenue   378
pro-cyclical   391

STUDY GUIDE

Study Tips

1. Students sometimes have difficulty understanding the concept behind the word "pro-cyclical." It simply means a tendency to push things further in the direction that they are already moving. Try this: assume that, early in the morning, it has been determined that there are 100 new forest fires in a particular area as a result of a thunderstorm the previous evening. If the rest of the day turns out to be sunny and very hot with some wind, the weather will certainly add to the size of the fires; that is, it will be pro-cyclical. On the other hand, if the day turns out to be cool, with some rain and no wind, then the weather will be counter-cyclical.

2. You should realize that all governments have some kind of fiscal policy. Just what kind of policy a government has depends on its attitude toward spending, taxation, and budgets. Few governments would ever set out to deliberately make an economy already in a recession even worse with a pro-cyclical policy that pushed down GDP and raised unemployment even more. However, if a government decided to balance its budget regardless of cost, pursuing a policy of reducing government spending (or increasing taxation) when the economy is in recession, then it would have the *effect* of doing just that.

3. It is probably useful to state outright that the cause-and-effect relationship between a change in taxes and GDP operates both ways. A change in the level of taxation will certainly have an impact on GDP. But it is also true that if GDP changes, then the tax revenue received by the government will change. To keep these effects clear, you need to focus on which is the cause and which is the effect. However, it's no different from saying that a change in income will affect consumption but also that a change in consumption will affect income. The distinction between induced and autonomous consumption and taxes is important here.

Key Problem

Figure 11.8 shows the aggregate expenditures and government budget line for the economy of Mahdis. The full employment level of real GDP in Mahdis is $1500. The economy is in equilibrium but suffering a recessionary gap of $500.

FIGURE 11.8

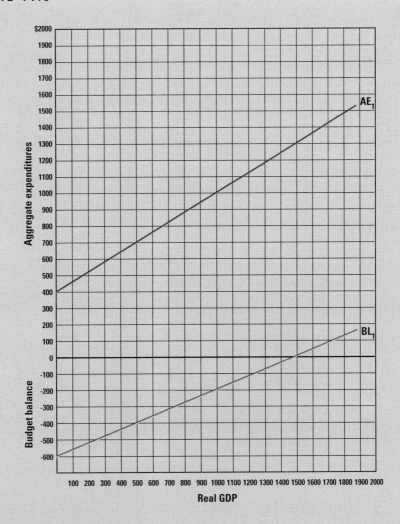

a) What is its level of real GDP?

Answer: _____.

b) Does the government have a budget deficit or surplus? How much?

Deficit or surplus? _____; amount: _____.

c) If the government wished to move the economy to full employment, should it increase or decrease government spending? How much?

Increase or decrease: _____; amount: _____.

d) Draw the new aggregate expenditure curve (AE$_2$) and new budget line (BL$_2$) in Figure 11.8.

e) What is the value of the multiplier in Mahdis?

Answer: _____.

f) What is the value of the government's budget at the new full-employment equilibrium?

Deficit or surplus: _____ ; amount: _____ .

g) Suppose that, given the original AE and BL curves in Figure 11.8, the government of Mahdis decided to balance the budget at the present level of equilibrium income. It would therefore need to increase or decrease government spending. By how much?

Increase or decrease: _____ ; amount: _____ .

h) Draw the new aggregate expenditures curve (AE_3) and new budget line (BL_3) in Figure 11.8.

i) What is the value of the resulting equilibrium GDP?

Answer: _____ .

j) What is the value of the resulting recessionary gap?

Answer: _____ .

k) What is the value of the government's budget balance?

Deficit or surplus: _____ ; amount: _____ .

More of the Same

Figure 11.9 shows the aggregate expenditures and government budget line for the economy of Kalam. The full-employment level of real GDP in Kalam is $4800. The economy is in equilibrium but suffering an inflationary gap of $1600.

FIGURE 11.9

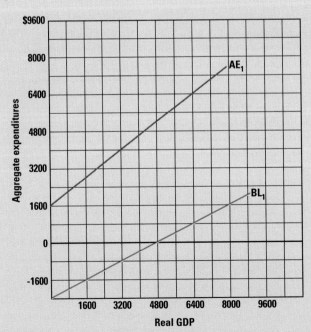

a) What is its level of real GDP?

   Answer: _____.

b) Does the government have a budget deficit or surplus? How much?

   Deficit or surplus? _____; amount: _____.

c) If the government wished to move the economy to full employment, should it increase or decrease government spending? How much?

   Increase or decrease: _____; amount: _____.

d) Draw the new aggregate expenditure curve (AE$_2$) and new budget line (BL$_2$) in Figure 11.9.

e) What is the value of the multiplier in Kalam?

   Answer: _____.

f) What is the government's budget at the new full-employment equilibrium?

   Deficit or surplus: _____; amount: _____.

g) Suppose that, given the original AE and BL curves in Figure 11.9, the government of Kalam decided to balance the budget. It would therefore need to increase or decrease government spending. By how much?

   Increase or decrease: _____; amount: _____.

h) Draw the new aggregate expenditures curve (AE$_3$) and new budget line (BL$_3$) in Figure 11.9.

i) What is the value of the resulting equilibrium GDP?

   Answer: _____.

j) What is the value of the resulting inflationary gap?

   Answer: _____.

k) What is the value of the government's budget balance?

   Deficit or surplus: _____; amount: _____.

Translations

Explain in words the graph in **Figure 11.10**, assuming that the shift in aggregate demand from AD$_1$ to AD$_2$ is a result of fiscal policy.

FIGURE 11.10

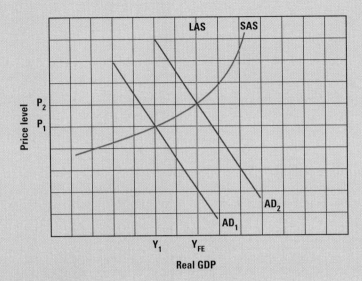

_____

_____

Are You Sure?

Indicate whether the following statements are true or false. If false, indicate why they are false.

1. The national debt is the sum of the federal government's past budget deficits less its surpluses.

   T or **F**   If false: _____

   _____

2. Monetizing the debt is the action by the government of borrowing from the central bank to finance spending.

   T or **F**   If false: _____

   _____

3. If aggregate demand increases as a result of counter-cyclical fiscal policy, prices will rise and GDP will fall.

   T or **F**   If false: _____

   _____

4. Counter-cyclical fiscal policy aimed at closing an inflationary gap is illustrated graphically by the aggregate demand curve shifting to the left.

   T or **F**   If false: _____

   _____

5. Both net tax revenues and government spending on goods and services are a function of GDP.

   T or **F**   If false: _____

   _____

6. A decrease in government spending on goods and services will lead to a decrease in net tax revenues.

   T or **F**   If false: _____

   _____

7. A decrease in autonomous taxes would pivot the NTR line down.

    T or **F**   If false: _____

    _____

8. Counter-cyclical fiscal policy is aimed at balancing the budget, whereas a balanced-budget fiscal policy is aimed at balancing the economy.

    T or **F**   If false: _____

    _____

9. If government spending on goods and services is increased by exactly the same amount that taxes are increased, the level of GDP will not change.

    T or **F**   If false: _____

    _____

10. In trying to cure a recession, counter-cyclical fiscal policy may crowd out both private investment and export spending.

    T or **F**   If false: _____

    _____

Choose the Best

11. What is fiscal policy?
    a) It is the government's approach toward its own spending and taxation.
    b) It is the central bank's approach to interest-rate policy.

12. Which of the following would close an inflationary gap?
    a) An increase in government spending.
    b) An increase in taxes.

13. The largest portion of the national debt is owed to what group?
    a) The Canadian public, that is, individuals, businesses, and banks in Canada.
    b) Foreign individuals, banks, and businesses.

14. What is net tax revenue?
    a) It is the total of all taxes collected by government less spending by government on goods and services.
    b) It is the total of all taxes collected by government plus transfer payments.
    c) It is the total of all taxes collected by government less transfer payments.

15. What is a budget deficit?
    a) It is government spending of all types in excess of net tax revenue.
    b) It is government spending on goods and services in excess of net tax revenue.
    c) It is government spending of all types plus net tax revenue.

16. What is true about the national debt since the 1960s?
    a) It has grown both absolutely and as a percentage of GDP.
    b) It has grown absolutely but has declined as a percentage of a GDP.
    c) It has grown absolutely but remained constant as a percentage of GDP.

17. What is the effect of a counter-cyclical fiscal policy?
    a) It intensifies changes caused by the business cycle.
    b) It dampens changes caused by the business cycle.
    c) It has no effect on changes caused by the business cycle.

18. Which of the following statements concerning a budget deficit is true?
    a) It is smaller if the economy is in the midst of a severe recession.
    b) It is smaller if the economy is experiencing strong aggregate demand.
    c) It has no effect on the size of the national debt.
    d) It can be measured in terms of the amount of unemployment that it causes.

Refer to **Figure 11.11** to answer questions 19, 20, and 21.

FIGURE 11.11

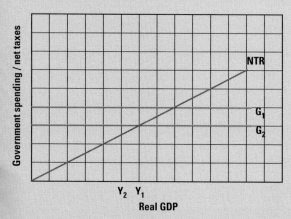

19. Refer to Figure 11.11 to answer this question. Which of the following statements is verified by the graph?
    a) A budget surplus exists if government spending is G_1 and real GDP is Y_1.
    b) A budget deficit exists if government spending is G_1 and real GDP is Y_1.
    c) If government spending was reduced from G_1 to G_2, the budget surplus at Y_2 would be larger than it was at Y_1.
    d) NTR is a function of the level of government spending.

20. Refer to Figure 11.11 to answer this question. What is most likely to happen if the level of GDP is Y_1 and the government reduces its spending from G_1 to G_2 in an attempt to balance its budget?
    a) The budget would be balanced at the new GDP level Y_2.
    b) GDP would remain at Y_1, but the budget would be in deficit.
    c) GDP would be Y_2, and the budget would be in deficit.
    d) GDP would be Y_2, and the budget would be in surplus.

21. Refer to Figure 11.11 to answer this question. If government spending is G_1 and GDP is Y_1, why won't a reduction in government spending by the size of the budget deficit eliminate the deficit?

a) Because NTR will decrease as a result of the decrease in government spending.
b) Because government spending is a function of income.
c) Because income will rise as a result of the decrease in government spending.
d) Because NTR will rise as a result of the decrease in government spending.

22. Suppose that an economy is simultaneously experiencing a budget deficit and an inflationary gap. If the government attempts to balance the budget, what will be the effect?
    a) Real GDP will increase, and the deficit will increase.
    b) Real GDP will increase, and the deficit will decrease.
    c) Real GDP will decrease, and the deficit will increase.
    d) Real GDP will decrease, and the deficit will decrease.

23. Suppose that counter-cyclical fiscal policy pushed up interest rates and the economy has a flexible exchange rate. Which of the following would be true?
    a) The exchange rate would fall, and exports would rise.
    b) The exchange rate would fall, and exports would fall.
    c) The exchange rate would rise, and exports would rise.
    d) The exchange rate would rise, and exports would fall.

24. What is the effect of counter-cyclical fiscal policy on the price level?
    a) It will increase in the case of a recessionary gap.
    b) It will increase in the case of a inflationary gap.
    c) It will decrease in the case of a recessionary gap.
    d) It will have no effect in the case of a recessionary gap.
    e) It will have no effect in the case of an inflationary gap.

25. An increase in government spending can result in crowding-out. Which of the following is a correct statement of the process?

a) It leads to a decrease in savings, which leads to a decrease in investment spending.

b) It leads to an increase in the money supply, which pushes interest rates up and causes a decrease in investment spending.

c) It causes bond prices to increase, which pushes interest rates up and leads to a decrease in investment spending.

d) It increases GDP and the demand for money, which causes interest rates to increase and investment spending to decrease.

e) It leads to an increase in GDP and in savings, which increases investment spending.

26. What would cause the aggregate demand curve to shift to the right?
   a) An increase in taxes.
   b) A decrease in government spending on goods and services.
   c) An increase in net tax revenues.
   d) Counter-cyclical fiscal policy and a recessionary gap.
   e) Counter-cyclical fiscal policy and a inflationary gap.

27. What is the meaning of the phrase: "The national debt is also a national credit"?
   a) Only interest payments on the national debt constitute an economic burden.
   b) What is owed must equal what is owned.
   c) The national debt is equal to the physical assets owned by the government.
   d) The national debt is a government debt held by the Bank of Canada, and both of these are public institutions.
   e) Official figures seriously understate the size of the national debt.

28. If counter-cyclical fiscal policy causes crowding-out, which of the following statements is correct?
   a) The crowding-out enhances the effectiveness of fiscal policy by pushing up interest rates and reducing private investment spending.
   b) The crowding-out reduces the effectiveness of fiscal policy by pushing up interest rates and reducing private investment spending.
   c) The crowding-out reduces the effectiveness of fiscal policy by lowering interest rates and reducing private investment spending.
   d) The crowding-out enhances the effectiveness of fiscal policy by lowering interest rates and increasing private investment spending.
   e) The crowding-out reduces money demand and thereby reduces the effectiveness of fiscal policy.

29. Which of the following statements about counter-cyclical fiscal policy is correct?
   a) It is appropriate in situations of a recessionary gap but not when an inflationary gap exists.
   b) It is appropriate in situations of an inflationary gap but not when a recessionary gap exists.
   c) It involves only higher government spending and/or lower taxes.
   d) It involves only lower government spending and/or higher taxes.
   e) It is the use of spending or taxation policies by the government to push the economy in a direction opposite to the way it was leaning.

30. Which of the following is true if the government attempts to balance its budget when the economy is in a recession and the government is running a budget deficit?
   a) Inflation would result.
   b) The unemployment rate would decrease.
   c) Either taxes or government spending would have to increase.
   d) GDP would increase.
   e) The action would be pro-cyclical.

Other Problems

31. Suppose that the government of Osiris decides that it can achieve its predetermined budgetary target over a seven-year cycle by maintaining its spending at $150 billion per year with a MTR of 0.25. **Table 11.6** gives the level of GDP in each of the first six years of the cycle in column 2.

TABLE 11.6

(1) Year	(2) GDP ($ billion)	(3) Deficit/Surplus if Target Met	(4) Actual Deficit/Surplus
1	600	_____	−2
2	580	_____	−7
3	560	_____	−12
4	612	_____	+1
5	620	_____	+1
6	608	_____	+2

a) Fill in column (3), which is the deficit/surplus that will be achieved if the government's budgetary target is met in each year.

Column (4) shows the actual levels of deficit/surplus achieved by the government. Assume that the estimate for the level of GDP in year 7 is $600 billion.

b) What level of government spending (assuming no change in the tax rate) is necessary for the government of Osiris to end the seven-year cycle with its budgetary goal on target?

Answer: _____

c) Alternatively, what change in the tax rate (assuming no change in government spending) is necessary for the government of Osiris to end the seven-year cycle with its budgetary goal on target?

Answer: _____

32. Assume that the parameters of for the economy of Tindor are:

$a_0 = 60$ $b = 0.8$
$I_0 = 600$ $t = 0.25$
$X_0 = 700$ $m = 0.2$
$T_0 = 200$

Further, assume that the government is constrained by law to maintain a balanced budget, that is, $G = T_0 + tY$.

a) What is the value of equilibrium income?

Answer: _____

b) What are the values of G and T at equilibrium income?

Answer: _____

c) What is the value of the multiplier in this economy?

Answer: _____

d) Is the multiplier derived in c) bigger or smaller than it is in an economy where G is autonomous?

Answer: _____

33. Answer the questions below for the economy of Motak using the graph in **Figure 11.12**.

FIGURE 11.12

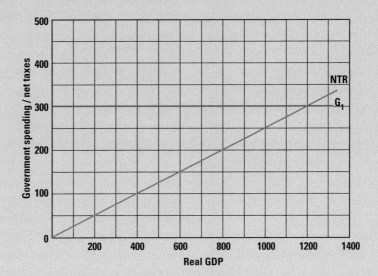

a) If GDP is $800 and government spending is G_1, what is the size of Motak's budget deficit?

Answer: _____

b) If government spending is decreased by the size of the deficit in a), and the multiplier is 2, what is the new level of equilibrium GDP?

Answer: _____

c) What is the size of Motak's deficit at this new level of equilibrium GDP?

Answer: _____

34. Government spending in Robok is an autonomous $140 billion, and its marginal tax rate is 0.35.
   a) Assuming there are no autonomous taxes, what is the balance on the government's budget at a GDP level of $360 billion?

Answer: _____

   b) What is the balance on the government's budget at a GDP level of $500 billion?

Answer: _____

   c) At what level of GDP will the economy of Robok have a balanced budget?

UNANSWERED QUESTIONS

Short Essays

1. Explain the circumstances under which a balanced budget fiscal policy will be pro-cyclical.

2. Give two reasons why net tax revenues decline as GDP falls.

3. Explain what is meant by the crowding-out effect.

4. What has happened to Canada's national debt as a percentage of GDP since the early 1930s?

5. List and discuss five potential problems associated with the national debt.

6. Explain some of the problems associated with a counter-cyclical fiscal policy.

7. Explain some of the problems associated with a balanced-budget fiscal policy.

Analytical Questions

8. Using a graph, illustrate the effects on aggregate expenditures and the budget line of:
   a) an increase in government spending;
   b) an increase in taxation.

9. If the government follows a cyclically balanced-budget fiscal policy over an extended period of time, what would you expect to happen to the size of the national debt? (For simplicity, assume there is no interest on the debt.)

10. We owe the national debt to ourselves. Therefore it isn't, and never will be, a problem. Discuss.

11. Suppose that a federal election is called at the time when the economy is experiencing a recessionary gap and the federal government's budget deficit is large. The leader of Party A promises, if elected, to immediately balance the budget by slashing government spending. The leader of Party B promises, if elected, to stimulate the economy with a tax decrease. What is the effect of each party's proposed policy on each of the following:
    a) The level of GDP.
    b) The level of NTR.
    c) The level of unemployment.
    d) The budget deficit.

12. For advocates of a balanced-budget fiscal policy, which economic problem would be more serious—high unemployment or a budget deficit? Is it possible for fiscal policy to reduce the intensity of both these problems at the same time?

13. Explain the effect on national income and the government's budget if the government were to increase both taxes and government spending by the same amount.

Numerical Questions

14. Assume that, in the economy of Ladush, the MPC is 0.75 and the multiplier is 4, and that both government spending and autonomous taxes are increased by 100. By how much, and in what direction, will equilibrium GDP change?

15. **Figure 11.13** depicts the economy of Trimac, where the government's budget would be balanced at full-employment equilibrium income.

FIGURE 11.13

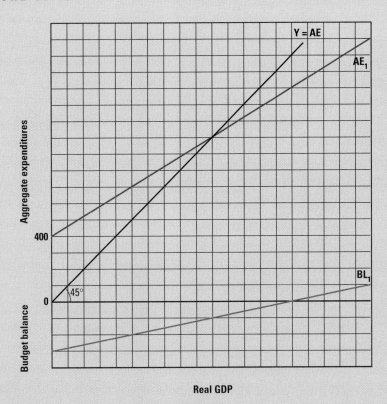

a) What is the value of equilibrium GDP in Trimac?
b) What is the size of the GDP gap at equilibrium?
c) What is the size of the budget balance at equilibrium?
d) What change in government spending is necessary in order to balance the budget at the present equilibrium level of GDP?
e) What change in government spending is necessary to close the GDP gap?

16. Figure 11.14 depicts the economy of Bodar.

FIGURE 11.14

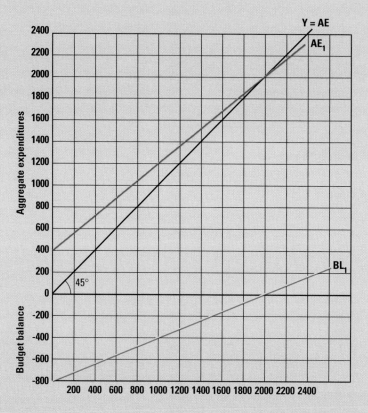

a) What would be the level of equilibrium real GDP if export spending were to decrease by 200?

b) Would there be a budget deficit or surplus at this new equilibrium level of real GDP? How much?

17. The aggregate demand and supply for Cancum are shown below. Full-employment GDP is $1500 billion.

Price	Aggregate Quantity Demanded	Aggregate Quantity Supplied
105	1600	400
110	1500	800
115	1400	1100
120	1300	1300
125	1200	1400
130	1100	1500
135	1000	1600
140	900	1650

a) Draw the AD, SAS, and LAS curves.

b) If the economy is in equilibrium, is the economy experiencing an inflationary or recessionary gap? How much?

c) Suppose the government uses counter-cyclical fiscal policy to close the gap. By how much and in what direction might AD change in order to achieve full employment?

d) As a result of this change, what will be the inflation rate?

18. The economy of Morin is shown in **Figure 11.15**.

FIGURE 11.15

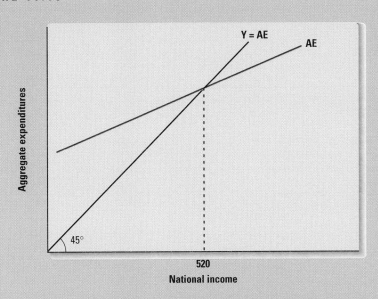

a) If full-employment GDP is $600, and the economy is in equilibrium, is there an inflationary or recessionary gap? How much of a gap?

b) Suppose that the government successfully closes the gap by increasing government spending by $40. What is the value of the multiplier?

c) Suppose, initially, that the government had a budget deficit of $50. If the marginal tax rate in Morin is 0.25, what will be the government's budget deficit at the new full-employment equilibrium?

19. Given the following data for the economy of Moksha:

$C = 40 + 0.75Yd$ $G = 160$
$T = 20 + 0.2Y$ $X = 55$
$I = 60$ $IM = 0.1Y$

a) Calculate equilibrium GDP.

b) Calculate the multiplier.

c) Calculate the size of the budget deficit or surplus.

d) Now cut taxes, or cut government spending, by the size of the surplus, or deficit, in an attempt to balance the budget. Calculate the new equilibrium income.

e) Calculate the budget surplus or deficit resulting from the new income level.

20. Return to the equilibrium GDP level that you calculated in question 19 a).

a) Assume that full-employment GDP is $700 billion. In what direction and by how much would government spending have to change to achieve full-employment GDP?

b) What is the budget deficit/surplus at full-employment GDP?

21. Given the following data for the economy of Potan:

$a_0 = 80$ $b = 0.75$
$I_0 = 620$ $t = 0.2$
$X_0 = 750$ $m = 0.1$
$T_0 = 200$
$G = T$

a) What is the level of equilibrium GDP?
b) What is the amount of government spending?
c) Assume now that G remains at the same level as in b), but T is allowed to change. If exports decrease by 30, what is the new level of equilibrium GDP?
d) Assuming that G must remain equal to T, if exports decrease by 30 what is the new level of equilibrium GDP?

 # Web-Based Activities

1. Go to **http://www.tdbank.ca/tdbank/Research/Economic_Reports/ROCGF/1998/roggf-10.gif** and **http://www.reform.ca/babb/dividen7.html** to answer the following questions:
   a) What was the average rate of growth in the total (provincial plus federal) debt over the period 1994–98?
   b) What are the interest costs on the debt per Canadian?
   c) Now, read **http://www.pei-intl.com/Research/ECONOMY/DEBTSOLU.HTM.** According to the author of the article, what is the real problem associated with government debt? What solutions does the author propose?

2. According to the author of **http://www.netizen.org/Progressive/wespa/articles/progressive.html,** how must traditional Keynesian fiscal policy be changed to effectively deal with the current problems facing the Canadian economy?

Monetary Policy

What's ahead... We start this chapter by looking at the agency responsible for monetary policy, the Bank of Canada, and examine some of the tools it has available to effect changes in the nation's money supply. We then proceed to discuss what is appropriate monetary policy by exploring the pro-active approach to policy making. This approach has two versions—one uses monetary policy to attempt to achieve full-employment equilibrium in the economy, and the other uses it to achieve stability in the value of the currency. The other approach, that of the neutralist school, is then discussed. The chapter closes with a brief discussion of stagflation and the resulting need for policies beyond those of fiscal and monetary policy.

Have you ever watched one of the many business or money shows on TV? Did you notice the emphasis that the analysts put on interest rates? "I expect that stock market to remain strong, as long as interest rates stay low, " is a sentiment that was often expressed in the late 1990s on these shows. Low interest rates are certainly good for the stock market, but are they also good for the economy and for you and me? Generally the answer is yes. So, if low interest rates are so important, why aren't they always kept low? Is it because they have to be kept up with those in the United States? Why is this? This chapter will help answer questions like these.

monetary policy:
economic policy designed
to change or influence the
economy through changes
in the money supply.

I n Chapter 8 we saw that changes in the money supply can bring about real changes in the economy and move it toward full-employment equilibrium. The Bank of Canada is the main agent that effects such changes in the money supply, a process called **monetary policy**. And what is the appropriate goal of monetary policy—what should these changes be aimed at? Not many years ago the stated mandate of the Bank of Canada was "to assist the economy in achieving a full-employment, non-inflationary level of total output." Then a perceptible shift in this mandate began to emerge. Today, the Bank's stated goal is:

> **"To preserve the value of money... [since] stability in the value of money (a low rate of inflation) promotes economic prosperity by providing a framework in which households and businesses can make sound economic decisions."**

The Bank of Canada nowadays sees the role of monetary policy as a means of providing an environment that will assist the economy in achieving the goals of low inflation and low unemployment. We will be examining the role of monetary policy in greater detail later in this chapter, but first we look at the Bank of Canada's functions and the tools it uses to carry out monetary policy.

Functions of the Bank of Canada

In general, the Bank of Canada operates in a way similar to that of most other central banks throughout the world. Some central banks are state owned (for example, the Bank of Canada, the Bank of England); others are privately owned (such as the American central bank, known as the Federal Reserve Board). However, for all intents and purposes, ownership is unimportant. What is important are the things that central banks have in common. The following comments about the Bank of Canada apply equally, therefore, to most central banks.

As we noted in Chapter 7, one traditional function of the Bank of Canada is that it is the *sole issuer of currency*. In this regard, it tends to act as a reservoir, in that it will issue more currency to the banks when needed (just before Christmas, for instance) and at other times it will take back any surplus above the banks' and the public's

A visitor to the currency museum in the Bank of Canada building in Ottawa looks at a half-burnt Canadian dollar. The display illustrates how old money is disposed of.

requirements (just after the Christmas holiday season). You may recall that only the portion of the outstanding currency that is in the hands of the public is considered part of the money supply; the portion in the banks is excluded.

A second traditional function is that the Bank of Canada acts as the *government's bank*. It is the institution that looks after the government's banking needs. More recently, however, individual government ministries have been given authority to deal with whichever commercial bank they choose, making this function of the Bank of Canada less important. However, the Bank of Canada also *manages reserves of foreign currencies* (and gold) on behalf of the government. This includes the buying and selling of Canadian dollars and other currencies, in consultation with the government and consistent with its policies.

Just as the Bank of Canada traditionally acted as the government's bank, so too did it act as the *bankers' bank*, in that each of the commercial banks has an account with the Bank of Canada. The central bank stands prepared to make extraordinary loans to a commercial bank that is experiencing a liquidity problem to avert a loss of depositor confidence. In this respect, it is often known as the "lender of last resort."

The Bank Act also charges the Bank of Canada with the responsibility of acting as *auditor and inspector of the commercial banks*, and the latter are required to submit periodic reports to the Bank of Canada and to open their books and accounts for inspection and audit.

The final function of the Bank of Canada is the most important, and that is to *regulate the money supply*. It is interesting to note in this regard that although the federal government, through Parliament, has the power and the responsibility to effect fiscal policy, it does not itself directly control monetary policy: this is the prime function of the governor and the board of directors of the Bank of Canada. It is possible, therefore, at least in theory, for the government and the Bank of Canada to be in conflict regarding the direction in which they want to move the economy. In fact, there was such a conflict between the two in the late 1950s. Generally speaking, however, this does not happen often, not because the two always agree, but because a conflict in policies would be regarded as something of a political failure and thus something which the policy makers wish to avoid. In summary, the functions of a central bank, such as the Bank of Canada, are to act as:

- the issuer of currency
- the government's bank and manager of foreign currency reserves
- the bankers' bank and lender of last resort
- the auditor and inspector of commercial banks
- the regulator of the money supply

ADDED DIMENSION

The Bank of Canada and the Government

It is worth emphasizing that although the governor and directors of the Bank of Canada are appointed by the federal cabinet (through the governor general), their roles are meant to be non-political. Appointments are not politically motivated by patronage, but rather based on merit and expertise. In addition, their seven-year terms exceed the life of a government, and the governor's appointment can be terminated only by an act of Parliament. In these ways it is hoped that the bank will operate independently of government and pursue monetary policy without needing to consider short-term political considerations. The government could, through the minister of finance, attempt to formally dictate to the governor what policy it wished him (so far, all governors have been men, including the present governor, Gordon Thiessen) to follow. However, being forced to act openly in this manner signals a marked political failure for the government and is therefore seldom done.

Let's now look now at the way in which the Bank of Canada carries out monetary policy.

Tools of Monetary Policy

expansionary monetary policy: a policy that aims to increase the amount of money in the economy and make credit cheaper and more easily available.

contractionary monetary policy: a policy in which the amount of money in the economy is decreased and credit becomes harder to obtain and more expensive.

open-market operations: the buying and selling of securities by the Bank of Canada in the open (to the public) market.

Let's assume that the Bank of Canada wishes to effect an **expansionary monetary policy** (also called an easy money policy). This involves increasing the money supply. How could this be done? Well, we know from Chapter 7 that if the Bank could increase the amount of cash reserves held by the commercial banks, then any reserves that banks consider in excess of their target reserves would be loaned out and, through the money multiplier process, would lead to an increase in demand deposits (the main portion of the money supply). **Contractionary monetary policy** (or a tight money policy) would imply the opposite.

One simple way for the Bank of Canada to increase the commercial banks' cash reserves would be simply to give them additional amounts of reserves. However, some of us might complain about a free gift of cash to the banks. The Bank of Canada therefore has to use a more subtle and businesslike process known as **open-market operations**, so called because it involves the Bank of Canada (or at least its agent) in buying or selling bonds in a market that is open to anyone. In other words, the Bank of Canada buys and sells government bonds in the same way that any individual or corporation might do.

To better understand just how this market works, we need to understand the role of treasury bills. These are a type of bond, or fixed-term debt, issued by the Bank of Canada acting as the government's agent. Fortunately, from time to time, corporations, commercial banks, life insurance and pension fund companies, and other organizations find themselves with excess cash. Usually, this cash will be needed by these organizations in the near future, so the question of what to do with, say, $2 million for 60 days can arise. One of the most popular revenue-earning assets are treasury bills, or T-bills, which can be bought for either a three- or six-month term. These bills can be bought and sold quickly and easily in various amounts. They differ from bonds in that they are short-term and do not pay interest. Instead, the return is earned on them because they are purchased at a discount (at a price below the face value) but are then redeemed at the end of the fixed term at face value.

If it wished to increase the amount of cash reserves of the commercial banks, the Bank of Canada would buy T-bills. The sellers of the T-bills would receive a cheque from the Bank of Canada, which they would then deposit in their bank accounts. At the end of the day, these banks would look to the Bank of Canada for collection. This could be effected by the Bank of Canada transferring the required amount of reserves to the commercial bank in question. Rather than doing this, however, the Bank of Canada simply credits the account of the appropriate commercial bank at the Bank of Canada. It, in effect, tells the commercial bank that the amount of credit it has "on reserve" at the Bank of Canada has been increased. The commercial banks' reserves have therefore increased, and this recently acquired surplus will be loaned out, thus leading to a multiple expansion of money in the economy, as we discussed in Chapter 7.

To reduce the money supply, the Bank of Canada would of course do the opposite and would sell bonds to whoever wished to purchase them. These people would have to make payment to the Bank of Canada, and their bank account balances would be thus reduced, and so would the reserves of the commercial banks. As a result of this, banks would be forced to call in loans, and this would reduce the amount of money in the economy.

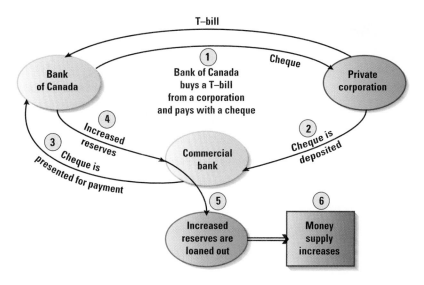

Open-market operations are not the only tool of monetary policy, but they are a frequently used and important method. This is because they can be initiated on short notice, take effect quickly, and can be done in any amount.

SELF-TEST

1. In terms of the banking system's ability to create money, what difference, if any, does it make if the Bank of Canada buys bonds from a commercial bank, rather than buying them from a member of the public?

ADDED DIMENSION

The Bank of Canada's Balance Sheet

The operations of the Bank of Canada affect the economy, but they, of course, also affect the balance sheet of the bank itself. The following table shows the Bank of Canada's balance sheet in simplified form as at December 1997. All figures are in billions.

Assets		Liabilities	
Treasury bills of Canada	$14.1	Notes in circulation	$30.5
Other securities	13.0	Government of Canada deposits	0.4
Advances to banks, etc.	0.4	Deposits of banks	0.6
Other assets	4.2	Other liabilities	0.2
Total	31.7	Total	31.7

The biggest asset of the bank is its holdings of government bonds and treasury bills, and it is the sale and purchase of these that we term open-market operations. Notice also that the advances (loans) to members of the Canadian Payments Association (abbreviated as "banks, etc."), are the short-term loans, mentioned in Chapter 7, that banks take from time to time. The major liability of the bank, as you can see, is the amount of notes in circulation. Although these notes are assets to members of the public that own them, they represent a liability to the issuing bank, the Bank of Canada. The other major liability is the reserves that the commercial banks lodge with the Bank of Canada. Such reserves are, of course, an asset to the commercial banks, but a liability to the Bank of Canada.

Source: Adapted from the *Bank of Canada Review*, Spring 1998, table B1.

SELF-TEST

2. Below are the simplified and hypothetical balance sheets for the commercial banking system and for the Bank of Canada (all figures are in billions):

All Commercial Banks		Bank of Canada	
Assets		**Assets**	
Reserves:		Securities	$80
In vaults	$ 70		
On deposit with the Bank of Canada	10		
Securities	120		
Loans	600		
Totals	800		80
Liabilities		**Liabilities**	
Deposits	800	Notes in circulation	65
		Deposits of banks	10
		Other liabilities	5
Totals	800		80

A) Show the effects on the balance sheets of both the Bank of Canada and the commercial banks as a result of the Bank of Canada buying $2 billion worth of securities directly from the commercial banks.

B) If the target reserve ratio is 10 percent, what effect does this have on the money-creating ability of the commercial banks?

C) If the bonds were bought directly from the public, again show the effects on both balance sheets. What effects does this have on the banks' money-creating potential?

bank rate: the rate of interest payable by the commercial banks on loans from the Bank of Canada.

The second tool of monetary policy is a change in the **bank rate**. The bank rate is the official rate of the Bank of Canada and is the rate charged on loans it makes to the commercial banks. It is an "announced" rate that stays in effect until it is changed by the Bank of Canada and generally influences all other interest rates in the economy so that it is closely watched. To the average consumer who is considering the purchase of a new house or car, the interest rate is one of the most important of all economic statistics. It has the power to shape the future of most of us, whether we are interest earners or interest payers. To a firm thinking of new capital investment, a change in interest rates will often tip the decision of whether or not to go ahead.

A commercial bank must pay the bank rate to the Bank of Canada on any loans it takes out to cover a temporary shortage of reserves. Commercial banks regard this rate as a penalty rate, and any increase in it would cause them to want to restrict the amount of any such loans. Therefore, Canadian commercial banks have historically tried to keep these loans to an absolute minimum, regardless of the level of the bank rate. Because of this, changes in the bank rate serve more as a psychological signal than anything else.

It is important to realize that the bank rate is just one of many rates that make up the whole interest-rate *structure*. For example, the rate that commercial banks charge their best customers, the prime rate, is a little higher than the bank rate. Moving up the scale, the mortgage rate would be next and then, above that, the personal loan rate. All the various rates on savings would be below the bank rate, with the rate on large sums of money that are committed for a long time paying the highest savings rate and small sums for short periods the lowest. When we speak of a change in the interest rate, we are referring to the whole interest-rate structure.

A drop in the bank rate signals expansionary policy, which, we just saw, means that credit is more freely available and cheaper. Contractionary policy, which means less money in the economy, is reflected in a higher bank rate. What this means is that:

> The supply of money and interest rates are inextricably linked, and it is impossible to change one without at the same time changing the other.

ADDED DIMENSION

Bond Prices and Interest Rates

To understand the connection between the price of bonds and interest rates, consider the issuance of a T-bill at the face value of $100 000 that will be redeemable in 91 days from issuance for the same amount. Since no one would pay $100 000 for a bill that will give them $100 000 later, these bills are sold at a discount.

A bill that is sold at a discounted price of $97 500 and is worth $100 000 in 91 days means that anyone purchasing this bill would earn a return of $2500 in just three months. As a percentage of the investment outlay this represents ($2500/$97 500) × 100, or 2.56 percent. Annualized, this comes to 2.56 × 4, or an annual rate of 10.24 percent. Now, what would happen if the purchaser had received a bigger discount and only had to pay $96 000 for the bill? In this case, she would be earning a return of ($4000/$96 000) × 100 × 4, or 16.67 percent per annum. From this, it can be seen that the lower the price (the higher the discount), the greater will be the rate of return (in effect, the rate of interest) that can be earned.

Another feature of treasury bills is that they can be bought or sold, through a broker, at any time during their 91-day life. In fact, a particular bill may have gone through three, four, or more owners between its original purchase and the time of redemption. The closer the maturity date, the closer to the face value will be its selling price. Thus, institutions that have excess cash will be T-bill buyers, and 20 or 40 or 60 days later when they need the cash they will be T-bill sellers.

A bond shares many of the characteristics of a treasury bill. A bond is another type of IOU issued by the government (and others). It differs from a T-bill in that it has a longer term and pays interest annually. A prospective buyer of a previously issued bond will take into account the interest receivable as well as the possible increase or decrease in the value of the bond. A purchaser willing to pay only $98 for an 8 percent, $100 bond redeemable in one year will therefore receive a $2 capital appreciation as well as $8 in interest. The return (the effective rate of interest), therefore, is $10, or 10 percent. If that same purchaser were forced to pay $103 for the bond, then the rate of return would only be approximately 5 percent (a capital loss of $3 plus interest of $8). Again, the actual rate of interest earned depends on the price of the bond. A higher bond price means a lower rate of interest.

Another way in which the Bank of Canada can affect the money supply is by *switching government deposits*. If the Bank of Canada wants to contract the money supply, for instance, then it can, with approval of the finance ministry, transfer some of the government's deposits from a commercial bank to the Bank of Canada. It does this by, in effect, writing a cheque on the government's account at the commercial bank made payable to the Bank of Canada. The effect of switching deposits is similar to open-market operations. In both cases, demand deposits and reserves are affected. Switching deposits has become an increasingly popular monetary tool for the Bank of Canada.

SELF-TEST

3. Suppose that the banking system's target reserve ratio is 10 percent and the Bank of Canada switches $100 million of government funds from the government's account with the Bank of Canada to an account at a commercial bank. Since neither the government's accounts with commercial banks nor the commercial banks' reserves are considered to be part of the money supply, how could such a switching of funds have any effect on the money supply?

A final tool of monetary policy is given the euphemistic title of *moral suasion*. This simply means that the Bank of Canada informs the financial community, by way of pronouncements, public or private discussions, and by other means, of the direction it would like to go. The heads of financial and government agencies constitute a relatively small and fairly exclusive group. Communication among them is ongoing and informal, so it is not difficult for the Bank of Canada to let members of this community know the direction it would like them to proceed. Usually, the banks are happy to concur. Even if they are not happy, they usually concur! In summary, the four tools of monetary policy are:

- open-market operations
- setting the bank rate
- switching government deposits
- moral suasion

By these various ways the Bank of Canada is able, directly and indirectly, to determine the supply of money in the economy. Changes in the *supply* of money, as we saw in Chapter 8, will lead to important changes in the economy. We will now turn to an examination of the way changes in monetary policy can affect various macroeconomic aggregates.

REVIEW

1. List the functions of the Bank of Canada.
2. What is the biggest asset of the Bank of Canada? What is its biggest liability?
3. What do we mean when we say a bond is sold at a "discount"?
4. What are the four tools of monetary policy?
5. Describe what is meant by the term *open-market operations*.
6. If the Bank of Canada switches government bank balances from itself to a commercial bank, would the money supply increase or decrease?

Is Monetary Policy Needed?

In Chapter 7 we looked at some of the characteristics of money and noted that it should be reasonably scarce (stones or sea shells would not be a good form of money) but not so scarce that people had to wait their turn to use it. What this means is not only that an economy can have too much money but that it is also possible for it to have too little money. Let's look at this aspect in more depth by asking:

> What would happen if the Bank of Canada increased the money supply too much?

You will recall from Chapter 8 that an increase in the money supply will reduce the interest rate, which will, in turn, raise the level of investment spending. The increase in investment spending will increase the level of aggregate demand. As aggregate demand increases sufficiently to push the economy to full employment and beyond, real GDP would be unable to rise any further and the full impact of the increase in the money supply would be on the price level. What this means is something most people are well aware of:

Gordon Thiessen, governor of the Bank of Canada, discusses the contents of the bank's monetary policy report.

If the money supply is increased too much, the result will be inflation.

Remember that this is what we earlier characterized as too much money chasing too few goods—a description of demand-pull inflation. History is filled with examples of what happens when a nation's money supply is increased too fast, resulting in serious inflation. For example, in the seventeenth and eighteenth centuries, European countries tied their money supply to the amount of gold reserves held by government. Thus, when shipload after shipload of Spanish bullion began arriving from the New World, inflation was triggered and continued for a long time. In the 1920s, because of the treaty that ended World War II, Germany's Weimar Republic felt it had little choice but to increase the money supply very rapidly in order to pay its bills. This triggered the hyper-inflation that we looked at in Chapter 4. A contemporary example is that of the Russian government, which began a rapid increase in its money supply in late 1998 after the collapse of its fixed exchange rate, which, as this book was being written, looked certain to trigger inflation on a grand scale.

If such increases result in these types of problems, why increase the money supply at all? In other words, let's now turn to the other side of the question and ask:

What would be the effect of the Bank of Canada not increasing the money supply?

We know that increases in the level of real GDP increase the demand for money. In other words, normal economic growth results in increased demand for money. If, at the same time, the money supply does not increase but, instead, is held constant, the result will be a higher interest rate. This will reduce investment spending, and thus aggregate demand, which brings the economy's growth to a halt and, in extreme cases, could cause real GDP to fall. Something like this in fact happened in the early 1930s, when the American Federal Reserve Board *contracted* the money supply in the face of falling aggregate demand. This, of course, made the fall in GDP even worse. In addition, we would also expect the price level to fall. This is in fact what happened in both the United States and Canada in the early 1930s. In Canada's case, the decrease in prices between 1929 and 1933 was 23 percent. This leads us to the conclusion that:

If the money supply is not increased sufficiently, the result will be a recession and low economic growth.

These two examples bring out something very fundamental. The economic health of an economy depends on the money supply growing but not too quickly nor too slowly. Since it is the Bank of Canada that controls the growth of the money supply through its actions, it is clear that some kind of monetary policy is needed. This being the case, what kind of policy should this be?

In Chapter 11, when we asked what kind of fiscal policy should be used, we saw that there were two distinct schools of thought on the question. Exactly the same

Source: *Money and Monetary Policy in Canada.* Toronto: Canadian Council for Economic Education, 1994. Cartoon by Kelly Brine.

The Bank of Canada's policies can influence the money supply, interest rates, and the exchange rate. The bank's goal is to create the right mix appropriate for the economy.

situation applies here to the question of what kind of monetary policy should be used. The first school of thought we will call the pro-active school, which is analogous to the interventionists of the previous chapter, and the second we will call the neutralist school, which is analogous to the non-interventionists.

The Pro-Active Approach to Monetary Policy

There are two versions of pro-active monetary policy. The first is Keynesian monetary policy, which, until approximately 20 years ago, dominated most monetary policy making. The second version is anti-inflationary monetary policy, which surfaced in the late 1970s and early 1980s. We will look at each in turn.

Keynesian Monetary Policy

The pro-active approach to monetary policy envisions an active process of setting goals and then adjusting policy to achieve those goals. As an example, the Bank of Canada used *Keynesian monetary policy* for some time after it was established in 1935. Its mandate then was:

> to regulate credit and currency in the best interest of the nation... and to mitigate by its influence fluctuations in the general level of production, trade, prices, and employment.

As you can see, implied here is the use of monetary policy to assist in achieving four separate goals:

- steady growth in real GDP
- an exchange rate that ensures a viable balance of trade
- stable prices
- full employment

However, it is clear that no single policy tool can be expected to simultaneously achieve multiple goals. Thus, we can see that in this situation what was called "policy making" often involved deciding which goal, or goals, should be given priority. For three or four decades following World War II, most economists and policy makers took it for granted that monetary policy should be pro-active. They felt that the two goals it, along with counter-cyclical fiscal policy, should focus on were stable prices and full employment.

SELF-TEST

4. Which of the above goals are in conflict with each other, and which are compatible?

Achieving these twin goals seemed reasonable enough at the time, since unemployment and inflation were seen as opposite ends of the spectrum. That is to say, if aggregate demand was too low to achieve full employment, then there would be little or no inflationary pressure. Similarly, if aggregate demand was so high as to create inflation, then there would be little or no unemployment. In short, it was believed that an economy might suffer from an unemployment problem or from an inflation problem, but never from both problems at the same time. It followed then that monetary policy could be used to address the one problem that was present at that time, be it inflation or unemployment. This point is illustrated in the next two figures.

FIGURE 12.1 The Effect of Contractionary Monetary Policy

Given an aggregate demand of AD_1, there exists an inflationary gap equal to the distance $Y_E - Y_{FE}$. If contractionary monetary policy reduced aggregate demand to AD_2, then the inflationary gap would be closed.

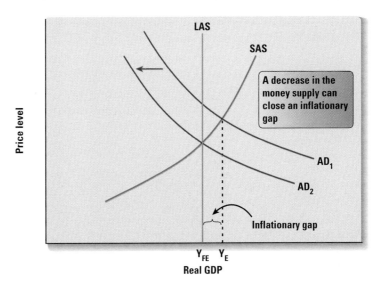

In **Figure 12.1**, If aggregate demand is AD_1 and full-employment national income is Y_{FE}, then there is an inflationary gap equal to $Y_E - Y_{FE}$. Keynesian monetary policy would call for contractionary monetary policy in this case. You will recall that this means reducing the money supply and making credit tighter, which increases the interest rate. The higher interest rate means a lower level of investment spending. Furthermore, the higher interest rate will encourage foreigners to send their savings to Canada, which increases the demand for the Canadian dollar on the international money markets and pushes the exchange rate up. This leads to a decrease in exports, which reinforces the decrease in investment spending. The combined effect of lower investment spending and lower exports reduces the level of aggregate demand to AD_2 and closes the inflationary gap.

SELF-TEST

5. If the Bank of Canada wanted to decrease the money supply, should it buy or sell government bonds?

Let's now turn to **Figure 12.2**. Once again, the level of aggregate demand is AD_1, and equilibrium national income is Y_E. However, in this situation there is a recessionary gap, since Y_E is less than Y_{FE}, the full-employment level of national income. Here, Keynesian monetary policy would call for the use of expansionary monetary policy, which means increasing the money supply and making credit more readily available. This would lower the interest rate, which would increase the level of investment spending. In addition, a lower interest rate discourages foreigners from holding Canadian bonds and savings-account balances and encourages Canadians to send their savings abroad in search of higher interest rates. This pushes down the exchange rate, which increases exports. The combination of higher investment spending and higher exports would increase aggregate demand, from AD_1 to AD_2, and this would close the recessionary gap by increasing national income from Y_E to Y_{FE}.

FIGURE 12.2 The Effects of Expansionary Monetary Policy

Given AD_1, a recessionary gap equal to the distance $Y_{FE} - Y_E$ exists. Expansionary monetary policy that increases aggregate demand to AD_2 would close the recessionary gap.

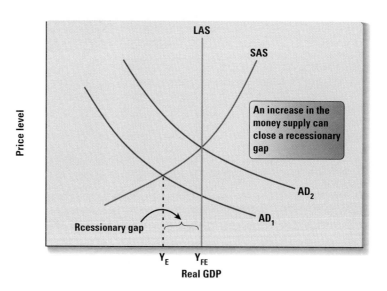

In summary, Keynesian monetary policy aims to keep the level of spending in the economy stable. If the economy is under-spending and a recessionary gap exists, then expansionary monetary policy would be used to raise spending. Similarly, if the economy was over-spending, then contractionary monetary policy would be used to reduce spending.

Criticisms of Keynesian Monetary Policy

The major problem with Keynesian monetary policy, as economists later came to realize, is that the twin goals of full employment and stable prices are incompatible and it is probably impossible to achieve them together. This point was first explored in the early 1960s by A.W. Phillips, a British economist, who explored the possibility of an economy achieving both goals simultaneously. He concluded that there was no evidence of this occurring in Britain in all of the previous century. In fact, it seemed to him that there was a "trade-off" between the two goals. This means that while it may be possible to achieve full employment, it would only be at the expense of higher rates of inflation. Similarly, stable prices could be achieved, but only at the cost of higher unemployment. Under these circumstances, the best that a central bank can do is achieve a delicate balance between the two without ever attaining either goal. For instance, it might be able to help the economy achieve a modest amount of inflation combined with a not-too-high level of cyclical unemployment. Any attempt to reduce inflation further would likely provoke unacceptably high rates of unemployment. Similarly, expansionary monetary policy designed to reduce unemployment would cause an acceleration in inflation rates. A central bank is caught therefore between "the devil and a hard place."

ADDED DIMENSION

The Phillips Curve

In 1958, British economist A.W. Phillips confirmed what many economists had long suspected, namely, that curing the twin evils of unemployment and inflation simultaneously may be not only difficult, but, in fact, impossible. Phillips did a time-series analysis of unemployment and inflation rates (actually, yearly changes in wage rates) for the British economy for the previous 100 years. He discovered that there were very few years of both low unemployment and low inflation rates. In fact, it seemed to be the case that when there was low unemployment, inflation was high; and vice versa—when inflation was low, unemployment was high. Furthermore, there appeared to be a "trade-off" between the two. A simple table of hypothetical data will illustrate the idea:

Unemployment Rate	Inflation Rate
4%	12%
6	8
8	5
10	3
12	2

Not only are low unemployment rates associated with high inflation rates and high unemployment with low inflation, but the cost of trying to fully achieve either of these goals becomes more and more expensive for society. In other words, to reduce unemployment by 2 percentage points when the economy is suffering 12 percent unemployment "costs" society a 1 percentage point increase in inflation, from 2 percent to 3 percent. But to reduce unemployment by a similar 2 percentage points when the economy is close to full employment, say from 6 percent to 4 percent, "costs" the country 4 percentage points in inflation.

While the idea seemed like a major breakthrough at the time, in hindsight, the Phillips curve does nothing more than confirm the shape of the short-run aggregate supply curve: that it is upward-sloping and gets steeper as we approach the full-employment level of GDP. You can validate this in your own mind by picturing what would happen as aggregate demand increases. The answer is that it would result in both higher GDP (lower unemployment) and higher prices (inflation). Additionally, as you move closer to full-employment GDP, the increase in the price level is greater than the increase in GDP.

Over the last two decades, the Bank of Canada, along with a number of other central banks around the world, have concluded that the task of simultaneously curing both unemployment and inflation simply isn't possible. As a result, the bank has refocused its mandate toward the more attainable goal of maintaining the value of the Canadian dollar.

Anti-Inflationary Monetary Policy

In contrast to Keynsian monetary policy, the Bank of Canada now sees its role as preserving both the internal and external value of the currency. This means that the bank uses monetary policy to keep inflation in Canada at a minimum. Recently this has meant an inflation rate of less than 2 percent per year. This is in stark contrast to the experience of most of the 1970s and 1980s. Following the OPEC-imposed oil price increases of the early 1970s, inflation rates around the world, including Canada, were in the range of 8 to 12 percent per year. In addition to holding the rate of inflation down, the bank is also concerned with the external value of the currency (the exchange rate), with an eye to maintaining stability in this market.

Those who support this new role for monetary policy argue that the underlying purpose of preserving the internal and external value of a country's currency is to create the right atmosphere for investment. If investment is high, it follows that price stability is the key condition in maintaining the highest possible levels of productivity, real incomes, employment, and global competitiveness. This is because, as we saw in Chapter 4, the worst enemy of new investment is uncertainty. High rates of inflation, or even unpredictable changes in the inflation rate, create an atmosphere of uncertainty. Foreign investors in particular need the assurance that both the external value (the exchange rate) and the internal value (the price level) of a currency will not be changing dramatically in the near future. Sudden, unpredictable changes in either are undesirable. In short, uncertainty and the lower levels of investment spending that go with it reduce the rate of economic growth and the prosperity of the nation.

Given this, the federal government and the Bank of Canada made a joint statement in December 1993 attempting to generate confidence in the economy. They announced their objective of keeping inflation within a target range of 1 to 3 percent for the period 1995 to 1998. Later, in February 1998 it was announced that this inflationary-control target was extended to the end of 2001. Furthermore, the government and the bank made it clear that more target-range announcements would be forthcoming in the future.

Using this new goal for monetary policy still involves a pro-active approach, but clearly the emphasis has changed. Where once the Bank of Canada's role was to help achieve full employment and price stability, it now attempts to control inflation and maintain a steady exchange rate.

We have already seen that controlling inflation means preventing aggregate demand from becoming too strong, and this is done by keeping the pace of monetary expansion in line with economic growth and, occasionally, by using contractionary monetary policy.

Let's now turn to the other part of the Bank of Canada's new mandate—preserving the value of Canada's flexible exchange rate. Is this possible if the bank is focused primarily on an anti-inflationary monetary policy ? In fact, not only is it possible, but these two goals are quite compatible. The most noticeable effect of a tight monetary policy is a higher interest rate. These same higher interest rates also encourage foreigners to hold Canadian securities, which increases the demand for the Canadian dollar and strengthens its value on international money markets. We know that a higher Canadian dollar will decrease Canadian exports and cause an increase in imports. Net exports, then, will decrease. Because of flexible exchange rates, monetary policy becomes a far more effective anti-inflation tool. Schematically, this can be shown as follows:

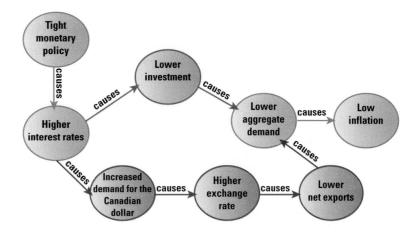

We have just seen how pro-active monetary policy is quite effective under a flexible exchange-rate regime. But what happens if a country has a fixed exchange rate? Can it still use monetary policy to preserve the internal and external value of its currency? Well, the policy of a fixed exchange rate takes care of the latter task, since its value is being held constant by decree. But there is a price to pay for this. As we saw in Chapter 10, if an economy operates on a fixed exchange rate, then its central bank is obliged to maintain that value by buying and selling its own currency and its holdings of foreign currencies on the international money market. This leads to a serious problem if the central bank attempts to fight domestic inflation. As we have seen, the normal procedure would be for it to dampen down spending through contractionary monetary policy. This means that the central bank reduces the money supply and in doing so pushes up interest rates. But while higher interest rates might dampen domestic real investment, they act as a magnet to foreign investors, which results in a big inflow of funds into Canada. These foreign investors will be selling their own (foreign) currency and demanding (buying) Canadian dollars. This means that the Bank of Canada will have to increase the supply of money to satisfy this increased demand.

ADDED DIMENSION

A Fixed Exchange Rate for Canada?

In the fall of 1998, professors Tom Courchene of Queen's University and Richard Harris of Simon Fraser University proposed that a small country like Canada has a better alternative to flexible exchange rates, which is a fixed exchange-rate regime with its major trading partner. They recognized that fixing Canada's exchange rate to the U.S. dollar would essentially let U.S. monetary conditions set Canadian interest rates and would give Canada a long-term inflation rate equal to that in the United States. However, they argued that since the U.S. business cycle drives the Canadian business cycle anyway, monetary independence is overrated.

And what would be the advantage of such a policy? Stability and the encouragement of investment in plant and equipment and in human capital. Such investment is undermined by large swings in the Canadian–U.S. exchange rate. For example, following the 12–14 percent fall in the exchange rate in 1998, many, mostly young, highly skilled Canadians migrated to the United States, where wages, measured in U.S. dollars, were much higher. If these people do not return to Canada, this will prove to be a serious loss to Canada for the next 40 years.

Harris and Courchene pointed out that Austria and the Netherlands have done with Germany exactly what they proposed that Canada do with the United States. They noted that these two fixed exchange rates held, even under the most turbulent of conditions including the global inflation crisis of the early 1980s.

This defeats the object of the policy, which was to contract the money supply. Furthermore, the increase in the money supply will push the interest rate back toward its original level. What all this means is that when a country is on a fixed exchange rate, it gives up control of its money supply. Therefore, monetary policy cannot be used to bring about change in the domestic economy.

SELF-TEST

6. Explain what will happen to the interest rate and to aggregate demand if the Bank of Canada increases the money supply and the country has a fixed exchange rate.

Criticisms of Anti-Inflationary Monetary Policy

The most serious criticism of anti-inflationary monetary policy is that because the Bank of Canada is overly concerned about controlling inflation it will lose sight of other equally valid goals such as economic growth and low unemployment.

An example of this concern can be found in a study done by professor Pierre Fortin of the University of Quebec, who points out that between 1981 and 1989 real short-term interest rates were about 1 percent higher in Canada than in the United States, but between 1990 and 1996 the gap rose to 3.6 percent. He attributes these higher interest rates to the zeal with which the Bank of Canada pursued an anti-inflationary monetary policy. Further, Fortin and others argue that these high interest rates cost the Canadian economy dearly in the form of lost GDP and higher unemployment. Along the same lines, a recent U.S. study argues that a modest amount of inflation, say 2 percent to 3 percent, is a necessary lubricant for economic growth.

The second criticism involves the question of lags. For example, if monetary policy is being used to fight inflation, then the question of timing becomes important. As with fiscal policy, there is a considerable lag before monetary policy finally has its full impact on the economy. It is not particularly difficult for the Bank of Canada to expand or contract the money supply, but it does take some time before the change in the reserves of the banking system is translated into a change in the amount of loans. And, it takes even longer for this change to show up in the overall performance of the economy.

Perhaps more seriously, other critics of pro-active monetary policy, especially critics of the Keynesian version, have argued that monetary changes have an uncontrollable impact on the economy. They therefore suggest that the money supply should not be left in the hands of central bank authorities, to be changed at their whim in an effort to fine-tune the economy. Instead, they feel that certain monetary rules should be followed. Let's explore this idea further.

The Neutralist School

A number of economists of the monetarist school that we looked at in Chapter 8 view the use of pro-active monetary policy with alarm. They believe that because changes in the money supply can have such a powerful effect on the economy and are subject to significant lags, it is better if the central bank's role is restricted to that of following certain established rules. The focus of this group, the neutralist school, is on ensuring that the quantity of money supplied is kept equal to the quantity of money demanded. This would imply a constant interest rate. This is illustrated in **Figure 12.3**.

FIGURE 12.3   Monetary Policy Aimed at Achieving Constant Interest Rate

Money demand will increase over time as a result of economic growth, as seen by the shifts from MD_1 to MD_2 to MD_3. If monetary policy accommodates each of these increases in demand with equal increases in supply, as seen by the shifts from MS_1 to MS_2 to MS_3, then the interest rate will remain unchanged at r_1.

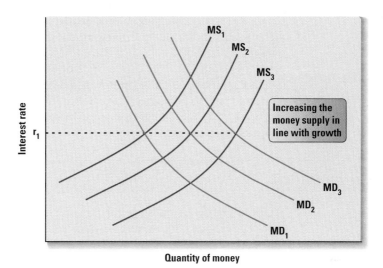

Figure 12.3 shows increases in the demand for money as illustrated by the shifts from MD_1 to MD_2 to MD_3. These increases are an inevitable result of growth in real GDP, since higher levels of income imply a higher transaction demand for money. If the monetary policy of the central bank is to maintain a steady interest rate, then it would accommodate each of the increases in demand with equal increases in the supply of money, as seen by the shifts from MS_1 to MS_2 to MS_3.

Advocates of a fixed interest-rate policy think that not only should rates be held constant but that the target rate should be announced to the world. They believe that a stable interest rate will allow people and businesses to make rational decisions about savings, investment, and spending that will maximize the benefits to both individuals and to society. Thus, they believe that the appropriate monetary policy for the central bank to pursue is to continuously adjust the growth in the money supply in order to maintain a constant, pre-announced interest rate.

A variation on this same approach would be for the central bank to maintain a constant, pre-announced pace of monetary expansion and have the interest rate adjust to maintain the balance between the quantities of money supplied and money demanded. Advocates of this variation argue that this will result in maximum growth in the economy.

Irrespective of which of these two variations is used, the underlying philosophy of the neutralist school is that the central bank should take what amounts to a very passive role in making monetary policy by setting either an interest-rate target or a money-supply-growth target. Either of these variations, they feel, would enhance the performance of the economy by allowing it to adjust to these well-known, long-term targets. Just how well an economy can adjust to changes is a subject that we will look in detail in Chapter 13.

Criticism of the Neutralist School

We have just seen that advocates of monetary rules suggest that this is the best way to achieve a degree of stability and predictability for the economy. Critics of setting fixed rules argue that, on the contrary, while the objective is stability in money markets, the result may well be instability in the economy. The reason for this is that fixing the growth in the money supply is not of much use if you cannot also control the demand for money. And a changing money demand will cause interest rates to change unpredictably. In short, a stable money supply might cause an unstable interest rate. Nor does it make much difference if the interest rate, rather than the money supply, is targeted for stability. A fixed interest rate of 6 percent, for instance, is neither a good or bad target in itself. If the economy is in a recession, 6 percent might well be too high a rate and help to prevent a recovery. But if, on the other hand, the economy is suffering from inflation, it might be that 6 percent is far too low a rate and is not doing enough to help dampen spending.

Beyond Fiscal and Monetary Policy

stagflation: the simultaneous occurrence of high inflation and unemployment.

We need first to set the stage for this discussion. In 1973, OPEC (the Organization of Petroleum Exporting Countries), which controls a large portion of the world's oil output, put quotas on the amount of crude oil being exported from member countries. This reduction in supply led to a quadrupling of the price of crude oil on world markets. Since most of the major industrial nations were net importers of oil, this rise in price increased the cost of production of most goods and services. The effect of this was to usher in a period of **stagflation**—simultaneous stagnation (high unemployment) and inflation. Until 1973, governments generally had only to deal with one of the twin evils at a time. Now Canada, along with most other countries, found itself fighting an economic war on both the inflation and unemployment fronts.

In terms of our aggregate demand–supply model, there is only one explanation of what could cause stagflation: a decrease in the short-run aggregate supply, as shown in **Figure 12.4**.

FIGURE 12.4 The Cause of Stagflation

A significant increase in the price of imported resources (such as oil in 1973) will decrease short-run aggregate supply, causing it to shift left as seen by SAS_1 to SAS_2. The result will be a higher price level P_1 to P_2 and a lower level of real GDP, Y_1 to Y_2.

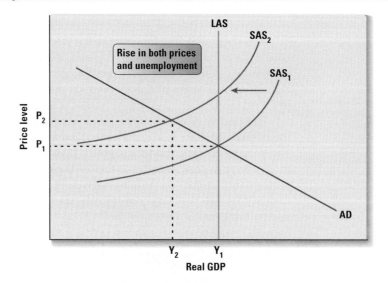

The 1973 increase in the price of imported oil caused a decrease in the short-run aggregate supply as seen by the shift from SAS_1 to SAS_2, in Figure 12.4. The result of this was to increase the price level in Canada, from P_1 to P_2, and cause unemployment to rise, as is seen by the drop in real GDP from Y_1 to Y_2.

Inflation and unemployment rates remained high in Canada throughout the 1970s and early 1980s, peaking in 1982, when inflation was 10.8 percent and unemployment was 11 percent. What was most alarming about stagflation when it first appeared was the fact that no one, including economists, was able to explain it, or offer remedies to cure it. The reason for this failure was the fact that the majority of economists were wedded to the idea that economic events could only be explained in terms of changes in *aggregate demand*. Although economists recognized the existence of aggregate supply, it was thought to be a very passive ingredient in the economy. After all, firms would never produce unless there was a demand for their products. If demand increased, firms would meet the increased demand by producing more; if demand decreased, firms would react by producing less. What more needs to be said about supply?

Unfortunately, this blind spot of most economists in the 1970s meant that they were unable to correctly diagnose the problem of stagflation and, worse, offered the wrong sort of remedies. This can be seen in **Figure 12.5**.

FIGURE 12.5 Aggregate Demand and Stagflation

The economy is in a stagflationary situation with a high price level, P_1 (inflation), and a low level of real GDP, Y_1 (high unemployment). Expansionary policy, either fiscal or monetary, will shift the aggregate demand curve from the present AD_1 to AD_2. The result will be a higher level of GDP, Y_2, but unfortunately this will cause even higher prices, P_2. Alternatively, the government could use contractionary policy to curb inflation. This will result in a leftward shift in aggregate demand from the current AD_1 to AD_3. This will cut prices to P_3 but with the unfortunate result of reducing real GDP to Y_3, thus causing even higher unemployment.

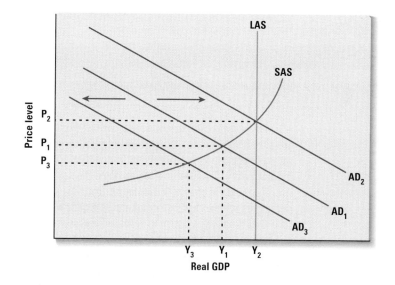

Neither expansionary fiscal nor monetary policies are able to cure the simultaneous problems of high unemployment and inflation. Such policies will increase aggregate demand, as shown by the rightward shift in the aggregate demand curve, from AD_1 to AD_2 in Figure 12.5. This will increase real GDP and therefore reduce unemployment. Unfortunately, it will also have the effect of pushing up prices, from P_1 to P_2. Contractionary fiscal or monetary policy is no better. It will cause a decrease in aggregate demand, from AD_1 to AD_3, which will reduce prices from P_1 to P_3. It will also cause an increase in unemployment, since GDP will fall.

Faced with this apparent failure of traditional policies, governments were forced to propose alternative policies. It is these we now turn to.

Direct Controls

Direct controls take the form of specific laws, rules, and regulations designed to modify the way people behave. Often these controls tend to have an impact on the supply side of the market, though in some cases they may also affect the demand side.

Direct-control policies can be grouped into three different categories, all of which are thought to help make the economy work more competitively and more productively. The first of these are called *tax incentive programs*. These include any tax changes that help stimulate people's incentives to work and save, and businesses to invest more. They include such things as reductions in personal and corporate income taxes, a decrease in capital gains tax, tax changes to allow bigger depreciation allowances (allowing firms to write off assets over a shorter period, thus stimulating investment), and bigger write-offs for spending on research.

The effect of a reduction in tax rates may well induce some people to work longer hours, take second jobs, postpone retirement, or remove themselves from the unemployment rolls. For others it could mean that they now need to work fewer hours than before to earn the same income. Economists are divided on whether such tax reductions cause people to work more or to work less; it really depends on the income level, the size of the tax cut, and the condition of the economy at the time. In addition, while people may have the desire to work more as a result of tax cuts, they may not have the opportunity unless an appropriate tax cut has similarly induced firms to invest more, increase output, and thus hire more people.

SELF-TEST

7. Will a cut in taxes affect aggregate demand or aggregate supply? Why?

The second category of direct-control policies are termed *pro-competition policies*. These are aimed at loosening the power of big corporations and trade unions in order to make the marketplace more competitive and enable it to more easily and rapidly adjust to the changing pattern of demand and technology. Particular policy proposals in this area include anti-monopoly or anti-combine legislation. A similar approach would be the increased deregulation of industry to make it easier for new firms to enter and compete; or the privatization of many government services so as to make them open to competition. Also, we need to mention the policy option that is becoming more significant as international trade continues to grow in both volume and in people's awareness. There is no question that freer trade results in greater competition within the economies involved. For example, both the Canadian and the Mexican economies are more competitive as a result of NAFTA.

The third category of direct-control policies available to government are called *employment policies*. These include policies designed to increase the amount of employment and to reduce the natural rate of unemployment. Specific programs in this area include improved job retraining and allowances to help workers relocate, a better system of making unemployed people aware of job and career prospects through better information, and legislation to promote equality of job opportunities and the outlawing of any type of discrimination in the workplace. All of these, it is thought, will help to reduce the amount of time people spend looking for jobs.

In summary, the three categories of direct controls are:

- tax-incentive policies
- pro-competition policies
- employment policies

Finale

This chapter and Chapter 11 complete our look at the two significant policies available to governments: fiscal and monetary policies. The efficacy of these tools involves a degree of both economic and political faith. How well, if at all, we can expect these policy tools to work depends essentially on how we think the economy operates. Those who advocate interventionist fiscal policy and pro-active monetary policy believe that the economy is essentially unstable and needs the direction of policy to steer a course of successful, healthy economy. Other economists believe in the ability of the economy to automatically adjust to problems that arise and argue that the fiscal and monetary policy should be non-interventionist and neutral. In addition, they argue that unless changes are made to the basic structure of an economy, the effects of interventionist, pro-active policies will not be sustainable and may even be harmful. They would argue that increases in productivity as a result of the application of improved technology, better capital equipment, and a more adaptable and better-educated work force are likely to produce bigger dividends for the economy in the long run. The question of whether the economy is self-adjusting and the contrast in policy prescriptions between those who think it is and those who do not is the subject of the next chapter.

REVIEW

1. What is the effect of a too-rapid pace of monetary expansion?
2. Explain how expansionary monetary policy works to affect the economy.
3. Why does contractionary monetary policy imply a leftward shift in the aggregate demand curve?
4. Explain the two versions of pro-cyclical monetary policy.
5. How effective is monetary policy for an economy operating with a fixed exchange rate?
6. What might be an undesirable by-product of anti-inflationary monetary policy?
7. What are the two different targets of the neutralist school of monetary policy?
8. What does *stagflation* mean?
9. What are the three types of direct controls?

Chapter Highlights

The chapter begins by defining monetary policy and then looks at five functions of the Bank of Canada. Next, both expansionary and contractionary monetary policy are defined and the four tools of monetary policy are discussed. Since open-market operations are the most important tool, this receives most of the discussion.

Next, the chapter explains why too large an increase in the money supply would result in inflation and why too small an increase would result in slow growth and high unemployment. This leads to the conclusion that all economies need a policy to determine the appropriate growth in the money supply; that is, monetary policy.

Two versions of the pro-active approach to monetary policy are then explored. The first version, Keynesian monetary policy, looks at how changes in the money supply can be used to either stimulate or constrain aggregate demand and thereby guide the economy toward full employment with stable prices. The major criticism of this version, that it may be impossible to achieve the twin goals of full employment and stable prices at the same time, is then discussed. The second version, the anti-inflationary approach, is then investigated. This approach sees monetary policy's role being redefined to that of preserving both the internal and external value of the currency. The chapter emphasizes that this might well be successful under a system of flexible exchange rates, but will almost certainly not be successful with fixed exchange rates. This new role for monetary policy is then criticized by pointing out that it seems to encourage an overemphasis on price stability at the expense of economic growth and unemployment.

Next, a second approach to monetary policy, that of the neutralist school, is explored. This approach involves setting monetary rules such as a preannounced interest-rate target, or, alternatively, a money-supply target. However, it too is seen to have a major defect, in that the process of keeping money markets stable may cause instability in the economy.

The chapter then moves beyond monetary policy by examining the causes and consequences of the stagflation of the 1970s. This is done to establish the point that monetary policy—irrespective of approach or version—is aimed at aggregate demand. If the economy's problems are rooted in aggregate supply, then monetary policy is unlikely to be effective. Direct controls that do mainly affect aggregate supply are then briefly looked at.

New Glossary Terms

bank rate   420
contractionary monetary policy   418
expansionary monetary policy   418
monetary policy   416
open-market operations   418
stagflation   432

STUDY GUIDE

Study Tips

1. Though the idea of open-market operations at first seems unnecessarily subtle and complicated, it involves nothing more than the transfer of cash for bonds between the Bank of Canada and anyone who wants to buy or sell bonds. But since the central bank is doing the buying and selling, the effect is a little different from normal trading. For instance, if I buy a bond from you, I will have less money but you will have more. The net effect on the economy's money supply is zero. However, when money goes into the Bank of Canada the money supply is reduced, and when money comes out the money supply is increased.

2. Try not to confuse the primary sale of bonds (or any other security) and the secondary sale of bonds. When an institution (including the government) "floats" a new issue, that institution receives the proceeds of the sale. Any subsequent sale of the same bond is a private transfer and, apart from registering the name of the new owner, does not involve the issuing institution at all. The sale of government bonds by the Bank of Canada is a primary sale, and the proceeds go to the government. Open-market operations involve the buying and selling of "pre-owned" bonds; that is, it is a secondary sale.

3. Do not interpret the fact that there are two approaches (one with two versions) to monetary policy as evidence that economics is unnecessarily complicated or that economists never agree with each other. What you are seeing is a natural evolution in policy making as economic circumstances change over time.

Key Problem

The country of Corona has, over the last two decades, achieved vigorous growth with stable prices and full employment (at a natural rate of unemployment of 4 percent), while the interest rate has been a constant 5 percent. Corona's economy in 1997 is in equilibrium and is depicted in **Figure 12.6**.

FIGURE 12.6

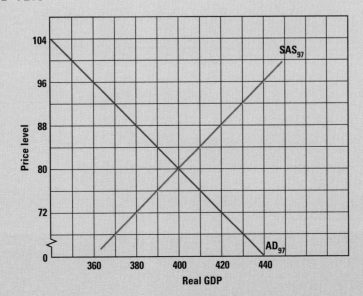

a) Draw in and label Corona's long-run aggregate supply curve.

However, in 1998, as the result of a very big increase in the price of imported malt, a resource on which many of its industries depend, Corona experiences stagflation for the first time in its history. Inflation of 10 percent and a negative 5 percent growth rate seriously depress the economy.

b) Show the new curves, labelled with the prefix 98, to denote Corona's 1998 economy. What are the new level of real GDP, the new price level, and the amount of the recessionary gap?

New level of real GDP: $_____; new price level: _____;

recessionary gap: $_____.

Alarmed at events in the republic, the president of Corona calls in the governor of the Bank of Corona and the secretary of the Corona Labour Congress and asks for their advice. The governor wants to focus on prices and suggests that the way to bring them down to the 1997 levels would be through the use of contractionary monetary policy. As a result of research done at the bank, he has concluded that for every 1-percentage-point change in interest rates, aggregate demand will change by $10 billion.

c) What new interest rate would bring price levels back to the 1997 level?

New interest rate _____%.

The secretary of the labour congress, while not disputing these figures, vehemently denounces the governor's plan. She argues that if successful, the contractionary monetary policy would undoubtedly cure inflation but it would further exacerbate the unemployment problem. The secretary points out that, according to Okun's Law, for every $2\frac{1}{2}$ percent that the actual GDP falls below full-employment GDP, unemployment rises by 1 percentage point.

d) If the secretary's fears are well-founded, what will be the rate of unemployment in Corona if the governor's plan is adopted?

Unemployment rate: _____%.

Instead, the secretary implores the president to stimulate the economy so as to get the unemployment rate down. She recommends that the government of Corona should immediately embark on expansionary fiscal policy, which will have a multiplier effect on the economy. The aim, she suggests, should be to boost aggregate demand by $40 billion. The governor of the Bank of Corona is outraged at the idea. To him, it means simply throwing taxpayers' money at the problem. He agrees that an increase in aggregate demand of $40 billion will indeed produce full employment. It will, however, he adds pointedly, also increase prices even more.

e) What will be the effect on the level of real GDP and the price level of increasing the 1997 aggregate demand by $40?

New level of real GDP: $_____; new price level: _____.

The president, angered by what he feels to be petty bickering and lack of consensus between the two (and also concerned that this Key Problem is getting far too long), dismisses them both. Unacquainted with Okun and other esoteric economic laws, he feels that the solution to the problem of stagflation is simplicity itself. The Coronan people must take a pay cut. The effect of this would be to shift the short-run aggregate supply curve.

f) What shift in the SAS is necessary to return the economy to full employment, and what will be the resulting price level?

Shift in the SAS curve: $_____; price level _____.

More of the Same

The country of Anoroc has, over the last two decades, achieved vigorous growth as well as price stability. It is at full employment (at a natural rate of unemployment of 7 percent), and its interest rate is 10 percent. Its president, impressed with the success enjoyed by the president of Corona, decides that her country's future lies in increasing the level of productivity. Furthermore, she is convinced that success requires hard work. She therefore issues a presidential decree that forthwith the workers of Anoroc will work a six-day week (they now work a four-day week).

a) Assuming that this change causes an increase in aggregate supply of 300, draw the new curve (SAS$_2$) on **Figure 12.7**.

b) What will be the new equilibrium level of GDP and the price level as a result of this shift?

FIGURE 12.7

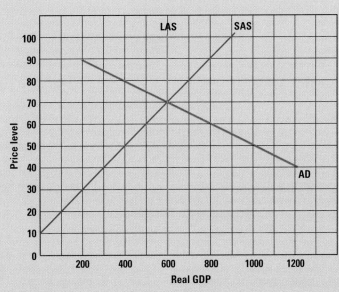

Three months later, the president of Anoroc is visited by the angry governor of the Bank of Anoroc and by the secretary of its labour congress. They point out to the president (politely, of course) that her actions, far from leading the country to prosperity, have instead led it into a recession.

c) Are they right? Is there a recession in Anoroc? How much of a recession?

The secretary of the labour congress points out that although most people are working harder than ever, there are now more people unemployed than before. Assuming that in Anoroc for every 2 percent that actual GDP falls below full-employment GDP, unemployment is 1 percentage point above its natural rate.

d) What is the present unemployment rate in Anoroc?

Furthermore, the governor of the bank points out, prices have taken a tumble. For once, the governor and the secretary are in agreement. They both insist that demand must increase in order to boost prices and to encourage firms to hire more workers. Monetary policy must be effected immediately, they insist. Interest rates need to fall. In Anoroc, the governor informs them, a 1-percentage-point change in interest rates changes aggregate demand by $100 billion.

e) What interest rate is necessary to bring the country back to full employment?

Translations

Figure 12.8 depicts the economy of Kirin in 1998. In 1997 Kirin had full employment and the price level was 90. Explain in words what happened between 1997 and 1998.

FIGURE 12.8

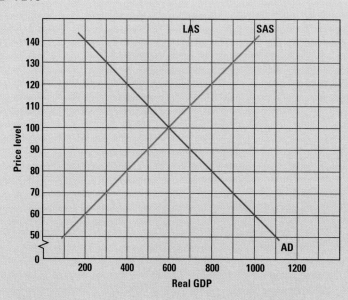

_____

_____

_____

Are You Sure?

Indicate whether the following statements are true or false. If false, indicate why they are false.

1. The most important function of the Bank of Canada is to regulate the money supply.

   T or F   If false: _____

   _____

2. One way that the Bank of Canada can increase the money supply is to purchase bonds in the open market.

   T or F   If false: _____

   _____

3. The biggest asset on the balance sheet of the Bank of Canada is notes in circulation.

   T or F   If false: _____

   _____

4. A decrease in the bank rate is part of contractionary monetary policy.

   T or F   If false: _____

   _____

5. Pro-active monetary policy can take two forms.

   T or **F**   If false: _____

   _____

6. Contractionary monetary policy will result in a rightward shift in the AD curve.

   T or **F**   If false: _____

   _____

7. Expansionary monetary policy is more effective with a fixed rather than a flexible exchange rate.

   T or **F**   If false: _____

   _____

8. Policies aimed at influencing the level of aggregate demand include monetary but not fiscal policy.

   T or **F**   If false: _____

   _____

9. Stagflation means an increase in both inflation and unemployment levels.

   T or **F**   If false: _____

   _____

10. Direct controls usually affect aggregate supply.

    T or **F**   If false: _____

    _____

Choose the Best

11. What type of monetary policy leads to an increase in the rate of interest?
    a) Contractionary policy.
    b) Inflationary policy.

12. Stagflation is the simultaneous occurrence of both:
    a) A recession and deflation.
    b) A recession and inflation.

13. With which exchange rate regime is pro-active monetary policy ineffective?
    a) Fixed exchange rates.
    b) Flexible exchange rates.

14. What is the name of the interest rate that the Bank of Canada charges to the commercial banks?
    a) The prime rate.
    b) The commercial rate.
    c) The bank rate.

15. In Canada, who controls the supply of money?
    a) The Department of Finance.
    b) The Bank of Canada.
    c) The market.

16. Suppose that the government wishes to affect the level of aggregate demand in the economy. Which of the following are *not* consistent policy measures?
    a) A tax increase and an increase in the money supply.
    b) A tax reduction and an increase in the money supply.
    c) An increase in government spending and an increase in the money supply.

17. Suppose that the demand for money decreased and the Bank of Canada wanted to keep interest rates unchanged. What would be its best policy?
    a) Switching government deposits into the commercial banks.
    b) Selling bonds in the open market.
    c) Lowering the bank rate.

18. Which of the following is the most important function of the Bank of Canada?
    a) The collection and clearing of cheques among commercial banks.
    b) Regulating the supply of money.
    c) Holding the reserves of commercial banks.
    d) Issuing new currency.

19. Suppose that the Bank of Canada buys $5 million of government bonds from the commercial banks and the target reserve ratio is 10 percent. What will happen to the reserves of the commercial banks as a result?
    a) They would decrease by $5 million.
    b) They would increase by $5 million.
    c) They would increase by $4.5 million.
    d) They would increase by $50 million.

20. Do open-market operations change the nation's money supply or the reserves of the commercial banks?
    a) The money supply but not the reserves.
    b) The reserves but not the money supply.
    c) Both the money supply and the reserves.
    d) Either a) and b), depending on circumstances.

21. If Canada wishes to maintain the value of the dollar relative to the American dollar, then what should it do?
    a) Keep the money supply constant.
    b) Continually adjust the money supply to keep interest rates in line with American rates.
    c) Increase the money supply whenever the American dollar starts to appreciate against the Canadian dollar.
    d) Purchase American dollars.

22. What effect does expansionary monetary policy have on the aggregate demand curve?
    a) It causes it to shift right.
    b) It causes it to shift left.
    c) It causes a movement down the aggregate demand curve.
    d) It causes a movement up the aggregate demand curve.

23. All of the following, *except one*, are direct controls. Which is the exception?
    a) Interest-rate policies.
    b) Tax-incentive programs.
    c) Pro-competition policies.
    d) Employment policies.

24. All of the following, *except one*, are possible tools of monetary policy. Which is the exception?
    a) Switching government deposits between commercial banks and the Bank of Canada.
    b) Moral suasion.
    c) Changing the bank rate.
    d) Changing tax rates.
    e) Open-market operations.

25. What happens when the Bank of Canada buys government bonds from the commercial banks?
    a) The demand deposits of the commercial banks remain the same, but their reserves increase.
    b) The demand deposits and the reserves of the commercial banks both decrease.
    c) The demand deposits of the commercial banks remain the same, but their reserves decrease.
    d) The demand deposits and the reserves of the commercial banks both remain the same.
    e) The demand deposits and the reserves of the commercial banks both increase.

26. What is the purpose of a tight money policy?
    a) To increase investment spending.
    b) To raise interest rates and restrict the availability of credit.
    c) To increase aggregate demand.
    d) To fight recessions.
    e) To lower the exchange rate.

27. Which of the following best describes the consequences of contractionary monetary policy?
    a) An increase in the interest rate, an increase in investment spending, and an increase in nominal GDP.
    b) An increase in the interest rate, an increase in investment spending, and a decrease in nominal GDP.
    c) An increase in the interest rate, a decrease in investment spending, and a decrease in nominal GDP.
    d) A decrease in the interest rate, an increase in investment spending, and an increase in nominal GDP.
    e) A decrease in the interest rate, a decrease in investment spending, and a decrease in nominal GDP.

Figure 12.9 refers to a closed, no-government economy (investment is the only injection, and savings is the only leakage).

FIGURE 12.9

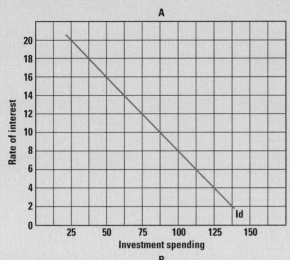

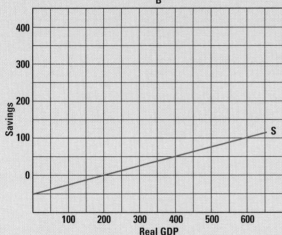

28. Refer to Figure 12.9 to answer this question. If the full-employment level of GDP in this economy is $400, what action should the central bank take?
    a) Set the interest rate at 8%.
    b) Set the interest rate at 10%.
    c) Set the interest rate at 14%.
    d) Set the interest rate at 16%.
    e) It is impossible to say without more information.

29. Refer to Figure 12.9 to answer this question. If the full-employment level of GDP in this economy is $600, what action should the central bank take?
    a) Set the interest rate at 8%.
    b) Set the interest rate at 10%.
    c) Set the interest rate at 14%.
    d) Set the interest rate at 16%.
    e) It is impossible to say without more information.

30. Refer to Figure 12.9 to answer this question. In this economy, by how much will GDP change as a result of a 1 percent change in the interest rate?
    a) $12.50.
    b) $25.
    c) $50.
    d) $100.
    e) It is impossible to say without more information.

Other Problems

31. **Table 12.1** a) shows abbreviated balance sheets for the central bank in the country of Beckland, and 12.1 b) for its whole commercial banking system. The target reserve ratio for the banks is 10 percent. (All figures are in $ billions.)

TABLE 12.1

a) Central Bank of Beckland

Assets		(1)	Liabilities		(1)
Treasury bills	189.5	_____	Notes in circulation	183.0	_____
Advances to banks	0.5	_____	Government deposits	4.5	_____
		_____	Deposits of banks	2.5	_____

b) Beckland's Banking System

Assets		(1)	(2)	Liabilities		(1)	(2)
Reserves: in vaults	7.5	___	___	Deposits	100.0	___	___
in Bank of Beckland	2.5	___	___				
Securities	30.0	___	___	Advances from Bank of Beckland	0.5	___	___
Loans to customers	70.0	___	___	Equity	9.5	___	___

a) Suppose that the Bank of Beckland buys $250 million ($0.25 billion) of government securities (T-bills) from the commercial banks. Show the immediate effects of this transaction on the balance sheets in columns (1) of Table 12.1 a) and b).

b) What effect does this transaction have on the money supply of Beckland?

Change in the money supply: (+/−) _____ of $_____.

c) What effect does the transaction have on the banking system's excess reserves?

_____

d) If the banks were to fully loan up, show the result in column (2) of the banking system's balance sheet.

e) By how much has the money supply now changed?

Change in the money supply: +/− _____ of $_____.

32. **Table 12.2** shows the effect of changes in various economic variables in two countries, Pabst and Kokanee.

TABLE 12.2

	Pabst	Kokanee
For every $10 million change in money supply:	Interest rates change by 1% point.	Interest rates change by 2% point.
For every 1% point change in interest rates:	Investment spending changes by $10 million; and net exports change by $5 million.	Investment spending changes by $5 million; and net exports change by $5 million.
For every $10 million change in expenditures:	Aggregate demand changes by $40 million.	Aggregate demand changes by $30 million.
For every $10 million change in aggregate demand:	The price index changes by 1 point; and real GDP changes by $5 million.	The price index changes by 2 points; and real GDP changes by $3 million.

a) What is the effect on the price level and the level of real GDP in both countries of an increase of $20 million in the money supply?

Pabst: price change: _____; GDP change: _____.

Kokanee: price change: _____; GDP change: _____.

b) If each country wishes to decrease real GDP by $45 billion, what change in the money supply is necessary, and what effect will this have on the price level?

Pabst: Δ money supply: (+/−) _____ $ _____; Δ price level: (+/−) _____ $_____.

Kokanee: Δ money supply: (+/−) _____ $ _____; Δ price level: (+/−) _____ $_____.

33. The economy of Carlsberg is at present in a recession and is depicted in **Figure 12.10**.

FIGURE 12.10

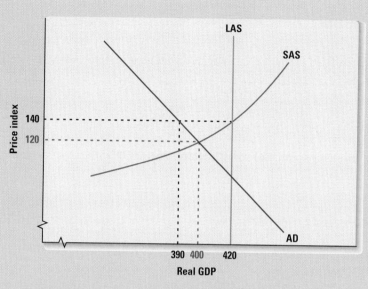

The government of Carlsberg is introducing an expansionary monetary policy to get the economy back to the full employment level of real GDP.

a) What increase in aggregate demand is necessary to achieve this?

Answer: _____.

b) If successful, what will be the growth rate?

Answer: _____.

c) If successful, what will be the inflation rate?

Answer: _____.

34. Suppose that the commercial banks' target reserve ratio is 2.5 percent and the Bank of Canada buys $100 million in bonds directly from the commercial banks. What immediate impact does this have on the money supply? What effect does it have on the money-creating potential of the banking system? Answer the same questions assuming that the Bank of Canada brought the bonds directly from the public.

Answer: _____

_____

UNANSWERED QUESTIONS

Short Essays

1. Explain how a change in the money supply can bring about changes in investment, real GDP, and the price level.

2. Explain the main functions of a central bank. Which is the most important of these, and why?

3. What are the main tools of monetary policy?

4. Explain the goals of both the Keynesian and anti-inflationary monetary policies.

5. Why might monetary policy be ineffective in combating stagflation?

6. Why might policies other than fiscal and monetary policies be needed?

Analytical Questions

7. If an economy is on a fixed exchange-rate system, what action, if any, must its central bank take if foreign interest rates fall?

8. Assuming that the Bank of Canada wishes to use contractionary monetary policy, explain what action it could take if it used both open-market operations and switching deposits.

9. Would Keynesian monetary policy be more effective in dealing with a recessionary gap or an inflationary gap? Why?

10. Explain how monetary policy could reduce the crowding-out effect associated with expansionary fiscal policy.

11. Explain the exchange-rate conditions that make monetary policy extremely effective.

12. How effective would expansionary fiscal policy be, and what would happen to the interest rate if:
    a) the Bank of Canada holds the supply of money constant.
    b) the Bank of Canada "accommodates" the fiscal policy by also increasing the supply of money.

13. Explain why the effect of expansionary monetary policy on net exports might be ambiguous.

14. A country with fixed exchange rates cannot have a monetary policy. Explain.

Numerical Questions

15. Assume that the original price of a three-month treasury bill with redeemable value of $100 was $96, and one month later it was sold for $96. What is the change in the rate of return on this bill?

16. Table 12.3 shows the aggregate demand and short-run aggregate supply for the economy of Stella Artois, which is in full-employment equilibrium:

TABLE 12.3

Price	Aggregate Demand	Aggregate Supply
$ 90	1000	700
95	950	750
100	900	800
105	850	850
110	800	900
115	750	950

a) What are the values of equilibrium GDP and the price level?
b) Assume that the money supply expands, causing an increase in aggregate demand of $100 at every price level. What will be the new equilibrium level of GDP and the price level? Assuming flexible wages, what will be the long-run values of GDP and the price level?
c) Starting from the initial values in a), assume there was an increase in the price of imported resources leading to a $100 change in aggregate supply at every price level. What will be the new equilibrium level of GDP and the price level? Again, assuming flexible wages, what will be the long-run values of GDP and the price level?

17. Assume that, given the initial values of aggregate demand and supply in question 16, the economy of Stella Artois is in equilibrium and policy-makers want to reduce the price level to 95 but maintain the economy at its full-employment level of GDP of $850. What type of policies must they pursue to achieve these goals? Graph the results.

18. The economy of Kronenburg is at present in a recession and is depicted in **Figure 12.11**.

FIGURE 12.11

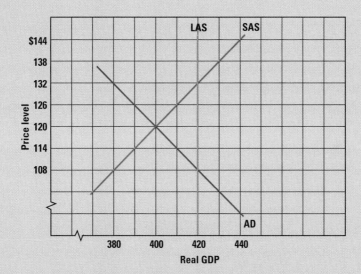

The governor of the Bank of Kronenburg favours a recovery program increasing the money supply. However, he insists it is in the long-run interest of the economy to keep inflation low. His target is a 5 percent inflation rate. What growth rate in the economy would this permit?

19. Use Figure 12.11 to answer this question. The opposition party in Kronenburg also favours a recovery program. But it feels that it is possible to achieve full employment and yet keep inflation down to 5 percent by a judicious mixture of aggregate demand and aggregate supply policies. What shift in each curve does it recommend?

20. **Table 12.4** shows the effect of changes in various economic variables in two countries, Beckland and Heineken.
a) What is the effect on the price level and the level of real GDP in both countries of a decrease of $10 million in the money supply?

TABLE 12.4

	Beckland	Heineken
For every $10 million change in money supply:	Interest rates change by 1% point.	Interest rates change by 2% point.
For every 1% point change in interest rates:	Investment spending changes by $10 million; *and* net exports change by $5 million.	Investment spending changes by $5 million; *and* net exports change by $5 million.
For every $10 million change in expenditures:	Aggregate demand changes by $40 million.	Aggregate demand changes by $30 million.
For every $10 million change in aggregate demand:	The price index changes by 1 point; *and* real GDP changes by $5 million.	The price index changes by 2 points; *and* real GDP changes by $3 million.

Beckland: price change: _____;

GDP change: _____.

Heineken: price change: _____;

GDP change: _____.

b) If each country wishes to decrease the price level by 5 points, what change in the money supply is necessary, and what effect will this have on the real GDP?

Beckland: Δ money supply: (+/−)

_____ $ _____;

Δ real GDP (+/−) _____ $ _____.

Heineken: Δ money supply: (+/−)

_____ $ _____;

Δ real GDP (+/−) _____ $ _____.

Web-Based Activities

1. Read the article found at **http://www.bmo.com/economic/special/bocwatch.htm**. Briefly explain what factors the Bank of Canada monitors to help it determine monetary policy.
   a) Now, read **http://www.cdhowe.org/eng/word/word-6.html**. What changes to monetary policy do the authors of this article see as necessary to make monetary policy more effective?
   b) Finally, read **http://www.bank-banque-canada.ca/english/spherm.htm**. According to the Bank of Canada, what action has it taken to reduce the uncertainty that may exist about its behaviour in the financial markets?

2. Should price stability be the only goal of the central bank? Read **http://www.worldbank.org/fandd/english/1296/articles/0101296.htm**, **http://www.euro-emu.co.uk/pubs/abnamro2.pdf** and **ftp://ftp.bank-banque-canada.ca/pub/publications/techreports/tr83.pdf** and write a short essay on the pros and cons of making price stability the primary goal of the central bank.

A Walk Through the Twentieth Century

What's ahead... This chapter examines the evolution of economic theory by looking at specific periods of the twentieth century. We begin by looking at the classical world of Say's Law in context of the first years of the 1900s. We then move to the World War I and its aftermath, which saw the evolution of neoclassical thought and its belief that economies are capable of self-correction. Keynesian economics emerged with the Great Depression and prevailed until the 1970s. Then we look at the stagflation of the 1970s and the rise of supply-side economics. This approach is given a boost with the development of the theory of rational expectations in the 1980s. Finally, we look at Canada on the cusp of the millennium.

Imagine that you are looking for an entry-level job as a graphic artist. Given your training and background, you decide to ask for $15 per hour. After three months of job searching, you have gotten nowhere: not a single interview, let alone a job offer. What went wrong? Do you think that the cause of your problem is personal, because you don't have the right qualifications or perhaps are asking for too high a wage? Or is it the fault of business in not being willing to create enough jobs? Or is it, instead, a problem to be laid at the doorstep of the government for not pursuing policies that would ensure that the economy created enough jobs?

W e want to do two things in this chapter. Using the Canadian experience, we want to examine the way in which contemporary events and economic theory are interrelated. We will look at six significant periods in the twentieth century, each of which had a profound influence on economic thinking and on the evolution of economic theory. At the same time, we will look at how these same economic theories, and the policies they generated, later helped shape some of the major events of this century.

The second thing we want to do is to refocus on a question that we have touched on throughout this text and that has claimed the attention of political commentators, economists, and many others for over two centuries:

> **What is the appropriate role of government in ensuring a successful economy?**

In answering this question, we will discover that there are two schools of thought, with different views on the question. Let's now turn to the first of our six time periods.

Canada at the Turn of the Twentieth Century

At the beginning of this century, Canada stood at the threshold of a new era, one filled with the promise of growth and prosperity. A major source of that confidence was the Canadian Pacific Railway, which had linked the East and the West. More especially, the railway had opened up the vast prairie lands of the West, and new immigrants were pouring in. All this led Prime Minister Wilfrid Laurier to declare: "A new star has risen upon the horizon. And it is to that star that every immigrant...now turns his gaze." The "Canadian miracle," as it was called, led to the construction of more railways in the West (the Canadian Northern, the Grand Trunk, and the National Continental), to a huge increase in wheat production and wheat exports, and to the birth of two new provinces, Alberta and Saskatchewan, in 1905. Fuelled by British and American investment, the economy of this "new star" boomed. A rapid growth in the demand for Canadian products and the low transportation costs—especially declining ocean-freight rates—caused so many things to increase: production, incomes, jobs, and immigration. Perhaps the most significant statistic was that in the first 20 years of the century, Canada's population grew from just over 5 million to almost 9 million.

Classical Economics and Say's Law

If Canada was prospering, so too was the rest of the world. The new century was alive with promise, and this was echoed in the ideas of economists. Despite some earlier gloomy predictions, capitalism was alive, well, and flourishing. Although there was a certain amount of government intervention, this was a period in which laissez-faire was dominant. Economists, policy makers, and indeed most of the public believed that the government that governed least governed best. Furthermore, the prevailing belief was that those who earned above-average incomes deserved them because they must somehow be better than most; otherwise they would not have earned those high incomes. Similarly, the majority believed that the poor suffered from some failing of character or were unwilling to work hard enough to avoid poverty. In short, people probably took on responsibility for many things for which they were not responsible.

However, a laissez-faire economy also meant an unplanned economy, and this was a source of disquiet for some. They wondered if it wasn't possible for such lack of planning to result in an economy producing more than people would be willing and able to consume. They asked: Isn't capitalism likely to experience periodic bouts of overproduction? And wouldn't such overproduction, and the resulting increase in inventories, result in firms reducing output and laying-off workers? In short, isn't capitalism prone to recessions?

Almost a century before, the loud and clear voice of David Ricardo, one of the giants of the classical school, answered "no" to these questions. Ricardo's answers relied on what is known as **Say's Law**, which states, "Supply creates its own demand." What this means is that:

Say's Law: the proposition that "supply creates its own demand"; that is, production (supply) creates sufficient income and thus spending (demand) to purchase the production. (Attributed to French economist Jean-Baptiste Say.)

- **The act of production (supply) requires the use of factors of production, which must be paid.**
- **Such payments are incomes to those who supply the factors, and these incomes are subsequently spent.**
- **This spending automatically creates enough demand to buy the supply.**

This is actually a restatement of the simple circular flow of income that we looked at in Chapter 3. Supply creates income, and this income creates enough demand to purchase the supply. If supply increases, then, income and thus demand increase by an equal amount. Furthermore, if supply decreases, incomes and demand would also fall. That is, *supply is active*, and demand is the passive result.

With Ricardo's endorsement of Say's Law, the prevailing view of the classical economists was that it ensured that all that was produced would be bought. In short, equilibrium (the equality of supply and demand) in the economy was both automatic and normal.

This last statement does need some qualification. It was conceded that if demand patterns changed, then temporary surpluses and shortages of specific goods were possible. For example, if demand changed so that a shortage of beaver hats and a surplus of cloth hats occurred, then there would be unemployment among those who made cloth hats and an increase in the demand for labour to make beaver hats. This would lead to wage rates and prices in the cloth industry quickly falling while those in the beaver-hat industry rose. That is, a surplus in one industry will create a shortage in another industry, but there is a normal adjustment between the two. Thus, we can again state the conclusion of the majority of classical economists of the nineteenth century:

Equilibrium occurs automatically and is the normal state of affairs in a market economy.

This optimistic view was shared by most economists in the first decade of the twentieth century. This sense of confidence was, however, shaken by "the war to end all wars" (or so it was believed): the "Great" War.

World War I and Its Aftermath

In 1914, Canada entered the war as one of the Dominions of the United Kingdom. But because of the enormous contribution Canada made to the Allied war effort, the

This World War I poster encouraged Canadian citizens to invest in the struggling economy.

country ended the war four years later a far more confident nation with a more independent frame of mind. Furthermore, relatively cheap credit, combined with a pent-up demand for consumer goods that had been in limited supply, fuelled an immediate postwar boom during which prices rose.

Despite the boom, the transition to a peacetime economy proved difficult, and when the bubble burst it led to a rapid contraction of the economy and a drop in prices. Returning soldiers, and workers who had been forced to make big sacrifices for the war effort, found that the promised rewards of victory were scant and a long time coming. A widespread and bitter strike broke out in Winnipeg, followed later by strikes in Halifax and Vancouver. Particularly hard hit were the Prairies and the Maritimes as the price of wheat, for example, fell by 60 percent. By December 1923, unemployment reached 17 percent and many workers were forced to roam the country in search of work—a taste of what was to come less than a decade later.

Then, slowly, the Canadian economy improved in tandem with a worldwide economic recovery. Fuelled by American investment (which surpassed that of Britain by 1921), Ontario in particular experienced a boom in industrial investment. Quebec saw a dramatic increase in the development of hydroelectric power, while the West enjoyed a recovery in world prices of grains and other resources. By the mid-1920s, the production of newsprint became the second-largest industry, next to agriculture, in Canada. It seemed like the long-awaited time of plenty had arrived, and Canadians were determined to make the most of it.

Neoclassical Economists and Aggregate Demand and Supply

Neoclassical economists of the time could rejoice in the recovery taking place and remained as confident as Ricardo that market economies could recover quickly from dislocations, even those caused by world wars. In short, they believed that market economies were self-adjusting. In fact, they went even further, and with the addition of three specific propositions they built an argument that concluded that prolonged recessions were an impossibility in a market economy.

The first of these propositions we already examined in Chapter 6. In terms of aggregate supply and demand analysis, neoclassical economists believed that any temporary overproduction (surpluses) or underproduction (shortages) would disappear through price changes. That is, flexible prices would ensure that the quantities demanded and supplied in an economy would be equal. Surpluses cause prices to drop; shortages cause prices to increase. This flexibility means that any change in aggregate demand will translate into a change in the price level but not a change in real GDP. This is illustrated in **Figure 13.1**.

FIGURE 13.1 A Change in Demand in the Neoclassical Model

An increase in aggregate demand will cause a rightward shift in the aggregate demand curve from AD_1 to AD_2. The effect will be an increase in the price level from P_1 to P_2, but the level of real GDP will remain unchanged at Y_{FE}.

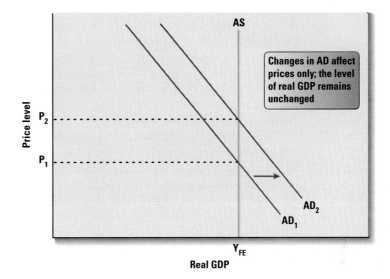

Changes in AD affect prices only; the level of real GDP remains unchanged

If prices are truly flexible, then aggregate supply would be determined by resource availability, productivity, and the current state of technology. This is to say, the current price level for goods and services, or any change in that price level, would have no effect on aggregate supply. Thus, an increase in demand, from AD_1 to AD_2 in Figure 13.1, would increase the price level and consequently wage levels, but it would not change aggregate supply. Similarly, a decrease in aggregate demand would decrease the price level and the wage level, but not change aggregate supply. In short, since prices and wages adjust rapidly, neoclassicists make no distinction between the long and the short run. In terms of our Chapter 6 model, such an increase in aggregate demand would immediately cause a decrease in short-run aggregate supply as the wage rate rises to adjust to the higher prices. The net result of this immediate adjustment of wages to prices is that there is only one supply curve, which is vertical, and its position is fixed at full employment. Of course, any change in resources, productivity, or technology would change aggregate supply, and this would shift the AS curve to the left, or to the right. However, it would always be vertical. In short,

> In the neoclassical model, the level of real GDP is unaffected by changes in aggregate demand.

SELF-TEST

1. Why did the neoclassical economists feel that the aggregate supply curve is vertical at the full-employment level of GDP?

Theory of Loanable Funds

To understand the neoclassicists' second proposition, we need to return to Ricardo's support of Say's Law. His argument also contained the proposition that any funds that were saved would automatically be invested, that is, spent in a different form. Recall that Ricardo wrote in context of the early nineteenth century, where most savers were profit-earning business owners who were quite willing to turn their savings into investment with an eye toward even greater profits in the future. However, by the early twentieth century, the incomes of a large percentage of working people had risen sufficiently so that savers (householders) and investors (businesses) had become different groups with different motivations.

This led some to ask: How could we be certain that savings and investment would be equal in a modern market economy? Surely their equality could come about only by coincidence? Not so, replied the neoclassical economists. After all, buyers and sellers of goods and services are different groups with different motivations, yet they are still able to "come together." And what brings them together? A commonly agreed upon price of the product. And what is the price of savings, or as they called them, loanable funds? The answer is the rate of interest.

Since there is only one rate of interest at which the quantity supplied (savings) and the quantity demanded (investment) for loanable funds is equal, if interest rates are truly flexible, the market will find this equilibrium rate automatically. For example, if the demand for loanable funds increases, then the interest rate would rise, and this increase in the interest rate would result in an increase in the quantity of savings to satisfy the higher demand. Thus, in a competitive market with flexible interest rates, what is saved must equal what is invested.

SELF-TEST

2. According to neoclassical economists, what two things could cause a decrease in interest rates?

The Supply of and Demand for Labour

The third and final proposition of neoclassical theory in support of the idea that an economy is capable of self-adjusting was the claim that any unemployment that might exist is temporary. This conclusion was arrived at by applying supply-and-demand analysis to the labour market. It was reasoned that there is only one equilibrium wage level at which the quantity supplied and the quantity demanded for labour are equal. Once this rate is achieved, there would be no surplus or shortage of labour, that is, no unemployment. Then how can the fact that unemployment exists be explained? As **Figure 13.2** illustrates, unemployment can occur only if the prevailing wage rate is above the equilibrium wage rate.

FIGURE 13.2 A Surplus of Labour

If the wage level is above equilibrium, there will be a surplus of labour. At wage level W_2, the number of workers demanded by firms, quantity a, would be less than at equilibrium. On the other hand, the number of workers seeking jobs would be higher, quantity b. The distance ab therefore, represents the surplus of labour, that is, unemployed labour.

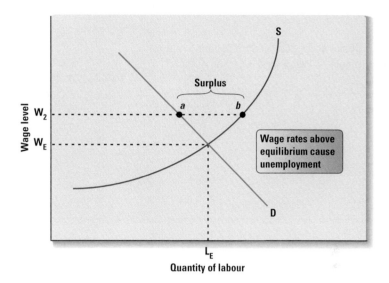

At wage rate W_2, the number of workers demanded and therefore employed is quantity a. The number of workers who would like a job at this rate, however, is quantity b. The distance ab then represents the quantity of unemployed labour, those people who would like jobs but are unable to obtain them. We can see that unemployment is a result of the prevailing wage rate being above equilibrium. However, such unemployment cannot continue indefinitely. Competition for jobs among the employed and the unemployed will force wage rates down and in doing so will induce firms to hire more workers. Flexible wage rates therefore ensure full employment. This means that if there are unemployed workers, then they must be voluntarily unemployed, because if they were willing to offer their services at a lower wage, they would be able to obtain a job. If, instead, they are holding out for a better wage, they must be doing so voluntarily.

In summary, neoclassicists built their view of how the macroeconomy works on four pillars:

- the validity of Say's Law
- the flexibility of prices
- the flexibility of interest rates
- the flexibility of wages

Given these four factors, neoclassical economists were convinced that serious or long-lasting recessions were an impossibility. Flexible prices, flexible wages, and flexible interest rates would all ensure that the macro market would quickly return to its normal equilibrium, and, further, this equilibrium was at full employment, or what we could also call capacity production. This view remained the prevailing view of most economists until the Great Depression of the 1930s.

SELF-TEST

3. The following table shows the labour demand and supply in a hypothetical economy:

Labour Demand (in millions)	Wage Rate ($)	Labour Supply (in millions)
12.8	6.00	11.0
12.4	6.50	11.5
12.0	7.00	12.0
11.6	7.50	12.5
11.2	8.00	13.0
10.8	8.50	13.5
10.4	9.00	14.0
10.0	9.50	14.5

A) What is the equilibrium wage rate, and how many workers would be employed?

B) Suppose that the wage rate increases to $8.50. How many workers are employed? How many are unemployed? How many of the unemployed are workers who have lost their jobs? Why is this figure less than the total number of unemployed?

C) What is the (numerical) relationship between the wage rate and the numbers unemployed?

The Great Depression

In the fall of 1929, Wall Street's stock market crashed and, during the next three years, the American economy experienced such a severe depression that many observers at the time felt that it signalled the death throes of capitalism itself. Production in the United States dropped by 42 percent between 1929 and 1933, 85 000 businesses failed, 5000 banks closed their doors, and unemployment increased from 3 to 25 percent. The American experience spread quickly to Canada and was soon repeated in economies around the world. Something clearly had gone wrong with the market economies.

What had caused such a calamity? It is easy to point the finger at the Wall Street crash, but the North American economies were in trouble before the crash. In Canada, the main reason for this was the fact that a significant expansion in world production capacity in several of Canada's key industries in the last half of the 1920s had depressed commodity prices. The first reaction of neoclassical economists to the sudden downturn was that whatever had caused this drastic turn of events, the prognosis was clear and obvious: the economy should be left alone to cure itself. They felt that prices would soon drop, which would encourage people to buy more, and this would stimulate production; that interest rates would soon fall, thus stimulating investment; and that wage rates would soon drop, encouraging firms to increase hiring. The Canadian experience in these early years of the Great Depression can be used to show how right and how wrong the neoclassicists were. Between 1929 and 1933, prices in Canada did drop by 23 percent. But production continued to fall. Wage rates also dropped by approximately 20 percent, but unemployment continued to hover around the 20 percent mark. Interest rates dropped to 2 percent, but gross investment remained low, and in 1933 net investment actually became negative.

It is difficult to overstate the fear and pain experienced by Canadians during these dark years. The beginnings of a social security net was in place, but this was hardly enough to cushion the fall into unemployment and poverty—no unemployment insurance, a very limited pension plan, very limited and localized welfare payments (with the exception of a national war-widows benefits plan), no baby bonus checks, no subsidized medical plan, and no subsidized housing. The freight trains that pulled into any one of many Canadian cities from the East had dozens of men, riding the empty

Canadian Press

Thousands of unemployed men from British Columbia, Alberta, and Saskatchewan climbed aboard freight trains in an on-to-Ottawa protest against conditions in depression-era job camps in 1935.

boxcars, in search of a new place that might have some work. The problem was that the trains leaving that same city heading in the other direction had just as many unemployed souls hoping that the next stop might offer something better. And it wasn't just the unemployed who were suffering. Those still working often faced the prospect of pay cuts, which they were in no position to argue about because it might be they who were laid off next. Even those in business faced falling sales and thus profits.

ADDED DIMENSION

Too Much or Too Little?

This extract from *Canada's Illustrated Heritage Series* neatly sums up the times: "The strange and terrifying thing about the depression was that there was too much of almost everything. Too much food. In Prince Edward Island, potatoes were left rotting in the ground, and on the prairies wheat was burned because it was not worth shipping. Too many houses. There were vacant houses on every street and you could rent a good-sized one for $10 a month. Too many automobiles. Factories could turn out 400 000 a year but only 40 000 were bought in 1932. Too many men for the jobs that needed doing. There was too much of everything, in fact, except jobs and money."

Through all this there was a nagging question that continued to go unanswered: why wasn't the economy adjusting in the way the neoclassicists thought it would? It took Keynes and his *General Theory* to finally provide some answers.

The Keynesian Response to the Neoclassicists

We have already studied the ideas of Keynes on how the macroeconomy works, but let's do a quick summary. Keynes disagreed with the neoclassical economists as to how the economy adjusts if production exceeds spending and a recessionary gap threatens. Where the neoclassicists saw prices falling, Keynes saw prices that were "sticky" and would fall only slowly, if at all. The reason why the neoclassicists and Keynes saw the question of the flexibility of prices so differently is because each built their models on different assumptions. The neoclassicists assumed perfect competition in both the product and the labour markets. Keynes, on the other hand, argued that the product market was dominated by large oligopoly firms who have the power to set their own prices. A more practical explanation of why prices are inflexible downward lies in the fact that for a firm to change prices is both time-consuming and expensive since existing labels, catalogues, advertisements, inventory valuations, and billing codes all have to be changed in order to institute a price change.

Given this, what was the economy's response to a decrease in demand? The answer is that firms would cut back on production and lay people off. This increases the level of unemployment but does not lead to much downward pressure on wages because, like prices, they too are "sticky downwards." The reason for sticky wages, Keynes argued, was the existence of trade unions, which had the power to resist wage cuts. But even non-union workers would resist the idea of wages that fluctuate along with the employer's fortunes, since in the modern world most wages are fixed in the short run and are reviewed only periodically, say once a year. In short:

> **Keynes saw the adjustment process in terms of a fall in production and employment rather than in a fall in prices and wages.**

To emphasize the contrast between the neoclassical and Keynesian viewpoints, we can use a metaphor. Suppose there are two firms, Classical Cookies and Keynesian Kandies, both of whom face a downturn in business. The manager of Classical Cookies calls a meeting of her staff and informs them that she has some good news and some bad news: "Despite the 20 percent reduction in orders this month, you'll be pleased to learn that we are proposing no layoffs. You will all keep your jobs. Unfortunately, we have no choice in the circumstances but to reduce your pay by 20 percent. We will, however, maintain production levels, but it does mean—please note, sales department—that in order to do so, we will be cutting prices by 20 percent starting tomorrow."

Meanwhile, over at Keynesian Kandies, another meeting is taking place between its manager and staff and, similarly, there is both good and bad news: "Despite the 20 percent reduction in orders this month, you'll be pleased to learn that we are not proposing any pay cuts for our staff. Unfortunately, we have no choice in the circumstances but to lay off 20 percent of you, starting tomorrow. We will, however, maintain present prices, but it does mean—please note, production department—that production levels will be cut by 20 percent."

On another point we should also mention that Keynes also disagreed with the neoclassicists over the way in which the equality of savings and investment in the economy is brought about. To Keynes, this occurs as a result of a painful adjustment of production and income and not by changes in the interest rate, as suggested by the neoclassicists. If savings are greater than investment, the value of total production must be greater than aggregate expenditures. This will lead to a cut in production *and* income *and* savings until once more savings and investment are equal. This is a reflection of Keynes's belief that changes in the interest rate have very little effect on the level of savings, which are, instead, determined by the level of income. Finally, Keynes believed, as we saw in Chapter 8, that interest rates are determined by the demand and supply of money and not by the interaction of total savings and investment demand in the economy.

In summary, if, as Keynes believed, prices and wages do not adjust quickly, if at all, to a decrease in aggregate demand, then an economy can fall into a recession and remain there indefinitely. In these situations, only active government intervention will get the economy on the road to recovery. This point is illustrated in **Figure 13.3**.

FIGURE 13.3 A Recessionary Gap with Sticky Wages and Prices

Originally, the economy is at full employment equilibrium, as illustrated by point *a*. If aggregate demand decreases, then we have a shift from AD_1 to AD_2. If prices remain at (or near) P_1 and wages don't fall much either, then the economy could get struck at point *b* and income level Y_1. If prices fall to P_2 but wages remain sticky downwards, then equilibrium at point *c* and GDP level Y_2 could become a permanent state of affairs. Point *d* occurs only if wages are completely flexible, which would shift the SAS curve to the right.

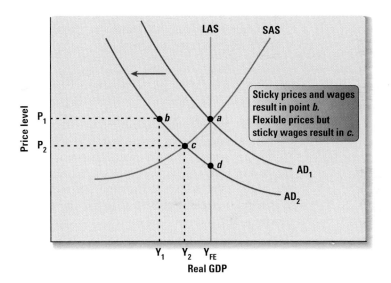

Let's begin with the economy at full-employment-equilibrium income, Y_{FE}, with a price level of P_1. As the recession worsens, aggregate demand decreases from AD_1 to AD_2. If the price level is sticky downwards and remains at P_1, and if wages exhibit the same resistance to falling, then the economy could get stuck at *b* with a GDP level of Y_1. But we know that prices and wages in the Great Depression did fall some. However, if wages don't fall enough, then the intersection of SAS and AD_2 at point *c* is an equilibrium that could persist indefinitely. What we have just described is, of course, the recessionary-gap situation that we looked at in Chapters 11 and 12.

Since Keynes reasoned that sticky wages prevent aggregate supply from shifting to the right and achieving full employment GDP at point *d*, then the only way out of such a recessionary trap was for aggregate demand to increase, enabling the economy to return to *a*. And if the circumstances of fear, uncertainty, high unemployment, and excess plant capacity results in neither households nor businesses being likely to increase their spending, and if exports don't go up, then the only way to increase aggregate demand is through increased government intervention and spending.

5. According to Keynesian theory, will an increase in aggregate demand cause an increase in real GDP, nominal GDP, or both?

In a sense, Keynes put Say's Law on its head by proposing that demand creates its own supply. The engine of change for Keynes was aggregate demand. If people are willing to spend, firms will be happy to produce. Therefore, anything that cuts spending will simply worsen a recession. In other words, instead of cutting back during a recession, people should spend more. Yet, this seemed to go against common sense. It would mean, for instance, that firms working well below capacity and in danger of being forced out of business should start to spend more on investment. Or, alternatively, it implied that governments should cut tax rates or increase their own level of spending at a time when they were already facing big budget deficits as a result of falling tax revenues. You can see why Keynes was regarded as a heretic. He was suggesting that when times are bad, people should spend more; and when they are good, they should spend less. Of course, as we have seen in earlier chapters, there is a lot more to the basic expenditure theory than this, but:

> Spending and *aggregate demand* lie at the heart of Keynesian analysis.

So how did governments initially react to these ideas of Keynes? In most cases the reaction was negative. It is true that the Canadian government did spend more to provide some limited relief for many of its impoverished citizens. For example, in 1932, the government established work camps run by military officers and under the control of the Department of National Defence. However, this was as much to stem the possibility of violent protest as to aid the unemployed. Wearing army fatigues, the mostly young men worked on roads, bridges, historic sites, and so on. They received food, clothing, lodging, and 20 cents a day. Needless to say, the camps were not too popular. There was also some direct relief in the form of money or vouchers, but the amounts were small. In rural Quebec, for instance, a family of five received a food allowance of $3.25 per week. Despite the small amounts, the government was often criticized for its generosity. In a 1934 article, for instance, *Maclean's* magazine complained that total spending of all governments—municipal, provincial, and federal—had reached the incredible figure of $1 billion! Despite all this, the Canadian government did not spend a fraction of what would have been needed to pull the economy out of the depression. Furthermore, most governments of the time regarded Keynes as a radical who had dangerous ideas about the economy. Validation of his theory had to await the arrival of an event even more traumatic than the Great Depression: World War II.

World War II and Its Aftermath

Canadians entered World War II in a far more sombre mood than they had entered World War I. They had lived through a decade of despair, and the easy patriotism of the earlier age had given way to a grimmer realization that the task ahead, necessary though it was, might not yield a quick and easy victory.

War meant mobilization on all fronts. The Canadian government, in line with other governments around the world, suddenly opened the spout, and out flowed massive government spending on military goods, all in the name of the defence of democracy. Economies responded very quickly to this dramatic increase in aggregate demand. In Canada, the war quickly converted a surplus of labour into a shortage. By 1941, the unemployment rate had fallen from the double-digit rates of the 1930s to 4.1 percent, and by 1944 it was down to 1.2 percent. Factories that had been standing idle for years were now humming, turning out Bren guns, military aircraft, tanks, and ships. The rate of growth of GDP hit double digits, 14.1 percent in 1940 and a whopping 18.6 percent by 1942. In addition, as Keynesian theory would suggest, such increases were accompanied by inflation: from the deflation of 0.9 percent in 1939, prices rose by 4 percent in 1940 and 6.3 percent in 1941. This is illustrated in **Figure 13.4**.

FIGURE 13.4 Return to Full Employment

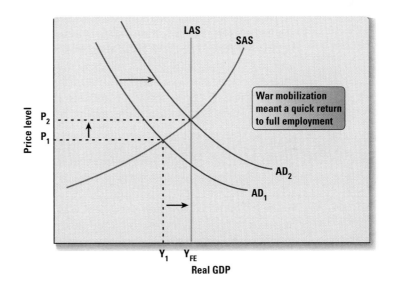

The increased government spending on the war effort greatly increased aggregate demand, as illustrated by the shift of the aggregate demand curve from AD_1 to AD_2. In addition, the price level increased from P_1 to P_2.

The depression was over, and it was massive increases in government spending that had ended it. This fact resulted in a growing recognition that Keynes was probably right about how the macroeconomy works.

Keynesian Economics in the Postwar Years

Following the end of World War II, there was a widespread sentiment among politicians, a growing number of economists, and a majority of the population that the experience of the Great Depression should never be allowed to happen again. Prime Minister Mackenzie King, who had led Canada in wartime, was re-elected in 1945 partly on the strength of his "New Social Order," which promised social and economic policies to prevent a reoccurrence of the economic woes of the 1930s. The cautious beginnings of Keynesian counter-cyclical policies, which had started in 1940 with the introduction of an unemployment scheme, were augmented by a system of family allowances that, combined with the Old Age Pension Plan, lay the foundation for the welfare state. In addition, measures were introduced to promote home building, to provide work for demobilized war veterans, and to increase aid to health care.

Such measures were not unique to Canada. In fact, governments around the world passed legislation that could be described as "full-employment acts." It was becoming accepted ideology that governments had a responsibility to use policy making to ensure that the economic goal of full employment and stable prices was maintained. The doctrine of laissez-faire was replaced with the ideology of interventionism dressed in the clothes of Keynesian economics.

For the 25 years following World War II, the ideas of Keynes reigned supreme in most countries in Europe and North American. Economies were now "managed" by governments using counter-cyclical fiscal and monetary policy to "fine-tune" them. During this time, the Canadian economy entered a period of remarkable stability. Between 1945 and 1970, apart from four years, the unemployment rate was never above 6 percent and inflation was consistently held below 5 percent. The trick, it seemed, was to steer the ship of state at a steady pace while not getting too close to the banks of inflation or the reefs of unemployment. If the economy was a little sluggish and in danger of falling into a recession, then a dose of expansionary fiscal and/or monetary injection was called for. If, on the other hand, it looked like the economy was overheating and a period of inflation threatened, the solution was a measure of contractionary fiscal and/or monetary policy.

It became apparent that economic stabilization might be even more effective if the two policies were operating in tandem. After all, one of the drawbacks of using expansionary fiscal policy is the fact that it crowds out both private investment and net exports by pushing up interest rates. This makes fiscal policy less effective. But what if interest rates could be held down in the face of the increased demand for money? Then the crowding-out effect would be eliminated. And how could this be achieved? Simply by increasing the money supply. This combination of fiscal and monetary policy produced a very powerful mixture and was used often in Canada. Occasionally, however, a conflict of policies occurred, as in the late 1950s, when the government wanted to pursue expansionary fiscal policy while the Bank of Canada was intent on using contractionary monetary policy. Fortunately, such instances proved to be rare.

Nonetheless, as successful as Keynesian policy was in reducing both unemployment and inflation in postwar Canada, it became clear, as a result of the work of Phillips (which we looked at in Chapter 11), that achieving both goals *simultaneously* may not be possible. As **Figure 13.5** shows, there definitely seemed to be a trade-off between the two. For instance, the low unemployment rates in 1947 and 1948 were accompanied by high rates of inflation, and the low inflation rates of 1958 through 1961 were achieved at the cost of the highest unemployment rates since the World War II. Apart from the single year of 1953, Canada had never seen inflation below 2 percent and unemployment below 4 percent *at the same time.*

FIGURE 13.5 Unemployment and Inflation in Canada, 1946–69

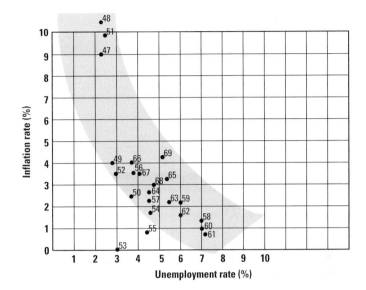

Using actual data from the Canadian experience, it is clear that a trade-off existed between the level of inflation and that of unemployment in this period.

In summary, the quarter century following the end of World War II was a period of comparative prosperity for Canada in which the size of the public sector grew significantly. However, the Phillips curve analysis meant that economists were beginning to realize that perhaps there were limits to what could be achieved with Keynesian policy. Its supremacy was to be challenged further by events in the early 1970s.

The Age of Anxiety: Canada in the 1970s and 1980s

By the early 1970s, the certainties of the postwar era started to fade. The United States devalued its currency by abandoning a fixed gold price at about the same time that its defeat in Vietnam seemed inevitable. The countries that would later be called the Asian Tigers were beginning to challenge established industries in both Canada and the United States. And in Canada, despite strong exports of prairie wheat to the USSR as well as of British Columbia and Alberta coal to Japan, total exports began to falter. This was also the time when three million baby boomers began entering the labour market.

Then, in 1973, the Arab-state-dominated Organization of Petroleum Exporting Counties (OPEC), angered by the falling value of the dollars that its members received for their oil and by the West's support for Israel during the Yom Kippur War, decided to reduce its exports of oil. The result was a quadrupling of prices in less than sixteen months. The shock was felt around the world. The Liberal government of Pierre Trudeau tried to insulate Canada from this shock by providing subsidies for eastern Canadian oil imports financed by a special tax on western Canadian oil exports to the United States. Needless to say, this created intense antagonism in the West and seriously intensified regional tensions in Canada.

The main problem facing the Canadian government, as well as other governments around the world, was how to deal with the OPEC-induced stagflation. With the increase in both inflation rates and unemployment rates, Canadian policy

On March 22, 1976, thousands of union people came together in Ottawa for a mass demonstration to protest the government's wage and price controls.

makers faced a dilemma they had never experienced before. Unemployment rose from a low of 4.1 percent in 1967 to over 7 percent by the mid-1970s. Worse still, inflation reached double digits and stood at 12.6 percent in 1974. Feeling that the latter was the more serious of the two problems, the Trudeau government introduced wage–price controls in October 1975, whereby the newly created Anti-Inflation Board could roll back the price and wage increases it felt were excessive. However, despite the best of intentions, this was a little like trying to control inflation by making it illegal! The problem with this approach, called incomes policies, is that, although it may curb inflationary expectations, it is really treating the symptoms rather than the disease itself.

In another attempt to protect Canadians from the ravages of inflation, the government tied the wages it paid, government pensions benefits, and welfare payments to a rising consumer price index. Furthermore, it also indexed tax exemptions to that same price index, which guaranteed that tax revenue would not rise as fast as government spending. These measures laid the groundwork for the huge budget deficits that followed in the late 1970s and 1980s.

We saw in Chapter 12 that trying to cure stagflation through traditional fiscal and monetary policy is impossible. As a result of this failure, many turned to a new school of thought that came to prominence: supply-side economics.

The Rise of Supply-Siders

This new school of thought felt that the Keynesian approach put far too much emphasis on curing economic problems solely through manipulating aggregate demand, an approach that had come to be known a demand management. They argued that the only cure offered by the interventionists was to throw more money at the problem, whatever the problem might be. While at times this might be an effective approach, especially in the short run, in many situations it simply created more problems by stifling investment and international competitiveness by burdening the country with large budget deficits. In the period following the OPEC-induced stagflation, these supply-side economists felt that attention must be focused on the underlying malaise crippling North America's economies: falling rates of productivity. Supply-siders argued that it is only through increased productivity that a country can lay the foundation for dealing with both inflation and unemployment.

Like the neoclassicists earlier in the century, supply-side economists believed that the aggregate supply was not simply a passive element that responded to changes in aggregate demand but was itself a prime mover of economic activity. Their diagnosis of the stagflation of the 1970s was straightforward. It was caused by the high price of imported oil and further accentuated by declining productivity rates. Both of these factors caused a decrease in aggregate supply. Similarly, they felt that the cure was equally straightforward: an increase in aggregate supply. This is shown in **Figure 13.6.**

FIGURE 13.6 Increasing Aggregate Supply to Fight Stagflation

Assume that the economy is at a price level of P_1 and a GDP level of Y_1. An increase in aggregate supply will shift the aggregate supply curve from SAS_1 to SAS_2. The result will be a lower price level, P_2, as well as a higher level of GDP, Y_2, the latter implying a lower unemployment rate.

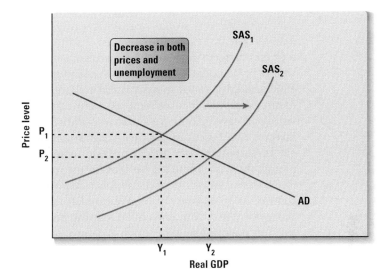

An increase in aggregate supply shifts the aggregate supply curve from SAS_1 to SAS_2. This results in a reduction in the price level from P_1 to P_2 *and* an increase in GDP from Y_1 to Y_2, which will result in reduced unemployment. Supply-siders believed that modern governments had stifled initiative and productivity through high levels of taxation and government bureaucracy. At different times in the 1980s, this argument caught the attention of a number of governments around the world, including the Brian Mulroney government in Canada, the Ronald Reagan government in the United States, and the Margaret Thatcher government in the United Kingdom.

What policies might be used to increase aggregate supply and stimulate the production of goods and services? The first was the *privatization* of many functions of government in the name of exposing these functions to the competition of the marketplace and thereby improving their efficiency. It was during this time, for example, that Air Canada and Canadian National ceased to be crown corporations and were privatized. Second, a policy of *deregulation* was instituted, which aimed, again, at using the competitive market place to increase efficiency. The most dramatic example here is that of the deregulation of the airline industry in the United States, which resulted in some long-established airlines going broke and other new airlines entering the industry. Most would argue that this has proved successful because it has resulted in the lowering of airfares and increased consumer choice on the most popular routes. (However, on other, less travelled routes, higher fares resulted.) Canada also deregulated both its airline and trucking industries, but not so completely.

A third policy aimed at increasing aggregate supply was the *contracting out* of specific government services in the name of reducing the costs of these services and saving the government, and taxpayers, money. An example of this was the contracting-out by Canada Post of its retailing function to firms that put this service into local drugstores and convenience shops.

The fourth and most significant plank in the supply-siders platform focused on *cutting tax rates* on business profits and on individual incomes. The aim was to increase incentives for people to work more, save more, and invest more. The result, it was believed, would lead to an increase in aggregate supply. If income tax rates were cut, many workers would work longer hours, since high marginal tax rates tend to deter people from working overtime. Additionally, many unemployed workers would seek employment with more enthusiasm, while some homemakers and retired people would be tempted to return to the labour force. These results would be further enhanced if the social security net of welfare payments, unemployment coverage, and lifetime disability income were restructured to aid those in real need rather than providing an easy income for those who didn't deserve it. Furthermore, savings would increase, since a cut in personal taxes would increase disposable income. Likewise, a cut in corporate taxes would provide increased profits for firms, who would then plough them back into the business in the form of new investment.

In short, advocates of the supply side position saw the above policies as necessary steps to undo 40 years of interventionist polices that, they believed, had sapped the economy of its vigour and ability to grow, prosper, and adjust to change. In summary, the four major policies of supply-side proponents are:

- the privatization of crown corporations
- the deregulation of industry
- the contracting-out of government services
- the reduction of tax rates

The promised benefits of all of this are very attractive. Greater competition, more work effort, increased investment spending, and greater willingness to accept risk would result in higher economic growth, thus creating jobs, lowering unemployment, increasing output, and easing inflation.

There was a fly in the ointment, however. In advocating lower tax rates, supply-siders did leave themselves open to accusations that they too (like the Keynesians) were proposing big government deficits as a way of curing stagflation. It was at this point (the late 1970s) that a Californian economist named Arthur Laffer put forward the intriguing argument that a cut in tax rates in North America would increase, rather than decrease, the government's tax revenue.

Laffer curve: the graphical representation of the idea that in terms of tax revenue there is an optimal tax rate; above or below this rate, tax revenue would be less.

The Laffer Curve

The essentials of Laffer's argument are contained in **Figure 13.7**. The curve (henceforth known as the **Laffer curve**) shows the amount of tax revenue received by the government at various tax rates.

FIGURE 13.7 The Laffer Curve

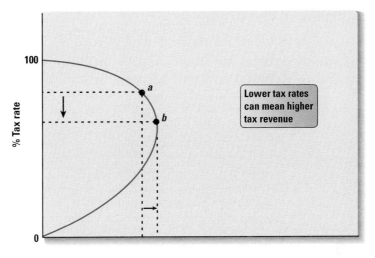

If the economy is at point *a* on the Laffer curve, then a drop in tax rates will cause an *increase* in tax revenues, pushing the economy to position *b*.

With a tax rate of 100 percent, presumably no one would work, and tax revenue would be zero. Obviously, revenue is also zero if the tax rate is zero. In between these extremes, there is a particular relationship between the tax rate and tax revenue. Over the years of Keynesian-type interventionism, tax rates had been pushed higher and higher, so that many countries found themselves at a point represented by *a* in Figure 13.7. What was needed, argued Laffer, was a massive cut in tax rates, which would increase incentives so that production and therefore income would increase so much that tax revenues would actually go up to, say, a point represented by *b* on the Laffer curve. So although tax rates are lower, tax revenues are higher.

SELF-TEST

6. Shown here are several different average tax rates (ATRs) associated with various levels of GDP. Calculate the total tax revenue at each level of GDP and indicate the tax rate that would maximize the government's tax revenue.

ATR	GDP	Tax Revenue
0.30	$2000	_____
0.35	1900	_____
0.40	1700	_____
0.45	1500	_____
0.50	1300	_____
0.55	1100	_____

If Laffer's argument was correct, then a government could, figuratively speaking, have its cake and eat it too. Appropriate tax cuts could increase work, savings, and investment and thereby slash both unemployment and inflation. And on top of this, the government's budget deficit would be also be reduced. It sounded very persuasive. The pity of it all was that many advocates of supply-side economics didn't stop there. Among other things, they also pushed vigorously in the United States for massive cuts to social programs (but leaving the military budget untouched), and for curtailing the power of trade unions (in the name of increased competition). Needless to say, this led to a backlash, both within and outside the economics profession.

Outside the economics profession, this backlash took on a political character. Within the discipline, however, the dispute centred on the supposed stimulative effect of tax cuts. Many commentators criticized the supply-side argument on the grounds that a tax cut was likely to have a bigger impact on spending than on productivity. The average person in receipt of a higher disposable income is more likely to spend most of it, rather than work more hours so as to obtain an even bigger income. In economic terms, this means that the substitution effect of a pay raise will likely exceed the income effect of such an increase. Similarly, firms with higher after-tax profits are just as likely to pay higher dividends as they are to use the increased earnings to reinvest in their companies. In short, the criticism of many economists was not that tax cuts do not provide incentives to people, but that the effect on spending and aggregate demand will be far greater than the effect on the supply side. All this means that aggregate demand would rise more than aggregate supply, and not only would GDP increase but so too would inflation. Nonetheless, the supply-side position, which was calculatedly laissez-faire, was given a boost by a relatively new idea in economics in the late 1970s: rational expectations.

SELF-TEST

7. Supply-side economists say that a cut in tax rates will lead to an increase in real GDP. Keynesians agree with this but for different reasons. In what ways do they differ?

Rational Expectations

Many of the adherents to this theory were later labelled "new" classicists. Their main focus was a dissatisfaction with the prevailing view that people's future expectations are solely guided by past experience. As an example of this prevailing view, suppose that wage contracts were based solely on recent experience, and inflation rates had been running at 10 percent. Logic would dictate that unions would attempt to negotiate wage increases in excess of 10 percent. If these wage demands were successfully achieved, inflation would intensify and the chances of ever reducing people's inflationary expectations would seem remote. This led to many arguing that inflation might well have a self-generating aspect to it and therefore could only be cured by a strong dose of unemployment. In other words, the only way of reducing inflation would be for the government to intervene with contractionary fiscal or monetary policy.

Adherents of the theory of rational expectations felt that such a conclusion is misguided and that the expectations of consumers, investors, and firms are formed not only by recent experience but also by their predictions of the likely response by the government and the central bank. In other words, they felt that rational individuals make use of all available information when making future plans. Thus, if the current rate of inflation is 10 percent, it does not mean that everybody expects it to remain at that level. People will take into consideration other indicators, such as unemployment levels, as well as their predictions of possible policy action to be taken by policy makers. This might well result in their lowering their expectations of future inflation rates. What all of this suggested was that inflation might be cured more quickly and less painfully than many economists believed. If this is so, then the economy could return to its "natural" state of full employment with stable prices, without the need for heavy-handed, recession-creating action by government.

Canada at the Turn of the Twenty-first Century: A Time of Uncertainty

The decade of the 1990s may well go down in history as one of the most significant of the twentieth century. It began with the collapse of the Soviet Union and, with it, the birth of a dozen new nations plus a well-spring of hope as well as some anxious expectations. This was the time when China began seriously experimenting with the market system and the world witnessed the enormous success of the Asian Tigers. All of this seemed to clearly say that the market system was likely to reign supreme forevermore.

Equally significant was the fact that the market was undergoing a transformation from being industry-based to knowledge-based. Globalization became the new buzzword. Yet, by the end of the decade, doubts and fears re-emerged as the "Asian flu" crippled the Tigers and the Russian economy faltered badly. These economic troubles threatened to engulf Latin America as well.

For Canada, the decade began with a brief but sharp recession that affected Ontario, Quebec, and the Maritimes more than it did the West. Once again, as with the much more serious recession of the early 1980s, some economists felt that this was a recession induced by the very tight money policy of the Bank of Canada, which seemed almost obsessed with holding inflation rates below 2 percent. For this reason, the then governor of the Bank of Canada, John Crow, was not a popular man in the eyes of many Canadians. Thus, one of the first things that a new Liberal government did when it came to power in 1993 was to take advantage of the fact that Crow's first term as governor had just expired and replace him with Gordon Thiessen. Many thought this might signal a new direction for monetary policy. As events transpired, the change of governors didn't produce any change in policy. The Bank of Canada remained transfixed at fighting inflation by keeping interest rates high.

On the fiscal side of policy, the big issue of the day was the federal government's budget deficits. The federal government had been running budget deficits for nearly 20 years straight, and these deficits were increasing year by year. The reasons for these huge deficits were at least threefold. First was the government's own attempt to shield Canadians from the effects of the inflationary 1970s, and the second was unusually high interest rates in the early 1980s. Third was the simple fact that the size of government was much bigger than just 20 years earlier. All this led to a growing chorus of political commentators joined by some economists who called for reduced deficits, or even balanced budgets, regardless of the costs of achieving this. Finance Minister Paul Martin responded by instituting massive cuts in federal government transfers to the provinces, in the form of cuts to health and education spending. By the fiscal year 1997–98, the federal government's budget showed a modest surplus followed by an even larger one in the 1998–99 budget year.

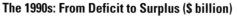

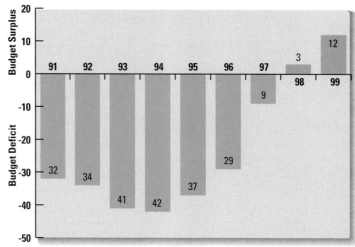

Despite the strong exports, the Canadian dollar was on the decline for most of the decade and fell to historic lows in 1998. A long-term downward trend in commodity prices and an economic crisis in Asia were certainly two reasons for this. Perhaps more significant was the fact that long-term foreign investment into Canada slowed considerably in the mid to late 1990s. The reasons for this include the political uncertainty about Quebec and a growing international perception that Canada had a restrictive business environment and high taxes.

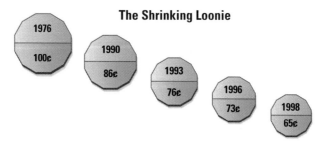

One thing that this brief overview of the twentieth century shows is that the economic goals that Canadians are concerned with are a reflection of the times they live in and are very much subject to change. At the beginning of the century, the problems of nation building and economic growth were at centre stage. By the 1920s there was growing concern that the benefits of economic growth were not always shared equitably among people. The 1930s understandably put full employment at the top of everyone's list of economic goals. The postwar period saw the balancing of the twin goals of full employment and stable prices come into sharp focus. In the 1970s, Canadian concerns went in two very different directions. First there was increasing anxiety about stagflation, and second there was an increasing worry over resource depletion and environmental degradation. In the 1980s, bigger government deficits and debt became the major issue for many. This worry continued into the 1990s, then faded to be replaced alarm over the depreciating Canadian dollar.

There is a clear message in all this: what is seen as the most important goal today is unlikely to remain as important tomorrow. Problems arise and then get dealt with, only to be replaced with some new problem that attracts people's concerns and attention. That is why the study of economic principles must remain broad and flexible. Too much focus on any one problem or any one issue is myopic and could prove to be dangerous.

Chapter Highlights

There are two main themes in this chapter. The first is an examination of how economic theory and contemporary events are interrelated, and the second revolves around the question of the appropriate role for government. Both of these themes are developed in context of six specific periods of time. The first period is Canada at the turn of the twentieth century—a time of optimism and hope for the country and the dominance of Say's Law in economic theory. We then turn to the end of World War I and its aftermath, which required a difficult economic adjustment but one that did lead to better times in the 1920s. It was at this time that Say's Law evolved into full-blown neoclassical theory, which argued that a market economy was capable of automatic full employment through the self-adjustment of prices, wages, and interest rates.

Next, we look at the Great Depression and Keynes's response to the neoclassicists. Both the Great Depression and Keynes's diagnosis heralded a fundamental shift in people's attitude toward market economies and in how economists looked at the workings of the macroeconomy.

We then note that the end of World War II launched 30 years of economic prosperity in Canada as well as the widespread acceptance of Keynesian economics. The idea that good times could be achieved through the policies of demand management seemed to be verified by the economy's performance. However, Phillips had raised concerns that perhaps the achievement of full employment might not be compatible with stable prices.

Next, we look at how the early 1970s ushered in serious inflation followed by long bouts of stagflation—something economists could not, at first, explain. In the face of this uncertainty, we see the rise of the supply-siders who offered an economic prescription of how to make things right again. Their views found favour with the Reagan government in the United States and, to a lesser extent, the Mulroney government in Canada. By the end of the 1980s, supply-side economics as a school of thought became integrated into mainstream economics.

Finally, the chapter concludes by suggesting that both the problems we consider most urgent and the goals that we believe to be the most important are ever-changing. That is why the study of economics needs to remain broad and flexible.

New Glossary Terms

Laffer curve   466
Say's Law   451

STUDY GUIDE

Study Tips

1. It is important to realize that the different schools of thought examined in this chapter are products of their times: neoclassical theory is rooted in an era of buoyant growth and low unemployment; Keynesian theory was the product of the depression years, when unemployment was, by far, the most serious economic issue, and supply-side economics came into existence as a result of mainstream economics being unable to offer any real solutions to the problem of stagflation.

2. It would be a mistake to leave this chapter with the idea that every economist, past or present, "belongs" exclusively to one or another of these schools of thought. The different schools are clearly delineated in order to clarify their contrasting viewpoints. In reality, the majority of economists seldom give their total allegiance to any one school.

3. In a similar vein, the different schools of economic thought are often characterized in political terms, with the Keynesians leaning left on the political spectrum and the other schools leaning to the right. But, as usual, all generalizations can be misleading (including this one?). It is possible to be a Keynesian and also to be concerned about the size of the national debt, or to be a neoclassicist and still have compassion about the underprivileged and so on.

Key Problem

The economy of Copland is in eqiulibrium but is suffering a recessionary gap of $10 billion. Its aggregate demand and supply curves are shown in **Figure 13.8**.

FIGURE 13.8

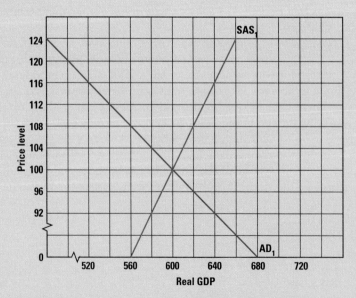

Both demand-side and supply-side economists in Copland have been advising the government to reduce taxes in order to cure the recession. Independent economic research has determined that for every 1 percent change in taxes, aggregate demand changes by $20 billion.

a) Assuming that the government decides to cut taxes by 6 percent, and that aggregate supply is unaffected, draw in and label the new curve AD_2 in Figure 13.8.

b) At the new equilibrium, by *how much* has real GDP and the price level changed?

Change in real GDP: (+/-) $_____; change in price level: (+/-) _____.

Independent economic research has also determined that in Copland every 1 percent cut in tax rates, because it stimulates productivity, will increase aggregate supply by $5 billion.

c) For the same 6 percent cut in taxes, draw in and label the new short-run aggregate supply curve, SAS_2 and the LAS_2, in Figure 13.8.

d) Assuming that aggregate demand *did not* change, by how much would real GDP and the price level change?

Change in real GDP: (+/-) $_____; change in price level: (+/-) _____.

e) Finally, assuming that the change in tax rates affect *both* aggregate demand and aggregate supply, add together the changes in b) and d):

Total change in real GDP: $_____; total change in price level: (+/-) _____.

f) Is Copland's economy now at full employment? If there is a gap, what sort is it, and how much?

Type of gap: _____ of $_____.

More of the Same

The economy of Bruchland is in equilibrium but is suffering a recessionary gap of $10. Its aggregate demand and supply curves are shown in **Figure 13.9**.

FIGURE 13.9

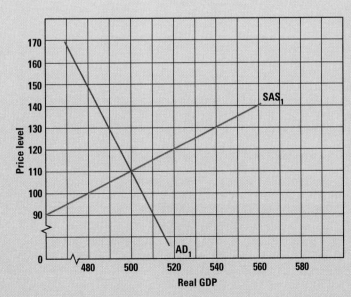

Both demand-side and supply-side economists in Bruchland have been advising the government to reduce taxes in order to cure the recession. Independent economic research has determined that for every 1 percent cut in taxes, aggregate demand increases by $5 billion.

a) Assuming that the government of Bruchland decides to cut taxes by 10 percent, and that aggregate supply is unaffected, draw in and label the new AD curve, AD_2, in Figure 13.9.

b) At the new equilibrium, by *how much* has real GDP and the price level changed?

Independent economic research has also determined that for every 1 percent change in tax rates, aggregate supply changes by $5 billion.

c) Assuming the same cut in taxes, draw in and label the new SAS (SAS_2) and LAS (LAS_2) curve in Figure 13.9.

d) Assuming that aggregate demand *did not* change, by how much would real GDP and the price level change?

e) Finally, assuming that the change in tax rates affect *both* aggregate demand and aggregate supply, add together the changes in b) and d). By how much would real GDP and the price level change?

f) Is the economy of Bruchland now at full employment? If there is a gap, what sort is it, and how much?

Translations

Assume that **Figure 13.10** is referring to the 1930s. Describe in words what actually occurred that enable the economy to return to full-employment equilibrium. Then assume the figure is referring to the 1970s. Describe in words what the supply-siders would advocate as a way of returning to full-employment equilibrium.

FIGURE 13.10

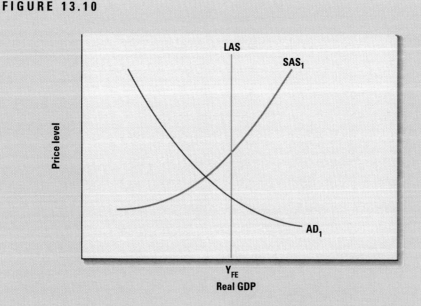

Are You Sure?

Indicate whether the following statements are true or false. If false, indicate why they are false.

1. Say's Law suggests that supply creates its own demand.

   T or F   If false: _____

   _____

2. Neoclassical economists were strong advocates of government intervention.

   T or F   If false: _____

   _____

3. According to neoclassical theory, the aggregate supply curve is horizontal at the prevailing price level.

   T or F   If false: _____

   _____

4. According to neoclassical theory, an increase in the level of saving will cause the rate of interest to fall.

   T or F   If false: _____

   _____

5. According to Keynesian theory, a change in aggregate demand might have little or no effect on the price level.

   T or F   If false: _____

   _____

6. Stagflation was a problem in both the 1930s and the 1970s.

   T or F   If false: _____

   _____

7. Neoclassical economists believe that market economies can achieve full employment through self-adjustment.

   T or F   If false: _____

   _____

8. Aggregate demand policies are effective in curing the problems of stagflation.

   T or F   If false: _____

   _____

9. The Phillips curve is based on the stable relationship between tax rates and the amount of tax revenue.

   T or F   If false: _____

   _____

10. One of the major criticisms of the supply-siders' emphasis on using tax cuts to stimulate the economy is that such cuts affect aggregate demand more than aggregate supply.

    T or F   If false: _____

    _____

Choose the Best

11. Which of the following is a statement of Say's Law?
    a) Demand creates its own supply.
    b) Supply creates its own demand.

12. Which school of thought believed that long-run equilibrium occurs automatically and is the normal state of affairs in a market economy?
    a) Keynesians.
    b) Neoclassicists.

13. What do Keynesians believe?
    a) Savings depends on the level of the interest rate.
    b) Savings depends on the level of income.

14. What will be the effect of a decrease in aggregate demand, according to neoclassical theory?
    a) An increase in the price level, but a lower level of GDP and employment.
    b) A reduction in GDP and employment, but no change in the price level.
    c) A reduction in the price level but, no change in GDP or employment.

15. What ensures the equality of savings and investment according to neoclassical theory?
    a) Flexible prices.
    b) Flexible interest rates.
    c) Flexible wages.

FIGURE 13.11

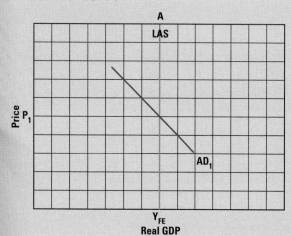

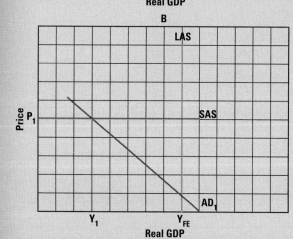

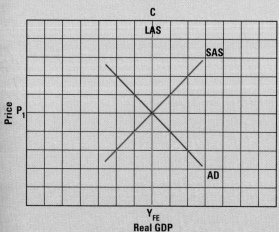

Refer to **Figure 13.11** to answer questions 16 and 17.

16. Refer to Figure 13.11 to answer this question. Which diagram best portrays neoclassical theory?
    a) Diagram A.
    b) Diagram B.
    c) Diagram C.

17. Refer to Figure 13.11 to answer this question. Which diagram best portrays Keynesian theory?
    a) Diagram A.
    b) Diagram B.
    c) Diagram C.

18. Which of the following did neoclassical economists believe?
    a) That the leakage of savings from the circular flow would always be matched by an equal amount of investment.
    b) That if savings exceed investment, the interest rate will fall.
    c) That surplus output would lead to a fall in prices.
    d) All of the above.

19. All of the following except one occurred during the Great Depression. Which is the exception?
    a) Real GDP and prices decreased.
    b) The average wage rate decreased.
    c) Government spending was increased in an attempt to stimulate aggregate demand.
    d) Both investment and exports decreased.

20. How might policy be used to overcome the crowding out effect?
    a) Contractionary monetary policy used together with expansionary fiscal policy.
    b) Contractionary monetary policy used together with contractionary fiscal policy.
    c) Expansionary monetary policy used together with contractionary fiscal policy.
    d) Expansionary monetary policy used together with expansionary fiscal policy.

Refer to **Figure 13.12** to answer question 21.

Refer to **Figure 13.13** to answer question 23.

FIGURE 13.12

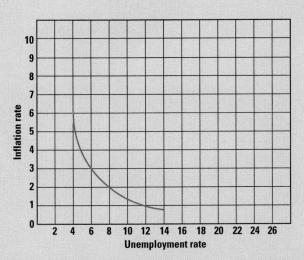

FIGURE 13.13

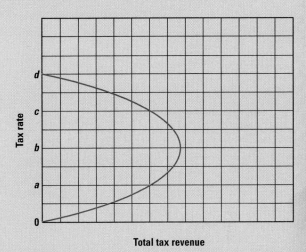

21. Refer to Figure 13.12 to answer this question. What is the name of the curve shown here?
a) Phillips curve.
b) Aggregate supply curve.
c) Laffer curve.
d) Production possibilities curve.

22. Which of the following represents one of the basic problems portrayed by the Phillips curve?
a) That the inflation rate tends to decrease as the economy moves closer to full employment.
b) That the inflation rate tends to increase as the economy moves closer to full employment.
c) That the unemployment rate tends to decrease as the economy moves toward price stability.
d) That high levels of unemployment tend to accompany high rates of inflation.

23. Refer to Figure 13.13 to answer this question. According to supply-side economists, at what level are present tax rates in Canada?
a) At some level like O*a*.
b) At some level like O*b*.
c) At some level like O*c*.
d) At O*d*.

24. According to neoclassical economists, what would happen if total spending was less than total output?
a) Product prices would rise, but wage rates would fall.
b) Product prices would fall, but wage rates would rise.
c) Nominal GDP would rise, but real GDP would remain constant.
d) Both product prices and wage rates would fall.
e) Both product prices and wage rates would rise.

25. All of the following, *except one*, are aspects of neoclassical economics. Which is the exception?
    a) The level of savings depends upon the rate of interest.
    b) Full employment is the normal state in laissez-faire capitalism.
    c) Wages and prices are rigid and do not adjust rapidly.
    d) The interest rate adjusts to ensure that saving equals investment.
    e) Supply creates its own demand.

26. According to Keynes, what determines interest rates?
    a) The level of savings.
    b) The level of investment.
    c) The velocity of money.
    d) Both savings and investment.
    e) The intersection of the demand and supply of money.

27. All of the following except one are pillars on which neoclassical theory is built. Which is the exception?
    a) The flexibility of production.
    b) The validity of Say's Law.
    c) The flexibility of prices.
    d) The flexibility of interest rates.
    e) The flexibility of wages.

28. According to supply-siders, what is one of the keys to curbing stagflation?
    a) Increasing the money supply and cutting government spending.
    b) Using income policies to increase productivity.
    c) Shifting the AD curve to the right.
    d) Convincing people to buy domestic rather than foreign-produced goods.
    e) Lowering taxes.

Refer to **Figure 13.14** to answer questions 29 and 30.

FIGURE 13.14

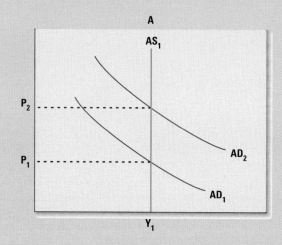

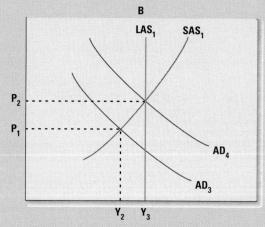

29. Refer to Figure 13.14 to answer this question. According to neoclassicists, which of the following is true?
    a) The horizontal axes of both graphs A and B show nominal GDP.
    b) It is not possible for an economy to be at Y_2 in graph B.
    c) The shift from AD_3 to AD_4 is caused by an increase in the price level.
    d) Graph A illustrates that changes in aggregate demand have no effect on the price level.
    e) Graph B illustrates a Laffer-curve-type trade-off.

30. Refer to Figure 13.14 to answer this question. According to the Keynesians, which of the following is true?

a) The horizontal axes of both graphs A and B show nominal GDP.

b) The shift from AD_3 to AD_4 illustrates what should have happened in the 1930s but did not.

c) Graph B illustrates a Phillips-curve-type trade-off.

d) A shift from AD_1 to AD_2 is the result of contractionary fiscal and monetary policy.

e) The economy is always automatically at income level Y_1

Other Problems

31. **Figure 13.15** shows the savings and investment functions for the very classical economy of Gluckland.

FIGURE 13.15

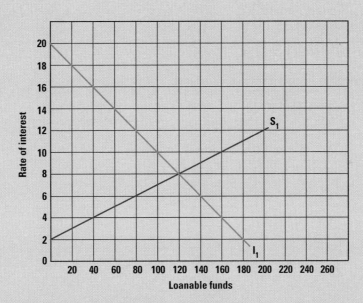

a) What is the equilibrium rate of interest in Gluckland?

Rate of interest: _____%.

b) According to the graph, what rate of interest would induce the people of Gluckland to save $100 billion?

Rate of interest: _____%.

c) According to the graph, what rate of interest would induce the firms of Gluckland to invest $100 billion?

Rate of interest: _____%.

d) What change in savings would reduce the interest rate to 6 percent, and how much would savings and investment be as a result?

Change in savings: $_____; new level of savings/investment $_____ .

e) Starting at the original equilibrium in Figure 13.15, what change in investment would reduce the interest rate to 6 percent, and how much would savings and investment be as a result?

Change in investment: $_____; new level of savings/investment $_____ .

32. Match each item in the left-hand column with a related idea or event in the right-hand column by placing a letter in each blank.

A. laissez-faire   1. Keynesians   _____
B. demand management   2. 1930s, early 1980s, and early 1990s   _____
C. tax cuts as a stimulus to aggregate supply   3. OPEC-induced oil price increases   _____
D. stagflation   4. supply-siders   _____
E. supply creates its own demand   5. peoples' reactions to changes in policy   _____
F. recessions   6. Say's Law   _____
G. rational expectations   7. neoclassicist   _____
H. the level of savings depends on interest rates   8. theory of loanable funds   _____

33. In the queendom of Frankland, GDP is currently $500 million. Production in Frankland is unaffected by changes in tax rates until the rate hits 35 percent. Thereafter for each 5 percent increase in the tax rate, GDP drops by $40 million.
a) Complete **Table 13.1** for the government of Frankland.

TABLE 13.1

% Tax Rate	GDP	Tax Revenue
0	$500	_____
5	_____	_____
10	_____	_____
15	_____	_____
20	_____	_____
25	_____	_____
30	_____	_____
35	_____	_____
40	_____	_____
45	_____	_____
50	_____	_____
55	_____	_____
60	_____	_____
65	_____	_____
70	_____	_____

b) In **Figure 13.16**, graph Frankland's tax revenue curve.

FIGURE 13.16

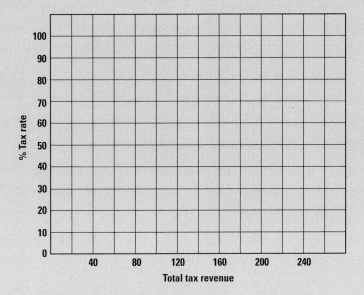

c) At what tax rate will the tax revenue be maximized? What will be the amount of tax revenue?

% tax rate: _____; tax revenue: $_____ .

UNANSWERED QUESTIONS

Short Essays

1. What can cause a change in aggregate demand, according to Keynesian theory? What are the effects of such a change?

2. What can cause a change in aggregate supply, according to neoclassical theory? What are the effects of such a change?

3. According to neoclassical theory, full employment is guaranteed because the market economy is self-adjusting. What is it that adjusts, and what is the effect of these adjustments?

4. Explain the major grounds on which Keynes disagreed with neoclassical theory.

5. Why do supply-siders feel that neither fiscal nor monetary policy is able to cure stagflation?

6. Explain how a decrease in tax rates might increase the government's tax revenue.

7. Explain how the theory of rational expectations reinforces the philosophy of non-intervention.

Analytical Questions

8. An upward-sloping supply of labour implies that the quantity of labour increases as the wage rate increases. Do you think this means the number of hours worked increases, or the number of workers increases or both?

9. Explain the circumstances in which economic policy might increase real GDP without affecting the price level.

10. If you were a Keynesian, how would you explain the effect of an increase in savings? What if you were a neoclassicist?

11. Explain the main differences between neoclassicists and supply-siders.

12. How might a Keynesian argue that fiscal policy could be made effective despite the existence of the crowding-out effect?

13. Both Keynesians and supply-siders agree that if taxes are cut, then GDP will rise. So what is the difference between the two concerning the effect of a decrease taxes?

14. Both neoclassicists and Keynesians agree that savings is the source of investment and that in equilibrium, in a simple economy, the two are equal. However, they disagree about how this equality is brought about. Explain how each theory describes the adjustment process that takes place if:
    a) firms decide to invest more;
    b) households decide to save more.
    How would income levels be affected in both cases?

15. According to neoclassicists, what would happen to the level of savings if the interest rate decreased? To the level of investment? How does this affect the equality of savings and investment?

Numerical Questions

16. **Figure 13.17** shows the demand for and supply of loanable funds in Handel.

FIGURE 13.17

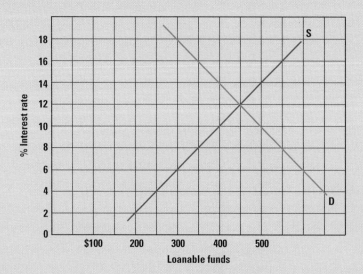

a) What is the equilibrium interest rate?

b) What rate of interest will induce savers to supply $400 million?

c) What rate of interest will induce firms in Handel to borrow and invest $400 million?

d) What change in savings would reduce the interest rate to 8 percent? What change in investment would reduce the interest rate to 8 percent?

17. The data below is for the economy of Haydn.

Price Index	AD	SAS
94	860	740
96	840	760
98	820	780
100	800	800
102	780	820
104	760	840
105	740	860

Suppose that in year one, the economy of Haydn is in equilibrium and experiencing a recessionary gap of 60 and inflation of 1 percent. In year two, aggregate demand increases by 40. The natural rate of unemployment is 6 percent, and for each $10 of recessionary gap, cyclical unemployment is 1 percent.

a) What is the unemployment rate and the inflation rate in years one and two?

b) Construct a Phillips curve from your answers in a).

18. **Figure 13.18** shows the aggregate demand for the economy of Bachland. Its full-employment level of GDP is $350, and its present price level is 110.

FIGURE 13.18

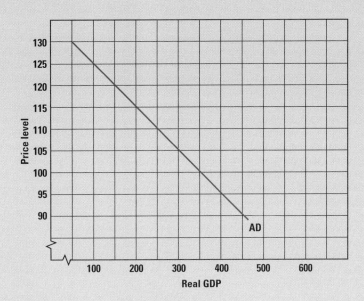

According to neoclassical theory:

a) Is the economy of Bachland currently in equilibrium? If not, what might happen?

b) If the economy of Bachland were in equilibrium at a GDP of $350 and price level of 100, what would happen to GDP and the price level if aggregate demand were to increase by $50?

According to Keynesian theory:

c) Is the economy of Bachland in equilibrium? If not, what might happen?

d) If the economy of Bachland were in equilibrium at a price of 110 and a GDP of 250, what would happen to GDP and the price level if aggregate demand were to increase by $50?

19. Using three AD/AS curve graphs, illustrate the effects on GDP of a general tax cut. Show how prices could rise, fall, or remain unchanged. What happens to GDP in each case?

Web-Based Activites

1. Go to **http://www.imf.org:80/external/pubs/ft/survey/pdf/060898.pdf** and read the article "Structural Reform and Market-Based Policies Heighten Need for Policy Coordination." What are the reasons for monetary and fiscal policy coordination? In terms of the impact on the economy, is there a clear distinction between monetary and fiscal policy? (For those who wish to go into this issue in greater detail, go to **http://www.imf.org/external/pubs/ft/wp/wp9825.pdf** for the entire working paper on policy coordination.)

2. Financial innovation tends to alter the velocity of money and, therefore, make any monetary policy rule less reliable over time. Is this true about electronic currency? With the growth of Internet commerce and the creation of e-money, will the debate surrounding rules versus discretion finally be settled— rules are no longer useful in the conduct of monetary policy! Is this assertion true? Go to **http://www.cato.org/pubs/books/money/money13.htm** and **http://www.stls.frb.org/general/speeches/970425.html** to help you answer these questions.

A Look into the Future

What's ahead... In this chapter we do something quite different that is both risky and exciting—we look into the future. We begin by looking at the new paradigm, which has symbolic knowledge at its core. Next, we examine the changing nature of the factors of production and of the wealth-creating process. We argue that the distinction between goods and services is becoming blurred, while at the same time national economic boundaries are also becoming blurred. Finally, we revisit Chapter 1's discussion of economic goals.

You probably live in or close to a large urban centre. It's likely that you drive a car and own a computer and a CD player. In all likelihood you will probably be looking for a career that will be quite different from your father's or mother's and, given your many years of education, it is unlikely to be in agriculture or manufacturing. All of this says that your lifestyle is very different from what it would have been 50 years ago. The only thing certain about your lifestyle 50 years from now is that it will be vastly different from what it is now. Will you be able to adjust to those coming changes well, or not so well? In this chapter we speculate on some of the possible future changes to our present ideas about work and earning a living—changes that are already underway.

We are all aware of the Industrial Revolution, which, beginning in about 1750, swept around the world and resulted in almost everything changing—people's lifestyles, the means of producing wealth, transportation systems, forms of government, prevailing customs, values, and much more. This enormous transition took place over a period of approximately 150–200 years.

A growing number of people today are convinced that the rise of the information age, and the concurrent fading of the industrial age, signals a second revolution that will prove to be just as significant as the first revolution. The difference this time, however, will be that we are probably looking at a transition of only 50 years or so. Let's turn our attention to the future. Before we do, however, we must emphasize that the following discussion should be read in the spirit of an attempt to stimulate thought and challenge conventional wisdom on various important issues. This discussion should not be interpreted as prediction, for this is simply not what we are trying to do.

A Look at the Future

paradigm shift: a significant change in pattern or in the model that one is looking at; in this case, a change in the economic system itself.

Let's accept the premise that our society is at the threshold of a whole new age. The industrial age is fast fading before our very eyes. The information age has arrived, with the result that our economy is undergoing profound changes that are equivalent to a **paradigm shift** that will ultimately affect almost every aspect of everyone's life. It is nearly impossible to overemphasize the significance of the way that the nature of wealth creation, the organization of production, and work itself is changing. It is entirely possible that:

> **The next 50 years will prove to be historically more profound than the two-century-long Industrial Revolution we all studied in secondary school.**

The New Paradigm

Let's now take a look at, and try to understand better, the nature of this paradigm shift and see how it affects our discussion of the economy's economic goals.

The Industrial Revolution took production out of the rural cottage and into the urban factory. Steam power, the electric motor, and other major innovations created the possibility for massive economies of scale in production, from which sprang the large corporation as the primary organizational form for the wealth-creation process. A vast array of durable goods then became affordable for ordinary consumers, and manufacturing became the driving force behind the powerful, rich economies of the world. This was the *old paradigm*.

But things are changing. We will develop our discussion of the *new paradigm* by focusing on four effects:

- the changing nature of the factors of production
- the changing nature of work and production
- the blurring of the traditional distinction between goods and services
- the globalization of the production process

The old paradigm.

symbolic knowledge: knowledge that encompasses data and information that is then systematically improved and refined into a form that has direct application to defining problems or creating solutions.

symbolic analyst: an individual who uses symbolic knowledge to identify problems, create solutions, and then present those solutions in a systematic form.

To accomplish our task better, we will make extensive use of two concepts. The first, used by Alvin Toffler in his work *Power Shift*, is called **symbolic knowledge**, and the other is what Robert Reich, in *The Work of Nations*, refers to as the **symbolic analyst**.

Symbolic knowledge is defined as facts and data that have been classified into meaningful categories and refined into a form that has direct application to defining problems or creating solutions. Much of today's symbolic knowledge comes in the form of symbols—either in mathematical form, or computer configurations, or in the form of new words and phases that convey a unique combination of ideas. Like the more conventional concept of knowledge, symbolic knowledge is infinitely expandable and can be applied in many places at the same time. But unlike the more conventional knowledge, symbolic knowledge puts data and information into new associations that previously were unimaginable. Symbolic knowledge juxtaposes ideas in ways that force us to re-examine our perspective. The result is that our perceptions change, and with changed perception comes a broadening of horizons and a growing awareness of new possibilities.

Symbolic knowledge is unleashing an explosion of practical applications of new ways of doing old things as well as a profound leap in creative thinking about new solutions to problems that we not long ago considered beyond our reach. An example can be found in the use of computer-aided design (CAD). The Boeing Company in Seattle, Washington, is in the process of producing a new aircraft called the 777. The very first one produced was sold as a functional flying machine. That is to say, Boeing no longer has to produce a mock-up aircraft, which would have to be test-flown and modified and then tested again. The time-consuming and expensive requirement needed to produce a prototype prior to mass production has been made redundant by a sophisticated computer-aided process that enables engineers to work out all the design bugs before actual production.

Finally, symbolic knowledge is expanding at breakneck speed and is being shared and exchanged nearly as fast. The result is that the old paradigm's bureaucratic managers are in fast retreat from a growing army of risk-taking, creative symbolic analysts who exhibit an entrepreneurial spirit outside the world's multinational corporations.

Reich's symbolic analysts are those individuals who, using symbolic knowledge, make a living identifying problems of technique, efficiency, information gathering, or interpretation, then create solutions for those problems, and, finally, present those solutions in some systematic form. An example here is that of a young woman who has successfully combined the technique of designing questionnaires and the analytical ability to interpret answers with the intuition needed to draw conclusions, such that her market research for clients produces valuable information that previously simply was not available.

From the mundane perspective of economics, the most significant aspect of the growing importance of both symbolic knowledge and the work of the symbolic analyst is the inability of anyone to control, restrict, or own knowledge, at least for very long. In the old paradigm, capital was at the centre of production, and capital could be accumulated and controlled and then transformed into the basis for monopoly control: one family, or even one individual, could control, say, a huge steel mill. In the new paradigm, symbolic knowledge is at the centre of the wealth-creation process, and it cannot be amassed and controlled in the same way as capital. No single firm, and certainly no individual, can control desktop publishing.

All of this has very interesting implications for where the centres of power in society lie. When the Industrial Revolution and the system of capitalism first started to sweep across Europe, we witnessed a struggle for power between the established landed gentry and the young, spirited, rising capitalists. As capitalism matured and production became organized around, and concentrated in, large corporations, we saw the struggle between capitalist and labour emerge. In the new paradigm, capital is waning in importance and, therefore, so too is the power of the large corporations as well as that of organized labour, whose members are centred within such corporations. Just who the protagonists will be in the future power struggles isn't clear, but the symbolic analyst will surely be involved.

REVIEW

1. **What is a *paradigm shift?***
2. **Define the term *symbolic knowledge*.**
3. **What is a *symbolic analyst?***

The Changing Nature of the Factors of Production

Given the emerging information age and the rise in importance of symbolic knowledge, it is clear that our conventional categories of the four factors of production—land, labour, capital, and enterprise—are no longer adequate. Further, the significant importance of symbolic knowledge, from an economist's point of view, is that it is very rapidly becoming the most important input in the wealth-creating process itself. Bearing both of these points in mind, let's look at some specific examples of how symbolic knowledge is being substituted for other inputs.

The first example is the substitution of symbolic knowledge for financial capital. The widespread use of computers has allowed business to adopt just-in-time inventory-control systems, with the result that the amount of materials that producers must carry has been reduced to a minimum. As a result, tens of billions of dollars worth of inventory, once financed with borrowed money (the interest on which is added to the cost of production), is simply no longer needed.

What about symbolic knowledge as a substitute for real capital? Here, the examples are almost endless. Robotics are reducing the capital–output ratio in thousands of different contexts. Fibre-optic cables are reducing the amount of needed capital per transatlantic phonecall. Superconductivity and giant batteries are eliminating the need for extra power plants that handle peak-load demand. Fuel cell technology, which will replace the internal combustion engine in automobiles as well as generate clean power, is only a few years away. More significant than any one example, however, is what Robert Thurow in *Head to Head* describes as the emerging reality of new *process technology* starting to replace *product technology*. In the old paradigm, changing a product was expensive. It required large inputs of highly paid machinists and tool-and-die makers and lots of downtime with no production. Hence the reliance on the production of standardized products that were mass-produced in order to capture economies of scale. In the new paradigm, computer-driven manufacturing technology and just-in-time inventory-control systems are producing customized products aimed at niche markets. As an example, one U.S. shoe manufacturer offers 32 different semi-customized shoe designs for each size of an individual customer's foot as measured in the retail outlet by a computer.

The products are changing, but the process of making them is changing even faster as firms target niche markets and substitute *high-value-added production* for *high-volume production.* What's more, these customized semi-personal products are not so expensive as to be beyond the budget of most consumers. To an increasing extent, customers are willing to pay a (not-so-high) premium for products that exactly meet their needs, and because such products cannot be easily duplicated by high-volume competitors, high-value output is where the new-paradigm firm's competitive advantage lies. In short:

> **Just as the Industrial Revolution shifted production from small-scale handicraft production to standardized mass production, the information revolution is reinventing the handicraft product in customized form.**

In a sense, this shift from an emphasis on product technology to process technology is being forced on firms in the advanced economies. Product technology can be easily copied by firms in the newly industrial countries, such as South Korea, Taiwan, Hong Kong, and Singapore (the four Asian Tigers), where routine labour is cheap. To survive, the firms in the advanced economies of Europe, North America, and Japan must begin to do different things that cannot be easily copied.

Let's move on and look at some examples of symbolic knowledge as a substitute for energy and other natural resources. It is a fact, surprising to most, that between 1979 and 1990 the U.S. economy used less energy in each year than in the previous year despite rising levels of GDP and population. Some of this was due to good conservation practices, but much of it was due to the application of new knowledge in production processes and product quality—from computer-assisted heating systems to fuel-efficient auto design. Another fact: the United States used less steel in 1990 than it did in 1960, despite a two and one-half time increase in GDP. This is an illustration of a materials-science revolution that will probably do to product manufacturing what the green revolution did to agricultural production. Raw-material prices the world over are, after correction for inflation, below what they were in the middle of the Great Depression of the 1930s. This has occurred despite significant increases in demand. The explanation can be found only in the application of symbolic knowledge to new-materials development as well as the more efficient use of traditional raw materials.

Symbolic knowledge is also being substituted for space and transportation. Here miniaturization is paramount. Products are increasingly becoming smaller (think of a 1940s radio that you may have seen in your grandmother's home), greatly saving warehouse space and reducing the weight per unit shipped. In fact, advanced information processing systems and highly efficient delivery systems ("by 10:30 A.M. the next day, guaranteed") will probably render huge warehouses and the related wholesaling function obsolete. (Later in the chapter, we will look at how symbolic knowledge is being widely substituted for labour.) All of this leads to the inevitable conclusion that we must add symbolic knowledge as the fifth factor of production.

Let's review what we have so far:

- Natural resources are fading in importance as the new-materials revolution forges ahead.
- Real capital is still important, but less so with process technology than with product technology.
- The application and importance of symbolic knowledge as a new factor of production is increasing everyday.

Now consider what Robert Thurow sees as some of tomorrow's key industries:

- microelectronics
- biotechnology
- the new-materials industries
- civilian aviation
- telecommunications
- robotics
- computer software

These are all brain-power industries that will employ a large percentage of the symbolic analysts. Almost all the firms in these categories and the jobs that go with them could be located anywhere in the world. There is little natural advantage to any particular location, as there was in the old paradigm. These jobs will go to those societies that organize themselves around the realities of the new paradigm and are also able to offer the individuals involved the most desirable lifestyle opportunities.

In the *old* paradigm, a nation's comparative advantage lay in:

- abundant natural resources
- a high level of capital accumulation
- a disciplined labour force that was experienced in product production so that economies of scale could be captured

The *new* paradigm's comparative advantage is entirely human-made.

In today's global markets, old and new products of a standardized nature can be easily reproduced by competitors located around the globe. The new comparative advantage comes from new-process technologies that concentrate on high-value

Problem solving exemplifies the new paradigm.

output. This involves identifying a customer's unique needs and then designing and engineering a customized product to meet those needs. Thirty years ago, few countries could match Canada, the United States, Britain, and Germany in terms of the mass production of standardized products. Today, these same countries no longer have this advantage. Many other countries are now able to compete. The new comparative advantage for every advanced country lies in producing customized products that meet unique needs. Such production relies heavily on the symbolic analyst for value added, while the value added by the actual manufacturing of any product becomes less and less important. This is at the heart of the reason for the decline in the relative importance of real capital in production and the rise in the importance of symbolic knowledge and the symbolic analyst.

The Changing Nature of Work and Production

The French physiocrats of the eighteenth century were sure that wealth sprang from land. Marx, in the nineteenth century, was sure that it sprang from labour. Neoclassical economists, at the turn of the twentieth century, emphasized the role of capital formation in increasing an economy's production possibilities. As we move into the twenty-first century, knowledge, information, and human creativity will play the key role in creating wealth.

Let's now look at ways in which symbolic knowledge acts as a substitute for labour and at the profound implications this has on the changing nature of work. Alvin Toffler reports that the Florida plant of a large electronics firm turns out customized radio pagers in production runs as small as one of a kind. Twenty-seven robots do the physical work. Of the 40 employees at the plant, only one actually touches the product. It is interesting to note that 24 highly specialized symbolic analysts worked (in teams and at very odd hours and on weekends) for 18 months to design the product, engineer the plant and equipment, and plan the strategy for the marketing of the product. Their work done, this group was shuffled and reassigned to other similar projects.

There are hundreds of other similar examples, but the point is that the nature of work itself is changing. Here, we will rely on Reich for our framework once again. He sees three broad categories of work emerging in the new paradigm. The first is *routine production services*, which range from blue-collar assembly-line workers to supervisors who do repetitive checks on subordinates' work to the makers of computer circuit-boards. This group makes up about 25 percent of today's work force, but this percentage is declining. The second category is *in-person services*, ranging from retail sales workers to bank tellers to nursing aides to real estate agents. This category makes up about 30 percent of the labour force and is growing. The third category is that of the *symbolic services*, which includes all problem-identifying, problem-solving, and strategic-brokering activities that involve the manipulation of data, words, and oral or visual representations. Like the products produced by the routine production workers but unlike those of the in-person service worker, the output of the symbolic analyst can be traded worldwide. Examples of occupations in this category are design engineers, public relations consultants, film editors, energy consultants, systems analysts, and textbook authors. They make up about 20 percent of today's work force. The remaining 25 percent of the work force is in agriculture and mining and in government employment. To some extent, those within government could be put into the same three categories. In summary, Reich's three categories of work are:

- routine production services
- in-person services
- symbolic services

Focusing on these three categories of work, one can discern certain future trends in employment. Routine production workers may well have to accept lower real wages or see their jobs disappear. In-service production work may be either very routine and low paid (waiters), or specialized and fairly highly paid (realtors or nurses). Systems analysts will be specialized, highly skilled, and well paid. Increasingly, workers will have only two things to sell: cheap routine labour or highly specialized skills. Often, those in the latter category will shun employment with large corporations and, instead, form small, highly specialized businesses of their own, and thus we find the number and variety of firms multiplying and forming clusters around a specific function or type of service.

Such clusters are held together by the free flow of information and data transfer and by the stimulus to creativity that personal interaction brings. Often, a major educational institution is at the core of such clusters. This last point emphasizes the fact that today's comparative advantage is human-made and not naturally endowed. This leads to an important conclusion:

> **Firms, industries, and economies with the best environment for symbolic analysts to work in will be the successful ones.**

Physical products, whatever they may be, can be manufactured anywhere in the world, and here the cheapest labour will win out. But the process that identifies the unique needs of the customers and designs a specialized response to those needs will capture most of the value added in production.

To say it again: in the old paradigm, capital was concentrated and owned by capitalists who hired interchangeable units of labour, who in turn produced standardized goods. In the new paradigm, capital is less important and less concentrated because of its mobility and abundance and because of the decreasing importance of standardized production. The most powerful wealth-creating tools are the symbols, ideas, and imagination inside the heads of the symbolic analysts. These workers, therefore, own a critical, often irreplaceable, share of the means of production.

Home-based offices are becoming more common. This symbolic analyst's journey to work consists of a 20-foot commute from his bedroom.

Returning to Robert Reich's three categories of work, tomorrow's successful economies will undoubtedly see the percentage of their labour force employed in routine production services continue to fall, while the in-person services category is likely to hold its percentage or grow slowly. More significantly, the number of people in symbolic services will grow more rapidly. Most of the individuals in this latter category will be employed by very small firms or even work on a self-employed contract basis. The possibility of this latter point could have significant implications on where people choose to live. Many symbolic analysts can, given home computers, modems, and communications systems such as the Internet, live and work at home and still be plugged in to the people and information needed for them to do their work. They will probably still tend to cluster, but such clusters could be almost anywhere. Could this be the prelude to seeing the 250-year-old trend of urbanization beginning to reverse itself?

SELF-TEST

1. List some of the factors that would be of importance to a systems analyst who is thinking of where to relocate.

The Distinction between Goods and Services

The evolution of the paradigm shift is resulting in the traditional distinction between goods and services becoming very blurred. For example, Reich reports that fewer than 20 000 of IBM's 400 000 employees are hands-on production workers. Thus when one looks at an IBM PC, one is looking at far more than a physical product. In fact, only about 10 percent of the price of the computer is actual manufacturing costs. The other 90 percent of the price goes to cover the costs of research, design, engineering, sales, follow-up servicing, and, of course, profit. Once again, most of the work associated with the 90 percent involves the work of the symbolic analysts. So does IBM sell a good (computer), or does it sell a service (the application of computing systems to a particular function)?

To extend this latter point, it is becoming increasingly impossible to identify a product as, for example, Canadian, American, or Japanese. A classic example of this point is provided again by Reich, who chronicles the case of the U.S. Department of Commerce, which was trying to define what was is meant by an *American* forklift. A Japanese firm was exporting forklifts to the United States, but, upon investigation, it turned out that a significant percentage of its added value was contributed by firms operating within the United States (as well as other countries). Furthermore, the same investigation revealed that the Portland, Oregon, firm that had launched an **anti-dumping regulation** complaint against the Japanese firm had a lot of Japanese (and other countries) value-added services and components in its own forklift. In a typical, and unfortunately bureaucratic, fashion, the U.S. Commerce Department ended up defining an American forklift as one whose frame was made within the U.S. borders. A fitting end to this story would be for a Canadian firm to jump into the market, buy U.S. frames (probably about 10 percent of the total cost of a completed forklift), import these frames to, say, an Ontario plant, stamp "made in the USA" on the product, and begin an aggressive sales campaign in the United States. To ask the question: What is an American forklift? is akin to asking: What is a Canadian movie?

Let's pull things together. To an increasing extent, goods are mostly services. Natural resources and real capital are becoming less important. Brain power, owned

anti-dumping regulation: a law or regulation found in most countries that prohibits the importation of any good at a price below the cost of production.

by the individual possessing it, is becoming the most important input in production and in the determination of comparative advantage. No wonder the very nature of our economic system of capitalism is changing. In fact, what we have is a whole new wealth-creating system. We will probably continue to call it capitalism, but people from the mid-twentieth century will barely recognize the version we will see in 2025.

SELF-TEST

2. Using the conventional view that the economy produces two categories of products, goods and services, into which category do each of the following items belong?

A) Nursing care.
B) An apple.
C) A commercial movie.

D) A textbook.
E) An automobile.
F) Auto maintenance.
G) Household furniture.

Now, using the three categories of production services, in-person services, and symbolic analyst services, go through the list again.

The Globalization of the Production Process

The new wealth-creation system is both global and local. International trade continues its phenomenal increases of the last 30 years as routine production services move out of North America, Europe, and Japan to the low-wage countries that offer relative stability and security for investment. This includes such countries as Asia's Four Tigers, but maybe not a country like Ecuador, where political instability persists. This global market is increasingly populated by small (sometimes very small), specialized firms that use new information technologies to plug into a global production process web.

ADDED DIMENSION

Growing World Trade

The accompanying figures are the annual percentage increases in the volume of world trade from 1989 to 1998.

Year	Increase
1989	7.4%
1990	5.5%
1991	4.0%
1992	5.1%
1993	4.0%
1994	9.5%
1995	9.5%
1996	6.3%
1997	7.7%
1998	6.8%

Source: International Monetary Fund, *World Economic Outlook*, October 1997.

In Chapter 4, we mentioned Joseph Schumpeter's work in the area of economic growth. The driving force behind Schumpeter's cycles of boom and bust is the pace of innovation and the diffusion of new technology. Our discussion of today's paradigm shift is evidence that the world is on the edge of a Schumpeter boom. In terms of the manufacture of products, the whole world is rapidly becoming the market. The services that the symbolic analysts offer for sale are also increasingly being traded on a worldwide basis. Financial capital flashes around the globe as if there were no national borders.

ADDED DIMENSION

Joseph Schumpeter

Joseph Alois Schumpeter (1883–1950) was born in Moravia (now part of the Czech Republic) and studied law and economics at the University of Vienna. He practised law and lectured in economics and for a brief period became the Austrian minister of finance. In 1924, after the bank of which he was president collapsed with the great inflation in Germany, he returned to academia. From 1932 until his death he taught at Harvard University. Although a strong opponent of Marxism, he nevertheless was impressed by Marx's emphasis on the nature of economic growth and change and believed, like him, that profits, the source of capitalism's great success, might also be the cause of its eventual demise. His generally iconoclastic views are best contained in his early work, *The Theory of Economic Development.*

The trend toward globalization can also be seen in the economic policy coordination that is increasingly happening between nations. In the 25 to 30 years following World War II, the U.S. economy was large enough relative to the rest of the world that it alone could act as the world's economic locomotive. Fiscal and monetary policy expansion in the United States translated into expansionary policy in much of the rest of the world. However, the U.S. economy itself just can't do this any more. Together the United States, Japan, and the European economies are certainly large enough to be the locomotive pulling the world economy, but this, of course, implies policy coordination. Not only is there this apparent need for international policy coordination, there are also economic pressures that lean in the same direction. Alvin Toffler estimates that $200 billion worth of currencies are traded *every day* in London, New York, and Tokyo alone. This makes it difficult for any single central bank to push its economy's interest rates in a direction opposite to the one prevailing in the world market. The acceptance of the need for monetary coordination will probably be forced on governments as a result. It is for this reason that many economists predict that the world will see similar interest rates around the world becoming the norm. In the same vein, no nation is going to be able to tax its firms or its citizens significantly more than what is done in other postindustrial countries for fear of losing some of its symbolic analysts and firms that have integrated into the global web.

The following quote from Robert Thurow emphasizes the tremendous opportunity that he believes presents itself to the post–Cold War world but, at the same time, doesn't leave the impression of anything being easy.

> At temperatures near absolute zero, and now at much higher temperatures in some ceramic materials, superconductivity occurs. The rules that govern the propagation of electricity suddenly change. Old constants are no longer constant. New rules suddenly apply. Resistance disappears, and electrical devices that could not be previously built can now be built, but the currents that are unleashed are difficult to control.
>
> Much the same is happening in the world economy. New players, technologies, and rules are coming together to generate an economic form of superconductivity. Old

constants will have to be discarded. Suddenly, new rules will emerge in a very different game. Potentially, much more productive economies can be built, but controlling the currents that will be unleashed will be equally difficult.[1]

Implications for Canada

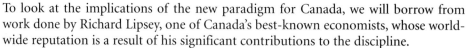

To look at the implications of the new paradigm for Canada, we will borrow from work done by Richard Lipsey, one of Canada's best-known economists, whose worldwide reputation is a result of his significant contributions to the discipline.

According to Lipsey, Canada's resource industries are under enormous pressure from new sources of existing materials (globalization) and from new materials emerging from the materials-science revolution (the new paradigm). The real price that Canadian resource producers will receive for their output in the future will probably continue to fall, and only dramatic increases in productivity will keep these producers in business.

The prospects for the Canadian agriculture industry are equally challenging for the same reasons. The simple fact is that the world can now produce more food than is currently demanded. Despite this fact, many nations around the world—from France to Japan to Canada to the United States—continue to subsidize farmers to produce far more food than is sold. The reason for this is that no government is anxious to move toward policies that will force large numbers of its farmers to leave agriculture. Yet, that is exactly what will have to happen at some point in the future. The boost to agricultural output that is coming from new biotechnology applications will probably force this issue sooner than many want to believe.

Globalization of the markets for unskilled production-service jobs has already resulted in the permanent loss of many formerly high-paying blue-collar jobs in Canada. This trend will continue. Organized labour worries a great deal about this trend, but raising tariffs to try to reduce the Canadian economy's exposure to the rest of the globalized world would almost certainly condemn the Canadian economy to the backwater of a fast-moving and growing world economy. Most of the world's economies are integrating themselves into a global unit, and any country that deliberately opts out of this process will face a very uncertain future.

Finally, the growing importance of the high-value, small but flexible new-paradigm firm has resulted in the permanent loss of many jobs in the middle-management level of the large corporations as these institutions lose their dominance over production. This trend will likely continue.

Economic Goals Revisited

Just as the new paradigm is changing the very structure of the economy, so will it change what are perceived to be the important economic goals. Let us give some tentative indications of how these are likely to change in the future.

As we have seen, the goal of full employment hinges on the very definition of employment and on what constitutes work. In the machine age, full employment usually meant working away from home for a 40-hour week, Monday to Friday, for a single

---

[1] Robert Thurow, *Head to Head* (New York: William Morrow, 1992), p. 66.

employer, at a fixed wage on a long-term basis. In the information age, none of these parameters will remain fixed. Further, the relative importance of capital is fading, and along with it the need for a large, disciplined, regimented labour force will also diminish. Instead, more and more people will be working flexible hours at home on short-term contracts for a number of companies located around the world. This is not to suggest that all traditional forms of employment will disappear; there will still be a demand for routine production services, but even these types of jobs are bound to feel the effect of change.

Turning now to the goal of economic growth, the conventional view of growth will likely evolve into something quite different. The shift from the high-volume production of standardized products to high-value customized products that better meet the specific requirements of the individual buyer is well underway. This is a reflection of increased affluence and more discriminating taste being expressed on an individual level in the private markets. If this trend begins to express itself on a more collective level, we could see a growing concern about the composition of overall production. People could well begin to be more concerned about *how* growth meets their wants rather than just in growth itself. Product quality and uniqueness could be more important than just more of the same. Improvements in more abstract goods, such as access to skiing and jogging trails or unique cultural and entertainment events, could become more important than another factory or more trees allocated for logging. In short:

> **We can see some definition of the right *kind* of growth beginning to take precedent over the size of the growth *rate*.**

Another way of looking at this is that just as we are seeing a paradigm shift in the wealth-creation process, we can also see a paradigm shift in what gets produced. Tied up in all this will undoubtedly be a growing awareness of what we are doing to our environment.

Currently we are witnessing a debate between those conventionalists who put the economy and jobs first and the environment second, and those environmentalists who do the exact opposite. The debate is often heated and unproductive. For example, those in the former category would point out that the generation of electricity is a highly desirable output, and that no matter how it is done problems arise. The use of coal brings acid rain. Nuclear power leads to radioactive wastes. Hydroelectric power floods valleys and scars the landscape with power lines. The use of oil and natural gas creates air pollution and depletes a valuable resource. The use of solar cells require enormous amounts of space and copper and creates arsenic waste. In short, every technique carries environmental costs, but, the conventionalists point out, the benefits are worth it. In contrast, environmentalists tend to focus on acid rain, natural-resource depletion, radioactive wastes, and lost valleys and argue that increased conservation should be substituted for more output.

In time, one can hope that this growth-versus-environment debate will evolve into a concerted effort to allow the economy to grow in an environmentally sound manner. What we are really saying here is that it may be possible in the future that people will no longer see growth and maintaining a liveable environment as separate goals to be traded off one for the other. Instead, these two goals may merge into the one goal of fostering growth in ways that preserve a liveable environment and better meet the more abstract needs of people that go far beyond the accumulation of even more material goods.

Let's turn now to the future prospects of maintaining an equitable distribution of income. As we mentioned earlier, it may well be the case that some Canadians will do very well in the new information age, but others probably will not. This could easily translate into a widening income gap among those who reach the status of symbolic analyst and those who get mired in the status of routine-production-service worker, or low-skilled in-person service worker, or, even more seriously, those who become unemployable. Will government policies of income redistribution be able to counter any such tendency so that all Canadians will benefit from the success of some? To try to answer this question would propel us into a detailed discussion of perceived moral responsibility, political philosophy, and some sort of perceived sense of fairness as well as analysis of new power structures. All of this is, indeed, a slippery slope. To put it bluntly, the question will become, does a successful software designer in Toronto, for example, have an obligation to subsidize an unemployed East Coast fisher? Suffice it to say that:

> **The issue of an equitable distribution of income and, in fact, the very definition of this term are likely to be at the centre of public consciousness and debate.**

And what of the other three conventional economic goals—the control of inflation, maintaining a viable balance of payments, and the national debt?

It is more than likely that concern over these goals will start to fade, not so much because of changed perceptions, but simply because they become less pressing in comparison to the goals of employment, income distribution, and ensuring a liveable environment. Inflation has been tame for several years now and, in the absence of policy mistakes or war, we see this trend continuing. A truly flexible exchange rate can take the possibility of balance-of-payments problems off the table. A manageable national debt depends on the success of government policies in keeping increases in government spending rates below increased revenues. The accomplishment of this goal in Canada has recently been achieved, and we see no reason for it slipping away.

Finale

So what might be your future?

The very optimistic scenario is one that sees inflation, the national debt, and balance-of-payment concerns fading into non-issues, while robust economic growth better allows us to redefine, and then deal with, the problems of unemployment, maintaining an equitable distribution of income, and creating a liveable environment.

To achieve this golden age will take imaginative government policies, a strong faith in human ingenuity, and a will to succeed that is free from rigid ideology. Above all, it will require all of us to take responsibility for our own actions as they affect both our fellow human beings and this small planet we call home.

We hope that you now have gained enough confidence in your study of economics to better accept such responsibility and to begin to appreciate this most challenging and fascinating discipline.

REVIEW

1. What was the source of all wealth, according to the French physiocrats?
2. In the new paradigm, what are the three categories of workers?
3. What is likely to happen to comparative interest rates between countries in the twenty-first century?
4. What is happening to many blue-collar production-service and middle-management jobs in Canada today?
5. In what way will our present definition of full employment be less relevant in the future?
6. In what way is the goal of economic growth likely to change?
7. Which is likely to be more pressing in the years to come: the goal of an equitable distribution of income or the goal of effectively managing the national debt?

Chapter Highlights

This chapter is unlike any of the previous chapters, in that we take a look into the future and try to analyze the dramatic changes taking place in today's world economy and then engage in some speculation about the consequences of these changes. We begin by examining the paradigm shift from the industrial age to the information age that is currently taking place. The heart of this new paradigm is symbolic knowledge. The important role of symbolic knowledge in four major trends is then investigated. The first of these is the changing nature of the factors of production. Here we suggest that symbolic knowledge has become a fifth factor of production. We also suggest that process technology is replacing product technology as the primary method of creating wealth. The second trend is the changing nature of work and production itself. We argue that tomorrow's successful economies will be the ones that best create an environment that encourages the work of the symbolic analyst. The third trend is the blurring of the traditional distinction between goods and services. The fourth is the globalization of the production process. We hypothesise that the world may well be on the edge of a Schumpeter-type explosion in economic growth but also warn that to accomplish this will require the co-ordination of economic policies among the world's leading economies. Next we take a brief look at the implication of all of this for Canada and the re-examine the definitions of our economic goals. The big conclusion here is that the problem of an equitable distribution of income is likely to be the most elusive goal of the next half century.

New Glossary Terms

anti-dumping regulation   493
paradigm shift   486
symbolic analyst   487
symbolic knowledge   487

STUDY GUIDE

Study Tips

1. This chapter is meant for you to enjoy and to stimulate your imagination more than to study in the same way that earlier chapters required. The ideas in the chapter are not presented to try to convince you of their validity but rather to appeal to your wonder of it all.

2. There is a great deal of pessimism about the future among young people today. This comes out in the form of questions such as, will there be any jobs left when I am ready to enter the labour force full-time, and will I be able to earn enough income to live at least as well as most people today? We think that this pessimistic outlook is misplaced. The world is entering a very exciting period in which opportunities for eager, creative, self-motivated young people will be greater than at any time in history. Finding those opportunities will not be easy, and those who try will inevitably make mistakes, but the rewards in terms of creative outlet, income, and a sense of accomplishment will be enormous. Oh, to be young again!

Translations

Below you will find six concepts associated with the old paradigm. What corresponding concept would fit the new paradigm?

product technology: _____

standardized production: _____

large corporations: _____

national markets: _____

high-volume output: _____

economies of scale: _____

Are You Sure?

Indicate whether the following statements are true or false. If false, indicate why they are false.

1. Both the Industrial Revolution that ushered in the machine age and the emergence of the information age are paradigm shifts.

   T or F   If false: _____

   _____

2. The information age is likely to spawn a rebirth of entrepreneurial spirit.

   T or F   If false: _____

   _____

3. It is likely that monopoly tendencies in the economy will intensify with the maturing of the information age.

   T or **F**   If false: _____

   _____

4. Although there are many examples of symbolic knowledge being a substitute for labour and real capital, it is not a substitute for natural resources or financial capital.

   T or **F**   If false: _____

   _____

5. The distinction between what is a good and what is a service is becoming more blurred.

   T or **F**   If false: _____

   _____

6. While the value of world trade has been growing, the volume has not.

   T or **F**   If false: _____

   _____

7. In the old paradigm, a nation's comparative advantage lay in abundant natural resources, a high level of capital accumulation, and a disciplined labour force.

   T or **F**   If false: _____

   _____

8. In the new paradigm, in-service production workers will be the lowest-paid.

   T or **F**   If false: _____

   _____

9. An anti-dumping regulation (or law) prohibits the importation of any good at a price below the cost of production.

   T or **F**   If false: _____

   _____

10. The achievement of an equitable distribution of income is, probably, the least contentious of Canada's economic goals.

    T or **F**   If false: _____

    _____

Choose the Best

11. Which of the following products has the least input of a symbolic analyst?
    a) A textbook.
    b) A pair of beach thongs.

12. What is true about economic policy coordination?
    a) It is becoming increasingly less relevant.
    b) It is becoming increasing more relevant.

13. What will most likely be true about employment in the future?
    a) It will rely more on a disciplined, regimented labour force.
    b) It will involve much more flexible working hours and locations.

14. Which statement about symbolic knowledge is correct?
    a) It is associated with Adam Smith and the *Wealth of Nations*.
    b) It can be used to differentiate between product technology and process technology.
    c) It comes in the form of new words or phrases but not in mathematical forms.

15. In what area will the manufacturing of standardized products tend to concentrate?

a) In areas with abundant natural resources.
b) In areas where symbolic analysts are concentrated.
c) In areas where routine labour is paid the lowest wage rates.

16. What was the basis for monopoly control in the old paradigm?
a) Capital accumulation.
b) Knowledge.
c) Process technology.
d) Land.

17. Which of the following statements about the source of wealth is correct?
a) Marx said that it was land.
b) The French physiocrats said it was capital.
c) The neoclassicists said it was labour.
d) Those who embrace the new paradigm say it is knowledge, information, and human creativity.

18. All of the following statements, *except one*, are correct concerning the world's agriculture industry. Which is the exception?
a) It enjoys significant government subsidies in many countries.
b) It is bound to become more efficient as a result of biotechnology.
c) The number of producers within it must be reduced sooner or later.
d) It is poised for a new "golden age" of high producer income.

19. Which of the following is true about symbolic analysts?
a) They need to be generalists.
b) They will eventually replace all service workers.
c) They concentrate on high-volume production more than high-value-added production.
d) They make up the fifth factor of production.

20. Which of the following characterizes the new paradigm?
a) The changing nature of the factors of production.
b) The changing nature of work and production.
c) The blurring of the distinction between goods and services.
d) The globalization of production.
e) All of the above.

21. Which of the following statements is correct about symbolic knowledge?
a) While it is powerful, it adds to the costs of production.
b) It is bound to make mass markets even larger.
c) It will shift the emphasis of production to product technology.
d) It often proves to be a substitute for real capital.
e) It has been most widely adopted and used in the newly industrial nations such as Asia's Four Tigers.

22. All of the following, *except one*, are associated with the industrial age. Which is the exception?
a) Steam power and the electric motor.
b) The computer.
c) Economies of scale.
d) The large corporation as the primary organizational form.
e) Manufacturing as the driving force behind the rich economies of the world.

23. All of the following, *except one*, make Thurow's list of "industries of tomorrow." Which one is the exception?
a) Microelectronics.
b) Biotechnology.
c) Medicine.
d) Robotics.
e) Telecommunications.

Problems

24. Decide which of Reich's three categories of work (routine production services, in-person services, or symbolic services) each of the following occupations best fits into.

    a) Coffee house waiter: _____

    b) Pulp mill worker: _____

    c) Cable TV installer: _____

    d) Computer systems consultant: _____

    e) Auto plant supervisor: _____

    f) Market research analyst: _____

25. Make a list of five products that you wish our economy would produce more of. Now, make a list of five products that you wish were produced in smaller quantities. Looking over your two lists, do you think the *kind of growth* is more or less important than the rate of growth?

UNANSWERED QUESTIONS

Short Essays

1. Within the past few hundred years, we have seen the wealth-creation process shift from agriculture to manufacturing to information. Identify the groups who were at the centre of the power struggles that took place in these shifts.

2. Compare product technology with process technology.

3. Which is the driving force behind economic growth in Schumpeter's eyes? If he is right, do you think economic growth will become easier or harder for an economy to achieve in the information age?

Analytical Questions

4. As production becomes more and more globalized, and it becomes increasingly difficult to identify any particular product with a country of origin, do you think people will become more or less attached to the country in which they live?

5. As of 1995, the provision of cable TV service to individual households is by a cable company that has a local monopoly granted by the CRTC. Can you imagine two different ways competition could be introduced into this industry?

6. When the authors were in college/university, few people questioned the popular concept that "bigger is better" and almost everything subsequently got bigger—cars, houses, corporations, cities, incomes, GDP, and so on. We see many examples from the information age in which smaller is considered better. Is this fact likely to alter our perceptions about other things too?

7. Location theorists in economics and geography argue that the location of (almost) every city in the world has a specific explanation involving either a national transportation factor (for example, two rives merging) or the presence of a nearby natural resource such as a coal or iron ore deposit. What do think might replace these factors as the main determinant of the fastest-growing population centres in the informational age, and what areas in North America do you think will grow the quickest?

8. The Canadian trade-union movement has consistently opposed various steps toward the liberalization of trade barriers between countries. Why do you think this has been the case?

9. As world trade expands and the global network widens, do you think the purchasing power parity theory will become more or less true? Explain.

10. According to Schumpeter, what are the sources of economic growth? Do you think that the information age encourage an increase in economic growth rates?

 ## Web-Based Activities

1. As the labour force ages, productivity and production costs will be affected. The important question for macroeconomists is how will productivity changes affect the economy and, specifically, the product market? Will potential GDP be adversely affected? What about short-run aggregate supply? Go to **http://www.oecd.org//subject/ageing/awp4_1e.pdf** to determine the impact that aging will have on productivity. Illustrate the impact in an aggregate demand–supply diagram. What policies should the federal government begin to enact today to offset the negative consequences of an aging population?

2. As we move into the twenty-first century, governments are asking themselves how to best position national economies so that citizens of their nation will prosper in the coming century. Questions surrounding debt and deficits, regulation, and fiscal and monetary policies are only a few of the many questions being looked at.
   a) Having completed this course, what changes in macroeconomic policy do you consider necessary so that Canada can prosper in the next century?
   b) Now read a speech by the Honourable Paul Martin found at **http://www.fin.gc.ca/newse98/98-074e.html.** What does Mr. Martin see as necessary changes required so that Canada can prosper?
   c) Finally, read **http://www.cdhowe.org/pdf/group22.pdf** and summarize what this "group of 22" proposes.

Glossary

aggregate demand: the aggregate quantity of goods and services demanded by all buyers at various price levels.

aggregate expenditures: total spending in the economy, divided into the four components: C, I, G, and (X – IM).

aggregate supply: the aggregate quantity of goods and services produced by all sellers at various price levels.

anti-dumping regulation: a law or regulation found in most countries that prohibits the importation of any good at a price below the cost of production.

arbitrage: the process of buying a commodity in one market, where the price is low, and immediately selling it in a second market where the price is higher.

asset demand for money: the desire by people to use money as a store of wealth, that is, to hold money as an asset.

assets: the part of a company's balance sheet that represents what it owns or what is owed to it.

automatic stabilizers: government policies and programs that automatically change with the state of the economy so as to stabilize the economy.

autonomous consumption: the portion of consumer spending that is independent of the level of income.

autonomous spending: the portion of total spending that is independent of the level of income.

balanced budget: the equality of net tax revenues and government spending on goods and services.

balanced-budget fiscal policy: the belief that a government's budget should be balanced each budget period.

balance of payments: an accounting of a country's international transactions that involves the payment and receipts of foreign currencies.

balance of trade: the value of a country's exports of goods and services less the value of its imports.

bank rate: the rate of interest payable by the commercial banks on loans from the Bank of Canada.

bank rate: the rate of interest that the Bank of Canada charges a commercial bank for a loan.

budget deficit: government spending on goods and services in excess of net tax revenues.

budget surplus: net tax revenue in excess of government spending on goods and services.

business cycle: the expansionary and contractionary phases in the growth rate of real GDP.

capital: all human-made resources that can be used to produce goods and services.

capital account: a subcategory of the balance of payments that reflects changes in ownership of assets associated with foreign investment.

change in demand: a change in the quantities demanded at every price, caused by a change in the determinants of demand.

change in supply: a change in the quantities supplied at every price, caused by a change in the determinants of supply.

change in the quantity demanded: the change in the quantity that results from a price change. It results, graphically, in a movement along a demand curve.

change in the quantity supplied: the change in the amounts that will be produced as a result of a price change. This is shown as a movement along a supply curve.

commodity money: a type of money that can also function, and is useful, as a commodity.

comparative advantage: the advantage that comes from producing something at a lower opportunity cost than others are able to do.

complementary products: products that tend to be purchased jointly and whose demands, therefore, are directly related.

consumer goods and services: products used by consumers to satisfy their wants and needs.

consumer price index: an index of the changes in the prices of goods and services based on the cost of those same items in a base period.

consumption: the expenditure by households on goods and services.

contractionary monetary policy: a policy in which the amount of money in the economy is decreased and credit becomes harder to obtain and more expensive.

cost–push inflation: inflation caused by an increase in the costs of production or in profit levels, with the effect being on the supply side.

counter-cyclical fiscal policy: deliberate adjustments in the level of government spending and taxation in order to close recessionary or inflationary gaps.

crowding-out effect: the idea that government borrowing to finance a deficit crowds out private investment because it causes interest rates to rise.

currency appreciation: a rise in the exchange rate of one currency for another.

currency depreciation: the fall in the exchange rate of one currency for another.

current account: a subcategory of the balance of payments that shows the income or expenditures related to exports and imports.

cyclical unemployment: unemployment that occurs as a result of the recessionary phase of the business cycle.

cyclically balanced-budget fiscal policy: the use of counter-cyclical fiscal policy to balance the budget over the life of the business cycle.

demand: the quantities that consumers are willing and able to buy per period of time at various prices.

demand–pull inflation: inflation that occurs when total demand for goods and services exceeds the economy's capacity to produce those goods.

demand schedule: a table showing the various quantities demanded per period of time at different prices.

devaluation: the re-fixing by government of an exchange rate at a lower level.

direct investment: the purchase of real assets.

dirty float: an exchange rate that is not officially fixed by government but is managed by the central bank's ongoing intervention in the market.

discouraged worker: an individual who wants work but is no longer actively seeking it because of the conviction that no opportunities exist.

disposable income: the personal after-tax income of people.

economic growth: an increase in an economy's real GDP per capita or an increase in the economy's capacity to produce.

employed: those who are in the labour force and hold paid employment.

enterprise: the human resource that innovates and takes risks.

equation of exchange: a formula that states that the quantity of money times the velocity of money is equal to nominal GDP (price times real GDP).

equilibrium: a state of balance of equal forces with no tendency to change.

equilibrium price: the price at which the quantity demanded equals the quantity supplied such that there is neither a surplus nor a shortage.

equilibrium quantity: the quantity that prevails at the equilibrium price.

excess reserves: reserves in excess of what the bank wants to hold as its target reserves.

exchange controls: government-imposed restrictions limiting the amount of foreign currencies that can be obtained.

exchange rate: the rate at which one currency converts into another.

expansionary monetary policy: a policy that aims to increase the amount of money in the economy and make credit cheaper and more easily available.

expenditure equilibrium: the income at which the value of production and aggregate expenditures are equal.

exports: goods and services produced in one country and sold to another country.

factor market: the market for the factors of production.

factors of production: the productive resources that are available to an economy, categorized as land, labour, capital, and enterprise.

financial security: any claim on assets that usually takes the form of a bond or certificate of deposit or similar financial instrument.

fiscal policy: the government's approach toward its own spending and taxation.

fixed exchange rate: a currency exchange rate pegged by government and therefore prevented from rising or falling.

flexible exchange rate: a currency exchange rate determined by the market forces of supply and demand and not interfered with by government action.

foreign-trade effect: the effect that a change in prices has upon exports and imports.

fractional reserve system: a banking system whereby banks keep only a small fraction of their total deposits on reserve in the form of cash.

frictional unemployment: that part of total unemployment caused by the fact that it takes time for people to find their first job or to move between jobs.

full employment: the situation in which there is only frictional and structural unemployment, that is, where cyclical unemployment is zero.

GDP deflator: a price index based on a representative bundle of GDP goods and services.

GDP gap: the difference between potential GDP and actual GDP.

gross domestic product (GDP): the value of all final goods and services produced in an economy in a certain period.

gross national product (GNP): the total market value of all final goods and services produced by the citizens of a country regardless of the location of production.

human capital: the accumulated skills and knowledge of human beings.

imports: goods and services that are bought from other countries and that reflect a leakage from the circular flow of income.

income: the earnings of factors of production expressed as an amount per period of time.

induced consumption: the portion of consumer spending that is dependent on the level of income.

induced spending: the portion of spending that depends on the level of income.

inferior products: products whose demands will decrease as a result of an increase in income and will increase as a result of a decrease in income.

inflation: a persistent rise in the general level of prices.

inflationary gap: the difference between actual real GDP and potential real GDP when the economy is temporarily producing an output above full employment.

injection: any spending flow that is not dependent on the current level of income.

interest: the payment made and the income received for the use of capital.

interest-rate effect: the effect that a change in prices, and therefore interest rates, has upon investment; for example, higher prices cause higher interest rates, which leads to lower investment.

investment: spending on capital goods.

investment demand: the relationship between investment spending and interest rates.

labour: human physical and mental effort that can be used to produce goods and services.

labour force: members of the labour-force population, whether employed or unemployed.

labour-force population: the total population in a country, excluding those under 15 years of age, inmates of institutions, those in the armed forces, and residents of Indian reserves or the territories.

labour productivity: a measure of the amount of output produced per unit of labour input (per unit of time).

Laffer curve: the graphical representation of the idea that in terms of tax revenue there is an optimal tax rate; above or below this rate, tax revenue would be less.

land: any natural resource that can be used to produce goods and services.

law of increasing costs: as an economy's production level of any particular item increases, its per unit cost of production rises.

leakage: income received within the circular flow that does not flow directly back.

liabilities: the part of a company's balance sheet that represents what it owes.

loanable funds: the portion of wealth that is available for loan through financial intermediaries.

long-run aggregate supply: the aggregate quantity of goods and services produced after all prices and wages have adjusted; that is, the full-employment level of real GDP.

M1: currency in circulation plus demand deposits.

M2: M1 plus all notice and personal term deposits.

M3: M2 plus non-personal term deposits known as certificates of deposits.

macroeconomic equilibrium: a situation in which the quantity of real GDP demanded equals the quantity of real GDP supplied.

macroeconomics: the study of how the major components of an economy interact; it includes the topics of unemployment, inflation, interest rate policy, and the spending and taxation policies of government.

marginal leakage rate: the ratio of change in leakages that results from a change in income.

marginal propensity to consume: the ratio of the change in consumption to the corresponding change in disposable income (MPC) or national income (MPC*).

marginal propensity to expend: the ratio of the change in expenditures that results from a change in income.

marginal propensity to import: the ratio of the change in imports that results from a change in national income.

marginal propensity to save: the ratio of the change in savings to the corresponding change in disposable income (MPS) or national income (MPS*).

marginal tax rate: the ratio of the change in taxation as a result of a change in income.

market demand: the total demand for a product by all of its consumers.

market supply: the total supply of a product offered by all producers.

medium of exchange: something that is accepted as payment for goods and services.

microeconomics: the study of the outcomes of decisions by people and firms through a focus on the supply and demand of goods, the costs of production, and market structures.

monetarism: an economic school of thought that believes that cyclical fluctuations of GDP and inflation are usually caused by changes in the money supply.

monetary policy: economic policy designed to change or influence the economy through changes in the money supply.

monetizing the debt: the action by government of borrowing from the central bank to finance increased spending.

money: anything that is widely accepted as a medium of exchange and therefore can be used to buy goods or to settle debts.

money multiplier: the increase in total deposits that would occur in the whole banking system as a result of a new deposit in a single bank.

multiplier: the effect on income of a change in autonomous expenditures.

national debt: the sum of the federal government's budget deficits less surpluses.

national income equilibrium: that level of income where total leakages from the circular flow equal total injections.

national income (Y): total earnings of all the factors of production in a certain period.

natural rate of unemployment: the unemployment rate at full employment.

near-banks: financial institutions, like credit unions or trust companies, which share many of the functions of commercial banks but are not defined as banks under the Bank Act (they are also known as non-bank financial intermediaries).

net domestic income: incomes earned in Canada (equals the sum of wages, profits, interest, farm, and self-employed income).

net exports: total exports minus total imports of goods and services which can be written as (X – IM) or as Xn.

net national product (NNP): gross national product less capital consumption (or depreciation).

net tax revenue: total tax revenue received by government less transfer payments.

net worth: the total assets less total liabilities of a company—also called equity.

nominal GDP: the value of GDP in terms of prices prevailing at the time of measurement.

nominal income: the present-dollar value of a person's income.

normal products: products whose demand will increase as a result of an increase in income and will decrease as a result of a decrease in income.

Okun's law: the observation that for every 1 percent of cyclical unemployment an economy's GDP would be 2.5 percent below its potential.

open-market operations: the buying and selling of securities by the Bank of Canada in the open (to the public) market.

opportunity cost: the value of the next-best alternative that is given up as a result of making a particular choice.

paradigm shift: a significant change in pattern or in the model that one is looking at; in this case, a change in the economic system itself.

participation rate: the percentage of those in the labour-force population who are actually in the labour force.

personal income: income paid to individuals before the deduction of personal income taxes.

pro-cyclical: action by the government that tends to push the economy in the same direction that it is leaning.

product market: the market for consumer goods and services.

production possibilities curve: a graphical representation of the various combinations of maximum output that can be produced.

profit: the income received from the activity of enterprise.

protectionism: the economic policy of protecting domestic producers by restricting the importation of foreign products.

portfolio investment: the purchase of shares or bonds representing less than 50 percent ownership.

purchasing power parity theory: a theory suggesting that exchange rates will change so as to equate the purchasing power of each currency.

quota: a limit imposed on the production or sale of a product.

real-balances effect: the effect that a change in the value of real balances has on consumption spending (the value of real balances is affected by changing price levels).

real GDP: the value of GDP measured in terms of prices prevailing in a given base year.

real income: the purchasing power of income, that is, nominal income divided by the price level.

real interest rate: the rate of interest measured in constant dollars.

real wage: nominal wage divided by the price level; that is, the amount of goods and services that can be bought from a given nominal wage.

recessionary gap: the difference between actual real GDP and potential real GDP when the economy is producing below its potential.

rent: the payment made and the income received for the use of land.

savings: the portion of income that is not spent on consumption.

Say's Law: the proposition that "supply creates its own demand"; that is, production (supply) creates sufficient income and thus spending (demand) to purchase the production. (Attributed to French economist Jean-Baptiste Say.)

short-run aggregate supply: the quantity of goods and services produced at various price levels assuming that factor prices remain constant.

stagflation: the simultaneous occurrence of high inflation and unemployment.

store of wealth: the function of money that allows people to hold and accumulate wealth.

structural unemployment: the part of total unemployment that results from structural changes in an economy's industries.

subsidy: a payment by government for the purpose of increasing some particular activity or increasing the output of a particular good.

substitute products: any product whose demand varies directly with a change in the price of a similar product.

supply: the quantities that producers are willing and able to sell per period of time at different prices.

supply schedule: a table showing the various quantities supplied per period of time at different prices.

symbolic analyst: an individual who uses symbolic knowledge to identify problems, create solutions, and then broker those solutions in a systematic form.

symbolic knowledge: knowledge that encompasses data and information that is then systematically improved and refined into a form that has direct application to defining problems or creating solutions.

target reserve ratio: the portion of deposits that a bank wants to hold in cash.

tariff: a tax (or duty) levied on imports.

terms of trade: the average price of a country's exports compared with the price of its imports.

transactions demand for money: the desire of people to hold money as a medium of exchange, that is, to effect transactions.

transfer payments: one-way transactions in which payment is made, but no good or service flows back in return.

transmission process: the Keynesian view of how changes in money affect (transmit to) the real variables in the economy.

the spread: the difference between the rate of interest a bank charges borrowers and the rate it pays savers.

unemployed: those who are in the labour force and are actively seeking employment, but do not hold paid employment.

unemployment: the situation in which persons 15 years old and over are actively seeking work but do not have employment.

unemployment rate: the percentage of those in the labour force who do not hold paid employment.

unit of account: the function of money that allows us to determine easily the relative value of goods.

unplanned investment: the amount of unintended investment by firms in the way of a build-up or run-down of inventories.

value of production: the total receipts of all producers.

velocity of money (or circulation): the number of times that the average unit of currency is spent (or turns over) buying final goods or services.

voluntary export restrictions (V.E.R.s): an agreement by an exporting country to restrict the amount of its exports to another country.

wages: the payment made and the income received for the use of labour.

wealth: the sum of all valuable assets less liabilities.

wealth effect: the effect of a change in wealth on consumption spending (a direct relationship between the two).

Index